DEBATES IN FAMILY LAW AROUND THE GLOBE AT THE DAWN OF THE 21ST CENTURY

European Family Law Series

Published by the Organising Committee of the Commission on European Family Law

DEBATES IN FAMILY LAW AROUND THE GLOBE AT THE DAWN OF THE 21ST CENTURY

Edited by

Katharina Boele-Woelki

intersentia
Antwerp – Oxford – Portland

Distribution for the UK:
Hart Publishing Ltd.
16C Worcester Place
Oxford OX1 2JW
UK
Tel.: +44 1865 51 75 30
Fax: +44 1865 51 07 10

Distribution for Switzerland and Germany:
Stämpfli Verlag AG
Wölflistrasse 1
CH-3001 Bern
Switzerland
Tel.: +41 0 31 300 63 18
Fax: +41 0 31 300 66 88

Distribution for the USA and Canada:
International Specialized Book Services
920 NE 58th Ave Suite 300
Portland, OR 97213
USA
Tel.: +1 800 944 6190 (toll free)
Tel.: +1 503 287 3093
Fax: +1 503 280 8832
email: info@isbs.com

Distribution for other countries:
Intersentia Publishers
Groenstraat 31
BE-2640 Mortsel
Belgium
Tel.: +32 3 680 15 50
Fax: +32 3 658 71 21

Debates in Family Law around the Globe at the Dawn of the 21st Century
Katharina Boele-Woelki (ed.)

ISBN 978-90-5095-875-2
D/2009/7849/5
NUR 822

PREFACE

In June 2008, the Utrecht Centre for European Research into Family Law (UCERF) organized an expert meeting of the authors of this volume. Upon the editor's invitation they had contributed to a special volume of the Utrecht Law Review dealing with comparative family law. All these contributions are compiled in this book. They address three issues that at the dawn of the 21st century have provoked passionate discussion. With regard to these issues legislative measures are being taken, judicial decisions vary also within singular jurisdictions, and arguments in legal literature are being exchanged. The topics concern:

(1) (Compulsory) arrangements regarding children
(2) Registration schemes for same-sex couples: new jurisdictions
(3) The effectiveness of the *pater est* rule

The thematic contributions are preceded by two introductory articles. The historical introduction addresses the 'cultural constraints argument' which, according to a few legal scholars, prevents both spontaneous and the deliberate harmonization of family law. Is family law indeed embedded in unique national (legal) culture? What lessons can be learned from the past? The methodological introduction offers some general ideas as to how comparative family law is perceived and what it should entail, whereby a comparison is made between more recent developments in Europe and the United States of America. At the end a comparative synthesis of the discussions has been included.

The two-day expert meeting was positively evaluated. With no more than 30 participants it provided an excellent opportunity to really exchange and express ideas, opinions and concerns. The authors were all well prepared and familiar with the views of their colleagues as expressed in the respective contributions. In addition, the mix of experienced and young, but advanced family law experts, also turned out to be stimulating. All in all, the Utrecht debates on family law around the globe were successful from both a professional and a personal perspective.

Katharina Boele-Woelki
Utrecht, December 2008

LIST OF AUTHORS

Antokolskaia, Masha
Professor of Private Law, Faculty of Law, VU University, Amsterdam

Blauwhoff, Richard J.
LLM, MA, PhD Candidate at the Molengraaff Institute for Private Law, Utrecht University

Boele-Woelki, Katharina
Professor of Private International Law, Comparative Law and Family Law at the Molengraaff Institute for Private Law, Utrecht University, Chair of the Commission on European Family Law

Bonini Baraldi, Matteo
EU Research Adviser, Law, Political Sciences & Economics, Università di Bologna

Curry-Sumner, Ian
Senior University Lecturer and Researcher, Private International Law, Comparative Law and Family Law, UCERF and Molengraaff Institute for Private Law, Utrecht University

Curry-Sumner, Scott
University Lecturer, Common Law Systems, Private Law Department, Maastricht University

Einhorn, Talia
Professor of Law, Sha'arei Mishpat College of Law / Tel-Aviv University Faculty of Management

Glennon, Theresa
Professor of Law, Temple University Beasley School of Law, Philadelphia

Granet, Frédérique
Professor at the Robert Schuman University of Strasbourg, Director of the Department on Private Law in charge of the Master on Family Law

Jeppesen de Boer, Christina G.
University Lecturer and Researcher at the Molengraaff Institute for Private Law, Utrecht University

Martins, Rosa
Assistant Lecturer at the Family Law Centre, Faculty of Law, University of Coimbra

Maxwell, Nancy G.
Professor and Director of International Legal Programs, Washburn University School of Law, Topeka, Kansas

Schrama, Wendy M.
Senior University Lecturer and Researcher in Family Law at the Utrecht Centre for European Research into Family Law (UCERF) of the Molengraaff Institute for Private Law, Utrecht University

Singer, Anna
Associate Professor, Faculty of Law, Uppsala University, Uppsala

Szeibert-Erdő, Orsolya
Assistant Professor of Family Law, ELTE University of Budapest

Vonk, Machteld
University Lecturer and Researcher at the Molengraaff Institute for Private Law, Utrecht University

De Vos, Pierre
Professor of Constitutional Law, Law Faculty, University of the Western Cape, Bellville, Cape Town

TABLE OF CONTENTS

REGISTRATION SCHEMES FOR SAME-SEX COUPLES: NEW JURISDICTIONS

IS THE UNION CIVIL? Same-sex marriages, civil unions, domestic partnerships and reciprocal benefits in the USA

COMPARATIVE SYNTHESIS

THE ISSUES OF TODAY IN PERSPECTIVE

WHAT COMPARATIVE FAMILY LAW SHOULD ENTAIL

Katharina Boele-Woelki*

Regardless of whether globalization is to be applauded or condemned, it has had the undeniable effect of bringing more people and cultures together. The result for the family law practitioner is a world of new and challenging legal issues as well as new possibilities prompted by the cross-fertilization of legal ideas.[1]

1. PRELIMINARY REMARKS

The editing of the contributions about 'Debates in Family Law around the Globe at the Dawn of the 21st Century' provides an exciting opportunity to reflect on the elements, aspects, dimensions, scope and method of comparative family law.

This introductory contribution consists of four parts. Information about the selection of the authors is provided in this first section. Subsequently, in the main body of the article, some general ideas as to how comparative family law (methodology) is perceived and what it should entail are presented whereby reference is made to more recent developments in Europe and the United States. Thirdly, information is proffered about the thematic approach of the contributions and the underlying ideas in respect of the selection of the topics that have been addressed by the authors in this issue. Finally, in the concluding section some reflections introduced in the main part of this contribution are taken further.

---

* Professor of Private International Law, Comparative Law and Family Law at the Molengraaff Institute for Private Law of Utrecht University (The Netherlands), email: K.Boele@law.uu.nl. Since 2001 she has been the Chair of the Commission on European Family Law (CEFL), see http://www.law.uu.nl/priv/cefl. In 2007, she established the Utrecht Centre for European Research into Family Law (UCERF). Research for this contribution has been carried out at Columbia Law School in New York where the author was a visiting scholar from January until March 2008. Special thanks to Professor Elizabeth Scott of Columbia Law School for her interest and guidance and to Professor Nancy Maxwell of Washburn University School of Law for commenting upon the analysis of US family law.

1 See D. Blair & M. Weiner, *Family Law in the World Community, Cases, Materials, and Problems in Comparative and International Family Law, Introduction to the Study of Family Law in the World Community*, 2003, p. 3.

Sixteen other authors have contributed to this volume. Upon invitation they all showed an immediate and great interest in contributing to the current debates in family law. In addition to renowned legal scholars many authors in the category 'young, yet advanced' researchers have been asked to contribute. Repeatedly, they have demonstrated that they are (almost) prepared to take the lead. All contributions were anonymously peer reviewed by other family law experts from many other jurisdictions. Also their comments for improvement and clarification were highly appreciated. It is to this author's great pleasure that six authors belong to the Utrecht Centre for European Research into Family Law (UCERF).[2] This publication enables them to showcase the work that goes on within the Centre.

Right from the outset it was this author's initial aspiration that the invited authors should be provided with the opportunity to discuss their contributions with each other in order to get direct feedback from colleagues interested in the field. Besides, face-to-face meetings provide an excellent opportunity to establish or extend one's own personal network. The G.J. Wiarda Institute for Legal Research of Utrecht University, and the Royal Netherlands Academy of Art and Sciences have granted financial support for the organization of an expert meeting in which all authors participated.[3] This was of course highly appreciated.

2. FRAMING COMPARATIVE FAMILY LAW

This part is dedicated to the question as to how comparative family law could be framed. Which components should it comprise? Are there any general guidelines and trends? Is it possible to draw a roadmap? How can it be outlined without drawing the lines too narrow or even putting it into a straightjacket? In an attempt to answer these questions the following instructive definition of 'framing' has been used as a guideline:

> 'Framing is the art of presenting an argument by strategically revealing certain information while concealing other information and hopefully presenting the package in a way that is sufficiently beautiful that no one notions (or objects to) the absence.'[4]

---

2 For more information about UCERF objectives and activities: www.ucerf.nl.

3 The expert meeting took place from 27–28 June 2008 in Utrecht. In addition to the authors of this volume several other family experts from The Netherlands and abroad were invited. See also the final contribution "Research questions in family law derived from a comparative synthesis of general developments and trends".

4 Explanation of the objects 'Framing' at the exhibition of Barbara Bloom (8 January – 4 May 2008) at the International Center of Photography, New York. The explanation starts with: 'Framing is frequently an act of cunning. Lawyers succeed by how they "frame the question"; politicians succeed by how they "frame the issue." Detective stories frame clues, novelists frame plots, criminals frame fall guys.' See also the exhibition at the Statens Museum for Kunst, Copenhagen, 'Frames, State of the Art' (8 March – 8 September 2008): 'The frame is

2.1. THE SUBJECT MATTER

Which issues are addressed by those who discuss comparative family law? In trying to discover answers to this question three recent publications of well established authors in the field of comparative family law have been selected. Firstly, Harry Krause's article in the *Oxford Handbook on Comparative Law* about 'Comparative Family Law';[5] secondly, Masha Antokolskaia's contribution to the book *Comparative Law: A Handbook*, entitled 'Comparative Family Law: Moving with the Times?'[6] and thirdly, Mary Ann Glendon's substantive and long awaited introduction to the *International Encyclopedia of Comparative Law* on 'Family Law in a Time of Turbulence'.[7] At present all three publications belong to the most up-to-date and comprehensive overviews, which at least those who teach comparative family law should be familiar with. The analysis provided, the trends identified and worries of the authors focus not only on developments in Europe with its great variety of family law systems (Antokolskaia), but also comprise a general, instructive and pointed comparison of the American and European family law systems by taking a mezzo-perspective (Krause), and eventually take into account – as far as this has been possible – all family law systems in the world (Glendon).

Glendon indicates the major social, political and legal trends of family relations during the last three decades by reviewing the topics that since 1971 have been addressed in specific chapters by several comparative family law specialists, being Persons, Formation of Marriage, Interspousal Relations, Creation of Relations of Kinship, Children, Parents and Guardians, Family in Socialist and Post-socialist Countries and Family in Religious and Customary Laws. This review – while brief – is of precious value since the majority of the chapters and some of their parts were finalized more than almost twenty years ago.[8] From there, she identifies the major issues confronting the family at the dawn of the 21st century. Whereas ideas of individual freedom, equality and women's rights influenced family law in the past, advances in bio-technology and genetic science will influence family law in the future. She concludes that the present legal ordering of the family surveyed in the family volume of the *International Encyclopedia* is composed of the accumulated wisdom, accidents, and inventions of the past. Today,

---

what concentrates the focus on something, shows off and demarcates what has a special value or status.'.

5 In M. Reimann & R. Zimmermann (eds.), *Oxford Handbook on Comparative Law*, 2006, pp. 1099–1132.

6 In D. Nelken & E. Örücü (eds.), *Comparative Law: A Handbook*, 2007, pp. 241–262.

7 In A. Chloros *et al.* (eds.), *International Encyclopedia of Comparative Law, Persons and Family*, Vol. 4, 2007, pp. 1–27.

8 Generally it is to be regretted that it takes the editorial board of the *International Encyclopedia of Comparative Law* on average almost three years to publish the chapters and parts that have been submitted.

lawmakers in every corner of the world are in the process of adding their own contributions, determining which parts of that inheritance can be usefully developed and which should be reconsidered or rejected.[9] Truly speaking her closing remark properly emphasizes one of the major functions of comparative family law: a comparative approach is indispensable if we want to learn lessons from the past and the present. Expectedly, Krause supports this view by further pointing to the fact that family laws are unfolding in similar directions: 'For all their very real differences, nations around the world find themselves facing fundamentally similar dilemmas in defining and regulating the modern family. Accordingly, it makes sense to take stock of what has been tried and what has – or has not – worked elsewhere. Comparative family law's days as an unlikely pioneer are over.'[10]

Now comes the work of tilling the soil and seeing what will grow. He explains what in the field of comparative family law has been, and is being, done and who is doing it. Further he questions what it means to compare – and how one should compare, and in so doing takes a critical stance towards the 'West' as a monolithic culture.[11] Subsequently, he presents the 'Great Debates' of yesterday, today and tomorrow by referring to contrasting examples derived from the family law systems in Europe and the United States. In particular in finding explanations as to why the approaches, solutions and methods are similar or differ, Krause's comparison is highly illuminating. Antokolskaia, finally, focuses on the development of the European family law systems in respect of marriage, divorce and non-marital relationships. In complementing Krause's and Glendon's contributions, she adds a new point of discussion that recently has emerged in Europe: namely the deliberate harmonization of family law to which the activities of the Commission on European Family Law (CEFL) are contributing.[12] She describes this issue as highly controversial whereas the progress of harmonization activities only has made the debate sharper and could only have started in spite of serious opposition.[13] Whether this characterization is accurate, however, should definitely not be assessed by someone who is – like this present author – heavily involved in the CEFL activities. At any rate it pinpoints a new development, which was not even conceivable a decade ago.

---

9 See Glendon, *supra* note 7, p. 25.

10 See Krause, *supra* note 5, pp. 1099–1132, p. 1101.

11 In particular he warns us (*supra* note 5, p. 11) that if Europeans loudly profess not to understand American (prudish? Victorian?) attitudes regarding sex and the political power of fundamentalist (intolerant?) interpretations of religion, Americans do not understand the Europeans' preoccupation with ideology and their (mostly unpleasant) ethnic/nationalistic history.

12 See K. Boele-Woelki, 'The Principles of European Family Law: its aims and prospects', 2005 *Utrecht Law Review* 2, pp. 160–168.

13 See Antokolskaia, *supra* note 6, p. 258.

In exploring the subject matter of comparative family law another issue needs a little further discussion. Frequently, family law courses, for instance, which look beyond national boundaries, combine both comparative family law and international family law.[14] Is it possible to distinguish the one from the other? A brief explanation of both terms might be useful. Usually, comparative family law refers to the comparison of (domestic) substantive and procedural family law rules and norms applicable in two or more particular states or jurisdictions. A whole range of relationships belong to family law: the personal status, name law, formalized (marriage, registered or civil partnership) and non-formalized (cohabitation) relationships, rights and duties of spouses and partners, dissolution of these relationships (divorce and dissolution), property distribution, spousal, partner and child maintenance, parental responsibilities, adoption, domestic violence, assisted conception and reproductive assistance, abortion, assisted suicide, incapacitated (elderly) persons etc. All these family relations might extend beyond national boundaries and the answers to questions such as 'which court decides?', 'which law applies?' and 'is a decision of a foreign court or a status obtained abroad to be recognized?' are provided by private international rules, which might be either of an international, European or national origin. Evidently, the comparison of private international law solutions in family matters also falls under comparative family law.[15]

The term 'international family law' has two meanings. It entails both the rules for cross-border family relations,[16] on the one hand, and the body of international and (European) instruments and decisions of supranational courts which regulate family relationships, on the other. Sometimes both 'elements' are covered which is the case in respect of the Hague Conventions on Private International Law, many of which address cross-border family law issues. Hence, the importance of international family law is dramatically increasing. Recently, it has been sensibly demonstrated that within roughly the last two decades, the global migrations of capital and the vast migrations of labour that have accompanied it, have torn families apart, created new families and radically changed the meaning of family.[17] As a

14 Teaching material for American law schools is, for instance, provided by Blair & Weiner, *supra* note 1. See for Europe: W. Pintens & K. Vanwinckelen, *Casebook European Family Law*, 2001. This book contains an introduction into the Europeanization of family law and a compilation of a number of cases, annotated with brief references from the European Court of Human Rights, the European Court of Justice and a series of English, French and German judgments that can be considered as representative for the various tendencies in the field of family law in Europe.

15 See, for example, K. Boele-Woelki & C. González Beilfuss, *Brussels IIbis: Its Impact and Application in the Member States*, 2007.

16 Defined as private international law rules or according to the Anglo-American approach the conflicts of law rules.

17 See B. Stark, 'When Globalization Hits Home: International Family Law Comes of Age', 2006 *Vanderbilt Journal of Transnational Law*, pp. 1551–1603, p. 1555: 'Borders have become more porous, allowing adoptees and mail order brides to join new families and women fleeing

result international family law has evolved and become a subject of its own whereas not that long ago it was merely studied as part of a course on family law or as part of a course on conflicts of law.[18] For some time, globalization has primarily been discussed from an economic and a political viewpoint.[19] This development which envisions – among other things – worldwide growth within one united market rather than in separate geographic and political economies, which leads to a greater connectedness of peoples around the world in terms of communication and transportation, which causes cultural homogenization such that more people share similar cultural experiences,[20] and which increases the migration of individuals and families,[21] is also transforming family law;[22] as Barbara Stark metaphorically has typified, 'hits home'.[23] As a result, each domestic family law problem eventually has an international dimension, for instance the human rights and/or the cross-border perspective.[24] In addition, the internationally shared or agreed rules and norms are based on comparative family law studies.

In this authors' experience international family lawyers commonly are aware of the fact that comparative family law is an essential component of international

domestic violence to escape from old ones. People of different nationalities marry, have children, and divorce, not necessarily in that order. They file suits in their respective home States or third States, demanding support, custody, and property. Otherwise law-abiding parents risk jail when they try to abduct their children from foreign ex-spouses. Local laws alone cannot resolve these matters. Rather, lawyers increasingly draw on a wide range of international treaties, national laws, religious laws, and local traditions.'.

18 See Stark, *supra* note 17, p. 1559: 'Globalization transforms families in three major ways. First, the increase mobility of families, or some family members, reconfigures families. Second, income shifts among different families, and among the individuals within families, alters social relations. Third, globalization transforms culture, and culture changes everything. The transformation of families, in turn, places new demands on international family law.'.

19 See generally R. Michaels & N. Jansen, 'Private Law beyond the State? Europeanization, Globalization, Privatization', 2006 *American Journal of Comparative Law*, pp. 843- 890.

20 See for an attempt to define globalization: M. Birnhack, 'Global Copyright, Local Speech', 2006 *Cardozo Arts and Entertainment Law Journal*, pp. 491–547, pp. 497–498.

21 See also N. Dethloff, 'Familien- und Erbrecht zwischen nationaler Rechtskultur, Vergemeinschaftung und Internationalität, Perspektiven für die Forschung', 2007 *Zeitschrift für Europäisches Privatrecht*, pp. 992–1005.

22 See A. Estin & B. Stark, *Global Issues in Family Law*, 2007, pp. 1–6 who explain how the globalization of the family is transforming family law and why it matters to lawyers as well as to their clients.

23 See B. Stark, *International Family Law: An Introduction*, 2005, p. 1.

24 See J. Masson, 'International Families: Making New Relationships at Home and Away', in R. Probert (ed.), *Family Life and the Law*, 2007, pp. 181–196. She concludes: 'The impact of increased travel and migration on families is being recognized with the development of international laws which regulate arrangement and protect the parties, particularly children. However, these have yet to adapt to the challenges which changing families will bring. Whereas laws and practices in Europe are likely to become more similar, there is little to suggest that liberal family laws will be developed in much of the rest of the world. This gulf will make it more difficult to secure the co-operation necessary to cope with the internationalization of family life.' (p. 196).

family law,[25] whereas those who are more specialized in substantive and procedural family law occasionally might overlook the importance of the private international approach that is chosen in either international or European instruments. The following example may illustrate the interaction between the one and the other.

The child's right to be heard is a fundamental human right that is laid down in the United Nations Convention on the Rights of the Child (UNCRC). It includes the right to be informed, consulted and grants the child the right to express his or her opinion in all matters concerning him or her. In Europe, this generally accepted principle of hearing the child in disputes over parental responsibilities is, however, frequently not applied in practice. If national legislatures want to improve the child's position by introducing a rule that lowers the age of the child at which it must be heard from, for example, 12 to 7, a comparative family law study would reveal, at least in respect of European jurisdictions, that in the majority of jurisdictions more relevance is given to the age and maturity of the child in determining whether he or she should be heard,[26] rather than set age limits. Moreover, in particular EU Member States should take into account that according to Article 23(b) of the Regulation concerning jurisdiction and the recognition and enforcement of judgments in matrimonial matters and matters of parental responsibilities (Brussels II *bis*),[27] a judgment of a Member State court relating to parental responsibility shall not be recognized if it was given, except in case of urgency, without the child having been given an opportunity to be heard, in violation of fundamental principles of procedure of the Member State in which recognition is sought. This latter State might have the rule that the hearing of children is decided on the basis of the child's maturity and the child's ability to assess the issue at hand. Consequently this might be considered as being a fundamental principle which is violated if a specific age limit in the country where the decision is rendered is set.[28]

---

25 The crucial question to what extent and according to what framework the European legislator can and should act in the field of international family law has been addressed by leading authors in: J. Meeusen *et al.* (eds.), *International Family Law for the European Union*, 2007.

26 See K. Boele-Woelki *et al.*, *Principles of European Family Law Regarding Parental Responsibilities*, 2007, Principles 3:6 and 3:37, pp. 49–55 and pp. 239–252.

27 Regulation (EC) no. 2201/2003 of 27 November 2003, *OJ* L 338/1, 23.12.2003.

28 According to, for instance, the decision of the Bezirksgericht Wien, 23 February 2006, (4P 14/06y), a Belgian decision on parental responsibilities was not recognized in Austria because the child of six year old was not given any opportunity to be heard: 'Gerade im vorliegenden Fall, wo die Fragestellung sich nicht auf die Frage Vater oder Mutter beschränkt, sondern die Frage "Aufwachsen in Belgien oder Österreich" im Raum steht, erscheint dem Gericht die Nichtbefragung der Minderjährigen als so schwerwiegend, dass die Anerkennung der belgischen Entscheidung versagt wird. Auch kleine Kinder können aufgrund der unterschiedlichen Sprache der Mitmenschen, des Kindergarten- bzw. Schulsystems und der ganzen Eigenheiten eines Landes (Klima, Essen, etc.) schon gut zwischen Ländern unterscheiden. Da das Kind in einem Obsorgeverfahren eigentlich "Subjekt" und nicht "Objekt" der Entscheidung

More illustrations which demonstrate the interconnectedness between comparative family law and international family law can easily be provided. Those jurisdictions – to provide another example – which currently consider addressing issues of same-sex relationships through legislation might not only compare different same-sex regulatory schemes that since 1989 have been introduced around the world,[29] but initially should answer private international law questions such as, are foreign nationals also allowed to enter into the formalized relationship? Will a relationship established abroad be recognized? In addition, human rights instruments and – where applicable – European instruments, communications and resolutions,[30] should be taken into account.

Since the subject matter of comparative family law has been more or less delineated the following question immediately arises: How to do comparative family research?

2.2. THE METHOD

A huge amount of literature on the methods of comparative law is available.[31] Can something different and substantial be added from a family law perspective? As a starting point it is submitted that generally the same rules, advice and steps apply; the same chances and pitfalls are present, the same problems and challenges are apparent. Irrespective of how we perceive comparative law – as a method or as an autonomous direction in legal research – today it has become a reality; it has acquired a firm standing and won universal application in all legal sciences. In addition, the comparative method does not differ either according to the legal discipline or the branches of law to which it is applied. As a result there is no separate comparative method depending on the nature of the field under research. Hence, a specific comparative family law method which is distinct from the methods in other legal fields does not exist. However, a concise explanation of what the comparative method generally demands might be useful in getting an overall pic-

sein sollte, erscheInt es dem Gericht notwendig, dass das Kind zu dieser bedeutenden Frage gehört wird.'.

29 See K. Boele-Woelki, 'The Legal Recognition of Same-Sex Relationships within the European Union', 2008 *Tulane Law Review* (forthcoming).

30 See, for instance, the European Parliament's resolution which was adopted on 18 January 2006, P6_TA(2006)0018.

31 See R. Michaels, 'The Functional Method of Comparative Law', in M. Reimann & R. Zimmermann (eds.), *Oxford Handbook on Comparative Law*, 2006, pp. 339–382; G. Dannemann, 'Comparative Law: Study of Similarities and Differences', *ibid.*, pp. 383–419 both with further references. See also E. Örücü, 'Methodological Aspects of Comparative Law', 2007 *European Journal of Law Reform*, pp. 29–42.

ture of the elements and aspects of comparative family law. This is provided in the subsequent section.[32]

2.2.1. *Definition, four steps and preliminary questions*

The commonly accepted definition of the comparative research process applies also through as large a field of learning as comparative family law:

> Comparison is a scholarly process in which specific 'objects' of at least two jurisdictions are set against each other in order
> (1) to determine their similarities and differences;
> (2) to explain the causes of the similarities and differences and
> (3) to evaluate the solutions.[33]

This definition necessitates the comparative researcher to distinguish between the following four steps.

The *first step* consists of the finding of similarities and differences. In this stage two methodological rules are to be applied. Firstly, the subject matter must be divided into different aspects or part problems. In comparative law the breaking up of the problem into smaller part problems is known as the Cartesian method.[34] The division of the subject matter into part-problems is usually done by drafting a list of questions.[35] Later, the order of these questions and their respective answers determine the structure of the comparative research report. Secondly, the subject for comparison is to be re-integrated into its own environment by discovering the relationship of the subject with other institutions, norms etc. of the same legal system and by studying and determining the relationship between the subject and its background, whereby legal and non-legal factors might be relevant. If, for instance, assisted reproduction techniques have been

32 According to K. Zweigert & H. Kötz, *Introduction to Comparative Law*, 1998, p. 33, however, a detailed method cannot be laid down in advance; all one can do is to take a method as a hypothesis and to test its usefulness and practicability against the results of actually working therewith. Even today it would be extremely doubtful whether one could come up with a logical and self-contained methodology of comparative law which had any pretensions of being perfect.

33 This is a slightly modified version of the definition provided by D. Kokkini-Iatridou, 'Some Methodological Aspects of Comparative Law', 1986 *Netherlands International Law Review*, p. 155.

34 See R. Descartes, *Discours de la méthode*, 1637, Chapter 2: '(...) de diviser chacune des difficultés que j'examinerois, en autant de parcelles qu'il se pourroit, et qu'il seroit requis pour les mieux résoudre.' ((...) to divide each of the difficulties under examination into as many parts as possible, and as might be necessary for its adequate solution).

35 Examples as to how (extensive) questionnaires in the field of family law can be drafted are provided by the CEFL, see http://www.law.uu.nl/priv/cefl.

chosen as our field of research we have also to take into account the rules governing health insurance, medical law, the law of parentage and human rights.

The *second step* is dedicated to the effort of providing an explanation for the similarities and differences that the analysis of the comparison has revealed. Which factors have been influential? A whole range of historical (including the reception of law), social, economic, political, geographic, religious factors might be of relevance, but also conventions and within the European Union the communitarian instruments. What are, however, exactly the similarities and differences? Should the findings also encompass converging and diverging tendencies which the researcher was able to detect and which also need to be elucidated? The answer to this question is positive; however, neither similarities and convergence, on the one hand, nor differences and divergence, on the other, should be used as synonyms.[36] They have different meanings. Convergence and divergence indicate a certain development of the law. Speaking of convergence means that certain developments are coming together – they are progressing towards a common goal or developing towards a common result – whereas in the case of divergence the developments are moving away from each other – in other words they are becoming more dissimilar. In addition, convergence and divergence are signalling developments in either this or that direction, whereas similarities and differences merely indicate a factual situation. Generally speaking, the term development is neutral; it can have positive or negative effects, although these connotations allegedly contain a value judgement. As a result, developments can, for instance, either be characterised as leading to expansion, improvement and progress or to restriction, control and constraints. Additionally, it should be stressed that even if national solutions differ, which by the way is always the case, convergence may be attained if the different solutions are pointing in the same direction. For instance, the national legislature allows, to a greater or lesser extent, party autonomy in the field of divorce. The spouses may not only agree that their marriage should be dissolved, but they may also agree on the consequences of the divorce. In that respect, the national law may – to provide another example – require more or less public intervention by the competent authority regarding the consequences of the divorce as far as, in particular, children are concerned. Another example is – illustrated also in this special issue – the increasing number of jurisdictions which have recently introduced new institutions for same-sex relationships which, despite their differences (there are no two identical schemes),[37] evidently confirm the modern trend, that in addition to the traditional concept of marriage, other

---

36 According to E. Örücü, *The Engima of Comparative Law*, 2004, p. 34, the cognition of the legal, social and cultural environments in which we live can best be done not just by discovering resemblances between similars or even similarities between differents, but more fundamentally by finding and explaining similarities among differents, and differences and divergences among similars.

37 See the contributions to this special volume.

relationships between two persons should be recognised by the law regardless of their gender.[38]

The *third step* is dedicated to the evaluation of the legal solutions. It is the essential part of the comparative research process. Kokkini-Iatridou convincingly argued that the researcher who has undertaken the comparative study has the duty to provide an evaluative judgment. In her view an assessment of the values inherent in every legal order[39] – though in different degrees – and expressed by the legal institutions, legal solutions, and norms of the various legal orders must take place. The question arises whether it really matters that apparently there is no universally accepted hierarchy of values, and thus no objective standard for the evaluation. Consequently, some degree of subjectivity in the evaluation process cannot be avoided.[40] However, despite the awareness that evaluating solutions and taking positions can never be made without any subjectivity it is at any rate essential to reveal the kind of evaluation criteria which are considered to be decisive for the choices that are made or the solution that is either criticized or favoured.[41] Nonetheless, the researcher should be aware of that the value judgement only has a relative character. It depends on the period in which it was made, the object that was studied and the legal systems that were selected. It permits the comparatist to take part in the legal discourse whereas it enables others to confirm, disapprove or criticize the findings.

The *fourth* and *final step* consists of the research report and its presentation. Here a choice is to be made – no system requests preference – to present the findings either successively[42] or simultaneously.[43] Also a combination of both ways of presenting is possible; however, this should be justified.

Before, however, commencing upon comparative research, important preliminary steps are to be taken. In particular, the following questions are to be answered: What should be compared? Are the selected objects comparable? What is the aim and objective of the comparative study? Which legal systems will be compared? Why are they selected? Are primary sources available? If not, are secondary sources reliable? Who will do the research, a (national) expert of the selected jurisdiction or a legal scholar who has received his/her education in a

---

38 See for other examples, K. Boele-Woelki, 'Building on Convergence and Coping with Divergence in the CEFL Principles on European Family Law', in M. Antokolskaia (ed.), *Convergence and Divergence in European Family Law*, 2007, pp. 253–269.

39 Such as party autonomy, equality of partners, protection of the weaker party, certainty, flexibility, discretion of a competent authority or the free movement of persons (within the EU).

40 See Kokkini-Iatridou, *supra* note 33, p. 191.

41 See Zweigert & Kötz, *supra* note 32, p. 47.

42 According to the successive method an individual report covering all legal aspects for each legal system is provided.

43 According to the simultaneous method a report per legal question containing the answers of the legal systems is provided.

different jurisdiction? How are the language skills of the researcher? How much time is available?

2.2.2. *The comparative family law method: some examples*

The definition used above of what is comparative law raises the question which kind of research is covered. Do studies which deal with foreign law also fall within the ambit of comparative research? In the following an attempt is made to answer these questions by looking more specifically at comparative family law studies which were undertaken in Europe and the United States. Given the fact that this author has already published extensively about European developments[44] more attention is given to the development in the latter jurisdiction. A few examples for the different stages of the comparative family law process will be provided whereby the following distinction is made: the usefulness of national reports (descriptive stage), the determination of similarities and differences (analytical stage), the discovery of the reasons that clarify the developments and that allow the classification of the solutions in those which are either similar or different (explanatory stage) and, finally, the assessment of the legal solutions presented and compared (evaluative stage) which parenthetically belongs to the most exciting steps in the comparative research process. Whereas in Europe family law experts decidedly contribute to the comparative methods debate, similar discussions seemingly do not take place in the United States. It should, therefore, be examined why this is the case.

Europe

Noticeably, the discussions concerning the method to be applied when comparing family law rules, solutions and systems surfaced when the CEFL commenced its activities in 2001.[45] In particular its founders had to establish a clear and efficient method as to how the CEFL could achieve its results which consist of the drafting of Principles of European Family Law.[46] These Principles are aimed at contributing to the process of harmonizing family law in Europe and they may be used as a framework or model for legislatures and courts alike. CEFLs method

44 See K. Boele-Woelki, 'Comparative Research-based Drafting of Principles of European Family Law', in M. Faure *et al.* (eds.), *Towards a European Ius Commune in Legal Education and Research*, 2002, pp. 171–189 and K. Boele-Woelki, 'The Working Method of the Commission on European Family Law', in K. Boele-Woelki (ed.), *Common Core and Better Law in European Family Law*, 2005, pp. 15–38.

45 See W. Pintens, 'Europeanisation of Family Law', in K. Boele-Woelki (ed.), *Perspectives for the Unification and Harmonisation of Family Law in Europe*, 2003, pp. 3–33.

46 See K. Boele-Woelki *et al.*, *Principles of European Family Law Regarding Divorce and Maintenance Between Former Spouses*, 2004 and Boele-Woelki *et al.*, *supra* note 26.

has been discussed extensively, not only by those who question its legitimation.[47] In this author's opinion the CEFL apparently does not need any legitimation, because the comparative research is carried out by legal scholars who only have to meet scientific standards, in particular accuracy. In this respect the family and comparative legal scholars involved in the CEFL have fulfilled the requirements. Apart from this difference in perception, however, the comparative family law method discourse is blooming. In particular in respect of the solutions to be favoured and finally adopted, sparking ideas and arguments[48] have been proffered. Admittedly, the evaluation depends on the aims and objectives of the comparative research and consequently the selected criteria, guidelines and perspectives may differ. The CEFL, for example, where to date 22 European jurisdictions are represented, opted for both the common core method and the better law approach when evaluating and finally drafting its principles.

United States

In searching for specific ideas, trends or guidelines for the method to be applied in comparative family law little can be found in the American legal literature while from the outset American lawyers are comparatists. By drawing upon examples and opinions of other states American lawyers always compare. Moreover, by definition family law requires a comparative exercise, since this field of law has developed separately in each state by its own local courts and local legislature: 'As a result, American family laws vary significantly in both substance and procedure from one state to another.'[49] Uniform

---

47 See D. Bradley, 'Family Law', in J. Smits (ed.), *Elgar Encyclopedia of Comparative Law*, 2006, pp. 259–272; M.-Th. Meulders-Klein, 'Towards a Uniform European Family Law? A Political Approach', in M. Antokolskaia (ed.), *Convergence and Divergence of Family Law in Europe*, 2007, pp. 271–281.

48 See in general I. Schwenzer, 'Methodological Aspects of Harmonisation of Family Law', *supra* note 45, pp. 143–158 and in particular M. Antokolskaia, 'The "Better Law" Approach and the Harmonisation of Family Law', *ibid.*, pp. 159–182; also published in 2005 *European Journal of Law Reform*, pp. 159–179.

49 See L. Wardle & L. Nolan, 'United States of America' (latest update 1998), in W. Pintens (ed.), *International Encyclopedia of Laws*, Vol. 4, Family and Succession Law, no. 11, p. 37: 'Of course, no state has developed its family law entirely independently. However, there are many homogenizing cultural influences in the United States that create a tendency of similarity, if not harmony and consistency. For example, persuasive sister-state judicial opinions, new legislation enacted in other states that proves to be effective or popular, proposals for uniform legislation, programs of federal government providing support and incentives for states to take particular policy position, federal constitutional standards, the national news and entertainment media, and special interests that operate nationally have produced many multi-state and national trends in the family laws of the various states. Due to the homogenizing influences, students and teachers of family law in the United States often – look for and find – trends, and general principles that are shared and prevailing rules and practices (...)'.

legislation is only available in a few areas which, however, must be enacted at state level.[50]

It is a continuing challenge to be informed and be updated about the family law systems of the 50 states and federal territories. The comparisons of these systems belong to the daily practice of those who teach and do research in family law in the United States. Extremely helpful information is provided by the special volumes of the Family Law Quarterly which annually contain a Review of the Year in Family Law consisting of analytical reports, case digests and charts.[51]

In the following, three publications are analyzed with the aim to discover the answer to the question as to how American family law experts reflect on and perceive the methodological aspects of comparative family law. These publications caught this author's interest and were selected because they represent different aims and objectives: an individual study of a legal scholar, a teamwork project and materials for students to study comparative family law.

1) One of the most eminent and reflective American comparative family law scholars is Mary Ann Glendon. In her famous book on *The Transformation of Family Law: State and Family in the United States and Western Europe*,[52] she reminds us that the study of foreign experiences can also be a fertile source of inspiration and ideas. Even when it would not immediately move the comparatist into a new stage of thinking, it nearly always affords a deeper understanding of and a more balanced perspective on one's own law.[53] Specific attention to the

50 Adoption of Uniform Acts: Uniform Child Custody Jurisdiction and Enforcement Act (47 states); Uniform Marriage and Divorce Act (8 states); Uniform Premarital Agreement Act (26 states); Uniform Marital Property Act (1 state); Uniform Parentage Act 2000/2002 (7 states); (the 1973 version: 14 states); Uniform Interstate Enforcement of Domestic Violence Protection Orders and the 2001 amendments to the Uniform Interstate Family Support Act (17 jurisdictions); Uniform Mediation Act (9 states). In July 2006, the National Conference of Commissioners on Uniform State Laws adopted two new acts in the family law area: the Uniform Child Abduction Prevention Act and the Uniform Representation of Children in Abuse, Neglect and Custody Proceedings Act. See L. Elrod & R. Spector, 'A Review of the Year in Family Law: ERISA, Jurisdiction, and Third-Party Cases Multiply', 2007 *Family Law Quarterly*, pp. 545–589, pp. 552–553.

51 For a number of years these overviews have been coordinated and compiled by L. Elrod and R. Spector. See http://www.abanet.org/family/flq/archives.html. There was an annual review of adoption law for the first 5 years that the *Family Law Quarterly* was published, starting in 1967. There are reviews of specific areas of family law for a 10 year period, but no real overview like the current overviews. The first 'Law in the 50' was published in the *Family Law Quarterly* in 1977 as 'Divorce Law in the 50 States'. The next one was published in 1979 and then in 1982–83 it became 'Family Law in the 50 States'.

52 See M. Glendon, *The Transformation of Family Law: State and Family in the United States and Western Europe*, 1989. The predecessor of this book is: *State, Law and Family*, 1977.

53 *Ibid.*, p. 4. See also M. Glendon, 'Irish Family Law in Comparative Perspective: Can There be Comparative Family Law?', 1987 *Dublin University Law Review*, pp. 1–20 in which she compared Ireland (which at that time did not allow spouses to obtain a divorce and also forbid abortion) with 20 other Western countries: 'I believe comparative analysis *can* contribute to

method to be applied or the method that she has used in analyzing, synthesizing and finally presenting her comparative findings are not elaborated. Surprisingly, however, in her review of Glendon's book Inga Markovits assessed the author's approach from a truly methodological perspective.[54] In her brilliantly drafted evaluation two different methods suggest themselves:

> 'You can *either* zoom in on the essential patterns you discover, outline the common concerns or convictions running like colored threads through the entire fabric of family law, and use concrete examples only to illustrate overall themes. *Or*, you can describe the developments in different areas of family law, highlight in each area those details which manifest common strands of thinking, and in the end pull these strands together to arrive at a meaningful picture. The *first approach* will require you to articulate your themes at the outset, will allow you to pick and choose your supportive evidence, will encourage theoretical speculation, and thus is likely to produce forceful and consistent results. But it will also tempt you to overstate your case, will make it easier to disregard conflicting evidence, will hide from your readers how you discovered your themes in the first place, and thus will make criticism and disagreement more difficult. The *second approach* will require extensive description, obliging you to spend much time on matters only tangentially related to your search for common patterns of development, will limit occasions for analytical speculation, and will produce more conflicting results. But it will also guard against theoretical overstatements, will put your cards on the table, and will educate readers sufficiently about the field to allow them to make up their own minds.' (emphasis added KBW)

Markovits' characterization of the *first approach* is sound. It is a dangerous endeavour to pick and choose solutions, examples and arguments at random and present them without little structure, but more importantly merely with the intention to promote ideological or political ideas.[55] Furthermore it is indeed difficult to enter into a discussion about the author's findings, if the study does not indicate the aim of the comparison, if it does not systematically present differences and similarities, if explanations for these are not provided and if the criteria which determine the evaluation are not specified.

Glendon applied the *second approach* which resulted in an excellent analysis and synthesis of mainly four family law systems: England & Wales, France, West Germany and the United States. She already noticed the remarkable change in family life that has taken place in the United States and in Europe in the last three or four decades. Hardly any other field of law has experienced such profound and

current Irish discussions (...) Nevertheless, the types of regulation of divorce and abortion needed, desired, or tolerated by larger, more heterogeneous, urbanized and affluent societies may be highly inappropriate for Ireland.'.

54 See I. Markovits, 'Family Traits', 1990 *Michigan Law Review*, pp. 1734–1758, p. 1735.

55 See L. Wardle, 'Global Perspective on Procreation and Parentage by Assisted Reproduction', 2006 *Capital University Law Review*, pp. 413–464.

deep social and demographic changes as family law in this short period of time: an explosion in the divorce rates and extramarital cohabitation and the resulting increase in the number of children born out of wedlock; women joining the paid work force *en masse*, influencing, among other things, parental roles and property relations among partners; and – more recently – the growing social acceptance of same-sex relationships and new techniques of artificial insemination are just a few important features of this development. We are in the middle of a 'silent revolution' in family life, and while these transformations take place, we experience a vast cross-border movement of people.[56] For those who are seeking information about the current state of family law in Europe and the United States it is absolutely advisable to consult more recent publications, but Glendon succeeded in portraying the most striking lines of West European and American family law as they were apparent in the late eighties in a way that could perfectly function as a model for other researchers.

2) An American Restatement on Family Law does not exist; instead in 2000, Principles of the Law on Family Dissolution were finalized under the auspices of the American Law Institute (ALI).[57] This enormous project which started in the early nineties is aimed at harmonizing certain aspects of family law in the United States[58] because the wide discretionary power in family disputes has been perceived as causing uncertainty and inequality. According to ALI Chief Reporter Ira Mark Ellman,[59] 'alimony, custody, and even property allocation are effectively governed in most states by family law's version of Rule 1: decide as you see fit. The legislatures and appellate courts leave basic policy choices up to the trial judge

56 See K. Boele-Woelki & T. Sverdrup, 'Preface', in: K. Boele-Woelki & T. Sverdrup (eds.), *European Challenges in Contemporary Family Law*, 2008, pp. v-vi.

57 American Law Institute (ALI), *Principles of the Law on Family Dissolution: Analysis and Recommendations, as Adopted and Promulgated by the American Law Institute on May 16, 2000*, 2002. According to its drafters 'the work is described as "Principles" rather than "Restatement" because 'Principles' is the better designation for a project that carefully explores and clarifies the fundamental assumptions – about the best interests of children, fairness to divorcing wives and husbands, and the legitimate economic claims of unmarried partners – upon which the legal rules must rest. Many of these Principles, nevertheless, restate and clarify present law, while others recommend directions for implementation by courts, legislatures, and other appropriate decision makers. The result is a coherent legal framework, sensitive to both the traditional value systems within which most families are formed and the nontraditional realities and expectations of other families, a framework the earlier drafts of which have already begun to influence both courts and legislatures.' Online available via Lexis (FAMDIS file within the 2NDARY and FAMILY libraries) and via Westlaw in the ALI-FAMDISS database.

58 See R. Fretwell Wilson, 'The Harmonization of Family Law in the United States', in Boele-Woelki & Sverdrup (eds.), *supra* note 56, pp. 27–49, p. 34.

59 See I. Ellman, 'Inventing Family Law', 1999 *U.C. Davis Law Review*, pp. 855–886, pp. 870–871. Interestingly he mentions child support rules which in his view only exist 'because they were pushed on the states by Washington lawmakers concerned primarily with their potential value in reducing the federal contribution to welfare payments' (p. 856).

deciding each case. Most people think there is something unfair about having the governing legal principles change from judge to judge and from case to case.'

He concluded about a decade ago that rules of largely limitless discretion are common in family law, and that their prevalence is not a good thing, whereas proponents of the discretionary system urged the importance of providing customized justice in each case. Given their extensive experience with family law, the drafters of the ALI Principles had no illusions about the difficulty of their task and they admitted that indeed it would be rather surprising if they really would have got it right. Their more modest hope was that they might nudge the law in a more fruitful direction.[60] Apparently, all states' family laws have been taken into account. They were thoroughly analyzed, scrutinized, compared and classified. The black letter text of each principle is followed by comments, illustrations of cases and reporter's notes which contain references to state legislation, literature and cases. A methodological motivation of or an explanatory introduction into the working method, however, is not provided. When the Principles were finalized in 2000 and published in 2002 the ALI clarified that no state's law is precisely that of the Principles,[61] instead they 'can be found in the current law of some states, as well as in that of other countries with a common-law tradition. In seeking to accommodate both important traditional values and the reality of modern conditions, the Institute has borrowed profitably from both domestic and foreign experience.'[62] Indeed sporadically references are made to the laws of Australia, Canada, England and New Zealand. The ALI Principles of the Law of Family Dissolution contain recommendations as to how the law in this field could be harmonized. They have been praised because of their breadth, depth, and novelty. Six years after their publication little has happened at the harmonization front though. To date, they have not been adopted in any state; however judges frequently rely on the Principles for guidance whereby ALIs prestige might also play a major role. As Robin Fretwell Wilson expresses: 'They have begun to filter into American law.'[63] It may very well be that the Principles will find their way more rapidly into case law but will not be enacted into statutory law. Since the subject matter of the Principles is considered to be of enormous significance – they address divorce, custody, child and spousal support, property division, agreements and domestic partnerships – leading intellectuals in family law recently meticulously examined their content.[64] The overall conclusion based on the

60 *Ibid.*, p. 872.
61 See on the nature of the Principles the Chief Reporters Foreword, *supra* note 57.
62 Press release dated May 15, 2002; see www.ali.org/ali/pr051502.htm.
63 See the reference provided in the following footnote.
64 See R. Fretwell Wilson (ed.), *Reconceiving the Family, Critique on the American Law Institute's Principles of the Law of Family Dissolution*, 2006. See the Editor's Introduction, pp. 2–3. A similar study has been undertaken in respect of the CEFL Principles regarding Divorce and Maintenance between Former Spouses by E. Örücü & J. Mair (eds.), *Juxtaposing Legal Systems*

majority of the contributions is a critical one; many characterize the ALI Principles as a failed effort of law reform.[65]

3) In their magnificent and voluminous compilation of cases, materials and problems in comparative and international family law entitled *Family Law in the World Community*[66] Marianne Blair and Merle Weiner specifically address the question: What is Comparative Family Law? They do not provide a specific answer, but illustrate the needs of comparative family law by framing the problem with the famous *Marckx* v. *Belgium* case which was decided by the European Court of Human Rights in 1979. Additionally, they refer to John C. Reitz's article on *How to Do Comparative Law*[67] which offers nine principles about comparative law scholarship and the closely allied field of foreign law.[68] These principles make no

---

and the Principles of European Family Law on Divorce and Maintenance, 2007. They empirically tested whether they are indeed acceptable and/or regarded as an improvement on existing national laws.

65 See *e.g.* D. Westfall, 'Unprincipled Family Dissolution: The ALI's Recommendations for Division of Property', in: Fretwell Wilson, *supra* note 64, pp. 176–194, p. 193.

66 See Blair & Weiner, *supra* note 1. The book consists of more than 1200 pages.

67 See J. Reitz, 'How to Do Comparative Law', 1998 *American Journal of Comparative Law*, pp. 617–635.

68 These principles are:

1. Comparative law involves drawing explicit comparisons, and most non-comparative foreign law writing could be strengthened by being made explicitly comparative.
2. The comparative method consists in focusing careful attention on the similarities and differences among the legal systems being compared, but in assessing the significance of differences the comparatist needs to take account of the possibility of functional equivalence.
3. The process of comparison is particularly suited to lead to conclusions about (a) distinctive characteristics of each individual legal systems and/or (b) commonalities concerning how law deals with the particular subject under study.
4. One of the benefits of comparative analysis is its tendency to push the analysis to broader levels of abstraction through its investigation into functional equivalence.
5. The comparative method has the potential to lead to even more interesting analysis by inviting the comparatist to give reasons for the similarities and differences among legal systems or to analyze their significance for the cultures under study.
6. In establishing what the law is in each jurisdiction under study, comparative law (and, for that matter, studies of foreign law, as well) should (a) be concerned to describe the normal conceptual world of the lawyers, (b) take into consideration all the sources upon which a lawyer in that legal system might base her opinion as to what the law is, and © take into consideration the gap between the law on the books and the law in action, as well as (d) important gaps in available knowledge about either the law on the books or the law in action.
7. Comparative and foreign law scholarship both require strong linguistic skills and maybe even the skills of anthropological field study in order to collect information about foreign legal systems at first hand, but it is also reasonable for the comparative scholar without the necessary linguistic skills or in-country experience to rely on secondary literature in languages the comparatist can read, subject to the usual caution about using secondary literature.
8. Comparative law scholarship should be organized in a way that emphasizes explicit comparison.
9. Comparative studies should be undertaken in a spirit of respect for the other.

distinction between comparative studies and the study of foreign law, they address without any logical order different stages which the comparatist experiences, and they necessitate neither an attempt to explain differences and similarities, nor an evaluation of the legal solutions studied. The outsider who might criticize other solutions is, however, encouraged to show respect and is reminded of being careful.[69]

At any rate, in Blair and Weiner's Casebook guidance is provided to those who intentionally study international family law and family systems of different jurisdictions, whereby insight is provided into predominately contrasting solutions which are available in different parts of the world regarding many family law issues. The authors distinguish numerous potential benefits to engaging in comparative legal analysis, such as fostering open mindedness, providing ideas for improvement of one's own law, assisting in crafting international legal solutions, advising about foreign family law in case of cross-border relationships and advocating a specific solution.[70] Distinctively they state that 'comparative law has not been used much to harmonize family law'[71] nor 'do (they) expect students to become proficient in harmonizing the law, assuming such harmonization is a beneficial process in the family law area.'[72] From a European point of view mainly the first statement is mistaken in view of the many international instruments of international and European organizations that have unified and harmonized certain fields of family law – many of them have been prepared by comparative studies – and particularly in view of the harmonization projects of family and succession law in Scandinavia.[73] In addition, the current activities of the Commission on European Family Law, which results are aimed at contributing to either spontaneous or deliberate harmonization of family law, illustrate the opposite.

Although the three examples derived from the American family law literature totally differ from each other as regards their aims and objectives, they exemplify that relatively little reflection is given to the method to be applied in comparative family law. This can be explained by the fact that the American family lawyer is

69 From a methodological point of view it might be interesting to compare Reitz's principles with the earlier provided definition, which also requires that during the comparative research process different steps are to be taken.

70 See Blair & Weiner, *supra* note 1.

71 *Ibid.* They explicitly refer to two contributions delivered at the Centennial World Congress on Comparative Law which took place in 2000 in New Orleans: D.S. Clark, 'Nothing New in 2000? Comparative Law in 1900 and Today', 2001 *Tulane Law Review*, pp. 871–909 and X. Blanc-Jouvan, 'Closing Remarks', 2001 *Tulane Law Review*, pp. 1235–1244.

72 See Blair & Weiner, *supra* note 1, p. 6.

73 See P. Lødrup, 'The Reharmonisation of Nordic Family Law', in Boele-Woelki & Sverdrup (eds.), *supra* note 56, pp. 17–26; I. Lund-Andersen, 'Approximation of Nordic Family Law within the Framework of Nordic Cooperation', in Antokolskaia (ed.), *supra* note 38, pp. 51–61; J. Scherpe, 'The Nordic Countries in the Vanguard of European Family Law', in Scandinavian Studies in Law Volume 50, *What is Scandinavian Law? – Social Private Law*, 2007, pp. 265–287.

educated in developing a comparative instinct. This may sound contradictory since comparing is one way of finding the law. A justification or explanation as how to do it is not deemed to be necessary; on the contrary it is the common approach to be applied. The exploration of non-American jurisdictions is more or less done in the same spirit. Seemingly, no distinction is made between interstate and out-of-state comparisons. In respect of the latter, however, comparisons with jurisdictions with a common-law background are preferred, at least in the harmonization-through-principles-project of the ALI. In contrast, the Casebook provides mainly opposing and contrasting solutions from jurisdictions where cases and writings of legal scholars are available in the English language.

2.3. THE USEFULNESS OF NATIONAL REPORTS

Being concerned with comparative law and undertaking research into foreign law is not synonymous. Comparative research is not carried out in the case where this author, for instance, who received her legal education in Germany, writes about Dutch law in the English language even if the trouble is made to try and understand the readers' way of thinking and imagine the breadth of their knowledge.[74] No matter how systematically it is executed, research cannot be described as being 'comparative research' if it does not compare 'objects' of at least two different jurisdictions. Logically, it cannot provide an 'explanation' of similarities and differences and an evaluation of different solutions is not possible. Presenting one's own (family) law in a different language is, however, often done in the form of national reports.[75] These contributions, which fall under the category of *Auslandsrechtskunde* are, however, extremely valuable in order to gain vital information about foreign (family) law solutions. Many national reports about family law are available. They are repeatedly drafted under the auspices of, for instance, the International Academy of Comparative Law,[76] the International Society of Family Law,[77] the Commission on European Family Law[78] and the bi-annual conferences

74 See Kokkini-Iatridou, *supra* note 33, p. 157.

75 All contributions belonging to this special issue fall under this category except Antokolskaia's article and this introductory contribution.

76 See, for instance, the compilation of the latest national reports on the family law topic to the 17th Congress of Comparative Law by the general rapporteur I. Schwenzer, *Tensions between Legal, Biological and Social Conceptions of Parentage*, 2007.

77 The books also contain an annual review of International Family Law: Conventions of the UN, Council of Europe, Hague Conference on Private International Law, European Union and case law of the European Court of Human Rights. More information about ISFLs publications is available at www.law2.byu.edu/isfl/publications.php.

78 22 national reports on divorce, maintenance between former spouses and parental responsibilities are available at: www.law.uu.nl/priv/cefl.

in Regensburg on European Family Law.[79] These national reports are written for those who, in principle, are not familiar with a particular jurisdiction. Consequently, elliptical presentations are to be avoided. Sometimes, supplementary explanations concerning, for instance, typical institutions or recent phenomena[80] must be included in order to avoid cryptically drafted exposés which can only be understood by lawyers from the same jurisdiction. In short, compiling a national report calls for a great deal of sensitivity towards the addressee who generally has a different legal background. It is to be regretted that in the future at least in The Netherlands, national reports on Dutch law written in another language will not be valued anymore as academic publications,[81] whereas they require extensive research and a good presentation. In particular, these kinds of publications contribute to the legal market of solutions which provides the tool for any further development of the law at the national, European and international level. For projects which are aimed at harmonizing or unifying the law, national reports constitute the building blocks.

Another interesting example which demonstrates the usefulness of national reports has been carried out by young legal scholars. It concerns the research project of 37 students of Yale University, New Haven. Between July 2004 and December 2005 they compiled information and resources on how children's voices are heard in child protective proceedings in the 194 signatories to the United Nations Convention on the Rights of a Child and in the United States.[82] Their study focused on how different countries' practices relate to Article 12 of the UNCRC, which guarantees children's right to express views freely in all matters concerning them, and particularly to be heard in all judicial and administrative proceedings that concern them. To that end they provided not only national reports for each jurisdiction, but also comparative charts.[83]

---

79 See D. Schwab & D. Henrich (eds.), *Entwicklungen des europäischen Kindschaftsrechts*, 1994; *Der Schutz der Familienwohnung in europäischen Rechtsordnungen*, 1995; *Familiäre Solidarität- die Begründung und die Grenzen der Unterhaltspflicht unter Verwandten im europäischen Vergleich*, 1997; *Eheliche Gemeinschaft, Partnerschaft und Vermögen im europäischen Vergleich*, 1999; *Familienerbrecht und Testierfreiheit im europäischen Vergleich*, 2001; S. Hofer *et al.* (eds.) *Scheidung und nachehelicher Unterhalt im europäischen Vergleich*, 2003; *From Status to Contract? Die Bedeutung des Vertrages im europäischen Vergleich*, 2005; A. Spickhoff *et al.* (eds.), *Streit um die Abstammung⊠ein europäischer Vergleich*, 2007. All volumes are published by Gieseking Verlag.

80 For examples about the French *prestation compensatoire* and the Dutch *lightning divorce*, see Boele-Woelki, *supra* note 44, p. 24.

81 In contrast to specialist publications which are considered to be less important. See R. van Gestel *et al.*, 'Rechtswetenschappelijke artikelen', 2007 *Nederlands Juristenblad*, pp. 1448–1461. To the present author's opinion national reports should be assessed on a case-by-case basis, as either being specialist or academic publications.

82 The project includes in total 250 different jurisdictions.

83 See Representing Children Worldwide, http://www.law.yale.edu/rcw. See also about 'The Child's Voice in Legal Proceedings', A. Griffith, *Working for Justice: Comparative Reflections*

3. CURRENT DEBATES IN FAMILY LAW AROUND THE GLOBE

As indicated above (§2.1) family law covers many subjects. For this special issue a selection has been made of three topics that have currently provoked passionate discussion. Legislative measures are taken, judicial decisions vary also within a jurisdiction, and arguments in legal literature are exchanged. By way of introduction family law issues of today are put into a historical and a more methodological perspective. The latter is provided in this contribution.

3.1. THE ISSUES OF TODAY IN PERSPECTIVE

The second contribution of this special issue addresses the 'cultural constraints argument' which according to a few legal scholars prevents both spontaneous and deliberate harmonization of family law. Is family law indeed embedded in unique national (legal) culture? What lessons can be learnt from the past? Due to her pioneering study on the harmonization of family law in Europe in which she takes a historical approach dating back approximately 200 years,[84] Masha Antokolskaia[85] has been the predestinated author for this contribution. She concludes that today the assumption that family laws are embedded in unique and unchangeable national cultures cannot be maintained. History illustrates that in respect of family law, unique national cultures do not exist, but that it is possible to distinguish between a pan-European conservative and a pan-European progressive culture in which political factors determine the evolution of family law. As a result the 'cultural constraints argument' is beyond redemption. National family laws are determined by fluid political factors, rather than relatively consistent cultural factors. The question arises whether this conclusion characterizing the family law systems in Europe,[86] also applies to, for instance, the great variety of family law systems in the United States where self-determination and individual freedom are highly valued features of the American culture. These ideals are frequently expressed by politicians and applied by State Governments and are also reflected

on Family Law, Inaugural Lecture University of Edinburgh, 30 January 2007, http://www.law.ed.ac.uk/file_download/series/7_inaugurallectureofprofessorannegriffiths.pdf.

84 See M. Antokolskaia, *Harmonisation of Family Law in Europe – A Historical Perspective*, 2006.

85 See M. Antokolskaia, 'Family law and national culture – Arguing against the cultural constraints argument', 2008 *Utrecht Law Review*, no.2, pp. 25–34.

86 See also S. Cretney, 'Breaking the Shackles of Culture and Religion in the Field of Divorce?', in Boele-Woelki (ed.), *supra* note 44, pp. 3–14: '(...) the 'shackles' restricting our freedom to divorce law and its reform are no longer primarily those of religion and culture; they are those of psychology of individuals and groups.' (p. 14).

in family law. Looking at family law in the United States reveals a very colourful picture which to a certain extent is dependent on and determined by either progressive or conservative political forces.[87] David Bradley in his review of the book *Cross Currents* – edited by American and English family experts[88] –, which contains the tentative prediction that English family law may follow American developments, wonders why developed countries – not least those with common legal traditions – vary in their response to social change when comparing family law. He too finally reaches the conclusion that the answer lies in the differences in political culture and objectives that have determined the response to issues such as transsexualism, legal recognition of same-sex couples, marriage formalities and divorce law.[89]

The following three sections address the selected issues which belong to today's family law discourse around the globe. Most of them fall under the category national report whereas others – like Christina Jeppesen de Boer's,[90] Ian and Scott Curry-Sumner's[91] and Richard Blauwhoff's[92] contributions – took more than one jurisdiction into account. Based upon the provided information deriving from various jurisdictions the comparison can take place.

3.2. (COMPULSORY) ARRANGEMENTS REGARDING CHILDREN

Whereas in predominately Western family law systems in the case of a divorce or a separation up until about twenty years ago parental responsibilities were usually only granted to one of the parents, the conviction has steadily gained ground that neither divorce nor a separation between the parents should affect the joint

87 See also Wardle & Nolan, *supra* note 49, p. 38: 'Notwithstanding many homogenizing influences the various family laws of the American states remain remarkably diverse in policy and practice. Family law is a prime example of the 'different laboratories' idea of how federalism usually generates solutions to social problems much more quickly, how it preserves valuable cultural pluralism much more effectively and how it fosters individual liberty much more than do centralized forms of governments.'.

88 See S. Katz *et al.* (eds.), *Cross Currents: Family Law and Policy in the United States and England*, 2000.

89 See D. Bradley, 'Comparative Law, Family Law and Common Law', 2003 *Oxford Journal of Legal Studies*, pp. 127–146, pp. 145–146.

90 C. Jeppesen de Boer, 'Parental relocation – Free movement rights and joint parenting', 2008 *Utrecht law Review*, no. 2, pp. 73–82.

91 See I. Curry-Sumner & S. Curry-Sumner, 'Is the union civil? – Same-sex marriages, civil unions, domestic partnerships and reciprocal benefits in the USA', 2008 *Utrecht Law Review*, no. 2, pp. 236–278.

92 See R. Blauwhoff, 'Tracing down the historical development of the legal concept of the right to know one's origins – Has "to know or not to know" ever been the legal question?', 2008 *Utrecht Law Review*, no. 2, pp. 99–116.

exercise of parental responsibilities. Hence joint parental responsibilities on the part of the spouses automatically continue after divorce or separation.[93] Consequently, the exercise of parental responsibilities as such is not affected by the fact that the marriage or other formal relationship of the holders of parental responsibilities has been dissolved or annulled or that they have legally or factually separated. When the parents do not live together they have to jointly decide on the residence of the child. Increasingly the child resides with both parents on an alternate basis. Joint parental responsibilities, now common, require that the parents communicate and make important decisions concerning their children together. One of the possible consequences following an alternating residence of the child is the issue of relocation which limits the geographic mobility of residential parents.[94] The overall questions are: Which factors should be relevant in order to evaluate whether an alternating residence is in the best interest of the child and whether relocation should be permitted? Answers to these pressing problems are provided by Anna Singer[95] for Sweden, Frédérique Granet[96] for France,[97] Theresa Glennon[98] for the United States of America and Christina Jeppesen de Boer for Denmark and The Netherlands.[99] A variety of solutions and results have been presented and seemingly uncertainty and unpredictability play centre stage when these highly sensitive kinds of disputes are to be decided. In this context the Principles regarding Parental Responsibilities of the CEFL may be used as a frame of reference. They also address both alternating residence and relocation.[100] CEFLs solutions are innovative due to the fact that legislation is exceptional and judicial decisions differ to a great extent.[101] Admittedly, only by empirical testing in a

93 See also C. Jeppesen de Boer, *Joint Parental Authority, A Comparative Legal Study on the Continuation of Joint Parental Authority after Divorce and the Breakup of a Relationship in Dutch and Danish Law and the CEFL Principles*, 2008.

94 See Th. Glennon, 'Mobility and the Post-Divorce Family: Resolution of Relocation disputes in the U.S', in Boele-Woelki (ed.), *supra* note 44, pp. 193–215.

95 See A. Singer, 'Active parenting or Solomon's justice? – Alternating residence in Sweden for children with separated parents', 2008 *Utrecht Law Review*, no. 2, pp. 35–47.

96 See F. Granet, 'Alternating residence and relocation – A view from France', 2008 *Utrecht Law Review*, no. 2, pp. 48–54.

97 See also L. Talarico, 'The *Coparentalité* in French Law', in Boele-Woelki (ed.), *supra* note 44, pp. 217–223.

98 See Th. Glennon, 'Divided parents, shared children – Conflicting approaches to relocation disputes in the USA', 2008 *Utrecht Law Review*, no. 2, pp. 55–72.

99 Legal and sociological research under the supervision of this author and professor Tanja van der Lippe (Sociology, Utrecht University) which also involves Dutch law has been selected as one of the twenty-three research projects that from 2008 onwards will be undertaken within the framework of Utrecht's multidisciplinary research program 'Family Matters'. Its predecessor entitled 'Changing patterns of interdependence and solidarity in family relations' started in 2003.

100 See Boele-Woelki *et al.*, *supra* note 26, Principles 3:20 and 3:21.

101 See K. Boele-Woelki, 'The CEFL Principles Regarding Parental Responsibilities: Predominance of the Common Core', in Boele-Woelki & Sverdrup (eds.), *supra* note 56, pp. 63–91.

number of legal systems, however, it can be demonstrated whether the Principles are acceptable and/or an improvement on existing laws.

3.3. REGISTRATION SCHEMES FOR SAME-SEX COUPLES: NEW JURISDICTIONS

For more than a decade the legal recognition of same-sex relationships has gained considerable attention around the globe.[102] The substantive discussion about whether to permit same-sex couples to formalize their relationship is one of the most contested issues which becomes even more disputed and complicated in the case of cross-border situations due to the fact that the private international law approaches in respect of same-sex relationships differ to a large extent.[103] The contributions of this part of the volume belong to the so-called 'new jurisdictions'.[104] They recently introduced a new institution and/or opened marriage for same-sex couples.[105] Pierre de Vos[106] and Orsolya Szeibert-Erdős[107] inform us about the choices and experiences of the South African and Hungarian legislature respectively. In contrast to these two jurisdictions the American landscape analyzed by Ian and Scott Curry-Sumner[108] looks totally different. Here we are confronted with a variety of approaches and regulations such as the federal Defense of Marriage Act (DOMA) of 1996, the mini-DOMAs of 41 states, different same-sex relationship schemes in the form of marriage (only a few) or civil unions and domestic partnerships acts which are available in a few states. They all differ considerably, although uniform patterns are perhaps discernible. Most importantly

102 See I. Curry-Sumner, *All's Well that Ends Registered? The Substantive and Private International Law Aspects of Non-marital Registered Relationships in Europe. A Comparison of the Laws of Belgium, France, The Netherlands, Switzerland and the United Kingdom*, 2005 and I. Curry-Sumner, 'European Recognition of Same-Sex Relationships: We Need Action Now!', 2008 *International Family Law* (forthcoming).

103 See Boele-Woelki, *supra* note 29 and I. Schwenzer, 'Convergence and Divergence in the Law of Same-sex Partnerships' in Antokolskaia (ed.), *supra* note 38, pp. 145–157.

104 In contrast the following jurisdictions can be indicated as 'old jurisdictions': Andorra, two provinces of Argentina (Buenos Aires City and Río Negro), one state in Australia (Tasmania), Belgium, one region in Brazil (Rio Grande do Sol), Canada, Czech Republic, Denmark, Finland, France, Germany, Iceland, Luxemburg, The Netherlands, New Zealand, Norway, Slovenia, Spain, Sweden, Switzerland and the United Kingdom. In these jurisdictions same-sex couples are permitted to either conclude a marriage and/or a registered partnership. Regarding the latter, however, the rights and obligations of the partners differ.

105 Only Uruguay where since January 2008 same-sex partners can also register their partnership is not represented.

106 See P. De Vos, 'A judicial revolution? – The court-led achievement of same-sex marriage in South Africa', 2008 *Utrecht Law Review*, no. 2, pp. 162–174.

107 See O. Szeibert- Erdős, 'Same-sex partners in Hungary – Cohabitation and registered partnership', 2008 *Utrecht Law Review*, no. 2, pp. 212–221.

108 See Curry-Sumner & Curry-Sumner, *supra* note 91.

the officials and courts of the different states do not know whether and how they should recognize same-sex relationships that have been concluded out-of-state not to speak of those established in a foreign jurisdiction. The courts in New York recently decided that same-sex marriages concluded in Canada are to be recognized in the state of New York in the absence of legislation to the contrary;[109] in other words, no rule prohibits residents of New York to enter into marriage in a jurisdiction where it is permitted. However, this is only *one* of the many different approaches within the United States, where the conflict of laws issue has been overlooked to a very large extent.

What about the other three jurisdictions that have been selected for this part? Italy, comprehensively analyzed by Matteo Bonini Baraldi,[110] where bills to introduce a same-sex registration scheme have been submitted to parliament; Portugal, extensively investigated by Rosa Martíns,[111] where a request of a same-sex couple to enter into marriage currently is under revision of the constitutional court and finally, Israel, critically scrutinized by Talia Einhorn,[112] where the Supreme Court has ordered to enter a same-sex marriage concluded abroad into the population registry, whereas under Israeli substantive law same-sex couples cannot obtain a marital status? However, does such a registration in Israel also imply recognition? Have the 'new jurisdictions' learned or are they learning any lessons from the 'old jurisdictions' or did they reinvent the wheel? Which role, if any, has comparative law in this area played?

3.4. THE EFFECTIVENESS OF THE PATER EST RULE

The tensions between legal, biological and social conceptions of parentage which currently belong to the most interesting questions in family law have been addressed at the 17th World Conference on Comparative Law in 2006 by Ingeborg Schwenzer as general rapporteur and 16 national rapporteurs.[113] The four contributions to this special volume specifically focus on the *pater est* rule.

Who is the father of the child? According to the *pater est* rule it is the man to whom the mother is married at the time of the child's birth. He shall be regarded

109 2008 WL 275138 (N.Y.A.D. 4 Dept., 42 Employee Benefits Cas. 2692, 2008 N.Y. Slip Op. 00909, Supreme Court, Appellate Division, Fourth Department, New York, Patricia MARTINEZ v. COUNTY OF MONROE, Feb. 1, 2008 and Beth R. v. Donna M., No. 350284/07, N.Y. State Supreme Court Justice Laura E. Drager, N.Y. County of Feb. 25, 2008.

110 See M. Bonini Baraldi, 'Family *vs* solidarity – Recent epiphanies of the Italian reductionist anomaly in the debate on *de facto* couples', 2008 *Utrecht Law Review*, no. 2, pp. 175–193.

111 See R. Martins, 'Same-sex partnerships in Portugal: from *de facto* to *de jure*?', 2008 *Utrecht Law Review*, no. 2, pp. 194–211.

112 See T. Einhorn, 'Same-sex family unions in Israeli law', 2008 *Utrecht Law Review*, no. 2, pp. 222–235.

113 See Schwenzer, *supra* note 76.

as the legal father of the child. This worldwide acknowledged presumption applies to all children born within marriage. Presumably, many children still grow up together with their parents with whom they are genetically, intentionally and legally related. However, the married (nuclear) family is gradually losing it's dominate position as the traditional family form and as a result family structures have changed considerably. The contributions falling under this section address the following three developments which at present are challenging the effectiveness of the *pater est* rule. Firstly, the increasing number of children who are born in informal relationships (Wendy Schrama[114]), secondly, assisted conception (Machteld Vonk[115] and Nancy Maxwell[116]) and thirdly the right to know one's genetic parentage (Richard Blauwhoff). In respect of informal relationships which in view of their function are similar to formalized relationships, it is essential to indicate the underlying principles of the law of parentage. Seemingly, at least in Dutch society, there is little awareness among cohabiting couples that the child who is born into such an informal relationship needs to be recognized in order to establish a legal link between the begetter and the child. From the Dutch law perspective Schrama analyzes three elements of parentage: the meaning of procreational responsibility, the right to have two parents and legal certainty. The crucial question is whether it is possible to extend the *pater est* rule to informal relationships. Obviously where parents have not formalized their relationship it is more difficult to presume that the male partner was the begetter of the child, but Schrama[117] finally succeeds in drawing a roadmap as to how the gap may be bridged between formal and functional relationships.

When it comes to assisted conception we have – in respect of the *pater est* rule – to distinguish between unknown and known sperm donors. Does the sperm donor have any rights? If so, which rights? Does the distinction between known and unknown donors make a difference? How does he obtain these rights? Should merely visitation rights be granted? Are the birth mother and the sperm donor free to contract about his position? Is an oral agreement sufficient or should it be in writing? Even if an agreement is made what is the value of it? Can it be set aside, should it be executed? Can you dispose on parentage? Does each of the parties have the right to dissolve the contract? Will courts take an agreement into account when a dispute arises? Which role does the female partner play who lives with the birth mother in a formalized or informal relationship? What happens if the lesbian couple splits? Should a known sperm donor be allowed to assert parentage

---

114 See W. Schrama, 'Family function over family form in the law on parentage? – The legal position of children born in informal relationships', 2008 *Utrecht Law Review*, no. 2, pp. 83–98.

115 See M. Vonk, 'The role of formalised and non-formalised intentions in legal parent-child relationships in Dutch law', 2008 *Utrecht Law Review*, no. 2, pp. 117–134.

116 See N. Maxwell, 'The Kansas case of *K.M.H.* – US law concerning the legal status of known sperm donors', 2008 *Utrecht Law Review*, no. 2, pp. 135–161.

117 See Schrama, *supra* note 114.

rights against the wishes of an 'unmarried' woman also in cases where lesbian couples were trying to create a family?

All these questions have been extensively addressed by Vonk[118] and Maxwell[119] by investigating Dutch law[120] and the law of the United States. In respect of the latter jurisdictions the recent *Kansas case* is highly illustrative. The mother asserted she did not intend for the sperm donor to have a parental relationship with the child whereas the sperm donor claimed he assumed, or the parties agreed, he would be the child's father and have certain parental rights concerning the child born of the assisted insemination by donor (AID). If a dispute is to be decided, the following aspects are of essential importance. Which intention did the birth mother and the known sperm donor have? Further, how can this intention be proved? Moreover, which role, if any, does a (written) agreement play?

Currently, statute law and case law of the jurisdictions that are presented by Vonk and Maxwell do not provide clear-cut solutions and one should also bear in mind that each case is different and complex. Certain striking parallels, however, can be discerned. Before the assisted conception takes place all persons are more or less 'in agreement', although during this period the perceptions already differ and often both the birth mother and the known sperm donor 'avoid the subject'. During the pregnancy, but at least when the child is born and during his or her early childhood things change. The birth mother slowly but surely withdraws whereas the donor immediately or steadily claims more rights. The problem whether or not agreements should be enforceable touches upon ethical and moral values. Nevertheless – as Vonk[121] recommends – drafting such an agreement may at any rate help all parties involved to envisage the consequences of the adventure that they are embarking upon. And at a later stage also mediation might be useful.

In many countries in Europe[122] anonymous sperm donation is not permitted because children should be able to obtain information about their biological fathers. The right to know one's genetic parentage has been addressed by Blauwhoff.[123] He presents an analysis of the problem by analyzing the case-law of the European Court of Human Rights. He goes on to focus on recent German law reform that became effective on 1st April 2008. As the first country in the world, Germany has introduced a 'purely informational paternity procedure', which the

118 See Vonk, *supra* note 115.

119 See Maxwell, *supra* note 116.

120 See also M. Vonk, *Children and their Parents, A Comparative Study of the Legal Position of Children with Regard to their Intentional and Biological Parents in English and Dutch Law*, 2007.

121 See Vonk, *supra* note 115.

122 Identification of the donor by the child should be possible in, for instance, Austria, Finland, Italy, The Netherlands, Norway, the United Kingdom, Sweden and Switzerland.

123 See Blauwhoff, *supra* note 92.

Federal Constitutional Court requested in 2007.[124] The new law recognizes the legal father's right to have his biological fatherhood ascertained, a claim enforceable against the child and the mother, and if necessary, with the use of the required physical compulsion to conduct a DNA test. Indisputably, this new procedure contributes to the debate about the (in)effectiveness of the *pater est* rule.

4. CLOSING REMARKS

This contribution to the special issue on 'Current Debates in Family Law around the Globe' consists of two main parts. The last part (§3) provides an introduction into the topics addressed by the authors of the other 15 articles. The first part (§2) which is aimed at framing comparative family law constitutes the heart core of this exposé. As a result these concluding remarks essentially focus on some of the thoughts reflected there, whereby two aspects instantly come into sight. First the scope of comparative family law, which should also include its international dimension, and second the attempt to get hold of and compare the European and the American approaches in comparative family law. Which meaning has comparative family law for comparatists from both sides of the Atlantic?

4.1. COMPARATIVE FAMILY LAW INCLUDES INTERNATIONAL FAMILY LAW

Since the beginning of the 21st century several comparative family law projects and publications have been completed within Europe and the United States. Most of the projects that have been briefly discussed in this contribution apply an integrated approach of family law including both the comparative and international perspective.[125] Hence, comparative family law is blooming.[126] Since globalization is not only restricted to economic and political relationships, but literally 'hits home' it has become indispensable to look beyond national boundaries and to

124 See M. Wellenhofer, 'Das neue Gesetz zur Klärung der Vaterschaft unabhängig vom Anfechtungsverfahren', 2008 *Neue Juristische Wochenschrift*, pp. 1185–1189.

125 This approach has been applied by Blair & Weiner, *supra* note 1 and Stark, *supra* note 23 in their books. See also the CEFL Principles on European Family Law Regarding Parental Responsibilities, *supra* note 26, which took all relevant international and European instruments in the field of parental responsibilities into account. They significantly influenced the final result.

126 See the increasing number of publications listed at CEFLs website: http://www.law.uu.nl/priv/cefl and since the establishment of the European Family Law series in March 2003, for instance, 22 books have been published. They include comparative legal studies and materials as well as studies on the effects of international and European law making within the national legal systems in Europe.

take international developments into account. In particular the comparative perspective not only provides a window into other jurisdictions, but exposes the often unquestioned assumptions of one's own law,[127] whereas the international perspective expresses the commonly shared values and norms which in many areas of family law have been accepted as guiding principles. The increasing number of cross-border relationships, finally, amount to challenges in respect of certainty and predictability. Will these goals more effectively be achieved if the private international law rules are unified? In this author's opinion an affirmative answer can be given. Currently, we are witnessing rapid legislative activities at the European level in respect of cross-border family matters[128] whereas at the global level the Hague Conference for Private International Law plays an active and naturally the central role in this process. Its international family law conventions belong to the most important and successful achievements in the field of the unification of law. Their application in practice is supported by bi-annual Conferences on Cross-Frontier Family Law Issues – co-organized by the Hague Conference[129] – at which judges and experts exchange their experiences and address their problems. These meetings lead to a better understanding of each other's rules and procedures and comparative family law and international family law are literally intertwined. For the enhanced functioning of the conventional rules in each country this exchange of views is of vital importance and this example of good practice should be taken over by the European Union Member States in respect of their cross-border family law instruments.

4.2. HARMONIZATION: WHY AND HOW?

During the last decade the question whether and how substantive family law should be harmonized has been frequently posed in Europe. The answers vary. In this debate one should bear in mind that the EU Member States transferred their

127 See Stark, *supra* note 23, p. 1.

128 The uniform conflicts of law rules for maintenance and divorce proposed by the European Commission in 2005 and 2006, however, have their drawbacks. See Th. De Boer, 'The Second Revision of the Brussels II Regulation: Jurisdiction and Applicable Law', in Boele-Woelki & Sverdrup (eds.) *supra* note 56, pp. 321–341 and M. Hellner, 'The Maintenance Regulation: a Critical Assessment of the Commission's Proposal', *ibid.*, pp. 343–378. See further M. Jänterä-Jareborg, 'Jurisdiction and Applicable Law in Cross-Border Divorce Cases in Europe', in J. Basedow & H. Baum & Y. Nishitani (eds.), *Japanese and European Private International Law in Comparative Perspective*, 2008, pp. 317–343 and V. Lazić, 'Recent Developments in Harmonizing 'European Private International Law' in Family Matters', 2008 *European Journal of Law Reform*, pp. 75–96.

129 In 2004 and 2006 these conferences took place in Malta. See http://www.hcch.net under news and events.

competence to legislate cross-border family matters to the European legislature,[130] but retained their competence in the field of substantive family law. It is to be expected that in the long run the dissimilarities among the EU family law systems, on the one hand, and the communitarian uniform private international law rules regulating family matters, on the other, will cause frictions, such as forum shopping, which may only be smoothed if the differences become less pronounced.

In Europe, a supranational legislative body that suggests model laws or adopts uniform acts in order to harmonize the family law systems does not exist. This is left to academic initiatives, whereas national courts and legislatures decide about the rules to be applied and adopted. The situation is entirely different in the United States, where the American Law Institute and the National Conference of Commissioners on Uniform State Laws are well-established and respected rule-making bodies. It is however, up to the States themselves to decide whether or not in whole or in part to adopt their Principles or Uniform Acts. In addition, not only the formal adoption of certain Uniform Laws has a harmonizing effect. The Uniform Marriage and Divorce Act (UMDA), for instance, was not widely adopted by the state legislatures, yet the wave of state legislatures adopting the concepts accepted and codified in this act had a significant impact on the trends within US family law.[131] Maybe this past history of the UMDA portends any sort of attempt at harmonizing family law in the United States. A comprehensive project dealing with general principles of family law historically has not been doing well in whole-scale adoption, but discrete Uniform Acts, such as the Uniform Parentage Act, have been far more successful. Is this because the general substantive principles of family law have, for so long, been seen as state-specific and that US family lawyers have existed with these differences without 'a second thought'? Are US family lawyers so comfortable with the comparative analysis of the substantive differences that they don't see the need for harmonization? If this is the case, does this account for the lack of a comparative methodology[132] and their propensity to look for differences rather than similarities? It is also interesting that the Federal Government must 'force' the harmonization in the area of child custody jurisdiction, interstate compacts on adoption and the enforcement of child/spousal maintenance in order for harmonization to occur. It is the threat of the loss of federal funds that seems to be the driving force in any harmonization in the United States.

130 See S. Bariatti, *La famiglia nel diritto internazionale private comunitario, L'Italia e la vita giuridica internazionale*, 2007 and A. Malatesta & F. Pocar & S. Bariatti (eds.), *The External Dimension of EC Private International Law in Family and Succession Matters*, Studi e pubblicazioni della Rivista di diritto internazionale privato e processuale, 2008.

131 See N. Maxwell, 'Unification and Harmonization of Family Law Principles: The United States Experience', in Boele-Woelki (ed.), *supra* note 44, pp. 249–267.

132 Why develop a methodology if the goal, harmonization, is not valued?.

4.3. COMPARATIVE RESEARCH PROJECTS COVERING EUROPE AND THE UNITED STATES

It is striking to note that extensive comparative research projects that cover both European and American jurisdictions are – as far as this author was able to verify – relatively exceptional. Here, American legal scholars are taking the lead. Krause's article in the *Oxford Handbook on Comparative Law* (2006) and Glendon's book (1989) and her introduction to the Person and Family Volume of the *International Encyclopedia of Comparative Law* (2003) represent the main exceptions. To these examples the contributions to the book edited by Sanford Katz, John Eekelaar and Mavis Maclean on *Cross Currents: Family Law and Policy in the United States and England*[133] can be added as well as the Utrecht dissertation of 1998 which addresses *The Influence of the European Convention of Human Rights on Dutch Family Law and the Influence of the United States Constitution on American Family Law.*[134] From the American perspective other common-law systems are usually selected when it comes to the comparison of solutions whereas from the European perspective it might be a little threatening that essentially 'American family law' does not exist, instead more than 50 different jurisdictions have to be taken into account. The latter is a complicated and time-consuming factor which might prevent European family lawyers to include the family systems of the United States in their comparative research.[135]

4.4. ALI AND CEFL PRINCIPLES

At the level of common principles and their potential harmonizing effect, however, the above mentioned concerns are of less importance. It might be challenging to contrast the ALI Principles of Law of Family Dissolution with the CEFL Principles regarding Divorce, Spousal Maintenance and Parental Responsibilities. They are comparable. Such a project could, for instance, include a case-oriented comparison, inquiring into how the cases provided in the illustrations of the ALI Principles would be solved if tried according to the CEFL Principles. Apart from this, the objectives of both projects differ. The ALI Principles are aimed at reforming the law. States are free to adopt (part of) these solutions. Family law in the United States primarily develops on case to case basis, as one of the

---

133 Katz *et al., supra* note 88.

134 G. Kleijkamp, *Family life and family interests: a comparative study of the influence of the European Convention of Human Rights on Dutch family law and the influence of the United States Constitution on American family law*, 1999.

135 But see N. Maxwell & C. Forder, 'The Inadequacies in US and Dutch Adoption Law to Establish Same-Sex Couples as Legal Parents: A Call for Recognizing Intentional Parenthood', 2004 *Family Law Quarterly*, pp. 623–662.

main characteristics of the common law system. Hence, in the absence of extensive statutory legislation of all family law issues US courts easily can – if necessary – refer to and apply the solutions suggested by the ALI, which is a highly renowned and respected law-making body. In contrast, an institution such as the ALI does not exist in Europe. It is up to legal scholars to initiate and propose models that might be useful in the harmonization of the law process. These frames of reference – they are also available for the law of obligations[136] – are primarily addressed towards national, European and international legislatures in their potential quest to reform a specific area of the law. In respect of those issues, however, which, for instance, in many jurisdictions are not (yet) regulated by statute, such as the alternating residence of the child after the breakup of the relationship of the parents or the request of one of the parents to relocate with the child in case parental responsibility is held jointly, national courts in Europe might be inspired by the solutions proposed in the CEFL Principles.[137] In order to find and further develop the law they provide guidance.

4.5. HOW FOREIGN FAMILY LAW SHOULD BE APPROACHED

A final general remark should be made in respect of the 'dos and don'ts' in comparing different family law systems, in particular how foreign solutions should be approached. In this respect it has been submitted that 'comparative analysis of family laws requires an *acknowledgement of difference*. It has limited application to the function envisaged by Zweigert and Kötz that "the law student will understand his own law better... [and develop] the critical standards which might lead to its improvement"' (emphasis KBW).[138] This advice should not be overvalued. Allegedly, differences can always be detected, but they should not only be categorized as conflicting, incompatible or irreconcilable but might – in view of the final result – also be classified as being almost alike, bridgeable and inspiring. In venturing comparative family law narrow-mindedness and prejudice are to be avoided. Instead openness, neutrality, curiosity and flexibility are required.

---

136 This process already started in the mid seventies of the previous century. See Study Group on a European Civil Code Former Research Group on EC Private Law (Acquis Group), *Principles, Definitions and Model Rules of European Law*, 2008 and European Group on Tort Law, *Principles of European Tort Law*, 2005.

137 See the recent decision of the Dutch Supreme Court, Hoge Raad 25 April 2008, LJN BC5901 where the Advocate General referred to Principle 3:21 of the CEFL Principles on Parental Responsibilities.

138 See D. Bradley, 'Comparative Law, Family Law and Common Law, Review Article', 2003 *Oxford Journal of Legal Studies*, pp. 123–146, p. 145.

FAMILY LAW AND NATIONAL CULTURE
Arguing against the cultural constraints argument

Masha Antokolskaia*

INTRODUCTION

'Family laws are embedded in unique and cherished national cultural heritages of particular countries' – this is the core of the so-called 'cultural constraints argument'.[1] The 'Cultural constraints argument' further suggests that this cultural and historical diversity is unbridgeable and therefore family laws are not spontaneously converging and cannot be deliberately harmonised. Otto Kahn-Freund reflected upon the common negative attitude towards the harmonisation of family law, by proclaiming the unification of family law 'a hopeless quest'.[2] This scepticism was rooted in the alleged fundamental unsuitability of family law for harmonisation due to the strong cultural and historical constraints, resulting in the lack of shared values and objectives. The notion of the cultural and historical embedment of family law originates from family law scholars. As early as in the 1968, Wolfram Müller-Freienfels wrote, 'family law concepts are especially open to influence by moral, religious, political and psychological factors; family law tends to become introverted because historical, racial, social and religious considerations differ according to country and produce different family law systems'.[3] Most scholars engaged in harmonisation activities in other areas of private law have rather uncritically adopted the same attitude. Even the political institutions of the EU have been susceptible to this assumption. For instance, the European

* Professor of Private Law, Faculty of Law, VU University, Amsterdam (The Netherlands), email: m.v.antokolskaia@rechten.vu.nl.

1 On the use of this argument see, for instance: G. de Oliveira, 'A European Family Law? Play it again, and again ... Europe!', 2000 *Tijdschrift voor familie- en jeugdrecht*, pp. 272–277; M. Hohnerlein, 'Konturen eines einheitlichen europäischen Familien- und Kindschaftsrecht – die Rolle der Europäischen Menschenrechtskonvention', 2001 *European Legal Forum*, no. 4, p. 252.

2 O. Kahn-Freund, 'Common Law and Civil Law – Imaginary and Real Obstacles to Assimilation', in M. Cappelletti (ed.), *New Perspectives for a Common Law of Europe*, 1978, p. 141.

3 W. Müller-Freienfels, 'The Unification of Family Law', 1968 *The American Journal of Comparative Law*, p. 175.

Council has quite recently stated that family law is 'very heavily influenced by the culture and tradition of national (or even religious) legal systems, which could create a number of difficulties in the context of harmonisation'.[4]

Accordingly, family law has for quite some time been regarded as unsuitable for deliberate harmonisation, without substantial scrutiny of the merits of the cultural constraints argument.[5] As a result, the issue of the harmonisation of family law has long remained on the fringes of the discussion surrounding harmonisation of private law.[6]

Nonetheless, since the late 1990s the attitude towards the harmonisation of family law has become increasingly, albeit it gradually, more positive.[7] The most tangible result of this development was the establishment of the Commission on European Family Law (CEFL) in 2001, aimed at elaborating non-binding Principles for family law in Europe. However, in spite of the growing amount of literature[8] and the thriving drafting activities of the CEFL, harmonisation of family law remains a highly controversial issue and the discussion whether it is at all possible is far from being closed case.[9] The reason for this is that the cultural constraints argument has not been overcome, but rather circumvented.

The notion that family law is strongly embedded in national culture has long been taken for granted without having been analysed thoroughly by either proponents or opponents of the cultural constraints argument. Even those who try to

4 Council report on the need to approximate Member States' legislation in civil matters of 16 November 2001, 13017/01 justciv 129, p. 114.

5 For instance I. Kon, *Sexual'naia kul'tura v Rossii* (Sexual Culture in Russia), 1997; T. Koopmans, 'Towards a New "*Ius Commune*"', in B. de Witte & C. Forder (eds.), *The common law of Europe and the future of legal education*, 1992, pp. 43–51; K. Kerameus, 'Problems of Drafting a European Civil Code', 1997 *European Review of Private Law*, no. 4, pp. 455–481, p. 479; G. Alpa, 'European Community Resolutions and the Codification of "Private Law"', 2000 *European Review of Private Law*, no. 2, p. 326; J. Basedow, 'Codification of Private Law in the European Union: the making of a Hybrid', 2001 *European Review of Private Law*, no. 1, pp. 35–37.

6 Rather illustrative in this respect is a remark by Ole Lando, the 'father' of the first harmonisation project, made in 2006: 'The family laws of the European Union are a fascinating subject. One would think that each of the laws reflect the national character, the dominant religion, the tradition, the family matters, which are linked to the economic and social conditions of each country. For these reasons I thought that there could never be any rapprochement of family laws and notably not in the laws of divorce. The more the laws are linked to persons and passions, I thought, the more they would differ and remain different.' O. Lando, 'Can Europe Build Unity of Civil Law Whilst Respecting Diversity?', 2006 *Europa e diritto privato*, no. 1, p. 8.

7 K. Boele-Woelki, 'Comparative Research-based Drafting of Principles of European Family Law', in M. Faure, *et al.* (eds.), *Towards a European Ius Commune in Legal Education and Research*, 2002, pp. 175–177; W. Pintens, 'Europeanisation of Family Law', in K. Boele-Woelki (ed.), *Perspectives for the Unification and Harmonisation of Family Law in Europe*, 2003, pp. 4 *et seq.*

8 D. Martiny, 'Is Unification of Family Law Feasible or Even Desirable?', in A. Hartkamp *et al.* (eds.), *Towards a European Civil Code*, 2004, pp. 328–333 and the CEFL website: http://www2.law.uu.nl/priv/cefl/ under the rubric 'publications'.

9 Martiny, *supra* note 8, pp. 307–333.

put this argument into perspective have not investigated it in any depth. The most common counter-argument is that certain peculiarities of the family law of the country in question cannot be explained by cultural factors. For instance, Ewoud Hondius doubts that the fact that The Netherlands is the only European country that still has a total community of assets as the legal regime for matrimonial property could be explained by the particularities of Dutch national culture.[10] Others point out that certain changes in long-standing family law concepts have not brought about any cultural shocks.[11] The most elaborate criticism thus far is that some culturally-imbedded rules do not coincide with the modern notion of human rights;[12] that tradition is not 'holy' and should not be protected at any rate; and that even culturally-laden family rules are not an end in themselves, but rather a means by which to promote a desired regulation of human relations.[13]

In my earlier work[14] I tried to make a first step in the direction of a more fundamental qualification of the cultural constraints argument, by bringing to light the common historical roots of family law that all European countries have in common. This endeavour inspired me to undertake a five-year study into the convergence and divergence of family law in Europe.[15] I was challenged by the idea of exploring the main objection to family law harmonisation, the so-called 'cultural constraints argument'. This study revealed that the 'cultural constraints argument' has a number of various dimensions. In this article, I will summarise my findings regarding one of its core dimensions: the cultural embedment of family law.

10 E. Hondius, *Naar een Europees burgerlijk recht, preadvies Vereniging Burgerlijk recht*, 1993, p. 180.

11 The introduction in Belgian family law of the notion of *mater semper certa est*, is used as an example thereof, pp. 785–794. W. Pintens & C. Vanwinckelen, *Casebook European Family Law*, 2001, p. 15.

12 G.-R. de Groot, 'Op weg naar een Europees personen- en familierecht?', 1995 *Ars Aequi*, no.1, p. 29.

13 See for instance Pintens & Vanwinckelen, *supra* note 11, p. 15: '(...) law, even if imbedded in our culture, is primarily an instrument to regularize human relationships and is not a purpose in itself.'.

14 M. Antokolskaia *et al.*, *Naar een Europees Familierecht, Report for the Netherlands Comparative law Association*,1999.

15 This study, financed by the Dutch Royal Academy of Sciences and Arts, resulted in a monograph *Harmonisation of Family Law in Europe: A Historical Perspective. A Tale of Two Millennia*, 2006.

1. IS FAMILY LAW EMBEDDED IN UNIQUE NATIONAL CULTURE?

The assumptions constituting the cultural constraints argument can be summarised as follows. Firstly, it is suggested that laws are ingrained in the culture of the countries in which they operate. Secondly, it is assumed that each country has its own particular national culture that influences the respective law. Thirdly, it is presupposed that each of these national cultures is unique to the country concerned and that these national cultures are not moving any closer to one another. The final reckoning is that due to their embedment in the unique national cultures, laws are not converging spontaneously and cannot be harmonised deliberately.

Culture can be defined in many different ways. A general definition of culture could be that it is the 'heritage of art, science and ideas'.[16] The issue is to what extent such heritage should be considered 'national' when it comes to the elements that are relevant to family law. Pierre Legrand and many others clearly perceive the 'cultureness' of law from a national perspective.[17] Laurence Friedman, for instance, has extensively explored the concept of 'legal culture' and tends to believe that each country has its unique particular culture.[18]

1.1. ARE NATIONAL FAMILY CULTURES INTERNALLY HOMOGENEOUS?

The first relevant issue is to what extent the national cultures within Europe are internally homogenous. It is has rightly been noted that the culture of a given country 'may be understood as a vast diversity of overlapping cultures; some relatively local, some, more universal'.[19] Laurence Friedman speaks in this respect of 'a dazzling array of cultures' within a single culture[20] One of the important points of distinction between these sub-cultures is their ideological affiliation. Thus, Friedman delineates the conservative culture and the liberal culture and 'all sorts of variants and subgroups' between them.[21]

---

16 S. Hicks, 'A Model of Society for the Comparative Study of Law', in *Monismus oder Pluralismus der Rechtskulturen?* Proceedings of the 13th World Congress, *Rechtstheorie*, 1997, p. 215.

17 Legrand speaks in this sense of the 'Frenchness' of French law. P. Legrand, *Fragments on Law-as-Culture*, 1999, p. 5.

18 L. Friedman, *The Legal System: A Social Science Perspective*, 1975, p. 199.

19 R. Cotterrell, 'The Concept of Legal Culture', in D. Nelken (ed.), *Comparing Legal Cultures*, 1997, p. 20.

20 L. Friedman, *The Republic of Choice: Law, Authority and Culture*, 1990, p. 213.

21 L. Friedman, *Total Justice*, 1985, p. 98.

This internal cultural diversity is especially manifest in family ideology and the discourse on family legislation. Ever since the Enlightenment, an ideological conservative/progressive discord has divided political life in Europe. All ideological trends since the Enlightenment, such as the Restoration, nineteenth century liberalism, socialism, feminism etc., are of a pan-European nature. All these trends generated their own sets of values with regard to family and family law. The corresponding progressive-conservative dichotomy does not coincide with State boundaries, but is instead prevalent in every European country. This does not refer to the growing multi-culturalism resulting from immigration from non-European countries.[22] What is meant is that the innate population in each particular European country is split into various different 'cultures' that are affiliated to corresponding ideologies. A clear example is France. Max Rheinstein noticed that since the 1789 Revolution, France has been split up into '*les deux Frances*', a progressive France and a conservative France, and has shown how much the subsequent history of French family law has been affected by the struggle between those two camps.[23] Describing the 1975 reform of French divorce law, Mary Ann Glendon concludes that at the end of the twentieth century French society was still divided into the same '*les deux Frances*'.[24] Italy is also a good example. As Valerio Pocar and Paola Ronfani have stated: 'It is important to remember that Italy today still presents major contrasts in culture and daily usage between industrialized zones and those with a predominantly agricultural economy, between town and country, between North and South. As result there are many different family structures, which cannot be integrated into a single abstract model. The same consideration applies to the whole discourse on family legislation.'[25]

Everywhere in Europe, the modernity of family patterns and family culture differs greatly from one social environment to another. The ideas that a highly educated, urban family of young professionals have about family and family law, differ significantly from the corresponding ideas of a rural family of middle-aged traditional farmers in any European country, be it Italy, Sweden, Malta or The Netherlands. Franz Rothenbacher concisely labelled this phenomenon 'the contemporaneity of the noncontemporaneous'.[26] Each country has, of course, a predominant ideology regarding family law matters, which is generally the ideas of

22 On this and other aspects of multiculturalism see: E. Örücü, *The Enigma of Comparative Law. Variations on a Theme for the Twenty-first Century*, 2004, pp. 123–132.

23 M. Rheinstein, *Marriage Stability, Divorce, and the Law*, 1972, p. 195.

24 M.A. Glendon, 'The French Divorce Reform Law of 1976', 1976 *The American Journal of Comparative Law*, p. 201.

25 V. Pocar & P. Ronfani, 'Family Law in Italy: Legislative Innovations and Social Change', 1978 *Law and Society Review*, no. 4, p. 629.

26 F. Rothenbacher, 'Social Change in Europe and its Impact on Family Structures', in J. Eekelaar & T. Nhlapo, *The Changing Family: International Perspectives on the Family and Family Law*, 1998, p. 21.

the majority of the population or the *élites dirigeante*.[27] Thus the pertinent family law is either a reflection of the predominant values of the majority, or a compromise between the values of the various groups.

Sometimes the ongoing struggle between the conservative and progressive 'cultures' in the field of family law reaches the point of ideological confrontation. The Irish and Italian divorce referendums are good illustrations of this phenomenon.[28] The history of family law reform shows that most confrontations finally result in compromise legislation. Only every now and then is one side able to clearly overpower the other. For example, the conservatives did manage to turn back the clock with the abolition of divorce in France after the Restoration in 1816 and in Spain under Franco in 1939. More often it is the progressive side that manages to achieve a certain breakthrough, for example with the introduction of divorce on demand in Sweden and Spain, and same-sex marriage in The Netherlands, Belgium and Spain.

It is worth noting that there is an objective difference between 'conservative' and 'progressive' family law that is relevant here. Family law built upon a conservative 'culture' is often rather restrictive. Population groups representing minority 'cultures' are also subjected to the restrictions of that law, although they do not share its underlying convictions. A good example is the first Irish divorce referendum of 1986, when 63.5% of the electorate voted against the introduction of divorce and 36.5% voted in favour.[29] As the legal possibility to obtain a divorce does not compel anyone to divorce, the result of the referendum meant that the majority of the Irish population denied not only themselves, but also the dissenting minority the right to dissolve their marriage. Therefore, these minorities often have the feeling that their rights are being infringed upon in an undemocratic manner.[30] Such is also the in the infamous *Johnston* case, where the plaintiffs maintained that the impossibility of obtaining a divorce in Ireland infringed upon their right to family life and the right to marry – protected under Articles 8 and 12 of the European Convention on Human Rights.[31] Family law built upon a progressive 'culture', however, is generally more permissive. This means that cultural groups representing a more conservative ideology are left enough room to

27 I am indebted to Esin Örücü for this term. See her E. Örücü, *Critical Comparative Law: Considering Paradoxes for Legal Systems in Transition. Report for the Netherlands Comparative law Association*, 1999, p. 86.

28 See for instance: M. Dillon, *Debating Divorce. Moral Conflict in Ireland*, 1993.

29 C. James, 'Cead Mile Failte. Ireland Welcomes Divorce: The 1995 Irish Divorce Referendum and the Family (Divorce) Act of 1996', 1997 *Duke Journal of Comparative and International Law* 8, no. 1, p. 175.

30 As Will Kymlicka has noted, 'the state unavoidably promotes certain cultural identities, and thereby disadvantages others'. W. Kymlicka, *Multicultural Citizenship: A Liberal Theory of Minority Rights*, 1995, p. 108.

31 See: *Johnston and others* v. *Ireland*, ECtHR, Judgment of 18 December 1986, Series A, No. 112, and the dissenting opinion of Judge De Mayer.

arrange their family life in their own way. They have, of course, to accept the existence of permissive legislation, which is sometimes met with difficulty. For instance, not everyone in The Netherlands was happy with the opening of civil marriage to same-sex couples, as some felt that this also involved the deterioration of 'their marriage'.[32] Still, providing more options for everyone is a relevant advantage of permissive law above restrictive law in this 'multicultural' context.

1.2. THE PAN-EUROPEAN CHARACTER OF NATIONAL CONSERVATIVE AND PROGRESSIVE 'SUBCULTURES'

If one accepts that the culture of each particular country is not internally homogeneous, the question arises to what extent the subcultures, in which national cultures are divided, are unique to the countries concerned. Analysing family law history, allows one to draw the conclusion that ever since the Enlightenment Europe has been split by the ideological discord between the 'progressive' camp (seeking modernisation of family law under the influence of the ideas of the Enlightenment), and the 'conservative' camp (opposing this modernisation in the name of 'traditional' family values).[33] The 'subcultures' relevant to family ideology and law generally correspond with this divide. Both the 'conservative' and 'progressive' family ideologies are clearly of a pan-European nature, since they both have their own rank and file in each European country. Sometimes this is a majority, sometimes a tiny stratum. The countries with modern family laws also have population groups with a conservative family 'culture' and the countries with conservative family laws always have population groups that represent the most modern views on family life. Laurence Friedman notices that adherents of specific attitudes 'tend to cohere, to hang together, to form clusters of related attitudes'.[34] The members of the affiliated cultural groups understand each other across the borders, often looking abroad to support their ideas, and they repeatedly call on the European courts to adjudicate their confrontations with their compatriot opponents.

Thus, the elements of national culture that are relevant to family law are, in general, anything but unique. On the other hand, as the influence of different

32 M. van Mourik, 'Wettelijke en contractuele vormgeving van affectieve relaties,' in *Het familierecht in het perspectief van de 21e eeuw*, 1999, pp. 67–68.

33 It is worth noting here that in domestic debates the cultural constraints argument is by far more popular in the 'conservative' camp. Rodolfo Sacco has mentioned that 'The ideology of cultural self-sufficiency is merely the name given to the ideology of cultural delay'. R. Sacco, 'Diversity and Uniformity in the Law', 2001 *The American Journal of Comparative Law*, p. 177.

34 L. Friedman, *Total Justice*, 1985, p. 98.

(sub)cultures varies from country to country,[35] national differences in prevailing family ideology and law certainly cannot be disregarded. Yet, it seems clear that in the field of family ideology and law there are few unique national cultures, but instead pan-European conservative and progressive cultures, and a wealth of variety in between. There are of course all kinds of national peculiarities that contribute to the rich cultural, ideological and political fabric that is Europe, but their significance as a determinant of family policy and law pales into insignificance in light of the dominance of pan-European conservative and progressive ideological trends.

2. IS FAMILY LAW EMBEDDED IN UNIQUE NATIONAL LEGAL CULTURE?

If the other elements of national culture that are relevant to family law are not, or at least not predominantly, of a unique national character, the question arises whether perhaps *legal* culture is. The proponents of the cultural constraints argument seldom directly refer to the embedment of family law in culture in general. It more often suggested that family laws are embedded in one particular element of culture, namely legal culture. Thus, Pierre Legrand speaks of the embedment of law in a subjective component of legal culture: legal *mentalité.* Marie-Thérèse Meulders-Klein suggests that family law constitutes the hard core of any legal culture.[36] This reference to legal, rather than general culture, allows the suggestion that, while general family 'cultures' are not unique to particular European states, the legal cultures are. This possibility calls for some inquiry into the notion of legal culture.

2.1. WHAT IS LEGAL CULTURE? DEEP AND SURFACE LEVELS OF LEGAL CULTURES

Legal culture is a particular element of general culture: a sort of translation of general culture into the language of legal concepts, techniques and ideas. The issue of legal culture has received substantial attention recently and a lot of literature has been devoted to the topic.[37] I will confine myself to only a few remarks.

35 Roger Cotterrell has rightly noticed that legal ideology is more strongly linked with social power than other elements of legal culture. Cotterrell, *supra* note 19, p. 23.

36 M.-T. Meulders-Klein, 'Towards a European Civil Code of Family Law? Ends and Means', in K. Boele-Woelki, (ed.), *Perspectives for the Unification and Harmonisation of Family Law in Europe*, 2003, p. 109.

37 For an overview see: D. Nelken, 'Comparing Legal Cultures: An Introduction', in D. Nelken, (ed.), *Comparing Legal Cultures*, 1997, pp. 1–9.

As was mentioned above, the concept of legal culture has been extensively explored in various works of Laurence Friedman. Friedman defines legal culture as 'ideas, attitudes, values and opinions about law, the legal system, and legal institutions of some given population'.[38] Within a legal culture Friedman primarily distinguishes between the professional and the common (lay) legal culture.[39] Mark van Hoecke and Mark Warrington introduce the concept of 'paradigm' in order to describe the hard core of legal cultures more specifically.[40] To such 'paradigmatical' aspects of legal culture they attribute: (1) a concept of law; (2) a theory of valid legal sources; (3) a methodology of law; (4) a theory of argumentation; (5) a theory of legitimation of law; and (6) a common basic ideology.[41]

Within those paradigms of legal culture, Van Hoecke and Warrington distinguish between different levels. The 'common ideology, common moral convictions form the *deep* level, which eventually comes to dominate the other levels.'[42] On the basis of this differentiation they further distinguish between differences amongst legal cultures, which manifest themselves at the surface and the deeper levels. The differences on the deep moral and ideological level are of paramount importance. The differences on the surface level (for example legal rules, legal concepts and legal techniques) are less important.[43] It is justly pointed out that 'once the moral choices have been made, legal techniques are used in such a way as to reach the desired result.'[44] In a similar way Hugh Collins remarks with regard to the contemporary harmonisation activities, that technical aspects of the differences in legal cultures are relatively easy to reconcile, while overcoming differences, based on dissimilar moral values 'encounter[s] a general tension between the project of harmonisation and respect for cultural diversity in Europe.'[45] This proposition strongly applies to family law, where almost every rule 'represent[s] a symbolic endorsement of particular moral ideas.'[46] The emphasis on the political and ideological aspects of legal culture laid by Van Hoecke, Warrington and Collins is narrowly related to the idea of the embedment of family law in the political aspects of society, put forward by Otto Kahn-Freund and David Bradley and

38 L. Friedman, 'Some Thoughts on Comparative Legal Culture', in D. Clark (ed.), *Comparative and Private International Law. Essays in Honour of J. H. Merryman on his Seventieth Birthday*, 1990, p. 53.

39 L. Friedman, *The Legal System: A Social Science Perspective*, 1975, p. 223.

40 M. van Hoecke & M. Warrington, 'Legal Cultures, Legal Paradigms and Legal Doctrine: Towards a New Model For Comparative Law,' 1998 *International and Comparative Law Quarterly*, p. 513.

41 *Ibid.*, pp. 514–515.

42 *Ibid.*, p. 519.

43 *Ibid.*

44 *Ibid.*

45 H. Collins, 'European Private Law and the Cultural Identity of States', 1995 *European Review of Private Law*, p. 363.

46 *Ibid.*

amply supported by the results of the examinations in my aforementioned book.[47]

2.2. THE LEGAL CULTURES OF COMMON LAW AND CIVIL LAW

According to Pierre Legrand, the most important differences between the legal cultures in Europe lie across the axes of the common/civil law dichotomy.[48] Legrand postulates an irreconcilable discord between the civil law and the common law *mentalités*.[49] He suggests that 'there exist[s] both [a] common law and [a] civil law *mentalité* – two different ways of thinking about the law, about what it is to have knowledge of law and about the role of law in society'.[50] Legrand presents the history of the relationship between common and civil law systems as a kind of perpetual 'epistemological war'.[51] Consequently, he resolutely denies any possibility of the evolution of common and civil law cultures towards each other and claims that even evident examples of growing proximity between legal solutions provided in civil and common law systems should be dismissed as illusions based on a fallacious reduction of law to legal rules.[52]

In contrast to Legrand's contentions, several authors[53] assert that convergence of civil and common law systems, albeit gradual and patchy,[54] has taken place on various levels. Basil Markesinis notes convergence on both the functional (similar

---

47 See my *Harmonisation of Family Law in Europe: A Historical Perspective*, 2006.

48 L. Moccia has traced the historical routes of this 'mental obsession with presumed division between Civil and Common law' in the 'oversimplified as well as nationalistically biased' attitude that emerged, in L. Moccia, 'Historical Overview of the Origins and Attitudes of Comparative Law', in B. Witte & C. de Forder (eds.), *The common law of Europe and the future of legal education*, 1992, pp. 611–619.

49 P. Legrand, 'European Legal Systems Are Not Converging', 1996 *International and Comparative law Quarterly*, p. 62.

50 P. Legrand, 'Against a European Civil Code', 1997 *Modern Law Review*, p. 45.

51 For which he received a well-deserved acquisition of selective and tendentious 'rétrodiction' of legal history. A. Chamboredon, 'The Debate on a European Civil Code: For an "Open Texture"', in M. van Hoecke & F. Ost (eds.), *The Harmonisation of European Private Law*, 2000, p. 68.

52 P. Legrand, *Fragments on Law-as-Culture*, 1999, pp. 83–84.

53 *E.g.* X. Lewis, 'The Europeanisation of the Common Law', in R. Jagtenberg *et al.* (eds.), *Transfrontier Mobility of Law*, 1995, pp. 47–61; R. Zimmermann, 'Roman Law and European Legal Unity', in A. Hartkamp *et al.* (eds.), *Towards a European Civil Code*, 1998, pp. 34–35; J. Merryman, 'On the Convergence (and Divergence) of Civil Law and Common Law', in M. Cappelletti (ed.), *New Perspectives for a Common Law of Europe*, 1978, pp. 195–233; B. Markesinis (ed.), *The Gradual Convergence. Foreign Ideas Foreign Influences and English Law on the Eve of the 21st Century*, 1994.

54 B. Markesinis, 'Learning from Europe and Learning in Europe', in B. Markesinis (ed.), *The Gradual Convergence. Foreign Ideas Foreign Influences and English Law on the Eve of the 21st Century*, 1994, p. 30.

solutions to similar problems) and the formal level (for example, convergence in the sources law; and a growing rapprochement of judicial views).[55] My research has shown that there is not much difference between the common law and civil law rules on marriage, divorce, cohabitation, the position of extramarital children, and even matrimonial property.[56] John Merryman has accurately pointed out that similarity of rules alone 'is in most cases an unreliable indicator of convergence or divergence of legal systems.'[57] Yet, even he admits that similar rules often provide 'outward evidence of a deeper legal similarity'. A 'more convincing measure of convergence' has to be found, according to Merryman, 'in the extent to which legal systems in Civil and Common Law nations play out the fundamental values of Western culture.'[58] Application of this criterion reveals that the common and civil law families 'are moving along parallel roads, towards the same destination.'[59] Mark van Hoecke and Mark Warrington conclude that 'there are still differences between common law and civil law, but they are very close to a point where there will no longer be *paradigmatical* differences. What will ultimately remain is some degree of difference, although not of a fundamental nature.'[60]

These conclusions apply all the more to family law. My research has made it clear that there are no more differences on the level of legal ideology in respect of family laws, between the common and civil law cultures than between the civil law countries internally.[61] If one takes as a starting point that legal ideology is the most important element in determining the differences and similarities between legal cultures, one must conclude that the alleged fundamental difference between common and civil law legal cultures, whatever its merits for other fields of law, does not apply to family law. The history of family law clearly shows that the choices that were made in the context of family law reforms, and the political debates surrounding these reforms, have always been and still very much are the same on the continent as on the British Isles. Moreover, not only the ideological, but also the formal elements of legal culture in family law are no different in common and civil law countries. The explanation for this is that the bulk of family law in the whole of Western Europe, with the only notable exception being matrimonial property law, is embedded in a common legal past: the medieval uniform canon law. The two systems even share the same conceptual language. For a common law lawyer terms like 'separation of bed and board', 'annulment' or 'illegitimate child' sound as familiar as for his continental colleague. There is not even

55 *Ibid.*
56 See M. Antokolskaia, *Harmonisation of Family Law in Europe: A Historical Perspective*, 2006.
57 Merryman, *supra* note 53, p. 230.
58 *Ibid.*, pp. 232–233.
59 *Ibid.*, p. 233.
60 Van Hoecke & Warrington, *supra* note 40, p. 501.
61 See M. Antokolskaia, *Harmonisation of Family Law in Europe: A Historical Perspective*, 2006.

much difference with respect to the legal sources, as even in the common law countries family law is mainly an area of codified law.[62]

2.3. CONCLUSION

In the context of the cultural constraints argument, only differences in legal culture on the 'deep' level of legal ideology and moral convictions could be truly relevant, as differences on the 'surface' level of legal rules, concepts and techniques are relatively easy to overcome. Studying the history of family law allows one to draw the conclusion that with respect to family law, the general similarity at the level of ideologies and morals between all countries in Europe is overwhelming. Due to the shared common past stemming from the application of medieval uniform canon law, the differences on the 'surface' level are also less than in any other field of private law. It is clear that the conclusions presented above in relation to the alleged fundamental differences between the legal cultures of common law and civil law can also apply to the civil law countries when compared to each other. The conclusion of this brief excursion into legal culture is therefore that with regards family law, legal cultures in Europe do not possess a unique national character, at least not in such a way that this should affect the conclusion previously drawn with regards the other elements of national culture relevant to family law, namely that in the field of family ideology and law, there is so such thing as a unique national culture, but rather a pan-European conservative and a pan-European progressive culture, and a plethora of variety in between.

3. IS THERE A COMMON EUROPEAN FAMILY CULTURE?

The conclusion remains that the elements of national culture that are relevant to family law are generally anything but unique. Modernisation goes on everywhere in Europe, albeit sometimes at a very different pace, and both the driving and opposing forces that shape this evolution are of a pan-European character. Does this mean that we can speak of a common European family culture?

The proponents of the cultural constraints argument firmly postulate the uniqueness of national cultures, while their opponents tend to see the particularities of the national cultures within Europe within the broader context of a common European culture. Even Laurence Friedman, who generally believes in

[62] Kahn-Freund, *supra* note 2, p. 150.

the uniqueness of national cultures,[63] acknowledges the existence of such general phenomenon as modern culture or the culture of modernity.[64] Although there is no definite agreement concerning the principal characteristics of the common European culture, some characteristics thereof are more or less unambiguous. Such common features include, for instance, individualism and rationalism,[65] personalism and intellectualism,[66] rights-consciousness and dissolution of traditional authority,[67] and respect for human rights.

However, these are only very general characteristics. They are not enough to constitute a general ideological consensus on particular issues of family law. As we have seen, on some of those issues consensus does exist. The best examples are the above mentioned common ideological standpoints on the equality of spouses and of children born in and outside of marriage. Yet, it is abundantly clear that on many other issues such consensus does not exist. The consensus-forming potential of the European human rights instruments and courts is limited by the fact that they generally tend to go no further than the level of consensus that already exists among the Member States. Therefore there is not much hope that in the near future a shared notion of European human rights will form a basis of common ideology for the whole of family law.

The point is that the pan-European character of family law culture and ideology is most evident if examined from a historical perspective, removed from any particular point in time. However, if one considers the family law culture and ideology of the various countries of Europe as they stand at a certain point in time only, it is the differences, rather than the similarities, that tend to be most prominent. It was concluded above that these are caused merely by the differences in the pace and profundity of the modernisation of family law that takes place everywhere in Europe. Yet it is clear that in the context of an evaluation of the cultural constraints argument, the national differences in prevailing family culture and ideology that exist at present, and in one form or another will most probably continue, and thus cannot be disregarded altogether. It is therefore very plausible to speak of a common European family culture, but not in the sense that the cultural constraints argument could be dismissed altogether because in reality there are no relevant differences among the national family cultures and ideologies in Europe. Such differences are definitely present, and the analysis of convergence

63 L. Friedman, *The Legal System: A Social Science Perspective*, 1975, p. 199.

64 L. Friedman, *The Republic of Choice: Law, Authority and Culture*, 1990, pp. 198–199.

65 Van Hoecke & Warrington, *supra* note 40, p. 503.

66 F. Wieacker, 'Foundations of European Legal Culture', 1990 *The American Journal of Comparative Law*, pp. 1–29.

67 L. Friedman, 'Some Thoughts on Comparative Legal Culture', in D. Clark (ed.), *Comparative and Private International Law. Essays in Honour of J. H. Merryman on his Seventieth Birthday*, 1990, p. 57.

tendencies in the preceding sections suggests that for the foreseeable future, they will not disappear.

4. CONCLUSION

It is clear that the core assumption of the cultural constraints argument – the alleged embedment of family laws in unique and unchangeable national cultures – cannot be maintained. History plainly shows that in the field of family ideology and law one cannot really talk of unique national cultures, but rather of a pan-European culture, which is not homogeneous but an amalgamation of pan-European 'conservative' and pan-European 'progressive' cultures. The relative influence of these two opposing family 'cultures' varies from country to country and from time to time. Examinations of history of family law made in my aforementioned study suggest that there are the differences in the balance of political power between 'progressive' and 'conservative' forces, rather than national culture that determines the pertinent family laws.

The cultural constraints argument cannot be saved by the suggestion that national politics is just an element of national culture; this is not because such classification is impossible in principle. Although a more precise description of the relationship between culture and politics would of course depend on the adopted definition of both concepts, it seems obvious that national culture can be considered an important determinant of the political affairs of a country, and perhaps the same can be said of the reverse relationship. The cultural constraints argument cannot be saved by such reasoning, because it is not so much the element of 'culture' that is essential to it, but the elements of uniqueness and unchangeability. These are the elements that lie at the heart of the assumption that convergence and deliberate harmonisation of national family laws is impossible, not the contention that family law is determined by culture. As we have seen, the political factor that is the main determinant of the evolution of national family law is the balance of power between the local adherents of predominantly pan-European 'progressive' and 'conservative' family ideology. This balance of political power is obviously neither unique nor unchangeable. On the contrary, there are few things so variable as the political vicissitudes of a country and the outcome of democratic elections. Although one could of course say that a particular country generally has a more or less continuous 'conservative' or 'progressive' political character (for instance, when comparing Malta to Sweden or Ireland to The Netherlands), the example of Spain opening civil marriage to same-sex couples soon after the electoral victory of the social-democrats under Rodríguez Zapatero is a clear example that the political determinants of the evolution of family law are very changeable indeed. One never knows how long such a statement will remain valid when it comes to family law.

All things considered, the conclusion can be none other than that the cultural constraints argument is beyond redemption. Its core assumptions cannot be upheld. Family law is not so much embedded in unique national culture and history, but rather in a pan-European culture and history. Pertinent national family laws are determined by political, rather than cultural factors, and these are fluid. Every now and then family laws do converge spontaneously. However, it remains to be seen what all this means for the deliberate harmonisation of family law.

(COMPULSORY) ARRANGEMENTS REGARDING CHILDREN

ACTIVE PARENTING OR SOLOMON'S JUSTICE?

Alternating residence in Sweden for children with separated parents

Anna Singer*

1. ALTERNATING RESIDENCE – ACTUAL OCCURRENCE

Alternating residence for children with separated parents has become increasingly popular in Sweden over the course of the last few decades. The first reported statistics on children with alternate living stem from the public child support system. In 1992/1993 an estimated 4% of all children with separated parents were living alternating with both parents. In 2001/2002 the corresponding number was 18%.[1] In 2005 it was estimated that 21% of the approximately 500,000 children living in Sweden with separated parents were living alternately with both.[2] Closely related to alternating residence in practical terms is when the child is formally living with one parent, but has extended visits with the other parent. It is estimated that approximately 10% of children with separated parents live permanently with one of the parents, but stay with the non-residential parent for periods of time exceeding what could be labelled as traditional visitation, *i.e.* more than every other weekend and every other holiday.

Alternating residence is in most cases the result of an agreement between the parents. However, according to Swedish law, the courts have the possibility to order alternating residence, even against the will of one parent. This indicates that alternating residence is a solution generally considered to be in the best interests of the child.

* Associate Professor, Faculty of Law, Uppsala University, Uppsala (Sweden), email: Anna.Singer@jur.uu.se.

1 Government Report SOU 2005:43, *Vårdnad – Boende – Umgänge. Barnets bästa, föräldrars ansvar* (Custody – Residence – Access. Best Interest of the Child, Parents' Responsibility) Part A, p. 158.

2 SCB (Statistics Sweden), *Barn och deras familjer* (Children and their families), 2006, p. 270.

In the article, a brief background will be presented to the use of alternating residence in Sweden. Relevant legislation will be described and some of the problems noticed in connection to this kind of living arrangement will also be discussed.

2. JOINT CUSTODY FOR SEPARATED PARENTS – A BACKGROUND

2.1. INTRODUCTION

A brief summary of the developments of the Swedish legislation on custody for separated parents is useful in order to understand the rather widespread use of alternating residence for children. An explicit objective in Swedish family law has, for a long time, been to ensure that children have good contact with both parents after the parents' separation. This can also be described as making it easier for both parents to have access to their child, even when not living together. Regardless of how ones looks at the matter, it is easy to establish that one way of facilitating fulfilment of the goal of active parents has been to adjust the rules on custody, allowing for parents to have joint responsibility also after separation. This development has most likely promoted the use of alternating residence.

The first modern regulation on custody of children was introduced in the beginning of the 1900s. According to the 1917 Act on Children Born Outside of Wedlock, the unmarried mother had sole custody of her child. This was motivated by practical considerations; since she was unmarried it could be assumed that she lived alone and took care of the child on her own. Hence, she was given sole right to decide in matters concerning the child's personal affairs. Married parents, on the other hand, were thought to live together and consequently presumed to take joint responsibility for the care and upbringing of the child. The 1920 Act on Children Born during a Marriage consequently gave both parents joint custody. This, at the time rather radical, solution of putting both parents on equal footing as custodians was mainly motivated by egalitarian goals and not primarily justified with reference to the child's interests. If the married parents divorced, on the other hand, it was thought that both parents could not suitably exercise custody together; legal responsibility for the care of the child had to be vested in one of them. Decisive for the allocation of custody was in this situation the actual care of the child. Since the mother in most cases took care of the child she also became sole custodian. The non-custodian parent, in most cases the father, had an explicit right to have access to the child. The law stated that a father or a mother, who was not the custodian, should not be deprived of the right to access to the child, unless there were certain special circumstances.

2.2. JOINT CUSTODY IF BOTH PARENTS CONSENTED

The 1920 Act remained in force for many years. Towards the beginning of the 1960s, the law on custody and access began to appear outdated, in part due to the fact that divorce had became more common. Most children with separated parents lived with the mother. Since custodial responsibility as a general rule was given to the parent who had the actual care of the child, the mother in most cases became the sole custodian. Many fathers as a result lost contact with their children after separating from the child's mother. It appeared that access rights were not enough to rectify this. The fact that only one of the parents was entitled to be vested with custody after the divorce also generated many disputes in court concerning custody, even if the mother in most cases was eventually vested with sole custody.

The solution to the problem of the 'disappearing' father was the introduction in 1976 of a possibility for divorced parents to retain joint responsibility after divorce.[3] At the same time it also became possible for unmarried parents to be vested with joint custody. Joint custodial responsibility entailed a joint right and obligation to decide in all matters concerning the child. A prerequisite for joint custody was that the parents agreed. Joint custody after separation could in other words be decided only at the request of both parents. All matters concerning the child required a joint decision by the parents with one exception: If an agreement was not reached, the parent not living with the child could be obliged by the court to pay child maintenance.

The 1976 reform of the custody rules, making it possible for separated parents to have joint custody, and thereby a joint right to decide, was from a principal point of view a significant step in the development of custody as a legal concept in Swedish law. It was no longer necessary to have the actual care of the child in order to have the right to decide in all matters concerning the child. The fact that legal responsibility and actual care in a formal sense were separated from one another and thereby perceived, at least to some extent, as independent aspects of parenthood, indicates that the relationship between the child's right to care and the obligation to provide that care was weakened. Legal custody of a child became a right to decide in all matters concerning the child, without a responsibility to actually care for the child. In this way legal custody appeared more as a right for the parents than an obligation towards the child. This thought can be illustrated by a comment in the *travaux préparatoires* where it is stated that in many cases the circumstances are such that a parent can relatively easily accept that the other parent takes care of the child, if he [*sic*] can remain legal custodian.[4] This state-

[3] Government Bill (*Proposition*) 1975/76:170, *Faderskap och vårdnad* (Paternity and custody).

[4] Government Bill 1975/76:170, p. 143. This statement is repeated in the following reforms in support for expanding the possibilities to decide on joint custody for separated parents. See

ment also illustrates one of the other main goals of the reform, *i.e.* to minimise the number of custody disputes in court.

In 1982 joint custody for separated parents became the main rule and the parents were required to renounce joint responsibility if they did not want it. In other words, consensus between the parents remained a precondition for joint responsibility, but now demonstrated by both parents refraining from asking for sole custody.

2.3. JOINT CUSTODY IF TOLERATED BY A RELUCTANT PARENT

Joint custody seemed to promote children's contact with a parent they did not live with.[5] For that reason the law was changed again in 1992, stating that if it was considered to be in the best interests of the child that the parents had joint custody, this could be decided even if one of the parents preferred sole custody.[6] It was now enough that the reluctant parent would tolerate joint responsibility. Only in those cases where one of the parents was explicitly against joint responsibility could sole custody be vested with one of them. This reform can be seen as another landmark in the development of the custody rules in that it was no longer required that the parents agreed on joint responsibility and the resulting joint right to decide on matters concerning the child. Since it was foreseen that the parents in this situation might not be able to solve questions concerning visitation rights, a possibility for the court to decide on this matter was introduced, despite the fact that joint custody presupposed joint decision making in all matters concerning the child.

The 1992 reform resulted in joint custody becoming the most frequently chosen solution also for separated parents who could not reach an agreement on custody. One reason for this could have been that many parents were afraid to explicitly oppose joint custody since that entailed a risk of losing custodial responsibility altogether. The courts also deemed joint custody to be in the best interests of the child and often chose this solution. Maybe not surprisingly, most children with separated parents still stayed with the mother who remained the

---

Government Bill 1990/91:8, *om vårdnad och umgänge* (about custody and access), p. 32 and Government Bill 1997/98:7, *Vårdnad, boende och umgänge* (Custody, residence and access), p. 51.

5 Follow up studies showed that children with parents with joint custody had better and more frequent contact with the non-residential parent than when one parent had sole custody, Government ministry report, Ds 1989:52, pp. 48–49.

6 Government Bill 1990/91:8.

primary care-provider.[7] Since one of the key reasons for changing the law to make joint custody the main rule was the assumption that this form of custody encouraged the child's contact with the parent not living with the child – in particular the father. It is interesting to note that no real follow up was conducted after this reform regarding contact frequency. Available data, however, indicate that contact between children and the parent they were not living with did not increase, rather the opposite.[8] The reasons behind this were never investigated. The general opinion seems to have been that joint custody for separated parents is in the best interest of the child and this did not need evaluation.

2.4. JOINT CUSTODY AGAINST THE WILL OF ONE PARENT

Considering the development of the custody rules in the 1980s and 1990s it is maybe not surprising that the law was amended once more in 1998 in order to promote the use of joint custody, a form of custody that was considered to be 'an important part in the development taking place towards a stronger emphasis on the child's interests'.[9] Consequently it was made possible for the courts to decide that custody should be shared between the parents even if one of them was explicitly opposed to this.[10] An important limitation, however, was that joint custody should be decided only if it was in the best interests of the child. Furthermore, it could not be ordered if both parents were against it. The Supreme Court stated in a leading case the following year that the law should be interpreted as meaning that sole custody should be given to one of the parents only when there were particular circumstances contradicting joint custody.[11] In practice the new rule was used as a presumption for joint custody, a presumption that had to be counter proven if sole custody was to be decided. The result was that parents, as long as one of them was in favour, even when they had such a deep disagreement on custody that they actually had turned to the court for a decision, were given joint custody, and thereby a joint right and obligation, to decide in all matters concerning the child.

In order to facilitate out-of-court agreements between parents a possibility to have their agreement on questions concerning custody, access or residence con-

7 Statistics from 1992 showed that after separation the parents had joint custody for 82% of the children. The mother had sole custody for 17% of the children and the father for 1 %. According to the estimates 91% of the children lived with the mother. SCB (Statistics Sweden), *Demografiska rapporter* (Demographic reports) 1994:2, p. 39.

8 A comparison between the statistics on contact between children and the non-residential parent shows a decrease in contact frequency between the years 1984–85 and 1992–93. SCB (Statistics Sweden), *Barn och deras familjer* (Children and their families) 1992–93, p. 25.

9 Government Bill 1997/98:7, p. 49.

10 The Parental Code, Chapter 6, Section 5.

11 Supreme Court decision NJA 1999, p. 451.

firmed by the Social Welfare Committee was introduced with the 1998 reform. The confirmation of the agreement makes it valid as a court decision. The agreement can be confirmed only if what is agreed is not obviously detrimental to the best interests of the child.[12] The most remarkable feature of the 1998 reform was, however, the introduction of a possibility for the courts to decide on alternating residence for the child, even against the will of one parent. This will be further explored below in the following sections.

2.5. RESTRICTING THE USE OF JOINT CUSTODY

Joint custody against the will of one parent was put into extensive use by the courts following the Supreme Court decision in 1999. This practise was soon criticised by many, among them the Swedish Children's Ombudsman. Investigations of court practice after the 1998 reform indicated that the possibility to decide on joint custody was used in cases where there were good reasons to question if it was in the best interests of the child.[13] Parents that could not reasonably be expected to co-operate in a way that would give the child good living conditions were still given joint custody. The law concerning joint custody was consequently changed again in 2006. The Parental Code now states that when assessing the best interests of the child, the social authorities and the court must take into account, in particular, the risk of the child or any other member of the family being abused, or of the child being unlawfully abducted, retained or otherwise being harmed. A provision stating that the courts should pay particular attention to the parents' ability to co-operate before deciding on joint custody has also been introduced in order to prevent, or at least limit, the use of joint custody where this would not be appropriate. There are reasons to believe that this provision will limit the use of joint custody against the will of one parent.[14] Limiting the use of joint custody against the will of one parent will also limit the possibilities to decide on alternating residence in cases when the parents do not consent.

However, alternating residence has become a widely accepted form of living arrangement for children with separated parents. The efforts of the Swedish legislature underlining the importance of parents taking joint responsibility for their children after separation has no doubt contributed to this. Many parents have also found this way of organising life after separation very satisfying and it is not likely that this will change as a result of the legslative emphasis that this option

12 The Parental Code, Chapter 6, Section 6.

13 Barnombudsmannen (The Children's Ombudsman), *När tryggheten står på spel* (When Security is at Stake), BO2005:02.

14 Supreme Court decision NJA 2007, p. 382.

should only be used when the parents are able to co-operate. Alternating residence is certainly here to stay.

3. ALTERNATING RESIDENCE

3.1. LEGAL BACKGROUND

As was mentioned above, the possibility for the court to decide on alternating residence was introduced in 1998, together with the possibility to decide on joint custody against the explicit will of one of the parents. However, joint custody against the will of one parent meant that parents with great difficulties would be forced to reach joint decisions in matters concerning the child. This could prove to be problematic in certain cases. There was an obvious risk that some parents would not be able to reach an agreement even on the most basic questions concerning the child, such as where the child was to live. It was therefore necessary to create a method to resolve disagreements between the parents concerning the child's residence. Such an option was also seen as a way to facilitate the use of joint custody since it, again, was assumed that it could be easier for a parent to accept the child living with the other parent than sole custody being given to that parent.[15] Since most children with separated parents live with their mother, the parent referred to was in most cases the father. The lawmaker in other words assumed that fathers would settle for joint right to decide, but would not demand to have the actual care of the child. However, there were already indications that some fathers also wanted to exercise actual care of the child. As was indicated earlier, even in 1992/1993 it had been estimated that approximately 4% of children with separated parents were alternating living with both of them.[16] It was, in other words, apparent that there were fathers who would not settle for only having part of the legal responsibility. This insight might partly explain that the courts were given the option to decide on alternating residence even when the parents had joint custody against the will of one of them.[17]

It is obvious that if the parents agree on joint custody and alternating residence, court decisions regarding the alternating residence can be a useful option in order to confirm the parents' agreement, thus thereby provide a binding way to regulate some practical questions. The legal regulation acknowledges this. However, with respect to the child, the court can only confirm the parents' agreement

---

15 Government Bill 1997/98:7, pp. 51, 57.

16 SCB (Statistics Sweden), *Barn och deras familjer 1992–93* (Children and their families 1992–93), p. 24.

17 The Parental Code, Chapter 6 Section 5. In the Government Report preceding the change of the law, nothing is mentioned about this particular consequence of the possibility to decide on living, Government Report SOU 1995:79, pp. 88–90.

if what agreed on is considered to be in the best interests of the child. An agreement between the parents is usually seen as a guarantee of this.

However, making it possible to decide on alternating residence against the will of the one parent would appear to make alternating residence a goal in and of itself. It is remarkable that this option was given in addition to the possibility to decide on joint custody against the will of one parent. Even more remarkable is the fact that this was done without any discussion whatsoever. In the *travaux préparatoires* there is no advice concerning under what circumstances the option of deciding on alternating residence is to be used and no clarification of what factors to consider. All that is said is that the courts' decision can entail the child living with one of the parents or alternating with both.[18] The impression is that alternating residence without closer analysis became an automatic step in the development of the rules concerning custody of children. If the legal responsibility is shared between the parents, so should the actual care. In addition, dividing the child's time equally between the parents when they cannot reach an agreement is an easy way of reaching an equitable solution.

3.2. DEFINING ALTERNATING RESIDENCE

In legal terms there are some difference between alternating residence and extended visitation. A court decision on residence can only be given when both parents are custodians.[19] A decision on residence states that the child shall live with one of the parents. The term alternating residence is not used in the Parental Code. A decision on alternating residence thus states that the child is to live with both parents.

Visitation, on the other hand, can be determined regardless of the custodial status of the persons involved, *i.e.* when both parents have custody, but also if one of them has sole custody.[20] In reality the difference between alternating residence and extended visitation might not be visible, since it is possible to decide that the child shall reside with one parent and visit the other parent up to 50% of the time.

In practice, it has been determined that when both parents have custody and the child spends more than 40% of the time with one parent and slightly less than 60% of the time with the other it is alternating residence.[21] It is also required that this arrangement has some permanency or is intended to become more permanent. Consequently, if the child spends less than 40% of his or her time with one parent, it is regarded as involving extended visits. If only one of the parents has

18 Government Bill 1997/98:7, p. 56.

19 The Parental Code, Chapter 6, Section 14 a.

20 The Parental Code, Chapter 6, Section 15 a.

21 See *e.g.* Supreme Court decision NJA 1998, p. 267 and Court of Appeal decision RH 1993:64.

custody of the child, it is never regarded as alternating residence, even if the child spends half of the time with each parent.

4. FOLLOW-UP ON ALTERNATING RESIDENCE

4.1. ALTERNATING RESIDENCE IN PRACTISE

There has been some, albeit limited, follow-up on alternating residence for children in Sweden in recent years. In 2000, the National Board of Health and Welfare conducted a study. The purpose was to find out how alternating residence was put into practice, its advantages and disadvantages and how children were influenced by alternating residence.[22] The results of the study indicated that parents who had opted for alternating residence were positive to this way of organising life after separation. Children who had experienced alternating residence emphasised as positive that they were given the opportunity to develop close and good contact with both parents. However, they also pointed out that it sometimes was stressful not to have a stable place of their own. Some of the children expressed a wish that their living arrangements could change from time to time, but stated that they were afraid to take this up with their parents.[23]

Parents who had had alternating residence imposed by a court decision were, maybe not surprising, not as positive. Many of them pointed out that they had not been able to co-operate prior to the decision and were also not able to do so afterwards. It was also noted that in many cases the arrangement with alternating residence was not implemented; one year after the court decision, alternating residence was practiced in only one out of every two cases.[24]

One conclusion from the study was that alternating residence is in itself neither good nor bad. It depends on how the arrangements are handled by the parents. A prerequisite for a workable solution is that the parents manage to avoid conflict. It is also important that they live close to one another in order to facilitate that the child can attend school and retain the same friends even when the residence is changing. The parents also have to be very flexible and sensitive to the wishes of the child. Alternating residence can without doubt burden the child. As it is said in the report from the National Board of Health and Welfare, the child pays a price in order to have equal access to both parents.[25]

22 Socialstyrelsen (The National Board of Health and Welfare), *Växelvis boende. Att bo hos pappa och mamma fast de inte bor tillsammans* (Alternating residence. To live with dad and mum even when they are not living together), 2004, p. 7.

23 *Ibid.*, p. 8.

24 *Ibid.*, p. 8.

25 *Ibid.*, pp. 8–9.

4.2. RE-EVALUATING ALTERNATING RESIDENCE AS A LEGAL OPTION

Following the study by the National Board of Health and Welfare, in 2002 a governmental committee was given the task to evaluate the 1998 custody reform. This involved studying the consequences of the new regulation for joint custody and residence. The committee studied 249 district court cases from the first half of 2002. In 125 of these cases the parents were engaged in conflict regarding the child's residence. In 51% of the cases it was decided that the child should live with the mother, in 34% of the cases with the father and the remaining 15% of the cases it was decided that the child should alternately live with both parents. In 66 out of the 125 cases there was a claim by one of the parents for alternating residence. The courts rejected three out of four of these claims and decided on alternating residence only in 19 cases. However, in 15 out of these 19 cases the decision on alternating residence was against the will of one parent.[26] The reasons for deciding on alternating residence was in one out of every two cases that such an arrangement was justified with regard to the child's need for close and good contact with both parents. The child's own desire to live alternately with the parents was given as a reason in almost every other case. In many cases it was also stated that the parents did not have severe difficulties co-operating and that the parents lived close to one another. In two cases it was also stated that alternating residence had been the previous arrangement and that the child's need for continuity spoke in favour of continuation of the arrangement.[27]

The evaluating committee organised several hearings on the subjects of its investigation, among them alternating residence. The committee found that in general the possibility for the court to decide on alternating residence against the will of one parent was seen as positive, even if a restrictive use was recommended by many. The committee declared that it considered alternating residence as a living arrangement that under the right conditions could function quite well and could provide the child a natural and unstrained contact with both parents in the different events of everyday life that is not possible when the child lives with one parent. In its final report the committee took the opportunity to elaborate on the preconditions for deciding on alternating residence since this form of living arrangement demands that certain requirements are met.[28]

The child's own opinion is of great importance. The committee stated that the child's own opinion on how the living arrangements should be organised must, with increasing age and maturity, be respected and, for the oldest children, even decisive. It was also pointed out that for many children it is more self-evident to

---

26 Government Report SOU 2005:43 Part B, pp. 757–761.

27 *Ibid.*, p. 761.

28 Government Report SOU 2005:43 Part A, pp. 157–163.

have an opinion on where to live, than on the question of custody, thus underlining the importance of consulting the child.[29] Another factor to consider before deciding on alternating residence for a child is, according to the committee, if one of the parents is against such an arrangement. A basic requirement that needs to be met prior to considering alternating residence is whether the parents have the ability to co-operate with regard to the issue of the custody of the child and that they do not let their own conflict influence the child's situation. Experience indicated that joint custody and alternating residence against the will of a parent does not work as a means to force the parents to co-operate in matters concerning the child. Studies and experiences from child psychiatry has also shown that if the parents cannot co-operate or if there are serious conflicts between them, there is a risk that this affects the conditions for alternating residence. This form of living then becomes a source for continuous conflict that negatively affects the child. If one of the parents is guilty of violence or other degrading treatment of family members, the committee was of the opinion that neither joint custody nor alternating residence should be considered.[30]

Moreover, the commission found that the ability of the parents to be flexible is vital for the success of alternating residence. The needs of the child must always be paramount. Few grown-ups would accept to have their lives strictly and irrevocably planned for a long time in advance. Depending on the child's activities the parents must be able to adjust their schedules to fit the child's needs. Alternating residence cannot be a question of absolute fairness between the parents and should not be seen as a way of equally dividing the child's time between the parents or as a tool to achieve equality in the relationship between parent and child. On the contrary, it is necessary for the conditions of the child to develop continuously to accommodate for the child's needs and wishes. The child's time with each respective parent must be allowed to vary from one time to another.[31]

The committee did not find a specific age when alternating residence could be said to benefit the child. There had been discussions of a three-year age limit, indicating that younger children should not be subject to alternating residence. Even if such an age limit was based on well-founded reasons, according to the Committee, it could not be said to be absolute. The conditions for the individual child could differ greatly. If the child had lived with one parent for a long time, even maybe his or her whole life, a change to alternating residence could be dramatic also for an older child. The same could be true for a child who had lived with both parents but having had one of them as the primary care giver. On the other hand, in many families today, both parents take an active part in the child's

29 *Ibid.*, p. 159.
30 *Ibid.*, p. 160.
31 *Ibid.*, pp. 160–161.

life and care and the preconditions for alternating residence could in such cases be good.[32]

The committee also emphasised that the parents must live reasonably close to another if alternating residence is to be considered in the best interest of the child. Cases had been reported where children had alternating residence also when the parents lived far away from one another, in some cases more than 1000km. Even if the parents are in agreement on such arrangements, and co-operating parents in general can be assumed to provide good care of the child, it was difficult, according to the committee, to get away from the impression that these arrangements had more to do with the parents desire to have equal share in the child's life, than a genuine desire to see to what was best for the child.[33]

In summary it can be said that the committee underlined the importance of carefully judging the circumstances in the individual case before deciding on alternating residence, whether this was decided by the parents themselves or by the court. As a reminder to the courts it was emphasised that alternating residence should not to be decided when the parents had difficulties co-operating and should not be used as a way to create something adjacent to equal sharing of a child between the parents. Alternating residence was not discussed extensively in the subsequent government bill. The government stressed that alternating residence should not be used when the parents had problems co-operating, but saw no reason to abolish the possibility for the court to decide on alternating residence for the child against the will of one of the parents altogether.[34]

5. EMERGING PROBLEMS WITH ALTERNATING RESIDENCE

5.1. CHILD SUPPORT AND ALTERNATING RESIDENCE

The practical implication of whether the child has alternating residence or is just visiting with one parent becomes apparent when determining child support. According to the Parental Code parents are to provide maintenance for the child according to what is reasonable having regard to the needs of the child and their collected resources.[35] This means that each parent should have a share in the costs for the child proportional to his or her economic ability. If one parent has 80% of the total earnings of the parents, that parent should pay 80% of the costs for the child's support. Parents living with the child fulfil their maintenance obligation

---

32 *Ibid.*, pp. 161–162.

33 *Ibid.*, pp. 162–163.

34 Government Bill 2005/06:99, *Nya vårdnadsregler* (New custody rules), pp. 52–53.

35 The Parental Code, Chapter 7, Section 1.

by taking care of the child and catering to the child's needs in day to day life. A parent not permanently living with the child should pay maintenance allowances, regardless of whether he or she has custody.[36] The obligation to pay maintenance allowances can be determined by means of an agreement between the parents or by the court. A parent who lives permanently with the child may only be compelled by the court to provide special maintenance payments if he or she neglects the duty to maintain the child. This option, however, is never used in practice, seemingly because it is assumed that a parent living with the child automatically fulfils his or her maintenance duty.

Due to the wording of the law there are no legal grounds for obliging a parent to provide special maintenance payments when the child is living alternating with both parents. The reason is that the child is considered to live permanently with both parents. In this situation both parents are thought to fulfil their duty by virtue of their actual care of the child. Grounds for such an assumption may be present when both parents share a similar economic level, when they share the child's costs equally and when they co-operate. As is well known separated parents do not always manage to collaborate in the best possible way. In these instances, and when one of the parents has a greater economic ability – which means that he or she according to the main rule should cover a greater part of the child's economic needs – there is limited support for the assumption that the costs of the child is naturally divided between the parents according to the main rule of the law. For instance, the parent that is supposed to cover 80% of the child's economic needs cannot automatically be expected to do this in 40% of the time, thus compensating for the costs that are to be covered when the child is with the other parent. The parent who is supposed to cover 20% of the child's economic needs might find it difficult to manage when having the child in some cases more than half of the time.

The situation is further complicated by the fact that it is possible to receive maintenance support from the Swedish Social Insurance Agency. According to the Maintenance support law,[37] maintenance support can be paid to the parent with whom the child is living permanently, if the parent liable to pay maintenance fails to do so or simply as an advance payment of maintenance. The maintenance support is not means tested and is a fixed sum paid monthly. The Social Insurance Agency then endeavours to obtain reimbursement from the person liable to provide maintenance. If the full sum paid as maintenance support cannot be retrieved from the parent liable to pay maintenance, the difference is paid as a supplementary payment in order to guarantee the child a certain economic level. Since it is not possible to determine maintenance payments when the child has alternating residence, it is always possible to apply for maintenance support in these cases.

36 The Parental Code, Chapter 7, Section 2.

37 *Lag om underhållsstöd* (1996:1030).

When the child has alternating residence, however, the parent applying for maintenance support will receive half of the amount that would normally be paid. This sum is reduced in consideration of that parent's own capability to pay maintenance.

Without going into the rather complicated methods for calculating maintenance support, one can conclude that this system makes it possible to give public support to families that have alternating residence, which could not be paid to children in cohabiting families or to children who are living permanently with one of the parents.

5.2. THE REGISTRATION OF CHILD'S RESIDENCE

The registration of the child's residence in the national population register is another question that has been discussed in relation to children with separated parents with an alternating residence regime.[38]

The National Tax Board registers the child's residence independently of the custody of the child.[39] A parent with sole custody has the exclusive right to decide in all matters concerning the child and the child will consequently be registered with that parent. If the parents have joint custody, but are not living together the situation becomes more complicated. As a general rule a child should be registered at the address where he or she spends most nights. This is also the case when the child has alternating residence. If one of the parents remains in the previous family home this will be the registered address of the child. If both parents have moved, an independent assessment will be carried out. The parents' opinion, even if they are in agreement at which address the child should be registered, is of no relevance for the decision of the National Tax Board.[40] The result is that when the child has alternating residence it becomes very difficult to determine where the child is to be registered and from the parents perspective the decision can be perceived as arbitrary.

The question of where or with whom the child is registered is of importance for the child when it comes to, *inter alia*, access to health care. For any other treatment than emergency treatment, the child has to turn to a hospital in the area where the child is registered. If the child has alternating residence in two different areas, this could cause problems. Another practical question for both child and parents that has been discussed is the right to enrol in a school and free school

---

38 The questions concerning problems with social benefits in connection with alternating residence is discussed *i.a.* in A. Wickström, 'Barn som bor hos var och en av föräldrarna – skärningspunkt civilrätt/offentlig rätt (Children who live with each one of the parents – intersection of private/public law)', 2004 *Förvaltningsrättslig tidskrift*, pp. 329–356.

39 Government Bill 2005/06:99, p. 53.

40 Supreme Administrative Court decision RÅ 1997 ref. 8.

rides. A child has a right to go to school in the municipality where the child is registered. The decision in which school the child is to be enrolled has to be taken by the parents together. This has caused problems when parents are not in agreement in which school should be chosen and there are cases where the child has been enrolled in different schools. This problem is accentuated when the child has alternating residence and both parents would like for the child to be in a school close to his or her home. Parents with joint custody have to register the child in the school. When the parents are not in agreement the question of which school the child is to attend is decided by the registered address. Since the child with alternating residence can have to travel a long way to school half of the time, the cost for school rides can also cause problems. The municipalities will only pay for rides within the municipality. For the single parent it therefore can be of great importance to have the child registered at his or her address.

5.3. SOCIAL BENEFITS AND ALTERNATING RESIDENCE

The question of registration is not only of importance to the child. For a parent the registration of the child on his or her address can have great economic consequences since many forms of social benefits to children are paid to the parent living with the child. Social benefits are of great importance for single parents. Estimates show that around 30% of a single parent's disposable income consists of social benefits. For single mothers this percentage is almost 37%.[41] The system of paying social benefits to single parents has been reformed in recent years in order to decrease the importance of the child's registered residence. All children in Sweden are entitled to a state child allowance. When the child has alternating residence the parents can notify the Social Insurance Agency that half of the child allowance should be paid to each one of them. However, this requires consensus and the possibility is used infrequently. If no notification is made the child allowance is automatically paid to the mother.[42] Other social benefits, such as housing allowance, as well as families with children and childcare allowance paid to a parent taking care of a sick or disabled child at home, are paid to the parent registered as living with the child.

41 SCB (Statistics Sweden), *Income distribution survey 2005.*

42 There are suggestions that the child allowance always should be paid to both parents, but no legislation has been passed.

6. DISCUSSION – CONCLUDING REMARKS

All available information indicates that the most important prerequisites for alternating residence to function well is that the parents are not in conflict with one another and that they can co-operate. The question is whether this rather mundane requirement is addressed by the legal system. To solve conflicts between the parents, thus protecting the interests of the child, can be said to be one of the main purposes of the law concerning matters of custody and residence. A possibility to decide on joint custody and alternating residence against the will of one parent clearly contravenes such an ambition. There are no convincing arguments for introducing such an option or to retain it. The fact that it exists in Swedish legislation is difficult to understand, let alone justify. Mechanically dividing the time with the child equally between unwilling parents has nothing to do with justice or the best interests of the child.

Alternating residence when the parents are in agreement can, on the other hand, be encouraged, but only if the parents are co-operating the whole time that alternating residence continues. The aim for the legal system must therefore be to help parents to co-operate. In this respect improvements can be, and to some extent have been, made.

One factor to consider is the court process itself. There are indications that court proceedings concerning questions of custody and residence spur conflicts and efforts should, for that reason, be made to shorten the length of the process. It can be questioned if conflicts concerning custody and residence should be handled at all by the regular courts, as is the case in Sweden. If the goal is to improve co-operation between parents, a less formal way of handling conflicts would probably be more efficient. One way of doing this could be to develop the existing possibility for parents in conflict to turn to the Social Welfare Committee in their community to get help to reach an agreement. In their present form these talks are not sufficient.

Questions related to the economy for separated parents with alternating residence also need to be addressed. The lack of a possibility to have maintenance payments determined when the child has alternating residence is remarkable considering the general rule that each parent should take part in the costs for the child proportional to his or her economic ability. It is well known that economic questions are often at the core of conflicts between separated parents. The regulation of the division of costs for a child with separated parents must for that reason be perceived as just and the results as predictable. Consensus agreement should be encouraged and the rules should also be simple to put into practice. This can not be said about the Swedish system today. The result is that in some cases economical considerations are behind the decision to choose alternating residence for the child. Many parents have a – sometimes justified – impression that alternating residence for the child will improve the parent's economy. The parent with the higher income is provided an incentive to ask for alternating residence in order to avoid paying maintenance and the parent with the lower income has reasons to refuse alternating residence in order not to loose different kinds of social benefits or special maintenance payments.[43]

Furthermore the regulation concerning social benefits should to be amended in order to function well with alternating residence. It is apparent that the administrative system has not been able to adjust to the rapid increase of the use of alternating residence for children with separated parents. As it is today, the system is constructed for children living permanently with one parent, and the inadequacy of the regulation can cause conflicts between the parents when the child has alternating residence. A possibility to make equal, but divided, payments of different social benefits to both parents would probably alleviate some of the problems that are present today. Split child benefits would also indicate that both parents are equally important as parents. On the other hand, there is a risk that a division of social benefits could serve as an even stronger incitement for alternating residence for economical reasons than today, and possibly to an increase in court proceedings. This would not be in the best interests of the child. The ambition must be to create a system that does not prevent or hinder the parents to reach an agreement on alternating residence. But the system should not encourage alternating residence for economic reasons. A good starting point would be to look at who is actually paying the different costs of the child. Maybe it is reasonable that one parent has the main responsibility for paying, for example, the child's clothes or leisure activities, even when the child's residence is alternating. Splitting the benefits does not necessarily mean that each parent take equal part in all costs.

Last but not least, further research is needed to clarify children's experiences of alternating residence. The main argument in favour of alternating residence is that it is in the best interests of the child. It is being underlined that this is an arrangement that provides the child natural and unstrained contact with both parents in the different events of everyday life that is not possible when the child lives with one parent. But are there disadvantages seen from the child's perspective? Of this, very little is known. Before further encouraging the use of alternating residence a follow up should be done. It is quite noteworthy that this has not been done considering that it is a solution being promoted as a way to protect the best interests of the child.

43 The National Board of Health and Welfare (*Socialstyrelsen*), *Växelvis boende. Att bo hos pappa och mamma fast de inte bor tillsammans* (Alternating residence. To live with dad and mum even when they are not living together), 2004, p. 26.

ALTERNATING RESIDENCE AND RELOCATION

A view from France

Frédérique Granet*

INTRODUCTION

Alternating residence of children is regulated by the Act of 4th March 2002 and is based either on the basis of parental agreement or, if it is impossible, on a judicial decision. Of course, joint physical parental authority[1] implies appropriate material circumstances, but it also refers to the mutual respect of the parents for each other and to their capacity to communicate with each other, thus ensuring that the child is educated and raised in a harmonious environment.

However, this type of arrangement for the child can be altered at any time as and when new circumstances arise, for example when of one of the child's parents moves. The child's best interests must remain the paramount consideration in establishing, as well as when terminating an alternating residence arrangement.

Up until the 4th March 2002, legislation determined the scope of the joint exercise of parental authority. The Act of 4th March 2002 widened this ambit by establishing two additional rules. These rules apply to both married or unmarried parents equally, in accordance with the spirit of the United Nations Convention on the Rights of the Child (Article 18(1)).

The first rule is laid down by Article 372, French Civil Code (*Code civil*) which states that the 'father and mother shall exercise parental responsibility jointly'. This is the general rule, but it has been subject to a number of adjustments.

Firstly, the family judge (*juge aux affaires familiales*) can refuse to apply this principle in situations where its implementation would be impossible or contrary

* Professor at the Robert Schuman University of Strasbourg (France), Director of the Department on Private Law (EA 1351) in charge of the Master on Family Law, email: frederique.granet@urs.u-strasbg.fr.

1 Alternating residence is more than simple joint physical custody, since it not only means that the child spends *significant* amounts of time with both parents, but supposes *equal* amounts in an *alternating* manner, even if it does not systematically imply *strict shared* physical custody. Alternating residence can be seen as a sort of 'dual residence'.

to the child's best interests. In these situations, the judge can entrust the exercise of parental authority to either the father or the mother. This solution, which remains rare,[2] requires a motivated decision and, if it is pronounced at the request of one of the parents, the decision must elucidate the very serious reasons that prevent exercise of joint parental authority.[3] It must, however, be noted that the pure physical distance is not sufficient to prevent the exercise of joint parental authority and that neither a parent's sexual[4] nor religious orientation[5] may justify a denial of joint parental authority. If parental authority is exercised by a parent alone, the other parent has a right to contact (visiting and lodging rights), the terms of which are regulated by the judge. The parent who is not holder of parental authority cannot be deprived of these contact rights, except in exceptional cases.

Secondly, the scope of the general principle is restricted by Article 372(2), which applies to the children of unmarried parents after parentage has been established in respect of one of the parents and subsequently in relation to the other. This provision states that in two cases only one parent exercises parental authority, namely (a) if the parentage is initially established with respect to one parent and subsequently in relation to the other more than one year after the child's birth, the former remains the sole holder of parental authority and (b) if parentage with respect to the 'second parent' is established by a judgment. In these situations, Parliament has considered that it is non-expedient for the child to benefit from automatic joint exercise. However, Article 372(3) grants joint exercise of parental responsibility if both parents make a joint declaration before the court clerk of the court of first instance (*le greffier en chef du tribunal de grande instance*) (Article 1180-1, New Code of Civil Procedure (*Nouveau code de procédure civile*)). Moreover, one of the parents may submit a request to the family judge, who could also issue an order of joint parental authority in the child's best interests.

The second important rule is laid down by Article 373-2(1) and states that 'the separation of the parents has no consequence on the application of the rules concerning the allocation of parental authority. Consequently, the principle remains intact that parental authority is exercised jointly. Several new provisions form a common law of the exercise of parental responsibility by separated parents.

2 See Cass. civ. 1, 14th November 2006, No. 05-18.116.

3 See, for example, in case of a parent's manifest and continuous lack of interest towards the child: Cass. civ. 1, 21st April, JCP G 2001, I, 332, obs. H. Blosse-Platière; in case of one parent's systematically conflicting behaviour, of hostility to the other parent or of permanent denigration of the other one: CA Rouen, 19th October 2006, Juris-Data, No. 2006-317494; in case of an existing risk of international kidnapping: Cass. civ. 1, 17th January 2006, *Bull. Civ.* I, No. 10.

4 ECtHR, Judgment of 21st December 1999, *Salgueiro Da Silva Mouta* v. *Portugal*, 2000 *Dr. Fam.*, Comm. No. 45, note A. Gouttenoire; 2000 *RTD civ.*, p. 433, obs. J. Hauser.

5 ECtHR, Judgment of 23rd June 1993, *Hoffman* v. *Austria*, D. 1994, jur. p. 327, note J. Hauser.

Article 372–2, which applies whether the parents cohabit or are separated, states that 'towards any other sincere persons, each parent is deemed to act with the agreement of the other parent when solely making an usual act on issues of parental authority regarding the person of the child'. Mentioned in almost all European legal systems to facilitate the everyday exercise of parental responsibilities, this presumption only benefits 'other sincere persons' and may only be utilised for 'usual acts' concerning the child itself. These conditions can be appreciated in relation to the parents' former practice and to the fact that this act does not seriously affect the child's future (*e.g.* registration in a school, sporting club or musical lessons; normal medical or dental treatment, or even, according to the *Conseil d'État*, a request presented by a parent for the registration of the child on his/her passport – which can be criticised).[6] On the contrary, the father and mother must in principle reach agreement on important decisions.[7]

Despite all the facilities provided by this presumption and the principle of joint exercise of parental authority for divorced or separated parents and for unmarried parents, even if the latter do not live together or separated (Article 373–2(1)), the implementation of the parents' rights, obligations and responsibilities requires particular appreciation of the specificity of each situation. In any case, the law is concerned about the relationship between the child and both his/her parents when they separate. Since the child should not be deprived of any contacts with one of his/her parents, various measures have been established in order to preserve the principle of equality between parents (*e.g. coparentalité*). In this view, Article 373–2 states that 'each parent shall maintain a personal relationship with the child and respect his/her bond with the other parent'. Thus each parent has a dual obligation: an obligation towards his/her child and an obligation towards the other parent.

As for the European Court of Human Rights, it has also been considered that at any rate, the familial private life of both the child as well as each of his or her parents must be preserved after the divorce. This implies that the relationship between the child and each of the parents should be maintained.[8] This is the global context in which the alternating residence hypothesis (when the parents are jointly holders of parental responsibility) has to be examined, together with the issue of one of the parents' moving and relocation.

---

6 See *Conseil d'État*, référé, 4th December 2002, Defrenois 2003, p. 620, obs. J. Massip.

7 For example, participation of their children to a televised documentary: see CA Versailles, 11th September 2003, D. 2003, *AJ Famille*, p. 383, obs. F. Bicheron.

8 See, for example, ECtHR, Judgment of 30th June 2005, *Bove* v. *Italy*, No. 30595/02; ECtHR, Judgment of 28th June 2005, *Fourchon* v. *France*, No. 60145/00.

1. CONDITIONS OF SETTING UP AN ALTERNATING RESIDENCE FOR THE CHILD

Before the Act of 4th March 2002, in divorce cases, the spouses jointly determined the child's residence to be one of their homes. In the absence of any agreement, the child's residence was determined by the judge and the other parent was entitled to maintain a personal relationship with the child and to benefit from visiting and lodging rights. The Supreme Court strongly condemned shared residence, but some lower courts were not entirely opposed to such a solution if the parents could agree upon the solution. In order to reach a similar result, the courts granted the parent with whom the child was not living sizeable visitation rights.[9]

The Act of 4th March 2002 explicitly permits alternating residence either at the mutual behest of the father and mother, or by virtue of a judicial decision in spite of the absence of parental agreement. Article 373-2-9, paragraph 1 indeed states that 'the child's residence can be fixed on an alternating basis at both parent's domicile or at the domicile of one of the parents'. Parents can thus organize the consequences of their separation concerning the place where their child will live and, perhaps most notably, agree upon an alternating residence agreement without going to court.[10] However, they are also allowed to request judicial approval of a written agreement organizing the terms of the exercise of parental responsibility, *e.g.* a plan arranging the alternating residence for their child. The judge will officially authorise this agreement, unless it is contrary to the best interests of the child or if the consent of one of the parents was not freely given (Article 373-2-7 Civil Code).

Alternating residence can also result from a judicial decision pronounced in the child's best interest in cases of parental disagreement concerning the child's accommodation, since French law does not require parental agreement to implement an alternating residence arrangement. Under the Act of 4th March 2002, a temporary alternating residence arrangement can be imposed by courts, the duration of which is determined by the court. At the end of this period, the judge will determine the child's residence, either providing for the continuation of the alternating residence arrangement, or providing that the child live at the home of one of the parents (Article 373-9, paragraph 2 Civil Code). The alternating residence period is regarded as a trial period and as a 'litmus test' that can help parents to cease their conflict and adapt to the new circumstances.[11] Nevertheless,

---

9 See P. Hilt, 'La résidence alternée', 2001 *AJ Famille*, p. 43.

10 See for example: CA Bordeaux, 15th March 2005, 2005 *Dr. Famille* 2005, No. 130, note P. Murat.

11 See C. Moreau *et al.*, *La résidence en alternance des enfants séparés devant le juge aux affaires familiales, Enquête sur un échantillon de décisions prononcées par les JAF du 13 au 24 October 2003*, Ministère de la Justice, Cellule Études et Recherches, December 2003.

when facing parental disagreement with regards a child's alternating residence, the judge can also order such a measure without a trial period.[12]

In practice 80% of requests for an alternating residence arrangement are requested jointly by the parents and the judge agrees to these arrangement 95% of the time. On the other hand, when the parents disagree, an alternating residence arrangement is ordered in only 25% of the cases. Before deciding in such cases, judges generally order a social investigation in order to take the necessary precautions in order to implement their decision.

More concretely, an alternating residence arrangement obviously requires favourable circumstances. Parent's homes have to be close enough in order to ensure that regular and stable lifestyles are not disrupted. Only a few decisions have ordered an alternating residence arrangement for pre-school age children (*i.e.* under the age of six), although this solution does entail registration at two different schools. Moreover both parents have to be able to offer living and lodging conditions that are suitable for the child, as well as being willing to cooperate and communicate with each other in order to meet the child's educational needs. Furthermore, this sort of joint physical custody may neither be contrary to the best interests of the child, nor unbalancing for the child. The appreciation of the child's interest is also generally linked to his/her age and to the corresponding needs. As a consequence, an alternating residence arrangement is seldom ordered for very young children (*i.e.* younger than two or three). In this case, the residence is most often fixed at mother's home.

In case law, physical distance refers to the distance from one city to another, or from one neighbourhood to another,[13] but also a distance of ten to twenty kilometres between each of the parent's homes. The alternating residence arrangement can be organised according to each parent's professional situation, the school schedule or to the child's after school activities. The alternating residence arrangement can work on a weekly basis (every other week at each parent's home), on a monthly basis (every other month), on a yearly basis (every other year at each parent's home), or even on a daily one.[14] Finally, judges are also concerned about ensuring that affective links between the child and his/her half-brothers and sisters are maintained. For example, a court decided that it was in a boy's best interests to rotate between his parents' homes in order not to be separated from his half-brothers and sisters.[15] Sometimes the child him or herself will request such

12 See French Supreme Court, civ. 1, 14th February 2006, 2006 *Dr. Fam.*, Comm. No. 158, note P. Murat.

13 See for example CA Aix-en-Provence, 27th May 2004, Juris-Data No. 2004–251010.

14 See for example CA Lyon, 8th March 2005, Juris-Data No. 2005–273912, for a four-year-old child, when as a result of a parent's move the distance between their respective homes is more than 800 kilometres.

15 See CA Paris, 7th May 2003, 1st case, 2003 *Dr. Fam.*, Comm. No. 144, note A. Gouttenoire.

an alternating residence arrangement.[16] In these present circumstances, the only legal reference point is the best interests of the child criterion. The court pays great attention to this criterion. It is for this reason that one is only able to provide indications with regards the main tendencies, since one can find diverging decisions. When ordered, alternating residence obviously entails consequences with regards the evaluation of each parent's contribution to the child's maintenance.

The effects of an alternating residence in other fields, such as the fiscal and social fields, is also specified in special legislative provisions. With regards income tax, unless stated to the contrary, parents will share the benefit of the family general tax allowance (Article 196 of the French Tax General Code (*Code général des impôts*)). Under the Act No. 2006–1640 of 21st December 2006 concerning Social Insurance Financing (*JO* 22nd December 2006) the parents are allowed to share child benefit equally, unless they agree otherwise or if they cannot agree upon the beneficiary (Article L.521–1 of the Social Insurance Code (*Code de la sécurité sociale*)).

Similarly, if circumstances change and the alternating residence arrangement cannot be maintained, for example if it does not work properly,[17] this measure must be brought to an end. The same also applies when one parent decides to move. However, the mere change of the parent's residence does not imply the systematic cessation of the alternating residence arrangement; it all depends on concrete circumstances.

2. THE CONSEQUENCES OF THE CHANGE OF ONE PARENT'S RESIDENCE

The debate regarding the maintenance of the child's links with each of his or her father and mother when one of them moves was intense. According to Article 373-2-13, 'the rules contained in the approved agreement and all judicial decisions related to parental responsibility can be modified or supplemented at any time by the family judge on request of one or both parents, or of the prosecutor who can be called by a third person, child's relative or not'. Indeed, measures related to the exercise of parental authority are traditionally considered to be temporary, whether they are ordered by a judicial decision or included in a judicially approved agreement. They can therefore be changed at any time provided that circumstances require this to be done. This solution of course applies to judg-

16 See CA Paris, 7th May 2003, 2nd case, 2003 *Dr. Fam.*, Comm. No. 144, note A. Gouttenoire.

17 For example, because of young child's stress when separating from her mother: CA Dijon, 26th November 2002, Juris-Data No. 2002–199966; or because of need for stability of a ten-year-old child, whose school results were declining and whose behaviour expressed anxiety: CA Lyon, 6th June 2006, Juris-Data No. 2006–317910.

ments as well as to judicially approved agreements specifying the details of the child's residence.

The Act of 4th March 2002 aimed at preventing any difficulties, but it also invited the most diligent parent to submit a case to the family judge in cases of disagreement or dispute. This parent can request judicial amendment of the exercise of parental authority to the new circumstances, including the details of the child's accommodation, the fulfilment of the maintenance obligation and the payment of travel expenses due to the distance of one parent's home. To achieve this, it is stated in Article 373–2, paragraph 3:

> 'The parent who changes his/her residence, in so far as this modifies the way the parental responsibilities are exercised, shall inform the other parent in advance and in due time.
> In case of disagreement, the most diligent parent can call the family judge who will make a decision based on the child's best interest.
> The family judge decides on how parents share the travel expenses and consequently adjusts the contribution to the child's maintenance and education.'

The aim of this provision is to prevent a parent from attempting to appropriate the child and to remove him/her from the other parent.[18] This complies with the spirit of Article 373–2 stating that both the father and mother have the duty to respect the bonds between the child and the other parent. Some judgments punish an abrupt change of residence by one parent in cases of non-compliance with the law and without informing the other parent; judges will modify the child's residence and determine it to be at the other parent's home. The parent who disregards the child's right to contact with the other parent could furthermore be punished by a criminal court (Article L.227–6 Criminal Code (*Code pénal*)).

Nevertheless, as highlighted by case law, implementing an alternating residence arrangement 'cannot compel parents to live near each other', whether this was determined by a parental agreement or decided by judge,[19] since each of them has the right to freely choose the place where he or she lives.

As a result, when one parent moves to a place located too far away from the other parent, it is necessary to change the details of the exercise of parental authority in order to adapt them to the new situation. Most often the alternating residence is abandoned, simply because it has become impracticable due to the physical distance; if the circumstances favouring an alternating residence arrangement come to an end, more often than not this system will no longer be applied, regardless of each parent's educational abilities. The child's need for stability is the main consideration when determining his or her best interests. For example, it has been

[18] See Cass. civ. 1, 4th July 2006, *Bull. Civ.* I, No. 339.
[19] See CA Paris, 23rd February 2005, Juris-Data No. 2005–268955.

decided that a father moving forty kilometres away from his previous residence for a work-related transfer implied that the alternating residence had to be replaced by a permanent residence arrangement at the mother's home in order to preserve the child's lifestyle and education; the physical distance in this case became too important.[20] Similarly, when a mother planned to move hundreds of kilometres, the alternating residence of her four-year-old child was deemed to be no longer possible and his habitual residence was fixed at his father's home, after considering both the respective abilities of each parent, most notably the financial impact on and accommodation possibilities for the child, and this child's family and affective environment which was centralized at his father's residence.[21]

If this leads to litigation, judges must always decide in the child's best interest, even in cases of parental disagreement with regards to a change of the details of the residence. The motivation of their decisions is under the ultimate control of the French Supreme Court (*Cour de cassation*).[22] Judges considering the merits then specify, according to concrete circumstances, new circumstances of the child's life that ensure his or her stability, taking into account the maintenance of the relationship and the affective links between the child and the parent from whom he or she will no longer live with in the future.

More generally, the alternating residence arrangement is retained, despite a parent's move, only if the new homes of both of them are close enough to enable their school-age child to be registered at one school. In situations in which a parent's move brings him or her closer to the other parent's home and in which the habitual residence of the child has been previously fixed, an alternating residence may be implemented if all the circumstances of the case are favourable to this decision. This will be the case if the father and mother are able to communicate well and to agree on the educational needs of their child. On the contrary, when a parent moves far away from the other parent's home, replacing an habitual residence at one parent's home by an alternating residence has been sometimes considered as an appropriate solution to this new situation. In one particular case, this solution was approved in so far as it permitted a three-year-old child to preserve a close relationship with both his parents, which was deemed necessary for the development of his personality, and he was not yet of compulsory school age.[23]

20 See CA Douai, 16th October 2003, Juris-Data No. 2003–236164.
21 See CA Montpellier, 26th January 2005, Juris-Data No. 2005–278547.
22 See Cass. civ. 1, 13th March 2007, 2007 *Dr. Fam.*, Comm. No. 125, note P. Murat.
23 See CA Lyon, 8th March 2005, Juris-Data No. 2005–273912.

CONCLUSION

In conclusion, it has to be stressed, at first, that judges do not hesitate to approve any alternative residence arrangement agreed upon by the parents or, in the absence of agreement, to order such an arrangement if it does not destabilize the child and, moreover, enables him or her to be close to both parents. Nonetheless, judges do not hesitate to reprimand a parent who moves without previously informing the other parent or prevents the other parent from organizing new living arrangements and accommodation for the child, in accordance with his or her needs, as well as the affective relationships between the child and the other parent.

Judges deciding on the merits have in any case a 'sovereign power' (*pouvoir souverain*) when determining the facts of the case. Accordingly, the child's best interests are decided on a case-by-case basis in determining whether to implement an alternating residence arrangement, as well as whether to maintain this system or to replace it with a residence order at one parent's home and, at the same time, to adjust the details of his or her relationship with the other parent in the best possible way. The proximity of the parents' homes and the child's age (which in turn determines his or her schooling obligation) are important elements in the judicial determination. These issues can also be combined with any other specific circumstances. Nevertheless, the main consideration always remains the best interests of the child, in the spirit of the New York Convention.[24]

24 The author would like to thank Dr. Mélanie Schmitt, Researcher at the Robert Schuman University of Strasbourg, for her contribution to the case law research and the translation of this study into English.

DIVIDED PARENTS, SHARED CHILDREN

Conflicting approaches to relocation disputes in the USA

Theresa Glennon*

1. INTRODUCTION

Divorce and separation sets former partners, even those who share children, on diverging paths. These paths often involve remarriage, changes in employment, development of different circles of friends, and, in many instances, relocation to distant locations. The increasing disconnection of the lives of parents may make it difficult for parents to achieve the ideal 'bi-nuclear' family many policymakers envision for the children of divorced families. Custodial parents, however, may face special challenges as they seek to forge their own separate path, because non-custodial parents may seek judicial intervention to prevent their relocation.

Custody relocation disputes pose intractable dilemmas for courts. The cases often pit two well-intentioned parents against each other, in many cases undermining a prior history of inclusion of both parents in their children's lives. Non-custodial parents are often distraught at the thought of losing frequent access to their children. Custodial parents are similarly distressed to learn that their efforts to define their own lives are being thwarted by their previous partner in a now-defunct marriage. Each parent has a deep interest in the outcome of this dispute. The custodial parent seeks self-determination, freedom of movement and a continued custodial relationship with the child. The non-custodial parent seeks to remain in place and preserve a geographically close relationship with the child. Courts must identify the best interests of the children amidst these multiple and conflicting interests.

While courts grapple daily with children's best interests in custody disputes attendant to divorce and separation, relocation disputes are qualitatively different.

* Professor of Law, Temple University Beasley School of Law, 1719 North Broad Street, Philadelphia, Pennsylvania 19122 (USA), email: theresa.glennon@temple.edu, telephone 215.204.5430, fax 215.204.1185.

In these disputes, judges make decisions that could well determine the future course of custodial parents' lives. Judges may determine whether custodial parents will be able to remarry, follow their spouse to a new location, take a new career position, attend school, or rejoin family. A doctrinal approach that assesses only children's best interests ignores these key aspects of relocation disputes.

The United States is a highly mobile society. Almost 40 million people move to a new residence each year. While close to 25 million remain in the same county, 8 million move to a different county in the same state, and 5.7 million move to a different state.[1] Approximately 1.3 million move transnationally every year.[2] Movers are almost equally divided between males and females.[3] However, since the vast majority of custodial parents are mothers, most of those who need judicial permission to relocate with their children are women.[4] Thus, relocation doctrine impacts most men and women differently, with men often trying to keep their children geographically close to them and women typically seeking to move with their children. At the same time, most relocation after divorce or separation never reaches a court; geographical distance from one parent is now a common feature of childhood for many children of divorced or separated parents.

In this article I examine the challenges posed by relocation disputes. Section 2 discusses the varied state legislative and judicial approaches to relocation disputes in the United States, as well as proposed model statutes and principles for resolution of these disputes. As described more fully below, relocation doctrine exhibited a trend in the mid-1990s towards reducing legal barriers to relocation. However, more recent changes have gone in the opposite direction, imposing notice requirements and relieving the burden of proof on the non-custodial parent.[5] In addition to these legal standards, I also describe proposed model approaches to relocation, which themselves evidence the deep ambivalence reflected in the varied doctrinal approaches.

I review the academic literature concerning relocation disputes in the United States in Section 3. This scholarship has analyzed relocation disputes from a wide range of perspectives. These perspectives include: conflicting interpretations of the social science research about the best interests of children concerning relocation; competing ideologies of the post-divorce family; use of alternative dispute resolution strategies; constitutional rights of the parents; safety of domestic violence victims; and proposals to reshape relocation disputes to eliminate the geo-

1 US Census Bureau, Geographical Mobility, 2005–06, *Current Population Survey*, March, 2006, Table 1.

2 *bid.*

3 *Ibid.*

4 T. Glennon, 'Still Partners? Examining the Consequences of Post-Dissolution Parenting', 2007 *Family Law Quarterly*, p. 118 (noting that of 602 cases reviewed in the time period from June 1, 2001 to June 1, 2006, 90% involved custodial mothers seeking to relocate).

5 See Section 2, *infra*.

graphic presumption in favor of the current location and remedy the economic effect of a denial of permission to relocate. This literature demonstrates the complex nature of relocation disputes and suggests that relocation doctrine in the US should be realigned to address these complexities. The prevalence of post-divorce relocation also indicates that more important than fine-tuning relocation doctrine, states should take ameliorative steps to ensure that families are better prepared to support their children through the common experience of relocation and the many other changes that parental separation and divorce bring to the lives of children.

2. THE LAW OF PARENTAL RELOCATION: DOCTRINAL CHOICES IN THE STATES

The number of reported judicial decisions regarding relocation disputes has grown ten-fold over the past twenty-five years.[6] The outcome of these disputes is rarely predictable. In a recent study, I found that of the 602 custody relocation cases reported on a major electronic legal database, the custodial parent was granted permission to relocate in 41% of cases, denied permission in 43%, and the case was remanded for further proceedings in 16% of the cases.[7] Increased judicial intervention has also led to greater legislative activity by states, some of which have passed legislation concerning relocation within the last ten years.[8] These disputes have also drawn the attention of non-governmental bodies in the United States. The American Academy of Matrimonial Lawyers has proposed a *Model Relocation Statute*, and the American Law Institute has included resolution of relocation disputes in its *Principles of the Law of Family Dissolution*.[9] The National Conference of Commissioners of Uniform State Laws is currently drafting a proposed uniform law on the relocation issue.[10]

Researchers writing in the 1990s and early 2000s noted that relocation doctrine had been moving in the direction of reducing barriers to relocation by the custodial parent. High profile cases in New York and California in the mid-1990s

---

6 Glennon, *supra* note 4, p. 106.

7 *Ibid*., p. 123. Most trial court decisions are not available on Westlaw, the electronic legal database used for this research, so these figures mostly involve cases that reached the appellate level.

8 See Section 2, *infra*.

9 American Academy of Matrimonial Lawyers, 'Proposed Model Relocation Act of 1997', 1998 *Journal of American Academy of Matrimonial Lawyers*, pp. 1–24. Relocation has also received the attention of the Commission on European Family Law. K. Boele-Woelki, *Principles of European Family Law Regarding Parental Responsibilities*, 2007, Principle 3.21.

10 National Conference of Commissioners of Uniform State Laws, Drafting Committee on Relocation of Children Act, http://www.nccusl.org/Update/CommitteeSearchResults.aspx?committee=281.

seemed to establish a new norm. In *Tropea* v. *Tropea*, the New York Court of Appeals rejected its prior approach to relocation, which had required parents who wished to relocate to demonstrate 'exceptional circumstances.'[11] The Court instead adopted a 'best interests of the child' test that focuses on a range of factors related to the child's interests, including the effect of relocation on the child's relationship with the non-custodial parent and whether the child's life will be enhanced by the move.[12] The burden to demonstrate that the move is in the child's interests was placed on the parent who wishes to relocate.[13] That same year, *In re Burgess* provided the opportunity for the California Supreme Court to reject a standard requiring custodial parents to show that relocation is necessary.[14] California instead placed the burden of proof on the parent resisting relocation to demonstrate that relocation is detrimental to the children and requires a re-evaluation of custody.[15]

A wave of academic scholarship viewed these two cases as setting a clear trend favoring relocation.[16] Several other state courts and legislatures joined that trend. For example, the Colorado courts quickly followed and adopted a presumption in favor of relocation, and the Tennessee legislature adopted a similar presumption for parents with a significant majority of the residential time.[17] Not all states jumped on the liberalization bandwagon, however, and at least two states adopted more stringent requirements for relocation in the late 1990s.[18] The more recent trend appears to be away from a presumptive right to relocate towards a requirement that the custodial parent demonstrate that the move serves the best interests of the child. Since 2000, at least six state legislatures have adopted more stringent requirements for relocation, rejecting the more lenient standards adopted by their state courts.[19]

States currently employ two main types of approaches. One involves a test that determines whether the parent should be able to relocate with the child. The sec-

11 *Tropea* v. *Tropea*, 665 N.E.2d 145, 149 (New York 1996).

12 *Ibid.*, pp. 150–151.

13 *Ibid.*, p. 151.

14 *In re Burgess*, 913 P.2d 473, 481 (California 1996).

15 *Ibid.*, p. 482.

16 *See, e.g.*, C. Ford, 'Untying the Relocation Knot: Recent Developments and a Model for Change', 1997 *Columbia Journal of Gender and the Law*, pp. 1–53; E. Terry *et al.*, 'Relocation: Moving Forward, or Moving Backward?', 1998 *Journal of the American Academy of Matrimonial Lawyers*, pp.167–228.

17 *In re Francis*, 919 P.2d 776 (Colorado 1996); Tenn. Code. Ann. § 36-6-108 (2007).

18 In 1997, Louisiana and Arizona both passed legislation placing the burden of proof on the parent who wished to relocate. Ariz. Rev. Stat. § 25–408(G)(2008); La. Rev. Stat. § 9:355.13 (2007).

19 Ala. Code 1975 § 30-3-169.4 (2007)(adopted in 2003); Colo. Rev. Stat. § 14-10-129 (2008) (adopted in 2001); Conn. Gen. Stat. § 46b-56d (2008)(adopted 2006); Fla. Stat. § 61.13001(2008) (made more restrictive in 2002 and 2006); Ind. Code § 31-17-2.2-5 (2008)(adopted in 2006); Minn. Stat. § 518.175(3) (2008)(adopted in 2006).

ond, less common approach treats relocation as a possible basis for modification of custody to the non-relocating parent.

2.1. RELOCATION DOCTRINE: DETERMINING WHETHER TO PERMIT RELOCATION

Many states now explicitly require custodial parents who wish to relocate to provide notice of the proposed relocation to the other parent 60 days before the move.[20] If the other parent refuses consent, in some states, the custodial parent must then petition the court for permission to relocate.[21] In other states, the parent who opposes relocation must file within a certain timeframe to prevent the relocation, otherwise the custodial parent may move.[22] Even where there is no specific statutory notice requirement, courts are apt to penalize a parent who moves without giving such notice, so lawyers may advise their clients not to move without first giving timely notice to the other parent.[23]

Where a petition is filed with a court concerning relocation, the burden of proof varies greatly among the states. Some states place the burden of proof on the parent opposing relocation to demonstrate that the move is not in the child's best interests;[24] some employ a neutral best interests test; [25] while others place the burden of proof on the parent seeking relocation to demonstrate that the move is in the child's best interests.[26] In most states, courts will also consider the reasons for the proposed relocation to determine whether the proposed move is made in good faith, that is, whether it has a legitimate purpose or is designed to undermine the other parent's contact with the child, as well as assessing the other parent's reasons for opposing the relocation.[27]

For example, Arkansas employs a presumption favoring relocation for custodial parents with primary custody. In order to rebut the presumption, the non-custodial parent must demonstrate that relocation is detrimental to the child's

---

20 See, *e.g.*, Ariz. Rev. Stat. § 25–408(B)(2008); La. Rev. Stat. § 9:355.4 (2007).

21 See, *e.g.*, Nev. Rev. Stat. 125C.200 (2008).

22 See, *e.g.*, Ariz. Rev. Stat. § 25–408(D)(2008); Fla. Stat. 61.13001(5)(2007).

23 American Law Institute, *Principles of the Law of Family Dissolution: Analysis and Recommendations*, 2002, p. 375.

24 See, *e.g.*, *Hollandsworth* v. *Knyzewski*, 109 S.W.3d 653 (Arkansas 2003); Cal. Fam. Code § 7501 (2008); Wash. Rev. Code 26.09.520 (2008).

25 See, *e.g.*, Colo. Rev. Stat. § 14–10–129(2)(c) (2008); Conn. Gen. Stat. Ann § 46b-56 (2008); *Karen J. M.* v. *James W.*, 792 A.2d 1036 (Delaware Family Court 2002); *Bodne* v. *Bodne*, 588 S.E.2d 728 (Georgia 2003).

26 See, *e.g.*, Ala. Code § 30–3-169.4 (2007); Fla. Stat. Ann. § 61.13001(8) (2008); Haw. Rev. Stat. Ann. § 571–46 (2008); *Roberts* v. *Roberts*, 64 P.3d 327 (Idaho 2003); 750 Ill. Comp. Stat. Ann. 5/609 (2007); La. Rev. Stat. Ann. 9:355.13 (2007); Minn. Stat. Ann. § 518.175(3)(c)(2008).

27 See, *e.g.*, Wash. Rev. Code § 26.09.520(5); *Gruber* v. *Gruber*, 583 A.2d 434 (Pennsylvania Superior Court 1990).

best interests, or that the relocation is motivated by bad faith or a desire to interfere with the other parent's visitation.[28] In the state of Washington, the parent opposing the relocation must prove that 'the detrimental effect of the relocation outweighs the benefit of the change to the child and the relocating person.'[29] Indiana employs a shifting burden of proof, requiring the relocating parent to show only that the proposed relocation is made in good faith and for a legitimate reason. The opposing parent must then demonstrate that relocation is not in the best interests of the child.[30]

Some states, such as Colorado, have adopted a neutral best interests approach that requires the court to consider various best interests factors.[31] Other states employing a best interests test place the burden of proof on the relocating parent to demonstrate that the move is in the best interests of the child.[32] For example, Pennsylvania parents seeking to relocate must demonstrate that the move would substantially improve the quality of life for the parent and child, that they have a good faith motive to relocate, and that realistic, substitute visitation arrangements with the non-custodial parent are available.[33] Alabama disfavors relocation, and the parent who seeks to change the child's principal residence must rebut the presumption that relocation is not in the child's best interests.[34]

A few states vary the burden of proof based on the amount of parenting time of each parent. Tennessee permits a parent with substantially more of the parenting time to relocate with the child unless the relocation does not have a reasonable purpose, poses a threat of specific and serious harm to the child, or the relocating parent's motive is vindictive. If one of those criteria is met, or if the parents share substantially equal parenting time, the court must determine whether relocation is in the child's best interests.[35] West Virginia also explicitly varies the burden with the amount of parenting time each parent has. A parent who has a significant majority of the custodial responsibility (70% or more of the time) may relocate 'so long as that parent shows that the relocation is in good faith for a legitimate purpose and to a location that is reasonable in light of that purpose.'[36] If neither parent exercises custodial responsibility a significant majority of the time, then the court adopts a custody modification approach and must reallocate custodial responsibility based on the best interests of the child.[37]

28 *Hollandsworth* v. *Knyzewski*, 109 S.W.23d 653 (Arkansas 2003).
29 Wash. Rev. Code § 26.09.520.
30 Ind. Code Ann. § 31-17-2.2-5 (2008).
31 *In the Marriage of Ciesluk*, 113 P.3d 135, 140–41 (Colorado 2005).
32 *Matter of Groover* v. *Potter*, 792 N.Y.S.2d 693 (New York Appellate Court 2005); Vernon's Ann. Mo. Stat. 452.377(9)(2007); *Maynard* v. *McNett*, 710 N.W.2d 369 (North Dakota 2006).
33 *Gruber* v. *Gruber*, 583 A.2d 434 (Pennsylvania Superior Court 1990).
34 Ala. Code 1975, § 30-3-169.4 (2007).
35 Tenn. Code Ann. § 36-6-108(d),(e)(2008).
36 W. Va.Code § 48-9-403(d)(1)(2008).
37 W. Va. Code § 48-9-403(d)(3)(2008).

In some states, cases that involve joint custody are treated differently than cases involving sole custody. For example, New Jersey's relocation standard is viewed as favoring the relocating custodial parent. Custodial parents need show only that the move is proposed in good faith and is not 'inimical' to the child's interests.[38] However, where parents share custody, the New Jersey courts treat the relocation petition as a motion for a change in custody. This motion is decided under the best interests of the child standard, with the burden of proof equally shared by the parents.[39] North Dakota requires custodial parents to prove that relocation is in the best interests of the child. However, where parents have joint custody, courts must first assign primary custody, before making a relocation decision.[40]

2.2. THE CUSTODY MODIFICATION APPROACH

Several states use custody modification doctrine to evaluate relocation disputes.[41] A substantial move is generally considered a substantial change in circumstances that allows the court to determine whether there should be a change in custody.[42] Courts using the custody modification approach have resisted efforts to switch the focus to whether to permit the parent to relocate. The Alaska Supreme Court, for example, has admonished its lower courts that they are not to determine whether a parent is permitted to relocate. Rather, as long as the parent has a legitimate reason to relocate, courts must assume that the relocation will occur, and determine what custody arrangement is in the best interests of the child upon relocation.[43]

A custody modification approach may also place the burden of proof on the non-relocating parent. That burden may be heavy, as it is in Kentucky, where the parent seeking modification must show that the child is or will be endangered and that the advantages of a change in custody outweigh the harm that is likely to be caused by a disruption in the custodial arrangement.[44] Iowa places a lighter burden on the non-relocating parent seeking primary custody to prevent the child from relocating.[45] The non-custodial parent must prove that the move is a substantial change and that he has an ability 'to minister more effectively to the

38 *Baures* v. *Lewis*, 770 A.2d 214, 226 (New Jersey 2001).

39 *O'Connor* v. *O'Connor*, 793 A.2d 810 (New Jersey Superior Court 2002); see also *Lewellyn* v. *Lewellyn*, 93 S.W.3d 681, 686–87 (Arkansas 2002).

40 *Maynard* v. *McNett*, 710 N.W.2d 369 (North Dakota 2006); see also *Potter* v. *Potter*, 119 P.3d 1246, 1249 (Nevada 2005).

41 See, *e.g.*, *Latimer* v. *Farmer*, 602 S.E.2d 32 (South Carolina 2004).

42 See, *e.g.*, *Rowland* v. *Kingman*, 629 A.2d 613 (Maine 1993).

43 *Moeller-Prokosch* v. *Prokosch*, 99 P.3d 531 (Alaska 2004).

44 *Fenwick* v. *Fenwick*, 114 S.W.3d 767 (Kentucky 2003).

45 *In re Marriage of Thielges*, 623 N.W.2d 232, 235 (Iowa 2000).

children's well-being.'[46] In Kansas, a court should consider all factors in determining whether to modify custody, including the effect of the move on the best interests of the child and other affected parties and the increased costs of the exercise of visitation rights.[47] Wisconsin permits parents to choose between a petition to modify custody and a petition to oppose relocation.[48]

Courts using a custody modification approach join states that use relocation doctrine in treating joint custodial arrangements differently. For example, Vermont has a high threshold for removing custody from a relocating custodial parent. A parent with primary or sole custody will only lose custody if the non-custodial parent can prove that the children's best interests would be so undermined by the relocation that a transfer of custody is necessary.[49] However, where one parent in a joint custodial arrangement wants to move, the court considers the current custodial arrangement disrupted and allocates sole custody as in the best interests of the child.[50]

2.3. JUDICIAL INTERPRETATIONS OF CHILDREN'S BEST INTERESTS

Courts generally consider a wide range of factors in determining the child's interests in a relocation dispute. Courts will consider the quality of the relationship with each parent, as well as the child's relationship with other family and friends in their current and proposed locations. Courts also consider the child's age and development, and what the likely impact of relocation will be on the child, the child's preference, and whether the relocation will enhance the quality of life for the child and relocating parent. They also weigh the feasibility of alternative visitation arrangements to maintain the child's relationship with the non-relocating parent. Courts may order a new visitation and contact schedule if the relocation is permitted, and may also apportion the increased costs to maintain contact between the two parents.[51]

While precise doctrinal standards and burdens of proof vary widely, because courts in relocation cases consider a myriad of factors, they hear fact-intensive presentations by the parties.[52] Courts consider the amount of time the child spends with each parent, and the level of engagement in the child's activities,

46 *Ibid.*

47 Kan. Stat. § 60-1620(c)(2007).

48 Wisc. Stat. § 767.481(3)(2007).

49 *Lane* v. *Schenck*, 614 A.2d 792 (Vermont 1992).

50 *Hoover* v. *Hoover*, 764 A.2d 1192 (Vermont 2000).

51 See, *e.g.*, Fla. Stat. 61.13001(7)(2008).

52 The fact-intensive nature of presentations in relocation hearings is described in D. Hofstein *et al.*, 'A Moving Case for Staying Put', 2006 *Family Advocate* 25, pp. 25–29.

schooling and interests each parent has demonstrated. They also consider the extended family network available to the child in each location, and whether the child has a significant relationship with these relatives. Courts are much more reluctant to relocate children away from a community that is home to a supportive and involved extended family. Courts scrutinize the schooling arrangements, as well as participation in other community activities such as sports and religious organizations. If children have special educational needs, they will consider the ability of the schools in both locations to meet those special needs. They also consider whether a working parent will be able to stay home fulltime after relocation, and the economic situation of the family in both settings.[53]

Crucial to courts' analyses of these many factors relating to children's best interests, however, appears to be an underlying legislative or judicial policy determination favoring either the maintenance of the child's relationship with the non-custodial parent or the view that the child's custodial family takes precedence over the child's relationship with the non-custodial parent.[54] In later sections, this article explores the disputed social science and ideological bases for these differing views.

These varied state approaches have in common an emphasis on the best interests of the child. In many states, the court's only concern is the best interests of the child; the interest of the custodial parent in relocation is legally irrelevant.[55] In other states, even where the effect of the move on the quality of life for the parent as well as the child is a factor, courts may give it little or no attention.[56] In some states, however, the shared focus on the best interests of both the parent and child are given great weight. The Washington Child Relocation Act, for example, shifted judicial analysis from the best interests of the child to a shared focus on the child's and the parent's interests.[57] Some other states take the parent's well-being into account indirectly, by finding the child's interests to be interwoven with the interests of the primary custodial parent.[58] In many states, however, the focus is on the best interests of the child, and that focus often centers on the

53 *Ibid.*

54 *Fohey* v. *Knickerbocker*, 130 S.W.3d 730 (Missouri Court of Appeals 2004); *Curole* v. *Curole*, 828 So.2d 1094 (Louisiana 2002)(favoring relationship with non-custodial parent); *cf. Baures* v. *Lewis*, 770 A.2d 214 (New Jersey 2001) and *Rosenthal* v. *Maney*, 745 N.E.2d 350 (Massachusetts Court of Appeals 2001)(favoring needs of the custodial family).

55 See, *e.g.*, Ala. Code 1975 § 30-3-169.4; *Norris* v. *Heckerman*, 972 So.2d 1098, 1099 (Florida Court of Appeals 2008).

56 See, *e.g.*, *Speck* v. *Spadafore*, 895 A.2d 606, 614 (Pennsylvania Superior Court 2004).

57 Wash. Rev. Code § 26.09.520 (2008).

58 These courts have emphasized that the child indirectly benefits from the improvement of the general quality of life for the custodial parent. See, *e.g.*, *In re Marriage of Collingbourne*, 791 N.E.2d 532 (Illinois 2003); *Rosenthal* v. *Maney*, 745 N.E.2d 350 (Massachusetts Court of Appeals 2001).

possible disruption a move would cause to the child's relationship with the non-custodial parent.[59]

2.4. RECOMMENDATIONS OF PROFESSIONAL BODIES CONCERNING RELOCATION

Professional bodies share with US states the inability to agree on a common doctrinal approach to relocation. Two highly regarded professional legal organizations – the American Law Institute and the American Academy of Matrimonial Lawyers – have proposed methods for states to adopt to deal with relocation disputes. At this writing, the National Conference of Commissioners on Uniform State Laws is considering the adoption of a Model Relocation Statute, but has not yet published its recommendations.

2.4.1. The American Law Institute Principle for Relocation of a Parent

The American Law Institute (ALI) published *Principles of the Law of Family Dissolution* for the first time in 2002.[60] The ALI Principles deal with a wide range of subjects affected by dissolution, including the allocation of custodial and decision making responsibility for children. The Principles seek to reduce litigation by adopting firm rules that restrain judicial discretion and, it is hoped, decrease incentives for parents to engage in lengthy litigation. They favor relocation by a parent with a clear majority of the parenting time, but are neutral when parents more equally share parenting time.

The ALI Principles require a parent who wants to relocate to provide the other parent with sixty days' notice prior to the relocation. If the other parent opposes relocation, the Principles establish a three-tiered process. Where the relocation significantly impairs the other parent's exercise of responsibilities in accordance with an agreed upon or court-ordered parenting plan, the court should first try to revise the parenting plan to accommodate the change without changing the proportion of custodial time of either parent. If the circumstances of the relocation make it impossible to maintain the same allocation of custodial time, then the court should decide whether to permit the parent to relocate with the child. A parent who has a clear majority of custodial time is presumed to be permitted to relocate for 'a valid purpose, in good faith, and to a location that is reasonable in light of that purpose.' However, if neither parent has a clear majority of the custodial time, the court must modify the parenting plan to reflect the child's best

59 See, *e.g.*, La. Rev. Stat. § 355.13; Vernon's Ann. Missouri Stat. § 452.377(9); Wisc. Stat. § 767.481(5).

60 American Law Institute, *supra* note 23, p. xv.

interests. Whenever a court permits a parent to relocate, the court should minimize the disruption to the child's relationship with the other parent.[61]

2.4.2. *The American Academy of Matrimonial Lawyers Model Relocation Statute*

The American Academy of Matrimonial Lawyers has also proposed an approach to relocation disputes, but its approach differs greatly from the ALI Principles and is far less definitive than the approach adopted by the ALI.[62] The *Model Relocation Statute* requires sixty days' notice of a change in the principal residence of a child, and permits the non-custodial parent to object to the relocation. However, the members of the Academy were unable to reach agreement on the standard that should be applied to such a dispute, and instead, it provides states various options. For example, with regard to custody modification, the Act states that '[a] proposed relocation of a child [may] [may not] [shall] be a factor in considering a change of [custody]. States may choose any of the three options.'[63] The comments state that '[i]t is left for the states to debate and decide whether a custody proceeding should be tried in connection with the relocation request.'[64]

Members of the Academy reached agreement on the factors that courts should consider when determining whether to permit relocation, such as the child's relationship with each parent, whether the relocation would improve the quality of life of the child and the relocating parent, and the effect of relocation on the child's relationship with the non-moving parent.[65] It could not agree, however, on which party should bear the burden of proof with regard to those factors, or whether the burden of proof should shift from one parent to the other. Thus, the burden of proof is also left to states to determine.[66] The members of the Academy do reach agreement on one interesting factor that has gained little attention by courts. It states that courts should *not* consider whether the parent seeking relocation has declared that he or she will not relocate if relocation of the child is denied. This factor is designed to prevent courts from coercing parents to agree to give up their plans to relocate before they receive a judicial decision.[67]

61 *Ibid.*, pp. 354–356.
62 American Academy of Matrimonial Lawyers, *supra* note 9.
63 *Ibid*, p. 17.
64 *Ibid.*, pp. 17–18.
65 *Ibid.*, p. 18.
66 *Ibid.*, pp. 20–21.
67 *Ibid.*, p. 20.

3. THE ACADEMIC LITERATURE ON RELOCATION DISPUTES

3.1. THE UNRESOLVED SOCIAL SCIENCE DEBATE

As judges seek to determine the best interests of children, they often look to psychologists to conduct evaluations of the family situation or consider the social science literature concerning the effects of relocation after divorce on children. On occasion, courts have placed great reliance on social science findings, using them to determine aspects of the relocation doctrine itself. For example, courts that adopted rules that include consideration of the well-being of the custodial parent relied on social science research that linked children's well-being with that of their custodial parents.[68] Other courts have relied on research that focuses on the importance of the child's relationship with the non-custodial parent to place the burden on the parent who wishes to relocate to demonstrate that the move is in the child's interest.[69] Relocation disputes that reach state supreme courts now may include *amicus curiae* briefs by noted psychologists who have different interpretations of the social science literature.[70]

However, the social science literature supplies no easy answers to the relocation conundrum. The current state of the social science literature makes it difficult to clearly apply its findings to any area of custodial disputes, much less the more specific area of relocation disputes. In fact, only one very limited study directly addresses relocation, and no study compares outcomes for children whose custodial parents are denied permission to relocate with the outcomes for children whose custodial parents are permitted to relocate.[71]

In addition, children's outcomes are likely to be strongly affected by the context in which relocation or geographic stability takes place. Thus, a smooth relocation supported by both parents, in which the parents make efforts to encourage children to be emotionally close to the other parent, is a completely different

---

68 *In re Marriage of Goldman*, 725 N.W. 2d 747, 754 (Minnesota Court of Appeals 2007); *Baures* v. *Lewis*, 770 A.2d 214, 222–223 (New Jersey 2001); *In re Marriage of Burgess*, 913 P.2d 473, 483 (California 1996), *Hollandsworth* v. *Knyzewski*, 109 S.W. 3d 653, 660 (Arkansas 2003), *Scott* v. *Scott*, 578 S.E.2d 876, 880 (Georgia 2003); *In re Marriage of Pape*, 989 P.2d 1120, 1128 (Washington 1999).

69 *In re Marriage of Ciesluk*, 100 P. 3d 527, 531 (Colorado Court of Appeals 2004), reversed at 113 P. 3d 527 (Colorado 2005); *Mize* v. *Mize*, 621 So. 2d 417, 422–423 (Florida 1993); *Scott* v. *Scott*, 578 S.E.2d 876, 883 (Georgia 2003)(dissent).

70 When the California Supreme Court recently heard the case of *In re LaMusga*, 88 P.3d 81 (California 2004), *amicus* briefs were filed for the mother by Judith Wallerstein, law professors including Carol S. Bruch, and the California Women's Law Center. *Amicus* briefs for the father were filed by Richard Warshak and Leslie Ellen Shear, http://www.thelizlibrary.org/lamusga/.

71 K. Waldron, 'A Review of Social Science Research on Post Divorce Relocation', 2005 *Journal of American Academy of Matrimonial Lawyers*, pp. 342–343.

experience for children than a relocation that is disputed, creates stress and anger in the parents, and forces children to move between two different warring camps. Similarly, growing up with two parents who cooperate and each make sacrifices to remain in close proximity is quite different than being raised in a context in which one parent has been ordered by a court to forego an important employment or remarriage opportunity in order to remain in proximity to the other parent. Nevertheless, the social science literature, despite its conflicting and limited nature, continues to be widely cited in the legal academic literature to support directly conflicting views regarding relocation.[72]

The psychological needs of children whose parents divorce has gained importance in the development of legal rules because of an extensive literature that describes increased rates of various psychological disorders, emotional distress, and negative behaviors in children whose parents divorce. One longitudinal study, conducted over twenty years, identified continuing distress and negative behaviors in approximately 20% to 25% of adults whose parents had divorced, more than twice the 10% rate found for adults who had grown up with parents who remained married.[73] The negative behaviors included depression, and impulsive, irresponsible, and antisocial behavior.[74] These adults also demonstrated difficulty at work, and in romantic relationships.[75] Some studies demonstrate that many of these indicators of risk are present before divorce.[76] There is widespread agreement that children in families that experience divorce are subject to greater risks, and academics across viewpoints share an interest in designing legal rules to minimize those risks. Noted researchers split, however, on how best to ameliorate those risks in the context of divorce.

One set of literature draws upon research that focuses on the post-divorce role of the primary caregiver in the overall well-being of children. Led most publicly by Dr. Judith Wallerstein, a psychologist who followed a small group of children

---

72 Professor Carol Bruch believes that the current state of social science demonstrates that 'good parenting by the custodial parent is the most effective protection for a child's post-divorce well-being.' She claims that authors on the other side of the debate do not provide scientific basis for their statements and '[o]ften they are directly contrary to the credible scientific evidence. At best their reasoning constitutes wishful thinking. At worst, it relies on distortion.' C. Bruch, 'Sound Research or Wishful Thinking in Child Custody Cases? Lessons From Relocation Law', 2006 *Family Law Quarterly*, p. 297. On the other side of the debate, Robert Oliphant argues that there is little support for the view 'that what is good for the custodial parent is also good for the child.' He discusses research that describes children as thriving when they are able to maintain relationships with both parents. R. Oliphant, 'Relocation Custody Disputes: A Binuclear Family-Centered Three-Stage Solution', 2005 *Northern Illinois University Law Review*, p. 401.

73 E. Hetherington *et al.*, *For Better or For Worse: Divorce Reconsidered*, 2002, p. 228.

74 *Ibid.*

75 *Ibid.*

76 P. Amato *et al.*, 'Children's Adjustment to Divorce: Theories, Hypotheses and Empirical Support', 1993 *Journal of Marriage and the Family*, p. 31.

of divorce over a twenty-five year period, these researchers assert that the social science evidence identifies a healthy relationship between the primary caretaker and the child as the most important factor affecting the well-being of children after divorce.[77] They note that the deterioration in the parenting skills of custodial parents immediately following separation or divorce significantly impairs the well-being of their children.[78] The ability of custodial parents to recover quickly and assume an authoritative parenting role with their children is closely related to improving the well-being of their children.[79]

These researchers also argue that the available social science research does not support the view that the relationship with the non-custodial parent is a key factor in improving children's well-being.[80] To the more limited extent that the child's relationship with the non-custodial parent improves outcomes, they assert that it is the quality, not quantity, of time that is correlated to children's well-being.[81] They also highlight the detrimental effects of parental conflict on children.[82]

The conclusion Dr. Wallerstein and others have drawn from the close link between the custodial parent's parenting and children's well-being, the more limited value of increased time with non-custodial parents, and the detrimental effect of conflict, is that legal rules in the context of relocation should favor the well-being of the custodial parent.[83] This includes the custodial parent's interest in relocating without a renewal of legal discord concerning relocation. Dr. Wallerstein has not, however, applied her findings to cases in which the parents equally share custodial responsibility.

In stark contrast to this view are those who emphasize the significance of the child's relationship with the non-custodial parent.[84] The researchers who highlight this relationship do not dispute the importance of parenting by the custodial parent or the reduction of conflict between the parties. They argue that courts and policymakers have undervalued the child's relationship with a non-custodial parent, and they highlight the important benefits that a positive relationship with the

77 *Ibid.*, p. 126; J. Wallerstein *et al.*, 'To Move or Not to Move: Psychological and Legal Considerations in the Relocation of Children After Divorce', 1996 *Family Law Quarterly*, p. 311.

78 Hetherington *et al.*, *supra* note 73, pp. 130–133.

79 *Ibid.*, pp. 126–130.

80 *Ibid.*, pp. 133–134.

81 *Ibid.*, p. 558. (finding that the 'frequency of contact may be less important than other relationship dimensions, such as the strength of the emotional tie between children and fathers.'); Hetherington *et al.*, *supra* note 73, pp. 133–134; P. Amato *et al.*, 'Nonresident Fathers and Children's Well-Being: A Meta-Analysis', 1999 *Journal of Marriage & the Family*, pp. 557–573.

82 Amato *et al.*, *supra* note 76, p. 31.

83 Wallerstein *et al.*, *supra* note 77, p. 318.

84 R. Warshak, 'Social Science and Children's Best Interests in Relocation Cases: Burgess Revisited', 2000 *Family Law Quarterly*, p. 84; J. Kelly *et al.*, 'Using Child Development Research to Make Appropriate Custody and Access Decisions for Young Children', 2000 *Family and Conciliation Courts Review*, p. 298.

non-custodial parent brings to children.[85] Dr. Richard Warshak asserts that studies find that regular visitation with fathers improves children's well-being. He also cites studies that demonstrate that fathers who see their children frequently are more likely to provide economic support for their children.[86]

It is readily apparent that even if there were agreement on the basic premise of the importance of the non-custodial father-child relationship, relocation is likely to occur in most post-divorce families anyway. One large, longitudinal study found that 75 miles seems to be the distance where 'paternal inconvenience overcomes paternal guilt' and visitation declines, and that by the time the children are age 15, the average distance between children and their non-custodial parents was 400 miles.[87]

The only research study to attempt to answer directly questions regarding the effect of relocation of children of divorced parents had ambiguous findings.[88] The researchers surveyed a large number of college students whose parents had divorced. A strong majority (61%) had experienced relocation of more than one hour by one parent, almost evenly split between relocations by mothers and fathers. On most measured criteria, students who had relocated with their mothers showed no measurable differences from students whose parents had not relocated. These measures included personal and emotional adjustment, general life satisfaction, substance abuse, and levels of hostility. Statistically significant disparities did exist on some measures, including amount of parental financial support for college, inner turmoil and distress from the divorce, and global health.[89] The study did not measure the circumstances leading to the moves, the quality of children's relationships with both parents prior to the moves, or levels of pre-move conflict between the parents, so it is difficult to tell whether the disparities were caused by the relocations or were affected by other factors, including factors such as continuing parental conflict, which may have caused the relocation.[90]

Given the lack of evidence of causal connection between relocation and harm to children, it is difficult to know what conclusions to reach from these results. The highly disputed interpretations of various studies concerning which factors best assist children in successfully surviving divorce does little to assist policymakers to craft the legal rules that govern these disputes. Even where such conclusions have been proposed, they largely focus on which parent will bear the burden of

---

85 L. Trinder *et al.*, 'Measuring Up? The Relationship Between Correlates of Children's Adjustment and Both Family Law and Policy in England', 2005 *Louisiana Law Review*, pp. 1516–1517.

86 Warshak, *supra* note 84, pp. 93–94.

87 Hetherington *et al.*, *supra* note 73, p. 134.

88 S. Braver *et al.*, 'Relocation of Children After Divorce and Children's Best Interests: New Evidence and Legal Considerations', 2003 *Journal of Family Psychology*, pp. 206–219.

89 *Ibid.*, pp. 212–213.

90 *Ibid.*, pp. 214–215.

proof regarding the best interests of children involved in these disputes.[91] Both sides of this debate admit, however, that their interpretive approach provides little clear guidance to judges facing individual families with specific circumstances.[92] Nor, as at least one family court judge has pointed out, does the research enable judges, even with the use of psychological experts, to predict accurately which decision will ultimately best further children's development in individual cases.[93]

However, the extent to which relocation was a pervasive part of the lives of the college students who participated in the Arizona State relocation study, affecting close to two-thirds of the students whose parents had divorced, may indicate a need for policymakers to consider not simply what legal doctrine should apply to disputes in court concerning relocation, which are most likely a very small percentage of the total relocations. Rather, it may indicate a need to provide support to divorcing families as they make the various transitions that occur during and after divorce, including the apparently common experience of relocation by either the custodial or non-custodial parent. Relocation doctrine itself may be of little relevance to most post-divorce and post-separation families and children.

3.2. THE IDEOLOGY OF CO-PARENTING AND ITS EFFECT ON RELOCATION DISPUTES

Ideological changes concerning co-parenting may have a more profound impact on relocation doctrine than the social science literature. While the social science dispute continues unabated, many countries are currently experiencing a transcendence of the ideology of co-parenting after divorce and decreasing ideological support for the independence of the custodial family.[94] Professor Robert Oliphant has lauded the 'binuclear' family as the appropriate model for

91 Warshak, *supra* note 84, p. 111 ('If legislatures and courts believe that most children do best when their parents remain in close geographical proximity, this might result in presumptions, standards, tests, and burdens that discourage relocation.'); Oliphant, *supra* note 72, pp. 401–402 ('courts should give "greater weight to the child's separate interests" when deciding a relocation dispute.'); Bruch, *supra* note 72, p. 314 ('protecting continuity in the child's relationship with its primary caregiver and that person's decisions, including a choice to relocate.').

92 Waldron, *supra* note71, p. 342; Warshak, *supra* note 84, pp. 110–111 ('Neither research, nor this article, could possibly cover all the factors that might affect any individual child's adjustment to relocation. Children's adjustment after divorce has much to do with their own personalities and coping skills.').

93 W. Duggan, 'Rock-Paper-Scissors: Playing the Odds With the Law of Child Relocation', 2007 *Family Court Review*, p. 193; J. Bowermaster, 'Legal Presumptions and the Role of Mental Health Professionals in Child Custody Proceedings', 2002 *Duquesne Law Review*, pp. 295–301.

94 Glennon, *supra* note 4; P. Parkinson, 'Family Law and the Indissolubility of Parenthood', 2006 *Family Law Quarterly* pp. 242–247.

post-dissolution parenting.[95] 'A binuclear family is defined as a large, interconnected family, with one household headed by the ex-wife and the other household headed by the ex-husband, with the child being a member of both.'[96] He finds this term in a recent Georgia Supreme Court opinion, in which the concurring judge identified the benefits for children of this shared parenting approach.[97] Professor Oliphant contrasts the binuclear family concept with the view that he believes dominated in the 1960s and 1970s, a view he describes as the 'new family.' Under this view, courts would defer to the 'new' custodial family as the primary source of support for children. Professor Oliphant argues that dramatic shifts in the parenting role of fathers and the work involvement of mothers support the binuclear view of the post-dissolution family. The shifting focus towards post-dissolution co-parenting may account for the increase in the number of states that either prioritize or permit joint physical custody of children.[98] It is also reflected in the array of parenting books that encourage cooperative parenting after divorce.[99]

The ideology of co-parenting has also affected relocation disputes. As discussed in Section 2, recent legislative and doctrinal changes have largely emphasized the importance of non-custodial parents in the lives of their children by increasing the barriers to relocation.[100] In addition, increases in joint custody will likely increase the success of petitions to prevent relocation. Parents who have joint physical custody are able to more clearly demonstrate the benefits of their relationship to the child to prevent relocation.[101] While in most cases this distinction arises in the court's discussion of the facts of an individual case, at least two states have codified the distinction between situations in which one parent is the majority time parent and situations where the time is shared substantially equally.[102] Increases in post-dissolution co-parenting, now fostered in many ways, will significantly change the course of relocation disputes.

95 Oliphant, *supra* note 72, pp. 363–402.

96 *Ibid.*, p. 365.

97 *Bodne* v. *Bodne*, 588 S.E.2d 728,730(Ga. 2003)(Sears, J., concurring).

98 J. Murphy, 'Legal Images of Fatherhood: Welfare Reform, Child Support Enforcement and Fatherless Children', 2005 *Notre Dame Law Review* p. 337, n. 59 (collecting statutes concerning joint custody).

99 Glennon, *supra* note 4, p. 114, n. 48.

100 See Section 2, *supra*.

101 T. Glennon, 'Mobility and the Post-Divorce Family: Resolution of Relocation Disputes in the U.S.', in K. Boele-Woelki (ed.), *Common Core and Better Law in European Family Law*, 2005, pp. 193–215.

102 See Section 2.1, *supra*.

3.3. PROPOSALS TO EMPHASIZE PARENTAL COOPERATION

Articles have proposed adapting relocation doctrine to encourage parents to settle their disputes privately rather than seeking judicial intervention. Professors Lucy McGough and Robert Oliphant advocate the development of mandatory measures to encourage parents to cooperate to resolve the relocation issue privately before relocation disputes reach a judicial hearing in order to encourage the parties.[103] They note that open conflict between divorced or separated parents is a powerful stressor on children, and numerous studies have demonstrated that hostility between the parents may be the greatest risk factor for children of separation and divorce.[104] They hope that their proposed procedures will reduce this harmful parental conflict.

Professor McGough would require parents who want to relocate to not only provide written notice prior to relocation, but to include also a proposal for revised visitation arrangements to mitigate the potential damage of the relocation to their children's relationship with non-moving parents.[105] She would also require parents to attend a mandatory education program that addresses parenting strategies, including strategies to reshape the non-moving parent's relationship with the child after a relocation.[106]

Professor Oliphant would instead begin the process with a mandatory parenting plan meeting between the parents. This meeting would occur after notice of a proposed relocation is given, and the parents are to make reasonable efforts to resolve any dispute regarding the relocation.[107]

Most important, both authors would require parents to attempt mediation of the relocation dispute before reaching court. At least 33 states now require parents to attempt mediation prior to a judicial hearing on child custody disputes, and almost all others make mediation services available to assist parents to achieve resolution of their disputes. In mediation, the parents meet with an impartial third party who serves to facilitate an agreement between the parents. Although the authors realize that mediation will not prevent all relocation disputes from reaching the courts, they believe that it can resolve some of these disputes, and that the reduction in parental conflict and individual and judicial resources is well worth a requirement that parents attempt this strategy.[108]

---

103 L. McGough, 'Starting Over: The Heuristics of Family Relocation Decision Making, 2003 *St. John's Law Review*, pp. 291–343; Oliphant, *supra* note 72, pp. 395–397.

104 McGough, *supra* note103, pp. 323–325 (citing social science studies).

105 *Ibid.*, pp. 334–335.

106 *Ibid.*, pp. 336–337.

107 Oliphant, *supra* note 72, pp. 395–397.

108 McGough, *supra* note 103, pp. 337–341; Oliphant, *supra* note 72, pp. 397–399.

3.4. CONFLICTING CONSTITUTIONAL RIGHTS OF PARENTS

Both the right to travel freely and the constitutional rights of parents to the care and control their children have been raised in the context of relocation disputes. The exercise of judicial power to prohibit relocation by custodial parents arguably affects significant rights protected by the US Constitution. The Constitution has been interpreted to include a fundamental right to travel among the states as a liberty interest under the Due Process Clause of the Fourteenth Amendment. Travel is not the only asserted constitutional right at stake, however, as non-custodial parents have argued for recognition of a constitutionally protected liberty interest in the continuing care and control of their children. This liberty interest may apply to the interests of both custodial and non-custodial parents. To date few courts have addressed parents' interest in the care and control of their children in the context of relocation disputes.

The right to travel is clearly rooted in US constitutional law. In *Shapiro* v. *Thompson*, the US Supreme Court stated:

> 'This Court long ago recognized that the nature of our Federal Union and our constitutional concepts of personal liberty unite to require that all citizens be free to travel throughout the length and breadth of our land uninhibited by statutes, rules, or regulations which unreasonably burden or restrict this movement.'[109]

The Court did not identify the specific constitutional provision that supported this right, but found it to be a fundamental right. The Court found that legislation that significantly impaired the right to travel must serve a compelling state interest.[110]

Equally established is the constitutional right of parents to the care and control of their children. The US Supreme Court has stated that 'it cannot now be doubted that the Due Process Clause of the Fourteenth Amendment protects the fundamental right of parents to make decisions concerning the care, custody, and control of their children,' describing it as 'perhaps the oldest of the fundamental liberty interests recognized by this Court.'[111] However, courts have clearly held that while both parents have equal and fundamental rights at stake in custody determinations, it is constitutional for courts to make those decisions based on the best interests of the children.[112] They have thus rejected the argument that the parental rights of non-custodial parents require them to receive equal custodial

109 *Shapiro* v. *Thompson*, 394 U.S. 618, 629 (1969).

110 *Ibid.* at 634. The Supreme Court reiterated the fundamental nature of the right to travel in *Saenz* v. *Roe*, 526 U.S. 489 (1999).

111 *Troxel* v. *Granville*, 530 U.S. 57, 67 (2000).

112 M. Brinig, 'Does Parental Autonomy Require Equal Custody at Divorce?', 2005 *Louisiana Law Review*, p. 1358.

time with their children.[113] Some courts faced with 'equal custody' claims find that the rights of the parents cancel each other out.[114] Professor Margaret Brinig has viewed the state as having a compelling interest in the welfare of the children whose custody is disputed, which justifies judicial decision making in the best interest of the children.[115] Professor David Meyer has taken a different tack, asserting that state intervention is appropriate because each parent's rights are qualified by the competing interests of the other family members.[116]

Professor Arthur LaFrance, who himself married a woman who was unable to relocate to live with him after their marriage, argues strenuously against judicial interference with the rights of custodial parents to relocate. He asserts that courts may not interfere with the custodial parent's right to travel and other important interests, such as the right to remarry and establish a home with a new spouse, despite the interests of the non-custodial parent.[117] He believes that such interference is warranted only if the move endangers the child. Judicial intervention should be focused on ensuring reasonable visitation with the non-custodial parent.[118] The Wyoming Supreme Court has adopted this approach. In *Watt* v. *Watt*, the Wyoming Supreme Court stated:

> 'The right of travel enjoyed by a citizen carries with it the right of a custodial parent to have the children move with that parent. This right is not to be denied, impaired, or disparaged unless clear evidence before the court demonstrates another substantial and material change of circumstance and establishes the detrimental effect of the move upon the children.'[119]

Although other state courts are familiar with this approach, they have declined to follow it. One court has found that the deprivation of the right to travel is justified by the state's compelling interest in the best interests of the child.[120] Several courts have agreed that the right to travel is 'chilled' by the denial of the right of a 'majority time parent' to relocate with her children.[121] Other courts have identified the parents as having competing rights to travel and to continue to parent their child, and that the children have interests in their own well-being. Despite their recogni-

---

113 See, *e.g.*, *Arnold* v. *Arnold*, 679 N.W.2d 296 (Wisconsin Court of Appeals 2004), review denied, 679 N.W.2d 547 (Wisconsin 2004), certiorari denied, 543 U.S. 873 (2004).

114 D. Meyer, 'The Constitutional Rights of Non-Custodial Parents', 2006 *Hofstra Law Review*, pp.1478–1479.

115 Brinig, *supra* note 112.

116 Meyer, *supra* note 114, p. 1466.

117 A. LaFrance, 'Child Custody and Relocation: A Constitutional Perspective', 1995 *University of Louisville Journal of Family Law*, pp. 1–81.

118 *Ibid.*

119 *Watt* v. *Watt*, 971 P.2d 608, 615–616 (Wyoming 1999).

120 *LaChapelle* v. *Mitten*, 607 N.W.2d 151 (Minnesota Court of Appeals, 2000).

121 See, *e.g.*, *In re Marriage of Ciesluk*, 113 P.3d 135, 142 (Colorado 2005).

tion of the custodial parent's right to travel, however, these courts have determined that as long as the burden of proof regarding the best interests of the child concerning relocation is equal, the constitutional rights of all parties are protected.[122]

It is not clear that state court approaches to relocation adequately protect a custodial parent's right to travel. It is insufficient to claim that it is not the parent's right to travel that is at stake, but the parent's right to bring her children. This assumes that a court has determined that even if the parent moves, it would be in the children's interests to shift custody to the non-custodial parent. This is not always the case, however. In many cases, courts have ordered custodial parents to remain in their present area of residence, subject to a threat of loss of custody if they move. In some cases, they have threatened to transfer custody upon relocation without first determining that the children would be better served by living with the non-custodial parent rather than living with the custodial parent in the new setting.[123] This threat, which may be described as relocation blackmail, may violate the custodial parent's right to travel and right to the custody, care and control of the child, as well as children's best interests.

Another important factor in addressing the constitutional right of the custodial parent to travel is the uneven manner in which travel restrictions are imposed. In all jurisdictions, non-custodial parents are free to leave the jurisdiction and relocate wherever they wish, and they routinely do so.[124] They may initiate court proceedings to modify their visitation time to fit their new geographic circumstances, but no court has considered itself authorized to prevent the relocation itself. Thus, while a court will prevent a custodial parent from relocating in order to better protect the child's relationship with the non-custodial parent, it will not prevent relocation by a non-custodial parent in order to better protect that same relationship.[125] The uneven nature of these travel restrictions brings into question whether the custodial parents' right to travel is being unduly restricted, and whether these restrictions unfairly burden women, who most often have primary custody and are subject to such restraints.

Professor Thomas Oldham notes that while non-custodial parents are not prevented from relocating, they do face limits on their autonomy related to child support. Courts are generally reluctant to approve a reduction in child support payments based on voluntary changes in employment or withdrawal from employment.[126]

---

122 *Ibid.* See also *Jaramillo* v. *Jaramillo*, 823 P.2d 299 (New Mexico 1991); *Fredman* v. *Fredman*, 960 So.2d 52 (Florida Court of Appeals, 2007); *Baxendale* v. *Raich*, 878 N.E.2d 1252 (Indiana 2008).

123 Braver *et al.*, *supra* note 88 (suggesting that courts consider ordering relocation if a custodial parent insists on relocating in order to discourage such relocations).

124 *Ibid.*

125 M. Weiner, 'Inertia and Inequality: Reconceptualizing Disputes over Relocation', 2007 *University of California Davis Law Review*, p. 42.

126 T. Oldham, 'Limitations Imposed by Family Law on a Separated Parent's Ability to Make Significant Life Decisions: A Comparison of Relocation and Income Imputation', 2001 *Duke Jour-*

It is not clear, however, whether income imputation for purposes of child support work to restrict the non-custodial parent's autonomy as deeply as relocation restrictions, which may prevent a parent from accepting a new job or living with a spouse. As this discussion demonstrates, important and conflicting constitutional rights arise in relocation disputes; they demand more careful analysis by US courts.

3.5. RELOCATION AND DOMESTIC VIOLENCE

States have increasingly moved in the direction of explicitly requiring custodial parents to provide notice prior to relocation.[127] They also now mandate that if the other parent objects, relocation may not take place until after a hearing and a determination on the merits of the relocation. Professor Janet Bowermaster notes the dilemma relocation restrictions impose on mothers who are victims of domestic violence:

> 'Custodial parents attempting to escape abusive situations may actually be prevented from moving to another state, city, or even school district by state laws restricting the removal of minor children without the noncustodial parent's permission. These laws, which were designed to protect noncustodial parents' access to children after divorce or separation, contain no generally recognized exception for those custodial parents who are fleeing from domestic violence. Violation of these removal procedures can result in custody being transferred to the violent parent.'[128]

Thus, relocation statutes, which are intended to preserve the child's relationship with the non-custodial parent, can be used by perpetrators of domestic violence to continue to abuse and control their spouse or ex-spouse.[129] While one hopes that perpetrators of domestic violence are unlikely to be successful at a hearing, it can take a long time to get a hearing and final decision on relocation. Professor Bowermaster provides numerous other examples of relocation disputes in which domestic violence was a factor, and she describes in detail one case in which the process of receiving permission to relocate took two and one-half years, during

---

nal of Gender Law and Policy, pp. 333–341.

127 See Section 2, *supra*.

128 J. Bowermaster, 'Relocation Custody Disputes Involving Domestic Violence', 1998 *Kansas Law Review* p. 433.

129 The Hague Convention on the Civil Aspects of International Child Abduction raises similar concerns at a transnational level. Professor Merle Weiner has argued that the Convention needs to be strengthened to prevent its misuse to force victims to return to the community of the perpetrator. M. Weiner, 'Strengthening Article 20', 2004 *University of San Francisco Law Review*, pp. 701–744.

which time the mother was subjected to further abuse, harassment, and financial ruin due to her inability to leave her home safely.[130]

Clearly, relocation statutes need to be explicitly linked to laws protecting victims of domestic violence to ensure that victims may flee their attackers in a timely and safe manner. Victims of domestic violence should have a quick administrative or judicial process by which they can gain permission to withhold their new contact information from the other parent and relocate to safety.

3.6. RECONFIGURING RELOCATION DISPUTES

Scholars have recommended that relocation disputes be doctrinally altered away from a narrow focus on whether to permit the custodial parent to relocate with her children. These authors have challenged courts' failure to consider whether the objecting parent would be able to relocate to the new location, and whether custodial parents should have an economic remedy if they face a significant economic loss because of the denial of permission to relocate.

Professor Merle Weiner has challenged the binary nature of relocation disputes, which focus only on whether the custodial parent may or may not relocate. As part of their analysis, she believes that courts should also consider the non-custodial parent's potential mobility.[131] She argues that the failure to consider whether the non-custodial parent could relocate undermines children's best interests by ignoring what may be the best solution in particular cases. She explains that the failure to consider the possible relocation of the non-custodial parent also 'rests on outdated gendered assumptions and institutionalizes gender discrimination (...) [and] perpetuates stereotypes, fosters expectations of accommodation that are gendered, and sustains different degrees of mobility for custodial and noncustodial parents.'[132] She highlights the message that her proposal to reconfigure the relocation dispute would send to all divorced parents: that both parents have the responsibility to act in their child's best interests while respecting the long term interests of each parent.

In a recent article, I propose another factor that would also shift courts away from the yes/no nature of relocation disputes. I argue that the restrictions on the geographic mobility of custodial parents, together with imposition of the economic 'clean break' theory of divorce, have led to custodial parents, mostly women, facing significant economic hardship as a result of refusals by courts to permit relocations.[133] My review of all relocation disputes for the five-year period ending

130 Bowermaster, *supra* note 128, pp. 434–435.
131 Weiner, *supra* note 125, pp. 1–44.
132 *Ibid.*, p. 2.
133 Glennon, *supra* note 4.

July 1, 2006 revealed that many of the reasons that custodial parents sought to relocate had significant economic dimensions. Twenty-eight percent of custodial parents wanted to relocate to improve or maintain their own employment or their spouse's employment. Fifteen percent requested relocation for remarriage, and 11% wanted to relocate to live near family who would provide economic support or in-kind assistance. Another 21% sought to relocate for a combination of reasons that included employment, remarriage, or further education.[134]

These economic benefits could be significant, making the difference between a comfortable life style and ongoing financial difficulties. Since, overall, custodial parents received permission to relocate in only 49% of the cases reviewed that actually reached a final decision, custodial parents who want to relocate face great uncertainty and lengthy delays if the other parent refuses to consent to their relocation. The uncertainty and delays can prevent custodial parents from pursuing relocation or lead to withdrawn opportunities when potential spouses and employers decide they can no longer wait for a decision. Thus, when courts deny custodial parents permission to relocate, courts should have the explicit authority to grant an income-sharing economic remedy to the parent who is denied permission to relocate, thereby sharing the economic burdens of maintaining the child's close contact with both parents.

4. CONCLUSION

States within the US have failed to achieve any agreement over the fundamental issues involved in relocation disputes. They have adopted a wide range of approaches to this issue, underscoring the deep disputes within the social science literature and conflicting ideologies regarding post-divorce families. Most states have yet to fully grapple with the important constitutional rights of parents involved in these disputes, or the safety needs of victims of domestic violence. Scholars have proposed several important reforms, including the addition of mandatory alternative dispute resolution, deprivileging of the current location of the family, and the consideration of an economic remedy when thwarted relocation imposes significant economic losses on a custodial parent. Policymakers in this area need to carefully consider these issues to develop a legal doctrine more attuned to the needs of all participants in these disputes. They also need to recognize the pervasive nature of relocation after divorce and consider educational and other strategies to ensure that relocation is not a significant risk for children affected by parental separation and divorce.

134 *Ibid.*, p. 125.

PARENTAL RELOCATION
Free movement rights and joint parenting

Christina G. Jeppesen de Boer*

1. INTRODUCTION

As joint parental authority increasingly becomes the legal norm applied in situations where the parents do not live together, for example, after divorce or the breakup of a relationship, the settlement of disputes regarding the concrete exercise of parental authority gain increasing relevance. A common dispute concerns the relocation of the resident parent.

This article compares the approach towards parental relocation adopted by the European Commission on Family Law (CEFL) in their Principles Regarding Parental Responsibilities with the approach taken in Dutch and Danish law. Is relocation dealt with even-handedly between resident and non-resident parents? Do the same principles apply to relocation inside and outside the jurisdiction? First, however, this article takes a brief glance at the regulation of parental authority and residence in the chosen jurisdictions.

2. THE REGULATION OF PARENTAL AUTHORITY AND RESIDENCE

2.1. THE CEFL PRINCIPLES

The CEFL was established in Utrecht in September 2001 and has as its main objective the development of non-binding principles which may serve as an inspiration for the harmonisation of family law in Europe. The drafting of principles must be seen, according to the Principles themselves, in the context of a growing convergence of national family law in Europe, reflecting common European values, and the desirability and necessity of the harmonisation of family law in Europe in

* Christina Gyldenløve Jeppesen de Boer currently works at the Molengraaff Institute for Private Law, Utrecht University (The Netherlands), email: C.Jeppesen@law.uu.nl. In May 2008 she defended her PhD thesis: *Joint Parental Authority*, 2008.

order to facilitate the free movement of persons in Europe. The Principles on Parental Responsibilities also aim to contribute to common European values regarding the child's rights and welfare.[1]

According to the CEFL Principles legal parents hold parental responsibilities *ex lege* and their position is unaffected by divorce and the breakup of the relationship.[2] At the level of exercise parents should as far as possible exercise these jointly and are encouraged to come to an agreement.[3]

The determination of *residence* in the CEFL Principles is regulated through the general provisions applying to the settlement of parental disputes. The CEFL Principles provide in Principle 3:20 that the holders of parental responsibilities who are living apart should agree upon the child's residence. If the parents cannot agree, the matter will be deferred to the competent authority that will proceed according to Principle 3:14.[4] This Principle provides the general principle regulating parental disputes of a more important nature. Two alternative solutions to settle a dispute are offered. The competent authority may divide the exercise of parental responsibilities or decide the dispute. The principles consequently leave the choice open between two different solutions to national law considering that there is no common core. It may, however, be derived from the comments that the solution of establishing a residence with one parent is (probably) the preferred solution,[5] when it is also taken into account that a relocation is separately regulated in Principle 3:21.

The CEFL Principles provide for the possibility of *shared residence* based upon parental agreement and contemplate that such an arrangement may also be established when a parent resists such an arrangement subject to review by the competent authority.[6]

2.2. DUTCH LAW

Dutch law provides for the continuation of joint parental authority after divorce and the breakup of a relationship as the main rule. The termination of parental

1 K. Boele-Woelki *et al.*, *Principles of European Family Law Regarding Parental Responsibilities*, 2007, Preamble, p. 7 and Comments 1–4, p. 8–9, hereafter referred to as *Principles*.

2 *Principles*, Principle 3:8, p. 59 and 3:10, p. 79. Discharge from parental responsibilities is only possible in exceptional circumstances, Principle 3:32, p. 212.

3 *Principles*, Principle 3:11, p. 82, 3:13, p. 91 and 3:14, p. 95.

4 *Principles*, Principle 3:20(1), p. 130 and 3:14, p. 95.

5 *Principles*, Principle 3:14, p. 99, Comment 3. The principles states that: 'Authorising one of the parents to act alone will be preferable where it can be established that a specific, separable issue has to be resolved and one of the holders of parental responsibilities has a sufficient degree of competence or knowledge to pursue the best interests of the child concerning this question'. This statement would not seem to relate to a dispute concerning the residence.

6 *Principles*, Principle 3:20(2), p. 130.

authority is possible, however, subject to a strict criterion.[7] Presently joint parental authority continues after divorce in approximately 92% of cases.[8] Dutch law is currently under revision. The pending reform on 'continued parenting' strengthens equality through various means, for example, by means of an explicit norm for equal parenting within the concept of joint parental authority and further obliges parents to submit a parenting plan concerning the division of care and responsibilities together with the petition for divorce. This pending reform is aimed at implementing the 'child's right to be cared for by both parents'.[9]

In Dutch law either of the parents may apply to the court for a decision on the child's residence (*hoofdverblijf*).[10] Such a decision is given on the basis of the general dispute settlement provision contained in Article 1:253a of the Dutch Civil Code (*Burgerlijk Wetboek*).[11] While it is not required, most divorce decrees will contain a decision, if requested, or mention the agreement which the parents have reached concerning the child's residence.[12]

Parents may in Dutch law agree upon a shared residence. The establishment of a shared residence against the wishes of one parent is perhaps possible although there as yet are no final decisions establishing such a division.[13]

7 Art. 1:251(2) of the Dutch Civil Code. The termination of joint parental authority in Dutch law is only possible when there is a risk that the child is 'torn or lost', Supreme Court (*Hoge Raad*) 10 September 1999, *NJ* 2000,167.

8 Statistics Netherlands (*CBS*) concerning the year 2003.

9 Parliamentary proceedings (*Kamerstukken*) 2005–2006–2007, 30 145, adopted by the Dutch Parliament's Second Chamber (*Tweede Kamer*) and presently pending before the First Chamber (*Eerste Kamer*) as 30 145 A, *Wijziging van Boek 1 van het Burgerlijk Wetboek en het Wetboek van Burgerlijke Rechtsvordering in verband met het bevorderen van voortgezet ouderschap na scheiding en het afschaffen van de mogelijkheid tot het omzetten van een huwelijk in een geregistreerd partnerschap (Wet bevordering voortgezet ouderschap en zorgvuldige scheiding).*

10 As confirmed by the Supreme Court, Hoge Raad 15 December 2000, *NJ* 2001, 123 annotated by S.F.M. Wortmann.

11 Art. 1:253a provides that 'In the case of the exercise of joint parental authority, disputes between the partners in respect thereof may, on the application of both or either of them be submitted to the district court. The district court shall first attempt to reach an agreement between the parents prior to taking a decision. The court shall give such an order as it shall consider desirable in the best interests of the child.'.

12 The question of which effect the mentioning of the child's residence in the dictum has is not clear; M.J.C. Koens & C.G.M. van Wamelen, *Kind en scheiding*, 2001, pp. 58–59. The correlation between main residence and the child's registered address in the Council Administration is further unclear, see further the decision of the Court of Appeal, Gerechtshof 's-Gravenhage 18 October 2006, LJN AZ2072.

13 It has been presumed that the courts already have this competence in the Parliamentary proceedings (*Kamerstukken*) 2004–2005, 30 145, No. 3, p. 14. There is case law maintaining a shared residence where the parents initially agreed upon a shared residence; for example, Rechtbank Utrecht 12 April 2006, LJN AZ1191.

2.3. DANISH LAW

Danish law provides for the continuation of joint parental authority after divorce and the breakup of a relationship as the main rule. Since the Act on Parental Responsibility (*Lov om forældreansvar*) entered into force on 1st October 2007, the termination of joint parental authority is only possible subject to a strict criterion.[14] Presently joint parental authority continues after divorce in approximately 90% of cases.[15] The recent changes in Danish law have strengthened equality in various ways, for example, by providing that joint parental authority may no longer be terminated upon request of one parent and through the possibility of establishing a contact arrangement amounting to a shared residence in the sense of time allocation.[16] This Act aims to implement the principle that a child has the right to two parents.[17]

In Danish law the authority to establish the child's residence (*bopæl*) has been introduced with the 2007 Act on Parental Responsibility.[18] Article 17(1) of the Act provides that the court will decide with whom the child should reside in cases where the parents hold joint parental authority and disagree on the child's residence.[19]

Parents may agree upon a shared residence. It is not possible to establish or maintain a shared residence if a parent resists. However, it has become possible to establish a contact arrangement amounting to a shared residence since the 2007 Act on Parental Responsibility.[20]

2.4. FACTUAL RESIDENCE

While the vast majority of parents hold joint parental authority after divorce in The Netherlands and in Denmark children continue to reside primarily with the mother in both jurisdictions. In The Netherlands approximately 75% of children reside with the mother after divorce and the breakup of a relationship, 9% with

14 Art. 8, Act on Parental Responsibility, Act No. 499 of 6 June 2007. Termination is only possible in Danish law when there are 'weighty grounds'. Before this Act entered into force it was always possible to terminate joint parental authority upon request of one parent when the parents (no longer) lived together or intended to break off their relationship.

15 This percentage reflects upon the situation before the automatic continuation of parental authority was enacted in 2001 and must currently be expected to be higher, Explanatory notes to L 198, 2000, *Forslag til ændring af retsplejeloven og forskellige andre love*, p. 11.

16 Art. 11 and 21(2), Act on Parental Responsibility.

17 L 133, Comments to § 11.

18 Before this Act entered into force on 1 October 2007 a disagreement between the parents could only be solved through the allocation of sole parental authority to one parent.

19 The guiding criterion is the general 'best interests' principle contained in Art. 4 of the Act.

20 Art. 17(1) and 21(2), Act on Parental Responsibility.

the father and 16% are subject to a co-parenting (shared residence) agreement.[21] In Denmark 90% of children who do not live with both parents, including children born to unmarried parents, have their registered address with the mother and 11% with the father. Approximately 20% of all children spend more than one third of their time with one parent.[22]

These statistics indicate that the mother continues to be the primary carer after divorce in both The Netherlands and Denmark with, however, an increasing group of children who have shared residences. The statistics on children's residence with the mother or father are, however, not entirely comparable since the Danish statistics concern all children in Denmark including those born to single mothers, while the Dutch information is derived from research primarily concerning children whose parents have divorced.

3. REGULATION OF RELOCATION

3.1. THE CEFL PRINCIPLES

The CEFL Principles provide a specific regulation of parental relocation in Principle 3:21. A parent who wishes to relocate with the child must inform the other parent in advance.

In case the parents cannot reach an agreement on the matter each of the parents may seek a decision of the court. The CEFL Principles do not distinguish between relocation within or outside the jurisdiction. Consequently the parents must reach an agreement or seek a decision of any relocation according to the CEFL Principles.

The CEFL Principles provide a set of non-exhaustive consideration factors which the competent authority must take into account. These factors are:

(a) the age and opinion of the child;[23]

21 Co-parentage has been defined as encompassing children who spend more than 40% of their time with one parent. In 2001 the percentage of children subject to a co-parentage agreement was 4%; E. Spruijt, *Scheidingskinderen*, 2007, pp. 17–18. These data are based upon a group of children with divorced parents, including 17% of children whose parents had co-habited.

22 M. Heide Ottosen, *Samvær og børns trivsel*, 2004, p. 14 based upon statistics from Statistics Denmark. The percentage of children living with the father has decreased from 12 to 11% over the past 10 years probably due to the increase in shared residences from 4% at the end of the 1980s to approximately 20% in 2004.

23 The Principles do not contain a specific age requirement for the hearing of the child but depend upon the circumstances of the case and the age and maturity of the child. The hearing must take place *ex officio* and a decision not to hear the child must be reasoned so that the child's right to be heard is ensured and arbitrary refusals are avoided, *Principles*, Principle 3:37, Comment 2 and 3, p. 251.

(b) the right of the child to maintain personal relationships with the other holders of parental responsibilities;
(c) the ability and willingness of the holders of parental responsibilities to co-operate with each other;
(d) the personal situation of the holders of parental responsibilities;
(e) geographical distance and accessibility;
(f) the free movement of persons.

Although the Principles have as an objective the facilitation of the free movement of persons in Europe, the solution selected with respect to relocation is a balancing of interests with no clear starting point. This balancing of interests is formulated as concerning the child's right to maintain personal relationships with the other holder(s) of parental responsibilities and the right of the resident parent to move in pursuit of a 'valid purpose', for example in order to improve his or her professional situation or to accompany a new partner (free movement rights) taking account of the practical implications of a relocation.[24]

3.2. DUTCH LAW

There is no specific regulation of relocation in Dutch law. Each parent may apply to the court for a decision pursuant to the general dispute settlement provision contained in Article 1:253a Civil Code.[25] A child aged twelve or older will be heard in accordance with the general provision contained in Article 809(1) of the Civil Procedural Code (*Wetboek van Burgerlijke Rechtsvordering*).[26]

Since there is no specific regulation of relocation in Dutch law the guiding criteria concerning relocation must be derived from case law. In principle, any relocation probably requires the other parent's consent or the replaced consent of the court irrespective of the distance and regardless of whether a main residence has been established.[27] While there is no specific regulation of a duty to inform

24 *Principles*, Principle 3:21, Comment 7, pp. 141–142.

25 *Supra*, Section 2.2. with note 11.

26 Dutch courts generally provide the opportunity for children aged twelve or above to express their views by means of a letter addressed to the child, providing an invitation to appear before the court with the stated alternative to submit his or her views in writing. Children below the age of twelve may also be provided with an invitation to appear before the court or to state their views in writing. Generally, children are heard from the age of ten to twelve depending upon the court in question, A. van Triest, 'Het kinderverhoor in het resort Den Bosch onder de loep', 2004 *FJR*, pp. 16–26.

27 See, for example, Voorzieningenrechter Rechtbank Haarlem 14 August 2007, LJN BB1817 concerning an intended relocation (probably to a neighbouring council). It is, however, not evident from case law that relocation always requires consent; notable is the decision of Gerechtshof Leeuwarden 1 August 2007, LJN BB1198 where the Court of Appeal seemed to rely upon

the other parent it may be deferred from the case law that the resident parent has a duty to consult with the other parent.[28]

Until recently there was, as far as can be ascertained, no published case law which prevented the resident parent to relocate with the child within the jurisdiction (the European part of the Kingdom of The Netherlands, as opposed to Aruba and the Dutch Antilles) when the child had its main residence with this parent. A recent decision from Utrecht District Court (*Rechtbank*) did, however, disallow the mother of a child aged seven to relocate from the middle of The Netherlands to the south (approximately 100–150 kilometres). The mother wished to relocate to be with a new partner. The District Court found that it was not in the best interests of the child to relocate considering that the extensive contact arrangement (every weekend) with the father would have to be altered.[29]

This latter case may be viewed to reflect upon the case law pertaining to situations where the parents have agreed to a shared residence (co-parentage) arrangement. In this case the main rule inferred from the case law of the lower courts seems to be that a parent cannot relocate with the child when the other parent objects to the relocation. This seems to also apply in cases where, notwithstanding the co-parentage agreement, one parent emerges as the primary carer or when alongside the co-parentage agreement, a main residence has been established with this parent.[30]

The general trend concerning the resident parent's relocation outside the jurisdiction seems to be that this is only rarely allowed. A typical case is where the resident parent wishes to relocate to his/her country of origin. In 2001, Haarlem District Court delivered a decision in a case involving the relocation of the mother to Spain (although it was not explicitly stated, it would seem that the mother was a Spanish national). The parents had been married from 1992 to 2001 and had three children born in 1992, 1994 and 1998 respectively. They had lived in Spain prior to 1993 and from then onwards in The Netherlands. The divorce decree contained the provision that the parents continued to exercise joint parental authority after the divorce without mentioning the children's residence. The children, however, had had their main residence with the mother since the divorce and had contact on a regular and frequent basis with the father. Pursuant to the mother's announced intention to relocate to Spain by the end of the school year,

---

a right of the parent with whom the child had its main residence to determine the place of residence.

28 For example, Gerechtshof Arnhem 29 August 2006, LJN AZ5530 and Gerechtshof 's-Hertogenbosch 21 August 2007, LJN BB6006.

29 Rechtbank Utrecht 7 November 2007, LJN BB8272.

30 For example, Rechtbank Utrecht 12 April 2006, LJN AZ1191. However, in the only published case which reached the Supreme Court and where the decision of the Court of Appeal was upheld, the Court had allowed the mother to relocate by establishing the child's main residence with the mother, Hoge Raad 10 November 2006, LJN AY8773.

the father started proceedings claiming that he should be allocated sole parental authority supplemented at a later stage with a claim for main residence. The mother claimed sole parental authority or a decision allowing her to change the children's main residence to Spain where she considered that she had better work opportunities.

The Haarlem District Court rejected both parents' claim for sole parental authority, as well as the father's claim for a change in the main residence of the children dependent on, however, the mother's continued residence in The Netherlands. The mother was thus not allowed to relocate (with the children) to Spain. In case she decided to relocate the court would change the children's main residence so that they could be with the father.

On the other hand, the Leeuwarden Court of Appeal (*Gerechtshof*)[31] decided in its decision of 1st August 2007 that the mother could relocate to her country of origin, Brazil, with a daughter over whom the parents exercised joint parental authority and where the daughter's main residence with the mother had been established by the District Court in the course of the divorce procedure in 2004. In this case the father sought sole parental authority over the daughter and refused to consent to the mother's relocation and the issuance of a passport for the daughter. It was not possible for the mother to remain in The Netherlands because she no longer had a right to stay. The interesting aspect of this case is that the Court of Appeal seemed to rely upon a right of the parent with whom the child had its main residence to determine the place of residence.

Another type of case concerns the situation where the resident parent wishes to relocate to pursue a job abroad. In this situation relocation is typically denied. In the first case decided by the Utrecht District Court in 2005, the father of a child born in 2000 was denied the right to relocate to Dubai in the course of the divorce proceedings. The parents agreed upon the child's main residence with the father, but the mother did not consent to the relocation (the mother was being cared for in an institution).[32]

Furthermore, in a decision by Alkmaar District Court, the court denied the mother the right to relocate to Crete with a younger son who had his main residence with the mother since the parents' divorce. The mother wished to relocate to Crete with the son, two children from a previous relationship and her new partner in order to take over as manager of a restaurant. The mother had stated that she would go irrespective of the decision of the court. The court altered the main residence of the son so that he could be with the father. The court relied, *inter alia*, upon the fact that the parents had not shared the care of the son in a traditional manner (during the mother's part-time work, the father had cared some extra days during the week) and that although the relocation was well pre-

31 Gerechtshof Leeuwarden 1 August 2007, LJN BB1198.
32 Rechtbank Utrecht 26 January 2005, LJN AS 6703.

pared, also in respect of the children (schooling), the well-being of the son had not been the primary concern of the mother in her choice to relocate.[33]

Finally, the situation where the resident parent wishes to relocate in order to establish a new family in another country should be mentioned. In a case before The Hague Court of Appeal in 2003, the question was whether the court should substitute the father's consent to permit the mother to relocate to Australia.[34] The facts of the case were as follows. The parents had two children, born in 1989 and 1991 respectively. The parents divorced in 2001 and continued to exercise joint parental authority. The children's main residence was with the mother. In 2002 the mother requested permission from The Hague District Court to relocate to Australia. The mother wished to relocate to Australia in order to settle there with her new partner who could not obtain permission to reside in The Netherlands. The father would not consent to such a relocation and claimed that the children's main residence should be changed so that they could be with him. The District Court denied both parents' requests and the mother appealed the decision to The Hague Court of Appeal. The Court of Appeal reversed the decision of the District Court and permitted the mother to relocate to Australia. The Court of Appeal first considered that it was in the children's best interest to remain living with the mother given the fact that the parents had agreed to choose a traditional family pattern where the mother had been the primary carer both during the marriage and after the divorce. In light of this the Court considered that 'it is in keeping with this carer role that she should have sufficient room to fulfil that role, in principle also if she chooses to continue her life and the life of the children in another place'. The Court then considered whether the relocation was in the interests of the children, which it found to be the case taking into account that the mother had carefully planned the relocation and that the mother's new relationship was stable.

However, in most similar cases the mother is denied permission to relocate.[35] In a decision by the Arnhem Court of Appeal from 2006,[36] the court reversed the decision of Almelo District Court to allow the mother to relocate to the USA with three children who had resided with her since the divorce in 2004 and had contact with the father every second weekend, although this depended on the father's

33 Rechtbank Alkmaar 5 April 2006, LJN 8683, see also Rechtbank Haarlem 27 February 2007, LJN BA1742 where the mother was not allowed to relocate to Spain.

34 Gerechtshof 's-Gravenhage 5 March 2003, LJN AG1643.

35 Similar because they concerned the establishment of a new family abroad and the main residence was with the mother who was the primary carer, Rechtbank Rotterdam 23 July 2007, LJN BB0581 denied permission to the mother to relocate to Bonaire where she wished to marry. Further the Court of Appeal, Gerechtshof 's-Hertogenbosch 21 August 2007, LJN BB6006 denied the mother the right to relocate to Switzerland with two children where she wished to marry a man by whom she was pregnant.

36 Gerechtshof Arnhem 29 August 2006, LJN AZ5530.

work abroad.[37] The mother wished to relocate to the USA in order to be with her new husband who had settled there in 2005. The Arnhem Court of Appeal found that a main residence did not entail a right to relocate in a situation where the relocation would hinder frequent contact and where the other parent did not consent. The Court of Appeal further considered that the mother had not provided adequate contact possibilities after the relocation. The decision of the Court of Appeal provided that the children should continue to reside with the mother but have contact with the father every other weekend which would mean that the mother could not reside in the USA[38]

These decisions on relocation outside the jurisdiction (the European part of the Kingdom of The Netherlands) illustrate that each case is decided on its own merits and that there is no clear line to be derived. Most of the recent cases seem to depart from the starting point that the parent with whom the children have their main residence should be granted permission to relocate. However, often rejecting permission based upon an ascertainment of the contact possibilities of the other parent and child. If viewed in the context of the results of the decisions, relocation outside the jurisdiction was only permitted in two cases where the resident parent could be viewed as having a limited choice in respect of relocation. In one case because the parent (the mother) no longer had the right to remain in The Netherlands[39] and in the other because the mother's new partner could not obtain a permit to stay in The Netherlands.[40] Further, it appears that the co-operation potential of the resident parent in respect of consulting the other parent and the contact possibilities are important.[41]

---

37 The case before the District Court had been initiated by the father before the mother's factual relocation to the US. The father had requested that the children's main residence should be with him. Before the Court of Appeal the father stated that he did not wish to change the children's main residence with the mother considering that she had been the primary carer, also during the marriage, but he would not consent to the relocation.

38 The Court further added that 'needless to say' the mother had not requested permission to relocate pursuant to Art. 1:253a, Dutch Civil Code before the Court of Appeal. A somewhat odd addition considering that the District Court had allowed the mother to relocate. It is not clear whether or not the Court of Appeal considered this to be of importance. This case has been quashed by the Supreme Court for formality reasons and been remitted to another Court of Appeal for a new decision.

39 Gerechtshof Leeuwarden 1 August 2007, LJN BB1198.

40 Gerechtshof 's-Gravenhage 5 March 2003, LJN AG1643.

41 Gerechtshof Arnhem 29 August 2006, LJN AZ5530. In this case the mother had taken the decision to relocate without consulting the father and had not provided adequate contact possibilities. The Court of Appeal denied the mother the right to relocate to the US and the Court did not seem to depart from the starting point that permission should be granted.

3.3. DANISH LAW

It has only been possible to obtain a decision on residence or relocation since the 2007 Act on Parental Responsibility. Prior to this Act parents who held joint parental authority had to agree on the child's residence or relocation.[42] If the parents could not agree, the only option was to terminate joint parental authority. A number of cases concerning the termination of parental authority and the subsequent allocation of sole parental authority have, however, indirectly concerned the intended or factual relocation of the resident parent.[43] In these cases the courts have been obliged to allocate sole parental authority. This means that it has not been possible to prevent a resident parent's relocation. It has only been possible to allocate sole parental authority to the other parent requiring that this parent is able and willing to hold sole parental authority.

Decisions on the allocation of sole parental authority containing relocation as an element are concrete decisions in which, naturally, not only the relocation plays a role. From the published case law it seemed that the relocation or the intention to relocate did not in itself provide a reason to allocate parental authority to the other parent. This applied in respect of relocations within the jurisdiction[44] and presumably also in respect of relocation outside the jurisdiction.[45] Individual circumstances such as parental ability, contact obstruction and the child's own opinion could, however, provide a reason to allocate parental authority to the other parent.[46]

42 Factually, the parent could relocate, the registration of the child in the persons administration (*Folkeregisteret*) was based upon the child's factual residence irrespective of who held parental authority, Art. 8(1), *Lov om det Centrale Personregister*, Act No. 1134 of 20 November 2006.

43 Also a number of cases concerning the transfer of sole parental authority from one parent to the other have concerned the relocation of the parent holding sole parental authority, L. Frost, 'Ændring af forældremyndighedsdomme og –aftaler efter forældremyndighedslovens § 13', 2003 *TFA*, pp. 360–361.

44 For example, Eastern High Court (*Østre Landsret*) 15 September 2005, *TFA* 2006.450Ø where the child had previously had a shared residence with the parents. The mother was allocated parental authority (over a daughter aged 6) and intended to relocate to Funen which made no difference. See also Western High Court (*Vestre Landsret*) 24 August 2004, *TFA* 2004.535V where the father was allocated parental authority over two daughters aged 5 and 8 despite the fact that he would have to relocate within a few years.

45 For example, the decision of the Østre Landsret 16 February 2006, *TFA* 2006.238Ø and 14.02.2006, *TFA* 2006.227Ø. In these two cases, parental authority was allocated to the mothers who relocated to, respectively, Japan and Bulgaria with a young child. See also Vestre Landsret 4 June 2003, *TFA* 2003.395V where the father was not allocated parental authority despite his fear that the mother would relocate to Venezuela and, finally, Østre Landsret 28 May 2003, *TFA* 2003.392Ø where parental authority was allocated to the father who resided with the child in the Comoros.

46 Vestre Landsret 28 November 2003, *TFA* 2004.139V and 14.12.2001, *TFA* 2002.144V where the mother was allocated sole parental authority by the district court and relocated to The Netherlands. The Western High Court allocated parental authority to the father on appeal considering, amongst other things, problems relating to contact.

The present regulation of relocation draws a distinction between relocation within the jurisdiction (the geographical part of Denmark excluding the territories of Greenland and the Faeroe Islands) and outside of this jurisdiction. The resident parent (*bopælsforælderen*) has the right to relocate within the jurisdiction when the parents hold joint parental authority. Either parent who wishes to change his or her residence must notify the other parent six weeks in advance.[47] This provision applies to both legal parents whether they hold parental authority or not and whether the child resides with this parent or not. While the resident parent has the right to relocate within the jurisdiction, the Explanatory Notes to the Act specify that the relocation may provide a reason for changing the child's residence and the non-resident parent may consequently request a change of the child's residence.[48] A change of residence is possible, for example, when the initial decision on residence was based upon the presumption that the resident parent agreed to an extensive contact arrangement or where the resident parent may be viewed to obstruct contact or be lacking in parental co-operation.[49]

The new Act on Parental Responsibility is deemed to implement the 'child's perspective'. This has several consequences. In the first place Article 31 now provides that the child must always be involved in a case concerning parental authority or residence so that the child's perspective and views can be brought to light. This Article must be read in conjunction with Article 5 according to which the child's views must be taken into consideration in all matters, depending upon his/her age and maturity. A conversation will normally take place with a child aged seven or older, while the views of younger children will be brought to light through the use of child experts.[50]

A resident parent may only relocate outside of the jurisdiction if the parents holding joint parental authority agree or the court has decided that this parent may relocate with the child to a specified place abroad. It is consequently not sufficient to notify the other parent in this situation. The Explanatory Notes to the Act do not specify when such permission may be granted. Presumably, the present case law concerning the allocation of sole parental authority where a relocation does not in itself provide a reason to reallocate parental authority continues to be guiding. The circumstances relevant to the change of residence, for example, where the determination of residence was based upon the presumption of an extensive contact arrangement or the resident parent is viewed to obstruct contact or to be unco-operative may provide a reason to disallow the relocation or to change the child's main residence.

---

47 Art. 18, Act on Parental Responsibility. There are no direct sanctions if notification does not take place. A lack of or an incorrect notification may, however, be relevant in a subsequent case on parental authority or residence, L 133, Comments to § 18.

48 Art. 17(1), Act on Parental Responsibility, L 133, Comments to § 17.

49 L 133, Comments to § 17.

50 Art. 31, Act on Parental responsibility, L 133, Comments to § 31.

3.4. COMPARATIVE CONCLUSIONS

On a general level the CEFLs approach towards parental relocation providing a balancing of contradicting ideals concerning, on the one hand, the non-resident parents' right to maintain personal relationships with the child and, on the other, the resident parents' possibility to relocate in pursuit of a valid purpose is reflected in the Dutch and Danish approach.

However, the approach taken in Danish law and to some extent in Dutch law seem to provide a clearer starting point concerning the resident parent's possibility to relocate within the jurisdiction. The formal distinction between relocation inside and outside the jurisdiction in Danish law and the informal distinction in respect hereof derived from decisions on relocation in Dutch case law can be regarded as favouring the relocation opportunities of a resident parent within the jurisdiction. It is not surprising that the CEFL Principles do not favour such a distinction given the fact that they generally pursue free movement rights in a European perspective and the fact that they must serve as guidance to both small and large European countries, in a geographical sense.

As yet, Danish law seems more favourable to the resident parent who wishes to relocate outside the jurisdiction than in the equivalent situation according to Dutch case law. It is a point of interest to see if the changes to Danish law providing for a decision on relocation as opposed to an allocation or reallocation of sole parental authority will change this perspective.

On a technical level the CEFL Principles and Danish law provide a specific regulation of relocation while Dutch law relies upon the general dispute settlement provision. Nonetheless, the CEFL approach could be viewed to be closer to Dutch law because both provide for an individual assessment without formally relying upon a general starting point.

The duty to inform or notify the other parent formally contained in the CEFL Principles and in Danish law is also relevant in Dutch law where case law even indicates that the resident parent has a duty not only to inform but also to consult with the other parent.

The considerations mentioned in the CEFL Principles concerning geographical distance, accessibility and parental co-operation are clearly also central in Dutch case law and relevant in Danish law. With respect to the child's participation in the decision making process, the CEFL Principles and Danish law do not rely upon a specific age requirement as Dutch law continues to do. None of the jurisdictions clarify the importance attached to the child's opinion in a case on relocation as opposed to an interpretation of the child's best interests.

4. CONCLUSIONS

The legal regulation of parental relocation must accommodate contradicting ideals or legal principles, such as the free movement of persons and more equal parenting. These ideals point in the direction of an individual assessment in any concrete decision. The fact that the regulation is contained in the law regulating parental authority/responsibilities may, however, ensure that the decisions come more to reflect the current ideals underpinning this regulation. The approach taken in the CEFL Principles illustrate this point. While the Principles generally aim to promote the free movement of persons in Europe, the approach taken towards relocation relies upon a balancing of interests with no clear starting point. Furthermore, developments in both Dutch and Danish law could be viewed as increasingly limiting the relocation possibilities of the resident parent.

The continuation of joint parental authority and the strengthening of equality between the parents are often argued in the terms of the 'child's right to two parents' or 'right to maintain personal relations with both parents' rather than on the basis of an equal right of parental access to the child.

In the context of relocation the construction of 'the child's right to two parents' can be viewed as flawed considering that the regulation only deems to regulate the residence of the parent with whom the child has his/her primary residence, while the other parent is free to relocate. While the child is increasingly involved in procedures concerning the relocation of the primary carer and thereby may come into conflict with this parent, there is no clarification of the child's position, *i.e.* if the child has an autonomous position or a decision is made on his or her behalf in his or her best interests. As such the regulation cannot be viewed to support the notion of the child's right to two parents. Rather the regulation may be viewed to pursue an aim for the child involving more equal parenting which necessarily will come to disfavour the resident parents' relocation possibilities.

Considering that children most often reside with one parent, typically the mother, the effect is that this resident parent increasingly will be barred from relocating in pursuit of a new job, a better network, family support or in order to start a new family while the non-resident parent has the freedom to relocate. The parents may consequently be viewed to be in an unequal position in relation to an ideal favouring joint parenting.

THE EFFECTIVENESS OF THE PATER EST RULE

FAMILY FUNCTION OVER FAMILY FORM IN THE LAW ON PARENTAGE?

The legal position of children born in informal relationships

Wendy M. Schrama*

1. MY NEIGHBOUR RUUD

This article begins with a story about my neighbours Ruud and Leanne, who are highly-educated people. They had already informally cohabited for more than a decade when Rutger was born in 2005 and Nina in 2007. Being a concerned neighbour and family law specialist, I wondered whether Ruud had recognised his children and whether he exercised joint parental authority with Leanne. Ruud did, to my surprise, not know whether he was the legal father of Rutger and Nina, but in his view it did not matter anyway, since he loved them and cared for them. He told me, however, that he was happy that both children had his surname. At that point, I knew that he must be their legal father, since according to Dutch law children may only obtain the surname of their legal father. Accordingly, Ruud must have recognised the children.[1] Obviously, Ruud was not aware of this. He was also uncertain whether he shared parental authority over the children with Leanne. Although he thought it was probable, he thought it would be best to ask Leanne. Leanne was planning to take care of it, but as it did not appear urgent, the form and documents were still waiting to be sent to the court.[2]

In the case of Ruud and Leanne the function and the form of their family mostly overlap. The social unit of partners and children that operates in daily life as a family (the family function) is also formally recognised by the legal system as

* Dr. W.M. Schrama is a Senior University Lecturer and Researcher in Family Law at the Utrecht Centre for European Research into Family Law (UCERF) of the Molengraaff Institute for Private Law, Utrecht University (The Netherlands), email: W.Schrama@law.uu.nl. This article has been partially supported by an Innovative Research Grant from the Dutch Scientific Organisation. The author wishes to thank Laura Klaming for the analyses of the NKPS data.

1 Art. 1:5 (1 and 2) Civil Code (*Burgerlijk Wetboek, BW*).

2 A downloadable form, to be send to the registrar of the court with an abstract of the birth certificate, a copy of passport or identity card, and an original abstract of the registration in the Municipal Basic Administration from both the mother and the father.

a family (the family form), since Ruud and Leanne are both legal parents of their children. However, Ruud does not exercise parental authority with Leanne, so in this respect the formal aspects of the relationship do not correspond with Ruud's actual position as the person who takes care of the children. Although this informal relationship is therefore a functional equivalent of formally recognised relationships, this is not fully reflected in the corresponding formal status, which would be that Ruud formally exercises parental authority. The case of Ruud and Leanne is just one example, but as a result of social changes, there is a growing divergence in the form and the function of family and partner relationships.[3]

It will be demonstrated in this article that a divergence in family function and family form may result in problems for legal systems primarily based on formal relationships such as

marriage, registered partnership and formal family relationships. Such a discrepancy entails the risk of ignoring an increasing number of informal family and partner relationships. In this respect the sharp increase in the number of births outside formalised relationships makes one question the law on parentage in the context of non-formalised families. The aim of this article is to assess whether the law on parentage in informal relationships should be amended to cater for changing social conditions and to stimulate a debate between legal scholars and practitioners on this issue.[4] In fact, this issue has been virtually ignored by the legislature during the last decade.[5] Although the analysis is based on the Dutch legal system, the model and options might be of interest for other legal systems, in particular due to the underlying general debate on balancing family form and family function.

2. SOME SOCIOLOGICAL DATA

In order to put the question in a proper legal perspective, it is necessary to deal briefly with a number of social developments.[6] However, it is difficult to find reliable data. Surprisingly little demographic and sociological research has been carried out in The Netherlands which explores informal lifestyles.

---

3 A. Barlow *et al.*, *Cohabitation, Marriage and the Law*, 2005; N. Dethloff, 'Nichteheliche Lebensgemeinschaft und Kinder', in J. Scherpe *et al.*, *Die Rechtstellung nichtehelicher Lebensgemeinschaften*, 2005, pp. 137–162; W.M. Schrama, *De niet-huwelijkse samenleving in het Nederlandse en Duitse recht*, 2004, pp. 505–572.

4 The legal position of children born in informal relationships of same-sex couples will not be dealt with.

5 Although unsuccessful attempts have been made to improve the legal position of these children, for instance *Kamerstukken II* 2000–2001, 27 047, no. 10.

6 See also Barlow *et al.*, *supra* note 3.

In 2006, 63% of all children were born in wedlock[7] and 37% outside of wedlock (in total 68,500 children born outside of wedlock). In 1980 this was respectively 96% versus 4%.[8] The social trend is evident and every year the proportion of children born outside of marriage rises. On the basis of this data, one is unable to establish how many of the 68,500 children are born to unmarried cohabitants and what proportion to parents not living together. However, information is available with regards to the number of children in different family types. In 2006 680,000 children were living in 450,000 single parent families, 1.8 million children in 3.4 million married families and 420,000 children in 760,000 non-marital relationships. The issue at stake here regards the group of children who are *born* during non-marital cohabitation.[9] This number is very roughly approximately 300,000.[10] The other 120,000 children are stepchildren of one of the partners from an earlier relationship and are therefore not relevant for the current research question.

3. RELATIONSHIP STATUS AND THE LEGAL POSITION OF CHILDREN

3.1 WHY IS LEGAL PARENTAGE IMPORTANT?

There are substantial differences between the legal position of children born within and outside wedlock, not only regarding parenthood, but also with respect to parental authority. Before outlining these differences, the legal effects of both parenthood and parental authority will be dealt with. Legal parenthood is a cornerstone for all other legal areas in which interpersonal relationships are relevant. It brings about a number of important legal effects, which are attached only to the relationships of persons related by law. The legal status has direct effect with

7 The proportion of registered partnerships with children is roughly equal to that of marriages, but it not clear whether these children are of both partners or whether they are stepchildren: see M. Jansen *et al.*, *Huwelijk of geregistreerd partnerschap?*, 2007, p. 220, figure 19.

8 See the site of Statistics Netherlands: www.cbs.nl/statline and A. van der Meulen *et al.*, 'Samenleven en kinderen', *Bevolkingstrends*, 2e kwartaal 2006, pp. 24–27.

9 After the child's birth a proportion of the couples marries (one third). Five years after the child's birth about 50% is still cohabiting, one in five couples with children has split up: Van der Meulen *et al.*, *supra* note 8, pp. 24–27.

10 There is no data available, but an indicator is that about 72% of non-marital couples have never been married with someone else. It is presumed that the total number of children is evenly divided between the non-marital couples who have never been married and those who have. In addition, it is presumed that the children who are part of the non-marital families of never married partners are the children of both partners. See Schrama, *supra* note 3, p. 26.

respect to the parent-child relationship relating to name law,[11] maintenance,[12] parental authority,[13] and the right to contact and information.[14] Looking at the extended family, the status of a legal child results in the legal integration in the families of both parents. In family law, closely related family members are prohibited from marrying, they are the persons who may request for the application of court orders for the protection of vulnerable adult family members, and family members are under a duty to maintain a limited category of family members in need.[15] Outside the field of family law, legal parentage has far reaching results in inheritance law,[16] nationality law,[17] social security law,[18] income tax law,[19] succession tax law,[20] criminal law and criminal procedural law.[21]

An example may best illustrate this. If my neighbour Ruud would die before he had recognised Rutger and Nina, the children would not be entitled to a share of the estate, unless Ruud had made a will to this effect. If they would have been his legal children, they would each have been entitled to half of the estate. If the children would be entitled to a share on the basis of Ruud's will, they would be under a duty to pay a high amount of inheritance tax, which would be substantially less if he would have been their legal father.[22] These differences are therefore relevant not only during the child's minority, but have consequences throughout a child's entire life.

Parental authority, on the other hand, is only of a temporary nature, *i.e.* until the child attains the age of 18 and is aimed at the care and upbringing of the child. It does not have legal effects in other areas of law except issues concerning contact and the right to information.[23]

---

11 According to Dutch law, children can only obtain their father's surname if he is their legal parent. Art. 1:5 Civil Code.

12 Art. 1:392 Civil Code. However, also a begetter is under such a duty, even if he is not a legal parent: Art. 1:394 Civil Code.

13 The system of the Civil Code (*Burgelijk Wetboek, BW*) is based on the notion that only legal parents can exercise parental authority, although there is a minor exception, since a partner of a legal parent may under a number of conditions exercise joint parental authority with the legal parent. Art. 1:253t Civil Code, Art. 1:253sa Civil Code.

14 Art. 1:377a Civil Code for contact with a legal parent, Art. 1:377f Civil Code for a non-legal parent.

15 Art. 1:41 Civil Code, Art. 1:431 Civil Code, Art. 1:432 (1) Civil Code and Art. 4:435 (4) Civil Code; Art. 1:392 Civil Code.

16 Art. 4:10, 11 and 63 Civil Code.

17 Art. 3–6 Kingdom Act regarding Dutch Nationality (*Rijkswet op het Nederlanderschap*).

18 Art. 4 (a and b) Employment and Social Assistance Act (*Wet werk en bijstand*).

19 Art. 1.2 Income Tax Act 2001 (*Wet inkomstenbelasting 2001*).

20 Art. 24 Inheritance Tax Act 1956 (*Successiewet 1956*).

21 Art. 137, Art. 189 (2), 316, 334 and 338 Criminal Code (*Wetboek van Strafrecht*) and Art. 217 (3) Criminal Procedural Code (*Wetboek van Strafvordering*).

22 For smaller shares 5% tax for legal children, but 41% for unrelated persons. For big shares this is 27% for legal children and 68% for unrelated persons: Art. 24 Inheritance Tax Act 1956.

23 Art. 1:245–247 Civil Code. Art. 1:377a Civil Code for contact with a legal parent without parental responsibility and Art. 1:377h Civil Code for a legal parent with parental responsibil-

3.2. THE LEGAL PARENTS OF A CHILD IN INFORMAL RELATIONSHIPS

According to Dutch law the woman who gave birth to the child or who adopted the child is its legal mother.[24] The position of the child in relation to the man depends on whether at the time of the birth its mother and the man were married or had a registered partnership. The unmarried father, who lives together with the mother at the time of the child's birth, needs to formally recognise his child, with the mother's consent, in order to become its legal parent.[25] The same applies to male registered partners in a different-sex registered partnership, since a registered partnership does not have any consequences for the legal parentage of the male partner of the birth mother of the child.[26] The man, in contrast, who is married to the mother when the child is born, is the legal father by operation of law.[27] A marriage of a male cohabiting partner does not have any paternity effects with respect to children born before the marriage and thus he will still have to recognize the children. If a father is not willing to recognise his child, the mother or child may apply for a judicial determination of paternity.[28]

Even if an unmarried father recognises[29] his child with the consent of the mother, he does not automatically share parental authority with the mother.[30] Only the mother exercises parental authority by operation of law.[31] In order to exercise joint parental authority, the father and the mother have to be recorded in the parental authority register as exercising joint parental authority.[32] Although this request will generally be granted, the parents have to take certain steps.[33] If a father has not recognised his child, he cannot exercise parental authority with the mother.[34]

In contrast, married men have joint parental authority by operation of law. Therefore, almost all married men exercise joint parental authority, in principle

ity.

24 Art. 1:198 Civil Code.

25 The prior written consent of the mother is required when the child is under the age of 16 years: Art. 1:204 (1) (c) Civil Code.

26 Art. 1:198 Civil Code and Art. 1:199 Civil Code.

27 Art. 1:199 (c) and Art. 1:200 Civil Code respectively Art. 1:199 (a) Civil Code.

28 Art. 1:207 Civil Code. There are no empirical data on the number of judicial determinations of paternity.

29 Leaving aside the theoretical possibility that the biological father exercises joint parental authority with the mother ex Art. 1:253t Civil Code.

30 Unless the couple subsequently marries, in which case the parents exercise joint parental authority by operation of law. Courts sometimes find otherwise: Rechtbank Rotterdam, 11th October 2005, LJN AU4409.

31 Art. 1:253b Civil Code.

32 Art. 1:252 Civil Code.

33 Art. 252 (2) Civil Code.

34 K. Boele-Woelki *et al.*, *Dutch report on parental responsibility*, CEFL's site: http://www2.law.uu.nl/priv/cefl.

also after divorce.[35] The mother and father in a registered partnership share parental responsibility by operation of law over children born during the registered partnership, even if the male partner is not the legal father of the child.[36]

3.3. BREAK DOWN OF THE RELATIONSHIP

In intact families these issues will not cause immediate problems.[37] The problems occur when the relationship breaks down, a risk that is not entirely unrealistic since the number of separations of non-marital couples is estimated at 30,000–240,000 per year.[38] It is, however, unclear what proportion of these separations involves children. If the father has recognised the child and both parents exercise joint parental authority, issues 'only' arise with regard to the residence of the child, contact and maintenance. In principle, the parents will continue to exercise joint parental authority after they break up.[39]

If the father is not a legal father, but 'only' an informal biological father who wishes to recognise his child after the relationship has broken down, this may require more persistence. The mother's consent is necessary for the recognition of children under the age of 16, but in an emotional period of separation, in which conflicts between the partners might easily occur, it might not be easy to obtain the mother's consent.[40] The mother's consent can be replaced by the district court's permission upon request of the father. There is a whole body of case law in which fathers apply for permission from the district court to recognise their children. In most cases permission is granted, despite the mother's objections.[41]

---

35 Art. 1:251 Civil Code.

36 Art. 1:253aa and sa Civil Code. See also M. Vonk, *Children and their parents: A comparative study of the legal position of children with regard to their intentional and biological parents in English and Dutch law*, 2007.

37 Although the difference might cause problems in the field of nationality law.

38 L. Steenhof *et al.*, 'Ex-samenwoners', 2002 *Maandstatistiek van de Bevolking* 50 (3), pp. 17–20. Van der Meulen *et al.*, *supra* note 8, p. 26 suggest that children in informal cohabitation have a much higher chance of divorcing parents than children in formal relationships.

39 Hoge Raad, 28th March 2003, *NJ* 2003, 359.

40 The child's consent is required if it is at least 12 years old.

41 Hoge Raad, 16th February 2001, *JOL* 2001, 126; Hoge Raad, 16th February 2001, LJN AB0033; Rechtbank Maastricht, 1st November 2001, LJN AE0486 (consent not granted); Hoge Raad, 31st May 2002, LJN AE0745; Hof Den Bosch, 17th December 2002, LJN AF2802; Hof Den Haag, 26th March 2003, LJN AG1753; Rechtbank Zwolle, 31st December 2003, LJN AO1858; Hoge Raad, 9th April 2004, LJN AO1337; Hoge Raad, 18th November 2005, LJN AT6843; Rechtbank Haarlem, 19th July 2005, LJN AT8396 (consent not granted); Hof Den Haag, 10th May 2006, LJN AY6460 (consent not granted); Hof Den Haag, 14th June 2006, LJN AY5959; Hoge Raad, 16th June 2006, LJN AW1860 (*Hoge Raad* reverses the decision of the *Hof*, granting consent); Hof Den Haag, 4th October 2006, LJN AZ2437; Hof Den Bosch, 11th October 2006, LJN AZ1883; Rechtbank Den Haag, 3rd November 2006, LJN AZ2691; Rechtbank Groningen 20th February 2007, LJN BA1386; Hof Den Haag, 9th May 2007, LJN BA6656 (consent not

If the father succeeds in establishing legal family ties with his child by means of recognition, he still has to obtain parental authority. Generally, the mother will not be inclined to be registered as exercising joint parental authority with the father. In this case, the father will have to apply for sole parental authority with the mother. This is difficult to obtain if the mother is exercising sole parental authority. The application will only be granted if the court considers this to be desirable in the best interests of the child.[42] However, the Dutch Supreme Court has accepted that, contrary to the legal provisions, a legal father may ask the court for an order for *joint* parental authority with the mother.[43] It is not yet clear how the courts deal with these cases. A bill currently before the Dutch Parliament would introduce the option to unilaterally petition for joint parental authority.[44]

The legal position and status of children is therefore to a large extent determined by the relationship status of their parents. However, it is difficult to determine the significance of these differences in practice, since virtually no empirical data is available (see Section 5).

4. PRINCIPLES AND RATIO OF THE LAW ON PARENTAGE

It is important to identify underlying principles of the law of parentage.[45] Firstly, the principle of procreational responsibility is significant. This principle relates to the duty of the persons who decided to conceive a child to take responsibility for the child, in particular during its minority.[46] A second fundament of the law on parentage is the best interests of the child principle. Although it is difficult to assess what is in the best interests of the child, it is not a wild idea that it is in line with this principle that a child has a right to *two legal parents*. It would presumably be beneficial for the child both in social and economic terms to have two legal par-

granted); Rechtbank Alkmaar, 19th September 2007, LJN BB4179; Hoge Raad, 5th October 2007, LJN BA7643; Hoge Raad, 9th November 2007, LJN BB3765 (consent not granted); Hoge Raad, 9th November 2007, LJN BB3775; Hof Den Haag, 23rd January 2008, LJN BC4348 (consent not granted).

42 Art. 1:253c Civil Code.

43 Hoge Raad, 27th May 2005, *NJ* 2005, 485; Hoge Raad, 28th April 2006, LJN AV0656; Hoge Raad, 18th February 2008, LJN BB9669. See also Hof Den Haag, 23rd January 2008, LJN BC4346 ordering joint parental authority, even against both parents' wishes, in the interest of the child.

44 *Kamerstukken II* 2004–2005, 29 353, no. 8.

45 This is not an exhaustive list; other principles are of interest as well. The principle of equality in parentage law has been analysed in: W.M. Schrama, 'Is het Nederlandse afstammingsrecht in strijd met het gelijkheidsbeginsel?', 2007 *RM Themis* 3, pp. 86–94, resulting in the conclusion that this principle can probably not be used to enforce the application of a *pater est* rule in informal relationships.

46 Vonk, *supra* note 36, p. 252.

ents, not only because of all the rights and benefits connected to legal childhood, but also because of the fact that it is easier for two persons to organise the necessary financial and non-financial care, than one alone. Moreover, the child would be legally integrated into two extended families.[47] A third principle playing a role is legal certainty. It is important for the child, its parents and for third parties, including the State, that it is absolutely clear who is legally related and who is not.

Having regard to the marital presumption provision from this perspective, it is striking to notice that it is, on the one hand, almost perfect. It is a successful instrument to attribute legal paternity to those fathers who are in the majority of cases the biological, intentional and social parents of the children born during marriage.[48] It therefore automatically provides children with two legal parents. In doing so, it translates the principle of procreational responsibility of the father in his obligation to be a legal parent, thus improving the child's legal position and therefore being in its best interests. The provision is easy to operate and provides legal certainty about the legal status of the relationship. However, on the other hand, this rule is far from perfect in that it only operates within marriage, excluding children born during registered partnerships and non-marital cohabitation.

The ultimate goal of the law on parentage is to effectively deal with all relevant relationships of parents and children by protecting and regulating these relationships. The law on parentage should therefore *de lege ferenda* be designed to prevent a rise in the number of family relationships which are functional, but not formal equivalents. Such a system would operate along the lines of procreational responsibility, since biological and social fathers would be legal fathers, with all the related rights and duties, it would implement the interest of the child of having not only one, but two legal parents and could provide legal certainty. A system closely related to social conditions would also reflect people's expectations, would make it easier to become a legal father and could be cost efficient.

Nevertheless, one topic has to be considered before exploring the alternatives for the law of parentage in informal relationships: is there genuinely a problem with the legal system as it is at the moment?

5. IS THERE A PROBLEM?

If Dutch law on parentage would effectively result in a substantial proportion of fathers in informal cohabitation relationships without a full parental status, this would infringe upon the aforementioned principles. But is this the case? This is

47 Some doubts might be cast on a right to two parents in situations in which the parents are, even before the birth of the child, most unlikely to be able to communicate. It is beyond the scope of the article to deal with that issue.

48 See also Vonk, *supra* note 36, p. 254.

hard to ascertain. It is certain that a proportion of informal fathers is not the legal father and does not exercise parental authority. Unfortunately, there is almost no empirical data available on the number of fathers who for one reason or another do not recognise their children and on the proportion of the legal fathers who do not exercise joint parental responsibility with the mother. An exception is the data collected in the Netherlands Kinship Panel Study.[49] The NKPS is a multi-method panel study under over 8,000 respondents, aimed at analysing the nature of family relationships in The Netherlands. Of the total number of respondents, only 321 persons live together informally with their partner and one or more children. Questions were submitted about recognition, legal parenthood, parental authority, co-parenting, parental visitation and child maintenance.

90% of the children of the 321 respondents is the child of both partners and in about 10% of cases the child is a stepchild. It is noteworthy that the number of respondents who do not answer one of more of the questions relating to the parent-child relationship is substantial. For instance, only 222 of the 291 respondents answered the question whether the first child of both partners had been recognised by the male partner. It is not clear what the legal status is of the 69 parents who did not answer this question, but it might be expected that at least a number of the male partners did not recognise the child or if they did, are not really aware of it. In the remaining cases, about 95% of the children had been recognised.[50]

The next question is whether both parents are the legal parents of the child. One would expect that the data for this question correspond more or less with the data relating to the question on the recognition,[51] but they do not. It not clear how to explain this difference. It is possible that some parents did not answer the question on recognition, but did give an answer on the parenthood issue. However, one still wonders how it is possible that 228 out of 239 parents of a first child indicate that they are both the legal parents of the child (52 parents not providing an answer), while only 213 of the 222 respondents indicate that the first child has been recognised by the father. One can therefore doubt whether these data are reliable in all respects.

The results on the question on parental authority are really poor: only 10% of the 321 respondents provided information, although it is an issue that is relevant for all unmarried parents. It is not possible to ascertain whether the remaining data is reliable, but the numbers are so small that it is not useful to provide the results. This also applies for other interesting questions that were only answered by a relatively small number of persons. Although this research shows that a noteworthy proportion of informally cohabiting fathers are not fathers with a full

49 See the website: http://nkps.nl for more information on the methods.
50 This is the combined number for first, second and third children of the 321 couples.
51 A judicial determination of legal paternity is presumably only taking place in exceptional cases and would result in a higher number of legal parents.

parental status, further research appears to be necessary to understand what is really happening.[52]

Although empirical research does not give a really clear picture yet, there are other tendencies which seem to point in the same direction. There seems to be a growing body of case law concerning the replacement consent of the district court for the recognition of children by their biological fathers.[53] The number of published cases is not a realistic estimation of the total number of problems, since most of the conflicts do not result in court cases and most of the relevant court cases are not published. Sociological research on registered partners demonstrates that 10% of male registered partners do not recognise their first child.[54] If we would assume that between 5–10%[55] of the fathers in a non-marital relationship have not recognised their children, this would amount to a total number of 30,000 children who do not (yet) have a legal father. These fathers will generally not exercise parental authority. If this estimation would be correct, this would also imply that a proportion of the remaining 270,000 legal fathers do not exercise parental authority with the mother. Even if these actual figures would 'only' be half of these numbers, it would still be a considerable number of children. Problems are mostly likely to occur at the moment the relationship breaks down, but again, it is hard to estimate for which proportion of the group this is is relevant. In conclusion, it is clear that a problem exists, but it is unclear the exact extent of the problem.

6. SPECIFIC NATURE OF PARTNER AND FAMILY RELATIONSHIPS

The relationship between parents and children has some specific characteristics. Firstly, it is generally a relationship between at least three persons: the mother and the father, who should together take care of all the interests involved at the family level, and the child, who is not in a position to take care of its own interests. A relationship break down influences not only the relationship at the partner level,

---

52 Preferably a legal scholar should be involved in designing the interview and survey questions. For instance the NKPS survey contains a question on the '*voogdij*' (guardianship), but this is the old terminology of the repealed provisions of the Civil Code (*Burgerlijk Wetboek, BW*). This could create confusion for the respondents. One could also built in a check by adding a question on the surname of the child. Parents might not be aware of the exact legal position, but they do know the child's surname. If it is the male partner's, he must have recognised the children.

53 See *supra*, note 41.

54 Jansen *et al.*, *supra* note 7.

55 However, this could be less for non-marital couples, since due to the similarities of registered partnership and marriage, people might not expect to have to recognise a child in a registered partnership. It could, on the other hand, also be higher, due for instance to the fact that a part of the non-marital couples may be less concerned with 'legal formalities'.

but also affects the parent-child relationship. At that moment, individual interests of (mostly) the parents become more vital than the interests of the child. Secondly, the specific characteristic of a family relationship is its long-term nature, actually even an indissoluble tie between parents and children. Thirdly, it is an affection based relation as opposed to economically orientated ties. These particular features of close family relationships influence the behaviour of the parties. It could partially explain the sometimes rather irrational behaviour of relatives, for instance the fact that a proportion of fathers (and mothers) do not timely organise the legal aspects of family relationships. Ruud presumably refrained from taking the necessary steps assuming that his relationship with Leanne will not break down, even though he knows, as we all do, that many couples do split up. This specific nature might also result in fathers not being aware of the importance of recognising their children. In addition, it might explain why problems rise only after a relationship breakdown, when it is, due to the emotional aspects at the partner level, more difficult for fathers in informal relationships to provide a legal status for the affection based relationship with their children. This special nature presumably also contributes to the growing divergence between family function and family form. One should realize that although an ideal legal system should be directed at effectuating the best interests of the child, it is only to a limited extent possible within the scope of the legal system to effectuate a three party relationship at the partner level. The law cannot, against all social trends, prevent people from separating, it can only try to mitigate the consequences for the children involved. In rethinking the law of parentage, it is important to be aware of these effects of the special nature of this type of relationships on the behaviour of the parents.

7. HOW TO DEAL WITH A DIVERGENCE BETWEEN FORM AND FUNCTION?

Different options to deal with the divergence between formal and functional families spring to mind, but in the context of this article attention will be paid to the extension of the marital presumption rule. Before doing so, a number of alternatives will shortly be discussed: on the one hand a parentage law system based purely on genetic affiliation and, on the other, a legal system operating on the basis of optional parentage. A number of other options will not be dealt with, since they are not primarily aimed at solving the specific tension between law and society resulting from informal fathers not recognising their children.[56]

[56] See for those proposals: Nederlandse Gezinsraad, *Nieuw gezinsrecht, Rapport over ouderschap en partnerschap*, 1996; A. Henstra, *Van afstammingsrecht naar ouderschapsrecht*, 2002; J.A.E.

To begin with, some years ago a fundamental adaptation of the law on parentage was suggested in the Dutch doctrine based on genetic fatherhood as a prerequisite for legal paternity.[57] Such a system would probably result in a growing number of cases in which biological, social and legal fatherhood would diverge. Therefore such a change is not desirable, taking into account the principles laid down in Section 4.[58]

The second idea, proposed by Schwenzer in her *Model Family Code*, is to abolish the *pater est* rule all together and to replace it with optional parentage.[59] This option appears to be ignoring the fact that parents do not always arrange their family affairs adequately. The interests of the child would benefit from legal provisions aimed at providing children automatically with two legal parents most likely to be their biological and social parents. This is contrary to a system in which all fathers have to establish paternity. This proposal would provide all children with just one legal parent *ex lege*. The abolition of the marital presumption rule would most likely result in a decrease of the number of children with two legal parents, since a proportion of the parents will not take the required steps. This seems to be illustrated by the recent Dutch experiences on registered partnership. In addition, there will be more room for conflict between the mother and the partner in those cases where their relationship is unstable. The current Dutch system gives rise to a considerable number of conflicts that are brought before the court in which the male partner wishes to recognise the child. If paternity has to be accepted in all cases, this will undoubtedly result in an increase of the number of these conflicts, which is in no-one's interest. Although it would imply treating all children equally, regardless of their mother's relational status, it would throw many children out with the bath water. Thirdly, it would cause more problems and costs related to the practical operation of such a system. To make the exception the rule is thus not an idea which should be supported.

7.1. CREATING MORE AWARENESS

If empirical research would show that the number of couples that are not adequately dealing with the legal aspects of family relationships is low, it would not

van Raak-Kuiper, *Koekoekskinderen en het recht op afstammingsinformatie*, 2007; P. Vlaardingerbroek, *Ouder worden, ouder blijven*, 1998.

57 C. van Wamelen, 'Het tekort in het familierecht, in het bijzonder het afstammingsrecht', 1996 *NJB*, pp. 1093–1102. This author proposes to require parents to hand over a medical document at the registration of the birth of a child which proves that the father is the begetter or the life partner who consented to conception of the child. Critically: C. Forder, 'Biologisch ouderschap: vaders met of zonder keurmerk', 1997 *NJB*, pp. 19–21.

58 Unless parentage law will be structurally reformed and other legal consequences will be attached to it.

59 I. Schwenzer, *Model Family Code*, 2006, pp. 96–99.

be necessary to fundamentally change the law of parentage. In that case, a more simple solution could be of assistance. As the story of my neighbours Ruud and Leanne illustrates, one of the problems is the lack of knowledge on the rights and duties in the law on parentage. The point here is that people (often including highly educated people) are sometimes poorly informed about their legal rights and duties, in particular in situations in which it is not illogical to assume that no steps have to be taken. Maybe even more important is that partners do not really realize what the relevance of being a legal parent is. Moreover, it is likely that partners do not wish to acknowledge the risk of a relationship break down and the resulting implications in terms of the parent-child relationship. The specific nature of the triangular relationship in non-conflicting situations is partially responsible for this effect.

Nevertheless, the State provides sufficient legal information on legal parentage and parental authority, in particular on the Internet, such as the Ministry of Justice's site and *Postbus 51*, an information site operated by the State.[60] The point is, however, that more awareness could be created of the importance of legal paternity and parental responsibility. It should become part and parcel of people's understanding of what being a good parent involves: to deal with the legal aspects of the family relationship, even before the birth of the child. Information provided by the State could more than at the moment, stressing the importance of the legal relationship and the problems which might result from not dealing with the legal aspects adequately. Current information indicates the possibilities in a rather neutral way, but does not point out all of the potential consequences if no action is taken. Perhaps the information could include examples of two different couples, one regulating its legal affairs and the other one not, with special attention for the concrete consequences for both fathers and children in case of a relationship breakdown. If more awareness of the underlying interests is created, people might be more likely to take the necessary steps. Further, one could consider providing information to couples and to create more awareness during pregnancy courses and by consultation of midwifes, which play an essential role in the Dutch health care system. A major point of concern is that, given the specific nature of family and partner relationships, no miracles should be expected of this type of measures.

60 http://www/postbus51.nl.

8. EXTENDING THE PATER EST RULE TO INFORMAL COHABITATION

8.1. INTRODUCTION

An idea of a quite different nature is to extend the marital presumption rule.[61] This would result in a three-tier system of paternity: first, paternity by operation of law, in marriage, registered partnership and informal cohabitation; secondly, paternity by voluntarily recognition for all those fathers who are not an *ex lege* father, and thirdly, paternity against the begetter's will. Two options spring to mind: *ex lege* paternity for all informal cohabiting couples or for a limited category, such as informal cohabiting couples who subsequently marry (legitimisation of the child). The husband would then become the legal father of the children already born to the couple prior to their marriage.[62] This alternative will not be dealt with, since it will solve problems for only a limited group of children and fathers.

The core of this section incorporates an analysis of the advantages and disadvantages of an extension of *ex lege* paternity to informal cohabiting fathers, but this enquiry is of a rather exploratory nature. In doing so, it is hoped to initiate a debate on how parentage law systems could react to social trends. First, some practical difficulties of this idea will be analysed. The focus will then shift to the question when, having regard to the underlying rationale of the law on parentage, it is justified to extend the *pater est* rule. Finally, some general objections will be examined.

8.2. PRACTICAL PROBLEMS

Leaving aside for a moment the issue why a parentage law system should include a provision for informal fathers, the most problematic point is whether it could, having regard to the practical problems. The combination of, on the one hand, a far-reaching legal consequence having effect by operation of law and, on the other, the problems arising out of the informal nature of cohabitation is quite a challenge. It comes as no surprise that this is an objection put forward in the legal literature. It has been argued that if the paternity of the male partner would depend on the actual proof of the cohabitation, the rule would lose its principal argument for application, namely its *ex lege* effect.[63] It is certainly true that these

61 See also Vonk, *supra* note 36, pp. 254–255 who is of the opinion that it is vital to devise a connecting factor for the automatic attribution of legal parenthood to the unmarried biological or intentional father.

62 With the exception of the situation in which the children already have a legal father.

63 G. Verschelden, *Origineel ouderschap herdacht*, 2005, p. 338, no. 571. This point has also been put forward by M. Coester, 'Nichteheliche Elternschaft und Sorgerecht', 2007 *FamRZ* 2007, p. 1142 relating to joint parental responsibility for unmarried couples. See also: C. Forder *et al.*,

aspects require careful attention, in particular with an eye to legal certainty. The question is how to define informal cohabitation.

There are two basic techniques used to define informal cohabitation. Firstly, by means of a formal connecting factor, *i.e.* a factor that is recognised by the legal system without any verification, such as a marriage or the registration of a birth. Formal criteria are legal facts directly connected to the legal system itself. A formal definition of cohabitation would fit into the Dutch system based on formal legal parentage, in which parentage does not depend on a material connecting factor such as genetic affiliation or intention, but exclusively on a formality.[64] Alternatively, by means of a material connecting factor, *i.e.* a factor which cannot be ascertained exclusively on the basis of the legal system, but which has a factual component in reality, which needs to be verified.

The use of definitions based on material connecting factors for cohabiting couples is fairly common in the Dutch legal system, which is familiar with at least fifteen different legal terms, mostly variations on the concepts of 'joint household' (*gezamenlijke huishouding*), 'stable common household' (*duurzame gemeenschappelijke huishouding*), or 'life companion' (*levensgezel*).[65] In addition, other definitions are used, such as 'tax partners' and 'to live together as if they were married'.[66] Experience in the past demonstrates that legal certainty is not at stake in these areas of law. This applies even with respect to the more complex areas of law, such as social security law, where many cases have to be dealt with in a short period of time and where the risk of fraud is substantial.[67]

The Dutch Government expressed its aim to harmonise the diverging terminology in the different provisions. Definitions should be confined to either the term 'life companion' in provisions in which the emotional ties between the partners prevail or 'a joint household' in provisions in which the financial aspects of

---

The establishment of parenthood, Maastricht Working Papers 2007–01, p. 28; M. Antokolskaia (ed.), *Convergence and Divergence of Family Law in Europe*, 2007, pp. 169–235.

64 Forder *et al.*, *supra* note 63, p. 24.

65 See Schrama, *supra* note 3, pp. 128–212. The terms mentioned in the text are the most important ones, but in different acts small differences have been introduced, for instance 'durable joint household' instead of 'joint household' (in a number of social benefits provisions), different terms for 'tax partner', 'life partner' and 'other life partner' (many provisions, both private and public law and procedural law as well), and a number of different variants of '*duurzame gemeenschappelijke huishouding* (Art. 7:267 Civil Code; Art. 24 (2) (a) Succession Tax Act 1956; Art. 24 (2) (b) Succession Tax Act 1956; Art. 6:107 (2) (b) Civil Code as proposed in *Kamerstukken II*, 28 781), '*andere levensgezel met wie een gemeenschappelijke huishouding wordt gevoerd op basis van een notarieel samenlevingscontract*' (Art. 24 (2) (b) Succession Tax Act 1956), '*partner*' (pension legislation), '*ongehuwd tenminste drie jaren onafgebroken met een ongehuwde Nederlander in een duurzame relatie anders dan het huwelijk samenleeft* (Art. 8 (4) Kingdom Act regarding Dutch Nationality).

66 Art. 1:160 Civil Code. The effect is a termination of the right to maintenance due by the ex spouse in the event of an informal cohabitation, which has effect by operation of law.

67 See W. Schrama, 'The Dutch approach to informal lifestyles: Family function over family form?,' to be published in 2008 *IJLPF* 3.

the relation are most important.[68] Is one these terms useful? The term life companion does not require cohabitation. As a corollary, it is not an accurate concept for the issue at stake. In a number of legal areas, including social security law, the term joint household is used.[69] A joint household entails a situation in which two persons have their main residence in the same dwelling and in which they take care of each other by means of financial or non-financial contributions to the household.[70] This definition is not appropriate either, since the sole factor of cohabitation appears to be sufficient in the law on parentage, whereas this term requires much more.[71] A second objection is that it is rather difficult to attribute effect by operation of law if a civil registrar has to test complicated material conditions.[72] It would give room for interpretation and conflict. Therefore, material conditions are not very suitable in combination with the paternity presumption, in particular from the point of view of legal certainty. The same applies to 'stable common household' which is not an equivalent of 'joint household'. This term would require the registrar to check, for instance, the intention of the partners involved and the duration of the common household. The term 'tax partnership' requires the partners to chose whether they wish to be treated as a couple and the term 'to live together as if they were married implies having a joint household and thus demands a check of the material conditions. In conclusion, none of the existing definitions correspond with the actual situation in the law of parentage.

Therefore, it appears necessary to generate yet another definition of informal cohabitation, preferably one with a formal connecting factor. There are hardly any formal connecting factors, since informal cohabitation is characterised by a lack of State interference. There is no central register of couples living together like the civil status registers for married and registered partners. Using a cohabitation contract drawn up by a notary as a formal connecting factor would raise the objection that it would automatically exclude 50% of all cohabiting couples.[73] The registration of the partners at the same address in the Municipal Basic Administration provides a formal connecting factor representing the cohabitation criterion, which is in principle easy to operate. It seems unnecessary to complicate the system with requirements on a minimum duration of cohabitation or to demand a check on the content of their relationship. In further limiting the group of partners, the provision will be less effective, since it will exclude couples without good cause (see Sec-

68 Aanwijzing 72a, *Stcrt.* 1998, no. 45 p. 12 and *Kamerstukken II* 1995–1996, 22 700, no. 21, p. 3.

69 Art. 7:267 and 7:268 Civil Code.

70 Art. 3 (3 and 4) Employment and Social Assistance Act. The same argument applies to the term used in Art. 1:160 Civil Code.

71 Although, admittedly, in most cases where parents live together with a child, there will be a joint household.

72 See on the function of civil status registrars in this respect: Forder *et al.*, *supra* note 63, p. 28.

73 A. de Graaf, 'Helft samenwoners heeft samenlevingscontract,' *Webmagazine* 22 maart 2004, CBS, http://www.cbs.nl/nl/publicaties/artikelen/algemeen/webmagazine.

tion 8.3). However, the question arises whether cohabitation of the mother and father alone is sufficient to determine the group of children and fathers, for whom an *ex lege* presumption should apply. In order to deal with this issue, it is necessary to analyse the underlying aims of the marital presumption rule.

8.3. JUSTIFICATION FOR EXTENDING THE SCOPE OF APPLICATION

What is the rationale for linking the law of parentage and parental authority with marriage? Historically this question is uncomplicated, but as society and social attitudes to parentage and marriage itself have changed, the answer becomes more difficult. It is, even now, understandable to take marriage as a starting point for parentage and parental authority. It remains the prevailing family form and spouses are generally the biological, intentional and social parents of the children born during the marriage.[74] However, it is less obvious why the protection for children of married couples has not been extended to children of unmarried cohabitants. The issue here is under which conditions the law may justifiably presume that the male partner of the mother is the child's biological, intentional and social parent in the majority of the cases. It is not sufficient that a number of fathers meet these conditions; the majority of the fathers must meet these conditions before a rule of *ex lege* paternity should be considered. It is crystal-clear that male registered partners meet these conditions, and therefore the *pater est* rule should be extended to children born during a registered partnership.[75] The Government is currently, ten years after the Act on Registered Partnership came into force, planning to enact legislation to this effect.[76] This change causes no problems for the formal Dutch parentage system,[77] since registered partnership is a formal institution.

With regard to informal couples the question is far more delicate. The most important condition would be that the man who declares the birth of the child *cohabits* with the mother at the moment of the child's birth. Nevertheless, registration at the same address alone would be an insufficient guarantee that the male

74 See also Vonk, *supra* note 36, p. 253. See on the grounds for legal paternity: Forder *et al.*, *supra* note 63. Although it is generally accepted that either biology or intention is a ground for legal parenthood, it is important to realise that the husband is generally not only the biological father, but also the intentional and social father of the child born during his marriage. This would correspond with an idea of parentage law as a system to attribute parents to children on biological, intentional and social grounds.

75 W.M. Schrama, 'Is het Nederlandse afstammingsrecht in strijd met het gelijkheidsbeginsel?', 2007 *RM Themis* 3, pp. 86–94; K. Boele-Woelki *et al.*, *Huwelijk of geregistreerd partnerschap?*, 2007, pp. 271–272.

76 *Kamerstukken II* 2007–2008, 31 200 VI, no. 11.

77 Forder *et al.*, *supra* note 63, p. 24.

partner is the father and that *ex lege* paternity represents biology and the intention of the persons involved. Therefore, it is necessary to introduce an additional factor as well, namely that the man who is registered at the same address as the mother is also the one who registers the birth of the child at the civil registrar. The mother is allowed to register the birth of the child, but she is not under a legal duty.[78] A declaration by the mother is exceptional, partially due to the short period of only three days in which the declaration has to be made.[79] All legal fathers are under a duty to declare the birth of their children, and if the legal father is not present or not able to declare the birth of the child, any person who was present at the child's birth, such as the biological father, who is not a legal father.[80] Legal and biological fathers generally declare the birth of their child. The double condition of, on the one hand, the declaration of the child's birth and, on the other, the cohabitation of the declaring male partner with the mother seems to justify the presumption that this man is generally the child's biological, intentional and social parent.[81] This typology of non-marital cohabitation is presumably correct in a vast majority of cases, since it would seem likely that the group of men who declare the birth of a child and who cohabit with the mother, but who are not the child's father, is very small.[82] The legal system should provide this group with a possibility to opt-out, but the interest of this group of men is insufficient in order to hamper the extended scope of the paternity presumption.[83] A proposal for a new provision in the law of parentage could then read as follows:

> 'The father of a child is the male partner who declares the birth of the child at the civil status registrar if he is, at the moment of the child's birth registered at the same address as the mother of the child according to the Municipal Basis Administration.'

---

78 Art. 1:19e(1) Civil Code.

79 J. Kampers *et al.*, *Inleiding tot de burgerlijke stand*, 2006, p. 260.

80 Art. 1:19e Civil Code.

81 M. Coester, 'Nichteheliche Elternschaft und Sorgerecht', 2007 *FamRZ*, p. 1141 who comes to a similar conclusion, but then with respect to parental responsibility.

82 Couples not living together are not easy to categorise. There may well be male partners who declare the birth of the child and cohabit with the mother, who are the biological, intentional and social father of the child, but presumably there will also be partners who are not. The absence of an apparent typology of this group would make inclusion in the marital presumption unwise.

83 Secondly, the general conditions of the law of parentage should be applicable: the mother and the father should not be in a formal relationship with another partner and they should not be prohibited to marry each other. See Art. 1:204 Civil Code on the conditions for recognition, including a minimum age of 16 years of the father. Explicit consent of the mother is not required, since implicit consent can be presumed to be given, when the partners cohabit and the father declares the birth of the child.

The civil registrar should verify on the basis of the Municipal Basis Administration whether the father is registered with the mother at the same address.[84]

8.4. OBJECTIONS

This idea raises many questions and objections, with respect to its necessity, its effectiveness, and the problems it might create. It is clear that a fundamental change such as this one is only to be considered if the problem is sufficiently severe. This is not clear at the moment, due to a lack of reliable data on the actual divergence of family form and family function.

Would this particular solution really be effective, in particular having regard to alternatives? It is hard to predict, but a realistic concern is the unintended effect that such a change would generate confusion about the paternity system and consequently the status of parents and children. One could imagine that a system in which some informal fathers are legal fathers by operation of law and others not, creates uncertainty, which could finally result in a lower number of recognitions of those informal fathers who are not a legal parent by operation of law. For this reason, it is important to consider the way in which information could be provided by the registrar to the parents of the child on the status of both the child and the father.

Another sensible objection in terms of effectiveness concerns the reliability of the Municipal Basic Administration. It is not clear which percentage of the group of informal fathers who actually are living together with the mother, are not as such registered in the administration system. This has to be investigated further. In contrast, there may be problems caused by the registration of men at the same address as the mother, who are in fact not the father. This might not be a big issue, since the chance that a man who declares the birth of the child and who is incorrectly registered at the mother's address, but who is not the child's father, is more-than-likely not high. An opt-out procedure is therefore indispensable.[85]

Another argument that has to be reflected upon is the risk of abuse of this option for situations for which it is not intended. Probably this problem is not significant, in particular if the mother and the child have a right to lodge proceedings for the denial of paternity in cases where the *ex lege* legal father is not the biological or intentional father. Abuse of the system also seems unlikely in the context of the possibility of recognition, which is, in cases of abuse, a much easier way to accomplish a similar result.

---

84 The practical problems of this option fall outside the scope of this article, but should definitely be enquired.

85 See Art. 1:200 Civil Code on the denial of the marital paternity presumption for married men.

Finally, there is the practical and important issue of civil registrars who will be attributed with greater responsibilities: is this a desirable development

An argument of a quite different nature is the one put forward by the Dutch author Punselie in the context of whether automatic joint parental authority should be attributed to the mother and father at the moment of recognition by the father. She argues that the legal system should encourage parents to take responsibility for their children by marrying.[86] The author questions whether non-marital cohabiting couples take any mutual responsibility for the family as a whole; from a legal perspective, marriage is generally a more stable and safer lifestyle than non-marital cohabitation. The fact that parents do not wish to take responsibility for each other in good times, implies the risk that the children will suffer from the poor financial position of the caretaking partner after a relationship breakdown. If parents would obtain joint parental authority by operation of law, there would be no incentive whatsoever to consider the legal organisation of their family. Although the argumentation concerns parental authority, the author will presumably also have objections to an extension of the *pater est* rule. After all, it could be argued that if informal fathers will be legal fathers *ex lege*, the partners will be even less inclined to think about their family form.

It is true that formal relationships such as marriage and registered partnership offer more protection for the partner who takes care of the children.[87] A number of specific legal provisions compensate spouses for the negative effects of a traditional division of tasks, such as maintenance and property distribution. Such mechanisms are completely absent in the case of non-marital relationships.[88] Nevertheless, the argument that the gap between family function and family form could be reduced by not attaching consequences to an undesired lifestyle choice of the parents, which negatively affects the legal position of the child and the father, is not valid for a number of reasons. Social trends are hard to reverse by means of legislation. It is an overestimation of what law can do.[89] It also presupposes that people are informed about the different choices and the resulting different legal consequences. Moreover, it assumes that the legal aspects have an important impact on people's decision how to arrange their lifestyle. It is doubtful

86 L. Punselie, 'Kinderen van (ex-)samenwonenden', 2007 *FJR*, pp. 272–276.

87 W. Schrama, 'The Dutch approach to informal lifestyles: Family function over family form?' to be published in 2008 *IJLPF* 3.

88 See C. Forder *et al.*, *Gehuwd of niet: maakt het iets uit?*, 2005, pp. 553–555; W. Schrama, 'General lessons for Europe based on a comparison of the legal status of non-marital cohabitants in The Netherlands and Germany,' in K. Boele-Woelki *et al.*, *Common core and better law in European Family Law*, 2005, p. 263.

89 S.F. Moore, 'Law and social Change: the 'semi-autonomous social field as an appropriate subject of study', 1973 *Law and Society Review* 7, pp. 719–746; J. Griffiths, 'De sociale werking van recht', in J. Griffiths, *De sociale werking van het recht*, 1996, p. 469. See also: C.M. Klein Haarhuis *et al.*, *Legislation and reality, Findings from legislative evaluations*, 2008, www.wodc.nl/onderzoeksdatabase with an English summary.

whether these assumptions are correct. Dutch empirical research on formal relationships appears to point in a different direction.[90] Secondly, the effects of the specific nature of the three party familial relationship on people's behaviour seem to have been ignored. People will generally become aware of the legal organisation of their family only in discordant situations and not before. In addition, several alternatives have to be analysed: why not give the protection of marriage to non-marital families? Even assuming that we would wish couples with children to marry, there are other, possibly more viable alternatives, which have to be enquired first. Therefore, the argument that the law of parentage should not be changed to meet social conditions in order to reverse the current social trends of informal cohabitation and extra-marital births, is not convincing.

9. THE RESULT

In 1998 when the law on parentage was amended in order to abolish the distinction between children born within and outside wedlock, it was not contemplated to extend the rights relating to the children of married couples to children of unmarried couples. Issues arising out of informal different-sex parenthood have in fact almost completely been ignored. This is noteworthy, since social trends indicate a growing divergence between family form and family function, in particular as a result of the sharp increase in the number of extramarital births over the last few decades. The legislature needs to be aware of the growing divergence between social and legal developments, since this creates the risk of ignoring an increasing number of informal family relationships, which will not enjoy the protection of formal families.

The first action to be taken by the State is to invest money in empirical research. If one thing is clear, it is that empirical research is indispensable. Currently, there is a lack of empirical data on the legal organization of relationships between parents and children in informal families. In order to test if the legal system corresponds with social reality, we should first know which proportion of the parents take care of arranging their legal family relationships and for what reasons they do or do not.

If it would turn out that almost all parents in informal relationships adequately take care of the legal aspects of family relationships, there is no need to rethink the law on parentage. However, if such research would demonstrate that a considerable proportion of informal fathers does not possess full parental status,[91] the legislature should consider reforming the parentage law system. Legal debate and research should address the ways in which the principles of procreational

[90] Jansen *et al.*, *supra* note 7, pp. 206–217 and pp. 223–226.

[91] Not a legal parent, no parental authority or both.

responsibility, the best interests of the child and legal certainty can best be taken into account. In rethinking the law in this respect, the legislature and the legal doctrine should be aware of the fact that partner and familial relationships are affection based, three-party relationships with a specific nature, which makes people operate in legally ill-advised ways.

The idea of *ex lege* paternity is certainly one of the options to be considered, although it is obvious that the current contribution sketches merely a rough idea, which needs to be further investigated, using comparative law techniques. At first sight, a significant improvement of this alternative would be that a substantially larger group of children and fathers will have a formal legal relationship with each other and would enjoy such legal protection. Such a system would thus facilitate the duty of parents to arrange legal parenthood of their children.[92] Rutger and Nina would then have a legal father regardless of whether their parents happened to be aware of the importance of taking care of the legal aspects of familial relationships. Hopefully, a legal debate on the necessity of bridging the gap between formal and functional family relationships will inspire the legislature to keep an eye on social trends and their relevance for the law.

---

92 N. Dethloff, 'Nichteheliche Lebensgemeinschaft und Kinder', in J. Scherpe *et al.*, *Die Rechtstellung nichtehelicher Lebensgemeinschaften*, 2005, pp. 137–162; see also M. Coester, 'Nichteheliche Elternschaft und Sorgerecht', 2007 *FamRZ*, pp. 1137–1145.

TRACING DOWN THE HISTORICAL DEVELOPMENT OF THE LEGAL CONCEPT OF THE RIGHT TO KNOW ONE'S ORIGINS

Has 'to know or not to know' ever been the legal question?

Richard J. Blauwhoff*

1. INTRODUCTION

The informational interest persons may have in knowing their genetic parentage acquired a fundamental rights dimension almost two decades ago.[1] Thus, since 1989, Article 7-1 of the UN Convention on the Rights of the Child (CRC) recognises *'as far as possible, the right to know and be cared for his parents'*.[2] In Europe, that same year saw two cases of tremendous importance for the progressive international and national recognition of individuals' interest in knowing the truth

* R.J. Blauwhoff, LLM, MA, is a PhD Candidate at the Molengraaff Institute for Private Law, Utrecht University (The Netherlands), email: R.Blauwhoff@law.uu.nl.

1 Key publications from this 'early period' in this development towards constitutionalisation include: R. Frank, 'Recht auf Kenntnis der eigenen Abstammung', 1988 *Zeitschrift für das gesamte Handelsrecht und Wirtschaftsrecht*, pp. 113–120; E. Haimes, '"Secrecy": what can artificial reproduction learn from adoption?', 1988 *International Journal of Law and the Family*, pp. 46–61; B. Hassenstein, 'Der Wert der Kenntnis der eigenen Abstammung', 1988 *FamRZ*, pp. 120–123; K. O'Donovan, 'A right to know one's parentage?', 1988 *International Journal of Law and the Family*, pp. 27–45; K. O'Donovan, 'What shall we tell the children?', in R. Lee & D. Morgan (eds.), *Birthrights, law and ethics at the beginning of life*, 1989, pp. 96–114; D. Hodgson, 'The international legal protection of the child's right to a legal identity and the problem of statelessness', 1993 *International Journal of Law, Policy and the Family*, pp. 255–270; G. Stewart, 'Interpreting the child's right to identity in the UN Convention on the Rights of the Child', 1992 *Family Law Quarterly*, pp. 221–233; G. Van Bueren, 'Children's access to adoption records: state discretion or an enforceable international right', 1995 *Modern Law Review*, pp. 37–53.

2 The delegations of the United States and Germany insisted upon the insertion of the words 'as far as possible' in response to the original draft submitted by a few Muslim countries. UN Doc. E/CN.4.1989/48, 18–22. For a commentary on the UN Children's Right Convention, see in particular: S. Detrick, *A commentary on the United Nations Convention on the Rights of the Child*, 1999.

about their genetic descent as a fundamental right,[3] on the basis of the right to 'private life'[4] and the 'personality right' respectively.[5] Meanwhile, in legal scholarship, this 'right to know' has now also gained broad recognition.[6] As a fundamental right to 'know the biological truth', this recognition not only echoes the legal emancipation of the child that pervades the CRC, but also reflects developments towards greater certainty and availability of scientific parentage tests.[7]

Although there are now many uses of DNA identity tests, both media and legal interest in the West has concentrated to a great extent on their use in ascertaining paternity. Thus, as far as the 'paternity palaver' in the American popular media is concerned, legal sociologist Dorothy Nelkin has distinguished three repeated claims found in the media: that 'real' relationships depend on shared DNA, that uncertain paternity as a result of infidelity is so rampant that there are real reasons for suspicion and that accordingly there is a burning need, on both economical and emotional grounds, for persons to know the biological truth.[8]

For children, circumstances under which the issue may become relevant may range from displacement, adoption, artificial insemination and surrogacy. For reasons of brevity, this article shall not elaborate upon the disparities between legal and genetic parentage, but focus interest on the scope of the right to know in the context of socio-legally constructed paternity.[9] In discussing socio-legally constructed forms of paternity, it should be borne in mind that 'biology' is but

---

3 ECtHR, *Gaskin v. United Kingdom*, Appl. no. 10454/83, 7 July 1989; in Germany, by the Federal Constitutional Court (*Bundesverfassungsgericht, BVerfGE*) on 31 January: BVerfGE 79, 256 = *FamRZ* 1989, 255, on reference from the Amtsgericht Hamburg, 3 March 1987.

4 *I.e.* pursuant to Art. 8 of the European Convention on Human Rights.

5 The 'personality right' (*Persönlichkeitsrecht*) is protected in the German Federal Constitution or Basic Law (*Grundgesetz*) under Art. 1 I in conjunction with Art. 2 I. The basis of the right to know one's origins (*Recht auf Kenntnis der eigenen Abstammung*) is derived from the right to informational self-determination (*Recht auf informationelle Selbstbestimmung*) which is an aspect of this right. A 'personality right' is also regarded as the basis of the right to know one's origins in such jurisdictions as The Netherlands – 'implicit' in the Dutch Constitution in the *Valkenhorst II* case of the Dutch Cassation Court (*Hoge Raad*), 15 April 1994, 1994 *NCJM-Bulletin* no. 6, p. 652, and in Portugal, from which a 'a right to one's personal history' (*direito à historicidade pessoal*), protected under Art. 26 of the Portuguese Constitution, is derived.

6 O'Donovan 1988, *supra* note 1; Stewart 1992, *supra* note 1; Hodgson 1993, *supra* note 1; Van Bueren 1995, *supra* note 1; L. LeBlanc, *The Convention on the Rights of the Child: United Nations Lawmaking on Human Rights*, 1995; M. Freeman, 'The new birthright? Identity and the child of the reproductive revolution', 1996 *International Journal of Children's Rights*, pp. 273–297; J. Fortin, *Children's Rights and the Developing Law*, 2003; J. van Raak-Kuiper, *Koekoekskinderen en het recht op afstammingsinformatie*, (PhD thesis Tilburg University), 2007.

7 C. Forder, 'Het recht op afstammingsinformatie: "wilde speculations"', 1998 *Ars Aequi*, pp. 87–90.

8 D. Nelkin, 'Paternity Palaver in the Media; Selling Identity Tests', in M. Rothstein *et al.* (eds.),*Genetic ties and the family; the impact of paternity testing on parents and children*, 2005, p. 4.

9 This definition accordingly precludes further discussion on the contexts of donor insemination (or adoption). For reasons of brevity, the current discussion centres on paternity in different-sex families.

one 'fundament' next to the 'intention' to base legal parentage upon.[10] This contrasts with adoption and artificial insemination, situations wherein the establishment of legal paternity will as a rule only reflect the latter 'fundament'.[11] Paternity testing may confirm or shatter an identity; this applies to both a child and a legal father.[12] The fundamental right discourse, however, has only recently been acknowledged as extending to the informational interests of fathers as well, however, in particular biological fathers without parental status, whatever their motives may be.[13] This may be partly due to the fact that ascertaining biological ties to expose a mother's 'infidelity' may still be perceived by courts as an interest less worthy of legal protection than a child's personal identity-related concern.

Uncertain paternity has traditionally been considered a 'male problem'. In an alternate historical perspective on the establishment of paternity, nature in the pre-DNA age still forced 'informationally underprivileged' men to learn how to trust women not to deceive them about their paternity status.[14] Thus, a lack of clarity still existed about the true mechanism of fathering in some scientific circles until the 19th century.[15] This contrasts sharply with the contemporary ubiquitous availability of scientifically accurate DNA paternity tests,[16] notably via the internet, which does not fail to spark renewed legal debates on both the respective weight that should be attached to 'fundaments' of legal paternity, as well as the significance of 'knowing' in itself.

Notwithstanding greater scope for scientific certainty, across the world's various parentage law systems, legal presumptions of paternity remain *de rigueur*.[17]

---

10 M. Vonk, *Children and their parents; a comparative study of the legal position of children with regard to their intentional and biological parents in English and Dutch law*, 2007, p. 267.

11 It may be tentatively suggested that legislation oriented solely towards the realisation of the informational interest without loss of status may accordingly also be easier to realise in these specific contexts.

12 D. Scott-Jones,'Paternity testing, family relationships, and child well-being', in M. Rothstein *et al.* (eds.), *Genetic ties and the family; the impact of paternity testing on parents and children*, 2005, p. 50.

13 I. Schwenzer, 'Tensions between legal biological and social parentage', in I. Schwenzer (ed.), *Tensions between legal, biological and social parentage*, 2007, p. 7. Key publications regarding the reinforcement of the legal position of the biological father: P.Lødrup, 'Challenges to an established paternity: radical changes in Norwegian law', 2003 *International Society of Family Law*, pp. 354–361; A. Roth, 'Vaterschaftsanfechtung durch den biologischen Vater', 2003 *NJW*, pp. 3151–3160; N. Dethloff, 'Redefining the position of fathers in German family law', 2005 *International Survey of Family Law*, pp. 253–266; A. Nuytinck, 'Vernietiging door verwekker van erkenning door niet-verwekker Hoge Raad 24-11-2004, *JOL* 2004, *RvdW* 2004, 125', 2005 *Ars Aequi*, pp. 733–738.

14 W. Marsiglio, 'Artificial reproduction and paternity testing', in M. van Dongen *et al.* (eds.), *Changing Fatherhood: an interdisciplinary perspective*, 1995, p. 171.

15 K. Albrecht & D. Schultheiss, 'Proof of paternity: historical reflection', 2004 *Andrologia*, p. 33.

16 M. Anderlik 'Assessing the quality of DNA-based parentage testing: Findings from a survey of laboratories', 2003 *Jurimetrics Journal*, pp. 291–314. A probability of 99,9 % is attainable on the basis of an examination of the DNA of the putative father and the child.

17 Schwenzer 2007, *supra* note 13, p. 7.

Best known is the so-called marital presumption rule, which holds that the mother's husband is the legal father of the child.[18] Outside marriage, the establishment of paternity in most civil law traditions requires a voluntary acknowledgement. Since a prior (scientific) establishment of the biological truth is not a prerequisite, parentage law systems accordingly offer leeway for the creation of father-child relationships primarily based on a social reality and/or the man's 'intention' to be the child's parent. Most parentage law systems also foresee in procedures for both child and parents to deny an established paternity that is not in accordance with biological truth, albeit often subject to procedural time-constraints for reasons of legal certainty. If paternity has been denied effectively in court, this will result in the revocation of the legal relationship between the socio-legal father and the child.[19] An (unmarried) biological father, who is not a sperm donor may, in principle, in most systems also be forced to assume paternity by the child and/or the mother.[20] Such a judicial determination of paternity may also present itself as an alternative after the presumptive father's death if paternity could somehow not be established during his life, for example, because another man's paternity had to be denied first. In that respect, the scientific significance of reliable DNA-based paternity testing after the putative father's death can scarcely be overstated.

This contribution is intended, above all, as an attempt to identify – or 'uproot'– recurrent legal issues regarding the material scope of the right to know. On the basis of a concise, historical overview of the relevant case-law of the European Court of Human Rights (ECtHR), it is submitted that although this process has been far from linear, there has been a progressive recognition of the right under the case-law of the European Court of Human Rights in accordance with Articles 8 and 14 of the Convention, but some contradictions and ambiguities remain. Attention will also be briefly drawn to salient features of the legal discourse in Germany, the European jurisdiction in which the issue's fundamental rights implications, have without doubt most intensively been discussed at least in legal scholarship and, more debatably, also at the governmental level. In particular, the current scholarly debate in Germany which has recently resulted in the enactment of a legislative proposal[21] foreseeing in the creation of an 'exclusively informational' procedure for the legal father to ascertain his biological fatherhood, without this necessarily resulting in the revocation of his legal child-parent rela-

---

18 Commonly accepted to derive from the adage found in Roman law, *pater is est quem nuptiae demonstrant*, Paulus, *Digest* 2, 4, 5.

19 Therefore the German law proposal foreseeing in a 'solely informational' procedure warrants attention from a comparative law perspective. See below.

20 Schwenzer 2007, *supra* note 13, p. 7.

21 *BT-Drucksachen* 16/651, 16/6449 and 16/5370. Passed in the Bundestag on 20 February 2008, entering into force on 1 April 2008. Text available in PDF: http://www.bmj.de/files/3060/Gesetz%20zur%20Klärung%20der%20Vaterschaft%20unabhängig%20vom%20Anfechtungsverfahren.pdf.

tionship, will be of interest for comparatists. Finally, some evaluative, concluding remarks shall be made on the legal discourse as it now stands. First, however, it seems appropriate to highlight some of the most compelling questions affecting the right to know as a legal concept.

2. TOWARDS A DEFINITION OF THE LEGAL CONCEPT OF THE RIGHT TO KNOW ONE'S BIOLOGICAL ORIGINS: AN ON-GOING STORY

In the wealth of social science and legal literature that deals with access to information on genetic descent, it has remained a contentious issue whether (all) children should be able to know the truth irrespective of the circumstances of their birth.[22] Nonetheless, it seems safe to say that the justifications for providing such information have by now become widely accepted and understood. Two strands of thought have been important in this principled, moral recognition. Firstly, in the medical sense, in the prevention of hereditary diseases and incestuous relationships, and secondly, in the psychological sense, to enable a child to further develop her or his narrative identity.[23] In that latter sense, the moral basis underlying the fundamental right to know one's origins for all children has drawn especially on social science literature from the 1970s regarding the experiences of some adoptees, who, deprived of this information, may feel 'deracinated' or cut off from an essential part of themselves.[24] Still, the question at what age and how a child should 'ideally' be told has only been researched to a limited extent and

---

22 Disparities between socio-legal and biological parentage may vary from adoption, artificial insemination through an artificial donor, high and low technology surrogate motherhood, to socio-legally constructed forms of paternity. Social science studies concerning adoption: H. Sants, 'Geneaological bewilderment in children with substitute parents', 1964 *British Journal of Medical Psychology*, pp. 133–141; D. Schechter *et al.*, 'Emotional problems in the adoptee', 1964 *Archives of General Psychiatry*, p. 109. In the field of socio-legally constructed paternity: L. Van Kampen *et al.*, 'Onbekendheid met de biologische vader als een belemmerende factor in de identiteitsontwikkeling: een empirische exploratie', 1990 *Nederlands Tijdschrift voor de Psychologie*, pp. 283–288; on artificial insemination: R. Cook *et al.*, 'Disclosure of donor insemination: parental attitudes', 1995 *American Journal of Orthopsychiatry*, pp. 549–558; on drawing analogies between artificial insemination and adoption, in legal literature: E. Gibson, 'Artificial insemination by donor: information, communication and regulation', 1992 *Journal of Family Law University of Louisville School of Law*, pp. 1–43; Freeman 1996, *supra* note 6, p. 291; T. Helms, *Die Feststellung der biologischen Abstammung: eine rechtsvergleichende Untersuchung zum deutschen und französischen Recht*, (PhD thesis Freiburg), 1999, pp. 186–187.

23 O'Donovan 1988, *supra* note 1, pp. 29–30; Freeman 1996, *supra* note 6, p. 277.

24 J. Triseliotis, *In Search of Origins; the experiences of adopted people*, 1973; R. Hoksbergen & H. Walenkamp, *Adoptie uit de kinderschoenen*, 1983; Freeman 1996, *supra* note 6, p. 277; I. Cohen, 'Wagners Siegfried', 1998 *Psychologie*, pp. 29–31.

not in a manner which analyses the right's scope across the aforementioned different contexts.[25]

Notwithstanding the broad acceptance of the basic moral justifications, cumbersome issues concerning the material scope as a result of fundamental rights-level recognition remain. If the right is clearly not to be regarded an 'absolute right' on the basis of the UNCRC, it is nonetheless twenty years after ratification far from clear what enforcement 'as far as possible' could actually entail. To name but one example, the right to know is not exclusively guaranteed as a negative right that protects one's interests against active violations by State authorities, but also as a positive right offering protection against a passive omission of the State by preserving and opening access to birth data.[26]

There are further problems concerning the right's conceptual definition and moral basis. Thus, as a derivative of an individual's private life or 'personality right', the right to know has been understood as a (moral) claim to informational self-determination.[27] In that connection, it remains circumspect whether the right to know – as a right involving 'free' moral choice – could also encompass a right *not* to know.[28] As a possible conceptual gain of such an encompassing interpretation, the present author suggests that the legal discourse could in future move beyond utility-orientated assessments of the social and biological fundaments underlying the establishment of legal parentage. As such, in an autonomy-based view on the right to know, it may be preferable if legislatures looked beyond the traditional 'social' and 'biological' dichotomy as appropriate fundaments for establishing legal parentage, and instead departed from the idea that the informational interest represents a constitutional legal value for the person concerned having regard to the child's (progressive) autonomy. At the same time, it must be

25 H. Colpin, 'Opvoeding na kunstmatige voortplanting: de literatuur over kansen en risico's', 1992 *Gezin: tijdschrift voor primaire leefvormen*, p. 71, who suggests that if a child knows little about his biological father and is informed at a relatively late age, the more likely it will be that the child develops identity-related problems. F. Hajal & E. Rosenberg, 'The family cycle in adoptive families', 1991 *American Journal of Orthopsychiatry*, p. 78. These authors suggest that informing children about their origins should not be a single event, but involves an ongoing dialogue and changing requirements as the child develops.

26 S. Besson, 'Enforcing the child's right to know her origins contrasting approaches under the Convention on the Rights of the Child', 2007 *International Journal of Law, Policy and the Family*, p. 144.

27 Federal Constitutional Court (*Bundesverfassungsgericht, BVerfGE*) on 31 January: BVerfGE 79, 256 = *FamRZ* 1989, 255. Note, however, that the term 'informational self-determination' may also be inept in view of the 'fixed' character of the information, which links one generation to the next.

28 In defence of a personal autonomy-based, right not to know: G. Pennings, 'The right to privacy and access to information about one's genetic origins', 2001 *Medicine and Law*, pp. 1–16; C. Bohnert, 'Zur Zulässigkeit privater Vaterschaftstests', 2002 *Familie, Partnerschaft und Recht*), pp. 383–391; M. Wellenhofer, 'Die prozessuale Verwertbarkeit privater Abstammungsgutachten', 2005 *FamRZ*, pp. 665–668.; R. Zuck, 'Der heimliche Vaterschaftstest; Was kann der Gesetzgeber tun?', 2005 *Zeitschrift für Rechtspolitik*, pp.117–119.

conceded, that notions of '(progressive) autonomy' and 'informational self-determination' may become empty constitutional shells as long as the concerned individual remains ignorant of the underlying disparity. This prompts the question of enforceability as to who should be held accountable for 'telling'.

In connection to that question, it has been suggested that 'parents', whether socio-legal parents or biological, hold 'procreational responsibility' to tell children about their parentage. This concept has also been found useful in explaining why intentional and biological parents may be held responsible as parents for the child during her or his life.[29] According to Vonk, procreational responsibility before conception means, from the point of the child's right to know, ensuring that this information is available.[30] Still, it must readily be acknowledged that problematic situations remain in which the 'responsibility' argument may be difficult to sustain from an ethical – let alone, legal or procedural – perspective; suffice it to think of children born from legally incapable biological parents such as teenage pregnancies, children born out of incestuous relationships or rape, or from a gamete swap in a fertility clinic.[31]

Nonetheless, in the present author's view, procreational responsibility of parents may in most situations be regarded as a (meta-juridical, moral) justification for vesting primary legal responsibility on the (socio-legal) parents to tell.[32] From the viewpoint of legal enforcement, speaking in terms of responsibility may, however, have limited value. As such, in adoption, the public authorities already play an important role in the registration and disclosure of birth data. Moreover, in adoption by same-sex parents and of children ethnically different from the adoptive parents, the underlying disparity cannot be cloaked. Freeman refers to a child's 'right not to be deceived about one's true origins' with a corresponding duty incumbent upon socio-legal parents.[33] However, if it really were up to the

---

29 Vonk 2007, *supra* note 10, pp. 252–253.

30 *Ibid.*, p. 252.

31 C. Forder, *Legal establishment of the child – parent relationship constitutional principles in Dutch, English and German law having regard to the European Convention on the Protection of Human Rights and Fundamental Freedoms and other applicable international instruments*, (PhD thesis Maastricht), 1995, p. 132. Nonetheless, the Dutch Cassation Court (*Hoge Raad*), in the *Valkenhorst I* case, argued that the child's right prevailed on the basis of such a 'responsibility' argument, coupled with the child's 'vital interest in knowing', although the child had been born in wedlock and subsequently taken into care by a charitable religious foundation at a time when considerable stigma was still attached to non-marital births. Hoge Raad 15 April 1994, *NJ* 1994, 608. In the *Valkenhorst II* case, the mother also claimed that she did not wish to provide the information because she had been raped by the biological father. Hoge Raad 13 January 1997, *NJ* 1997, 451.

32 S. van de Goor, *Recht op afstammingsvoorlichting, moderne voortplantingstechnieken en het belang van het kind*, Nederlandse Gezinsraad Instituut voor Primaire Levensvormen 1988; E. Siberry Chestney, 'The right to know one's genetic origin: can, should or must a state that extends its right to adoptees extend an analogous right to children conceived with donor gametes?', 2001*Texas Law Review*, pp. 364–391.

33 Freeman 1996, *supra* note 6, pp. 290–291.

socio-legal parents to tell, the enforcement of the right may sometimes become illusory. Thus, there is some social scientific evidence which suggests that in artificial insemination the majority of (different-sex) socio-legal parents are not inclined to tell the 'truth'.[34] Since in socio-legally constructed paternity the underlying disparity may very well not be so apparent either, some parents may also wish to 'pass themselves off' as being the biological parents.

Furthermore, although the right to know involves a 'fixed' aspect of narrative identity,[35] on closer examination, references to '*the* objective biological truth' may also be seen as inept. This ineptness can be appreciated from the – apparent but nonetheless often overlooked – basic fact that the individualised narrative concerning the circumstances of conception necessarily precedes us. As such, an objective biological truth is unfathomable. Enabling children to accede to a birth certificate, a biological parent's name or the result of a DNA test may fall short of enforcing their right to know their 'origins'.[36] Paradoxically, then, our primary truth concerning our 'fixed' identity will remain 'unknowable', even for those of us who 'know'. The deeper question may therefore be what 'knowing' could actually involve: perhaps in discussing the rights' conceptual scope, a further definition is required because, admittedly, rather facetiously, 'to know or not to know' is not the question, as there are different types of information on genetic descent and degrees of familiarity.

In that respect, in determining the breadth of information, a distinction between the right to know in the strict, legal and a broader, ethical sense may have conceptual value. A rigorous division into ethical and legal discourses on the right's material scope may, however, be untenable, suffice, in that regard, to consider that the conceptual dividing line between the 'right to know' and the 'right to contact' with the biological parent may be narrow. Anyone searching for meaningful 'answers' regarding his or her personal identity will not be interested in disclosure of birth data alone, but also in meeting their biological parent (at least) once.[37] The release of closed birth records for adoptees and paternity testing may be understood as a means of enforcing the right to know in a strict, legal sense. A broader interpretation of the material scope is quite conceivable, though. From a more decidedly ethical perspective, the right to know *lato sensu* might be conceived of as a moral entitlement not to be left to one's own imagination as far as

34 M. Trommelen *et al.*, 'Bereidheid tot donatie van sperma bij opheffing van de anonimiteitswaarborg', SWOKA Instituut voor strategisch consumentenonderzoek 1999, pp. 30–31.

35 S. Wilson, 'Identity, geneaology and the social family; The case of donor insemination', 1997 *International Journal of Law, Policy and the Family*, pp. 270–297.

36 M. Dovy, *L'enfant et le droit de savoir: l'accès à ses origines familiales*, (PhD thesis Lyon), 2002, p. 397.

37 Helms 1999, *supra* note 22, p. 180. According to Besson 2007, *supra* note 26, p. 145, the right to know one's parents does *not* encompass a right to meet them (or to be with them), thereby denying such an extensive interpretation of the right to know and the right to contact.

the *story* surrounding the circumstances at conception and birth. In shifting attention to questions of procedural enforceability, then, it would appear that a realisation of the right to know in the broad, ethical sense must inevitably be preceded by an enforcement of the right to know *stricto sensu*. As a corollary, it is ventured, a discussion on the negative and positive obligations as regards the disclosure of birth data and scientific parentage testing, may do sufficient justice to the theme in a discourse centred on *legal* enforceability. In that respect, it should also be added that enforcement *stricto sensu* need not necessarily signify a less profound appraisal of the information that the persons may be looking for; thus, the evidence of a parentage test and access to the information on a birth record might be conceived of as something more 'personal' than an individualised story of the circumstances surrounding a person's conception, which, as cynics might add in an attempt to trivialise the objective value – if there is one – of the 'biological truth', involves a story so universal that it may be better learnt in biology class than in philosophy class or in court.

For adoptees, the right to know *stricto sensu* has now been ensured for considerable time in many jurisdictions by opening up access to birth records.[38] Following a Swedish example in 1985, laws allowing the disclosure of the identity of the anonymous sperm donor may also be found in a number of other jurisdictions.[39] In distinguishing between medical, non-identifying and identifying data concerning the donor, the Dutch donor information (donor insemination) act offers an interesting example of a legislative attempt at categorisation of information concerning biological parentage. Thus, this law suggests that enforcement in the child's interests may require a gradual process of disclosure, rather than revealing 'the whole story' at once. Whereas medical data may be claimed at any time from the public foundation that registers the data, non-identifying data, regarding the donor's physical description and professional and social background, may be claimed later.[40] At the age of sixteen, identifying data such as name and physical

---

38 Van Bueren 1995, *supra* note 1, p. 46. As this author suggests, this may fall short of enforcing the child's right to know (in a strict sense), notably as a corollary of the problem of 'false' birth certificates.

39 In The Netherlands, the 2002 Artificial Insemination (donor insemination) Act (*Wet Donorgegevens kunstmatige inseminatie*) identification of the donor's name and address is permitted when the child reaches the age of sixteen and in the United Kingdom at the age of eighteen following an amendment in 2005 of the Human Fertilisation and Embryology Act (HFEA) 1990. In Austria, Finland, Norway, Switzerland, and the Australian states of Western Australia and Victoria donor anonymity has also been waived, E. Bernat, 'Between rationality and metaphysics: the legal regulation of assisted reproduction in Germany, Austria and Switzerland: a comparative analysis', 1993 *Medicine and Law*, pp. 493–505; A. Lalos *et al.*, 'Legislated right for donor-insemination children to know their genetic origin: a study of parental thinking', 2007 *Human Reproduction*, pp. 1759–1768.

40 Art. 3(1) under (a) and (b) Dutch Artificial Insemination (donor insemination) Act.

address may be claimed.[41] Disclosure will in principle only be refused by the foundation if the donor's interests prevail.[42]

3. DEVELOPMENT OF THE RIGHT TO KNOW ONE'S ORIGINS UNDER ARTICLE 8 PRIVATE LIFE AND FAMILY LIFE OF THE EUROPEAN CONVENTION OF HUMAN RIGHTS

3.1. PHASE I. TOWARDS THE RECOGNITION OF THE RIGHT TO KNOW ONE'S ORIGINS

In tracing the emergence of a 'right to know' under Article 8 of the Convention, roughly three phases may be distinguished. It is defensible to take the decision *Gaskin* v. *United Kingdom*[43] as a starting point, as it was interpreted as bearing relevance for the issue throughout Europe.[44] This is not without irony, as the applicant in the *Gaskin* case, seeking the obtainment of information concerning his early childhood in childcare institutions from the Liverpool City Council to help him reconstitute his 'basic identity' and overcome psychological problems, knew who both of his biological parents were.

A few years after *Gaskin*, the Court decided in the paternity case of *M.B.* v. *United Kingdom*.[45] In this case, the presumptive biological father erroneously presumed that the mother would separate from her husband, the legal father, and come to live with him. Following the end of the extra-marital affair and the child's birth, the mother refused, however, to enter into a parental responsibility agreement with the applicant. The High Court decided that no order for tests determining paternity should be made, on the grounds that the applicant had never even seen the child and in view of the breakdown of the extra-marital relationship. Primarily, the High Court considered it unfair to expose a child to the risk of loss of the presumption of legitimacy. The High Court was therefore reticent to order a test 'at the behest of a stranger to the marriage' to satisfy that 'stranger's own desire to know the truth'. The man argued that the English courts had infringed his rights under Article 8 ECHR by denying him the truth about an aspect of his personal identity, which, incidentally, would mirror the child's interests in 'knowledge that would enable her to avoid marrying within the prohibited degrees of relationship and relevant to her health'. In that respect, the presumptive biological

41 Art. 3(3) Dutch Artificial Insemination (donor insemination) Act.
42 Art. 3(4) Dutch Artificial Insemination (donor insemination) Act.
43 ECtHR, *Gaskin* v. *United Kingdom*, Appl. no. 10454/83, 7 July 1989.
44 Forder 1998, *supra* note 7, p. 87.
45 ECtHR, *M.B.* v. *United Kingdom*, Appl. no. 22920/93, 6 April 1994.

father contended that Article 14 ECHR had been infringed, since the husband could assume parental responsibility by virtue of his marriage, whereas for him this had become impossible. In Strasbourg, the Commission concluded, however, that requirements of legal certainty and security of family relationships allowed States to apply a general presumption of paternity according to which a married man is regarded as the father of his wife's children and to require good cause before allowing the presumption to be disturbed. This case may accordingly be regarded as an early, unsuccessful attempt by a biological father to 'extrapolate' a child's right to know her or his origins in the pursuance of his *own* – but not necessarily, 'selfish' – interests in the establishment of paternity.

Only shortly after *M.B.* v *UK*, the Court was confronted with another case concerning the rights of a biological father. In *Kroon and Others* v. *The Netherlands*,[46] the case revolved around the impossibility under Dutch parentage law prior to the 1998 reform to challenge the paternity of the mother's (Moroccan) husband, whose whereabouts had been unknown for a prolonged period. Although the mother did not cohabit with the biological father, they had maintained a stable relationship from which a child, Samir, was born. Under Dutch parentage law as it then stood, the possibility for the mother of a 'legitimate' child to deny the paternity of her husband was only open, however, in respect of a child born within 306 days of dissolution of the marriage.

The applicants complained that under Articles 8 and 14 ECHR it was not possible for the mother to have entered in the Dutch register of births any statement that the missing husband was not Samir's father. This situation, accordingly, effectively prevented the biological father from establishing legal familial ties with Samir. The ECtHR addressed this situation under reference to a triple formula, holding that 'respect for family life' requires that 'biological and social reality prevail over a legal presumption (1) which, flies in the face of both established fact (2) and the wishes of those concerned without actually benefiting anyone (3)'.[47]

Debatably, then, this situation contrasted critically with *M.B.* v. *UK*, where the biological father in that case could neither substantiate the existence of a 'social reality' nor did his wish reflect a consensual wish of all parties concerned. In the *Keegan* case, which involved a biological father's opposition to an adoption order, the Court ruled that the rights of the biological father under Article 8 had been violated, however.[48] The Commission drew support from the fact that the period of in *Keegan* the couple had lived together for eleven months. As Forder has suggested, the relevant and important distinction between *M.B.* v. *UK* and *Keegan*

46 ECtHR, *Kroon and Others* v. *The Netherlands*, Appl. no. 18535/91, 27 October 1994.
47 ECtHR, *Kroon and Others* v. *The Netherlands*, Appl. no. 18535/91, 27 October 1994, para. 40.
48 ECtHR, *Keegan* v. *Ireland*, Appl. no. 16969/90, 26 May 1994, para. 44.

seems to have been that in the latter case the conception was planned, whereas in the former case it was not.[49]

Following *Kroon*, another paternity claim under Article 8, involving a rebuttal of the marital presumption rule, arose in *Ibrahim Yildirim* v. *Austria*.[50] The presumptive father in *Ibrahim Yildirim* v. *Austria*[51] contended that his impossibility to rebut the marital presumption under Austrian law was tantamount to a violation of the requirements of the *Kroon* formula. As in *Kroon*, the legal father had been missing for years on end. However, in this case it could not be held that this presumption did 'not benefit anyone', as the child had received child support. In that connection, the ECtHR affirmed that, once the period within which the applicant can deny paternity has come to an end, greater weight may be accorded to the interests of the child than to the legal father's interests in disproving paternity.

It was the decision in *Mikulić* v. *Croatia*,[52] however, which truly marked a transition in the Court's approach to the establishment of paternity in at least two significant ways. From the perspective of the realisation of the informational interest, it was significant that it was expressly recognised that the determination of parentage was an important issue in the development of individual identity. From the perspective that states are under an obligation to devise an equitable parentage law system, it was important in that certain procedural and temporal safeguards, setting significant restrictions to the discretion of the State in paternity proceedings, were now expressly built into the Court's line of argumentation. The ECtHR concluded that no fair balance had been struck in securing the right of the child to have her uncertainty as to her personal identity eliminated without unnecessary delay.

The applicant was a child born out of wedlock and was two months old when her mother filed a suit against the Zagreb Municipal Court so as to establish paternity of the putative father. Before the Croatian courts, the putative father had refused on no fewer than six occasions to undergo testing by invoking the *exceptio plurium concubentium*, thereby suggesting that the mother had sexual relations with a man other than him at the time of the applicant's conception. The applicant alleged that the paternity proceedings had not been concluded within a reasonable time. The ECtHR, reiterated that particular diligence is required in cases concerning civil status and capacity.[53] The ECtHR underlined that the applicant's right to have her paternity established (or denied) and to have her uncertainty as to the identity of her natural father eliminated, fell within the ambit of Article 6 (1) ECHR. As a consequence, Croatia was required to act with

49 C. Forder, 'Biologisch ouderschap: vaders met of zonder keurmerk', 1997 *NJB*, pp.19–21.

50 ECtHR, *Ibrahim Yildirim* v. *Austria*, Appl. no. 34308/96, 19 October 1999.

51 ECtHR, *Ibrahim Yildirim* v. *Austria*, Appl. no. 34308/96, 19 October 1999.

52 ECtHR, *Mikulić* v. *Croatia*, Appl. no. 53176/99, 7 February 2002.

53 ECtHR, *Bock* v. *Germany*, judgment of 29 March 1989, Ser. A no. 150, p. 23, para. 49.

particular diligence in ensuring the progress of the proceedings.[54] Furthermore, the ECtHR took note of the fact that the proceedings had been pending for over four years during which it had been impossible to adjourn a single hearing because of the applicant's conduct. The Croatian Government's submission that this delay was ascribable to the persistent refusal of the man to undergo testing, did not prevent the Court from concluding that Article 6(1) ECHR had been violated. In addressing the applicability of 'family life' under Article 8 ECHR, the Court reiterated that paternity proceedings also fall under that provision's scope. Clearly, the Court could not, however, base this on an applicant's wish to institute paternity proceedings aiming at the dissolution of existing family ties,[55] since the presumptive father was actually intent on eluding the establishment of his paternity by repeatedly refusing to undergo DNA tests.

Crucially from the perspective of the child's right to know, the Court stated that persons in the applicant's situation had a 'vital[56] interest, protected by the Convention, in receiving information necessary to uncover the truth about an important aspect of their personal identity.' Although these words echoed *Gaskin*, they were now applied in a rather different socio-legal context. Thus, the Court came to expressly acknowledge that disclosure of information concerning one's parentage has potentially strong formative implications for an individual's sense of identity.[57]

As a requirement of proportionality, the availability of an alternative means to enable an 'independent authority' to proceed speedily also echoed *Gaskin*, but applied in the distinct context of a judicial determination of paternity.[58] Notably, this requirement of efficiency left States a margin of appreciation to decide how paternity may be established. This measure of State discretion could also be inferred from the Court's statement to the effect that 'it must be borne in mind that the protection of third persons may preclude their being compelled to make themselves available for medical testing of any kind, including DNA testing.'[59] In that respect the Court took note of the variety of solutions that the States Parties to the Convention to address the legal problem of a presumptive father's refusal to comply with court orders to undergo testing.[60] The lack of (any) procedural measures under Croatian law to compel the presumptive father failed to meet proportionality requirements under both Article 6 and Article 8 of the Convention. Thus, it may be deduced from *Mikulić* that enforcement of the right to know (*stricto sensu*) does not require compulsory testing even though the legitimacy of

54 ECtHR, *Mikulić* v. *Croatia*, Appl. no. 53176/99, 7 February 2002, para. 44.
55 ECtHR, *Rasmussen* v. *Denmark*, Appl. no. 8777/79, 28 November 1984, para. 33.
56 ECtHR, *Mikulić* v. *Croatia*, Appl. no. 53176/99, 7 February 2002, para. 64.
57 ECtHR, *Gaskin* v. *United Kingdom*, Appl. no. 10454/83, 7 July 1989, para. 39.
58 ECtHR, *Mikulić* v. *Croatia*, Appl. no. 53176/99, 7 February 2002, para. 64.
59 ECtHR, *Mikulić* v. *Croatia*, Appl. no. 53176/99, 7 February 2002, para. 64.
60 ECtHR, *Mikulić* v. *Croatia*, Appl. no. 53176/99, 7 February 2002, para. 64.

such a legislative choice was also not expressly denied either. As a consequence, it can be stated that according to the Convention adverse inferences may also be drawn against a presumptive father persistently refusing to undergo testing to meet the proportionality and procedural efficiency requirements.

In *Haas* v. *The Netherlands,* the Court was faced with a claim under Article 8 involving the refusal of the courts to examine and recognise his claim to the estate of the deceased presumptive father over that of his nephew.[61] The applicant acknowledged that his interest in identifying his father, under the notion of *family life*, derived from his wish to claim inheritance rights. This frankness proved imprudent from a procedural point of view, since the Court refuted his claim under Article 8 because, in apparently regarding his claim foremost in terms of a less benign pecuniary motivated interest, it did not 'serve to resolve any doubts he may have on his personal identity', all the more so since he was 'convinced in his own mind' who his father was.[62]

3.2. PHASE II. RECOGNITION EXPRESSIS VERBIS OF THE RIGHT TO KNOW ONE'S ORIGINS AS AN ASPECT OF PRIVATE LIFE

In the case of *Odièvre* v. *France*,[63] the Court reacknowledged its *Mikulić* formula regarding the existence of a 'vital interest protected by the Convention in obtaining information necessary to discover the truth concerning important aspects of one's personal identity, such as the identity of one's parents'[64] under Article 8 ECHR. Nonetheless, the factual context between both cases contrasted sharply, the present claim being geared towards a disclosure of the identity of the birthmother of the applicant, who had been born under the French tradition of anonymous and secret birth (*accouchement sous X*). This tradition was defended by the French Government in the pursuance of perceived public interests as the prevention of infanticide and clandestine abortions. The applicant, Pascale Odièvre, born in 1965, had been adopted at the age of three. A full adoption order took effect in February 1969, in favour of Mr. and Mrs. Odièvre, whose surname replaced the applicant's surname, which was that figuring on the child's original birth certificate. The applicant maintained that her request for information about strictly personal aspects of her history and childhood fell within the ambit of Article 8 ECHR, not only as part of her 'private life', but also under the notion of 'family life' with her natural family, with whom she hoped to establish emotional ties.

61 ECtHR, *Haas* v. *The Netherlands*, Appl. no. 36983/97, 13 January 2004, para. 43.
62 ECtHR, *Haas* v. *The Netherlands*, Appl. no. 36983/97, 13 January 2004, para. 42.
63 ECtHR, *Odièvre* v. *France,* Appl. no. 42326/98, 13 February 2003.
64 ECtHR, *Mikulić* v. *Croatia*, Appl. no. 53176/99, 7 February 2002, paras. 54, 64.

It was not until the *Odièvre* case that the Court first came to acknowledge *expressis verbis* that 'people have a right to know their origins', that right being derived from a wide interpretation of the scope of the notion of private life'.[65] This is somewhat ironic since this effectively did not amount to more than a principled recognition of the right, as the Court concluded that France had not violated the applicant's right under Article 8 *private life*. Unlike in *Mikulić* it was unprecedented in the Court's case-law that the question of knowing one's genetic descent in *Odièvre* it could, however, not be said to have been subsumed into the legally more consequential issue of establishing legal parentage. However, in this sharply criticised case,[66] a slight majority of the judges decided in favour of 'a woman's interest in remaining anonymous in order to protect her health by giving birth in appropriate medical conditions.' In that respect, attention was drawn to the fact that the applicant was already a 38 year old adult and to the – further unspecified – interests of third parties, including those of the adoptive parents, who, incidentally, had lent their moral support to the applicant's claim. In assessing the breadth of the French Government's margin of appreciation, the Court had suggested that anonymous birth was not an isolated phenomenon in Europe, even though this argument can hardly be sustained by fact.[67] In striking a balance between the applicant's right and the countervailing interests, reference was also made to the new French law permitting mothers to waive their anonymity upon an application to a public organ charged *inter alia* with the centralisation of the identifying information regarding the mothers. As an argumentative non-starter, Judge Ress' added that 'persons who seek disclosure at any price, even against the express will of their natural mother, must ask themselves whether they would have been born had it not been for the right to give birth anonymously.'[68] As a result, and without acknowledging it, in Besson's view, the Court unduly gave the mother's right absolute priority thereby violating the child's right's 'inner core'.[69]

---

65 EctHR, *Odièvre* v. *France*, Appl. no. 42326/98, 13 February 2003, para. 44.

66 See, notably, T. Callus, 'Tempered Hope? A qualified right to know one's genetic origin', 2004 *Modern Law Review*, pp. 658–669; B. Mallet-Criout, 'Droit d'accès aux origines personnelles: l'embarras de la Cour europeénne des droits de l'homme', 2003 *Recueil Dalloz*, pp. 1240–1245; Besson 2007, *supra* note 26, p. 151.

67 ECtHR, *Odièvre* v. *France*, Appl. no. 42326/98, 13 February 2003, para. 19. In Europe, anonymous birth is only sanctioned under law in Italy, Luxembourg, the Czech Republic and Hungary, although it is condoned by the public authorities in Germany, Austria and Switzerland. For a comparative law approach to the phenomenon, see R. Frank, 'Rechtliche Aspekte der anonymen Kindesabgabe in Deutschland und Frankreich', 2001 *FamRZ*, pp. 1340–1349.

68 Concurring Opinion of Judge Ress joined by Judge Kūris, ECtHR, *Odièvre* v. *France*, Appl. no. 42326/98, 13 February 2003.

69 Besson 2007, *supra* note 26, p. 151.

3.3. PHASE III. THE JÄGGI AND THE PHINIKARIDOU CASES

In two decisions from 2006, *Ebrü*[70]and *Jäggi*,[71] the Court followed a more extensive interpretation, perhaps partly in response to the criticism on the *Odièvre* case.[72] Just like *Odièvre*, the *Jäggi* case involved a primarily informational identity-motivated claim rather than an interest in the establishment of legal parentage *per se*. The applicant, Andreas Jäggi, had been born in Geneva in July 1939. A person known as A.H. had been mentioned as the father by his mother before the civil status registrar. In old Swiss law, A.H. had been in a position to lawfully obstruct the paternity suits that had been lodged against him in January 1948 by claiming that other men might have also fathered the child. This procedural mechanism, known as the *exceptio plurium*, was preserved in Swiss law until 1976, which, incidentally, also happened to be the year that A.H. died. Following the initial 1948 proceedings Jäggi was placed in a foster family. Jäggi maintained that A.H. had had regular contact with him and that he received small sums of money from him during his childhood. Shortly after the death of his presumptive father, Jäggi provided a private laboratory with blood samples of himself and A.H. As the lease on the grave of A.H. drew to an end, Jäggi successfully filed for the acquisition and prolongation of the rights on the tombstone in 1997. The Court plainly referred to the applicant's 'right to know his genetic descent' linking it to an encompassing 'right to identity' also protected under Article 8 ECHR.[73] In performing its proportionality test between the various rights involved and favouring the applicant's right, the Court came to quite a different result, however, than in *Odièvre* by taking the applicant's adult age into account. Thus, the Court pointed out that the 'interest an individual may have in knowing her or his (genetic) descent does not decrease as one ages, *but rather on the contrary*'.[74]

Aware of the emotionally and culturally charged dimensions of *post mortem* determination of paternity, the Court juxtaposed the 'right to know' and the 'right to respect for the dead', but did not delve into the nature of that latter right, apart from observing that it has a 'temporary nature'.[75] The Court accordingly seemed to shy away from taking in any ethical position on the rights of dead persons, perhaps wisely so, by drawing attention rather to the fact that the lease on the tomb would expire by 2016, which would indicate that the respect for the dead

---

70 ECtHR, *Ebrü* v. *Turkey*, Appl. no. 60176/00, 30 May 2006. This case shall, for reasons of brevity, not be dealt with here, primarily because the legal issues differed little from the *Mikulić* case. In the *Ebrü* case, pursuant to Art. 6 and Art. 8 ofthe Convention, the Court concluded that the inability of the Turkish courts to settle the paternity issue in a timely manner had left the applicants in a prolonged state of uncertainty as to the child's individual identity.

71 ECtHR, *Jäggi* v. *Switzerland*, Appl. no. 58757/00, 13 July 2006.

72 Besson 2007, *supra* note 26, p. 151.

73 ECtHR, *Jäggi* v. *Switzerland*, Appl. no. 58757/00, 13 July 2006, para. 25.

74 ECtHR, *Jäggi* v. *Switzerland*, Appl. no. 58757/00, 13 July 2006, para. 40.

75 ECtHR, *Jäggi* v. *Switzerland*, Appl. no. 58757/00, 13 July 2006, para. 41.

lacked any lasting character.[76] Still, and curiously enough for a secular court, the Court followed the Swiss proceedings in attaching some weight to the fact that the relatives had not demonstrated any objections of a religious or philosophical kind. According to the dissenting opinion, the Court thereby unduly considered the fact that exhumation may very well also displease – indeed even appal – surviving close relatives, regardless of their moral convictions.[77]

The Court acknowledged that an exhumation could affect the living memory that close relatives may have of a deceased parent, if only because the procedure could strike them as something particularly morbid. As in *Odièvre,* the Court mentioned the possible interests of third parties, notably close relatives, in opposing a claim, but again, did not specify them further. As a *post mortem* paternity case, it was somewhat infelicitous following that rationale, to then go on and state that 'testing is not particularly intrusive'.[78] It remains circumspect whether the Court thereby also intended to claim that DNA paternity testing would be even less intrusive on a living putative father; this may be plausible, since this procedure doubtlessly involves a less contentious and emotionally charged situation than exhumation of a corpse. Even if this were so, it might sit uneasily with *Mikulić,* because the Court therein seemed to suggest that the use of physical compulsion in parentage testing, in view of the required infringement on the person's physical integrity, formed only one among many solutions for States to meet their obligations under Article 8.[79]

If the recognition of the applicant's claim in the *Jäggi* case is partially ascribable to the fact that it was of little consequence for the establishment of his legal parentage and appeared sufficiently 'ideologically motivated',[80] the Court's approach may for similar reasons have been more restrictive in some other recent paternity cases.[81] In *Phinikaridou* case, the Court established that 'a comparative examination of actions for judicial recognition of paternity reveals that there is no uniform approach in this field', while adding that a 'significant number of states do not set limitation periods for children' and recognising a 'tendency towards

76 ECtHR, *Jäggi* v. *Switzerland*, Appl. no. 58757/00, 13 July 2006, para. 41.

77 See the dissenting opinion of Judge Hedigan, to which Judge Gyulumyan also subscribed, ECtHR, *Jäggi* v. *Switzerland*, Appl. no. 58757/00, 13 July 2006.

78 ECtHR, *Jäggi* v. *Switzerland*, Appl. no. 58757/00, 13 July 2006, para. 41.

79 That states have been offered such relative leeway, may also be inferred from the case ECtHR, *Szarapó* v. *Poland*, Appl. no. 40835/98, 23 May 2002, para. 42. Thus, presumably, for states to comply with the requirements of *Mikulić* and *Szarapó*, adverse inferences could in a paternity case also be drawn against the putative father to the effect that his paternity could be established upon a (persistent) refusal to undergo testing. This solution is chosen in countries such as England, France, Italy and The Netherlands. See *inter alia* the various country reports in A. Spickhoff *et al.* (eds.), *Streit um die Abstammung: ein europäischer Vergleich*, 2007.

80 Compare, *mutatis mutandis*, ECtHR, *Haas* v. *The Netherlands*, Appl. no. 36983/97, 13 January 2004.

81 ECtHR, *Shofman* v. *Russia*, Appl. no. 74826/01, 24 November 2005; ECtHR, *Phinikaridou* v. *Cyprus*, Appl. no. 23890/02, 20 December 2007.

greater protection of the right of the child to have its paternal affiliation established'.[82] The Court also drew attention to the fact that 'it had not been shown how the general interest in protecting legal certainty of family relationships or the interest of the presumed father and his family outweighed the applicant's right to have at least one opportunity to seek judicial determination of paternity'.

It appears particularly significant that the Court drew a distinction '*between cases in which an applicant has no opportunity to obtain knowledge of the facts and, cases where an applicant knows with certainty or has grounds for assuming who his or her father is but for reasons unconnected with the law takes no steps to institute proceedings within the statutory time-limit*'.[83] Accordingly, the Court seemed to suggest that in a situation wherein an (adult) child remains passive while having more than an inkling of who his biological father could be, but fails to undertake procedural action, such an (adult) child should not be in a position to postpone paternity proceedings until he or she deems it fit. Perhaps this is because it would be akin to a calculating form of procedural inertia that the law need not condone. Conversely, the claim would be 'meritorious' if the expiry of a procedural time-limit to establish paternity were attributable to objective factors beyond her or his subjective control. Thus, a legal system may under circumstances have to interpret the time-limit it sets in the interests of legal certainty in a more flexible manner, because a child should be given a 'real' opportunity to ascertain paternity.[84] Furthermore, the *Phinikaridou* case is interesting in having recognised of what may be coined to be a form of 'procreational privacy' under certain circumstances as the claim becomes 'estopped' in the course of years.[85] The Court accordingly stated that 'a presumed father's interest in being protected from stale claims concerning facts that go back many years cannot be denied', in connection to the prevention of 'possible injustice if courts were required to make findings of fact that went back many years.'[86]

To this author, in distinguishing between degrees of (un)certainty as regards the identity of one's biological father with a view to the determination of the viability of the claim and the suggestion that it is legitimate to enquire into the legal nature of the applicant's motives in seeking the information, the Court may have

82 ECtHR, *Phinikaridou* v. *Cyprus*, Appl. no. 23890/02, 20 December 2007, para. 58.

83 ECtHR, *Phinikaridou* v. *Cyprus*, Appl. no. 23890/02, 20 December 2007, para. 63.

84 For the possibility of an effective claim to deny paternity by the legal father under Art. 8 in conjunction with Art. 6 of the ECHR, see also: ECtHR, *Mizzi* v. *Malta*, Appl. no. 26111/02, 12 January 2006, para. 134.

85 Contrast this with the mother's right to give birth anonymously in France considered reconcilable with the margin of appreciation accorded to the French state under Art. 8 of the Convention in *Odièvre* v. *France*, Appl. no. 42326/98, 13 February 2003.

86 ECtHR, *Phinikaridou* v. *Cyprus*, Appl. no. 23890/02, 20 December 2007, paras. 51 and 53. These interests were also acknowledged in: ECtHR, *Mizzi* v. *Malta*, Appl. no. 26111/02, 12 January 2006, para. 83, and ECtHR, *Shofman* v. *Russia*, Appl. no. 74826/01, para. 39.

taken an overtly restrictive view on the scope of the right to know. Moreover, it may also be impracticable for courts to determine whether the motives of the applicant relate primarily to the establishment of legal parentage and the consequences thereof, such as inheritance, or bearing an ideological dimension. The reasons for a child to choose not to cut legal ties with the socio-legal father may, after all, stem from a variety of legal and affective reasons. Especially in a situation wherein a biological father is not yet in sight following the expiry of the procedural time-limit for denying paternity, a child may, moreover, also find it appropriate to postpone the undertaking of judicial action. Furthermore, it may be considered unjust that the expiry of a procedural time-limit in establishing legal parentage necessarily results in a loss of the child's right to ascertain her or his biological fatherhood, whatever the degree of certainty as regards his identity the child may have, certainly if a court recognises that knowing may become more important as one matures.[87] In connection to that latter argument, as we shall see, the recent law proposal in Germany provides a singular example of a legislative attempt to bridge the gap between ideology and parentage law concerns.

4. RAMIFICATIONS OF THE SCHOLARLY AND LEGAL DEBATE OF THE RIGHT TO KNOW ONE'S ORIGINS IN GERMANY

4.1. THE SINGULAR HISTORICAL-LEGAL CONTEXT OF THE DEBATE ON THE SCOPE OF THE 'RIGHT TO KNOW' IN GERMANY

It goes beyond the scope of this article to give an overview of the constitutional development of the right to know in Germany. However, it is clear, from a comparative perspective that Germany has been a frontrunner in this development.[88] The right is based on the personality right doctrine[89] as well as §1618a, German Civil Code, incorporating a reciprocal duty of care for parents and children, which, at least theoretically, would involve a duty of the mother to inform the child on her or his genetic descent.[90]

---

87 ECtHR, *Jäggi* v. *Switzerland*, Appl. no. 58757/00, 13 July 2006, para. 40. See above.

88 BVerfGE 79, 256 = *FamRZ* 1989, 255. See also Spickhoff *et al.* 2007, *supra* note 79.

89 The personality right is inferred from Art. 2 I in conjunction with Art, 1 I Federal Constitution (*Grundgesetz, GG*). Also see above.

90 German Civil Code (*Bundesgesetzbuch, BGB*). On this duty, see in particular R. Frank & T. Helms, 'Der Anspruch des nichtehelichen Kindes gegen sine Mutter auf Nennung des leiblichen Vaters', 1997 *FamRZ*, pp. 1258–1263.

In Germany, persons may, except in case of medical necessity, in principle be obliged to comply with a court order to undergo parentage testing.[91] Controversially, this article stems from the national-socialist period, but this historical fact has not been considered to undermine its contemporary legitimacy, as it serves fundamental rights-related rather than eugenic or racist public policy concerns. Still, as Frank points out, 'on an international comparative level, it is a fascinating phenomenon that nearly all legal systems rank bodily integrity higher on a scale of values than biological truth, German law constitutes the exception.'[92]

Following the latest German parentage law reform in 1998, paternity is established in accordance with the marital presumption rule,[93] recognition[94] or a judicial determination of paternity.[95] Paternity may be denied by the man whose paternity has been established on the basis of marriage or recognition, by the mother, the child and since 2003 also the man who claims under oath that he had sexual intercourse with the mother during the conception period.[96]

This latter party, as the 'biological father', may deny an established paternity only if the child does not have a factual social-family relationship with his or her legal father,[97] and subject to the time-limit of two years from the day that he knows of circumstances speaking for his paternity.[98] As the socio-legal father will usually have such a factual relationship, it is presumed that this extension of the number of claimants in paternity proceedings may not be so significant.[99]

As a further feature of the German legal debate, from around the turn of the century, extra-judicial forms of testing entered the 'paternity market', provoking a much larger debate at the governmental and academic level than elsewhere in Europe.[100] An all-out ban on such forms of testing was first proposed, but so far this has not taken effect. German courts have, however, insisted on a requirement of preliminary indications of non-paternity to admit a paternity suit, thus aimed at thwarting 'frivolous' claims, as well as in the interests of legal certainty. This procedural requirement was re-acknowledged in two Federal Constitutional Court cases.

---

91 Pursuant to § 372a German Civil Procedural Code (*Zivilprozessordnung, ZPO*).

92 R. Frank, 'Compulsory physical examinations for establishing parentage', 1996 *International Journal of Law, Policy and the Family*, p. 210.

93 § 1592 I German Civil Code.

94 § 1592 II German Civil Code.

95 § 1592 II German Civil Code.

96 § 1600 (1) German Civil Code.

97 § 1600 (2) German Civil Code.

98 § 1600b German Civil Code.

99 Dethloff 2005, *supra* note 13, p. 258.

100 See in particular: C. Rittner & N.Rittner, 'Rechtsdogma und Rechtswirklichkeit am Beispiel so genannter heimlicher Vaterschaftstests', 2005 *NJW*, pp. 945–948; M. Wellenhofer, 'Die prozessuale Verwertbarkeit privater Abstammungsgutachten', 2005 *FamRZ*, pp. 665–668.

Finally, debate on the creation of an informational procedure for the verification of genetic descent has so far been confined largely to Germany. It is acknowledged that this must be accounted for, to some extent, as an response to the scholarly criticism on the insistence on preliminary indications of non-paternity, which are unique from a comparative law perspective.

4.2. THE NEW GERMAN LAW: IS AN 'EXCLUSIVELY INFORMATIONAL' PROCEDURE A LEGAL PANACEA?

In its 1989 landmark decision, the Federal Constitutional Court had called on the legislature to enquire as to how the child's right to know could best be effectuated. This appeal of the Federal Constitutional Court to the legislature descended into a debate on the desirability and legal feasibility of a so-called 'isolated' procedure,[101] in which solely the biological link would be established without a loss of status. In a case which followed in 1990, a child sought identification of his biological father.[102] The child maintained that he was not interested in breaking off the relationship and thus contact with his legal father, but that his interest derived from his wish to fill up narrative gaps in his personal history. His claim was found inadmissible as the relevant statutory time-limits for a status procedure had expired.[103]

In response a number of authors warmed to the idea of a 'solely informational' procedure.[104] Such a qualified procedure was already believed to exist in relation to adoptees, without this seemingly provoking any problems in the child's relationship to its socio-legal parents. Thus, the registration of data concerning the biological parents also served adopted children's informational needs without calling into question their status.[105] Rauscher dismissed this analogy, however, since the nature of adoption is *ab initio* fundamentally different.[106] Justifiably he pointed out that whereas adoption is geared 'openly' towards the creation of a legal relationship with parents other than the biological parents, a characterisa-

101 In German '*isolierte Abstammungsfeststellungsklage*'.

102 High Regional Court (*Oberlandesgericht, OLG*) Oldenburg, 17 July 1990, 1991 *FamRZ*, pp. 351–352.

103 In 1998, the High Regional Court of Hamm reached a similar conclusion in a case which involved a child's 'purely informational' interest. High Regional Court (*Oberlandesgericht, OLG*) Hamm, 7 August 1998, *FamRZ* 1998, p. 1365.

104 D. Mutschler, 'Emanzipation und Verantwortung – zur Neuordnung des Abstammungsrechts', 1994 *FamRZ*, p. 65; more skeptical: J. Gernhuber & D. Coester-Waltjen, *Familienrecht*, 2006, pp. 587–588.

105 D.Coester-Waltjen, 'Künstliche Fortpflanzung und Zivilrecht', 1992 *FamRZ*, p. 369.

106 T. Rauscher & J. von Staudinger, *J. von Staudingers Kommentar zum Bürgerlichen Gesetzbuch mit Einführungsgesetz und Nebengesetzen 4.Buch. Familienrecht*, 2004, § 1592, no. 4, pp. 227–228.

tion of a socio -legally constructed relationship based on a 'false' presumption of paternity as such would be untenable.[107]

Regarded by some as a threat to the time-worn principles of parentage law, the 'isolated' procedure also met with scepticism in the parliamentary debate on the children's law reform.[108] In particular, it was fathomed that, as a 'third parent', the biological parent's position would remain ambiguous with a view to the child's integration within her or his socio-legal family. In that connection, it was feared, too, that the socio-legal father's paternity, once bereft of its legal façade of biological truth, would be downgraded to a pitiable *Zahlvaterschaft*.[109]

Following a decision of the Federal Constitutional Court in 2007 the debate on an 'exclusively informational' procedure revived in earnest.[110] In the decision, the federal legislature was called upon to foresee in the creation of a legal procedure by the end of March 2008 for the enforcement of the father's constitutional right to know his progeny.[111] In October 2007, the Federal German Government submitted a legislative proposal regarding 'the ascertainment of paternity independent from proceedings involving a denial of paternity'.[112] Its Preamble affirms the aim of promoting 'dialogue within the family and society, to protect the family as a social institution and to prevent the intervention of courts as much as possible.'[113] The initial law proposal received sharp criticism for a number of reasons.[114] At a dogmatic level, the double-track character in itself was presumed to irretrievably provoke 'serious frictions' in parentage law.[115] In more concrete terms, the insistence on preliminary requirements of non-paternity in the status procedure would be difficult to reconcile with the ease of access to the biological

107 *Ibid.*

108 *BT-Drucksachen* 13/4899, p. 56.

109 *Zahlvaterschaft* = 'a fatherhood based on the handing out of money to the child'.

110 Federal Constitutional Court (*Bundesverfassungsgericht, BVerfGE*), 13 February 2007, 2007 *FamRZ*, p. 441.

111 Art. 2 1 in conjunction with Art. 1 1 Federal Constitution (*Grundgesetz, GG*). *Recht des rechtlichen Vaters auf Kenntnis seiner Nachkommenschaft (Nachwuchses).*

112 Entwurf eines Gesetzes zur Klärung der Vaterschaft unabhänging vom Anfechtungsverfahren, 4 October 2007, *BT-Drucksachen* 16/6561.

113 'Die hier vorgeschlagene Regelung (...) soll den Dialog in der Familie und der Gesellschaft fördern, die Familie in ihrem sozialen Besand schützen und die Einschaltung von Gerichten möglichts vermeiden', in: *BT-Drucksachen*. 16/6561, p. 10. The use of the word 'dialogue', interpreted in accordance with its Greek etymology, would suggest an ongoing process of communication and deliberation. As such, this choice of words was considered particularly inept in a humorous if merciless commentary on this law proposal written by D. Schwab, 'Abstammungserklärung leicht gemacht; Neuer Dialog in der Familie', 2008 *FamRZ*, p. 23.

114 R. Frank & T. Helms, 'Abhandlungen: Kritische Bemerkungen zum Regierungsentwurf eines "Gesetzes zur Klärung der Vaterschaft unabhängig vom Anfechtungsverfahren"', 2007 *FamRZ*, pp. 1277–1281; Schwab 2008, *supra* note 113, pp. 23–27.

115 Frank & Helms 2007, *supra* note 114, p. 1278 '(...) solche Zweigleisigkeit (...) zu gravierende Friktionen im Abstammungsrecht führen wird (...).'.

truth in the new procedure, causing frictions if the evidence used in the new procedure were admitted in a subsequent status procedure.[116]

In defiance of such criticisms, however, as of the 1st April 2008, §1598a (1), German Civil Code accords mother, father and child a temporally unrestrained right to have their biological parentage relationships[117] ascertained by a (private) laboratory that meets publicly sanctioned scientific standards. The mother and the legal father may now require the extraction of a genetic sample of the child before the court while the child may require such samples from both legal parents with a view to verification of the biological link accordingly. If any of these three family members refuses to co-operate, consent may be replaced by the family court.[118] However, the court may refrain from ordering a test if it considers that this may not be in the child's interests.[119] A rather extreme example is: a child in puberty suffers from an eating disorder and there is a risk that her or his health will worsen upon disclosure of the biological truth, possibly even entailing a risk of suicide. In such a case, the court should have to waive its competence to order the 'purely informational' test. Crucially, too, the legal regime to lodge status proceedings remains largely the same.

Accordingly, once the biological link has been disproved in the new procedure,[120] a subsequent denial of (legal) paternity within the previously already applicable procedural time-limits of two years for the legal parents will remain open. However, if the new procedure is first pursued, or if the person has been threatened not to deny paternity, the beginning of the statutory time-limit is deferred to that moment. A legal father or mother may therefore not 'calculatingly' await an opportune moment to deny paternity when they already know that the man is not the child's biological father. For the child, the period within which paternity has to be denied will not begin until six months after becoming a legally capable adult.[121]

The current law is its omission to reinforce the biological father's right to know. This was considered justifiable since he can now already demonstrate a willingness to assume parental responsibilities in the absence of a 'socio-familiar relationship' between the child and his legal father.[122] As Helms and Frank suggested, this omission fails to pay tribute to the rationale for creating a separate procedure geared towards a principled recognition of the need to clarify genetic

116 *Ibid.*

117 Ascertaining biological motherhood is therefore also possible but is likely to be more rare.

118 § 1598a III German Civil Code.

119 § 1598a III German Civil Code.

120 According to the law proposal the biological link is not disproved in 80% of the reported cases.

121 § 1600b V German Civil Code in conjunction with § 210 German Civil Code.

122 *BT-Drucksachen* 16/6561, pp. 12 and 19.

descent regardless of concerns associated with legal parentage.[123] Both authors acknowledge, however, that if the number of claimants of a constitutional right to know their origins were extended further, it could lead to even more claims.[124] Connected to such arguments is a weakness of the law which stems from the fact that the child will still not be able to first avail himself of the new procedure with regard to a presumptive biological father before contemplating status proceedings, as the child's right only applies with respect to his legal father and mother. Moreover, conceptual boundaries remain elusive: who can claim a 'right to know'? A half-sister and half-brother and a grandparent and grandchild might also have quite legitimate reasons to find out an important part of their biological legacy.[125]

Whereas a child may prefer to retain a legal relationship with the socio-legal father after his biological link has been disproved, it may be more circumspect whether legal fathers will content themselves with the negative results in the new procedure on the assumption that most legal fathers will not wish to uphold parental status in the absence of a biological link.[126] As private laboratories may conduct testing, the legal father may moreover be prevented from claiming expenses from the state in the new procedure; in order to obtain a substantiated 'initial suspicion' to deny his legal paternity the legal father may therefore first have to 'reach into his own pocket'.[127] A distinction between 'rich' and 'poor' fathers in denying paternity could accordingly not only become imminent, but the court may still see fit to order a new, judicial test.

5. CONCLUDING REMARKS: THE LEGAL NARRATIVE OF THE RIGHT TO KNOW, A STORY TO BE CONTINUED

The 'right to know' has gained progressive recognition under Article 8 ECHR in the context of socio-legally constructed paternity. The ECtHR has, however, also recognised the presumptive father's (conditioned) right to what may be coined a time-related right to 'procreative' privacy as well as the rights of third parties such as those of relatives. It falls within the margin of appreciation of states to establish paternity in an efficient manner. The German doctrinal idea of an 'exclusively informational' procedure for establishing genetic descent appears alluring since, at least in the abstract, in its realisation of the right to know *stricto sensu*, it could

123 Frank & Helms 2007, *supra* note 114, p. 1279.
124 Frank & Helms 2007, *supra* note 114, p. 1279; also Schwab 2008, *supra* note 113, p. 23.
125 Frank & Helms 2007, *supra* note 114, p. 1279.
126 *Ibid.*
127 *Ibid.*, p. 1280.

leave the fundaments of intention and social reality immanent in parentage law, intact. The new German law shows, however, that there are disadvantages that are not easily ignored. Nonetheless, as long as the informed consent may be obtained from all the persons involved, including that of a (sufficiently adult) child and that of the mother, there would appear little reason to deny that the informational interest could also be realised outside courts. For that reason alone, an all-out ban on extra-judicial tests seems disproportionate. Drawing a sharp distinction between extra-judicial tests as such and 'covert' forms of extra-judicial testing which dispense with consent requirements is therefore necessary. In situations in which parties have not agreed or could not agree on resorting to paternity testing, the legislature faces tougher choices. Leaving aside the possibility of DNA testing and registration of the child's biological father following birth, enforcement of the 'right to know' *stricto sensu* in the context of a 'false' socio-legally constructed paternity might be achieved either through the creation of an 'exclusively informational' procedure. If this latter course is chosen, this might very well mean that a legislator must also 'have the courage to point out to whoever seeks to ascertain relationships of biological parentage, that he must content himself with the realisation of his right to know his genetic descent and not seek advantages deriving from the establishment of legal parentage'.[128] This prompts further enquiries into the '*inner core*' of the right to know: could it not involve a right to trust rather than to identify who one's father if necessary with physical compulsion?[129] Thus, conceived as a right 'not to be deceived' about a vital part of our identity, for most it may sill be sufficient to believe rather than to know the 'truth'.

128 '(...) muss man auch den Mut aufbringen, denjenigen, der die Klärung der genetischen Abstammungsverhältnisse erzwingt, darauf zu verweisen, dass er sich mit der Befriedigung seines Rechts auf Kenntnis der eigenen Abstammung zufrieden geben muss und statusrechtlich hieraus keine Vorteile ziehen kann', in: Frank & Helms, 2007, *supra* note 114, p. 1281.

129 Compare § 372a German Civil Procedural Code (*Zivilprozessordnung, ZPO*), prescribing in such a duty to co-operate in parentage testing.

THE ROLE OF FORMALISED AND NON-FORMALISED INTENTIONS IN LEGAL PARENT-CHILD RELATIONSHIPS IN DUTCH LAW

Machteld Vonk*

1. INTRODUCTION

Families and family structures have changed since the last century. It is presumed that most children still grow up with their own genetic parents in a reasonably stable resident family.[1] However, a substantial number of children grow up in other kinds of families, be it unmarried families, stepfamilies, lone-parent families or same-sex families.[2] These developments are due to a number of factors including the advancement of assisted conception techniques such as IVF and the growing recognition of same-sex families. Whereas the assignment of parental status used

* Dr. Machteld Vonk is a University Lecturer and Researcher at the Molengraaff Institute for Private Law, Utrecht University (The Netherlands), email: M.Vonk@law.uu.nl.

1 There are no exact figures that prove this presumption is correct. However, considering the fact that most children grow up in a different-sex family and only about 10% of children live in a stepfamily, and given the fact that the majority of different-sex families do not make use of donor gametes (about 10% of different-sex couples have fertility problems, the majority of which will overcome these with the use of their own gametes in particular since the introduction of ICSE), moreover given estimates (J.R. Bellis *et al.*, 'Measuring paternal discrepancy and its public health consequences', 2005 *Journal of Epidemiology and Community Health*, pp. 749–754) that only about 3.7 percent of children are conceived during sex outside the relationship without the knowledge of the male partner, it may be relatively safe to conclude that the group of children that grows up with their biological parents is larger than the group of children that does not grow up with their two biological parents.

2 One in every ten families with children is at present a stepfamily (Stichting Stiefgezinnen Nederland). Furthermore, the number of children born outside marriage has increased from 3% of all live births in 1980 to 40% in 2007. (Eurostat 2004 and CBS 2008). There are no exact figures on the number of children growing up in same-sex families. However, in sociological publications reference is made to the lesbian baby boom following easier access to donor insemination as of the 1980s. 'In most Western industrialized societies the total number of lesbians who have given births to a child within a lesbian relationship amounts to several thousands.' (H. Bos, *Parenting in planned lesbian* families, 2004, p. 33). Some 9% of same-sex families have dependent children living with them (18% of the female same-sex couples and 1% of the male same-sex couples) CBS, *Bevolkingstrends* 2006 dl. 1, Heerlen/Voorburg, p. 6.

to be based largely on biology and relationship status, nowadays other factors such as intention and consent may play a role in assigning the status of legal parenthood. This article aims to explore the role that formalised and non-formalised intensions may play in the assignment of parental status to the parents[3] who are raising a child conceived by means of assisted conception in their family.

When couples make use of assisted conception, be it for instance IVF with their own genetic material, self-insemination with sperm donated by a friend or IVF surrogacy, the prospective parents need to undertake action (other than sexual intercourse) to realise their desire for a child. During the phase that precedes the actual conception of the child, they may have to find a hospital to carry out the procedure with their own genetic material or with the genetic material of a known or unknown donor, and the couple may in that case also have to find a donor or a surrogate mother. Before the conception of the child, all the parties involved (*i.e.* the prospective parents, the donors and the surrogate mother) have intentions with regard to the child.

The intentions of the parties may all be aimed at the integration of the child in the family of the prospective parents immediately after birth, or the intentions may differ. Parties may lay down their intentions in a contract, they may agree orally or simply assume that the other parties have the same intentions. The question that is posed in this article concerns the meaning of intentions, regardless of whether they are formalised, that exist prior to and lead up to the conception of the child, in the actual attribution of parental status to the parties involved. Do these intentions play a role and if so under what conditions and in which cases?

It is likely that in some cases intentions will be taken into account and in other probably not. Should they (always) be taken into account and what are the complicating factors? As in most jurisdictions,[4] a child under Dutch law can only have two legal parents. Where the law assigns two parents to a child by operation of law, it may be very difficult if not impossible to take the intentions of prospective parents into account, whereas in other cases the law may already have been adapted to base legal parent-child relationships on the intentions of the parties involved. In order to explore in which situations involving assisted conception the intentions of the parties may play a role and what the law does with these intentions, use will be made of the so-called Family Tree.[5] The Family Tree distin-

3 The term *parent* will be used as a generic term, which means that it includes all the adults who are either part of the child's resident family or have some kind of parental relationship with the child outside the *resident family*, this may be a genetic link, a gestational link or a social link based on parental responsibility. A child's *resident family* is the family in which the child spends the majority of her or his time A child may have more than one resident family if (s)he spends a substantial amount of her or his time in two different families.

4 I. Schwenzer (ed.), *Tensions between legal, biological and social conceptions of parentage*, 2007, p. 11.

5 The 'Family Tree' has been introduced in Chapter 2 of M. Vonk, *Children and their parents: A comparative study of the legal position of children with regard to their intentional and biological*

guishes between different familial categories on the basis of the genetic link between the child and the parents who are raising the child. It covers a wide spectrum of families, ranging from the traditional married family consisting of two persons both biologically related to the child, to the non-genetic family where neither of the parents is genetically related to the child(ren) raised within the family. With the help of the Family Tree the situations in which intentions play a role in the conception of the child will be inventoried.

2. AN INVENTORY OF INTENTIONS

2.1. THE FAMILY TREE

The Family Tree classifies families on the basis of whether a child is genetically related to the parent(s) in her or his resident family. Furthermore, the sex and the (legal) status of the relationship of the partners heading the family play a role in the sub-classification of these families, as will be explained below. Since the purpose of the Family Tree is to facilitate meaningful legal (comparative) research on the protection and recognition offered to children in their resident family, it is necessary to find criteria for the sub-classification of families that yield comparable units.[6] Given the fact that the existence of a genetic link has for a long time been one of the primary reasons for attributing parents with parental status, the existence or absence of such a link is a useful criterion for the main classification. The classification provides insight into the extent to which the law has come to accommodate families where, for one reason or another, there is no genetic link between one or both of the parents and the children they raise (the resident family).[7] However, the classification of families in the Family Tree not only allows for research into the protection and recognition of the child's resident family, but also takes account of the fact that a child may have a genetic link with one or more parents outside the resident family. Given the recent emphasis on the child's right to know its origins,[8] and European Court of Human Rights (ECtHR) case law on Article 8 ECHR, which may require a court to take the interests of genetic parents with family life into account,[9] this is indeed vital.

parents in English and Dutch law, 2007.

6 This article focuses on the situation in The Netherlands but comparative work on this topic is forthcoming.

7 Art. 7 of the Children's Convention requires the state to safeguard, as far as possible, the child's right to know and be cared for by its parents.

8 Donor data in cases of artificial insemination Act (*Wet donorgegevens kunstmatige bevruchting*), *Staatsblad* 2002, no. 240, and Art. 7, UN Convention on the Rights of the Child.

9 This may for instance include the right of a biological father with family life (ECtHR, *Keegan v. Ireland*, Appl. no. 16969/90, 26 May 1994) or a known donor with family life to be heard in the child's adoption proceedings.

Figure 1. The Family Tree

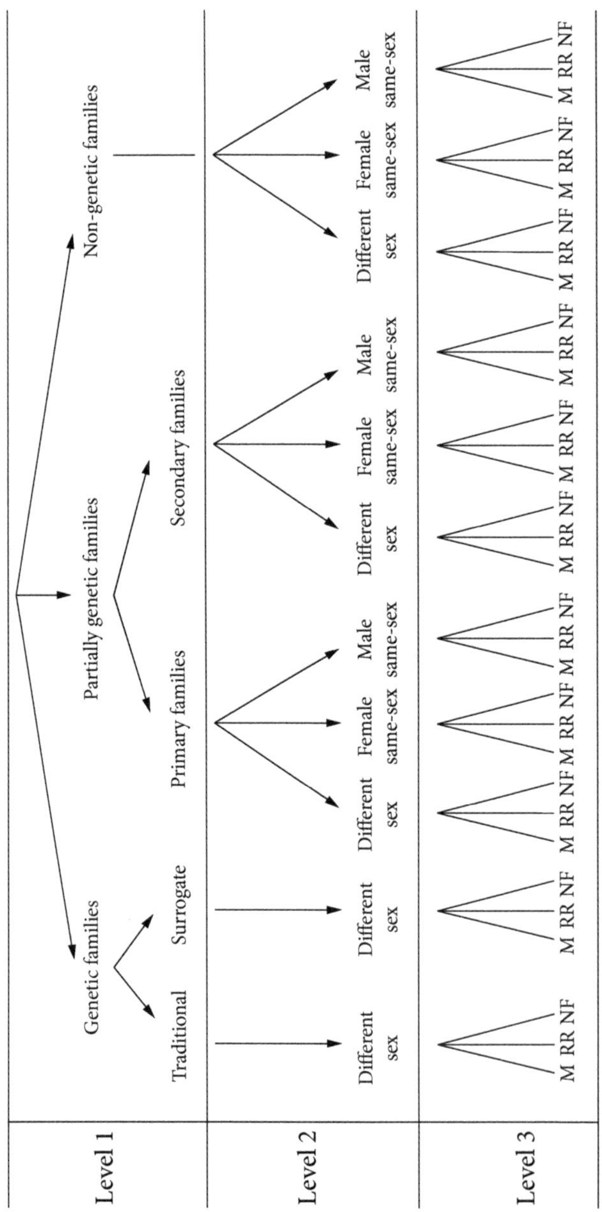

M = Marriage
RR = Non-marital registered relationship
NF = Non-formalised relationship

The Family Tree has three levels: main branches (level 1), sub-branches (level 2) and twigs (level 3).

(1) The classification of the main branches is based on the existence or absence of a genetic link between the child and the other family members: *genetic families*, where the child is genetically related to both parents in the resident family, *partially genetic families*, where the child is genetically related to one of the parents in the resident family, and *non-genetic families*, where the child is not genetically related to either of the parents in the resident family. Two of the main branches have a further classification on this level. The genetic families can either be classified as *traditional* genetic families, where the mother herself gives birth to her and her partner's genetic child, or as *surrogate* traditional families where the partners supply the genetic material for the child, but a third party, a surrogate mother, gestates and gives birth to the child. Moreover, the *partially genetic families* can either be classified on this level as partially genetic *primary* families, where the child is raised in the family it was originally born into, or as partially genetic *secondary* families, where the child is no longer raised in its primary family, but in a family that one of her or his parents has formed with a new partner. Partially genetic secondary families will not be discussed in this article.[110]

(2) On the second level, the partially genetic families and the non-genetic families in the family tree have the following sub-branches: different-sex families, female same-sex families and male same-sex families. Since a genetic family always consists of a different-sex couple and their children, the second level only concerns different-sex families.

(3) On the third level, the different family types are further classified on the basis of the legal status of the relationship of the parents (married, non-marital registered relationship or non-formalised relationship, which may range from long-term cohabitation to a one-night stand).

2.1.1. Family pictures

For the sake of clarity, the different family types – including the genetic or gestational parent who is not part of the child's resident family – will be depicted in the article with the help of the pictograms explained below. The *family pictures* consist of a number of icons (in incremental shades of grey to black) representing the parents and the children involved. The icons to the left form the child's resident family. The icon(s) to the right of the child represent the parent(s) outside the child's resident family. The different icons used for the mothers will be explained, then those used for the fathers and finally those used for the children.

10 For information on the legal relationship between parents and children in partially genetic secondary families see Vonk, *supra* note 5, pp. 93–130.

Mothers

A distinction has been made between four types of mothers:

- *Biological and genetic mother* = woman who supplies the ovum and gives birth to the child
- *Genetic mother* = woman who supplies the ovum, but does not give birth to the child
- *Gestational mother* = woman who gives birth to the child, but does not supply the ovum; and
- *Non-biological mother* = woman who raises the child but is neither genetically related nor has given birth to the child.

Where the term *birth mother* or *biological mother* is used, this includes both the *biological and genetic mother* and the *gestational mother.* Only where it is relevant for the understanding of the specific family situation, will a distinction be made between a biological and genetic mother, on the one hand, and a gestational mother, on the other.

Fathers

Fathers have been divided into biological fathers and non-biological fathers. There are only two types of fathers, because a father is either genetically related to a child or not; there is no other biological factor such as gestation that may need to be taken into account.

- *Biological father* = man who supplies the sperm
- *Non-biological father* = man who raises the child but is not genetically related

Children

For the children concerned two different icons are used, not on the basis of their genetic relationship to the parents in their resident family, but on the basis of the question whether the resident family is the child's primary or secondary family.

= the resident family is the child's primary family

or = the resident family is the child's secondary family

2.2. GENETIC FAMILIES

Genetic families consist of two parents who are both genetically related to the children they raise. This is more or less the standard family and in general it is presumed that the majority of families are genetic families. There are, however, two kinds of genetic families: the traditional genetic family and the surrogate genetic family. In the first kind of family the mother gives birth to her and her partner's own genetic child. In order to become pregnant they may have had to resort to assisted conception techniques such as artificial insemination (AI) or in-vitro fertilisation (IVF), but they have not made use of a third procreational party to conceive a child. This is the point at which the traditional and the surrogate genetic family differ; the surrogate family has come about with the help of a third procreational party, namely a surrogate mother. The surrogate mother is implanted with an embryo created with both the commissioning parents' gametes, which means that the child to whom the surrogate mother gives birth, is genetically related to both the commissioning parents (referred to in this article as full genetic or IVF surrogacy).

2.2.1. *Traditional genetic family*

Bio mother Bio father Child

The man and the woman are both genetically related to the child and the woman gives birth to the child herself. However, the child may have been conceived through IVF or artificial insemination with the male partner's sperm. The position of the mother is very straightforward under Dutch law; the woman who gives birth to the child is the child's legal mother. Depending on the relationship status of the parents, the father will either be the child's legal father by operation of law, may become the child's legal father with the mother's consent or may apply to the court to recognise the child if the mother refuses to give her consent.[111] The man who is married to the birth mother is the child's legal father by operation of law, because he is presumed to be the child's biological parent. This marital presumption of paternity has not been extended to different-sex registered partnerships or those involved in an informal cohabitating relationship. In these cases the biological father does not become a legal parent by operation of law, but he can recognise his partner's child if she consents. If the mother refuses to consent to the recognition, the man may ask the court to substitute the mother's consent, *provided that he is the child's genetic father and has begotten the child through sexual intercourse.*[112]

The way in which the child was conceived, through sexual intercourse or through assisted conception, is an important issue if the man concerned is not married to the mother. An unmarried man who resorts to assisted conception with his female partner with his own genetic material, for instance IVF with the

11 Arts. 1:199, 1:203 and 1:204 Civil Code (*Burgerlijk Wetboek, BW*).
12 Art. 1:204(3) Civil Code.

use of the genetic material of both the female and the male partner, is treated as a sperm donor. This means that he has no rights with regard to his child. He may, for instance, not apply to the court to recognise his child. However, it is very likely, given a recent judgement concerning sperm donation, that if such a man would apply to the court to replace consent to recognition, he would at the very least be heard by the court and, depending on the circumstances, might be given consent to recognise under the same conditions as any man who begets a child through sexual intercourse.[113]

If the unmarried father is unwilling to establish legal familial ties with the child, the child's mother or the child can ask the court to establish the father's paternity. This not only applies to child's genetic father, but also to the mother's male life partner who consented to an act that may have resulted in the conception of the child. Judicial establishment of paternity is a relatively new feature in Dutch family law which was introduced only as recently as 1998.[114] The biological father himself cannot apply to the court to have his fatherhood established.

In the context of this article, the most interesting situations are those where legal fatherhood does not come into being by operation of law. It may be assumed that where parents are married or have entered into a registered partnership that they both intended the conception of the child.[115] This may not always be the case, but it may be presumed that entering into a formalised relationship implies such an intention. Where parents are not married, it is more difficult to presume that both partners intended the conception of the child, in particular where the child is conceived during a very short or unstable relationship. However, with regard to the establishment of the legal fatherhood of a biological father in such a relationship, intention does not play a role. These men do not become legal fathers by operation of law, but they may, on the one hand, apply to have their legal fatherhood established through recognition and, on the other, their legal fatherhood may be established against their will. In short, it may be said that in the context of traditional genetic families intentions may play a role on the part of the parents before the conception of the child, but it is not a requirement for the establishment of the legal parenthood of the parents.

Contracts and the traditional genetic family

There are two issues that do not relate directly to the attribution of parental status, but may nevertheless be of interest in the context of traditional genetic

13 Hoge Raad 23 January 2003, *NJ* 2003/386 and possibly Hoge Raad 30 November 2007, LJN BB9094.

14 For an interesting discussion on attempts to introduce such an option almost a century earlier, see S. Sevenhuijsen, *De orde van het vaderschap: politieke debatten over ongehuwd moederschap, afstamming en huwelijk in Nederland, 1870–1900*, 1987.

15 Vonk, *supra* note 5, p. 253.

families, namely the embryo storage agreement[116] and post-mortal procreation. Where a couple undergo fertility treatment which involves the creation of embryo's outside the womb and more embryo's are created than can be used in one treatment cycle, the surplus embryos can be stored for later use. In the case of such storage, both partners will have to sign an embryo storage agreement, which among others includes clauses with regard to the storage and later use of the embryos. The embryos can only be used if both parties agree to such use. If one of the parties indicates that he or she no longer desires that the embryos be stored they will be allowed to perish. The fact that such requirements may have tragic consequences has become clear in the Evans case, a case that originated in England and was decided by the European Court of Human Rights in 2007.[117]

The second issue concerns post-mortal procreation. Where the male partner has consented to the use of his sperm or embryos fertilised with his sperm after his death, the legal fatherhood of the deceased father may be established after the birth of the child.[118] Article 7, Embryo Act (*Embryowet*) states that gametes can only be used after a person's death if he or she has explicitly consented in writing to such use.[119] The earlier mentioned embryo storage agreement contains a number of clauses that relate to post-mortal procreation. However, the validity of the consent given to post-mortal procreation and the consent to storage of embryos and consent to their use at a later date, is not found in the contract itself. The *Embryowet* requires the consent to be given in a certain form (namely in writing). Moreover, the Dutch Civil Code attaches consequences to the consent given: a life partner who consents to an act that may have resulted in the conception of the child may have his legal fatherhood established. The written consent embodied in the embryo storage contract is evidence of the fact that consent has indeed been given and the actions for which the consent has been given.

2.2.2. *Surrogate genetic family*

16 The Embryo Act (Model Regulation) (*Modelregelement Embryowet*) contains an example of such an agreement. This model is to be found on the website of the ministry of health, welfare and sport: www.minvws.nl/rapporten/ibe/modelreglement_embryowet.asp.

17 *Evans* v. *the United Kingdom* [2007] *ECtHR*, Appl. no. 6339/05, 7 March 2006 and 10 April 2007 (Grand Chamber).

18 Art. 1:207 Civil Code.

19 See also Art. 8 of the Model storage agreement (*Bewaarovereenkomst met betrekking tot embryo's*) included in the Embryo Act (Model Regulation) (*Modelregelement Embryowet*) mentioned in note 15.

The man and the woman are both genetically related to the child, but have made use of the services of a surrogate mother to carry and give birth to their child. It is very likely that it is the intention of all parties involved that the child carried by the surrogate mother will be integrated into the family of the commissioning parents. Parties may even have drawn up an agreement to this end.[220] Under Dutch law, the woman who gives birth to the child is the child's legal mother, whether or not she is also the child's genetic mother. This is a mandatory statutory provision from which parties cannot deviate.[221] Dutch law has no special procedure geared towards transferring parental rights and duties from the surrogate mother (and her husband) to the commissioning parents.[222] The commissioning couple will have to follow a number of complicated procedures, including an adoption procedure, of which the outcome is uncertain, in order to become the child's legal parents.[223]

2.3. PARTIALLY GENETIC PRIMARY FAMILIES

The sub-classification made for this family type is that the couple heading the family may be a couple of different sex, a female same-sex couple or a male same-sex couple. Despite the fact that in all these cases only one of the parents is a genetic parent, the legal consequences may differ considerably both for the child and its parents. Another important factor is that all these couples require the help of a third procreational party to have a child; this may either be a sperm donor, an egg donor or a surrogate mother. The legal status of this third procreational party may differ considerably and determines whether and how much manoeuvrability there is for the non-genetic parent to acquire (some) parental status with regard to the child.

---

20 One of the Dutch clinics that offers IVF-surrogacy services requires the couples involved to draw up a contract to this end. VUmc, *Hoogtechnologisch draagmoederschap*, http://www.vumc.nl/afdelingen/patientenfolders-brochures/zoeken-alfabet/D/hoog_technologisch_draagmoe1.pdf.

21 Rechtbank Den Haag 11 December 2007, LJN BB9844.

22 K. Boele-Woelki *et al.* (eds), *(On)geoorloofdheid van het draagmoederschap in rechtsvergelijkend perspectief*, 1999, pp. 25–44, and P. Vlaardingerbroek, 'Draagmoederschap: een gecompliceerde constructie', 2003 *Ars Aequi*, no. 3, pp. 171–178.

23 See Vonk, *supra* note 5, pp. 137–146.

2.3.1. *Sperm donation*

a. Different-sex and sperm donation

Bio mother | Non-bio father | Child | Bio father

Different-sex couples may consider using donated sperm to conceive a child, if the male partner is, for example, infertile or the carrier of a hereditary disease or condition. The woman may conceive through AI or IVF in a hospital, through self-insemination at home or through sexual intercourse with a third party (with or without her partner's consent or knowledge). In most of these scenarios it may be presumed that it is the intention of the couple that the child will be integrated into their family. This intention is recognised in Dutch law where the couple is married by granting the male partner the status of legal parent by operation of law, so long as he consented to the act that resulted in the conception of the child.[224] Where the couple is not married, the legal parenthood of the male partner may be established against his will where he consented to the conception of the child.[225] Consent is a broad concept; it need not have been provided in writing, it can have been given orally or simply by acting in a manner that implies consent. An interesting interpretation of 'consent to an act that may have resulted in the conception of the child' can be found in a case where the Dutch Supreme Court (*Hoge Raad*) stated that consent to an act that may have led to the conception of a child includes the situation where the birth mother's life partner consents to/induces her to work as a prostitute, if this results in the birth of a child.[226] It will be clear from this example that it may at times be difficult to establish whether consent was given, in particular where the conception of the child with third party genetic material does not take place in a hospital or clinic.

b. Female same-sex and sperm donation

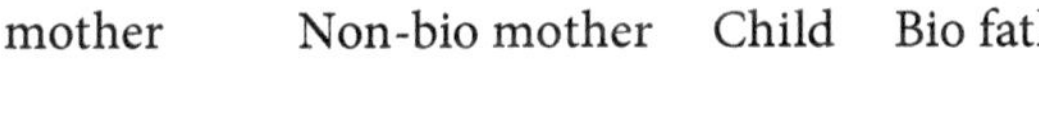

Bio mother | Non-bio mother | Child | Bio father

24 Art. 1:199 under (a) and 1:200(3) Civil Code.

25 See Vonk, *supra* note 5, pp. 152–163.

26 Hoge Raad 2 February 2003, LJN AF0444.

By definition female same-sex couples wanting a child need to make use of donor sperm. Conception may take place through AI or IVF in a hospital or through self-insemination at home.[227]

The intentions of the parties involved may vary in this case. It is probably most likely the intention of the female couple to integrate the child into their own family. Where a known donor is used the couple's intentions with regards the position of the donor in the child's life may range from completely banning him from the child's life to allowing him to become the child's legal father by means of recognition. It will be obvious that the intentions of the known donor may not correspond with the intentions of the female couple. The intentions of the parties may have been discussed to a greater or lesser extent detail and may even have been formalised in the form of a donor contract.[228]

The position of the non-biological mother in a same-sex relationship is not the same as that of a non-biological father in a different-sex relationship. Whereas the intentions of the non-biological father have been recognised by the law, those of the non-biological mother have not. The recognition of the intentions of a married non-biological father mentioned under §2.3.1.a has not been extended to married non-biological mothers. This means she will not become a legal parent by operation of law by virtue of her marriage to the birth mother, nor can her legal parenthood be established on the basis of the fact that she consented to the act that resulted in the conception of the child.[229]

2.3.2. Egg donation

a. Different-sex and egg donation

Different-sex couples may consider using donor eggs to conceive a child, for instance if the female partner does not have working ovaries or is the carrier of a hereditary disease or condition. She is, therefore, unable to conceive a child of her own, but may carry a pregnancy established with a donor egg to term. Since this procedure requires the egg donor to undergo invasive medical treatment and a synchronisation of the menstrual cycles of both women involved, it can only take place in a hospital. It will be the intention of all parties involved that the child will be raised by the gestational mother and her partner. The law recognises this inten-

27 Conception may also take place through sexual intercourse.

28 There are standard donor contracts available on the internet, for instance at the kidkids website: http://www.kidkids.nl/juridisch/contract.html.

29 See Vonk, *supra* note 5, pp. 163–180.

tion and the woman who gives birth to the child will be the child's legal mother by operation of law.

b. Female same-sex and egg donation

Gestational mother + Genetic mother | Child | Bio father

The most likely scenario for egg donation in a female couple is where one of the women supplies an egg, which is then fertilised with donor sperm and subsequently implanted into the other woman. It will quite likely be the intention of both women to become the child's parent. As IVF needs to take place in a licensed clinic, the donor will either be unknown or have been brought to the clinic by the mothers. It is very likely that the intentions of the parties involved have been discussed beforehand in the clinic. Nevertheless, the intentions of the women and the sperm donor may differ.

2.3.3. Surrogacy

a. Different-sex and surrogacy

In this section two examples of surrogacy with the gametes of one of the partners in a different-sex relationship will be discussed.

Non-bio mother + Bio father | Child | Bio mother (surrogate)

In the first case the surrogate mother is inseminated with the sperm of the commissioning father. For whatever reason the female partner of the commissioning couple cannot (or will not) carry a pregnancy to term. The couple may decide to use the services of a surrogate mother, who subsequently gives birth to her own genetic child conceived with the sperm of the commissioning father. In this case the surrogate mother is both the child's genetic and gestational mother. The commissioning father is the child's biological father. The commissioning mother, however, has no genetic relationship with the child. Of course, it is also possible that the couple use a donor egg, which is fertilised with the commissioning father's sperm and subsequently placed in the surrogate mother. In that case the surrogate mother is the child's gestational mother but not the child's genetic mother. [330]

30 For example, Rechtbank Rotterdam 8 February 2007, LJN BA0238.

The second case concerns an example of gestational surrogacy with donor sperm. The commissioning mother produces eggs, yet is unable or unwilling to carry a pregnancy to term. Furthermore, the commissioning father is infertile or the carrier of a hereditary disease or condition. The couple engage a surrogate mother who is implanted with an embryo created with the commissioning mother's egg fertilised with donor sperm. This means that the commissioning mother is genetically related to the child, the surrogate mother is the child's gestational mother and the commissioning father has no genetic link with the child.

b. Female same-sex and surrogacy

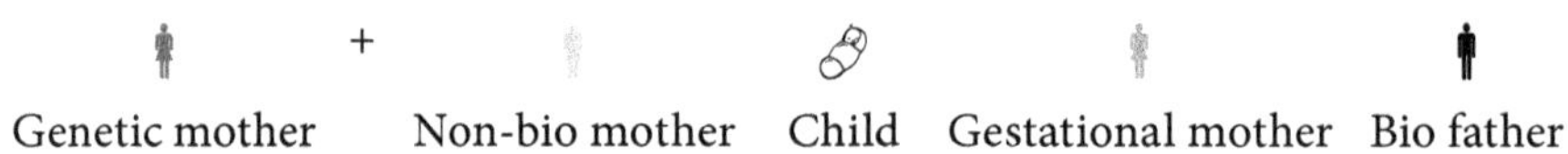

One of the women supplies the egg, which is subsequently fertilised with donor sperm. As neither of the women is able or willing to carry a pregnancy to term, they engage a surrogate mother to carry the child. This situation is not very likely to occur, since in most cases one of the women will be able and willing to become pregnant.

c. Male same-sex and surrogacy

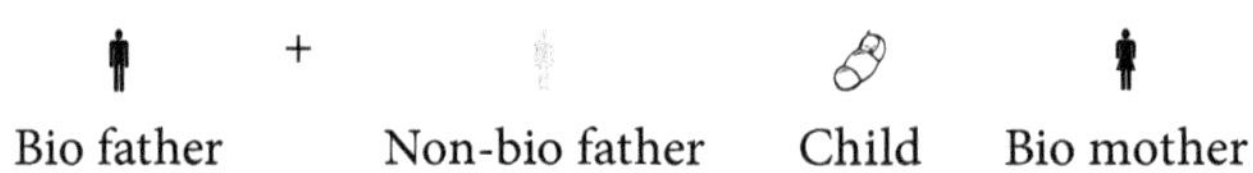

Male same-sex couples will always have to enlist the help of a surrogate mother if they wish to raise a child that is genetically related to one of them. The surrogate mother may carry a child of her own conceived with the sperm of one of the commissioning fathers in which case she is both the child's genetic mother and gestational mother (biological mother), or she may be implanted with an embryo consisting of a donor egg fertilised with one of the commissioning father's sperm in which case she is only the child's gestational mother.

In all the situations sketched above under (a), (b), and (c), it is very likely the intention of all the parties at the outset that the child will be integrated into the family of the commissioning parents. These intentions may or may have been formalised. Where the surrogate mother is also the genetic mother, insemination with the commissioning father's sperm may take place at home and no intervention by a clinic is required. In all the cases sketched above, the birth mother is the legal mother according to Dutch law.

2.4. NON-GENETIC FAMILIES

Neither the father nor the mother is genetically related to the child. The legal ties between the non-genetic parents and the child are forged through adoption.[331] The child may or may not have been conceived at the instigation of the non-genetic parents, but in the context of this article, the most interesting case is that where there is a surrogacy arrangement in place. Where the child is born as a result of such an arrangement, it will be the intention of the parties at the outset that the child is integrated into the family of the commission parents. These intentions may or may not have been formalised. As has already been mentioned the birth mother is the child's legal mother under Dutch law and a complicated procedure needs to be followed to transfer parental status from the birth mother to the commissioning parents.

3. SURROGACY AND DONOR INSEMINATION

The inventory of intentions made on the basis of the Family Tree has yielded a number of interesting situations in which formalised and non-formalised intentions play a role in the process leading to the conception of a child in assisted conception scenarios. In the remainder of the article, the focus will be on those situations where use has been made of a so-called third procreational party.[332] These cases are highly interesting, as they may give rise to tensions between biology/genetics, on the one hand, and intentions, on the other. From the previous sections it may be concluded that there are at least two important areas where formalised or non-formalised intentions play a role in the process leading to the conception of the child, namely surrogacy and sperm donation. It is now time to

31 There are exceptions, where only the non-biological mother has to adopt the child, and the non-biological father can become the child's legal parent through recognition, see Vonk, *supra* note 5, pp. 199–204.

32 A third procreational party may defined as a person who donates gametes to be used by others or who offers her gestational services to others.

consider whether these intentions also play a role in the attribution of parental status.

3.1. SURROGACY

3.1.1. Surrogacy contracts

There has been a lot of discussion regarding the validity of surrogacy contracts in The Netherlands.[333] Such contracts may contain many different kinds of clauses, ranging from the surrogate mother agreeing that she will not smoke during the pregnancy, to her agreement to abort the child if serious birth defects are discovered.[334] However, the main clause concerns the obligation of the surrogate mother to surrender the child to the commissioning parents after the birth. Whereas not all authors agree on the validity of the subsidiary clauses and the possibility for damages if the surrogate mother does not fulfil her obligations, they all agree that the main clause is void and cannot be enforced.[335] Under Dutch law, juridical acts (including agreements) that violate mandatory statutory provisions or are contrary to good morals will result in the agreement being regarded null and void, which means they are treated as if they never came into being and can thus not be enforced.[336] Contracts concerning the surrender of children after birth are considered to be a breach of good morals. Contracting about the legal position of children, for instance who will be the child's legal parent, may violate the mandatory statutory provisions of parentage law and parental responsibility which would render such a contract illegal and void.[337] Nevertheless there are authors who propose that under certain conditions surrogacy contracts should play a role

---

33 A. Broekhuijsen-Molenaar, *Civielrechtelijke aspecten van kunstmatige inseminatie en draagmoederschap*, 1991; J. Vranken, 'Contractualisering en draagmoederschap', 1997 *Tijdschrift voor Privaatrecht*, no. 4, pp. 1751–1761; Boele-Woelki *et al.*, *supra* note 21; J. Nieuwenhuis, 'Promises, promises', 2001 *Nederlands Juristenblad*, no. 37; S. Dermout, *De eerste logeerpartij: Hoogtechnologische draagmoedershap in Nederland*, 2001; Vlaardingerbroek, *supra* note 21, pp. 171–178; M. van den Berg *et al.*, 'Hoogtechnologisch draagmoederschap', 2004 *Nederlands Juristenblad*, no. 14; J. Klijnsma, 'De verzakelijking van het menselijk lichaam', 2008 *Ars Aequi*, no. 1, pp. 11–19.

34 See for instance Boele-Woelki, *supra* note 21, p. 23 for a list of such clauses; see also Asser-De Boer, *Asser's Handleiding tot de beoefening van het Nederlands burgerlijk recht, Deel 1: Personen- en familierecht*, 2006, no. 696 and Vlaardingerbroek *supra* note 21, p. 175.

35 For an overview of the discussion see Vlaardingerbroek *supra* note 21.

36 Art. 3:40(2) Civil Code.

37 See Asser-De Boer, *supra* note 33, no. 696. With regard to parental responsibility see for instance Art. 1:121 lid 3.

in the process of transferring parental rights from the surrogate mother to the intentional couple.[338]

At present, however, adults cannot legally enter into contracts concerning the status of legal parenthood if this deviates from mandatory statutory provisions and they cannot be obliged on the basis of a contractual provision to surrender 'their' child to the other contractual party. This does not mean that such contracts are completely without meaning. For instance, one of the licensed IVF centres that recently opened a surrogacy centre, requires the parties to draw up a contract.[339] The contract itself cannot alter the legal status of the parties involved, but the idea is that it can give a court supportive evidence about the intentions of the parties involved at the time the contract was drawn up and thus may facilitate decisions in the adoption process.

3.1.2. Surrogacy and the intentions of the parties in practice

What role do such formalised and non-formalised intentions play in practice? In order to answer this question, it may be useful to look at the different kinds of surrogacy. As can be deduced from the Family Tree there are at least three different kinds of surrogacy: surrogacy with the genetic material of commissioning parents, surrogacy with the genetic material of only one of the genetic parents and surrogacy with genetic material of others. Dutch law recognises none of these forms of surrogacy explicitly. However, full genetic surrogacy is more or less condoned and a very small group of hospitals have recently embarked upon offering this kind of surrogacy.[440] There is no specific procedure for transferring parental status from the surrogate mother to the commissioning parents for any of the forms of surrogacy mentioned. The child can only become the legal child of both commissioning parents through adoption.[441] In the following section, a number of recent cases concerning the abovementioned types of surrogacy will be discussed.[442]

---

38 Van den Berg, *supra* note 32, also Vranken, *supra* note 32, pp. 1760–1761 and Vonk, *supra* note 5, pp. 276–277.

39 See note 19.

40 For instance The Medical Centre of the Free University in Amsterdam (*VU medisch centrum, VUmc*). A couple of years ago a trial with full genetic IVF surrogacy was conducted with the approval of the government (Dermout, *supra* note 32). The trial was successful, but once it was over there were no hospitals in The Netherlands willing to offer such surrogacy services. Only recently the VUmc opened a surrogacy centre that offers IVF surrogacy services to married couples who have to bring their own surrogate mother. For more information see Vonk, *supra* note 5, pp. 137–140.

41 The steps necessary to transfer parental status from the surrogate mother to the commissioning parents are described in Vonk, *supra* note 5, Chapters 5 and 6.

42 For information about earlier case law see for example: A. Heida, 'Juridische perikelen rond het draagmoederschap', 1984 *Weekblad voor Privaatrecht,Notariaat en Registrstie*, no. 5716; E. Sutorius *et al.*, 'Het gezag van draagmoeders', 1997 *Nederlands Juristenblad*, no. 25, pp.

Full genetic surrogacy

The first recent decision by a lower court in The Netherlands concerns the adoption of a child by the commissioning parents after IVF surrogacy with the genetic material of the commissioning parents.[443] The surrogate mother lived and gave birth to a child in England. In the adoption decision the fact that both commissioning parents were genetically related to the child played an important role, as did the fact that the contract drawn up in advance clearly indicated that it was the intention of the surrogate mother to hand over the child after its birth. The genetic relationship between the commissioning parents and the child played such an important role that the rules for international adoption were deemed not to apply. According to the court these rules only apply in international cases where a child will grow up in another family than that of his or her 'parents'.[444]

Partially genetic surrogacy

In general, it may be far more difficult for partially genetic surrogate parents to acquire full parental status with regard to the child they are raising than it is for genetic surrogate parents. Whether a court would be as willing to set aside international adoption rules where only the commissioning father is genetically related to the child remains to be seen. This may be illustrated by another recent decision of a Dutch lower court. In this case only the commissioning father was genetically related to the child. The Court decided that transferring parental responsibility from the surrogate parents to the commissioning parents would be in breach of Article 7 UNCRC, because it would result in the child not being raised by his or her natural parents (*c.q.* birth mother).[445] The fact that the commissioning father was the child's biological father played no part in the decision, nor did the fact that the child concerned had been living with the commissioning couple since his or her birth.

Another case that demonstrates the relative unimportance of biological fatherhood in partially genetic surrogacy is a Dutch/Belgian case that was brought before the Dutch courts in recent years. The case concerns a Belgian surrogate mother who agreed to carry a child for a Belgian commissioning couple with the sperm of the commissioning father. Towards the end of the pregnancy, the surrogate mother informed the commissioning parents that she had miscarried. However, this turned out to be a lie. After the baby was born in February 2005 she

1116–1120; L. Kalkman-Boogerd, 'Ontheffing en draagmoederschap', 1998 *FJR*, no. 9, pp. 198–202.

43 Rechtbank Rotterdam 11 December 2007, LJN BB9844.

44 *Ouderlijk gezin.*

45 Rechtbank Rotterdam 8 February 2007, LJN BA0238.

handed the child over to a Dutch couple. The Dutch couple had informed the appropriate authorities that they would receive a new born baby into their family for the purpose of adoption, but not that it concerned a child from abroad. This is important, since the couple had not followed the necessary procedure for inter-country adoption. At the time the court was confronted with the question whether the child could stay with the couple despite the fact that the couple had not proceeded in accordance with the relevant provisions, the child had been living with the couple for some 7 months. The District Court in Utrecht (*Rechtbank Utrecht*) decided that there was 'family life' between the child and the couple on the basis of the fact that the child had been living with them since her birth. Accordingly, the child was allowed to stay with the couple for the time being.[446]

Meanwhile, the Belgian commissioning parents discovered that the surrogate mother had given birth to 'their' child. More than 2 years after the baby was born, DNA-testing revealed that the commissioning father was the child's biological father, a fact that had been contested by the surrogate mother form the start. The commissioning father subsequently started proceedings with the Dutch courts to have the child turned over to him and his wife. The case, which is still pending, gives rise to moral and legal questions concerning surrogacy, the freedom to have another couple raise your child, the meaning of 'family life' and the genetic link between a father and a child.

Non-genetic surrogacy

A recent case of non-genetic surrogacy concerns an arrangement where the 'surrogate' and biological parents promised to hand over the child after birth to friends.[447] After its birth the child was fraudulently registered as the child of the commissioning parents. A few months later, the biological parents regretted their decision to surrender the child to the surrogate parents and tried to reclaim the child. The court of first instance and the Court of Appeals ordered the commissioning parents to return the child to the biological parents. They both argued that parents have a right to raise their own child (there are exceptions where the child is at risk) and children have a right to be raised by their own parents (this right is encapsulated in Article 7 UNCRC). The intentions of the parties that resulted in the conception of the child and the agreements they made about the future of the child play no role whatsoever.

It is interesting to consider how the right of a parent to raise his or her own child and the right of a child to be raised by its own parents would be interpreted if the commissioning parents were the genetic parents of the child in case of conflict between the surrogate and the commissioning parents. In the first case, the

46 Rechtbank Utrecht 26 October 2005, LJN AU4934.

47 Hof Leeuwarden 6 October 2004, LJN AR3391.

court referred more-or-less to the genetic commissioning parents as the real parents of the child. Would this court have taken the same approach if the surrogate mother had refused to surrender the child? The application of these rights becomes even more difficult where the child has a genetic parent in both the surrogate family and the commissioning family. Nevertheless, on the basis of the case law discussed, which is by no means a comprehensive discussion, it would appear likely that the position of the birth mother will be far stronger than the position of the genetic father in conflict cases.

It may be concluded that intentions, whether formalised or not, that are formulated before the conception and birth of the child, do not play a very substantial role in the assignment or transfer of parental status after the child's birth. On the other hand, intentions of the parents at the time the transfer is to take place do play a role, if a conflict has arisen between the parties. In these cases it is likely that courts will not cooperate in transferring parental status (this may be different in case of full genetic surrogacy, but only time can tell). If there is no conflict and the child is doing well in the commissioning family, courts *may* be willing to participate in transferring parental status. However, since the *Hoge Raad* has never had the opportunity to adjudicate on a surrogacy case, this is not certain. In short both commissioning parents and surrogate parents are left in the dark about whether or not parental status will be transferred to the commissioning parents after the birth of the child.

3.2. SPERM DONATION

3.2.1. Different-sex relationships

Intention in different-sex relationships only plays a role if it takes the form of consent by the partner to the conception of the child with the genetic material of a third party. If there is no consent, there is no ground for the attribution of the status of legal parent to a non-biological parent non-biological parent with the status of a legal parent.[448] The consent of the male life partner covers any act that may have resulted in the conception of the child. This may range from consent to licensed fertility treatment with donor sperm, on the one hand, to consent to have sexual intercourse with another man to conceive a child, on the other. Consent as a basis for legal parenthood is not based on the notion of *double consent.* Only where the birth mother and her partner receive fertility treatment with donor

48 This does not mean that where there was no consent the non-biological father can never be regarded as the child's legal parent. If the couple concerned is married, the birth mother's husband will be presumed to be the child's legal father even where consent is lacking. Unless this presumption is challenged, the husband will in practice be regarded as the child legal parent. See Vonk, *supra* note 5, pp. 223–225.

sperm in a clinic, will the consent of the non-biological father be matched with the consent of the donor. For children conceived outside the fertility treatment context, this situation may or may not exist. The fact that double consent is not a requirement may be due to the categorisation of biological father into *begetters* and *sperm donors*. The latter category includes all biological fathers who are not in a relationship with the birth mother and have contributed to the conception of the child with their genetic material without sexual intercourse. In principle a *begetter* may acquire legal rights and duties with regard to his biological child, yet a *sperm donor* may not. However, if the birth mother is not married to the *begetter*, but is married to another man, the intentions of the birth mother's *husband* will determine whether the begetter may acquire a legal relationship with the child. The begetter in such a situation has no standing to challenge the legal parenthood of the birth mother's husband.

The legal implications of consent for establishing legal parenthood by operation of law depend on the legal status of the relationship between the partners. If the consensual non-biological father is married to the birth mother he will be a legal parent by operation of law. If he is not married to the birth mother he will not be the child's legal parent by operation of law. On the one hand, this may be due to the fact that marriage may be regarded as a commitment that includes the intention to take care of any children born during the marriage, whereas this may or may not be true for couples in non-formalised relationships. On the other hand, this may also be due to the fact that no distinction is made between fertility treatment with donor sperm in a licensed clinic and the use of a DIY sperm donor (who may incidentally be the birth mother's life partner). As a consequence, one cannot be certain that the supplier of the genetic material consented to the use of his material in this manner. This means that the partner will have to take action to establish his legal parenthood with maternal cooperation by means of recognition. He cannot establish his legal parenthood without maternal cooperation In contrast, the child or the child's mother may have the consensual father's legal parenthood established by court order, if the non-biological father consented to the conception of the child in this manner and may be regarded as the birth mother's life partner.

3.2.2. *Same-sex relationships*

Same-sex partners do not acquire the status of legal parent by operation of law, regardless of the legal status of their relationship or the kind of sperm donor they use. The partner's consent, which plays an important role for different-sex couples, is of no relevance for same-sex couples. The intentions of the female partner of the birth mother to become the legal parent of her partner's child is not recognised as such by the law. A number of years ago the law was amended so as to allow for a woman to adopt her female partner's child. However this is a far cry from the recognition offered to the intentions of different-sex couples.[449] Recently, the Minister of Justice and the Minister of Youth and the Family have established a commission to investigate possibilities for the automatic attribution of the status of legal parent to the birth mother's female partner.[550] This commission reported in October 2007 and found that, at the very least, the female partner of the birth mother should be permitted to recognise her partner's child.[551] This means that the female partner would be granted the same possibilities with regard to the child and vice versa as an unmarried intentional father has with regard to his child. Whether the position of the married female partner should be the same as that of a married intentional father is, according to the commission, a political choice.[552]

When discussing the role of intention in the context of donor insemination in same-sex relationships, not only the intentions of the biological and the non-biological mother play a role. The intentions of the sperm donor may also play a role, where the couple has called upon the assistance of a known donor to achieve pregnancy. The intentions of all three parties involved in this kind of donor insemination may or may not have been laid down in the form of a written agreement, such as a donor contract. Such a donor contract may, for instance, contain clauses as to the position of the donor in the child's life. In general such clauses will determine that the donor plays no role in the child's life and will not contact the child of his own accord. The value of such a contract is debatable. Where 'family life' develops between the child and the donor over the course of time, it may well be that the court grants him a contact order if conflict arises between the mothers and the donor on the basis of the right to family life encapsulated in Article 8 ECHR.[553] The existence of a contract in such a case is probably not very relevant for the court. A contract may provide an overview of what the intentions of the parties were when they embarked on the donor insemination process. However, drawing up a contract may help parties to consider all the possibilities and may help them become aware of what they are getting into.

---

49 Act of 21st December 2000 amending Book 1, Dutch Civil Code (Adoption for persons of the same sex)(*Wet van 21 december 2000 tot wijziging van Boek 1 van het Burgerlijk Wetboek (Adoptie door personen van hetzelfde geslacht)*), *Staatsblad* 2001, 10.

50 *Kamerstukken II* 2006–2007, 30 551, no. 8 and 9.

51 Commissie lesbisch ouderschap en interlandelijke adoptie, *Rapport Lesbisch Ouderschap*, Ministerie van Justitie 2007. For a critical evaluation of the report see M. Vonk, 'Duo-moeders en hun kinderen', 2008.

52 For more information on legal issues relating to lesbian motherhood see for instance also A. Henstra, *Van afstammingsrecht naar ouderschapsrecht*, 2002, and K. Saarloos, 'Duo-moederschap: op de grens van adoptie en afstammingsrecht', 2007 *Tijdschrift voor Familie- en jeugdrecht*, p. 60.

53 For instance: M. Vermeulen, 'Spermadonor eist vaderrol op', *De Volkskrant*, 12 March 2008, and M. Vermeulen, 'Zaad zoekt kind', *De Volkskrant*, 12 March 2008.

A recent decision that is of great interest in this context concerns the consequences of the intentions of a homosexual donor and a lesbian birth mother regarding their biological child.[554] The two were friends and had frequently discussed the possibility of his 'donating' sperm and his subsequent role in the child's life. During the pregnancy the woman and the donor disagreed with regards the extent to which the donor would be part of the child's life. This brought their friendship to an end and they stopped meeting. By the time the donor's request for a contact order reached the *Hoge Raad*, he had only seen the child once. The *Hoge Raad* had to decide whether there was family life between the donor and the child, in which case it would be possible under Dutch law to make a contact order. The *Hoge Raad* judged that there was family life between the donor and the child, despite the fact that they had hardly ever met. The *Hoge Raad* based its decision on basis of the long term friendship between the mother and the donor before the conception of the child and their joint intention to become parents. What may be gleaned from this case is that when trying to ensure that the intentions of the birth mother and her female partner in the attribution of parental status to the co-mother are given a more prominent position, it should be borne in mind that the donor may also have intentions with regard to the child. In particular where these intentions have been discussed and the parties have agreed upon the role that the donor will play in the child's life, these intentions should not be disregarded without proper justification.

An interesting question in this respect involves the case where the donor and the birth mother have agreed that the donor will be given consent to recognise the child after birth and the birth mother subsequently, for whatever reason, refuses to consent.[555] What is the status of such an agreement? Is the agreement void because it is against good morals? Is it contrary to a mandatory statutory provision? What is the relevance of the fact that there is no other person who is the child's other parent by operation of law, nor is there another person who has a prior claim to this consent? Nevertheless, it seems unlikely that such a contract will in itself replace the mother's consent, but it may well be that the existence of the contract will grant the donor access to the court to apply for the court to replace the mother's consent. The difference between the two routes is that the first route has no other requirements than the mother's consent, whereas the second route requires the court to investigate whether granting the donor consent to

54 Hoge Raad 30 november 2007, LJN BB9094. For a annotation of this case see A. Nuytinck, ' Het omgangsrecht van de spermadonor', 2008 *Ars Aequi*, p. 133.

55 A similar case came before the Dutch court a couple of years ago. In that case there was no written evidence that the birth mother promised the donor that she would consent to his recognition of the child. After the birth of the child the parties disagree whether such a promise was indeed made. See M. Vonk, 'One, two or three parents: Lesbian co-mothers and a known-donor with "family life" under Dutch Law', 2004 *International Journal of Law, Policy and the Family*, pp. 103–117.

the recognition of the child would negatively influence the relationship between the mother and the child.

4. CONCLUSIONS

Written contracts and oral agreements give the court a taste of the intentions of the parties before they embarked on the journey towards pregnancy. What importance should be attached to such intentions after the child is born and legal parenthood is to be assigned or transferred? A quote from an English judge, trying to decide on a known donor's application for parental responsibility, illustrates the problem at hand:

> 'One of the things that struck me most forcefully in this case was how, notwithstanding that they were all highly intelligent and self-possessed individuals, biology had ambushed all of the adults in one way or another, whether it be in the unexpected impact of the arrangements for D's conception or the unanticipated strength of emotions once D was born.'[556]

It may be very difficult to foresee, how the parties involved feel towards the agreements made before the conception of the child once the child is born. Should be forced to keep their promises or should their misgivings and possible changes of heart be taken seriously? One of the main problems in this question is that it does not only concern the (intentional) parents but a primary consideration in all matters pertaining to the legal and social position of children should be the best interests of the children themselves.[557] Should contracts and agreements be given a more prominent role in the attribution of legal parent-child relationships? Yes and no.

Intentions, whether or not they have been formalised, already play a (minor) role in the assigning legal parent-child relationships to non-biological parents. In particular in cases where all parties agree and the agreements made have been tested or approved for example by a judge, the fact that there is agreement might be an argument to devise specific (less lengthy) procedures for attributing legal parent-child relationships.[558] This is in fact what is happening where the legal position of co-mothers is concerned. Proposals have been made to facilitate the assignment of the status of legal parent to co-mothers. This may also be possible

556 The Honourable Justice Black in *Re D (Contact and PR: Lesbian mothers and known father) No. 2* [2006] EWHC 2 Fam, Para. 65.

557 Children's Convention Art. 3(1).

558 This has been proposed by Van den Berg, *supra* note 32, for surrogacy and in the context of donor insemination by M. Vonk, 'Kinderen, co-moeders en het afstammingsrecht', 2007 *Nederlands Juristenblad*, pp. 448–449.

for surrogacy, in particular where full genetic surrogacy is concerned and the child is genetically related to both commissioning parents. For cases where the child is the genetic child of the surrogate mother and the commissioning father, things may be more complicated, which is certainly true for cases of non-genetic surrogacy.

However, despite the fact that intentions and written or oral agreements do not play a substantial role in parent-child law at present, drawing up such an agreement may help all the parties involved envisage the consequences of the adventure that they are embarking upon. It may help them become aware of potential problems and conflicts that may arise once the child is born and possibly reconsider or restart the discussion. Even if drawing up an agreement only serves the purpose of helping the parties involved discuss and come to terms with all the issues involved in engaging a sperm donor or surrogate mother, this is by no means a small thing.

THE KANSAS CASE OF *K.M.H.*
US law concerning the legal status of known sperm donors

NANCY G. MAXWELL*

1. INTRODUCTION

On October 27, 2007, the Kansas Supreme Court issued its opinion in the case of *In the Interest of K.M.H and K.C.H*[1] *(hereinafter K.M.H.)*, joining the growing number of states that have determined the legal status of known sperm donors *vis-à-vis* their biological children born to women who are not in heterosexual marriages. This article examines the *K.M.H.* decision within the context of this increasing body of US case law, in an attempt to discern *K.M.H.*'s contribution to, and its place in, this 'nascent area of law which is changing on almost a daily basis.'[2]

The article begins with an explanation of parentage law in the United States, including a discussion of the constitutional ramifications of parental rights. Next the article examines the US court decisions involving known sperm donors asserting parental rights prior to the K.M.H. decision. The purpose of the case law examination is three-fold. First, under the common law system the courts have the authority to make law in the absence of statutory provisions that deal with a particular issue before the court. In the common law system the court decisions are the *law* and the inferior courts must follow the appellate court decisions. Consequently, in those situations in which there are no applicable assisted insemination

---

* Professor and Director of International Legal Programs, Washburn University School of Law, Topeka, Kansas, USA, email: nancy.maxwell@washburn.edu; B.A. (1972) and J.D. (1975) University of North Dakota; LLM (1979) Harvard University; licensed to practice law before state and federal courts in North Dakota and the United States Court of Appeals for the Eighth Circuit. Professor Maxwell gratefully acknowledges Washburn University School of Law for funding this article through a summer research grant. She also thanks Barbara Dye and Lynn Trevino, Class of 2008, Washburn University School of Law, for their excellent research assistance.
See also N.G. Maxwell, 'Taking the Side Exit in the United States', 2001 *Nemesis*, no. 1, pp. 14–22, which analyzes the US case law involving sperm donors from 1977 to 2000.

1 169 P.3d 1025 (Kan. 2007).

2 *Browne* v. *D'Alleva*, 2007 Conn. Super. LEXIS 3250, p. *28.

by donor (AID) statutes, the court decisions become the sole law on the subject of whether known sperm donors have parental rights. Second, even when the legislature has enacted AID statutes that address the parental rights of sperm donors, the courts have the authority to interpret those statutes and these interpretations become binding law until the legislature amends the statute. Finally, the courts in the United States have the authority to strike down statutes as violations of federal or state constitutional provisions, resulting in the statutes becoming unenforceable. Interestingly, all three of these possibilities occurred in US known sperm donor cases that were decided prior to the *K.M.H.* case.

The article proceeds with a synthesis of the cases that were decided before the *K.M.H.* case, attempting to find common themes among the cases. The article then details the four different opinions in the *K.M.H.* case and, in particular, lays out the discussion of the constitutional challenges to the Kansas sperm donor statute. Next the article discusses how the previous known sperm donor cases impacted the sperm donor's arguments in *K.M.H.*, and how these cases failed to support his claim for parental rights.

The article continues with a review of two more decisions, issued after the *K.M.H.* case, incorporating these cases into the evolving trends discerned in the recent court decisions. The article concludes by summarizing *K.M.H.*'s position within that evolution.

2. PARENTAGE LAW IN THE UNITED STATES

Although each state in the United States has the authority to determine the laws concerning a child's parentage, once parentage is established, the child's parent or parents have exclusive rights to exercise their authority over the child. As a general rule, if a child is born during a heterosexual marriage, then parentage laws create a presumption that the husband and wife are the child's legal parents and the couple shares parental authority. When the child is not born to a heterosexual marriage, however, the parentage rights of a biological father were unrecognized in earlier US cases, following the traditional common law rules. This changed, though, when unmarried fathers began to challenge the constitutionality of statutes that had prevented them from asserting parental rights concerning their biological children. State statutes that ignored unmarried fathers in custody or adoption actions were struck down as unconstitutional because the statutes violated either the equal protection or the due process clause, or both, of the United States Constitution.[3] One of the cases that is quoted and plays prominently in the K.M.H.

3 The due process clause appears in two places in the United States Constitution, in the fifth amendment, which applies to the federal government and the fourteenth amendment, which

case is *Lehr* v. *Robertson*.[4] There the United States Supreme Court held that, 'When an unwed father demonstrates a full commitment to the responsibilities of parenthood by coming forward to participate in the rearing of his child, (...) his interest in personal contact with this child acquires substantial protection under the Due Process Clause. (...) If he grasps that opportunity and accepts some measure of responsibility for the child's future' then the unwed father's constitutional due process rights must be protected.[5]

Based on this analysis, a father of a non-marital child must be given an opportunity to assert his parental rights and, if he has attempted to assume parental obligations, he cannot be excluded from the protections granted to other legal parent child relationships. These rights include the ability to petition a court for a custody/residency order or a visitation/contact order. Only a court-ordered termination of his parental rights, or an adoption of the child by a person other than his spouse, can cut off the biological father's status as a legal parent. Therefore, the question of whether a known sperm donor in an AID birth is the child's legal parent becomes extremely important, because conferring legal fatherhood to a sperm donor puts him on equal footing with the legal mother, regardless of whether they are married to each other.

3. EARLY CASE LAW

In 1977, a New Jersey court decided the first reported case dealing with the parental rights of a man who provided his sperm to an unmarried woman in the case of C.M. v. C.C.[6] As with many of the cases that were to follow, the testimony of the sperm donor and the mother were conflicting and contradictory. For example, in the majority of these cases, including the Kansas case of K.M.H., the mother asserted she did not intend for the sperm donor to have a parental relationship with the child. The sperm donor, on the other hand, claimed he assumed, or the parties agreed, he would be the child's father and have certain parental rights concerning any child born of the AID. In the facts of the New Jersey case, the mother testified that she told the sperm donor she wanted to have a child by donor insemination. The sperm donor suggested he would be willing to provide his sperm and the mother accepted his offer. The mother stated she did not intend for the sperm donor to have a parental relationship with the child. The sperm donor, on the other hand, testified he and the mother were dating each other and con-

applies to the state governments. The equal protection clause appears in the fourteenth amendment.

4 *Lehr* v. *Richardson*, 463 US 248 (1983).

5 *Ibid.*, at pp. 261, 262.

6 See generally *C.M.* v. *C.C.*, 377 A.2d 821 (N.J. Juv. & Dom. Rel. Ct. 1977).

templated marriage. He further testified the mother wanted to have a child by him, but she did not want to have intercourse before they were married. Consequently, the sperm donor provided sperm to the mother, who inseminated herself at her home, pursuant to a doctor's description of the insemination process. The parties stopped seeing each other three months into the mother's pregnancy, when they discovered they did not share the same assumption about the role the sperm donor would have in the child's life.

Because there was no applicable AID statute in New Jersey in 1977, the court relied on common law principles that had developed in New Jersey case law. The court first noted, under current law, a 'natural' father had visitation rights to his children, even though he was not married to the child's mother. The court framed the issue as one involving the definition of a 'natural' father. In doing so, the court looked at AID cases concerning married couples. The court determined these cases were factually distinguishable from the present case because the issue in those cases was whether the husband or a sperm donor was the child's legal parent. The present case, however, did not involve competing interests of two men. The court therefore analogized this case to conception by intercourse and stated the sperm donor was the only other parent figure in this case, and the fact that an unmarried woman conceived the child without intercourse was not relevant. In addition, the court stated the sperm donor did not waive his parental rights by donating his sperm. The court held that because (1) it was in the child's best interests to have two parents whenever possible; (2) there was no one else to assume the responsibilities of fatherhood; (3) the sperm donor was asserting those responsibilities; and (4) the sperm donor actively participated in the insemination, he should be considered the legal parent of the child. The court granted visitation rights against the wishes of the mother, who the court characterized as 'thwarting' the sperm donor's attempts to establish a relationship with the child. In a subsequent action, the court ordered the mother to sign the necessary documents to amend the child's birth certificate, changing the designation of the father from 'unknown' to the name of the sperm donor.[7]

4. CASES INTERPRETING STATUTES THAT REGULATE THE PARENTAL RIGHTS IN AID BIRTHS

As mentioned previously, each state in the United States has the authority to determine its laws concerning a child's parentage. However, the desirability of interstate uniformity and predictability concerning a child's parentage resulted in

[7] *C.M.* v. *C.C.*, 407 A.2d 849 (N.J. Juv. & Dom. Rel. Ct. 1977).

the National Conference of Commissioners on Uniform State Laws proposing the Uniform Parentage Act in 1973.[8] Although a state's legislature is not required to adopt a uniform act drafted by the Commissioners, many state legislatures do so because these acts are the product of much study and debate by the leading legal experts in a particular field of law. Consequently, the Uniform Parentage Act has been adopted in a number of the states within the United States.[9]

The Uniform Parentage Act creates presumptions of parentage. Many of the presumptions are based on the man and woman's marriage to one another. In addition, Section 5 of the Act addresses the parentage of a child born by AID. There are two subsections in Section 5 that work together in establishing who will be considered the father of the child. The first subsection specifically provides if a physician supervises the AID and the husband consents to the AID, then 'the husband is treated in law as if he were the natural father of a child thereby conceived.'[10] Subsection (b) of Section 5 then states that a man, who provides semen to a physician for AID 'of a married woman other than the donor's wife, is treated in law as if he were not the natural father of a child thereby conceived.'[11] The limitation of the 1973 Uniform Parentage Act, however, is that it only addresses parentage in an AID conception involving a heterosexual married couple. There are no specific provisions that address the rights of the persons who participate in AID if the woman does not have a husband. This can result in uncertainty when the AID involves a woman who is not in a heterosexual marriage, particularly if the procedure is not done under the supervision of a physician. Both of these factors have played an important role in the courts refusing to apply Subsection (b), resulting in a court determination that the sperm donor was the legal parent of the child.

The first case that interpreted a state's AID statute was a California Court of Appeals case, *Jhordan C. v. Mary K.*[12] *Mary K. and Victoria T.*, her female friend who lived in a nearby town, decided Mary would attempt to have a child, who the two women would raise together. After interviewing several possible sperm donors, Mary and Victoria chose Jhordan C. However, there was conflicting tes-

---

8 Unif. Parentage Act, 9B *U.L.A.* 287 (1987).

9 The 1973 version of the Uniform Parentage Act has been adopted in Alabama, California, Colorado, Hawaii, Illinois, Kansas, Minnesota, Missouri, Montana, Nevada, New Jersey, New Mexico, Ohio, and Rode Island. The 2000/2002 version has been adopted in Delaware, North Dakota, Washington, Wyoming, Oklahoma, Texas, and Utah. See 'Final Acts and Legislation-Parentage Act- Legislative Fact Sheet,' Uniform Parentage Act, at www.nccusl.org.

10 Unif. Parentage Act § 5, 9B *U.L.A.* 301 (1987).

11 Unif. Parentage Act § 5(b), 9B *U.L.A.* 301 (1987). The 2002 Uniform Parentage Act no longer requires the use of a physician. Section 702 states 'Parental Status of Donor. A donor is not a parent of a child conceived by means of assisted reproduction.' Unif. Parentage Act, § 702 (2002). The comments to this section acknowledge that married and unmarried women will use of AID and other forms of assisted reproduction.

12 *Jhordan C.* v. *Mary K.*, 224 Cal. Rptr. 530 (Ct. App. 1986).

timony about the parties' intentions concerning the involvement of the sperm donor beyond providing the semen for the insemination. According to Mary, she told Jhordan she did not intend for him to have an on-going relationship with any child who might be conceived with his semen, but she did agree that Jhordan could satisfy his curiosity concerning the physical appearance of the child by having an opportunity to look at the child. Jhordan, however, testified he and Mary agreed they would have an on-going friendship, he would have consistent contact with the child and he would care for the child as much as two or three times a week. Neither party consulted an attorney about their intentions or legal rights, nor were they aware there was a statute that addressed AID births.

Jhordan provided Mary with semen on several occasions. Mary did not use a physician for the insemination procedures and, instead, inseminated herself or Victoria assisted her with the insemination. After Mary became pregnant, she and Jhordan had several social contacts and Jhordan called her to tell her he had obtained baby furniture for the child; Mary responded by telling him to keep those items at his home. Jhordan also informed Mary he had started a trust fund for the child. However, when Jhordan asked for legal guardianship of the child in the case of Mary's death, Mary refused. On March 30, 1980, Mary gave birth to a baby boy, Devin. Although Mary permitted Jhordan to visit and photograph her and Devin at the hospital, Mary initially resisted Jhordan's request to visit Devin five days later. She then allowed the visit, but she told Jhordan she was angry about the request. During the visit Jhordan claimed a right to visit Devin. Mary responded by agreeing Jhordan could see Devin once a month. In August, 1980, after five monthly visits, Mary terminated the visits. Jhordan told Mary he would consult an attorney if Mary refused future visitation. Mary requested Jhordan sign a contract stating he would not assert paternity but Jhordan refused. In December, 1980, Jhordan filed an action against Mary to establish that he was Devin's parent and to assert visitation rights. Later he amended his petition and requested joint legal custody of Devin.

Mary supported Victoria's request to be considered a party to the action, joining in Victoria's request for joint legal custody of the child and court-ordered visitation. Victoria and Mary presented evidence at the time of trial to support their claim that Victoria was the child's de facto parent. At the parentage trial, the court found Jhordan was Devin's legal parent and granted both Jhordan and Victoria visitation rights, with the stipulation that Victoria's visitation was not to impinge on Jhordan's visitation schedule. Mary and Victoria appealed, arguing, among other points, that the trial court erred by not applying the AID provisions of the California parentage act. This provision states the 'donor of semen provided to a licensed physician for use in artificial insemination of a woman other than the donor's wife is treated in law as if he were not the natural father of a child thereby conceived.'[13]

The California Court of Appeals reviewed this statute by first noting this language originated from the Uniform Parentage Act, except that the California legislature had eliminated one word from the uniform act. The uniform act stated the semen donor was not the natural father of the child in the insemination of a 'married' woman. The California appellate court found the legislature, by eliminating this one word, intended the statute to apply to all inseminated women, regardless of marital status. However, the appellate court ruled the statutory provision did not apply to the facts in this case because the statute stated the donor was not the legal parent of the child if the semen was 'provided to a licensed physician for use in artificial insemination.' Because Jhordan did not provide the semen to a licensed physician, but rather provided the semen to Mary directly, the appellate court found the statute did not prevent Jhordan from asserting his legal parentage to Devin.[14] The appellate court upheld the trial court's order, finding Jhordan the legal parent of Devin.

Three years after the *Jhordan C. v. Mary K.* case was decided, the Colorado Supreme Court, in *In re R.C.*,[15] interpreted the Colorado AID statute, which contained language identical to the California statute. Like the two previously discussed cases, the Colorado case involved conflicting claims from the sperm donor, J.R., and the mother, E.C., regarding the parties' intention concerning the sperm donor's involvement with the child. J.R. claimed he donated sperm for E.C.'s insemination only because she promised him he would be the legal parent of the child. E.C., however, alleged she never promised J.R. he would be treated as the father of the child and she advised him numerous times to consult an attorney. Another similarity between this case and the earlier California case was that, at the time of insemination, neither party was aware that Colorado had an AID statute.

Although the case involved the same statutory language that was interpreted in the Jhordan C. case, in the Colorado case the mother's gynecologist performed the insemination. Since it was the failure to follow this statutory language that resulted in Jhordan C. succeeding in his parentage petition, one might expect when a sperm donor provided semen to a licensed physician, the semen donor would not succeed in his petition to assert parental rights to the child. However, the Colorado Supreme Court held the language of the AID statute, stating the

13 CAL. CIV. CODE § 7005(b) (West 1983), (repealed 1992, c. 162 (A.B.2650), 4, operative Jan. 1, 1994, and replaced with CAL. FAM. CODE § 7613 (2004)).

14 Although Mary argued that statutory language requiring the sperm donor to provide the semen to a physician was merely directory language, the court did not agree. The appellate court noted that the Commissioners of the uniform act deliberately added the use of a physician in later drafts of the act and that, therefore, it was an important statutory requirement.

15 775 P.2d 27 (Colo. 1989).

sperm donor would not become the father of the child when a physician performs the insemination, was 'ambiguous' when the mother knew the sperm donor. The court found the statute only applied when the sperm donor was anonymous. The Colorado Supreme Court stated if the mother knew the sperm donor, and the sperm donor alleged he and the mother had an agreement that he would be considered the father, then the statutory provision did not operate automatically to prevent him from having a trial on that issue.[16] Because the Colorado Supreme Court decided the case based on the interpretation of the statutory language, there was no need for the court to address the known sperm donor's due process and equal protection arguments.

These constitutional arguments, however, became important in an Oregon case, *McIntyre* v. *Crouch*,[17] in which Kevin McIntyre provided his sperm to an acquaintance, Linden Crouch, who used the sperm to inseminate herself. As in the previous cases, Mr. McIntyre alleged he had given his sperm to Ms. Crouch pursuant to an oral agreement that he would have an active role in the life of the child, but Ms. Crouch denied the existence of any agreement between the parties. There also was no indication the parties were aware of the existence of the Oregon statute dealing with AID.

Although not modeled after the Uniform Parentage Act, the Oregon AID statute was similar to the California statute because it provided for a physician to perform the insemination. It also stated:

> 'If the donor of semen used in the artificial insemination is not the mother's husband: (1) Such donor shall have no right, obligation or interest with respect to a child born as a result of the artificial insemination; and (2) A child born as a result of the artificial insemination shall have no right, obligation or interest with respect to the donor.'[18]

Mr. McIntyre alleged in his pleadings that because no physician was involved in the insemination and because he was a known donor, the provisions of the statute that excluded him from legal parenthood did not apply in this case. Unlike the California and Colorado courts, the Oregon appellate court rejected this argu-

16 However, the court was clear that this interpretation of the statute only applied if the woman did not have a husband. The court determined if the woman receiving the sperm had been married, then 'an agreement that the donor would be the natural father is *not* a relevant consideration when the recipient is married and her husband consents in writing to the artificial insemination.' *In re R.C.* 775 P.2d at 33 (Colo. 1989) (emphasis added). It appears that the presence of a husband protects a woman from a challenge of legal parenthood by the sperm donor, even if there is an agreement otherwise. For a detailed description of the different treatment of unmarried and married women who use AID to conceive children and suggested legislative changes to protect unmarried women, see Note, 'A Tale Of Three Women: A Survey Of The Rights And Responsibilities Of Unmarried Women Who Conceive By Alternative Insemination And A Model For Legislative Reform', 1993 *Am. J.L. & Med.* 285.

17 *McIntyre* v. *Crouch*, 780 P.2d 239, 83 ALR 4th 277 (Or. App. 1989), *rev. denied* 784 P.2d 1110 (Or. 1989), *cert. denied* 495 US 905 (1990).

18 Or. Rev. Stat. 109.239 (1977).

ment. The Oregon appellate court found the statute did not exclude the donor from its provisions if the parties failed to use a physician nor did the statutory language state the donor must be anonymous; the court held that to decide otherwise would 'rewrite the act.'[19]

The court next addressed Mr. McIntyre's constitutional argument that the statute violated equal protection and due process. The Oregon appellate court first determined the statute did not violate equal protection because of the biological differences between unmarried men, who contribute the sperm, and unmarried women, who conceive and bear the child. In addition, the court found the distinctions between unmarried men and unmarried women were rationally related to the purpose of the statute. The appellate court, however, struck down the statute as an unconstitutional violation of the due process rights of a sperm donor if the statute was an absolute bar preventing the sperm donor from alleging and proving he donated his sperm in reliance on an agreement with the mother that he would have an active role in the child's life. The court relied on the language of the United States Supreme Court in *Lehr* v. *Richardson*,[20] which held a biological father, who had 'grasped the opportunity' to 'participate in the rearing of his child,'[21] must be granted due process protections by including him as an interested party in litigation concerning the child. Therefore, the Oregon court found the Oregon AID statute, 'as applied to [the sperm donor], will violate the Due Process Clause of the Fourteenth Amendment if he can establish that he and [the mother] agreed that he should have the rights and responsibilities of fatherhood and in reliance thereon he donated his semen.'[22]

Three cases were decided in 1994 in which lesbian couples sought sperm from gay males. The first case from Ohio, *C.O.* v. *W.S.*,[23] was similar to the previous cases because it involved conflicting testimony concerning the role the sperm donor would have in the life of the child. The parties also disagreed on whether the insemination was done under the supervision and control of a physician. In addition, the parties disagreed on whether the sperm donor would have full parental rights, although the parties did agree the sperm donor would be considered a male role model and would be referred to as the child's father. Also there was no indication that the parties were aware of the Ohio AID statute, which stated '[i]f a woman is the subject of a non-spousal artificial insemination, the donor shall not be treated in law or regarded as the natural father of a child conceived as a result of the artificial insemination, and a child so conceived shall not be treated in law or regarded as the natural child of the donor.'[24]

19 *McIntyre*, 780 P.2d p. 243.
20 *Lehr* v. *Richardson*, 463 US 248, 103 S. Ct. 2985, 77 L.Ed.2d 614 (1983).
21 *Ibid.* pp. 261, 262.
22 *McIntyre*, 780 P.2d p. 244.
23 *C.O.* v. *W.S.*, 64 Ohio Misc. 2d 9, 639 N.E.2d 523 (1994).
24 Ohio Rev. Code Ann. § 3111.37(B) (1998).

At the time of the child's birth, the mother and her female partner refused the sperm donor's request for visitation and his offer to support the child financially. Six months later the sperm donor filed an action to determine parentage, including a request for custody, child support and visitation. Although the Ohio statutes on AID contemplated the insemination to be done by a physician, the statutes also provided that the physician's failure to follow certain provisions of the insemination statute did not affect the legal status of the child, who was not to be considered the child of the sperm donor. However, the Ohio appellate court, citing the earlier Colorado and New Jersey cases, determined the statute did not apply in situations in which the sperm donor was not anonymous and the donor alleged he and the mother had an oral agreement that the sperm donor would have a relationship with the child. The court also stated if its interpretation of the statute was erroneous, then, in any event, the statute was unconstitutional under a due process analysis. Citing the earlier Oregon case of McIntyre and the United States Supreme Court case of *Lehr* v. *Richardson*,[25] the Ohio court held that the due process clause protected a father who attempted to assume financial responsibility for his child and a statute that extinguished a father's efforts to assert his rights and responsibilities of being a parent was therefore unconstitutional. Pursuant to this finding, the court ordered an investigation of the two parties' homes and psychological evaluations of the parties and their partners in order to determine the residency of the child.

The second 1994 case, *Thomas S.* v. *Robin Y.*,[26] involving a New York court, is noteworthy because the parties agreed at the time of the insemination the sperm donor would not have parental rights. Both parties testified they orally agreed the sperm donor, Thomas S., was donating his sperm so the mother, Robin Y., and her female partner, Sandra R., would raise the child together,[27] without Thomas having any parental rights or obligations. Thomas did agree, however, to meet with the child if the child asked about his or her biological origin.[28] Robin performed several self-inseminations in California, Thomas's home state, and in her home state of New York. Robin became pregnant and gave birth to a daughter named Ry, while she and Sandra were temporarily living in California. Although Thomas and the mother's partner, Sandra R., were attorneys, neither party sought the advice of an attorney or attempted to put their agreement in writing.

25 *Lehr* v. *Richardson*, 463 US 248 (1983).

26 *Thomas S.* v. *Robin Y.*, 618 N.Y.S.2d 356 (App. Div. 1994), *rev'g* 599 N.Y.S.2d 377 (Fam. Ct. 1993).

27 Sandra R. had given birth to a daughter, Cade, two years earlier through AID with a different man. Sandra R. and Robin Y. intended to be co-equal parents to both children who they would treat as siblings in a two-parent household. Thomas was aware of, and agreed to, Robin and Sandra's intentions. See M. Brady, 'The Sorrow of a Donor Dad', 2000 *In the Family*, p. 14, which discusses how the dispute between Robin and Thomas resulted in Sandra terminating Cade's visits with Jack, the man who provided sperm to Sandra R.

28 *Thomas S.* v. *Robin Y.*, 599 N.Y.S.2d at 378.

Pursuant to their oral agreement, Thomas had little contact with Robin, Sandra and Ry during the first three years of Ry's life. Then Robin contacted Thomas to ask if he would be willing to see Ry, so she could meet the person 'who helped make her.' Over the next six years, Thomas and Ry saw each other anywhere from 60 to 148 days. All the parties were in accord, however, pursuant to their agreement, that Robin and Sandra had complete control over the terms of the visitation and, in particular, they requested they be present during all visits. In 1991, Thomas requested that Ry attend a family reunion with him, but since he was not comfortable introducing Robin and Sandra to his family, he asked that Ry be allowed to visit without them being present. Robin and Sandra denied Thomas's request, prompting him to file an action asserting he was the father of Ry and requesting visitation rights.

In the trial court decision, the judge noted the AID statutes in California and New York did not apply in this case to cut off a sperm donor's parental rights. Citing the earlier California case of *Jhordan C.* v. *Mary K.*,[29] the court stated the California AID statute required the sperm donor to provide the sperm to a physician in order for the statute to apply. The trial court did not apply the New York AID statute either because its provisions only referred to insemination of a married woman. Thomas argued the New York parentage statute was the applicable statute in this case. Under the parentage statute the court 'must' enter a finding of parentage if there is clear and convincing evidence that a man was the biological father of the child. Instead of entering the parentage order, however, the trial court applied the common law doctrine of equitable estoppel to prevent Thomas from asserting parentage rights. This doctrine prevents a party from asserting his or her legal rights if that party's prior conduct induces another person to rely on that conduct to his or her detriment, or if a party does not promptly assert his or her rights, and, because of the passage of time, it would be inequitable to permit the party to assert the rights. The court applied the equitable estoppel doctrine because Thomas agreed with Robin that he would not act as a parent to Ry and did not have any interaction with her for the first three years of her life.

Thomas appealed the trial court decision, and the appellate court reversed, instructing the trial court to issue an order finding Thomas the legal parent of Ry. The appellate court interpreted the parentage statute as requiring the trial court to issue the parentage order once blood tests proved Thomas was the father. But in an interesting twist of the facts, the appellate court applied equitable estoppel to Robin, characterizing her as the person who initiated the contact between Thomas and Ry and consequently, she could not now deny Thomas's right to the legal recognition of his relationship to Ry. Concerning the agreement between Robin and Thomas, the court held the oral agreement between Robin and Thomas was

29 224 Cal. Rptr. 530 (Ct. App. 1986).

unenforceable and against public policy.[30] The court also found that denying Thomas his right to a parentage determination would violate his constitutional due process rights.[31]

The third case decided in 1994, *Leckie & Voorhies,*[32] stands apart from the two previous cases for several reasons. First of all, it was the first case that ruled against the sperm donor's attempt to assert parental status. Second, it involved a court that had issued a decision in one of the earlier cases, the Oregon Court of Appeals. Third, and perhaps most importantly, the case involved a written agreement, one in which the sperm donor clearly acknowledged he understood he would have no parental rights with the child.

According to the facts in this case, a detailed agreement was signed by the sperm donor, Michael, the recipient of the sperm, Janet, and Janet's female partner. The agreement expressly waived the parties' rights to bring an action to establish the sperm donor as a legal parent and prohibited Michael from referring to himself as the child's father. However, the agreement also allowed Michael visitation with the child, allowed him to identify himself as a sperm donor with limited visitation rights and the agreement contained a statement that Janet and her partner 'are happy to include the donor in their lives, not as a father, but as a good male role model for their children.'[33] Pursuant to this agreement, when the child conceived by donor insemination was born, Michael exercised visitation with the child for the first three and one-half years of the child's life. For sixteen months during this time, Janet and the child actually lived in a house Michael owned, which was located on land adjacent to Michael's home. The child referred to Michael as 'Dad' without Janet objecting. When Michael attempted to be more involved in the child's life than was acceptable to Janet, however, Michael and Janet participated in mediation to resolve their dispute. The mediation resulted in Michael and Janet re-affirming their original written agreement and signing it a second time, with an additional provision that Michael could have six hours of visitation per month. Six months later Michael filed a petition to establish parentage, requesting court-ordered visitation, claiming that the parties' conduct implicitly modified their agreement, vitiating his waiver to bring a parentage action.

The trial court dismissed Michael's petition and the Oregon Court of Appeals affirmed the trial court. The appellate court found no facts supporting Michael's

30 Both the majority and dissenting opinions determined that an agreement, between biological parents in which one parent agrees to surrender legal parentage, is unenforceable under New York law.

31 Robin appealed the appellate court's decision. The appeal was abandoned, however, when Thomas withdrew his petition to establish legal parentage in spring of 1995. See N. Polikoff, 'The Social Construction of Parenthood in One Planned Lesbian Family', 1996 *N.Y.U. Rev. L. & Soc. Change* 203.

32 *Leckie & Voorhies*, 875 P.2d 521 (Or. App. 1994).

33 *Ibid.*, p. 522.

claim the parties' behavior vitiated his waiver, particularly since both parties reaffirmed the waiver in writing only six months earlier. The appellate court also stated Michael did not have a constitutional claim of a denial of due process, as did the sperm donor, Kevin McIntyre, in the earlier Oregon case.[34] The earlier case involved the constitutionality of the AID statute that stated the donor 'shall have no right, obligation or interest with respect to the child' when applied to the donor's assertion he and the mother had an agreement he could be the legal parent of the child if he donated his sperm. In this later case, the mother was not relying on the AID statute, but rather she argued the donor waived his right to assert parental rights in the written agreement. Because the donor was unable to present evidence that the parties' agreement had been altered by their conduct, the court enforced the terms of their written agreement.

In 2002, there were two cases that dealt with the legal status of known sperm donors. *Lamaritata v. Lucus*,[35] a Florida case, involved a written agreement that the donor would have no parental rights and obligations and both parties were 'foreclosed from establishing those rights and obligations by the institution of an action to determine the paternity of any such child or children.'[36] In addition, the Florida statute stated the 'donor of any egg, sperm, or preembryo, other than the commissioning couple or father who has executed a preplanned adoption agreement under s. 63.212, shall relinquish all maternal or paternal rights and obligations with respect to the donation or the resulting children.'[37] The court found the statute, which did not define 'sperm donor', applied to Mr. Lucas, who brought a paternity suit. The court made this determination by looking to the terms of the parties' agreement, which referred to Mr. Lucas as a 'donor.' The court also found the mother, Ms. Lamaritata, and Mr. Lucas were not a 'commissioning couple,' as defined in the statute. The parties 'joined forces solely for the purpose of artificially inseminating Ms. Lamaritata, an intent clearly set forth in the parties' contract.'[38] Based on the language of the Florida statute and the terms of the parties' agreement, the district court of appeals found the sperm donor was a 'non-parent.'[39]

The second case, *Tripp* v. *Hinckley*,[40] involved a lesbian couple and gay couple in New York. At the time of the insemination the sperm donor and the mother

---

34 *McIntyre* v. *Crouch*, 780 P.2d 239, 83 ALR 4th 277 (Or. App. 1989), *rev. denied* 784 P.2d 1110 (Or. 1989), *cert. denied* 495 US 905 (1990).

35 823 So.2d 316 (Fla. Dist. Ct. App. 2002).

36 *Ibid.*, p. 318.

37 FLA. STAT. § 742.14 (1997).

38 *Lamaritata*, 823 So.2d at 319.

39 This case was litigated a number of times because the parties entered into a visitation agreement. Ultimately the Florida District Court of Appeal held that since the sperm donor was a non-parent, the visitation order was unenforceable because, under Florida law, non-parents are not entitled to visitation rights. See *Lamaritata* v. *Lucas*, 827 So.2d 1049 (Fla. Dist. Ct. App. 2002).

40 *Tripp* v. *Hinckley*, 736 N.Y.S.2d 506 (App. Div. 2002).

agreed the lesbian couple would be the custodial parents of any child conceived and the sperm donor and his partner would have regular contact with the child. Two children were born, one in 1994 and another in 1996, using Mr. Tripp's sperm. After the birth of both children, Mr. Tripp signed acknowledgements of paternity, which authorized him to be named as the father on the children's birth certificates. The parties also entered into a visitation agreement. Mr. Tripp later filed an action for more visitation time when the lesbian couple ended their relationship.

The mother, Ms. Hinckley, objected to the increased visitation, alleging Mr. Tripp was merely a sperm donor who should be restricted to the terms of the visitation agreement. The court found, however, the case involved undisputed paternity, which creates a legal parent status. In addition, the court relied on the evidence of Mr. Tripp's 'regular contacts with the children since their births, as well as [Ms. Hinckley's] own testimony that the children view [Mr. Tripp] as their father and love him.'[41] The court also noted that visitation agreements were not binding and were enforced only if they were found to be in the children's best interests. Finally, the court did not accept Ms. Hinckley's assertions that Mr. Tripp waived his right to increased visitation and he was estopped from asserting this right. The circumstances of this case supported Mr. Tripp because he had been exercising his visitation rights pursuant to the parties' agreement. Consequently, this case did not deviate from the result of the earlier New York decision involving parental rights of a known sperm donor when the recipient was an unmarried woman, Thomas S. v. Robin Y.,[42] which the court cited in its opinion.

There were three more known sperm donor cases decided in 2005 and another one in 2006. Interestingly, two of these cases were decided by different panels of the Texas Court of Appeals, with each panel reaching the opposite conclusion on whether a sperm donor had standing to bring a parentage action under Texas law. In the first case, In re Sullivan,[43] the parties entered into a 'Co-Parenting Agreement' drafted by the sperm donor's attorney. The agreement explicitly stated both parties intended to be the parents of the child and the parties agreed 'that any child born as a result of the donor insemination procedure will be the child of BRIAN KEITH RUSSELL as if he and SHARON SULLIVAN were married at the time of the conception, and that BRIAN KEITH RUSSELL will be named as the father on the child's birth certificate.'[44]

Prior to the child's birth, however, the parties had a disagreement and when the child was born, Mr. Russell filed an action entitled 'Original Petition to Adjudicate Parentage, Suit Affecting the Parent-Child Relationship and Breach of Contract.'[45] Ms. Sullivan responded by asserting that Mr. Russell lacked standing

41 *Ibid.*, p. 508.

42 *Thomas S.* v. *Robin Y.*, 618 N.Y.S.2d 356 (App. Div. 1994), *rev'g* 599 N.Y.S.2d 377 (Fam. Ct. 1993).

43 157 S.W.3d 911(Tex. App. Ct. 2005).

44 *Ibid.*, p. 913.

45 *Ibid.*

to bring a parentage action because, under the Texas statute, he was a sperm donor without any parental rights. According to the Texas statutes relied upon by Ms. Sullivan, 'a donor is not a parent of a child conceived by means of assisted reproduction'[46] and a donor is defined as 'an individual who produces eggs or sperm used for assisted reproduction,' excluding 'a husband who provides sperm or a wife who provides eggs to be used for assisted reproduction (...).'[47] Mr. Russell, however, claimed the parentage act provided him with standing because it provided that 'a man whose parentage of the child is to be adjudicated'[48] could file a parentage action.

The Houston appellate court determined that because this section of the parentage act did not specifically exclude a male donor, particularly when other provisions of the Texas Family Code did exclude a male donor from being an 'alleged father,' then the intent was to allow the sperm donor standing to have his parentage adjudicated. The court specifically held, however, it was not deciding whether Mr. Russell was, in fact, a mere 'donor' under the parentage statute. It was deciding only whether the lower court had the jurisdiction to determine that issue, based on Mr. Russell having standing to raise the issue of his status. Consequently, the case was remanded to the trial court to determine the applicability of the sperm donor statute and the co-parenting agreement.

In the second Texas case, *In re H.C.S.*,[49] the San Antonio court of appeals panel decided a sperm donor did not have standing to bring a parentage action. The H.C.S. case involved a brother of one of the partners in a lesbian couple who donated his sperm so that his sister's partner could have a child. The donor, J.S., asserted he and the mother orally agreed he would be more than a mere donor and he would be involved in the child's life. The mother, K.D., disputed this fact, denying the parties made this agreement. When his sister and K.D. ended their relationship, J.S. filed a parentage action, alleging K.D. was denying visitation after having allowed visitation previously.

In ruling that J.S. lacked standing to bring the parentage action, the appellate court specifically rejected the holding in the *Sullivan* case:

> 'While we acknowledge the scholarly research reflected in the *Sullivan* opinion, we respectfully disagree with the court's conclusion that status as a donor is irrelevant to the question of standing to establish parentage. We likewise do not agree that donor status is more appropriately addressed at the merits stage of the litigation. To the contrary, based on the plain language of the Family Code (...) we conclude that J.S., as an unmarried man who provided sperm used for assisted reproduction and who did not

46 Tex. Fam. Code Ann. § 160.702 (Vernon Supp. 2004).
47 Tex. Fam. Code Ann. § 160.102(6) (Vernon Supp. 2004).
48 Tex. Fam. Code Ann. § 160.602 (Vernon Supp. 2004).
49 219 S.W.3d 33 (Tex. App. Ct. 2006).

> sign an acknowledgement of paternity, does not have standing to pursue a suit to determine paternity of the child born through the assisted reproduction.'[50]

The San Antonio appellate court then looked at the provisions of the Texas statutes affecting the parent-child relationship, which excluded a male donor from the definition of an 'alleged father'[51] thereby disqualifying J.S., under the parentage act, from being 'a man whose parentage is to be adjudicated.'[52]

The remaining two cases in 2005 came out of California. In the first case, *Steven S. v. Deborah D.*,[53] Steven, a married man, donated his sperm so Deborah, a single woman, could be artificially inseminated. The initial attempts at insemination, which were done through Steven providing sperm to a physician to inseminate Deborah, resulted in a miscarriage. Following the miscarriage, Steven and Deborah had a sexual relationship for several months. When the sexual relationship ended, Deborah and Steven returned to the physician to attempt another insemination, using the sperm Steven had originally provided to the physician. Trevor was born nine months later. After three years, during which time Steven developed a relationship with Trevor, who referred to Steven as 'Daddy Steve,' Steven filed a parentage action.

The first issue in contention at the trial court level was whether Trevor was conceived through insemination or sexual intercourse. The trial court found Trevor was conceived through the last insemination procedure. Deborah alleged Steven was not entitled to parental rights, relying on the California sperm donor statute, which stated the 'donor of semen provided to a licensed physician and surgeon for use in artificial insemination of a woman other than the donor's wife is treated in law as if he were not the natural father of a child thereby conceived.'[54] The trial court found that this statute, however 'did not preclude a finding of paternity because of the doctrine of estoppel prevents [Deborah] from denying [Steven] his rights as a biological father. [Deborah's] conduct clearly reflects that [she] intended [Steven] to be Trevor's father and to be a part of Trevor's life. It is also clear that [Steven] relied on [Deborah's] conduct to form his expectations of ongoing contact and visitation.'[55]

In reversing the trial court, the appellate court distinguished its earlier case of *Jhordan C.* v. *Mary K.*,[56] in which the appellate court found the sperm donor statute did not apply, because no physician was involved in the insemination. In the Steven S. case the appellate court held that, because the couple used a physician to

---

50 *Ibid.*, pp. 35–36.
51 Tex. Fam. Code Ann. § 101.0015(a) & (b) (Vernon 2002).
52 Tex.Fam. Code Ann. § 160.602(a)(3) (Vernon 2002).
53 *Steven S.* v. *Deborah D.*, 25 Cal. Rptr. 482 (Cal. App. Ct. 2005).
54 Cal. Fam. Code § 7613(b) (2004).
55 *Steven S.*, 25 Cal. Rpt.3d p. 485.
56 224 Cal. Rptr. 530 (Ct. App. 1986).

inseminate Deborah, the statutory language directly applied. Steven urged the appellate court to carve out an exception to the statute in a situation in which the parties had an intimate relationship and attempted to conceive a child by sexual intercourse. He based his argument on the public policy of California to favor paternity and the best interest of the child. The appellate court, however, found it was a legislative function to determine public policy and, in this case, the plain meaning of the statute prevented the court from reading an exception into the language of the statute. In addition, the appellate court rejected the estoppel argument, noting the legal theory had not been presented or argued at trial.

The second California case is unique in that it involved the donation of a woman's ova (eggs) rather than sperm. In *K.M.* v. *E.G.*,[57] two women, who had been in a lesbian relationship, were involved in litigation over the parentage of twins born to E.G. from ova donated by K.M. The parties disagreed about their intentions when K.M. donated her ova to E.G., who was having difficulty conceiving a child through anonymous insemination and in vitro fertilization (IVF). The doctor treating E.G. for fertility suggested that E.G. use K.M.'s ova for the next IVF procedure. The couple agreed to use K.M.'s ova, but at trial E.G. stated the agreement terms were that E.G. would be a single parent, whereas K.M. stated she agreed to provide her ova because the parties intended for both women to raise any child born to E.G.

There also was disagreement about the facts surrounding K.M. signing a document provided by the medical center entitled 'Consent Form for Ovum Donor (Known)'. The document stated K.M. waived any right and relinquished any claim to the donated ova. In addition it stated K.M. agreed not to attempt to discover the identity of the person who was receiving her ova. K.M. stated she thought parts of the form were 'odd' and did not apply, particularly the clause about not attempting to discover the identity of the recipient of her ova. She testified she did not intend to relinquish her parental rights and she thought she would be the parent of the child or children born from her ova.

When the twins were born, E.G. referred to K.M.'s parents as the children's grandparents and K.M's siblings as the children's aunt and uncle. When the children attended school, the school forms listed both women as the parents of the twins. The children's nanny also testified that both women were the twins' parents. E.G. and K.M. ended their relationship in 2001 and K.M. filed a parentage action shortly thereafter. Although the lower courts ruled in favor of E.G., the California Supreme Court reversed, finding K.M. was a parent, together with E.G.

The California Supreme Court rejected the argument that the sperm donor statute should apply to cases in which a woman 'supplied ova to impregnate her lesbian partner in order to produce children who would be raised in their joint

57 33 Cal. Rptr.3d 61 (2005).

home.'[58] The court distinguished the Steven S.[59] case, stating 'the semen donor in that case did not live with the impregnated woman, so the court did not address whether the statute would apply if the child was raised in the semen donor's home.'[60] Because the court found the sperm donor statute did not apply to the facts in the E.G. case, K.M.'s genetic connection to the children was sufficient to establish a mother and child relationship under the California version of the Uniform Parentage Act. In addition, the court found that K.M. could not waive her parentage rights by signing the Consent Form, analogizing it to attempts by parents to limit or abrogate their obligation to support their children. According to the court, K.M. 'cannot waive her responsibility to support [her] child. Nor can such a purported waiver effectively cause [K.M.] to relinquish her parental rights.'[61]

5. SYNTHESIZING THE CASE LAW INVOLVING KNOWN SPERM DONORS PRIOR TO THE K.M.H. LITIGATION

At first glance it may appear difficult to synthesize the cases that were decided prior to the appeal in the *K.M.H.* case because of the differences in facts and the statutory language. Some common threads, however, can be discerned in these cases. It appears in the earlier cases the courts were strongly inclined to allow a known sperm donor to assert parentage rights against the wishes of an 'unmarried' woman. When a state had no statutes dealing with sperm donation, as in the 1977 *C.M.*[62] case in New Jersey, the court allowed the parentage action because it was in a child's best interest to have two parents whenever possible. Sperm donors also were allowed to assert parentage rights, even when the sperm donor statute directly applied to unmarried women, if the parties deviated from the method of insemination contemplated in the statute, as in the 1983 *Jhordan C.*[63] case in California.[64] Because the couple did not use a physician to accomplish the insemination, the court found the statute cutting off the parentage rights of a sperm donor did not apply. Even when a physician performed the insemination, as in the 1989 *C.R.*[65] case in Colorado, the court found the statute was 'ambiguous' when applied

58 *K.M.*, 33 Cal. Rptr. 3d p. 71.
59 25 Cal. Rptr. 482 (Cal. App. Ct. 2005).
60 *Ibid.*, p. 70, n. 5.
61 *K.M.*, 33 Cal. Rptr. 3d p. 72.
62 377 A.2d 821(N.J. Juv. & Dom. Rel. Ct. 1977).
63 224 Cal. Rptr. 530 (Ct. App. 1986).
64 But see *Steven S.* v. *Deborah D.*, 25 Cal. Rptr. 482 (Cal. App. Ct. 2005), which found that when a physician does perform the insemination, the statute applies, even if the couple had a previous sexual relationship and the sperm donor had exercised visitation for a period of years.
65 775 P.2d 27 (Colo. 1989).

to a known sperm donor. The next case, the 1989 *McIntyre*[66] case in Oregon, rejected the distinctions drawn in these prior cases, finding the physician insemination was not essential and the statute was not ambiguous if the donor was known to the mother. Nonetheless, the court found that applying the statute to a sperm donor, who alleged he donated his sperm based on an oral agreement with the mother that he would be the father, would violate the sperm donor's constitutional due process rights.

Even in cases in which lesbian couples were trying to create their own families, the courts found a known sperm donor could assert parental rights. Thus, in the 1994 *C.O.*[67] case in Ohio, the court held the sperm donor statute did not apply to a known sperm donor, and even if the statute did apply, a sperm donor, who asserted he had an agreement with the mother to act as a parent, had a due process right to a parentage determination. In the second case involving a lesbian couple attempting to form a family, the 1994 New York case of *Thomas S.*,[68] the court also found the sperm donor statute inapplicable to cut off the parental rights of the sperm donor because the New York statute only applied to married women. Even in the face of both parties testifying they agreed at the time of insemination the sperm donor would have no parental rights, the court found the agreement unenforceable 'for failure to comply with explicit statutory requirements for surrender of parental rights.'[69] The court noted the termination of Thomas's parentage rights without strict adherence to the parentage statutes would be 'in violation of well established standards of due process and cannot stand.'[70]

In all of these earlier cases, the sperm donor was successful in obtaining parentage rights. These cases share the facts that, at the time of the insemination, none of the parties entered into a written agreement, the parties appeared unaware of the existence of a sperm donor statute, there were no allegations that the parties consulted an attorney and, except for the last case of *Thomas S.*,[71] the sperm donor and mother disagreed over whether the parties intended for the sperm donor to be a parent.

A noticeable shift occurs, however, when the evidence involves a written agreement at the time of the insemination,[72] coupled with the courts becoming

66 780 P.2d 239, 83 ALR 4th 277 (Or. App. 1989), *rev. denied* 784 P.2d 1110 (Or. 1989), *cert. denied* 495 US 905 (1990).

67 64 Ohio Misc. 2d 9, 639 N.E.2d 523 (1994).

68 *Thomas S.* v. *Robin Y.*, 618 N.Y.S.2d 356 (App. Div. 1994), *rev'g* 599 N.Y.S.2d 377 (Fam. Ct. 1993).

69 *Ibid.*, p. 361.

70 *Ibid.*

71 *Ibid.*, p. 359.

72 Two cases involving written agreements deserve mention. *Myers* v. *Moschella*, 677 N.E.2d 1243 (Ohio App. 1996) and *LaChapelle* v. *Mitten*, 607 N.W.2d 151 (Minn. Ct. App. 2000). In both cases the agreements granted visitation rights to the sperm donors, although the agreements specifically stated the sperm donors did not have parental rights. The mothers attempted to cut

aware of the widespread use of known sperm donors by 'unmarried' women, who wanted to become mothers. The first case involving a written agreement was the 1994 *Leckie*[73] case in Oregon, where the sperm donor signed an agreement, not only at the time of insemination, but also re-affirmed it six months prior to bringing a parentage action. The agreement stated '[e]ach party relinquishes and releases any and all rights he or she may have to bring suit to establish paternity.'[74] When the sperm donor brought a paternity action, the court found he was barred from doing so by his relinquishment of that right in the agreement. In addition, the sperm donor was unable to show that the parties conduct after the child's birth vitiated his waiver of parental rights. The court did not find, as courts in other states had found, that the sperm donor's visitation with the child equitably estopped the mother from arguing that the sperm donor does not have parental rights,[75] nor did it hold that an agreement relinquishing parental rights violated public policy.[76] In addition, the Oregon court held that its prior decision in *McIntyre* did not apply to the *Leckie* case because the mother in *Leckie* was not relying on the sperm donor statute and the written agreement prevented the sperm donor from asserting the due process violations mentioned in the *McIntyre*[77] case.

In the 2002 *Lamaritata*[78] case from Florida, the court enforced the parties' written contract, which stated the sperm donor agreed he would have no parental rights and both parties were foreclosed from bringing a parentage action. In addition, the court applied the language of the state's sperm donor statute, which provided a sperm donor relinquished all rights and obligations towards any children resulting from the donation.

In the 2002 New York case of *Tripp* v. *Hinckley*,[79] in which the court allowed the sperm donor to assert parental rights, the parties did not have a written agreement at the time of insemination. The mother, however, had signed acknowledgements of paternity, which allowed the sperm donor to be named as the father on the children's birth certificates. Signing the acknowledgements of paternity created a legal parent-child relationship with the sperm donor and two children, preventing the mother from later claiming Mr. Tripp was merely a 'sperm donor'

off the sperm donor's visitation, prompting the sperm donors to file parentage actions in order to secure their visitation rights. The issues on appeal in these cases did not involve the validity of the written agreements nor were the mothers appealing the lower courts' orders granting parentage rights to the sperm donors.

73 875 P.2d 521 (Or. App. 1994).

74 *Ibid.*, p. 522.

75 See *Thomas S.* v. *Robin Y.*, 618 N.Y.S.2d 356, 361 (App. Div. 1994), *rev'g* 599 N.Y.S.2d 377 (Fam. Ct. 1993).

76 See *K.M.* v. *E.G.*, 33 Cal. Rptr.3d 61 (2005).

77 780 P.2d 239, 83 ALR 4th 277 (Or. App. 1989), *rev. denied* 784 P.2d 1110 (Or. 1989), *cert. denied* 495 US 905 (1990).

78 823 So.2d 316 (Fla. Dist. Ct. App. 2002).

79 736 N.Y.S.2d 506 (App. Div. 2002).

and should be held to the terms of the parties 'visitation agreement' signed after the birth of the second child.

The first of the two Texas cases also involved a written agreement but, unlike the prior written agreement that cut off the sperm donor's parental rights, this agreement preserved his rights, stating he was to be treated as if he were married to the mother.[80] Although the mother asserted the Texas sperm donor statutes cut off the sperm donor's standing to file a parentage action, the Texas appellate court disagreed, granting the sperm donor standing, and advised the mother to raise the applicability of the sperm donor statutes within the context of that litigation. The second Texas case,[81] however, departs from the earlier cases involving oral agreements. As in the prior cases, the parties disputed whether they orally agreed, at the time of the insemination, that the sperm donor would be involved in the child's life. In addition, the mother allowed visitation with the child, which, in previous cases, could have estopped her from trying to prevent the sperm donor from asserting parental rights. Instead of following the path of the earlier cases involving oral agreements, the second Texas court held that the sperm donor statutes denied the sperm donor standing to bring a parentage action.[82]

The cases come full circle in the California case of *Steven S.*[83] Although the parties did not have any written agreement concerning the sperm donation, they followed the provisions of the California sperm donor statute by providing the sperm to a physician, for the purposes of the inseminating 'a woman other than the donor's wife.'[84] This case came nineteen years after the first California appellate court ruled in *Jhordan C.*[85] that the sperm donor statute did not apply if the parties did not use a physician for the insemination. In *Steven S.* the court not only found the statute directly applied to the parties, but did so even though the parties tried unsuccessfully to have children through sexual intercourse and the sperm donor exercised visitation with the child.[86]

Consequently, it appeared that in the more recent decisions, the courts were beginning to apply the sperm donor statutes to deny sperm donors parental rights if the facts, at the time of the insemination, matched the clear language of the statutes. In addition, when the parties executed a written agreement at the time of insemination, particularly an agreement that cut off the sperm donor rights, the

80 *In re Sullivan*, 157 S.W.3d 911(Tex. App. Ct. 2005).

81 *In re H.C.S.*, 219 S.W.3d 33 (Tex. App. Ct. 2006).

82 *Ibid.*, p. 36.

83 25 Cal. Rptr. 482 (Cal. App. Ct. 2005).

84 Cal. Fam. Code § 7613(b) (2004).

85 224 Cal. Rptr. 530 (Ct. App. 1986).

86 The final California case, *K.M.* v. *E.G.*, 33 Cal. Rptr.3d 61 (2005), which granted parental rights to an ova donor, is consistent with the other two California cases because the sperm donor statutory language did not apply to ova donations, the children had been raised over a period of years by the ova donor and the gestational mother, and the court found, in the absence of an applicable statute, the parties could not contractually waive their parental rights.

courts were willing to follow the parties intention at the time of the signing of the agreement. It also is worth noting that, in 1994, the year in which the first appellate court enforced a written agreement against a sperm donor who attempted to assert parental rights in contradiction to that agreement, the Kansas legislature adopted its present sperm donor statute.[87] This statute incorporates the requirement of a written agreement, but the agreement is one that acknowledges the parental rights of the sperm donor. The statute states: 'The donor of semen provided to a licensed physician for use in artificial insemination of a woman other than the donor's wife is treated in law as if he were not the birth father of a child thereby conceived, unless agreed to in writing by the donor and the woman.'[88] This was the legal landscape at the time of the Kansas *K.M.H.*[89]case.

6. THE KANSAS CASE: K.M.H.

6.1. FACTS AND PROCEDURAL HISTORY

The *K.M.H.* case involved S.H., an unmarried woman who was an attorney. She was friends with D.H., an unmarried man, who agreed he would provide S.H. with his sperm. The parties did not have a written agreement, at the time of the donation and insemination, addressing the expectation of the parties concerning D.H.'s parental rights. D.H. alleged the parties had an oral agreement that they would co-parent any children born from the insemination. S.H. denied there was a co-parenting agreement, arguing she intended to raise any children born from D.H.'s sperm as a single mother. It was undisputed, however, that the parties' agreement for S.H. to be inseminated with D.H.'s sperm was entered into in Kansas.

S.H. underwent two attempts at insemination, both of which were done by a physician in the state of Missouri. D.H. accompanied S.H. to Missouri for the first insemination attempt, where he provided his semen to medical personnel at the clinic. When this insemination attempt was unsuccessful, S.H. underwent a second insemination in Missouri. This time, however, D.H. did not accompany S.H. to Missouri, but instead he gave his semen to S.H. in a plastic container in Kansas and S.H. delivered the semen to the Missouri doctor for the insemination procedure. S.H. became pregnant and delivered twins, in Kansas, on May 18, 2005. The next day S.H. filed a Child In Need of Care (CINC) petition in the local Kansas district court. According to the facts in the Kansas Supreme Court's majority opinion, written by Justice Carol Beier, the 'petition identified D.H. as "[t]he minor children's father" and alleged that the twins were in need of care "as it relates to the father" and that "the [f]ather should be found unfit and his rights

87 Kan. Stat. Ann. § 38-1114(f) (2000).
88 *Ibid.*
89 169 P.3d 1025 (Kan. 2007).

terminated." The petition continued to refer to D.H. throughout as the twins' father.'[90]

On May 31, 2005, D.H. filed an answer to the *CINC petition*, and, in addition filed a parentage action in which he acknowledged his financial responsibility for the children and requested joint legal custody and visitation with the children. S.H. filed amended CINC petitions, for the first time asserting the sperm donor statute barred D.H.'s claim as a parent. The *CINC* case and the parentage action were consolidated and S.H. filed a motion to dismiss the parentage action, based on the Kansas sperm donor statute.

The trial judge requested the parties brief the issues concerning choice of law and the constitutionality of the sperm donor statute. According to S.H., Kansas law applied to the parties' dispute and the sperm donor statute was constitutional, thereby cutting off D.H. from asserting parental rights in the absence of a written agreement otherwise. D.H. argued that Missouri law applied, but if Kansas law did apply, then the sperm donor statute was unconstitutional, both on its face and as applied to the facts in the case. He also asserted that, because S.H. referred to him as the children's 'father' in the *CINC* petition, this was written evidence of the parties' intent that he not be a mere sperm donor, but a parent. The trial court ruled against D.H. on all points and granted S.H.'s motion to dismiss, finding that, as a matter of law, D.H. had no legal rights or responsibilities for the twins born to S.H.

6.2. ISSUES ON APPEAL

D.H. raised six issues on appeal to the Kansas Supreme Court:

> '(1) Did the district court err in ruling that Kansas law would govern? (2) Did the district court judge err in holding K.S.A. 38-1114(f) constitutional under the Equal Protection and Due Process Clauses of the Kansas and federal Constitutions? (3) Did the district judge err in interpreting and applying the 'provided to a licensed physician' language of K.S.A. 38-1114(f)? (4) Did the district judge err in determining that the CINC petition did not satisfy the requirement of a writing in K.S.A. 38-1114(f)? (5) Did K.S.A. 38-1114(a) grant D.H. parental rights and (6) Does equity demand reversal of the district court?'[91]

[90] *Ibid.*, p. 1029.

[91] *Ibid.*, pp. 1030-31.

6.3. STANDING AND STANDARD OF REVIEW

The *K.M.H.* opinion began with the statement that D.H.'s 'standing is not in serious doubt.'[92] According to the appellate court, because the district court considered more than the parties' pleading, the trial court's decision to dismiss the case should be viewed as a summary judgment. Consequently, on appeal the evidence must be viewed in the light most favorable to D.H., who objected to the case being dismissed. The court also noted the district court's judgment will only be affirmed 'if there is no genuine issue of material fact for trial and the case is appropriate for disposition in [S.H.'s] favor as a matter of law.'[93]

6.4. CHOICE OF LAW

D.H. argued that Missouri law should control in this case because Missouri was where the insemination took place. According to D.H.'s argument, because Missouri did not have a sperm donor statute that would apply to the facts in this case, he could assert parental rights to the children. The Kansas Supreme Court noted that the law in Kansas is the doctrine of *lex loci contractus*, which looks to the law of the state where the contract was made. In addition, Kansas judges tended to apply *lex fori*, the law of the forum, applying Kansas law unless there was a clear showing that another state's law applied. According to D.H., the last act in the contract formation was the insemination in the state of Missouri. The Kansas Supreme Court rejected D.H.'s argument because the facts overwhelmingly favored the application of Kansas law. The parties' agreement that D.H. would provide S.H. with sperm occurred in Kansas, D.H. provided his semen to S.H. in Kansas, the children were born in Kansas, and all the parties resided in Kansas. Based on the significant connections to Kansas, the Kansas Supreme Court determined that Kansas law applied.

6.5. CONSTITUTIONALITY OF K.S.A. §38-1114(F)

There are two ways to attack the constitutionality of a statute, either alleging the statute is invalid on its face or as it is applied to the particular facts in a case. In this case, D.H. challenged the constitutionality of the Kansas sperm donor statute as it applied to his situation, based on equal protection and due process grounds. In analyzing this claim, the court first set out the standard of review when a litigant has alleged that a statute is unconstitutional. Under this circumstance, a

92 *Ibid.*, p. 1031.
93 *Ibid.*

statute is presumed to be constitutional and all doubts must be resolved in favor of the statute's validity. In addition, a 'statute should not be stricken down unless the infringement of the superior law is clear beyond substantial doubt.'[94]

The Kansas Supreme Court then mapped the evolution of the Uniform Parentage Act and reviewed a number of the sperm donor cases from other jurisdictions. The opinion also discussed the enactment of the Kansas sperm donor statute, which was adopted from the 1973 Uniform Parentage Act. The Kansas legislature made two amendments to the Uniform Act, however. The original statute stated 'the donor of semen provided to a licensed physician for use in artificial insemination of a married woman'[95] would be treated in law as if he were not the father. The Kansas legislature removed the word 'married,' with the result that the statute applied to all women regardless of their marital status.

The second amendment was the addition of the language 'unless agreed to in writing by the donor and the woman.'[96] Although other states have a similar statutory requirement that the parties must have a written agreement in order for the sperm donor to obtain parental rights,[97] none of these states had determined their statute's constitutionality. Consequently, *K.M.H.* was the first case to address the issue of whether this requirement met constitutional muster.[98]

The court addressed D.H.'s equal protection challenge by noting that a denial of equal protection arises when similarly situated individuals are treated differently. According to D.H., he was being treated differently than S.H. because he could only obtain parental rights if S.H. agreed in writing to give them to him. The court stated, however, that based on the differences between a sperm donor's role, when compared to a woman who carries and gives birth to a child, 'we are skeptical that S.H. and D.H. are truly similarly situated.'[99] In addition, the court found there were legitimate legislative purposes for the difference in treatment. For example, the statute allowed both married and unmarried women to become parents without sexual intercourse, it protected donors from claims of child support and it protected women from donors asserting parental rights if there was no written agreement. The statute enhanced 'predictability, clarity, and enforceability' and it encouraged 'early resolution of the elemental question of whether a

94 *Ibid.*, p. 1033.

95 Unif. Parentage Act § 5(b), 9B *U.L.A.* 301.

96 Kan. Stat. Ann. § 38-1114(f) (2000).

97 See Ark. Code Ann. § 9-10-201 (2002); Fla. Stat. § 742.14 (2005); N.H. Rev. Stat. Ann § 168-B:3(I)(e) (2002); N.J. Stat. Ann. § 9:17-44(b) (2002); N.M. Stat. Ann. § 40-11-6(B) (2006).

98 Two amici briefs were filed in this case, both dealing with the constitutionality of the Kansas sperm donor statute. The first amicus curie brief was filed by the Washburn University School of Law Children and Family Law Center, with Linda Henry Elrod, Distinguished Professor of Law and Director of the Center, on the brief, arguing the sperm donor statute was unconstitutional. The other amicus curie was the Family Law Professors, with Timothy M. O'Brien on the brief, which took the position that the statue was constitutional.

99 *K.M.H.*, 169 P.3d, p. 1039.

donor will have parental rights.'[100] Therefore, the court found the statute did not violate equal protection.

As regards the due process challenge, the court noted D.H. failed to clarify whether he was making a procedural or substantive due process claim. It first dealt with the potential procedural due process challenge. The court disagreed with D.H.'s argument that the statutory requirement of a written agreement denied him 'a meaningful opportunity to be heard' on the issue of whether the parties had an oral agreement. Even assuming the parties did have an oral agreement to co-parent, the court found 'the statute merely sets up a burden of proof that [D.H.'s] own inaction before donating his sperm left him unable to meet.'[101]

Therefore, the court assumed D.H.'s claim that he has a fundamental right to the care, custody, and control of his children to be a substantive due process claim. In making that argument, D.H. focused on the United States Supreme Court case of *Lehr v. Robertson*.[102] The facts of the *Lehr* case, however, were not helpful to D.H. In that case, an unwed father, who had not developed a relationship with his child, did not realize that, in order to preserve his right to be notified of his child's adoption, he must register with the New York Putative Father Registry.

The *Lehr* court stated that a state would violate the due process rights of an unwed father, who demonstrated 'a full commitment to the responsibilities of parenthood,'[103] if a statute created an absolute bar from the father asserting his parental rights. Because the unwed father in the *Lehr* case had not developed a relationship with his child and because he could have protected his right to receive notice of the adoption if he had registered as a putative father, the Supreme Court did not find a violation of the unwed father's due process rights. The Court stated 'the mere existence of a biological link does not merit equivalent constitutional protection.'[104] In applying the *Lehr* case to D.H.'s situation, the Kansas Supreme Court noted that the sperm donor statute did not create an absolute bar to a biological parent from asserting parental rights, because the statute allowed a sperm donor to become a legal parent if he had a written agreement with the mother.

Next the court addressed D.H.'s argument that because the statute required the parties to have a written agreement to prevent him from being cut off as the legal father, this requirement transformed the otherwise constitutional statute into one that violated the due process rights of known donors such as him. The court stated that although it agreed

---

100 *Ibid.*

101 *Ibid.*, p. 1040. It appears, therefore, that D.H. lacks standing under this analysis, contradicting the court's earlier statement that D.H.'s standing was not in question. *Ibid.*, p. 1031. See also *In re* H.C.S., 219 S.W.3d 33 (Tex. App. Ct. 2006).

102 *Lehr*, 463 US 248 (1983).

103 *Ibid.*, p. 261.

104 *Ibid.*

> 'that one goal of the Kansas Parentage Act as a whole is to encourage fathers to voluntarily acknowledge paternity and child support obligations, the obvious impact of the plain language of this particular provision in the Act is to prevent the creation of parental status where it is not desired or expected. To a certain extent D.H. (...) evidently misunderstand[s] the statute's mechanism. It ensures no *attachment* of parental rights to sperm donors in the absence of a written agreement to the contrary. It does not *cut off* rights that have already arisen and attached.'[105]

Consequently, the court found the statute prevented the attachment of a known sperm donor's parental rights in the absence of an agreement, noting this statutory interpretation was in accord with the expectation of anonymous and unknown sperm donors. If a known sperm donor had a different expectation, the court pointed out the statute instructed him on how to become a father, by having a written agreement that stated that intention.

Although D.H. also argued the requirement of a written agreement allowed S.H. to be the 'sole arbiter' of whether he could become a legal father, the court pointed out that was the case only after the donation was made. Before the donation was made, however, 'a prospective donor has complete autonomy to refuse to facilitate an artificial insemination unless he gets an agreement in writing to his paternity terms. This is more than most fathers, wed or unwed to their children's mothers, can ever hope for.'[106] Consequently, the court held the requirement that the sperm donor and mother must have a written agreement in order for the sperm donor to become a legal father did not violate D.H.'s due process rights.

The court ended its analysis of the due process challenge by noting 'all that is constitutional is not necessarily wise.'[107] The court pointed out that children may benefit from having two parents, and those parents resources, available to them. In addition, other countries, such as Britain and The Netherlands, no longer have anonymous sperm donation, because children in these countries can obtain information about their biological fathers. The court stated it sympathized with AID children who want to know their biological fathers' identities. 'However, weighing of the interests of all involved in these procedures as well as the public policies that are furthered by favoring one or another in certain circumstances, is the charge of the Kansas Legislature, not of this court.'[108]

6.6. 'PROVIDED TO A LICENSED PHYSICIAN'

D.H.'s third argument was that the Kansas sperm donor statute required the semen to be provided *by the donor* to a licensed physician for use in artificial

105 *Ibid.*, p. 1041 (emphasis in original).
106 *Ibid.*
107 *Ibid.*
108 *Ibid.*, p. 1042.

insemination. According to D.H.'s interpretation of the statute, because S.H. provided the semen to the physician, the statute was not followed and consequently did not apply, similar to the California case of *Jhordan C.* The court rejected this argument using the 'plain meaning' rule. Only in the situation in which a statute was unclear and ambiguous would courts turn to rules of statutory construction or legislative intent. The court pointed out the Kansas statute stated '[t]he donor of semen provided to a licensed physician for use in artificial insemination', not 'the donor of semen to be provided *by the donor* to a licensed physician for use in artificial insemination.' Because D.H.'s interpretation of the statute would require that words be added to the statute, the court rejected D.H.'s interpretation and, instead, adopted the plain meaning of the statute. '[The statute] requires only that the donor's sperm be provided to the physician by an unspecified someone or something. The fact that S.H. was that someone here did not prevent application of the statute to this situation.'[109]

6.7. 'UNLESS AGREED TO IN WRITING'

D.H.'s fourth argument on appeal was that S.H.'s CINC pleadings, in which she referred to D.H. 56 times as the 'father' and D.H.'s parentage petition, in which he asserted his paternity, should be read together to form the written agreement required under K.S.A. §38-1114(f). The court rejected this argument, pointing out it was the *absence* of a parenting agreement which resulted in both pleadings. The court also mentioned S.H.'s use of a CINC petition to terminate D.H.'s parental rights was 'an odd procedural vehicle for effecting S.H.'s desire – a court order stating that D.H. never acquired any parental rights' but the court recognized this case was 'in uncharted waters.'[110]

6.8. PARENTAL RIGHTS UNDER K.S.A. §38-1114(A)(4)

D.H. also argued the general parentage act provisions should control in this case rather than the sperm donor statute. He relied on the language of K.S.A. §38-1114(a) (4) which states a man is presumed to be the father of a child if he notoriously or in writing recognizes paternity of the child. The Kansas Supreme Court rejected this argument, relying on the rule of statutory construction that a specific provision within a statute controls over a general provision. Because D.H. is a sperm donor, the specific sperm donor statutory provision applies to him, not the more general provision listing the presumptions of paternity.

109 *Ibid.* (emphasis in original).
110 *Ibid.*, p. 1043.

6.9. EQUITY

D.H.'s last argument on appeal was based on S.H.'s 'unclean hands' in this case. D.H. argued in his reply brief on appeal that S.H., a lawyer, told D.H. he did not need a lawyer or a written agreement that they would be co-parents of any children born of the insemination. He also asserted S.H.'s conduct violated her ethical duties as an attorney. The Kansas Supreme Court pointed out that D.H.'s equity claim was not raised in the lower court or in his opening appellate brief, and thus it was not preserved for appeal. In addition, the court stated it was prevented from dealing with this issue because D.H. did not have any evidence in the record to support his claims of S.H.'s deceit. In the lower court, D.H. only alleged he and S.H. had an oral agreement and he tried to provide support, not that S.H. deliberately deceived him. Although the court conceded there might be a case in the future in which a donor could prove deliberate concealment of the sperm donor statute, or fraudulent inducement not to obtain legal advice or not to enter into a written agreement, D.H. failed to allege and prove these facts. In the absence of these facts, D.H.'s ignorance of the sperm donor statute would not excuse him from its application. Consequently, based on the language of the Kansas sperm donor statute, D.H. was not a birth father and had no parental rights.

6.10. CONCURRING OPINION

Justice McFarland concurred in the court's decision. She noted the sperm donor statute was very specific in its language. She viewed the statute as allowing a woman to be a true 'single parent' regardless of whether she used sperm from an anonymous or a known donor. The statute 'appears to be aimed at protecting both parties from unwanted duties and/or obligations being imposed without their consent in the very limited factual situation to which it applies.'[111] Justice McFarland also noted, however, that she agreed with the majority 'that some factual situation might result in the statutory bar [against the donor becoming a legal parent] being held inapplicable under those specific facts.'[112]

6.11. DISSENTING OPINIONS

There were two dissents in the *K.M.H.* case, by Judge Caplinger and Judge Hill, both members of the Kansas Court of Appeals, who were appointed to sit with the Supreme Court on this case. These judges found the sperm donor statute was

111 *Ibid.*, p. 1045 (McFarland, C.J., concurring).
112 *Ibid.*, p. 1046 (McFarland, C.J., concurring).

unconstitutional as applied to D.H. because it violated his fundamental rights without due process of law.

Judge Caplinger objected to the majority's finding that due process was satisfied by the written agreement requirement and it was D.H.'s inaction in not getting a written agreement, before he donated his sperm, which resulted in him not having legal parentage. According to Judge Caplinger, '[t]herein lies the constitutional problem with the statute. Fundamental rights must be actively waived, rather than passively lost due to inaction.'[113] Judge Caplinger cited the United States Supreme Court, stating courts must 'indulge every reasonable presumption against waiver of constitutional rights',[114] requiring instead that a waiver must be 'an intentional relinquishment or abandonment of a known right or privilege.'[115] Because the Kansas sperm donor statute allowed a known donor to waive his fundamental right to parent through his 'inaction,' Judge Caplinger did not find the 'escape clause' of a written agreement saved the statute from violating due process.[116]

In addition, Judge Caplinger disagreed with the majority's position that 'ignorance of the law is no excuse.' In particular, she focused on the *Lehr* case by noting it involved the issue of whether the New York putative father registry protected a biological father's opportunity to form a relationship with his child. The United States Supreme Court found that the registry provided sufficient due process protections for a biological father in the context of an adoption, where an adoptive father 'was ready, willing and able to assume the responsibilities of parenthood'[117] and a previously absent biological father was attempting to block the adoption. In contrast, D.H. was not competing with a non-biological father figure after having failed to come forward. Instead he was attempting to participate, emotionally and financially, in raising his children. Because the record disclosed that D.H. was unaware of the sperm donor statute and its requirement that he enter into a written agreement with the mother in order to have rights as a legal parent, Judge Caplinger stated she 'would find the statute's requirement that a known sperm donor affirmatively take action to preserve his fundamental rights to parent constituted a violation of due process as applied to D.H.'[118]

Judge Caplinger also was not persuaded by the majority's position that the statutory requirement of a written agreement acknowledging the donor as a legal father enhanced predictability, clarity and enforceability. Although she acknowledged the Kansas sperm donor statute provided an efficient means to reject paternity claims, she pointed out it must, nonetheless, meet due process requirements. According to Judge Caplinger, in the case of a known sperm donor and an

113 *Ibid.*, (Caplinger, J., dissenting).
114 *Johnson* v. *Zerbst*, 304 US 458, p. 464 (1938).
115 *Ibid.*
116 *K.M.H.*, 169 P.3d, pp. 1047–1048 (Caplinger, J., dissenting).
117 *Ibid.*, p. 1049 (Caplinger, J., dissenting).
118 *Ibid.*, pp. 1049–1050 (Caplinger, J., dissenting).

unmarried woman, due process would require the sperm donor be given 'the opportunity for a hearing to establish his intent to be something other than a sperm "donor" – i.e. to establish his paternity and rights as a parent. Simply stated, I would find the statute's clarity does not justify its constitutional violation.'[119]

In addition, Judge Caplinger noted S.H.'s original CINC petitions could be perceived as supporting D.H.'s position that the parties had an agreement to co-parent the children. For example, S.H. filed the CINC petitions alleging D.H.'s parental rights should be terminated because, among other things, he failed to provide prenatal emotional and financial support, thereby implying S.H. expected D.H. to be more than a mere sperm donor. S.H. also did not mention the sperm donor statute at all in her original filings, which also could support D.H.'s version of the facts. It was over two weeks later, when S.H. filed amended CINC petitions, that she raised the sperm donor statute for the first time. Based on these facts, Judge Caplinger would remand the case to the district court for a hearing on the intention of the parties at the time D.H. donated his sperm. If the trial court were to find, on remand, the parties had an oral agreement that D.H. would co-parent the children, then Judge Caplinger would hold the sperm donor statute did not apply to D.H. and D.H. could proceed with his parentage action.

Judge Hill dissented in order to raise an additional concern he had with the Kansas sperm donor statute. Not only did he find the statute unconstitutional as applied to D.H., but he also objected to the statute because it cut off the ability of the court to determine the best interests of the children when a donor attempted to assert parental rights. 'None of the elaborate and meticulous safeguards our Kansas law afford parents and children in proceedings before our courts when confronted with questions of parentage have been extended to these children.'[120] Judge Hill believed the Kansas sperm donor statute fits the Ohio court's assessment of its sperm donor statute – when a donor and the mother have an oral agreement that the donor will be a legal parent, but the sperm donor statute absolutely extinguishes a father's efforts to assert his parental rights, the statute 'runs contrary to due process safeguards.'[121]

7. THE SIGNIFICANCE OF THE KNOWN SPERM DONOR CASES IN K.M.H.

One can readily recognize D.H.'s arguments in the *K.M.H.* case, based on the previous cases dealing with known sperm donors attempting to gain parental

119 *Ibid.*, p. 1050 (Caplinger, J., dissenting).

120 *Ibid.*, p. 1051 (Hill, J., dissenting) (emphasis in original).

121 *C.O.* v. *W.S.*, 64 Ohio Misc. 2d 9 p.12, 639 N.E.2d 523, p.524 (1994). (citing *Lehr* v. *Robertson*, 463 US 248 (1983).

rights when an unmarried woman was inseminated with their sperm. D.H. was asserting the statute should not apply to a known sperm donor, if the parties had an oral agreement at the time of insemination, that the sperm donor would be a parent to the children conceived from his sperm, similar to *C.M.*, *R.C.*, *McIntyre*, *C.O.* and *Steven S.* D.H. also was arguing the specific statutory requirements setting out how the semen was to be provided for insemination, by examining the language 'provided to a licensed physician' as was done in the *Jhordan C.*, *Thomas S.* and *Steven S.* cases. He also asserted constitutional questions that were raised in *R.C.*,[122] *McIntyre* and *C.O.* In addition, D.H. argued the general provisions of parentage statutes should be read to allow him to assert his parentage claim, similar to the sperm donors' arguments in the two Texas cases, *In re Sullivan* and *In re H.C.S.* Finally, D.H. argued equity and esptoppel, as was done in the *Thomas S.* and *Tripp* cases.

The problem, however, is the Kansas statute has one significant difference, setting it apart from the statutes in the previous cases. The Kansas statute states a sperm donor is not the birth father 'unless agreed to in writing by the donor and the woman.' This one clause significantly changes the nature of the arguments made in the prior cases, particularly those cases that found the sperm donor statutes did not apply to the parties because the parties had an oral agreement the sperm donor would be a legal parent. Because the Kansas statute requires a written agreement to that effect, it is difficult to argue that only an oral agreement is required.

The significance of D.H. relying on the presence of an oral agreement, however, is not fully understood until he alleges in his reply brief the facts surrounding the formation of the oral agreement. There D.H. asserted for the first time he relied on S.H. being an attorney, that she knew the law required him to have a written agreement to be considered the birth father and she entered into an oral agreement instead, because she 'knew that she could obtain the sperm and be safe from [D.H.] if he asserted claims.'[123] Even more specific was the affidavit D.H. unsuccessfully attempted to submit with his Motion for Re-Hearing, after the Kansas Supreme Court ruled against him. In this affidavit D.H. stated S.H. told him it was not necessary to consult an attorney about their co-parenting agreement, because S.H., herself, was an attorney, and oral contracts were binding in Kansas. It is only when one understands this context that D.H.'s insistence on the presence of an oral agreement between the parties becomes significant and the argument makes sense. For D.H., however, his assertion of these surrounding facts comes far too late. If he had asserted these facts and provided evidence to

---

122 Although the sperm donor, J.R., challenged the constitutionality of the Colorado sperm donor statute, the Colorado Supreme Court did not decide the case on that issue. See *In re R.C.*, 775 P.2d 27 (Colo. 1989).

123 Corrected Reply Brief of Appellant p. 3, *In re K.M.H.*, 169 P.3d 1025 (Kan. 2007).

support his allegations at the lower court level, it appears the majority opinion might have decided the case in his favor.[124]

8. KNOWN SPERM DONOR CASES DECIDED AFTER K.M.H.

After the decision in *K.M.H.*, two more cases have dealt with the issue of whether a known sperm donor is a legal parent.[125] The first case in Ohio, *In re R.A.S.*,[126] involved the mother, V.S., asking J.M., a person she knew through her employment, if he would donate sperm so she could have a child. V.S. alleged the parties had an oral agreement that J.M. would be considered a 'friend' or 'uncle' to the child. Before the child was born, however, J.M. changed his mind and told V.S. he wanted to be the child's father. Shortly after the child was born, J.M. filed a parentage action in the juvenile court. The juvenile court magistrate adjudicated J.M. as the natural father of R.A.S., based on paternity tests, and ordered a new birth certificate and birth record be issued, indicating J.M. was R.A.S.'s father. The parties were given 14 days to file written objections to the juvenile court's adjudication, but neither party filed any objections.

Some time later at a hearing on the issue of visitation, V.S. raised for the first time the Ohio sperm donor statute, alleging the statute precluded J.M. from being the child's natural parent. The magistrate ruled against the mother because she failed to present evidence of the method of insemination, noting the previous Ohio case of C.O. The magistrate also determined, based on the *C.O.* case, the sperm donor statute did not apply to a known sperm donor. This finding was affirmed by the juvenile court judge, who also noted the parties failed to comply with the statutory requirement that a physician perform the insemination. The appellate court not only agreed with the magistrate and the juvenile court judge, but, in addition, held the mother was foreclosed from raising the sperm donor

124 'There may be a case in the future in which a donor can prove that the existence of K.S.A. 38-1114(f) was concealed, or that he was fraudulently induced *not* to obtain independent legal advice or *not* to enter into a written agreement to ensure creation and preservation of his parental rights to a child conceived by artificial insemination. This is not such a case.' *K.M.H.*, 169 P.3d. p. 1044 (emphasis in original).

125 There was one other case that involved a known sperm donor, *Ferguson* v. *McKiernan*, 2007 WL 4555437 (Penn.). This case is distinguishable for the other known sperm donor cases, however, because Pennsylvania does not have a sperm donor statute, the case involved IVF rather than AID and the mother was married to another man at the time of the IVF procedure. The mother was seeking child support after five years of honoring the parties oral agreement that the sperm donor would not be treated as the legal father and he was released of any obligation of support.

126 2007 WL 4146828 (Ohio. App. 12 Dist.).

statute, in a hearing on visitation, after a final order granting parental rights to J.M. had become effective.

In adding this case to the synthesis of the previous cases involving known sperm donors, this decision is very similar to *Tripp* v. *Hinckley*.[127] In both cases, the parties had an oral agreement at the time of insemination that the donor would not be a legal parent. However, in both cases the mothers allowed, without timely objection, the filing of documents establishing the donor's status as a legal parent.

The second case decided after *K.M.H.* was *Browne* v. *D'Alleva*,[128] in the state of Connecticut. As in many of the previous cases, the donor agreed to provide sperm to the mother, but the parties later disagreed about the terms of the oral agreement they entered into prior to the insemination. The mother, Ms. D'Alleva, alleged she agreed with the donor, Mr. Browne, that she and her female partner would adopt any children born of the insemination and Mr. Browne and his male partner would have 'a role as secondary or "fun parents".'[129] Mr. Browne, however, claimed the parties agreed he would be a legal guardian and have 'a permanent and significant role' in the lives of any children born from his sperm. When the parties went to the health center where the insemination took place, Mr. Browne signed a standard form, stating he gave up 'all rights and claims' to any children born of his sperm.

When a child was born to Ms. D'Alleva, she signed an acknowledgement of paternity and Mr. Browne was listed as the child's father on the birth certificate. Mr. Browne later filed an action for custody and access to the child. Ms. D'Alleva responded with a motion to dismiss the action, based on the Connecticut sperm donor statute, asserting Mr. Browne lacked standing to bring the custody action. The sperm donor statute stated a 'donor of sperm used in AID, or any person claiming through him, shall not have any right or interest in any child born as a result of AID.'[130]

The Connecticut court relied on the *K.M.H.* court's analysis of several of the known sperm donor cases. Although the court noted these cases were not 'dispositive,'[131] it applied some of the rationale found in the various cases. First, the court pointed out the sperm donor statute was not clear and unambiguous, finding the language did not address known sperm donors and unmarried women, particularly because the statute was enacted in 1970 when 'it was not envisioned by our legislatures that the statute would apply to this unique fact situation.'[132] Thus the court held the statute only applied to married couples,

[127] 736 N.Y.S.2d 506 (App. Div. 2002).
[128] 2007 Conn. Super. LEXIS 3250.
[129] *Ibid.*, p. *2.
[130] Conn. Gen. Stat. §45a-775 (2004).
[131] *Browne* v. *D'Alleva*, 2007 Conn. Super. LEXIS 3250. p. *47.
[132] *Ibid.*

based on the intent of the legislature at the time of enactment. Second, the court noted that even if the statute were to cover a known sperm donor, it would violate the donor's due process rights if the effect of the statute was to cut off the donor's standing in a case in which he alleged he had an oral agreement with the mother to be a parent.

Based on these two rationales, the Connecticut case could be viewed as relying on the earlier known sperm donor cases, where the sperm donors were allowed to assert parentage rights when there was a dispute between the donor and the mother concerning the nature of the parties' oral agreement. However, the case has one more factor that is more compelling than the similarities with these earlier cases. In this case the mother signed an acknowledgement of paternity, naming Mr. Browne as the child's father. Under Connecticut law, a written acknowledgement of paternity 'has the same force and effect as a judgment of a court.'[133] It was this factor 'in particular'[134] that resulted in the court determining Mr. Browne, as a legal parent, had standing to apply for joint custody and visitation with the child. Consequently, similar to the facts in the *Tripp* and *R.A.S.* cases,[135] once a mother participated in the creation of documents that established the donor as a legal parent, all other facts become irrelevant, including the fact she was ignorant of the operation of the law and did not intend that result.

9. CONCLUSION

An examination of the known sperm donor cases reveals discernable trends in the US law, particularly among the most recently decided cases. In these cases, the courts applied the language of the sperm donor statutes if the statutory language was unambiguous and the legislature contemplated the possibility of a known sperm donor providing sperm to an unmarried woman. If the parties had an oral agreement that differed from the clear language of the sperm donor statute, the more recent court decisions have not allowed that agreement to override the application of the statute, unlike the earlier sperm donor cases. And, if the parties had a written agreement, the terms of which complemented the language of the sperm donor statute, courts have enforced the written agreement. Finally, although several recent cases appeared, at first blush, to have fallen back on the holdings of the earlier cases, where a sperm donor was able to avoid the application of the sperm donor statute by asserting he had an oral agreement with the mother that he would be a legal parent, these cases ultimately turned on the moth-

133 *Ibid.*, p. *49 (citing *Bleidner* v. *Searles*, 561 A.2d 954 (Conn. App. Ct. 1989)).

134 *Ibid.*, p. *50.

135 *Tripp* v. *Hinckley*, 736 N.Y.S.2d 506 (App. Div. 2002), *In re R.A.S.*, 2007 WL 4146828 (Ohio. App. 12 Dist.).

ers participating in the creation of legal documents that irrevocably established the donor as a legal parent.

K.M.H. is clearly aligned with the recent trends in the US cases. The Kansas case was unique because it was the first case to deal with a statute that specifically allowed a sperm donor to become a legal parent – if the sperm donor had a written agreement, he would fall squarely within the language of the sperm donor statute and his parental rights would be secured. Similar to the later sperm donor cases, the Kansas Supreme Court applied the plain meaning of the statute when the sperm donor, D.H., attempted to assert the terms of an oral agreement giving him parental rights. The clear language of the statute, however, prevented him from being able to raise that issue. In addition, because D.H. had the opportunity to become a legal parent through the operation of a written agreement, the statute also withstood his constitutional challenge based on due process. Ultimately D.H. found himself in the same situation as the mothers who were not allowed to argue that they did not intend to give sperm donors equal parental rights when they acquiesced in, or acknowledged, paternity – their ignorance of the law did not prevent it from taking effect. Unlike these mothers, however, who found themselves sharing their children with unintended co-parents, D.H. found he did not have any children at all. Perhaps this is the ultimate question that legislators should consider when drafting statutes that add or subtract potential legal parents – what will be the law's impact on all interested parties when individuals continually create children through assisted reproduction, completely ignorant of the law and its consequences?

REGISTRATION SCHEMES FOR SAME-SEX COUPLES: NEW JURISDICTIONS

A JUDICIAL REVOLUTION?

The court-led achievement of same-sex marriage in South Africa

Pierre de Vos*

1. INTRODUCTION

At the end of 2006 South Africa became the first country in Africa to extend full marriage rights to same-sex couples. After a successful Constitutional Court challenge[1] to the exclusion of same-sex couples from the common law definition of marriage and the failure of the Marriage Act[2] to provide for same-sex marriage, the South African Parliament reluctantly passed the Civil Union Act[3] to extend marriage rights to same-sex couples who were until then denied the right to marry. This would not have been possible if the South African Constitution[4] did not explicitly prohibit discrimination on the basis of sexual orientation[5] and if the Constitutional Court had not ruled in several cases[6] that this meant that same-sex relationships deserve equal protection and respect and that same-sex

* Professor of Constitutional Law, Law Faculty, University of the Western Cape, Bellville, Cape Town (South Africa), email: pdevos@uwc.ac.za.

1 In the case of *Minister of Home Affairs* v. *Fourie*, 2006(3) BCLR 355 (CC).

2 Act 25 of 1961. Marriage in South Africa has traditionally been regulated by the Marriage Act but this regulation was based on the common law definition of marriage as determined by the judiciary. While the Act therefore provided for the formal requirements of how to enter into a valid marriage, the common law as determined by judges determined who would be entitled to marry whom.

3 Act 17 of 2006.

4 Constitution of the Republic of South Africa Act 108 of 1996.

5 Section 9(3) of the Constitution states: 'The state may not unfairly discriminate directly or indirectly against anyone on one or more grounds, including race, gender, sex, pregnancy, marital status, ethnic or social origin, colour, *sexual orientation*, age, disability, religion, conscience, belief, culture, language and birth.' (my italics).

6 *National Coalition for Gay and Lesbian Equality* v. *Minister of Justice*, 1998(12) BCLR 1517 (CC); *Satchwell* v. *President of the Republic of South Africa and Another*, 2002 (6) SA 1 (CC); 2002 (9) BCLR 986 (CC); *Du Toit and Another* v. *Minister of Welfare and Population Development and Others (Lesbian and Gay Equality Project as amicus curiae)*, 2003 (2) SA 198 (CC); 2002 (10) BCLR 1006 (CC); *J and Another* v. *Director General, Department of Home Affairs, and Others*, 2003 (5) SA 621 (CC); 2003 (5) BCLR 463 (CC).

couples are equally capable of forming caring long-term relationships and of raising children in a loving and caring environment.

However, in order to accommodate objections from religious groups, Parliament opted not to extend marriage rights to same-sex couples by simply changing the common law definition of marriage and the relevant provisions of the Marriage Act in a way that would allow same-sex couples to get married under the Marriage Act. Instead Parliament adopted a separate Civil Union Act – open to both same-sex and different-sex couples – that extended the right to marry to all unmarried couples over the age of 18. In order to understand the full import of the Civil Union Act it is therefore necessary briefly to sketch the legal path that led to the adoption of this Act before exploring its specific provisions. I will then evaluate the Act and assess whether it really provides equal marriage rights for same-sex couples or not and whether problems might remain.

2. OVERVIEW OF THE CONSTITUTIONAL COURT JURISPRUDENCE

By the time that applicants challenged the exclusion of same-sex couples from the right to get married, the Constitutional Court had confirmed on several occasions that the prohibition on unfair discrimination on the basis of sexual orientation meant that the state had to respect and protect the human dignity of gay men, lesbians and other sexual minorities in South Africa. In the process, it developed a detailed set of assumptions that it said should guide any enquiry as to whether unfair discrimination[7] on the basis of sexual orientation had taken place. In setting out its understanding of same sex love and same-sex relationships, the Court rejected many of the stereotypical assumptions made about gay men and lesbians and their intimate relationships that are prevalent in South Africa and most other societies in the world.

---

7 Section 9 of the Constitution prohibits *unfair* discrimination on any ground including the sixteen grounds listed in Section 9 itself. The Constitutional Court has given this phrase a very specific meaning and has argued that where differentiation occurs between individuals belonging to different groups and where that differentiation is based on a listed ground, it would be assumed to constitute unfair discrimination. It would then be for the state or other role players trying to justify the discrimination to show that the discrimination was not unfair. In evaluating whether discrimination was unfair or not a court will take into account all relevant factors, including the position of the complainant in society and whether she or he belongs to a group that has been previously discriminated against; the purpose of the discrimination and whether it was aimed at rectifying past injustice or merely to perpetuate it and also whether the discrimination would be so serious as to affr5ont the human dignity of the complainant and the group he or she belongs to. See *Harksen* v. *Lane NO*, 1997 11 BCLR 1489 (CC); 1998 1 SA 300 (CC), pp. 1508–1511.

In the Constitutional Court judgment on marriage, these guiding assumptions were said to include that:[8]

- gays and lesbians in same-sex life partnerships are as capable as heterosexual spouses of expressing and sharing love in its manifold forms including affection, friendship, eros and charity;
- they are likewise as capable of forming intimate, permanent, committed, monogamous, loyal and enduring relationships; of furnishing emotional and spiritual support; and of providing physical care, financial support and assistance in running the common household;
- they are individually able to adopt children and in the case of lesbians to bear them;
- in short, they have the same ability to establish a *consortium omnis vitae*; and finally
- '(...) they are capable of constituting a family, whether nuclear or extended, and of establishing, enjoying and benefiting from family life which is not distinguishable in any significant respect from that of heterosexual spouses'.

The Constitutional Court thus concluded that the family and family life of gay men and lesbians were in all significant respects indistinguishable from those of heterosexual spouses and in human terms as important.[9] Where the law fails to recognise the relationship of same-sex couples 'the message is that gays and lesbians lack the inherent humanity to have their families and family lives in such same-sex relationships respected or protected. It serves in addition to perpetuate and reinforce existing prejudice and stereotypes. The impact constitutes a crass, blunt, cruel and serious invasion of their dignity'.[10]

When a female same-sex couple then challenged the legal exclusion of same-sex couples from the institution of marriage in the common, the Constitutional Court relied on these precedents to find in favour of the couple and declared invalid the common law definition of marriage which defined marriage as 'a union of one man with one woman, to the exclusion, while it lasts, of all others'.[11] It also found that the Marriage Act, which provided only for the legal mechanisms for different-sex couples to enter into a marriage, to contravene the equality guarantee in the Constitution. In considering its options to remedy the unconstitutionality of the South African family law as it relates to marriage, the Constitutional Court opted for an approach that would give Parliament a chance to correct

---

8 *National Coalition for Gay and Lesbian equality* v. *Minister of Home Affairs*, *supra* note 6, at 32F-33C, restated in *Fourie*, *supra* note 1, at 545F/G-546D/E.

9 *Fourie*, *supra* note 1, par. 54.

10 *Home Affairs*, *supra* note 6, par. 54; *Fourie*, supra note 1, par. 54.

11 This definition was provided by Chief Justice Innes in *Mashia Ebrahim* v. *Mahomed* Essop, 1905 TS 59, p. 61.

the defects in the law in an appropriate manner.[12] The South African parliament was therefore given 12 months to pass legislation that would either amend the existing Marriage Act or would create a new piece of legislation that would extend to same-sex couples the right to enter into a legally binding institution that would extend to same-sex couples the legal rights and duties as well as the same social status as that associated with marriage entered into by heterosexuals in terms of the existing Marriage Act. But the Court made it clear that Parliament was not free to fix this problem in any way it saw fit and thus circumscribed the way in which partnership rights had to be extended. Parliament could therefore not merely extend civil partnership rights to same-sex couples in a way that fell completely outside the marriage regime. It had to recognise same-sex relationships, said the Court, in a way that would not perpetuate the marginalisation and disrespect for same-sex couples. There are several aspects of the judgment that makes this conclusion inevitable.[13]

First, the court affirmed the importance of marriage in South African society. According to the *Fourie* judgment marriage was a unique institution that constituted 'much more than a piece of paper'.[14] This was because until recently marriage was the only institution in South Africa from which a number of socio-economic benefits would accrue. These included the right to maintenance, medical insurance coverage, adoption, access to wrongful death claims and post-divorce rights.[15] But the Court also made it clear that marriage was important because it bestowed a myriad of *intangible* benefits on those who choose to enter into it. As such, marriage entitled a couple to celebrate their commitment to each other at a public event so celebrated in our culture. Well aware of and affirming the centrality attributed to marriage and its consequences in South African culture, the Court held that to deny same-sex couples a choice in this regard 'is to negate their right to self-definition in a most profound way'.[16] The Constitutional Court thus asserted that to exclude same-sex couples from the benefits and responsibilities of marriage would not be:

> 'a small and tangential inconvenience resulting from a few surviving relics of societal prejudice destined to evaporate like the morning dew. It represents a harsh if oblique statement by the law that same-sex couples are outsiders, and that their need for affirmation and protection of their intimate relations as human beings is somehow less than that of heterosexual couples. It reinforces the wounding notion that they are to

12 *Fourie, supra* note 1, par. 134.

13 See generally P. de Vos & Jaco Barnard, 'Same-sex marriage, civil unions and domestic partnerships in South Africa: Critical reflections on an ongoing saga', 2007 *South African Law Journal*, p. 795; P. de Vos, 'The "inevitability" of same-sex marriage in South Africa's post-apartheid state', 2007 *SA Journal on Human Rights*, pp. 432–465.

14 *Fourie, supra* note 1, par. 70.

15 *Ibid.*

16 *Ibid.*, par. 72.

> be treated as biological oddities, as failed or lapsed human beings who do not fit into normal society, and, as such, do not qualify for the full moral concern and respect that our Constitution seeks to secure for everyone. It signifies that their capacity for love, commitment and accepting responsibility is by definition less worthy of regard than that of heterosexual couples.'[17]

Thus the exclusion of same-sex couples from marriage has both a *practical and symbolic* impact, which means that the unconstitutionality could not be rectified through the recognition of same-sex unions outside the law of marriage. In responding to the unconstitutionality of the existing marriage regime, both the *practical* and the *symbolic* aspects had to be addressed. According to the Constitutional Court it would therefore not be sufficient for the South African Parliament 'merely to deal with all the practical consequences of exclusion from marriage. It would also have to accord to same-sex couples a public and private status equal to that which heterosexual couples achieve from being married'.[18]

In order to reach this conclusion the Constitutional Court had to deal with arguments put forward by opponents of same-sex marriage who conceded that given the prohibition against sexual orientation discrimination in the South African Constitution, same-sex couples were entitled to legal protection of their relationships but that the remedy did not lie in radically altering the law of marriage, which by its very nature and as it has evolved historically is concerned with heterosexual relationships, but instead merely required Parliament to provide an alternative form of legal protection for such couples.

The Court first considered and then rejected the argument that the constitutive and definitional characteristic of marriage is its procreative potential and that marriage – properly defined and understood – could therefore never include same-sex couples. The Court's rejection of this argument was based on the insight that to base an understanding of marriage on the procreative potential of that marriage would be deeply demeaning to *heterosexual couples* (married or not) who, for whatever reason, either choose not to procreate or are incapable of procreating when they start a relationship or become so at any time thereafter. It would also be demeaning for couples who start a relationship at a stage when they no longer have the capacity to conceive or for adoptive parents. Although this view might have some attraction in the context of a particular religious world view, from a legal and constitutional point of view, the Court found, it could not hold.[19]

Second, the Court addressed an argument with a more obviously religious basis. According to this argument marriage was by its very nature a religious

17 *Ibid.*, par. 71.
18 *Ibid.*, par. 81.
19 *Ibid.*, par. 86–87.

institution and to change its definition would violate the freedom of groups whose religious identities are wrapped up in a heterosexual definition of marriage. This argument was in no uncertain terms rejected by the Court. Although the Court recognised that religious bodies played a large and important part in public life and are part of the fabric of our society,[20] it affirmed that in an open and democratic society contemplated by the Constitution there was a need for mutual respect and co-existence between the secular and the sacred. The Court thus pointed out that the acknowledgement by the state of the right of same-sex couples to enjoy the same status, entitlements and responsibilities as marriage that the South African law accords to heterosexual couples, would 'in no way [be] inconsistent with the rights of religious organisations to continue to refuse to celebrate same-sex marriages'. The two sets of interests involved were not in conflict, but rather they co-existed in a constitutional realm based on accommodation of diversity.[21] This was a logical consequence of the constitutional imperative that the religious beliefs of some could not be used to determine the constitutional rights of others.[22]

Applying these views to the facts, the court held that the exclusionary common law definition of marriage and aspects of the Marriage Act which provided only for heterosexual marriage were unconstitutional.[23] Instead of an immediate reading-in of words into the Marriage Act to remedy this unconstitutionality, the court suspended the its order for one year to give Parliament a chance to addresses the unconstitutional exclusion of same-sex couples from enjoying the status and entitlements coupled with responsibilities that are accorded to heterosexual couples by the common law and by the Marriage Act.[24] If Parliament failed to deal with this matter within the year stipulated, the common law and the Marriage Act would automatically be changed to allow same-sex couples to enter into marriage.

It is important to note that the Court did not give Parliament a wide discretion on the manner in which this defect in the law had to be fixed. Although it never explicitly stated that Parliament was constitutionally obliged to extend full *marriage* rights (as opposed to some lesser partnership rights) to same-sex couples, the Court made it clear that the remedy fashioned by Parliament had to provide the same legal rights as well as the same status that is traditionally associated with heterosexual marriage. In this regard, the Court expressly held that whatever the legislative measures Parliament took, it could not subject same-sex couples to new forms of marginalisation or exclusion by the law, either directly or indirectly.[25] The Court provided Parliament with 'certain guiding principles' to be kept in

---

20 *Ibid.*, par. 90–93.
21 *Ibid.*, par. 98.
22 *Ibid.*, par. 92.
23 *Ibid.*, par. 114.
24 *Ibid.*, par. 132–153.
25 *Ibid.*, par. 147.

mind when rectifying the injustice. The most important principle here was that Parliament had to be 'sensitive to the need to avoid a remedy that on the face of it would provide equal protection, but would do so in a manner that in its context and application would be calculated to reproduce new forms of marginalisation'.[26]

It would therefore be completely unacceptable for Parliament to adopt a 'separate but equal' approach and to provide same-sex couples with a separate legal institution that would not have the same status as traditional marriage because this would serve 'as a threadbare cloak for covering distaste for or repudiation by those in power of the group subjected to segregation.'[27] The Court referred to the notorious apartheid-era Appeal Court judgment of *S* v. *Pitje*[28] where the appellant, an African candidate attorney employed by the firm Mandela and Tambo, occupied a place at a table in court that was reserved for 'European practitioners' and refused to take his place at a table reserved for 'non-European practitioners'. The then Chief Justice upheld the appellant's conviction for contempt of court as it was '(...) clear [from the record] that a practitioner would in every way be as well seated at the one table as at the other, and that he could not possibly have been hampered in the slightest in the conduct of his case by having to use a particular table'.[29] Such an approach, the Court argued in the *Fourie* case, would be 'unthinkable in our constitutional democracy today not simply because the law has changed dramatically, but because our society is completely different'.[30] The Court warned explicitly against providing an apparently neutral remedy that could have a severe impact on the dignity and sense of self-worth of the persons affected. Although different treatment itself does not necessarily violate the dignity of those affected, as soon as 'separation implies repudiation, connotes distaste or inferiority and perpetuates a caste-like status it becomes constitutionally invidious':[31]

> 'This means that whatever legislative remedy is chosen must be as generous and accepting towards same-sex couples as it is to heterosexual couples, both in terms of the intangibles as well as the tangibles involved. In a context of patterns of deep past

26 *Ibid.*, par. 150.

27 *Ibid.*, par 150. Sachs J explained this view with reference to South Africa's apartheid past: 'The very notion that integration would lead to miscegenation, mongrelisation or contamination, was offensive in concept and wounding in practice. Yet, just as is frequently the case when proposals are made for recognising same-sex unions in desiccated and marginalised forms, proponents of segregation would vehemently deny any intention to cause insult. On the contrary, they would justify the apartness as being a reflection of a natural or divinely ordained state of affairs. Alternatively they would assert that the separation was neutral if the facilities provided by the law were substantially the same for both groups.'.

28 1960 (4) SA 709 (A).

29 *Ibid.*, p. 710.

30 *Fourie*, *supra* note 1, par. 151.

31 *Ibid.*, par. 152.

discrimination and continuing homophobia, appropriate sensitivity must be shown to providing a remedy that is truly and manifestly respectful of the dignity of same-sex couples.'[32]

3. FIRST DRAFT OF THE CIVIL UNION BILL

Many gay and lesbian activists and other members of the Lesbian Gay Bisexual Transgendered and Intersex (LGBTI) community were deeply upset by the remedy offered by the majority of the Court in the *Fourie* judgment, arguing that the majority of the Court failed to provide an effective remedy and condemned same-sex couples who wished to get married to another year in legal limbo.[33] Because the judgment never used the word 'marriage', there was also some anxiety that Parliament would try to avoid its responsibilities by providing a 'separate but equal' regime of legal protection in the form of partnership rights that would not comply with the letter and spirit of the majority judgment. It was therefore with some trepidation that LGBTI activists greeted the original version of the Civil Union Bill[34] when it was tabled in Parliament at the end of August 2006. The Bill proposed the creation of a separate institution for same-sex couples – called a civil partnership – which purported to bestow exactly the same legal rights on same-sex civil partners as on heterosexual married couples.[35] There were, however, three pivotal ways in which the proposed civil partnership differed from traditional marriage:[36] it would not be called a marriage (except at the ceremony if the partners so choose);[37] marriage officers employed by the state would have a right to refuse to solemnise a civil partnership;[38] and it would only be open to same-sex couples, not to heterosexual couples.[39]

LGBTI activists criticised the Bill, arguing that it represented an attempt to create a 'separate but equal' marriage regime that would 'protect' 'real marriage' from 'contamination' and 'defilement' by same-sex couples, while pretending to provide such couples with equal partnership rights. This move was deeply upsetting to many in the LGBTI community, not only because it failed to respect the

---

32 *Ibid.*, par. 153.

33 See De Vos, *supra* note 13, p. 458. As I have pointed out before, many of us who had criticized the majority in this regard, changed our minds. Although the public participation process that accompanied discussions about the adoption of the Civil Union Act was deeply flawed, it did open up a conversation about sexual orientation and provided an unprecedented platform in the media for those arguing in favour of respect of gay men and lesbians.

34 Draft Civil Union Bill, published in the *Government Gazette* No. 29169 of 31 August 2006.

35 *Ibid.*, Section 13.

36 De Vos, *supra* note 13, p. 458.

37 *Ibid.*, Section 11.

38 *Ibid.*, Section 6.

39 *Ibid.*, definition Section 1.

human dignity of gay men and lesbians which are protected in the Constitution, but also because, so it was argued, it obviously contradicted the very clear instructions set out by the Constitutional Court.[40]

This view was based on the fundamental assumption at the heart of the *Fourie* judgment that the institution of marriage indeed had a special *status* in our society and that access to the institution of 'marriage' would be the only way to truly give effect to the Constitutional promise of equality. The Bill, it was argued, created a separate and inferior regime and failed to recognise – as the Constitutional Court did – that both tangible legal consequences and intangible benefits flow from the act of entering a marriage. The problem, it was said, was clearly that a Bill that did not allow same-sex couples the right to get married and call their union a marriage, would not provide for an institution of equal *status*. It seemed to propose a remedy that on the face of it would provide equal protection, but would do so in a manner that in its context and application would be calculated to reproduce new forms of marginalisation. This was problematic, given the fact that the Constitutional Court made clear that 'separate but equal' partnership rights would not be good enough because it would serve as a threadbare cloak for covering distaste for or repudiation by those in power of the group subjected to discrimination.

LGBTI activists, assisted by the language deployed by the Constitutional Court, launched a sustained attack on the draft legislation.[41] By pointing out that the concept of marriage has a profound symbolic, emotional and political power in our culture that gives it a special status, it became easier for LGBTI activists and academics to show that by refusing same-sex couples the right to enter into an institution called 'marriage', the Bill would deprive same-sex couples of the right to access the status associated with the term 'marriage'. It was also easier to show how deeply problematic it was that civil partnerships were envisaged as being exclusively for same-sex couples who would still be prohibited from accessing the institution of marriage reserved for heterosexuals.[42] Civil partnerships entered into by same-sex couples would therefore continue to have a lesser status than traditional marriage and would infringe on the rights of such couples not to be discriminated against. Activists furthermore could point to the Constitutional Court warning that creating a special institution for same-sex couples would invariably send the signal that bringing same-sex couples under the umbrella of

40 De Vos & Barnard, *supra* note 13, pp. 808–811.

41 See for example P. de Vos, 'Gays and Lesbians now "separate but equal"', *Mail & Guardian*, 17 September 2006, accessed on 18 July 2007 at http://www.mg.co.za/articlePage.aspx?articleid=284218&area=/insight/insight__comment_and_analysis/.

42 See Parliamentary Monitoring Group *Report on the Portfolio Committee of Home Affairs on Peoples⊠ Public Hearings in Provinces on the Civil Union Bill, 20 September to 9 October 2006, and the Public Submissions*, accessed on 8 September 2007 at http://www.pmg.org.za/docs/2006/061031hearings.htm.

marriage law would taint those already within its protection. Such a move would endorse the view that homosexuals are somehow depraved, impure and tainted and that 'pure' heterosexual marriage must be protected from this abomination. As the Constitutional Court pointed out in the *Fourie* judgment, such a view – no matter how seriously and sincerely held – can only be based on prejudice against, or hatred of, homosexuals. And prejudice, the Court has said on many occasions, can never justify discrimination in our constitutional dispensation. It was furthermore argued that the effects of the Bill were potentially more severe because so many gay men and lesbians still experience tremendous oppression, marginalisation and vilification in our society. Some are still raped, assaulted or even killed because they are lesbians or gay. In this context, the creation of an apartheid style separate civil partnerships for same-sex couples, it was argued, would merely confirm that the law did not consider our relationships equal in status and worthy of equal concern and respect. In short, a doctrine of 'separate but equal' was deeply humiliating and insulting when applied to black South Africans. It remains humiliating and insulting (and now also unconstitutional) when applied to homosexuals.

The argument put forward by LGBTI activists resonated with some members of the ruling party, the Africa National Congress (ANC), exactly because it powerfully reminded them of the similarities with apartheid.[43] After political intervention, the ANC members of the relevant Parliamentary Committee decided at the last possible moment that it would be necessary to amend the first version of the draft Bill.

4. THE AMENDED CIVIL UNION ACT

4.1. GENERAL DESCRIPTION

Ultimately, arguments put forward by activists and academics were at least partly successful and early in November the National Assembly adopted a substantially amended Bill which provided for same-sex couples to enter into a Civil Union marriage which could be called either a 'marriage' or a 'civil partnership'. This was because a Civil Union is defined in the Act as 'the voluntary union of two persons who are both 18 years of age or older, which is solemnised and registered by way of either a marriage or a civil partnership, in accordance with the procedures

[43] I was told this personally by a member of the ANC caucus in Parliament who took part in the debate in the caucus on the Civil Union Bill on the condition that I would not mention his name. Similar sentiments were expressed to me by an advisor to the Minister of Home Affairs. See De Vos, *supra* note 13, p. 459.

prescribed in this Act, to the exclusion, while it lasts, of all others'.[44] The Act also makes it clear that those who enter into a Civil Union marriage would be accorded the same rights as those who enter a traditional Marriage in terms of the Marriage Act.[45] The Civil Union Act thus amended all existing legislation in South Africa in which references are made to 'marriage', 'husband', 'wife' or 'spouse', so that these Acts which bestow rights and privileges and duties on married heterosexual couples would now also apply equally to those couples – heterosexual or same-sex – who had registered a marriage or a civil partnership in accordance with the Civil Union Act. The Act thus now provided for the recognition of same-sex relationships in a way that extends to same sex couples the same rights and duties and the same status as that traditionally enjoyed by different-sex couples.

It is important to note that the amended Bill eventually passed by Parliament provided for both same sex and different sex couples to enter into a marriage or a civil partnership.[46] The Act also prescribed the formal requirements for entering into such a civil union marriage and in many ways mirrors the provision of the Marriage Act, which was not repealed or amended and remained open exclusively to facilitate marriage by heterosexual couples who chose not to get married in terms of the new Act. This means that the Act allows both same-sex and different-sex couples to register their relationship in terms of this legislation. It also means that it provides such couples a choice, either to register a 'marriage' or a 'civil partnership'. Whether one chooses to register a marriage or a civil partnership, the legal consequences would be exactly the same. At first blush, it seems somewhat perplexing that this choice was provided at all. Most couples would probably not choose to register 'civil partnerships' if they have the choice of registering a 'marriage', given the powerful symbolic power of entering into an institution called 'marriage' in our society and given the absence in the public discourse of a

---

44 Civil Union Act 17 of 2006, Section 1.

45 *Ibid.*, Section 13, which states:
'(1) The legal consequences of a marriage contemplated in the Marriage Act apply, with such changes as may be required by the context to a civil union.
(2) With the exception of the Marriage Act and the Customary Marriages Act any reference to –
(a) marriage in any other law, including the common law, includes with such changes as may be required by the context, a civil union: and
(b) husband, wife or spouse in any other law, including the common law, includes a civil union partner.'.

46 It has been suggested that Section 8(6) of the Act muddies the waters in this regard and may be interpreted as restricting marriage under the new act to same-sex couples. Section 8(6) states that: 'A civil union may only be registered by prospective civil union partners who would, apart from the fact that they are of the same sex, not be prohibited by law from concluding a marriage under the Marriage Act or the Customary Marriages Act.' I contend that it is clear from the context that this section does not prohibit different sex couples from entering a marriage in terms of the Civil Union Act. It merely states that such different sex couples would only be able to enter into a Civil Union marriage if they would also have been allowed to enter into a marriage in terms of one of the two other laws regulating marriage in South Africa.

critique of the institution of marriage. This choice was most probably retained as a compromise to placate more conservative critics. This is ironic because given the contested nature of heterosexual marriage and feminist critiques regarding the alleged patriarchal nature of the institution,[47] the inclusion of this option seems like a net gain for progressives because it allows both heterosexual and homosexual couples to enter into a civil partnership without having to call their union a 'marriage' but would nevertheless give such couples access to a union that will provide them with the full range of legal rights and duties associated with that institutions of 'marriage'. Some more conservative same-sex couples who view marriage as an institution exclusively associated with heterosexual relationships, may well also choose to enter into a civil partnership instead of a 'marriage'.

Some of the most important legal consequences associated with entering both the traditional marriage in terms of the Marriage Act, and a Civil Union marriage entered into in terms of the Civil Union Act are as follows.

(a) Changing of the status of spouses

Upon entering either a traditional marriage in terms of the Marriage Act or a marriage in terms of the Civil Union Act, the legal status of spouses changes. For example, neither spouse may marry anyone else while the marriage subsists.[48] When a valid marriage under either regime is concluded a right arise for a surviving spouse to inherit intestate from a deceased partner in the event where no will was made by the deceased.[49] Furthermore, where one of the partners to the marriage had children prior to the conclusion of the marriage, both spouses automatically become the legal guardians of the children[50] and the children are legitimated by the marriage.[51]

(b) Consortium omnis vitae

In South African law a marriage creates a *consortium omnis vitae* between the spouses.[52] This turn of phrase is supposed to capture in the abstract the 'totality of a number of rights, duties and advantages accruing to the spouses in a

47 See P. Ettelbrick, 'Since When is Marriage a Path to Liberation?', in R. Baird & S. Rosenbaum (eds.), *Same Sex Marriage: the Moral and Legal Debate*, 1997, pp. 164–168.

48 See Civil Union Act, *supra* note 3, Section 8 and D.S.P. Cronjé & J. Heaton, *South African Family Law*, 2004, p. 30.

49 Intestate Succession Act 81 of 1987, ss. 1(1)(a) and (c).

50 Guardianship Act 192 of 1993, s. (1(1).

51 Children's Status Act 82 of 1987, s. 4.

52 See generally Cronjé & Heaton, *supra* note 47, pp. 49–50.

marriage'.[53] As Cronjé and Heaton points out this includes, *inter alia*, companionship, love, affection, comfort, mutual services and sexual intercourse. The *consortium omnis vitae* is not directly enforceable in a court but is indirectly protected by the threat of divorce.[54]

(c) Maintenance of a spouse

In South African law marriage imposes a reciprocal duty of support on both spouses from the moment spouses enter into a marriage until the marriage is terminated – provided that the spouse who claims maintenance is in need of maintenance and the spouse from whom it is claimed is able to provide it.[55] Maintenance is generally assumed to include the provision of accommodation, clothing, food, medical services and other necessities.[56] This general duty of support will come to and end at the dissolution of the marriage – either because of the death of one of the parties or because of a divorce. But legislation does provide for spouses to claim maintenance even after the dissolution of the marriage. The Maintenance of Surviving Spouses Act[57] provides for the surviving spouse to claim for maintenance against the deceased spouse's estate.[58] Moreover when a couple divorces the court which grants the divorce order can make a maintenance order in favour of one of the spouses in terms of the Divorce Act.[59]

(d) The matrimonial home

During the marriage entered into in terms of the Marriage Act or the Civil Union Act both spouses are entitled to live in the matrimonial home and to use the household assets – such as furniture and appliances – irrespective of whether they are married in or out of community of property and irrespective of which spouse owns or rents the matrimonial home or household assets.[60] This is a right that is not conferred by one spouse on the other but arises automatically and as a rule the spouse who owns or rents the house may not eject the other spouse from the matrimonial home without providing him or her with suitable alternative accommodation. But the other spouse may also not eject the owning or renting spouse from the matrimonial home.[61]

53 *Grobbelaar* v. *Havenga*, 1964 (3) SA 522 (N) 525.
54 Cronjé & Heaton, *supra* note 47, p. 50.
55 *Oberholzer* v. *Oberholzer*, 1947 (3) SA 294 (O). See generally Cronjé & Heaton, *supra* note 47, p. 50.
56 *Ex parte Hugo*, 1960 (1) SA 773 (T).
57 Act 27 of 1990.
58 *Ibid.*, Section 2(1).
59 Act 70 of 1979, Section 7(1) and (2).
60 Cronjé & Heaton, *supra* note 47, p. 65.
61 *Badenhorst* v. *Badenhorst*, 1964 (2) SA 676 (T).

4.2. CRITICISM OF THE CIVIL UNION ACT[62]

The Civil Union marriage regime remains problematic in at least one important technical sense relating to the solemnisation of marriages in terms of the Act. In terms of the Marriage Act and the Civil Union Act marriages can be solemnised either by religious officials, or by public servants designated to fulfil this task. According to the Marriage Act, certain civil servants like magistrates and commissioners are, by reason of their office, automatically deemed to be marriage officers, while other state officials and diplomatic officers may be appointed as marriage officers by the relevant Minister.[63] In order to accommodate religious practices and beliefs, the Marriage Act also provides for another kind of marriage officer to be appointed to ensure that marriages are conducted according to 'Christian, Jewish or Mohammedan rites or the rites of any Indian religion'.[64] Thus officials from these religious groups may also be appointed as marriage officers. In practice, religious bodies of Christian and Jewish faith groups apply on behalf of the individual members who want to become marriage officers.[65] However, in terms of the Marriage Act religious marriage officers are not obliged to marry any couple who asks them to marry them because in terms of Section 31 of the Act they may object to conducting marriages which do not conform to the 'rites, formularies, tenets, doctrines or disciplines' of their religions. The Marriage Act does not provide for a similar exemption for civil servants who are marriage officers. Only religious marriage officers may therefore refuse to conduct marriages under the Marriage Act (which will always be heterosexual in nature) and they may only do so on the grounds of their religious beliefs.

Unfortunately the Civil Union Act deals with this matter in an entirely different – and constitutionally problematic – way. It distinguishes between religious marriage officers and non-religious marriage officers in the same way that the Marriage Act does. However, in respect of religious marriage officers the Act requires first, that a religious denomination or organisation must apply for approval to conduct civil unions.[66] Once the religious organisation has been approved, an official from the organisation may apply to be appointed as a marriage officer.[67] Individuals who belong to a specific religious order cannot apply individually to become religious marriage officers and it therefore seems that

62 See for example E. Bonthuys, 'The Civil Union Act: more of the same', in M. Judge *et al.* (eds.) *To have and to hold: the making of same-sex marriage in South Africa*, 2007, p. 171.

63 Marriage Act, *supra* note 2, Section 2.

64 *Ibid.*, Section 3(1).

65 Regulations under the Marriage Act GN R2207, *Government Gazette* No. 10500 of 24 October 1986, as amended, reg 2. Muslim religious officials do not act as marriage officers, because the common law still does not recognize Muslim marriages on the grounds that they are 'potentially polygamous'. See *Ismail* v. *Ismail*, 1983 (1) SA 1006 (A).

66 Section 5(1).

67 Section 5(4).

becoming a marriage officer to conduct marriages in terms of the Civil Union Act is more cumbersome than becoming a marriage officer in terms of the Marriage Act. In the case of civil union marriages, both the institution and the individual religious official must apply, while in the case of marriage in terms of the traditional Marriage Act, one application suffices.

But there are other anomalies in the Civil Union Act regarding religious marriage officers. The Act does not provide for such officers to refuse to conduct civil union marriages which do not comply with the dictates of the particular religion they belong to. This might be because both the religious institution and the individual marriage officer must apply to conduct civil unions and it could, therefore, have been assumed that the issue of conscientious or religious objection would not arise. However, this overlooks the situation where, for instance, a Jewish marriage officer is asked to conduct a civil union for a Christian same-sex couple. In such a case the Act would not allow a marriage officer in this position to refuse to conduct the marriage on religious grounds.

The Civil Union Act also provide for designated marriage officers to conduct civil union marriages in their capacity as civil servants. In terms of the Civil Union Act any marriage officer designated as such in terms of the original Marriage Act would also automatically become a marriage officer for the purposes of the Civil Union Act. However, it is highly problematic that the Civil Union Act allows these marriage officers – representing the state – to refuse to conclude a civil union marriage 'on the ground of conscience, religion and belief'.[68] This right to refuse to solemnise a marriage is not provided for in the Marriage Act dealing with traditional heterosexual marriages. This means, for example that a devoutly Christian civil servant may not object to marry a heterosexual couple in terms of the Marriage Act who are atheist or Muslim and a racist marriage officer may not object to marrying an interracial couple when a heterosexual couple chooses to marry in terms of the traditional Marriage Act. Civil servants may therefore only object to conduct marriages under the Civil Unions Act and, moreover, only to same-sex marriages under this Act. The only ground upon which they can object is therefore the sexual orientation of the couple.

This provision thus clearly endorses sexual orientation discrimination by state officials and will most probably be struck down by the Constitutional Court if challenged. But apart from the legal problem with this provision, it also represents a potential practical problem for same-sex couples who wish to tie the knot. This is because it may make it more difficult for especially less wealthy and less educated same-sex couples who live in small towns in South Africa to get married. Such a couple would typically go to the local magistrates court where the local magistrate would act as the state's designated marriage officer. When such a magistrate then refuses to marry a couple, they might not pursue the matter out

68 Civil Union Act, s. 6.

of ignorance or a lack of resources. This clause has therefore been strongly criticised by the activists in the GLBTI community.

5. RIGHTS OF NON-MARRIED SAME-SEX COUPLES

It is ironic that with the adoption of the Civil Union Act, same-sex couples will, in effect now have more legal rights than different sex couples. Over the past ten years the Constitutional Court has extended many of the rights enjoyed by married heterosexual couples to (obviously unmarried) same-sex couples in life partnerships.[69] These rights include the right of same-sex couples to jointly adopt children, to enjoy immigration rights, pension benefits and the right to inherit from a same sex life partner. Limiting these rights to heterosexual married couples were found to be discriminatory exactly because same-sex couples could not get married and were thus automatically excluded from enjoying these rights.[70] The question was raised whether unmarried same-sex couples who had gained these rights over the previous ten years would automatically lose these rights from the date that the Civil Union Act came into force on 1 December 2006. In *Gory* v. *Kolver and Others*, the Constitutional Court recently confirmed that these hard-won rights would not *automatically* be amended merely because same-sex couples are now allowed to get married. Even if same-sex couples do not get married they will have, for example, the right to inherent from their life partner – even where no will was left. But, as the Court pointed out, Parliament will have the right to amend this kind of legislation to take away the rights of non-married same-sex couples so that they are treated the same as heterosexual couples.[71]

6. CONCLUSION

Since the inception of the Civil Union Act at the end of 2006 there has not been a rush of same-sex couples to the marriage altar. Almost one year after the incep-

69 *National Coalition for Gay and Lesbian Equality* v. *Minister of Justice*, 1999 (1) SA 6 (CC); 1998 (12) BCLR 1517 (CC); *National Coalition for Gay and Lesbian Equality and Others* v. *Minister of Home Affairs and Others*, 2000 (2) SA 1 (CC); 2000 (1) BCLR 39 (CC); *Satchwell* v. *President of the Republic of South Africa and Another*, 2002 (6) SA 1 (CC); 2002 (9) BCLR 986 (CC); *Du Toit and Another* v. *Minister of Welfare and Population Development and Others (Lesbian and Gay Equality Project as amicus curiae)*, 2003 (2) SA 198 (CC); 2002 (10) BCLR 1006 (CC); *J and Another* v. *Director General, Department of Home Affairs, and Others*, 2003 (5) SA 621 (CC); 2003 (5) BCLR 463 (CC); *Gory* v. *Kolver NO and Others*, 2007 (3) BCLR 249 (CC).

70 *Gory* v. *Kolver*, supra note 69, par. 26–27.

71 *Ibid.*, par. 28.

tion of this Act, only 1,070 couples had tied the knot in terms of the new Act.[72] It is difficult to say why this is so. Perhaps because same-sex couples with access to resources and with the sufficient access to emotional and family support, already enjoy many of the rights associated with marriage in South Africa. It is also unclear to what extent the Court judgment in the *Fourie* case and the subsequent legal process that led to the adoption of the Civil Union Act may have contributed or will continue to contribute to changes in attitudes among the broader population about same-sex desire and those who experience it in South Africa.

In many ways the compromised reached by Parliament – by adopting a separate Civil Union Act that nevertheless extends full marriage rights to all qualifying same-sex and different-sex couples – is an inelegant one. It has unnecessarily complicated South Africa's family law regime by providing heterosexual couples with a choice to marry under the old or the new Act while providing same-sex couples only with the option of entering into a marriage or a civil partnership under the Civil Union Act. Moreover the new Act is silent on some difficult legal issues that necessarily flow from the fact that same-sex marriages are not gendered in nature. For example, in South African law when a family law dispute arise in terms of heterosexual marriages it is assumed that the legal solution will be found with reference to the country where the man who has entered in to the marriage presently resides. As no provision has been made for such an eventuality in the case of same-sex marriages, it is unclear how legal disputes about same-sex marriages will be resolved. At the same time it might be argued that the compromise reached by a democratically elected Parliament bestows the kind of legitimacy on same-sex relationships that would have been unthinkable only ten short years ago. Given the fact that South Africa is not a developed country and given, moreover, that attitudes towards same-sex desire amongst ordinary South Africans can hardly be described as enlightened, the adoption of legislation that now allows same-sex couples the choice of entering into a marriage seems little short of revolutionary.

72 M. Judge *et al.*, 'Introduction', in M. Judge *et al.* (eds.), *To have and to hold: the making of same-sex marriage in South Africa*, 2007, p. 14.

FAMILY *VS* SOLIDARITY

Recent epiphanies of the Italian reductionist anomaly in the debate on *de facto* couples

MATTEO BONINI BARALDI*

1. THE CONSTITUTIONAL DEBATE ON SAME-SEX FAMILIES

1.1. BACKGROUND

Taking family matters seriously is a distinct, internationally renowned trait of Italian culture. This often ignites fierce feelings, touching upon a bundle of deep-rooted, yet changing values, such as personal autonomy, masculinity, motherhood, reproduction, etc., which have significant implications on national identity itself.

In recent times, new influences have shown that such a bundle of values might sometimes be founded upon reactionary and discriminatory premises, and/or produce unacceptably hard consequences on those who do not conform to the predominant rule. Due to diffuse and diehard prejudices in many parts of Italy, men and women (whom we today call gays and lesbians) continue to face discrimination based on a personal characteristic such as (homo)sexual orientation. Discrimination which, for its traits, does not belong to the experience of those, heterosexual people, who are not normally marginalised on grounds of (hetero) sexual orientation. The stereotypes which branded the former with characteristics of unreliability or sickness still contribute to ensuring that same-sex couples

* PhD (2004), LLM (2002). EU Research Adviser, Law, Political Sciences & Economics, Università di Bologna (Italy), email: matteo.boninibaraldi@unibo.it. The author wishes to thank Mathias Möschel at the European University Institute in Firenze for his precious comments on an earlier draft of this paper. This paper was submitted for review in March 2008. The reader is advised that, after the general elections of April 2008, all bills discussed in this paper have been dropped by the new Parliament and that, although single opposition MPs have introduced new bills, the new political majority has already made it clear that it will not pursue the matter further.

remain at a distance from 'conjugality', the socially recognised place – whether we like it or not – for profound commitment and the most significant existential dynamics of love, care, and moral and material communion.

Despite an ongoing need to do so, in this paper I do not purport to discuss or demonstrate discrimination in family matters, nor to address (at least explicitly) the most openly homophobic discourses. Rather, my concern stems from the intrinsic discriminatory arguments present in the rhetoric of those who claim to favour the promotion of equal treatment and individual rights and liberties. Without any claim to thoroughness, I will briefly survey the debate surrounding constitutional values and principles relevant for the matter at hand, as well as the three main bills on *de facto* partnerships that have attracted public and institutional attention. The survey will serve a twofold aim: it will inform the reader both as to the content of the various proposals, and as to the cultural and political frame of reference within which the proposals found their origin.

By juxtaposing and comparing the three proposals, which have succeeded one another in a relatively short time, I hope to be able to show the reader the different, yet homogenous, political objectives and theoretical or cultural references which underpin each of them, in

addition to their material content. The three bills can be seen as the unique testimony of the profound implications of the 'pull-and-let-go' exercise typical of Italian society and politics. An exercise which, regrettably, mainly descends from the desire to please the wishes of the moderate (mostly) catholic sectors of the population, as well as the official religious predicaments based on clearly antiquated binary notions of right *vs* wrong, natural *vs* innatural, and moral *vs* immoral.

In my view, whilst the process of law reform and modernization should be welcomed if based on values such as personal autonomy and equality, the censoring temptations which have always contributed to the disappearance of same-sex couples, or to the (self)portrayal as something different and less worthy, must be taken seriously, and even more seriously when they propagate from progressive, left-wing narrations of equality and legal recognition. When the worth of family life of such couples is downgraded to a mere matter of competency for the population registry, or once again ignored through the segregation in hybrid legal schemes, it means that there is a severe gap in the ability to seriously question the reiteration of such concepts of 'family' and 'nature' which reinforce social and legal exclusion or marginalization. Therefore, every attempt at law reform in this sense should be regarded with utmost suspicion.

My conclusion is that the current Italian anomaly lies precisely in the fact that, masked by the promotion of the much cherished constitutional value of 'solidarity', there seems to be only one viable option for progressive political parties and scholars: the reductionist hypothesis. I use this formula to indicate the widespread and predominant incapacity or unwillingness to approach the matter of equality for same-sex couples in any other way that differs from that of diluting the specific problems into broader issues concerning all sorts of cohabiting arrangements based on solidarity or, as they are also called, 'reciprocal help'.

1.2. BETWEEN NATURE AND CULTURE

Article 29 of the 1948 Italian Constitution stipulates, among other things, that 'the Republic recognizes the rights of the family as a natural society based on marriage', and is still today interpreted as the highest source of the *favor matrimonii* principle, which characterises the Italian legal system.[1] Most scholars interpret this Article as preventing equal treatment of those couples that do not want to or cannot marry (*coppie di fatto*).

In a brilliant essay published in 2000, however, a prominent constitutional scholar remarked that the oxymoron expressed by Article 29 invited answers conceived in an essentially 'cultural' manner, as opposed to the echoes of an ideal 'nature' it still powerfully generates. Professor Bin warned that the concept of 'natural society' refers to 'that concept of family which derives from the past, of which our culture is imbued and which certainly does not ignore the values of the catholic religion'.[2] Such a perspective is clearly inspired not by an absolute and immutable axiology, but by the principle of the mutability of definitions depending on historical variables.[3] A similar viewpoint also characterizes Robby, an 11-year old boy who, on the day his two co-mothers got married in Canada, stated:

---

1 C. Grassetti, 'I principi costituzionali relativi al diritto familiare', in P. Calamandrei & A. Levi (eds.), *Commentario sistematico alla Costituzione italiana*, 1950, pp. 290 *et seq.*; C.M. Bianca, 'Famiglia (diritti di)', in *Novissimo Digesto italiano*, VII, 1961, pp. 68 *et seq.*; C. Grassetti, 'Famiglia (dir. priv.)', in *Novissimo digesto italiano*, 1965 (reprint 1981), p. 48 and in App., III, 1982, p. 637; P. Barcellona, 'Famiglia (dir. civ.)', in *Enciclopedia del diritto*, XVI, 1967, pp. 779 *et seq.*; M. Bessone, 'Rapporti etico-sociali, art. 29–31', in G. Branca (ed.), *Commentario alla Costituzione*, 1976, pp. 14 *et seq.*; A.M. Sandulli, 'Rapporti etico-sociali, art. 29', in G. Cian, G. Oppo, A. Trabucchi (eds.), *Commentario al diritto italiano della famiglia*, I, 1992, p. 3; M. Sesta, 'Privato e pubblico nei progetti di legge in materia familiare', in *Studi in onore di Pietro Rescigno*, II, 1998, p. 811; M. Bessone, G. Alpa, A. D'Angelo, G. Ferrando, M.R. Spallarossa, *La famiglia nel nuovo diritto*, 2002, p. 16.; M. Fortino, *Diritto di famiglia. I valori, I principi, le regole*, 2004, pp. 25 *et seq.*; L. Califano, 'La famiglia ed I figli nella Costituzione italiana', in R. Nania & P. Ridola (eds.), *I diritti costituzionali*, 2006, pp. 925–948; M. Sesta, 'Article 29', in M. Sesta (ed.), *Codice della famiglia*, 2007, p. 3.

2 R. Bin, 'La famiglia: alla radice di un ossimoro', 2000 *Studium Iuris*, p. 1067.

3 See V. Zagrebelski, 'Famiglia e vita familiare nella Convenzione europea dei diritti umani', in M.C. Andrini (ed.), *Un nuovo diritto di famiglia europeo*, 2007, p. 118; G. Ferrando, 'Matrimonio e crisi della famiglia – Note introduttive', in G. Ferrando (dir.), *Il nuovo diritto di famiglia*, 2007, p. 50.

'Nobody can say that their family is a real family and my family is just a bunch of people living in the same house'.[4]

It would certainly be interesting to know what, from the perspective of this young boy, distinguishes a family from just another bunch of people, or perhaps what is natural and what is 'against nature'. Taking this path would inevitably bring to the surface the problem of definitions, of the *ubi consistam* of the family and, with it, the problem of power relations between those who have always imposed, or posed, such definitions and those who have always borne the consequences of them. In the same way, it would bring to the surface the problem of the distinction of the family from other types of cohabiting arrangements or, even more importantly, that of the value to attribute to the criterion of self-representation, which returns the power to the hands of stakeholders to speak of themselves by themselves.

Although it is clear that the arguments proposed today for supporting the value of cultural (as opposed to natural) traditions – unity of the family, perpetuation of the species, children well-being, the community's benefit, and similar others – often mask the normative translation of certain moral beliefs, there appears to be a preoccupying lack of a sufficiently informed and broad vision able to remedy the ongoing situation of social exclusion and of limitation of individual prerogatives. Regrettably, extreme radicalization of right-wing and religious discourses have produced the perverse effect of imposing the inability to look beyond the lowest common denominator on the more progressive, yet fragmented, sectors of society.

Whilst marriage equality is an issue that, in contemporary Italy, is giving headaches to many, very few support the contention that because the construction of the 'legitimate family' (a term still widely used) finds its source in cultural traditions shaped by history, and not in an immutable idea of nature and 'naturality', then the *status quo* would need to be argued for at the level of principles. Very few are willing to recognise that traditional Italian values have often contributed to constraining the individual within clothes that were not really custom-made for those who were required to wear them, especially when one considers women, children, the disabled or homosexuals. Whereas most scholars and intellectuals recognise that the legal culture of our times conceives marriage principally as an individual prerogative, a free choice which reflects a life-plan imagined, built up, conquered for celebrating one's own affections and projects, for overcoming the many difficulties that a life together always presents, inside and outside the

4 E. Wolfson, *Why Marriage Matters. America, Equality, and Gay People's Right to Marry*, 2004, p. 85.

couple,[5] few would concede that society has little interest in keeping some of its members away from it.

This circumstance raises the question of justifiability of the *status quo*. The most refined thinkers have warned that every exclusion 'must give explanations, arguments: it must produce an argument that justifies it';[6] and it must do so if it wishes to avoid to be perceived as that 'French cook who, when asked to justify the cruelty with which she peeled off eels while still alive, answered "they are used to it": she had been doing it for thirty years'.[7] However, few have embraced such perspective thus far.[8] Meanwhile, recent medical research drew attention to the implications of the so called 'minority stress' suffered by lesbian and gay families by way of lack of legal recognition.[9]

1.3. INDIVIDUAL 'DESIRES' VS OBJECTIVE DISCOURSES

Freedom and equality are fundamental principles of law. The theme of same-sex and unmarried unions, and the problems posed by it, concerns precisely these two fundamental principles and values: equality and autonomy, equal treatment and respect for fundamental rights of the individual, the ban on discrimination and the promotion of personal development and identity.

Whilst these concepts have framed the debate elsewhere, both in Europe and overseas, in the boot of Europe they have not yet been able to limit the token of hypocrisy and deference which the legislature and intellectuals continue to pay to external and non-democratically appointed agents. Legal scholars or philosophers, in turn, have initially been very critical of any attempt to inject these elements into the legal debate. Even when they grant the individual a certain degree of autonomy within the private sphere, such critiques forcefully maintain that same-sex couples should not aspire to any kind of recognition in the public sphere. Concerning sexual orientation in general, even when they show tolerance towards certain dimensions linked to conduct, these scholars tend to limit it to a conduct of a merely erotic-sexual nature.

5 The Belgian Cour d'arbitrage, with its decision of 20 October 2004, no. 159 (on line at www.arbitrage.be) held that 'Au regard d'une telle conception du mariage (la création d'une communauté de vie durable), la différence entre, d'une part, les personnes qui souhaitent former une communauté de vie avec une personne de l'autre sexe et, d'autre part, les personnes qui souhaitent former une telle communauté avec une personne de même sexe n'est pas telle qu'il faille exclure pour ces dernières la possibilité de se marier'.

6 See the B. Constant's quotation in G. Zanetti, 'Le coppie di fatto tra diritto e morale', in G. Zanetti (ed.), *Elementi di etica pratica. Argomenti normativi e spazi del diritto*, 2003, p. 159.

7 *Ibid.*

8 See, however, as one attempt to raise the profile of alternative discourses on the family, various contributions published online at www.famiglienellacostituzione.it/spunti/1index.html.

9 V. Lingiardi, *Citizen gay: famiglie, diritti negati e salute mentale*, 2007.

The conclusion normally drawn from such premises is that sexual orientation is a characteristic that should be relevant only within the limits of the private sphere of the individual; therefore, any further expression of sexual orientation cannot rise to the level of a legally relevant phenomenon, deserving of protection. This line of reasoning, while accepting that today homosexuality is no longer a disease and the homosexual is no longer a deviant, emphatically reiterates that the homosexual is a person with an identity which should be respected, but only in the bedroom.

Following some elaborations – which embody the closest attitude – same-sex relationships are not, and should not be, relevant for the law because, by being indicators of 'subjective and individual desires', they belong to a pre-juridical experience which clashes with an 'objective discourse on the human person'.[10] This viewpoint seems to consider 'homosexual cohabitation' a 'thing' where sexual activity takes place which, albeit protected in the private sphere, does not deserve any public recognition. Those who admit a certain degree of 'respect for human dignity and private autonomy' see legal recognition of same-sex couples as a merely ideological statement, where 'homosexuals are not considered for what they are, but for what they would like and cannot be'.[11]

On the occasion of the approval of some regional laws granting same-sex couples access to public housing facilities, some have even argued that same-sex couples could not be denied such facilities, but should be considered 'following a proper order', that is to say 'in an inferior and subordinate position' when compared with married and unmarried different-sex couples.[12] Others have claimed that the family has 'intrinsic characteristics which cannot be defined or modified by the legal system'. These characteristics are monogamy, exogamy, and heterosexuality, and the argument produced is that if one is upset, such as difference of sexes, 'nothing can guarantee that in the future the others will not be modified', as demonstrated by a German case where brother and sister were subjected to criminal sanctions for living together as a couple.[13] Even more radically, some have argued that 'if homosexuality is not a sin, nothing is a sin. If homosexuality is not morally reprehensible, neither is paedophilia. The latter is nothing but a *species* of the former'.[14]

Apart from apocalyptic parallels between homosexuality and incest or paedophilia, the specifically problematic element is not really that of conceding tolerance towards certain social and even legal phenomena, when individual rights are

10 F. D'Agostino, *Una filosofia della famiglia*, 2003, p. 140.
11 F. D'Agostino, 'Le coppie omosessuali, problema per I giuristi', 1994 *Iustitia*, p. 83.
12 F. D'Angeli, *Il fenomeno delle convivenze omosessuali: quale tutela giuridica?*, 2003, p. 32.
13 L. Violini, 'Il riconoscimento delle coppie di fatto: praeter o contra constitutionem?', 2007 *Forum dei Quaderni costituzionali*, online at http://www.forumcostituzionale.it/site/temi-di-attualita/temi-di-attualita/diritti-e-liberta.html.
14 A. Donati, *La famiglia tra diritto pubblico e diritto privato*, 2004, p. 326.

at stake, but that of imposing on the 'objective discourse' concerning the human person a discourse aimed at the legitimation of a phenomenon in the family sphere, which is inherently sterile and, thus, fundamentally different. It is this difference which impedes that such subjective desires acquire dignity before the law, just as it happens for friendship, a situation existentially important, but legally irrelevant. Practically speaking, as it will be illustrated in the last section, a marriage contracted in The Netherlands by two Italian men has been considered radically non-existent and, thus, has not been registered in the national registry or births, marriages, and deaths.

1.4. SOCIAL FORMATIONS AND THE ROLE OF SOLIDARITY

Midway between the integralist views mentioned above and claims for full marriage equality lie some cautious theses which favour a limited recognition of *de facto* couples, irrespective of the partners' gender and, to be sure, of the intimate nature of the relationship. The focus of this paper is precisely on these views; more precisely, my aim is principally to provide some indications as to why they only favour *limited* recognition.

The dominant argument claims that Article 29 of the Constitution – by tracing a clear divide between marriage and *de facto* families – requires the legal scholar to 'raise the issue of the control of the border between family and non-family'.[15] Unmarried cohabitation is considered by many as a way for the individual to realise his or her personality, which nevertheless cannot lead to full equality with marriage.[16]

There is, thus, a deeply felt and shared need to reiterate the exclusivity of the family model supposedly foreseen by the Constitution. The argument normally concludes that it should be possible to embrace same-sex couples within the concept of 'para-family relations', which would seem to include every kind of cohabitation under the same roof and could be 'lightly' regulated under the auspices of Article 2 of the Constitution.[17] Article 2 guarantees inviolable human rights by connecting them both to the individual and to the 'social formations' where he or

---

15 F.D. Busnelli, 'La famiglia e l'arcipelago familiare', 2002 *Rivista di diritto civile*, p. 509. See also G. Bonilini, 'Il matrimonio', in G. Bonilini and G. Cattaneo (dir.), *Il diritto di famiglia*, I, *Famiglia e matrimonio*, 2007, p. 63; F. Santosuosso, *Il matrimonio*, 2007, p. 25.

16 See in general on unmarried cohabitation M. Dogliotti, 'Famiglia di fatto', in *Digesto delle discipline privatistiche, sezione civile*, 1992, p. 192; F.D. Busnelli & M. Santilli, 'La famiglia di fatto', in G. Oppo, G. Cian & A. Trabucchi (eds.), *Commentario al diritto italiano della famiglia*, VI, 1, 1993, p. 757; L. Califano, 'La famiglia ed I figli nella Costituzione italiana', cit., p. 937; L. Balestra, 'La famiglia di fatto', in M. Sesta & V. Cuffaro (eds.), *Persona, famiglia e successioni nella giurisprudenza costituzionale*, 2006, pp. 483–503.

17 Busnelli 2002, *supra* note 15, p. 509.

she develops his or her own personality; furthermore, it demands the execution of the non-renounceable duties of political, economic and social solidarity.[18]

These conceptions echo arguments that other experiences around the globe have had to face. They have informed both the French and the Spanish approach, to name but some neighbouring countries, where at some point the debate was dominated by those wishing to dilute the incumbent recognition by mixing it with broader issues dealing with personal relationships of 'reciprocal help'. In Italy, however, the distinct trait is that such attempts characterize the *maximum*, not the minimum, of protection that has been put on the table by the academic and political establishment and the lesbian, gay, bisexual and transgender (LGBT) movement alike. Why?

I believe that if constitutional scholars continue to claim (even recently) that it is 'imprecise', especially with regards to same-sex couples, to call them '*de facto* families' or 'non-traditional families', because they are in truth 'social formations within which solidaristic manifestations are realised',[19] this is because the family is assumed to be an immutable part of the debate. Starting from this often implicit assumption, all new phenomena must automatically fall under the other, the open, the variable element of the debate, the one referring to 'social formations' in general. My contention here is that few authors have been willing or able to emancipate from the binary logic which – in the Italian constitutional system – opposes the 'family' and 'social formations', a logic which descends from a limited reading of the constitutional text approved by the Constitutional Court.[20] This Court, in particular, has always held very clearly that 'cohabitation *more uxorio* is different from the matrimonial tie, and with the latter not automatically comparable in order to deduct the constitutional requirement to equal treatment: the former, in fact, lacks those characters of stability and certainty typical of the matrimonial tie, based as it is on day-to-day affection which can be freely and instantly withdrawn (...) Therefore it cannot be held unreasonable and arbitrary that (...) the legislature adopts diversified solutions for the family based on marriage, foreseen by Article 29 of the Constitution, and for cohabitation *more uxorio*: and this

18 A. Barbera, 'Principi fondamentali, art. 1–12', in G. Branca (ed.), *Commentario alla Costituzione, sub art. 2*, 1975, pp. 66 *et seq.*; D. Messinetti, 'Personalità (diritti della)', in *Enciclopedia del diritto*, XXXIII, 1983, p. 366; A. Baldassarre, 'Diritti inviolabili', in *Enciclopedia giuridica*, XI, 1989; A. Barbera, '"Nuovi diritti": attenzione ai confini', in L. Califano (ed.), *Corte costituzionale e diritti fondamentali*, 2004, p. 19; A. Barbera & C. Fusaro, *Corso di diritto pubblico*, 2006, p. 126; P. Lillo, *Diritti fondamentali e libertà della persona*, 2006, p. 79.

19 R. Alesse, 'Quando I "dico" non trovano "Pacs"', 2007 *Forum dei Quaderni costituzionali*, online at http://www.forumcostituzionale.it/site/temi-di-attualita/temi-di-attualita/diritti-e-liberta.html, p. 2.

20 See, for instance, Corte cost. 13–18 November 1986, no. 237, 1986 *Consiglio di Stato*, II, p. 1447; Corte cost. 26 May 1989, no. 310, 1991 *Foro italiano*, I, p. 446; Corte cost., 18 January 1996, no. 8, 1996 *Famiglia e diritto*, p. 107; Corte cost. 29 January 1998, no. 2, 1998 *Consiglio di Stato*, II, p. 3; Corte cost. 13 May 1998, no. 166, 1998 *Giurisprudenza italiana*, p. 1783.

because the former epitomises, as opposed to the latter, not only the need to protect individual affective relations, but also the need to protect the "family institution" based on stability of relations'.[21]

In this context, the permeability of the concept of solidarity and of social formations mentioned by Article 2 of the Constitution appears to many the maximum stretch allowed under the current system. As I mentioned, this is perhaps true only if the other side of the bar remains constant. Everything changes, of course, if the meaning of family and of marriage, and the content of their constitutional protection, is approached from a perspective capable of taking into account the theoretical references mentioned in the Paragraph 1.2 above and superbly illustrated by some of the most often cited judicial decisions around the globe.[22]

It is also interesting to note how the mainstream constitutional argument appears to be at odds with the more open teachings of the best *dottrina* of civil law, which stress that 'man does not simply have sexual instincts, but also and foremost, the essential need to realise himself in the family, as the first form of human living-together arrangement [so that] freedom of the family must be understood as freedom of the individual to set up the family in accordance with his own choices, and as freedom to develop in it one's own personality'.[23] Rather interestingly, very few constitutional scholars have considered that: (1) freedom to marry is a fundamental (human) right; (2) as a fundamental human right, it is protected by Article 2 of the Constitution; (3) freedom to marry entails the freedom of each individual to choose the person to be married; (4) gay and lesbian people cannot marry a person of their choice; and (5) gay and lesbian people suffer an interference with the sphere of personal freedom guaranteed by the Constitution.

This line of reasoning is still alien to many, who only see Article 2 as a (weak) way of counterbalancing the protection that Article 29 allegedly affords to the traditional family based on marriage. Instead of embracing the argument just outlined, a majority of the moderately progressive scholars support what I call the reductionist argument. The reductionist argument claims that: (1) *de facto* (same-sex or different-sex) couples are not a family based on marriage (a stronger version claims that this is because the family is 'natural' and therefore immutable as allegedly prescribed by Article 29 of the Constitution); (2) however, they *can* be

21 Corte cost. 25 July 2000, no. 352, 2001 *Cassazione penale*, p. 28.

22 Ontario Court of Appeal, *Halpern et al* v. *Attorney General of Canada et al.*, 10 June 2003, 2003 *Dominion Law Reports*, (4th), 225, p. 529, online at http://www.ontariocourts.on.ca/decisions/2003/june/halpernC39172.htm; Vermont Supreme Court, *Baker* v. *State of Vermont*, 20 December 1999, no. 98–032, 744 A.2d, 864 (Vt. 1999); Massachusetts Supreme Court, *Goodridge* v. *Department of Public Health*, 18 November 2003, SJC-08860, online at http://news.findlaw.com/hdocs/docs/conlaw/goodridge111803opn.pdf.

23 C.M. Bianca, *Diritto civile. La famiglia, le successioni*, 2, 2005, p. 15.

seen as a manifestation of functions of solidarity; (3) these functions are approved by the Constitution in its Article 2; and (4) regulating such social formations would not be unconstitutional *provided that the supremacy of the traditional family is left untouched* (this part is often left implicit).

There are no reasons to hide the fact that a similar approach has inspired, two decades ago, the first Danish law establishing a 'separate' scheme for same-sex couples. However, the Danish scheme, as well as many of the subsequent ones, also produced a substantive equalisation in rights and duties; it was separate, true, but (more-or-less) equal.[24] What is striking about the Italian situation is that mainstream, liberal discourses all focus on a separate *and* unequal scheme, while presenting it as a fair innovation.

In my view, an argument such as this one can be subject to a number of critiques, the main one being that it isolates from the debate precisely what needs to be debated: the immutability and the naturality of the traditional family. However, what I wish to emphasise here is the principle from which this position originates. In my view, as it will be clear, solidarity is *the* key word in contemporary Italian debate on *de facto* couples. It appears in the title of the bill drafted and supported by the Italian LGBT movement. It appears in a regional law of Apulie, which has addressed these matters. It appears in the Governmental Bill on 'Rights and Duties of Cohabitants' (DiCo), as well as in the title of the latest parliamentary bill, creating the 'contract of solidarity union'. It is, I conclude, the only (hypothetical) *laissez-passer* under the current circumstances.

The theoretical premises of the diverse Italian political establishment, notwithstanding apparent ideological distance, all converge into the concept of solidarity and have all had an immediately visible influence on the various legislative proposals that have been presented to the public opinion and to the decision makers. This conclusion is not contradicted by the fact that the real debate is much richer than this – especially at the fringes – and that there have even been parliamentary proposals for opening up marriage to same-sex couples. These are issues of, and for, the radicals, which bother mainstream élites to a negligible extent.

Clearly, solidarity is a very noble concept, but also very distant from what needs to be debated. Solidarity is a broad concept that can be found in a multiplicity of situations in life and that can acquire several meanings. In legal terms, it is very difficult to grasp its precise relevance.

It is my firm belief that solidarity is a concept that has been put forward because it allows one to gather political consensus around a central concept of both Christianity and socialist/communist views. The same concept also serves a more subtle purpose, because it allows one to pretend that the real problem of full

---

24 See, also for further developments, K. Waaldijk, 'Others May Follow: the Introduction of Marriage, Quasi-Marriage, and Semi-Marriage for Same-Sex Couples in European Countries', 2004 *New England Law Review*, no. 3, p. 569.

marriage equality for same-sex couples will disappear. Regrettably, the emphasis on solidarity also has the effect of reinforcing the shift of the debate from some of the central problems of Italian society: male chauvinism and machismo, homophobia and transphobia, lack of adequate public policies and programmes in support of minorities and for the promotion of diversities, lack of adequate welfare nets for the economically weak, lack of opportunities for the young and innovative sectors of society.

Overall, the widespread obsession on the constitutionality of an eventual parliamentary act on *de facto* couples obliges many to direct their efforts at demonstrating that the solidarity ties within these couples do make them constitutionally relevant and, thus, do ensure the legitimacy of an eventual act. This move, however, produces a progressive distancing from the problematisation of concepts of family and marriage in the 21st century, considerably reduces the room for discussion by strengthening the insulation and the immutability of such concepts and, thus, procrastinates the supremacy of the classical understanding that marriage is the only legitimate place for the exercise of sexuality, which should be orientated to procreation.

The proposals for new legislation, which will be discussed in the following sections, illustrate both how the shift from the crucial problems was implemented, and the impact this has had on the position of individuals and couples alike.

2. THE PROPOSAL ON THE *PATTO CIVILE DI SOLIDARIETÀ*: PHENOMENOLOGY OF A SELF-INFLICTED COMPROMISE

Even if the story begins at least a decade earlier, the theme of same-sex couples became a hot electoral issue only in the months prior to the 2006 parliamentary elections, following an intense campaign by political parties of the major Italian gay association (Arcigay). Prior to the 2006 elections the Chamber of Deputies had already addressed the issue with an analysis of the various proposals on the table. The main proposal to be discussed had rapidly become the one named '*Patto civile di solidarietà*' (Pacs), proposed by Franco Grillini MP on behalf of Arcigay. The Justice Committee of the lower Chamber held hearings on the matter, which made it possible to collect and put on parliamentary records various experts' views on same-sex couples.[25]

The 'Pacs' proposal has always been defended by its drafters as 'the lowest possible compromise', meaning that the proposal had already taken into account the peculiarities of the Italian situation by refraining from claiming full legal

25 See them on the website of the campaign www.unpacsavanti.it.

recognition, on an equal footing with marriage. This claim also meant that, notwithstanding the self-restraint exercise, the proposal was the best possible compromise under the circumstances of that time, for it actually sought to improve the situation to some degree.

The Pacs proposal, re-presented after the elections as Bill C-33, is accompanied by an introduction that goes out of its way to clarify what it is *not*. The need to downplay and 'disguise' the meaning of the bill vividly depicts the climate of misinformation and suspicion that characterised the political audience towards which it was directed. It also epitomizes the difficulties that the proposers had to face in order to defend an even incomplete recognition. The main character which illustrates this difficulty is symbolised by the choice of combining, from the very beginning, the position of different-sex cohabitants with that of same-sex couples. This monistic approach was then believed to avoid further singling out of sexual differences, and to be able to attract support from a larger population than just the gay and lesbian population. To this end, the lesbian and gay movement started or reinvigorated relations with some of those social sectors working on secularism, pluralism, diversity, and organised for a few years a national 'Pacs day' in Rome as an occasion to collectively press Parliament for change.

The choice of addressing the situation of all unmarried couples in a single bill, without focusing on the specificity of same-sex couples, had a clear negative impact on the intensity and the scope of the legal scheme proposed. Put simply, it is rather clear that if same-sex couples wish to obtain a legal scheme that closely resembles marriage in terms of legal effects, this does not necessarily hold true for different-sex couples aiming at an alternative scheme. Moreover, even if the scheme was conceived and proposed as an instrument to ensure better protection of the inviolable right to personal development, and it does indeed propose some interesting solutions, the majority of the choices made at the private law level were not entirely consistent with these lofty premises.

The first and main aspect which testifies to the self-inflicted exclusion from family law is exemplified by the fact that the new scheme is a contract, governed by contract law. By way of illustration, the explanatory notes written by the proposers state that 'today in Italy contracts must rigorously have a patrimonial content. Without this legislative reform two individuals cannot, under the current state of things, conclude agreements concerning the non-patrimonial issues of their cohabitation'.[26]

Clearly, a contract for regulating both the patrimonial and non-patrimonial issues of a life together already exists, and it is normally called marriage. Since it was chosen not to address marriage and marriage rights directly, though, the proposal sought to achieve as many practical results as it could whilst at the same time distancing the Pacs from the family as much as possible.

26 Explanatory Memorandum to Bill C-33, p. 4.

This dubious juggling exercise can also be deducted from Article 2 of the proposal, which defines the Pacs as 'the agreement between two people, also of the same sex, concluded in order to regulate the personal and patrimonial relations concerning their life together'. Moreover Article 6 stipulates that 'the *patto civile di solidarietà* is governed by the rules of the Civil Code on contracts, if applicable'.

Articles 3 to 5 are dedicated to the manner in which a Pacs can and should be established. The system tends to resemble the establishment of a marriage, as much as possible. In fact, it includes the impossibility to sign a Pacs between close relatives, or between individuals who are already bound by a marriage or a Pacs. Article 4, in particular, makes it clear that a Pacs can come to life only after a formalised procedure in front of the registrar (with the signature of the pact by both parties).

In terms of legal consequences, Article 7 stipulates a duty to contribute to the charges of the common life and Article 8 gives the parties the possibility to opt for the *comunione legale*, the matrimonial regime of common property between spouses foreseen by Articles 177 *et seq*, Civil Code. Furthermore, Article 11 makes it clear that, in case of intestate succession, the party to a *patto civile di solidarietà* will have exactly the same inheritance rights as a spouse. There are other important rights attached to the *patto*, albeit the proposal is by no means complete. The rest of the bill is devoted to regulating the termination of the pact, as well as issues of private international law; the final part modifies various laws and codes in order to make room for the new scheme.

The informed reader might be able to identify in this proposal some opportunities and suggestions for the new, light, minimal family law of the future, but will also conclude that the sanctity of the legitimate family cannot be challenged as easily as the 'homosexual lobbies' would like. For the reasons set out in the previous paragraphs, a bill such as this one might have started as the best possible compromise, but it ended up as something very close to a ghetto.

3. 'OUT OF THE FRYING PAN INTO THE FIRE': THE GOVERNMENTAL PROPOSAL ON RIGHTS AND DUTIES OF COHABITANTS

As mentioned, the theme of *de facto* couples became a hot electoral issue, and thus of public domain, only in 2006, with severe delay if compared to other European and non-European jurisdictions. The diverse and rather fragmented centre-left coalition headed by Mr. Prodi had managed to agree that, once in power, it would propose new legislation to improve the protection and the rights afforded to *individuals* living in a *de facto* cohabitation. When, at the beginning of 2007, the

Government chose to draft and publish its own proposal on the issue,[27] the public debate erupted uncontrollably. The Governmental proposal fuelled rampant opposition by the Catholic Church and conservative sectors of Italian society, which found a common reason to call for a large public demonstration in Rome in defence of the traditional family, called the Family Day, organised just weeks before an unprecedentedly huge gay pride parade took place in the same city. In between, the President of the Republic had called upon all political parties to refrain from exacerbating the deep fracture between *laici* and *cattolici*, between secular and Catholic views. The contrast, however, exploded in the streets and, thus, could not have been more evident.

The Government had attempted to craft a compromise proposal, refraining from any recognition of *de facto* couples but granting protection to the *individual* cohabiting with another person. The ruling coalition, composed of moderate Catholics, liberals, social-democrats, greens, communists and post-communists could only agree on this minimal standard which, as a matter of fact, largely corresponds to the views of mainstream, moderately liberal legal doctrine. I have sketched above the theoretical and legal reasons of this choice, such as the rigid dichotomy between family and other 'social formations' always upheld by the Constitutional Court.

An initial benchmark for assessing the nature and content of the Governmental Bill could consist in clarifying from which debate the DiCo Bill emanates. Did it originate from a political, cultural, and scientific debate on the problematisation of the dominant representation of the family? Did it originate from the problematisation of the prevalent narrations of the body, sexuality, pleasure, desire and reproduction? Did it originate from the renewed role of family functions and parental responsibilities in the 21st Century? I strongly believe that, if the DiCo Bill was indeed a product of such a broad reflection, it would already be a positive development in itself, even with its intrinsic (technical) limitations in terms of rights and benefits it entails.

Unfortunately, all indicators point in different directions. The obsessive and recurring governmental emphasis on the rights of the individual as a single person, the repeated assurances by the LGBT movement that its proposals would do nothing to change the family and its structures, the alarmed and recurrent comments made by the highest religious authorities, including the Pope, *vis-à-vis* the Catholic sectors of political forces, they all point to the conclusion that the core inspiration of the DiCo Bill, clearly reflected in most technical solutions adopted, is that of tracing a very visible and rigid line between the legitimate family and other living-together arrangements. As I tried to illustrate, this fundamental

27 Senate Bill no. 1339, *Diritti e doveri delle persone stabilmente conviventi*, by Ministers Pollastrini and Bindi

choice is consistent with the majoritarian views on the matter of both the political, the religious, and the scientific community in Italy.

From my point of view, however, the bill stands out, because it embodies the reductionist hypothesis taken to its highest level, as if a decade of European and global experiences had nothing to teach; or rather, as if the only teaching of such experiences was that full equality was indeed possible and, thus, a concrete and immediate danger urging solutions of a radically different nature. What happened with the DiCo Bill was inspired not only by plain reductionism, but by a reductionism so complexly inter-related with international developments to take the form of a race to the bottom growing faster, rather than slower, as full equality for same-sex couples became a more and more concrete reality elsewhere and, especially, in neighbouring countries, more comparable, and more interrelated with Italy (*e.g.* France and Spain). A reductionism so pronounced that it induced the Government to entirely reject any scheme based on a formal manifestation of party choice, because the danger of equating, from the formal point of view, marriage and cohabitation was too great.[28]

If compared with the Pacs proposal, the Governmental choice has produced a very significant downgrade of the scheme, and by consequence of the personal relationship which underpins it, from the (mildly) formal to the purely informal level. The way this 'cultural' and political premise was technically implemented was the involvement of a mechanism foreseen by the population registry, called to prove the existence of cohabitation by means of the data recorded. In other words, the population registry is used as a tool to prove cohabitation between two individuals, through a presumptive mechanism which allows contrary evidence as to the existence of the prerequisites, the initial or final date of cohabitation, etc. Nothing farther from a new legal scheme.

Notwithstanding the premises I recalled, the title of the Governmental proposal, 'Rights and duties of people stably cohabiting' (DiCo its short name) could seriously run the risk of pleasing some post-modern commentators. Here it is, finally, the light, minimal law, the law that speaks of and to persons with multiple and interchangeable identities, not of legal constructs or institutions. But is it really the family law of the future, the one that abandons the rigidity of the traditional status and allows for the broadest blossoming of personal autonomy, the law set by this proposal? Or, rather, such law is so 'minimal' that no one could reasonably dare to speak of family law at all, as, in fact, several reactionary critiques wished?

The way the nature of the union and the subjective requisites are conceived sends out a clear message. According to Article 1 (coldly called 'Scope and modalities of application'), 'Two people of age and not incapacitated, also of the same

---

28 M. Dogliotti & A. Figone, 'Famiglia di fatto e DICO: un'analisi del progetto governativo', 2007 *Famiglia e diritto*, p. 417.

sex, united by reciprocal affective ties, who cohabit stably and exchange assistance and moral and material solidarity, not tied by marriage, blood ties in the direct line within the first degree, in-law ties in the direct line within the second degree, adoption, affiliation, guardianship or protection, are entitled to the rights, duties and claims established by the present act' (unofficial translation).

First of all, a stylistic remark: if the Government has always defended the proposal arguing that it only protects the rights of individuals and not of couples, it is then ironic that the first word of the bill is 'two', 'two persons'. As is immediately clear by the cumbersome and inelegant definition cited above, the very essence of the type of relationship is precisely based on exchange of assistance and solidarity. Not the family, not conjugality, not cohabitation *more uxorio*, nor sexuality, but solidarity, an evergreen champion of good sentiments directed at the disenfranchised, the excluded, the 'minor'. Thus, the bill attaches rights and duties not only to individuals living in a marriage-like relationship (characterised by the *affectio maritalis*), but also to those who cohabit for affective reasons, with assistance and solidarity: old people, brothers and sisters, relatives or in-laws who remained in the same house after the once large family became thinner, students, etc.

According to the bill, cohabitants must not be already married. Furthermore, the bill does not exclude relations between close relatives, such as for instance brothers and sisters. Only first degree relatives in the direct line, that is parents and children, and second degree in-laws in the direct line are excluded from the definition of (potential) cohabitants. Apart from these cases, all other relatives living together could potentially fall under the scope of the law. There is, really, little need to comment why this is done the way it is. Past European, but also overseas experiences have shown that this option is a way of symbolically diluting the material object and, thus, of downplaying any potential comparison between such living-together arrangements and marriage.

There have been both political and scientific claims, in the global debate around the world, that this expansion beyond sexuality and conjugality might not be a negative development in itself. In this case, however, it becomes a very negative counter-revolution if seen as the product of the limited debate sketched above. In truth, in Italian politics there seems to be an omnipresent subtext, never expressly mentioned. An idea of the couple, of the cohabiting couple, of the conjugal but unmarried couple, which cannot be the object not only of recognition, but even of explicit representation. This is also evidenced by the fact that the Governmental Bill does not address one of the crucial problems of *de facto* families that of the fate of purchases made during the relationship and of the division of property upon its break-up.

At the centre of this bill are not people, single or coupled, but rights and duties, mere legal constructs which become, in the absence of a subject, nomad and empty ghosts 'in search of an author', to say it with Pirandello. There are laws that mould, shape, organise, foresee, guarantee; and, within the scope of these purposes, entrust certain subjective position to the individuals concerned. But this draft has the only declared purpose of 'attributing' rights and duties.

According to the bill, cohabitation does not begin with a formal act; simply, it is proven by the records of the population register. The second paragraph of Article 1 speaks only of an aseptic 'inscription' and of 'cancellation'. The population registry, according to the explanatory notes, allows the interested parties to 'demonstrate the existence and the duration of the cohabitation in order to exercise the rights foreseen by the Bill'.[29] The 'inscription' seems to follow a declaration given by the parties according to existing rules governing the population registry which, as maintained by the explanatory notes, already has the institutional mandate of 'ascertaining and certifying'.[30] To be sure, it was already a legal duty for everyone to declare to the population registry his or her eventual cohabitants. The bill even stipulates that when the declaration is made by only one party, he or she *must* inform the other of this circumstance by registered mail (Article 1(3)). There is, thus, nothing resembling a formal celebration.

In terms of legal consequences, Article 4 of the bill delegates to hospitals and other care facilities the regulation of the ways in which the cohabitant can exercise his or her visitation and assistance rights. This is another rather curious provision, without much attached to it; whilst delegation to the periphery is sometimes a good thing, in a diverse and contradictory country like Italy the law should at least set the general criteria and establish clear guidelines and principles for hospitals to follow. Otherwise, it is almost certain that a situation similar to that of abortion or contraception would arise, where doctors with conscience objections refuse to implement the law and to provide services or care to women in need.

The bill also addresses important issues such as residence permits for the partner of third country nationality, work carried out by the *de facto* partner in the partner's company, tenancy contracts, change of workplace, succession, maintenance in case of need. The common theme in all of these cases is that of underscoring the difference between cohabitants and spouses, either by making the exercise of rights for the former more cumbersome, or by crafting such rights in a more limited fashion both *ratione personae* and *ratione materiae*. As just one instance which testifies to this approach, it will be sufficient to mention that succession rights can only be acquired after nine years of cohabitation (Article 11).

In general, cohabitation must be 'actual, ongoing' in order for the parties to be able to exercise the rights and duties attributed by the bill. Ironically, thus, cohabitants must always stay together, at all times, as opposed to spouses who can each go their own way, since living apart is not a problem in marriage and certainly not

29 Relazione di accompagnamento, p. 14.
30 The system is regulated by Decreto del Presidente della Repubblica 30 maggio 1989, no. 223.

a condition for its existence. On closer examination, however, if one analyses other areas of human behaviour, it is not 'living under the same roof' in itself which justifies the attribution of rights and benefits (except for cases specifically and strictly linked to this circumstance, such as the right to housing or domicile). If this was true, I could issue a declaration of cohabitation with my cat: after all, we have mutual affective and solidarity links and we live together. It is, rather, the common life project, the interconnection of experiences and desires, of fears, of attempts, of property, it is the *comunione di vita*. Cohabitation is nothing, but one of the many possible epiphanies of this *comunione*, which is a central aspect in the lives of many and what should really matter: it is condescending to pretend that it is cohabitation alone what triggers the necessity of law reform.

Clearly, it is no secret that this view leads one to admit that there is no real difference between *de facto* and married couples. In fact, the Italian Constitutional Court has held on various occasions that the reason for upholding differential treatment lies precisely in a legal, non-factual difference (marriage is a relationship encapsulated in a legal scheme which guarantees certainty and stability, cohabitation is uncertain and unstable). Hence, this bill magically ensures that cohabitation between unmarried partners remains a *de facto* phenomenon, unable and unfit to pierce the juridical realm, the sanctuary of marriage and the traditional family. This is why it only 'attributes' rights and benefits, and why it attributes them only to disentangled individuals. The underlying fact is not a juridical fact, but a *brute* fact which penetrates the legal order as a mere fact, without any social meaning and worth. In a way, this bill treats the cohabitation experience as the legal system treats a car accident: a brute fact which triggers some legal protections and a need to distribute rights and duties between the various parties involved.

As it has been written by a highly respected scholar, 'juridification means (...) guarantee: setting up of protection and, thus, possibilities of defending one's own subjectivity or whichever aspect of it before a court, either civil, administrative, or criminal. It means, in other words, to bring back in society – in the form of court structures – the conflict which used to be resolved in a power game among single individuals, or between individuals and the group (or the state), where the weakest individual, either because mere individual or because socially marginalised, had to succumb'.[31] Unfortunately, it is difficult to conclude that the DiCo Bill could have such an empowering effect.

Finally, Article 13(2) stipulates that – when pension entitlements will be reorganised as envisaged by Article 10 – it still will not be possible to calculate pension rights based on the years of cohabitation which preceded the 'declaration'; for pension purposes, cohabitation only begins when the declaration is made. The bill

---

31 G. Alpa, *Status e capacità: la costruzione giuridica delle differenze individuali*, 1993, pp. 44–45.

is silent as far as termination of the relationship is concerned (or, rather more accurately, as far as termination of the possibility to exercise the rights and benefits is concerned). Only Article 13(6) concludes that patrimonial and succession rights, as well as other benefits foreseen by the bill, terminate upon marriage of one of the cohabitants. There is absolutely no mention of the implications of a relationship breakup: it is only said that 'rights terminate'.

4. THE PARLIAMENTARY COMPROMISE: TOWARDS A 'CONTRACT OF SOLIDARITY UNION'?

At the outset of this paper I claimed that the current situation allows the curious scholar to reconstruct, through the analysis of the three bills, the rapid and sharp variations which have accompanied the debate on rights and duties of cohabitants. I also claimed that, notwithstanding the apparently different cultural and political frame, some common traits – based on the concept of solidarity – constitute the backbone of all proposals. A demonstration can be found in the way Parliament chose to approach the matter.

In the spring of 2007, almost submerged by implacable opposition and brought to the edge of a crisis, the Government chose to bring to an end its involvement in the matter of *de facto* families. It claimed that Parliament was sovereign, and left the matter to the perils of parliamentary vicissitudes, so as to detach the uncertain fate of the coalition from the even more uncertain fate of the DiCo Bill. At that point the Senate Rapporteur, who was said to favour a rather more pronounced legal protection of *de facto* couples, decided to recast all proposals in a new, single proposal. What came out of this exercise was the bill on the Contract of Solidarity Union (*Contratto di unione solidale, CUS*). With this move, the rapporteur practically killed the Government Bill, by tabling the discussion of the Senate committee only on the new CUS Bill.

Whilst the DiCo Bill only 'attributes' rights and duties to a *de facto* situation (the declaration foreseen by the law is only intended as evidence of an existing cohabitation) which is and should remain informal, because the bill is only concerned with the protection of the *individuals*, the CUS Bill seeks to anchor the new scheme to a rather more formal, yet not really institutional, frame of reference.

Clearly, the bill could not have been too daring, given the premises set by the Pacs and the DiCo Bills. In fact, as the name already anticipates, the CUS is conceived as a contract; a contract for the 'organisation of life in common' (proposed new Article 455-*bis*, Civil Code). We know from the French experience that framing the issue in contractual terms mainly responds to the wish of maintaining intact the supremacy of the family and marriage, whilst being at the same time an attempt of ensuring some 'juridification' to a situation that is felt as socially and politically pressing. We also know that this 'light', separate, and unequal solution is a product of ambiguity (though some would call it realism) rather than vision, of prejudice rather than equality.

The novelty of the CUS Bill is that it would insert the new rules in the Civil Code, an option that has a profound symbolic meaning in civil law countries. The bill proposes to insert a new Title XV at the end of Book 1 of the Civil Code, the one dedicated to persons and family, as opposed to the Pacs which borrowed heavily from contractual theory. Most importantly, the scheme is certainly given a more pronounced family-like structure than the DiCo, since the contract cannot be concluded between relatives in the direct or *collateral* line until the *second* degree (Article 455-*bis*). Whilst this testifies to the slightly more open and progressive approach of the drafters, it remains rather evident that the contract of solidarity union resulted in a sinister hybrid regulated both by the specific rules of the bill inserted in Book 1 of the Civil Code, and by the general and specific rules on contracts of Book 4, as made it explicit by Article 455-*bis*(2) of the bill.

My negative stance towards the bill derives not only from the general theoretical principles from which it stems, but also from the very concrete and practical options chosen to substantiate the scheme. Firstly, the contract can only come to life through a 'joint declaration' made to the justice of the peace or a notary (Article 455-*ter*). Again, certainly not a normal conclusion of a normal contract (I can purchase or sell a diamond worth millions without a justice or a notary), more significant than a declaration made to the population registry as in the DiCo Bill, but not really a public ceremony as for marriage.

Once the contract has been 'declared', the two parties have a duty to provide reciprocal help, and to contribute to the needs of the communal life in proportion to their income, assets and work capacity, either professional or domestic (Article 455-*septies*). The contract may regulate the time frame and the modalities of the contribution. Up to this point, one might wonder whether the same objectives could not be realised by the couple by way of a simple cohabitation contract which, under Italian law, is considered valid according to Article 1322 Civil Code; this allows individuals to conclude so-called atypical contracts within certain bounds. The question, thus, becomes that of assessing whether the bill does indeed add anything to what private parties can already do under the general legal framework.

As far as reciprocal relations are concerned, it must be concluded that the added value is very little. For instance, the bill claims that both parties must state in the contract whether they wish to consider purchases made after the contract as subject to the ordinary rules on joint property even if the purchase is made by one party alone. Here, the law makes it possible for one partner to become co-owner even when he or she did not actually participate to the purchase; such co-ownership is, however, governed by the general rules on joint property and not by the rules on matrimonial joint property. In addition, the bill stipulates that both parties can be held responsible *vis-à-vis* third parties for the debts made by only one of them (Article 455-*septies*(2) Civil Code). The joint responsibility only exists when debts were made for the needs of the communal life including the joint home.

Regarding the rights and benefits attributed by a contract of solidarity union, the bill attempts to ensure some protection in some areas. According to Article 455-*nonies* a party to such a contract has the same rights and duties as first degree relatives in relation to hospital and prison assistance and information. After at least three years of cohabitation, the parties can have some benefits when it comes to change of workplace. Furthermore, in the lack of explicit choice, all decisions on health conditions, including organ donation and funeral services, are made by the other party to the exclusion of all relatives. Finally, some succession rights accrue to the party of a CUS, but only after nine years of formal cohabitation.

In conclusion, it is rather evident that, whilst the bill does attempt to ensure some legal protection, at least in the most sensitive areas, it operated as an arbitrary selection of rights and benefits, and even within the areas selected it requires unacceptable conditions based on length of cohabitation (three years for some rights, nine years for some others). Lastly, in order to avoid any possibility for more favourable foreign schemes to enter the Italian legal system, Article 455-*quinquies* sets the principle that the Italian citizen who concludes a 'contract of solidarity union' abroad *according to the formalities of the law of that country*, is still subject to the rules of the new title of the Civil Code. Thus, the Italian citizen registered abroad, even in countries that foresee schemes very similar to marriage, cannot acquire more rights and duties than those acquired by the Italian citizen who concluded a CUS in Italy.

5. GLOBAL ISSUES AND ITALIAN POLICIES TOWARDS FOREIGN REGIMES

Italian policies towards foreign schemes alternative to marriage have been, until recently, non-existent. Generally speaking the regulation of cases entailing a foreign element is left to the private international law rules contained in Law 31st May 1995, No. 218 which, nonetheless, is silent on the issue of registered partnership and other schemes. This has opened up an academic debate on the potential of the current rules, and on the limitations of the connecting factors foreseen by the relevant articles of that law.[32]

Briefly, matrimonial capacity and other conditions to marry are regulated by the national law of each party at the time of marriage (Article 27 of Law 218/1995). This means that, for instance, while a Spanish marriage between two Spanish citizens should hypothetically be considered valid because Spanish law applies, a Spanish marriage between a Spanish and an Austrian citizen would not be considered valid, due to the lack of matrimonial capacity for one of the two spouses (the Austrian). Of course, in the first case the public policy exception of Article 16 of Law 215/1995 would prevent the application of foreign law contrary to domestic fundamental values.

As to the formalities, Article 28 tends to be rather liberal, since it poses three alternative criteria: a marriage is valid in Italy if it is considered valid (a) by law of the place where it was contracted (*lex loci celebrationis*), (b) by the national law of at least one of the spouses at the time of marriage, or (c) by the law of the place of common residence at that time. Furthermore, personal relations between spouses are governed by the common national law or, in its absence, by the law of the place where matrimonial life is principally located (Article 29). Patrimonial relations are regulated by the same law applicable to personal relations, unless the parties have agreed in writing on the applicability of a different law, namely the law of the country of which at least one of them is a citizen or has his or her residence (Article 30(1) and (2)).

Whilst there have been isolated attempts[33] to argue that these rules should at least apply to foreign same-sex marriages and registered partnerships, because the private international law qualification of 'what is marriage' should be autonomous from the substantive law qualification, the majority of the legal doctrine considers that difference of sexes is a fundamental prerequisite which, if lacking, prevents the application of such rules *tout court*, let alone subsequent, eventual recognition according to the applicable law.[34]

An illustration of this point of view can be found in a recent court case. In 2005 an Italian court had to decide whether two male Italian citizens could register the marriage they had contracted in The Hague in Italy. After moving back to Italy, the two men had chosen to request the registrar of the city where they lived

32 M. Bonini Baraldi, *Le nuove convivenze tra discipline straniere e diritto interno*, 2005; G. Rossolillo, 'Registerd partnerships e matrimoni tra persone dello stesso sesso: problemi di qualificazione ed effetti nell'ordinamento italiano', 2003 *Rivista di diritto internazionale privato e processuale*, p. 363 *et seq.* See also S. Tonolo, *Le unioni civili nel diritto internazionale privato*, 2007; E. Calò, *La pianificazione delle vicende personali e patrimoniali. Dall'amministrazione di sostegno al testamento biologico. Rapporti patrimoniali tra coniugi e successioni nel diritto internazionale privato*, 2004.

33 Bonini Baraldi 2005, *supra* note 32, pp. 199 *et seq.*

34 See the authors cited in the two following notes and their bibliographies.

to record them as 'married' in the national registry of births, marriages, and deaths. Upon refusal of the registrar, who was also supported by an opinion of the Ministry of the Interior that he had requested, the couple sued the State. The local court rejected the claim,[35] and so did the Rome Court of Appeal. The marriage was considered non-existent under Italian law and contrary to Italian public policy.[36] The Court based its reasoning on the notion of 'family' which can be found in the 1948 Italian Constitution, thereby putting the debate on the highly contentious grounds seen at the outset of this paper. It concluded that the Italian Constitution refers only to the traditional marital relationship between people of different sex, and that this concept finds its justification 'in the sentiment, the culture, and the history of our national community' which precede the law books.

In this unsympathetic context it is not surprising that, on the specific problem of registration of foreign marriages, the central director of the Ministry of the Interior has felt the need to warn Italian registrars that they should always carefully check, when receiving foreign marriage certificates and multilingual forms, that the spouses be of different sex.[37]

If registration of foreign marriages appears to be a dead end, there has been an unreported case, which leaves fewer reasons for pessimism. The case was based on EC Regulation No. 44/2001[38] (Article 19(2)(a)) and on the Employment Equality Directive.[39] A public sector employee had been seconded indefinitely to the Brussels liaisons office of his employer. After he got married with a Belgian citizen in Belgium, he requested his employer to grant him honeymoon leave. After a long and not always smooth confrontation, the employer agreed with his submission that his Belgian marriage should have been recognised for the purposes of employment benefits. In this case, which made national headlines, the Italian citizen was able to obtain from his Italian employer the benefit normally awarded to newlywed personnel. From a political point of view, it is interesting to note how the debate on 'what is family' was influenced more by a European dimension than by a closed circuit of purely local values. Legally speaking, the worker was able to make 'portable' his personal status of being married.[40]

---

35 Tribunale di Latina, decree 10 June 2005, 2005 *Famiglia e diritto*, p. 411, with concurring comment of P. Schlesinger and with dissenting comment of M. Bonini Baraldi, and in 2006 *Nuova giurisprudenza civile commentata*, p. 86, with dissenting comment of F. Bilotta.

36 Rome Court of Appeal, decree 13 July 2006, 2007 *Famiglia e diritto*, p. 166, with concurring comment of M. Sesta.

37 Ministry of the Interior, Circolare no. 55 of 18 October 2007.

38 *OJ* L 12, 16.1.2001, p. 1.

39 Council Directive 2000/78/EC of 27 November 2000, establishing a general framework for equal treatment in employment and occupation, *OJ* L 303, 2.12.2000, p. 16.

40 On the concept of 'portability' see M. Bonini Baraldi, *Freedom and Justice in the EU: Implications of the Hague Programme on Lesbian, Gay, Bisexual, Transgender Families and their Children*, 2007, p. 21.

Alongside the very evident recognition problem and some fragmented openings in the employment field, Italian judges had previously addressed sexual orientation cases – in immigration or family law matters – with suspicion. As far as immigration cases are concerned, the *Corte di Cassazione* held in two instances that a deportation order of a third country citizen, illegally residing in Italy, could only be suspended in case of demonstrated persecution in the country of origin. Moreover, persecution can only be alleged if the criminal law of the country penalises homosexuality *per se*, not 'the manifestation of homosexual practices not conform to the public sentiment of that country'.[41] In other words, it held that criminalisation of homosexual acts which are felt to be against the public sentiment cannot amount to persecution if the person has the choice of being 'discreet'. The immediate (negative) consequence is that persecution can only be proved when 'being' homosexual is penalised, but not when sexual orientation is acted upon.

As mentioned, there is an accumulation of other preoccupying decisions dealing with sexual orientation and family matters. First, the *Cassazione* has confirmed the decision of a Sicilian court which had found the wife responsible for the marriage breakup because she had had a lesbian affair (the practical consequence being that, if entitled to maintenance, the spouse who is found responsible for breakup loses his or her entitlement to ex-spousal maintenance, Article 156 Civil Code).[42] Furthermore, a lower court in Brescia not only found the husband responsible for the marriage breakup on grounds of his homosexual affair, but also awarded € 40,000 to the wife in damages for a peculiar item of pain and sufferings (*danno esistenziale*). The amount awarded took into account the fact that the homosexual relationship was a circumstance which 'has created a situation of severe shock – due to the realistic suspicion of having been infected with some serious disease following sexual intercourse with her husband – which has certainly negatively altered the quality of life of Ms C. for a significant period of time'.[43]

Other courts have adopted more open approaches. Recently, a specialised court for child protection (*Tribunale dei minorenni*) was asked by the former lesbian partner of the mother of two children to grant her contact, since before breakup she had been taking part in their upbringing. The court could only conclude that, according to current Italian law, only (biological or adoptive) parents have standing in court for such requests. Therefore, it had to turn down the appli-

41 Cass. 16 April 2007, I civil section, no. 16417, unreported; see also Cass. 18 January 2008, I criminal section, no. 2907, unreported.

42 Cass. 1 March 2005, no. 4290, 2005 *Foro italiano*, I, p. 2994.

43 Tribunale di Brescia, 14 October 2006, 2007 *Famiglia e diritto*, p. 57, with comment of G. Facci, and in 2007 *Responsabilità civile e previdenza*, p. 81, with dissenting comment of F. Bilotta and P. Cendon. Confirmed on appeal by the Brescia Court of Appeal, 5 June 2007, forthcoming publication in 2008 *Responsabilità civile e previdenza*, with comment of Caterbi.

cation for contact on grounds of lack of standing.[44] However, the court also considered that, notwithstanding the lack of any inquiry into the merits, the best interests of the children could in the abstract require further action in order to ensure the continuation of their relationship with the applicant. The Court, thus, instructed the public prosecutor to assess whether there were grounds for activating further child protection proceedings.

Finally, in the context of separation proceedings, a court in Naples chose to attach no significance whatsoever to the husband's claim that his wife should be denied parental authority of their child on ground that she was lesbian.[45] The Court held very clearly that the husband's argument was only the product of 'pseudo-cultural stereotypes, expression of moralism and not of shared ethical principles'. Moreover, it stated that such prejudices have no legal foundation in light of the equality clause of the Constitution (Article 3).

6. CONCLUSION

Notwithstanding the development of advanced solutions in foreign countries, repeated recommendations of the European Parliament, and ongoing internal pressure, in Italy the inclusion of same-sex couples within the family is destined to find an insurmountable limitation in the constitutional concept of the 'natural family'. Now, if one concludes with this answer, which accurately summarises the *status quo*, it seems to me that the wrong question was asked. When this is the answer, it means that the theme of legal recognition of same-sex couples was addressed from the following perspective: can same-sex couples be understood as falling within the scope of the constitutional concept of the 'family'? This perspective, which is dominant among liberal scholars and politicians, places on same-sex couples the burden of demonstrating their family character as a condition for obtaining the right to be treated equally. Of course, difference of sexes is considered a natural and immutable trait of the family, so that the burden is (believed to be) insurmountable. Failing evidence, either no action should follow, or public action and new legislation could be legitimised only on grounds of the solidarity element present in a wide range of cohabiting arrangements. This second option epitomises what I called the reductionist solution which is predominant among liberal élites.

I believe that the reductionist solution is inadequate and that the correct question to be answered is a different one. This belief is motivated by the circumstance

44 Trib. Min. Milano, 2 November 2007, with comment of F. Bilotta, forthcoming publication in 2008 *Famiglia e minori*.

45 Tribunale di Napoli, 28 June 2006, 2007 *Famiglia e diritto*, p. 621, with comment of M. Iannaccone.

that Article 2 of the Italian Constitution (let alone Article 3, the equality clause) celebrates the centrality of the protection afforded to fundamental freedoms and human rights. Without forgetting that sexual orientation is a personal characteristic protected both by the Constitution and by the European Convention on Human Rights, it becomes crucial to motivate whether a prevailing State interest exists, which could justify the *prima facie* violation of a fundamental freedom. Briefly, the question to be addressed should be: is it possible to demonstrate a rational or even necessary link between the objective served by the *status quo*, and current exclusion of same-sex couples from marriage?

This question should lead to the precise identification of the objectives, and interests, which underpin the *status quo*. Since freedom to marry is a fundamental freedom of the individual, one must assess whether, apart from mere ideological declamations about the supremacy of a certain family model, the marriage ban can be justified on grounds of rational principles, as several court decisions around the globe have already recognised. When this discussion will finally become of public domain in Italy, perhaps the answers will follow, more easily than expected.

SAME-SEX PARTNERSHIPS IN PORTUGAL

From *de facto* to *de jure*?

Rosa Martins*

1. INTRODUCTION

In 2001 Portuguese legislature conferred, for the first time, legal effects on the relationship of two persons of the same sex who have lived together for more than two years in a *de facto* union (*Act 7/2001 of 11th May*).[1]

The legislature's intent in regulating same-sex partnerships was clear and can be seen, firstly, in the title of the Act and, secondly, in Article 1. In contrast with the title of previous Act,[2] Act 7/2001 is entitled *'Act to adopt measures for the protection of de facto unions'* and not of the '*de facto* union'. The use of the plural

* Faculty of Law, University of Coimbra (Portugal), email: rmartins@ci.uc.pt.

1 This assertion needs to be clarified. Same-sex partnerships were not entirely ignored by the Portuguese legal system prior to Act 7/2001. As Coelho and Oliveira have already remarked, such partnerships had no legal effects *per se*, but would be taken into account as far as a 'joint household economy' was concerned. In this way, if two persons of the same sex lived in a *de facto* union for more than five years in premises leased by only one of them, on the latter's death the surviving partner enjoyed the right to a new lease that the law granted to whomever had lived with the tenant for more than five years (Arts. 90 (1), (a) and (2) and 76 (1), (a), Urban Leasehold Regime – *Regime do Arrendamento Urbano*). The surviving partner benefited from the right to a new lease, not by living in a *de facto* union with the deceased, but by living with him in a 'joint household economy'. See F. Coelho & G. Oliveira, *Curso de Direito da Família*, Vol I, 2003, pp. 112–113; J. Pitão, *Uniões de Facto e Economia Comum*, 2006, pp. 55–56.
Until 2001, Portuguese law did not directly attribute any positive legal effects to same-sex partnerships, nor did the courts recognise any effect arising from such partnerships *per se*. Take, for example, the judgment of the Lisbon Court of Appeal of 28th June 1990 that denied the right to the survivor's benefit to the surviving member of a same-sex *de facto* union under the same conditions as a surviving spouse. The summary of this judgment may be found at http://www.dgsi.pt
Act 7/2001 does not contain any provisions that could apply to situations of same-sex *de facto* unions prior to its entry into force. The Act provides only for the future; in other words, it only applies to same-sex *de facto* unions already existing on that date. See Judgment of the Lisbon Court of Appeal of 11th July 2002 at http://www.dgsi.pt and Judgment of the Constitutional Court 513/2003 of 28th October 2003 at http://www.tribunalconstitucional.pt/tc/acordaos/20030513.html.

2 Act 135/99, of 28th August 1999, Act to adopt measures for the protection of *de facto* union.

indicates that the ambit of Act 7/2001 has been extended beyond different-sex *de facto* unions to same-sex *de facto* unions. Article 1 confirms this purpose of being also applicable to same-sex *de facto* unions stating 'the present law governs the legal status of two persons, regardless of gender, who live together in a *de facto* union for more than two years'.[3] Was this the first step on a journey from *de facto* to *de jure*? In my opinion, it was.

As far as cohabitation is concerned, one can detect two opposite, yet simultaneous trends. With regards different-sex cohabitation, there is a growing preference for this model of living together, which seems to support the idea that a 'privatisation' of the couple is underway.[4] Indeed, statistics show an increasing percentage of different-sex couples choosing to live together instead of entering the legal institution of marriage.[5] A movement towards the 'deinstitutionalisation'[6] of conjugal life is, therefore, noticeable. This trend also seems to point to an attitude of indifference, or even of rejection of, the need to legitimise cohabitation *vis-à-vis* the outside world.[7] Couples are now refusing to submit to predetermined values established by the Church or the State, no longer adhering to the 'institution of marriage'.[8]

Even though a demand for greater freedom to establish the terms of ones relationship[9] also appear to exist in Portugal, the Portuguese legislature insists in regulating that relationship. The State does not want this particular area of social life to become so private so as to exclude any sort of intervention. The State's intervention in different-sex non-marital cohabitation, however, is weaker than that with respect to different-sex marital cohabitation. Accordingly, laws on this subject confer the bare minimum level of protection on the partners. One can witness that the State is searching for a new balance between the autonomy of differ-

---

3 This was not the purpose of Act 135/99. According to Art. 1, the Act's purpose was to regulate the 'legal position of *persons of opposite sex* who live in a *de facto* union for more than two years'. Act 135/99 granted legal protection only to different-sex *de facto* union.

4 See S. Aboim, 'A formação do casal: formas de entrada e percursos conjugais', in K. Wall (ed.), *Famílias em Portugal*, 2005, p. 86.

5 See S. Leite, 'A União de Facto em Portugal', 2003 *Revista de Estudos Demográficos*, no. 33, pp. 115 and 132; S. Aboim, 'A formação do casal: formas de entrada e percursos conjugais', in K. Wall (ed.), *Famílias em Portugal*, 2005, pp. 85 *et seq.*; C. Saraceno & M. Naldini, *Sociologia da Família*, 2003, pp. 79 and 159.

6 J.-L. Renchon, 'Indisponibilité, ordre public et autonomie de la volonté dans le droit des personnes et de la famille', in A. Wijffles (ed.), *Le Code Civil entre Ius Commune et Droit Privé Européen*, 2005, pp. 285 *et seq.*

7 See I. Théry, *Couple, Filiation et Parenté Aujourdí hui. Le Droit face aux mutations de la famille et de la vie privée*, 1998, p. 32.

8 See S. Leite, 'A União de Facto em Portugal', 2003 *Revista de Estudos Demográficos*, no. 33, pp. 99–100; F. Coelho & G. Oliveira, *Curso de Direito da Família*, Vol. I, 2003, pp. 147–148.

9 See F. Coelho & G. Oliveira, *Curso de Direito da Família*, Vol. I, 2003, pp. 150.

ent-sex couples, who wish to define the rules of their private life and the State's interference with that definition.[10]

As regards same-sex relationships, the opposite trend seems to be becoming dominant.[11] A trend towards the public display of same-sex relationships can be observed. Indeed, due to the fact that same-sex relationships have achieved social recognition, the demand for increasing State intervention has risen to the top of the agenda. Same-sex couples are increasingly claiming outside legitimisation of their relationship; they claim for the institutionalisation of same-sex cohabitation by setting legal rules for its establishment, its legal effects and its termination. It amounts to a demand that *de facto* become *de jure*.

In the field of different-sex relationships, the trend appears to be that of deregulation, while in the field of same-sex relationships the opposite trend seems to be discernible.[12] In the words of Mary Ann Glendon: 'Regulation has thus been withdrawn where it was once taken for granted, and intensified where in the past it had been unknown'.[13]

Act 7/2001 was the first step in the path of granting same sex couples a legal status. What further steps will the Portuguese legislature have to take in the near future?

The legal recognition of same-sex relationships by means of regulation can take on different forms. In fact, this has not happened consistently throughout Western Europe.[14] Despite this divergence one can find three general models of State intervention: enacting a minimal legal regulation of the relationship of two

10 Bearing in mind the purpose of this study, this is not the appropriate place either to further consider this trend and to analyse its causes and effects in Portugal, or reflect on the correct attitude of Portuguese legislature should adopt. For an approach to the issue of cohabitation outside marriage from a historical, socio-demographic and legal-political perspective as well as for a critical analysis of legislative output regarding *de facto* unions in Portugal, see N. Cid, *A Comunhão de Vida à Margem do Casamento: entre o Facto e o Direito*, 2005.

11 Also pointing out these opposite trends Baronness Hale observes: 'Curiously, it may be that it is among the gay community that the unavailable legal status and commitment [of marriage] is increasing in attraction where everywhere else it is in decline', Baronness Hale, 'Unmarried Couples in Family Law', 2004 *Family Law*, pp. 420–421, *apud* N. Bamforth, 'Same-Sex Partnerhips: Some Comparative Constitutional Lessons', 2007 *European Human Rights* 1, p. 52.

12 See C. Saraceno & M. Naldini, *Sociologia da Família*, 2003, p. 159.

13 M. Glendon, 'Introduction: Family Law in Times of Turbulence', in M. Glendon (ed.), *International Emcyclopedia of Comparative Law: Persons and Family*, Vol. IV, 2006, p. 7.

14 See I. Schwenzer, 'Convergence and Divergence in the Law on Same-Sex Partnerships', in M. Antokolskaia (ed.), *Convergence and Divergence of Family Law in Europe*, 2007, p. 146.

persons of the same sex;[15] attributing 'quasi-matrimonial' status[16] to these relationships, or allowing same-sex marriages outright.[17]

This article aims, firstly, to give a brief description of Act 7/2001 as the first Portuguese Act that offered legal protection to same-sex relationships. Secondly, to reflect on the current legal situation in Portugal, and thirdly, to try to assess what the further steps the Portuguese legislature should take along the path of granting same-sex couples a legal status.

2. ACT 7/2001 OF 11TH MAY 2001: 'ACT ADOPTING MEASURES FOR THE PROTECTION OF *DE FACTO* UNIONS'

2.1. BACKGROUND TO ACT 7/2001

Act 7/2001 expressly repealed Act 135/99. One might suppose that the new legislation would contain new provisions regarding the regulation of *de facto* unions, however this did not occur. In fact, Act 7/2001 essentially reproduces the legislation it replaces. That is to say that the new law did not amend the definition of *de facto* unions,[18] their establishment, the conditions under which they can take effect, their effect on persons and property, their termination and its consequences.

15 For example, in France and Portugal. It should, however, be pointed out that although the two legal systems set a minimum legal status for same-sex partnerships, the same status is regulated in more detail in France (*Loi relative au Pacte Civil de Solidarité, Loi No.* 99–944, of 15 November 1999 and Arts. 515–1 to 515–7 French Civil Code) than in Portugal (Act 7/2001 of 11th May 2001). To better understand the distinction, see, on the PACS, J. Carbonnier, *Droit Civil. Introduction. Les Personnes. La famille, l'enfant, le couple,* Vol I, 2004, pp.1481–1490 and G. Cornu, *Droit Civil. La famille,* 2006, pp. 105–114, and on Act 7/2001 of 11th May, F. Coelho & G. Oliveira, *Curso de Direito da Família,* Vol. I, 2003, pp. 111–137; J. Pitão, *União de Facto e Economia Comum,* 2006, pp. 111–127.

16 As is the case in Denmark (Registered Partnership Act, Act No. 372 of 7th June 1989, in force as of 1st October 1989), Sweden (*Lag om registerat partnerskap,* Act 1994: 1117 of 23rd June 1994, in force as of 1st January 1995), Norway (*Lov om registreret partnerskap,* No. 40/1993, of 20th April 1993, in force as of 1st August 1993) of Finland (Registered Partnership Act, Act 950/2001, in force as of 1st March 2002), Germany (*Lebenspartnerschaftgesetz* of 16th February 2001 modified by the Law of 6th February 2005), the United Kingdom (Civil Partnership Act 2004, in force as of 5th December 2005) and, most recently, Switzerland (*Partnerschaftgesetz* of 18th June 2004, in force as of 1st January 2006).

17 As is the case in The Netherlands (Act Opening Marriage to Same-Sex Couples (*Wet openstelling huwelijk*) of December 2000 and Art. 1:30 Dutch Civil Code), Belgium (*Loi du 13 fevrier 2003* and Art. 143–1 Belgian Civil Code) and Spain (*Ley 13/2005,* of 1 July and Art. 44 Spanish Civil Code).

18 Act 7/2001 gives us no idea as to what should be understood by *de facto* union; nor, indeed, did Act 135/99.

Although we can say that *de facto* unions in Portugal, 'were somewhat institutionalised by Act 135/99 of 28th August',[19] the Portuguese legislature did not institute a systematic, unitary and substantially innovative regulatory structure for *de facto* unions.[20] Both Act 135/99 and Act 7/2001 appear to be little more than 'a mere summary of protective measures',[21] which had already been laid down in previous legislation. Indeed, Article 3, Act 135/99 referred in four of its eight paragraphs to 'measures to protect the *de facto* unions' to be found dispersed throughout existing legislation, largely in the fields of Social Security, Employment, Tax and Administrative Law.[22] Moreover, Act 135/99 refers itself, in Article 1(2), to standards laid down in other laws,[23] which confer to some extent legal consequences on *de facto* unions.

This being so, a few new departures from the previous legislation are discernible. However, none of these new departures include the legal protection of same sex relationships (Article 1 Act 135/99). Same-sex *de facto* unions remained almost irrelevant until 2001.

2.1.1. Constitutional Court's jurisprudence

Although there are a number of novelties in the act(s) referred to above, only a few of them can be considered really innovative. Indeed, some of these solutions have been anticipated by the Constitutional Court's jurisprudence.

Portuguese higher courts did not recognise *de facto* unions within the ambit of family law[24] and therefore did not analogously apply legal precepts relating to

---

19 F. Coelho & G. Oliveira, *Curso de Direito da Família*, Vol. I, 2003, p. 109.

20 On the need for and suitability of such regulations, see N. S. Cid, 'União de Facto e Direito: Indecisão ou Desorientação do Legislador?', 1994 *Economia e Sociologia*, no. 57, pp. 66–72; H.E. Hörster, 'Does Portugal Need to Legislate on the Facto Unions', 1999 *International Journal of Law Policy and the Family*, no. 3. p. 279; R. Xavier, 'Novas sobre a união "more uxorio" em Portugal', in J. Gomes (ed.), *Estudos dedicados ao Prof. Doutor Mário Júlio Almeida Costa*, 2002, pp. 1398 *et seq.*, N. Cid, *A Comunhão de Vida à Margem do Casamento: entre o Facto e o Direito*, 2005, pp. 759–789.

21 F. Coelho & G. Oliveira, *Curso de Direito da Família*, Vol. I, 2003, p. 109.

22 See R. Xavier, 'Novas sobre a união "more uxorio" em Portugal', in J. Gomes (ed.), *Estudos dedicados ao Prof. Doutor Mário Júlio Almeida Costa*, 2002, pp. 1398–1399.

23 Such as, for example, the Civil Code which, as regards maintenance, gives the surviving partner of a (different-sex) *de facto* union the right to require provision from the deceased's estate in cases where the union had lasted for more than two years and he or she could not obtain the same from a spouse, ex-spouse, descendants, ascendants or siblings (Art. 2020, Civil Code).

24 According to Article 1576, Civil Code only marriage, kinship, affinity and adoption are considered to be sources of family relationships. Since *de facto* unions were not on the exhaustive list of family relationships higher courts did not recognise *de facto* unions within the ambit of family law.
Even today case law and the predominating private law doctrine do not understand the *de facto* unions as a family relationship. See J. Castro Mendes, *Direito da Família*, 1990/1991, pp. 13 and 15; J.J. Almeida Lopes, 'A União de Facto no Direito Português', 1993 *Revista Española de Derecho Canónico*, no. 134, p. 246; P. de Lima & A. Varela, *Código Civil Anotado*, Vol. IV, 1992,

marriage. Thus, the Portuguese higher courts refused to attribute *de facto* unions with similar effects to those conferred on marriage by operation law.

Brief mention should, however, be made to several decisions of the Constitutional Court on this matter, where the solutions adopted have been accepted, in some cases, and even developed by the law.

Take, for example, the judgment of the Constitutional Court No. 359/91, of 9th July 1991,[25] where the Constitutional Court was asked to rule on the question of whether or not the transfer of the right to lease the family home was applicable upon the breakdown of a *de facto* union when there were minor children from that union. This right could be granted, by agreement of the spouses or ex-spouses, or, failing that, by court order, to the spouse or former spouse who was not the tenant in case of divorce or separation of persons with division of property. The issue here was to know whether the protection offered by the law could be analogously extended to the termination of a *de facto* union. The Constitutional Court declared the interpretation unconstitutional, which denied the analogous application to situations involving termination of a *de facto* union with minor children. However, the Constitutional Court did not directly address the controversial issue of equivalence of the *de facto* union to marriage for certain purposes. Instead, it developed a line of reasoning based on the constitutional principle of non-discrimination against children born outside marriage (Article 36(4) Constitution of the Portuguese Republic).[26]

A similar result was reached in the judgment of the Constitutional Court No. 1221/96 of 4th December 1996.[27] Here the Constitutional Court also ruled that an interpretation that reserved the application of Article 1793(1) Civil Code to cases of dissolution of the marriage, thus excluding the situations of breakdown of a *de facto* union with minor children, was unconstitutional. The provision referred to above provides that, at the request of one of the spouses, the court awards the

---

pp. 14–15; D. Leite de Campos, *Lições de Direito da Família,* 1997, p. 21; A. Varela, *Direito da Família,* Vol. I, 1999, p. 31; N.Cid, *A Comunhão de Vida à Margem do Casamento: entre o Facto e o Direito,* 2005, p. 505 (note 12), with extensive references to legal literature and case law.
However, as Coelho and Oliveira warn, although *de facto* unions are not seen as a family relationship for most legal purposes, 'we need to know if we are or not dealing with one of those exceptional areas where such a designation is merited', see F. Coelho & G. Oliveira, *Curso de Direito da Família*, Vol. I, 2003, p. 108.
Considering a *de facto* union as a family relationship see T. Carvalho, 'A União de Facto: A sua Eficácia Jurídica', in *Comemorações dos 35 Anos do Código Civil e dos 25 Anos da Reforma de 1977: Direito da Família e das Sucessões,* Vol. I, 2004, p. 226.

25 At http://www.tribunalconstitucional.pt/tc/acordaos/19910359.html.

26 On the principle of non-discrimination against children born out of wedlock as one of the constitutional principles of Portuguese Family Law, see F. Coelho & G. Oliveira, *Curso de Direito da Família*, Vol. I, 2003, pp. 172 *et seq.*; J. Miranda & R. Medeiros, *Constituição Portuguesa Anotada*, Tomo I, 2005, pp. 419 *et seq.*, J. Canotilho & V. Moreira, *Constituição da República Portuguesa Anotada*, Vol. I, 2007, p. 565.

27 At http://www.tribunalconstitucional.pt/tc/acordaos/19961221.html.

lease of the family home to one of them, irrespective of whether it is joint property or owned by one of them. The court should particularly consider the needs of both spouses and the children's interests.

Once again, the Constitutional Court avoided the problem of the legal consequences of *de facto* unions, basing its decision in the aforementioned principle of non-discrimination against children born out of wedlock.

Another 'irradiation'[28] of the same principle can be found in the judgement of the Constitutional Court No. 286/99, of 11th May 1999.[29] The question was whether or not to apply, by analogy, the rules of Articles 42(1) and 46 of *Decree-Law No. 18/88, of 21st January*. These rules established a 'conjugal preference' as a criterion to be used in the process for placement of teachers in public education in those situations where a teacher lived in a *de facto* union with another public official and with whom he or she had children. Faced with this question, the Constitutional Court again relied on the principle of non-discrimination against children born outside marriage. It held that the provisions under consideration were unconstitutional, since they excluded teachers who, though not married, lived in conditions similar to those of spouses and had children living with them. The Court held that such an exclusion prejudiced children who would thus be deprived of the chance of living together with their father and this constituted unjustified discrimination against children born outside marriage.

These solutions were incorporated into and even expanded upon by the law as will be seen below.

From the abovementioned cases, it can be concluded that both Act 135/99 and Act 7/2001 did not represent a substantial extension of the protection of *de facto* unions, but were above all of symbolic value. The public debate in Portugal was focused neither on the legal problems posed by the reality of *de facto* unions nor on developing a consistent family policy as would have been desirable.[30]

2.2. BRIEF ANALYSIS OF ACT 7/2001

This analysis purports neither to list nor analyse all the respects in which *de facto* unions can have legal consequences in the context of the Portuguese legal

28 See J. Canotilho & V. Moreira, *Constituição da República Portuguesa Anotada*, Vol. I, 2007, p 565.

29 At http://www.tribunalconstitucional.pt/tc/acordaos/19990286.html.

30 See R. Xavier, 'Novas sobre a união "more uxorio" em Portugal', in J. Gomes (ed.), *Estudos dedicados ao Prof. Doutor Mário Júlio Almeida Costa*, 2002, pp. 1401–1402. On the various draft laws that preceded the two laws and the parliamentary debate they gave rise to, see N. Cid, *A Comunhão de Vida à Margem do Casamento: entre o Facto e o Direito*, 2005, pp. 636–667; S. O. Pais, 'De Facto Relationships and Same-Sex relationships in Portugal'; A. Bainham (ed.), *International Survey of Family Law*, 2002, pp. 342–343.

system.[31] Reference will instead only be made to the general legal regime covering *de facto* unions as established by Act 7/2001.

2.2.1. Scope of the law

Act 7/2001 seeks to regulate the situation of two persons, regardless of gender, who have lived together in a *de facto* union for more than two years (Article 1(1)). However, it does not explain what a *de facto* union is.[32]

The absence of a legal definition can be justified by the difficulty, also experienced by scholars,[33] in accurately determining the legal contours of this 'multifaceted phenomenon'.[34] Despite such difficulties, one can say that the concept of *de facto* union embraces exclusive and enduring relationships between two persons, regardless of gender, who have 'made a life together under the same roof'.[35]

One must stress that a *de facto* union can only be invoked either by the partners (or by one against the other) or by third parties against them, if it has lasted for more than two years[36] (Article 3, Act 7/2001). Therefore, the determination of the beginning of the relationship is very important. However, the identification of that moment and the proof that the relationship exists are not easy tasks, consid-

31 See F. Coelho & G. Oliveira, *Curso de Direito da Família*, Vol. I, 2003, pp. 111 *et seq.*; A. Pitão, *União de Facto e Economia Comum*, 2006, pp. 71–328; T. Carvalho, 'A União de Facto: A sua Eficácia Jurídica', in *Comemorações dos 35 Anos do Código Civil e dos 25 Anos da Reforma de 1977: Direito da Família e das Sucessões*, Vol. I, 2004, pp. 239 *et seq.*

32 Neither did Act 135/99.

33 See N. Cid, *A Comunhão de Vida à Margem do Casamento: entre o Facto e o Direito*, 2005, p. 39.

34 See G. Cornu, *Droit Civil. La famille*, 2006, p. 85.

35 On this point, *see* F. Coelho & G. Oliveira, *Curso de Direito da Família*, Vol. I, 2003, pp. 84, 118; J. Pitão, *União de Facto e Economia Comum*, 2006, p. 76.
On the difficulties in choosing the appropriate terminology and of conceptual definition, *see* N. Cid, *A Comunhão de Vida à Margem do Casamento: entre o Facto e o Direito*, 2005, pp. 36 *et seq.*

36 A *de facto* union produces not only consequences favourable to the partners but also adverse effects. Although Act 7/2001 only provides measures for the protection of *de facto* unions and, accordingly, specifies only favourable consequences, the reality is that a *de facto* union produces more effects than those provided for in the statute and some of these are unfavourable to the two partners.
An example of the unfavourable effects is the joint and several liability of partners in a *de facto* union regarding debts incurred by one or the other as part of the normal outgoings of their life together. Scholars have maintained the view, in relation to *de facto* different-sex unions, that as the partners 'live together under the same roof', and thus create the appearance of marriage on which third parties rely, it appears reasonable to argue for the applicability of the regime concerning the debts of spouses provided for in Arts. 1691(1b) and 1695(1) Civil Code, by which the spouses are jointly responsible for debts incurred by either that represent the outgoings of normal joint life. On this point, see F. Coelho & G. Oliveira, *Curso de Direito da Família*, Vol. I, 2003, p. 106. For an argument that this regime should apply equally to homosexual de facto unions because of the expectations of third parties, see N. Cid, *A Comunhão de Vida à Margem do Casamento: entre o Facto e o Direito*, 2005, p. 571.

ering that the law does not provide any 'formalities' concerning the beginning of the relationship.[37] A *de facto* union comes into being 'when the partners in the relationship come together'.[38]

Although it is possible to prove the beginning and the existence of the relationship through documentary evidence, this means of evidence also presents difficulties. Indeed, neither a certificate from the council of the parish where the partners in a *de facto* union are resident, proving the existence of such a relationship between them, nor a statement made by them before the civil registrar at the time of registration of the birth of their child, affirming that they are living together 'as husband and wife' and that they wish to jointly exercise parental responsibilities (Article 1911(3), Civil Code), nor a contract made before the notary laying down their propertial relationship constitute full proof of the existence of the relationship or of when it came into being.[39]

It must be said that the possibility of seeking a declaration by the court to prove the existence of cohabitation between the members of a *de facto* union has also proved ineffective.[40] Thus, the protection offered by the law to *de facto* unions can end up being undermined since it ultimately depends upon witness evidence.

2.2.2. Circumstances that prevent de facto unions having legal effects

It is also necessary to add that not every instance of cohabitation between two persons that lasts for more than two years enjoys the protection of Act 7/2001. Cohabitation only produces the effects prescribed by this Act if none of the circumstances described in Article 2 pertain.

Situations that prevent *de facto* unions having legal effects include the following: if either of the parties is under the age of 16 (Article 2 (a), Act 7/2001);[41] visible dementia, even including lucid intervals, and incapacity or civil disability by reason of mental disorder (Article 2(b), Act 7/2001);[42] a subsisting previous

37 *De facto* unions are not subject to civil or even administrative registration.

38 See F. Coelho & G. Oliveira, *Curso de Direito da Família,* Vol. I, 2003, p. 110. On this point see also T. Carvalho, 'A União de Facto: A sua Eficácia Jurídica', in *Comemorações dos 35 Anos do Código Civil e dos 25 Anos da Reforma de 1977: Direito da Família e das Sucessões,* Vol. I, 2004, pp. 237–239, and J. Pitão, *Uniões de Facto e Economia Comum,* 2006, pp. 79–80.

39 See F. Coelho & G. Oliveira, *Curso de Direito da Família,* Vol. I, 2003, p. 110.

40 See the Judgment of the Lisbon Court of Appeal of 26th November 2006 which states in its summary: 'These legal proceedings are not intended to enable the parties to obtain evidence, but are intended to assert rights that are uncertain, threatened or violated (Arts. 2(2) CPCivil and 20(1) CRP)' at www.dgsi.pt.

41 For a critique of conferring legal consequences on *de facto* unions where the partners are minors, see N. Cid, *A Comunhão de Vida à Margem do Casamento: entre o Facto e o Direito,* 2005, pp. 644–645; J. Pitão, *Uniões de Facto e Economia Comum,* 2006, pp. 84–86.

42 For further observations on this impediment, see N. Cid, *A Comunhão de Vida à Margem do Casamento: entre o Facto e o Direito,* 2005, p. 645; J. Pitão, Uniões de Facto e Economia Comum,

marriage, except where the parties have been judicial separated and division of property has already been decreed (Article 2©, Act 7/2001);[43] kinship in the direct line or in the second degree of the collateral line or affinity in the direct line' (Article 2(d), Act 7/2001); a previous conviction of one partner for murder or attempted murder of the other partner's spouse (Article 2 (e), Act 7/2001).

It is interesting to note that this list copies the list of impediments to marry (Articles 1601 and 1602 Civil Code).

Taking into account the fundamental public interests that are the basis of impediments to marry, it is reasonable to assume that, by so doing, the legislature wished to avoid conferring favourable legal effects similar to those applying to marriage[44] on *de facto* unions of persons barred from marrying. Nevertheless, the legislature was not consistent with these aims.[45] Indeed, in dealing with *de facto* same-sex unions, this Act confers effects similar to those of marriage on the relationship of two people who cannot marry under Portuguese matrimonial law. A marriage celebrated between two people of the same-sex is non-existent pursuant to Article 1628(e) Civil Code.

2.2.3. *Legal effects of de facto unions*

In comparison with Act 135/99, Act 7/2001 did nothing more than extend the legal protection of *de facto* unions to include same-sex *de facto* unions. The legal regime of *de facto* unions has remained the same. All the rights that Act 7/2001 attribute to the partners of a different-sex *de facto* union are now equally attributed to the partners of a same-sex *de facto* union.[46]

Article 3 Act 7/2001 lists a series of measures for the protection of *de facto* unions. However, this list is not exhaustive. Under the Portuguese legal system, the legal consequences of *de facto* unions are not limited to the protective measures provided therein.[47] Indeed, this is acknowledged in Act 7/2001 itself where, in Article 1(2) it is provided that 'no rule of this statute shall affect the application of other laws or regulations in force seeking the legal protection of de facto unions (...)'. By this provision, the legislature seems to have wished to prevent a possible

2006, pp. 86–94.

43 For a critique of conferring legal consequences on adulterous *de facto* unions, see R. Xavier, 'Novas sobre a união "more uxorio" em Portugal', in J. Gomes (ed.), *Estudos dedicados ao Prof. Doutor Mário Júlio Almeida Costa,* 2002, p. 1399; N. Cid, *A Comunhão de Vida à Margem do Casamento: entre o Facto e o Direito,* 2005, p. 645.

44 For the argument that Art. 2 Act 7/2001 should be interpreted narrowly so that the occurrence of some of these impediments does not hinder the creation of adverse effects, see F. Coelho & G. Oliveira, *Curso de Direito da Família,* Vol. I, 2003, p. 117.

45 See F. Coelho & G. Oliveira, *Curso de Direito da Família,* Vol. I, 2003, pp. 116–118.

46 Except the right to full and jointly adopt a child.

47 See *supra*, 2.1.

restrictive interpretation of Act 7/2001 that would exclude the application of other legislative provisions not specifically mentioned in the statute.[48]

It should be emphasised that this provision does not imply any analogous application of the rules that apply to legal marriage; a *de facto* union has only the effects recognised by the law.[49]

2.2.3.1. Effects on persons

Act 7/2001 expressly recognises only one effect on persons who live in a *de facto* union: the right to adopt a child under the same conditions that law provides for married couples (Article 7 Act 7/2001 and Article 1979(1) Civil Code).[50] Act 7/2001, despite recognising direct legal consequences of same-sex *de facto* unions, retained the provisions of Act 135/99 in continuing to reserve the right to joint strong adoption to different-sex *de facto* unions. This being so only the partners of a different-sex *de facto* union enjoy that right. Moreover, two partners of a different-sex *de facto* union who want to qualify for joint strong adoption of the child must be over 25 years old and their relationship must have subsisted for over four years (Article 1979(1) Civil Code).

Even if two partners of a same-sex *de facto* union cannot jointly adopt a child, each one of them can qualify for strong adoption in the same conditions as unmarried people. That is to say, he or she must be over 30 years old (Article 1979 (2) Civil Code).

Other than the right to adopt, Act 7/2001 did not add anything to the effects on persons of *de facto* unions. There was no attempt to regulate personal relationships between the partners, such as establishing a catalogue of rights and duties similar to that applying to married couples (Articles *1672 et seq* Civil Code),[51] nor did it allow the partners in a *de facto* union the possibility of adding a partner's surname to one's own.

Act 7/2001 is also silent on the issue of nationality. However, the amendment of the Nationality Act (*Act 37/81 of 3rd October by Act 2/2006 of 17th April*) should be noted.[52] The Act provides that 'a foreigner who at the date of the declaration has been living in a *de facto* union for more than three years with a Portuguese

48 See J. Pitão, *União de Facto e Economia Comum*, 2006, pp. 82–83. For an interpretation of Art. 1(2) Act 7/2001 which considers the requirements set by the same law as minimum requirements for conferring favourable effects on *de facto* unions, see N. Cid, *A Comunhão de Vida à Margem do Casamento: entre o Facto e o Direito*, 2005, p. 644.

49 See F. Coelho & G. Oliveira, *Curso de Direito da Família*, Vol. I, 2003, p. 112.

50 On other effects on persons of *de facto* unions, see F. Coelho & G. Oliveira, *Curso de Direito da Família*, Vol. I, 2003, pp. 118–119; N. Cid, *A Comunhão de Vida à Margem do Casamento: entre o Facto e o Direito*, 2005, pp. 674–696.

51 The behaviour by a partner in the union that amounts to a breach of conjugal duties (respect, fidelity, cohabitation, cooperation and assistance) will have no legal consequences.

52 Published in *Diário da República*, I -Série-A, no. 75, 17th April 2006.

national may acquire Portuguese nationality, following an action in the civil court for the recognition of this situation' (Article 3(3)). Although this is one of those effects on persons provided for by outside legislation its novelty and significance justify it being referred to here.

Reference should also be made to the right to benefit from the legal regime on holidays, absences, leave and preferential placement enjoyed by officials of the Public Administration under the same terms as spouses (Article 3(b), Act 7/2001)[53] and the right to benefit from the legal regime on leave, public holidays and absences, as applied to individual employment contracts, on terms equivalent to those applying to married couples. Such rights cannot properly be characterised as effects on persons; they are rather measures of social protection that were intended by Act 7/2001 to extend to partners in *de facto* unions. They appear to evidence the law's recognition and protection of that special closeness which exists within a *de facto* union.

2.2.3.2. Effects on property

Since the Portuguese Civil Code does not recognize *de facto* unions as family relationships (Article 1576 Civil Code) cohabiting partners do not belong to each other's family: they are treated as strangers. The *de facto* union has no legal impact on the ownership of their property, that is to say that each partner remains the owner of the property that he/she has acquired prior to the *de facto* union, as well as the property that he/she has acquired during the *de facto* union. In addition, neither one of the partners acquires any right of ownership of the other's property, nor any right or duty to administer it. This being so, the property of each one is subject to the general regime of law of obligations and property law:[54] each partner is allowed, for instance, to sell or rent his/her movable or immovable property without the other's consent being required.[55] Moreover, partners are permitted to make between them sale, labour or loan contracts, among others.[56]

Act 7/2001 did not regulate these aspects, namely providing a property regime similar to the matrimonial property regime. Indeed, the statute neither provides a choice of property regimes, nor establishes rules covering the administration of assets and debts of the partners similar to those for married couples (Articles

---

53 As far as preferential placement of public administration officials is concerned, this measure was anticipated, by the Constitutional Court's jurisprudence for different-sex *de facto* unions with minor children, see above at 2.1. Act 7/2001 generalised this to cover different-sex *de facto* unions with or without children and same-sex *de facto* unions.

54 Note the exception in Art. 953, Civil Code.

55 In contrast, one spouse may have to ask for the other spouse's consent to sell his/her own property depending on the property regime, which applies to their marriage (Art. 1682 –A (1a), and (2), Civil Code).

56 There is no legal rule prohibiting them from making such contracts between them as there is for spouses (Art. 1714 (2), Civil Code).

1678–1697 Civil Code). Effects on property of *de facto* unions regulated by Act 7/2001 are thus also limited.

Even though the partners are treated as strangers, the fact is that living in a *de facto* union presupposes the sharing of resources in daily life and therefore some kind of mingling of ownership of movable assets of the two partners may occur.

Act 7/2001 does not permit the partners of *de facto* unions to freely set out the terms of their relationship; however it is also not prohibited. This being so, and taking into account the possible mingling of ownership of the partners' property, some authors have argued that so-called cohabitation contracts should be regarded as valid, although restricted to the field of property, and thus within the limits of the principle of private autonomy.[57]

The sole effect on property that Act 7/2001 effectively establishes is the application to the partners of the taxation regime of personal income established for cohabiting married couples (Article 3(e), Act 7/2001).[58]

2.3. TERMINATION OF THE RELATIONSHIP

According to the statute a *de facto* union can be terminated: on the death of one of the partners (Article 8(1a), Act 7/2001); by the decision of one of them (Article 8(1b), Act 7/2001),[59] and by the marriage of one of the partners to a third person (Article 8(1c), Act 7/2001).

Most of the protective measures of *de facto* unions contained in Act 7/2001 are directed towards moments of crisis. However, the regulation of these moments is not detailed; provision is only made for some of the consequences of the termination.[60]

One of the main problems in case of termination of a *de facto* union is the future of the joint home. In fact, the first of the protective measures listed in Article 3 specifically focuses on the attribution of the joint home (Article 3(a), Act 7/2001).

The statute provides different solutions to this problem and they depend on whether the *de facto* union is being terminated by breakdown or the death of one

57 See F. Coelho & G. Oliveira, *Curso de Direito da Família*, Vol. I, 2003, pp. 119–120; J. Pitão, *Uniões de Facto e Economia Comum*, 2006, pp. 174–175.

58 On other effects on property of *de facto* unions, see Pereira Coelho & G. Oliveira, *Curso de Direito da Família*, Vol. I, 2003, pp. 119–120; J. Pitão, *Uniões de Facto e Economia Comum*, 2006, pp. 315–321.

59 Or by agreement of both partners.

60 For instance, there are no rules covering the settlement and division of property acquired during a *de facto* union. On the difficulties that arise in this regard, with pointers towards a possible resolution, see F. Coelho & G. Oliveira, *Curso de Direito da Família*, Vol. I, 2003, pp. 120; J. Pitão, *Uniões de Facto e Economia Comum*, 2006, pp. 173–183.

partner, as well as whether the house is owned (by one or both of them), leased or rented.

For those situations involving breakdown of the *de facto* union where the joint home is leased or rented, Act 7/2001 provides the former partners the possibility to agree to the assignment of the lease from one partner to the other or from both to one of them (Article 4(3), Act 7/2001 which refers to Article 1105 Civil Code).[61]

If the partners are not able to agree, the court must decide the issue taking into account 'the needs of each [of the former partners], the interests of children and other relevant factors' and the landlord must be officially notified of that decision (Article 1105(2) and (3) Civil Code).

If the joint home is owned jointly by the partners or by just one of them, the act refers to Article 1793, Civil Code that governs the outcome for the joint home in cases of divorce where it belongs jointly to the spouses or to just one of them.

This provision allows either spouse to petition the court for the grant of a lease in the joint home. The court's decision must take into account the needs of each of the spouses and the interests of the children of the family (Article 1793(1) Civil Code).[62]

As referred to above, these provisions were anticipated by the Constitutional Court's jurisprudence[63] in cases of separation of the partners in a *de facto* union with minor children. Nevertheless, the protection that the statute now offers is broader in that it extends both to the possibility of agreement on which of the former partners will become the tenant, and to the ability of the court to grant one of them a lease of the joint home in cases where there are no minor children or no children at all.[64]

In case of the death of the owner of the joint home, the surviving partner has a right *in rem* to remain there[65] for a period of five years, as well as a preferential right in the sale of the property for an equal period (Article 4(1) Act 7/2001), provided that the deceased partner is not survived by a descendant aged less than one year old, nor by other descendants who lived with him or her for over a year and

---

61 Introduced by the Act 6/2006, of 27th February 2006, published in *Diário da República* I-Série-A, no. 41, 27th February 2006.

62 Once the court has granted to one of the spouses such application for a lease, the lease is then subject to the residential rent laws. Despite this, the court can set the terms of the contract, after hearing the spouses, as well as terminate the lease on the application of the landlord, when supervening circumstances so justify (Art. 1793(2), Civil Code).

63 See *supra*, 2.1.1.

64 Note that where a *de facto* union is terminated at the instigation of the partners, the termination must be declared judicially when any claim is made regarding rights that derive from the termination. A judicial declaration of termination of a *de facto* union should be made in an action where the alleged rights are exercised or in an action according to the procedural rules for status actions (Art. 8(2) Law 7/2001). See J. Pitão, *Uniões de Facto e Economia Comum*, 2006, pp. 327–328.

65 This does not give the partner the right to require that the contents be left for him or her use.

intend to continue living there, and in the absence of any testamentary disposition to the contrary (Article 4(2) Act 7/2001).

If the joint home was rented or leased and the deceased partner was the tenant, the tenancy is transferred to the surviving partner (Article 5 Act 7/2001 and Article 1006(1a) Civil Code).

In case of death of one partner, legal protection is not confined to the establishment of rules concerning the joint home. The death of one of the partners has other consequences that are reflected in the granting of a certain social protection to the surviving partner, namely: the right to the death grant and survivor's allowance (Articles 3 and 6, Act 7/2001),[66] the right to benefits for death resulting from an work related accident or occupational illness (Article 3(f), Act 7/2001) and the right to pensions for survivors of military personnel and for exceptionally meritorious services rendered to the country (Article 3(g), Act 7/2001).[67]

Departing from the principle that partners of a *de facto* union are treated as strangers, Act 7/2001 does not attribute one partner any kind of inheritance rights in case of death of the other. The surviving partner will continue to be treated as a stranger. He or she does not belong to the other partner's family and is therefore not considered to be one of his or hers legal heirs (Articles 2157 and 2133 Civil Code). So, unless one of the partners make a provision in his or her will in favour of the other, the latter will not acquire any assets or values from the first's estate.

3. SAME-SEX DE FACTO UNIONS AND ACT 7/2001

Act 7/2001 has given some legal visibility to same-sex *de facto* unions; it conferred important effects on them, but has not equalised their position as compared with different-sex *de facto* unions. The one does not coincide with the other in effective scope. This interpretation of the Act 7/2001 can give rise to increasing ambiguities,[68] which risk generating difficulties in the implementation of the statute due to the imprecision of language by the legislature and inadequacies of legislative technique. However, it does not seem possible to interpret the law other than as meaning that same-sex *de facto* unions do not produce the same legal effects as different-sex *de facto* unions.

Firstly, such equivalence seems not to have been the legislature's purpose: if that had been the legislature's intention, the legislature should have explicitly

66 On the interpretation of Art. 6, see J. Pitão, *Uniões de Facto e Economia Comum*, 2006, pp. 290–292; N. Cid, *A Comunhão de Vida à Margem do Casamento: entre o Facto e o Direito*, 2005, pp. 672–673.

67 For a more detailed description of these rights and the legal regime governing them, see F. Coelho & G. Oliveira, *Curso de Direito da Família*, Vol. I, 2003, pp. 127; J. Pitão, *Uniões de Facto e Economia Comum*, 2006, pp. 293–302.

68 See F. Coelho & G. Oliveira, *Curso de Direito da Família*, Vol. I, 2003, p. 113.

mentioned it – as they did, for example, in the case of the right to transfer residential leases (Article 5 Act 7/2001)[69] – and not simply omitted it. Secondly, Act 7/2001 itself makes the different sex of the parties an express condition for the only effect on persons that it recognises for *de facto* unions: the right to joint strong adoption of a child (Article 7, Act 7/2001),[70] Thirdly, the statute invokes by reference the provisions of other laws (Article 1(2), Act 7/2001) in which the difference of sexes is presupposed, either by the very nature of things – for example, in the functioning of the legal presumption of paternity in actions to establish the defendant's paternity when he and the child's mother have lived as husband and wife during the legal period for conception (Article 1871(1c), Civil Code) – or because the rules in question establish the difference in the sex of the parties as a requirement by specifying cohabitation 'in conditions similar to those of husband and wife' – such as Article 2020, Civil Code that accords to a person, who, had lived with the deceased (not married or legally separated in person with division of property) for more than two years under conditions similar to those of husband and wife, the right to ask for maintenance from the estate of the deceased, if he or she cannot obtain it from a spouse, ex-spouse, descendants, ascendants or siblings.

The effects of a same-sex *de facto* union can be summed up as those that Act 7/2001 explicitly confers on it (Articles 3 and 5, Act 7/2001) plus those that other laws, without requiring the difference of sexes, confer on *de facto* unions. There is therefore no legal basis for extending the scope of the effects of same-sex *de facto* unions in order to make it coincide with that of different-sex *de facto* unions.[71]

4. THE FUTURE OF SAME-SEX UNIONS IN PORTUGAL

From this brief description of Act 7/2001, one must conclude that the legal importance of same-sex *de facto* unions in the Portuguese legal system is limited. Though one may ask whether the partners in same-sex *de facto* unions after Act 7/2001 are left without legal protection to an extent that results in situations of profound injustice and consequently flagrant disrespect for the dignity of the human being demanding further legislative intervention.

Given the description above, it seems that, although the legal consequences of same-sex *de facto* unions are few, the statute covers a range of subjects (from the protection of the joint home to survivors' benefit) establishing a minimum of social protection of partners. This minimum of social protection ensures the ful-

---

69 See F. Coelho & G. Oliveira, *Curso de Direito da Família*, Vol. I, 2003, p. 114.

70 See *supra*, 2.2.3.1.

71 See F. Coelho & G. Oliveira, *Curso de Direito da Família*, Vol. I, 2003, p. 114.

filment of the imperative of respect for the dignity of the human being in a democratic State based on the rule of law (Articles 1 and 2 Constitution of the Portuguese Republic).

It is true that Act 7/2001 makes no mention of the issues concerning the ownership of assets and to the regime covering the consequences of possible mingling of ownership of movable assets during the lifetime of the relationship, nor of the recognition of inheritance rights.

These two aspects must be distinguished. With regard to the first aspect, it does not appear to be forbidden for partners, by means of a cohabitation contract, to determine the rules according to which their property will be governed.[72] With regard to the second aspect, as already mentioned, the rules of succession are mandatory and the surviving partner does not acquire any inheritance rights (Articles 2156, 2157, and 2133, Civil Code). Nevertheless, it should not be forgotten that the testator always has a margin of freedom, albeit within the *quota* available, of disposition of his or her assets by making provision in a will in favour of the other partner.

Is there a case for adding further (favourable) effects to a same-sex relationship, which has sufficient exclusivity and durability to amount to a 'life together under the same roof', in particular by recognising it as a familial relationship?

This question is not new in the debate on the legal status of same-sex relationships and therefore no major new line of argument is to be expected for or against more extensive protection of such relationships. It is, above all, a difficult and sensitive issue of social and family policy.[73]

This is not the place to attempt to propose a definitive solution. Therefore, only the most common arguments encountered in the debate will be dealt with here.

The benefit of such recognition is usually invoked by the following arguments, namely the greater visibility of same-sex relationships and the change of mentalities and attitudes towards homosexuality, which has increasingly gained social acceptance and is no longer prosecuted as a crime,[74] the progressive loss of the traditional functions of the family,[75] the absence of a single model of the family, the

72 See *supra*, 2.2.3.2.

73 See J.-L. Renchon, 'La Régulation par la Loi des Relations Juridiques du Couple non Marié', in J.-L. Renchon et al. (eds.), *Le Couple Non Marié à la Lumière de la Cohabitation Légale*, 2000, p. 13.

74 See S. Pais & A. Sousa, 'A União de Facto e as Uniões Registadas de Pessoas do mesmo Sexo – Uma Análise de Direito Material e Conflitual', 1999 *Revista da Ordem dos Advogados*, p. 707; A. Agell, 'The Legal Status of Same-Sex Couples in Europe – A Critical Analysis', in K. Boele-Woelki *et al.* (eds.), *The Legal Recognition of Same-Sex Couples in Europe*, 2003, p. 130.

75 On the causes of the progressive loss of the traditional functions of the family, see M. Glendon, *The New Family and The New Property*, 1981, pp. 1–2, 7; F. Coelho, G. Oliveira, *Curso de Direito da Família*, Vol. I, 2003, pp. 146–147; F. Swennen, 'O Tempora, O Mores! The Evolving Marriage Concept and the Impediments to Marriage', in M. Antokolskaia (ed.), *Convergence and Divergence of Family Law in Europe*, 2007, p. 123.

transformation of the concept of marriage into a relationship of emotional coexistence detached from the purposes of procreation and upbringing of children,[76] and finally, the argument of non-discrimination on grounds of sexual orientation.[77]

Against such recognition the following arguments are often deployed, namely the tradition that confines marriage to people of different sex,[78] the connection between marriage and procreation – though not necessarily a requirement, it is greater than a mere eventuality[79] –, the main functions of the different-sex family in the procreation, protection and socialization of children,[80] the 'intergenerational interest' of different-sex families and their importance for the reproduction of human society itself,[81] and, finally, a restrictive interpretation of the principle of equality.[82]

One may assume that, in the future, further legislative intervention will occur to extend the legal effects conferred on same-sex relationships due to the increasing social acceptance of those relationships, the discernable European trend towards a wider legal recognition of such relationships[83] and the legislature's intent to promote the integration of homosexuals into society.

---

76 See W. Eskridge, *The Case for Same-Sex Marriage: From Sexual Liberty to Civilized Commitment*, 1996, pp. 96 *et seq.*; D. Coester-Waltjen & M. Coester, 'Formation of Marriage', in M. Glendon (ed.), *International Encyclopedia of Comparative Law: Persons and Family*, Vol. IV, 1997, pp. 50–51; S. Oliveira Pais & A. Frada de Sousa, 'A União de Facto e as Uniões Registadas de Pessoas do mesmo Sexo – Uma Análise de Direito Material e Conflitual', 1999, *Revista da Ordem dos Advogados*, pp. 707–708; F. Swennen, 'O Tempora, O Mores! The Evolving Marriage Concept and the Impediments to Marriage', in M. Antokolskaia (ed.), *Convergence and Divergence of Family Law in Europe*, 2007, pp. 138, 139.

77 See W. Eskridge, *The Case for Same-Sex Marriage: From Sexual Liberty to Civilized Commitment*, 1996, pp. 153 *et seq.*, especially pp. 172 *et seq.*

78 See F. Swennen, 'O Tempora, O Mores! The Evolving Marriage Concept and the Impediments to Marriage', in M. Antokolskaia (ed.), *Convergence and Divergence of Family Law in Europe*, 2007, p. 137.

79 See R. Posner, 'Should there be homosexual marriage? And if so, Who should decide?', 1997 *Michigan Law Review* 95, p. 1583.

80 See F. Swennen, 'O Tempora, O Mores! The Evolving Marriage Concept and the Impediments to Marriage', in M. Antokolskaia (ed.), *Convergence and Divergence of Family Law in Europe*, 2007, pp. 140–141.

81 See A. Agell, 'The Legal Status of Same-Sex Couples in Europe – A Critical Analysis', in K. Boele-Woelki *et al.* (eds.), *The Legal Recognition of Same-Sex Couples in Europe*, 2003, p. 131.

82 See A. Agell, 'The Legal Status of Same-Sex Couples in Europe – A Critical Analysis', in K. Boele-Woelki *et al.* (eds.), *The Legal Recognition of Same-Sex Couples in Europe*, 2003, pp. 123–124; N. Cid, *A Comunhão de Vida à Margem do Casamento: entre o Facto e o Direito*, 2005, pp. 563–565. On the demand for non-discrimination on the grounds of sexual orientation, see J. Canotilho & V. Moreira, *Constituição da República Portuguesa Anotada*, Vol. I, 2007, pp. 333 *et seq.*, especially pp. 340–341 and pp. 349–350.

83 This trend is not equally established throughout Europe. This being so, some authors say that although the harmonisation or unification of family law in this area is desirable, it is not, however, feasible, see I. Curry-Sumner, *All's Well that Ends Registered?*, 2005, p. 518. Noting the lack of convergence in Europe in this regard, see M. Antokolskaia, 'Harmonisation of Family Law in Europe: A Historical Perspective', in M. Antokolskaia (ed.), *Convergence and Divergence of Family Law in Europe*, 2007, p. 17; detecting, however, a 'temporary divergence', see F.

It is thus the task of the legal scholar to determine which legal instrument better suits that purpose. It is incumbent on the legal scholar in the treatment of this problem, to develop a rational, logical and strictly legal and scientific discourse.[84]

There are two main models from which the legislature can choose:[85] the opening up of civil marriage to partners of the same sex, or the organization of a specific legal status for same-sex unions with more or less similar features as that relating to marriage, as registered partnerships.

4.1. MARRIAGE OF TWO PEOPLE OF THE SAME SEX

As stated in the introduction, there are calls for same-sex relationships to benefit from external legitimisation of the relationship. These calls often take the form of claiming the right to marry[86] with the symbolic value of marriage.[87] Furthermore, marriage is also seen as a means of access to a more 'advantageous' regime than that available to *de facto* unions, namely in the fields tax and inheritance.[88] Is this the correct legislative solution to adopt?

To answering this question one must, firstly, look at the terms in which the Portuguese legal system protects the right to marry and, secondly, assess whether that right embraces the possibility of marriage between two people of the same sex.

Swennen, 'O Tempora, O Mores! The Evolving Marriage Concept and the Impediments to Marriage', in M. Antokolskaia (ed.), *Convergence and Divergence of Family Law in Europe*, 2007, p. 137 *et seq.*

84 See A. Agell, 'The Legal Status of Same-Sex Couples in Europe – A Critical Analysis', in K. Boele-Woelki *et al.* (eds.), *The Legal Recognition of Same-Sex Couples in Europe*, 2003, pp. 122–123.

85 See A. Agell, 'The Legal Status of Same-Sex Couples in Europe – A Critical Analysis', in K. Boele-Woelki *et al.* (eds.), *The Legal Recognition of Same-Sex Couples in Europe*, 2003, p. 130. The author stresses the need to decouple the issue of organisational forms of cohabitation between people of the same sex from the forms of organization of cohabitation between people of different sex. The author asserts that, on the one hand, the social needs that the regulation of such relations must satisfy is not the same in the one case as in the other, and, on the other, that neither are the different roles that such relationships play in society.

86 See Judgment of the Lisbon Court of Appeal of 15th February 2007, which rejected the appeal and upheld the refusal of the Civil Registrar of a request for a marriage ceremony between T. and M. because they were two persons of the same sex. This was the first time a higher Portuguese court had pronounced on the issue of marriage between two persons of the same sex. See Judgment of the Lisbon Court of Appeal of 15th February 2007 at www.dgsi.pt. T. and M. were dissatisfied with that decision and have appealed to the Constitutional Court where a decision is pending.

87 See N. Cid, 'Direitos Humanos e Família: Quando os Homossexuais querem casar', 1998 *Economia e Sociologia*, no. 66, pp. 230–231; R. Posner, 'Should there be homosexual marriage? And if so, Who should decide?', 1997 *Michigan Law Review* 95, p. 1587.

88 See M. Glendon, 'Marriage and the State: the Withering Away of Marriage', 1976 *Virginia Law Review*, no. 62, p. 710.

4.1.1. The right to marry in the Constitution

The right to marry has constitutional support. Article 36(1) Constitution of the Portuguese Republic provides that 'everyone has the right to found a family and to marry on terms of full equality'. It is the unanimous view of scholars that this provision enshrines not one, but two fundamental rights: the right to found a family *and* the right to marry. Not unanimous, however, are the interpretations of the result of combining them.

The provision can be interpreted as meaning that the constitutional concept of family is not confined to the matrimonial family, but also covers the 'natural family' and the 'family created by adoption'. However, according to this interpretation, the right to found a family should be interpreted, firstly, as a right to procreate and, secondly, as a right to establish the corresponding parentage ties.[89]

According to a different interpretation, the consideration of the right to marry and the right to found a family as two different rights purports an implicit recognition of cohabitation outside marriage as a familial relationship. This being so, the right to found a family has to be interpreted as a constitutional expansion involving appreciation of how *de facto* unions can legally be recognised as familial relationships[90] and thus benefit from direct legal protection.[91]

In spite of those differences of interpretation, one can say that the Portuguese Constitution is open 'to the plurality and diversity of family relationships in our time'[92] and that constitutionally the worlds of *family* and *marriage* do not necessarily coincide.

The fact that these concepts do not coincide, however, does not appear to lead to the conclusion that of the acceptance of another model of the family within marriage or even the abandonment of the traditional concept of marriage as based on the difference of the sexes. Firstly, because Article 36(1) 2nd part Constitution of the Portuguese Republic enshrines not only a right to marry, but also includes an *institutional guarantee* of marriage. From this *institutional guarantee* follows a protection that amounts to a ban on the legislature modifying the concept and the legal regime governing marriage in a manner leading to its abolition or even to detraction from its main features.[93] The traditional concept of marriage itself delimits the right to marry, as can be seen in the prohibitions on polygamy and on

---

89 See F. Coelho & G. Oliveira, *Curso de Direito da Família,* Vol. I, 2003, pp. 162–166; J. Miranda & R. Medeiros, *Constituição Portuguesa Anotada,* Vol. I, 2005, pp. 399–401.

90 See J. Canotilho & V. Moreira, *Constituição da República Portuguesa Anotada,* Vol. I, 2007, p. 561.

91 See J. Miranda & R. Medeiros, *Constituição Portuguesa Anotada,* Vol. I, 2005, p. 402.

92 See J. Miranda & R. Medeiros, *Constituição Portuguesa Anotada,* Vol. I, 2005, p. 398. Similarly, see J. Canotilho & V. Moreira, *Constituição da República Portuguesa Anotada,* Vol.I, 2007, p. 567.

93 See F. Coelho & G. Oliveira, *Curso de Direito da Família,* Vol. I, 2003, pp. 159,160; J. Miranda & R. Medeiros, *Constituição Portuguesa Anotada,* Vol. I, 2005, pp. 396, 397.

the marriage of two people of the same sex.[94] Indeed, the constitutional concept of marriage is derived from the historical concept of marriage as a union of two people of different sex rooted in a communion of life. Therefore, we cannot, infer from Article 36(1) 2nd part Constitution of the Portuguese Republic 'a direct and compulsory recognition of same-sex marriages'.[95] The constitutional opening recognition of the different models of the family does not encompass same-sex marriage.

Secondly, the fundamental right to marry is not an absolute right[96] because it is limited by the impediments to marriage: marriageable age, insanity, prior marriage, certain degrees of kinships and affinity and the condemnation for murder of a prior spouse (Articles 1601, 1602, 1604 Civil Code). These impediments to marriage are considered to be in accordance with the right to marry provided they are based on fundamental public interests that express important societal interests.[97] The legislature may thus establish such impediments and set out a legal concept of marriage as the 'contract between two people of different sex who wish to found a family with a full communion of life' (Article 1577 Civil Code).

4.1.2. *The right to marry and the principle of equality*

Would such a solution violate the principle of equality which prohibits that anyone is 'privileged, benefited, harmed, deprived of any right because (...) of their sexual orientation'?[98]

The principle of equality, as the structuring principle of the social and democratic State based on the rule of law, has three strands: the liberal, the social and the democratic.[99] The dialectical combination of these strands has resulted in a broadening of the scope of protection of the principle of equality in the Portuguese constitutional system, resulting in the prohibition of arbitrariness and discrimination and in the obligation to differentiate.[100]

---

94 See F. Coelho & G. Oliveira, *Curso de Direito da Família*, Vol. I, 2003, p. 158; J. Miranda & R. Medeiros, *Constituição Portuguesa Anotada*, Vol. I, 2005, pp. 396–398; J. Canotilho & V. Moreira, *Constituição da República Portuguesa Anotada*, Vol. I, 2007, p. 562.

95 See J. Canotilho & V. Moreira, *Constituição da República Portuguesa Anotada*, Vol. I, 2007, p. 568.

96 See F. Coelho & G. Oliveira, *Curso de Direito da Família*, Vol. I, 2003, p. 158; J. Miranda & R. Medeiros, *Constituição Portuguesa Anotada*, Tomo I, 2005, p. 396; J. Canotilho & V. Moreira, *Constituição da República Portuguesa Anotada*, Vol. I, 2007, p. 562.

97 See F. Coelho & G. Oliveira, *Curso de Direito da Família*, Vol. I, 2003, pp. 158–159; J. Miranda & R. Medeiros, *Constituição Portuguesa Anotada*, Vol. I, 2005, p. 396.

98 See Art. 13, Constitution of the Portuguese Republic.

99 See J. Canotilho & V. Moreira, *Constituição da República Portuguesa Anotada*, Vol. I, 2007, pp. 337–338.

100 See J. Canotilho & V. Moreira, *Constituição da República Portuguesa Anotada*, Vol. I, 2007, p. 339.

For a complete answer to the question formulated above, one should clarify what the prohibition of arbitrariness and by the prohibition of discrimination mean. As to the former, the ban on arbitrariness is characterised in this way: neither shall what is essentially equal be arbitrarily treated as unequal, nor shall what is essentially unequal be treated as equal. The Constitution leaves to the legislature the task of defining, from an appropriate material base, the facts or relationships, which are to serve as points of reference for an equal or unequal treatment.[101]

When trying to discover if same-sex relationships are equal or different from different-sex relationships, one must focus not on the individuals themselves but on the relationship between them. Individuals involved in different-sex and same-sex relationships are persons and therefore citizens with equal right to the respect of their human dignity independent from their sexual orientation.

In spite of these relationships being equal with regards the 'intimate mutual love and affection and long-term commitment'[102] and the display of 'intimacy, stability and social and financial interdependence',[103] some differences remain. Besides the traditional argument of procreation, one must not forget another distinguishing factor: there are men and women involved. Even though men and women are considered to be citizens with equal rights and duties, the fact is that their real position before society and the labour market is quite unequal. It is often said that, in Portugal, a woman earns a half of what a man earns for the same work during the same time, a woman's career perspectives are quite inferior compared to those of a man. This difference between sexes has a great influence in the relationship of two persons of opposite sex. In fact, the Portuguese legislature when defining the legal regime of marriage took this into account establishing, for example, the principle of equality of rights and duties between spouses and the principle of joint orientation of the family life (Article 1671 Civil Code), the duty of contributing to the family expenses according to the each one's financial possibilities, which can also be fulfilled with the work done at home including the daily care and the education of the children of the family (Article 1676 Civil Code)[104] and establishing as criteria for the payment of maintenance between former spouses, namely, the professional qualifications of the spouses, each one's

---

101 See J. Canotilho & V. Moreira, *Constituição da República Portuguesa Anotada*, Vol. I, 2007, p. 339.

102 *Ghaidan* v. *Godin-Mendoza* [2004], UKHL 30, Lord Rodger of Earlsferry (126) at http://www.publications.parliament.uk/pa/ld200304/ldjudgmt/jd040621/gha-1.htm.

103 *Ghaidan* v. *Godin-Mendoza* [2004], UKHL 30, Baroness Hale of Richmond (139) at http://www.publications.parliament.uk/pa/ld200304/ldjudgmt/jd040621/gha-1.htm.

104 This specific way of accomplish the duty of contributing to the family expenses was thought for those situations of women staying at home caring and educating the children of the family while their spouses (men) were making progresses in their careers in the outside world.

employment possibilities, the time each one of them will spend with the care and education of their children.[105]

In same-sex relationships that difference does not exist and thus the above mentioned legislature's preoccupation does not seem to be justified under the same terms.

It follows that, given the substantive and objective difference in these situations, there being no right of marriage contemplated by the Constitution for same-sex couples does not seem to cause any incongruity in the constitutional system because it respects the prohibition on arbitrariness.

A similar conclusion is likely to be drawn in relation to the constitutional prohibition of discrimination. Regarding this prohibition, it should immediately be made clear that it does not impose absolute equal treatment whatever the concrete circumstances, nor prevent any differential treatment. From a constitutional point of view, different treatment is illegitimate where differences in treatment are not founded on the objective diversity of situations arising from consideration of one of the unlawful discrimination factors (Article 13(2), Constitution of the Portuguese Republic), did not pursue a constitutionally legitimate purpose and, finally, did not satisfy the requirements of necessity, appropriateness and proportionality.[106]

The lack of constitutional recognition of a right to marry for same-sex couples, in contrast to the position different-sex couples does not represent a violation of the prohibition on discrimination. Indeed, the denial of such a constitutional right is based in the first place on an objective distinction between situations; secondly, it is not based solely on sexual orientation as a reason for justifying the difference in treatment – the heart of the issue is not concerned with the sexual orientation of those seeking marriage, but in the institution of marriage itself, historically and sociologically oriented towards the legal regulation of different-sex relationships, and therefore an inappropriate instrument for legal regulation of the emotional relationship of two persons of same sex.[107] Thirdly, it is pursuing a constitutionally legitimate purpose in the shape of the *institutional guarantee* of marriage.[108] Finally, it is necessary, appropriate and proportionate to the pursuit of that objective, in that denying the right to marriage to persons of the same sex does not prevent the legislature from providing the legal effects of marriage to same-sex relationships and affording them the appropriate legal protection.

105 Once more one can find here a special worry with the situation of women.

106 See J. Canotilho & V. Moreira, *Constituição da República Portuguesa Anotada*, Vol. I, 2007, p. 340.

107 See M. Glendon, 'Marriage and the State: the Withering Away of Marriage', 1976 *Virginia Law Review*, no. 62, p. 677; S. Pais & A. Sousa, 'A União de Facto e as Uniões Registadas de Pessoas do mesmo Sexo – Uma Análise de Direito Material e Conflitual', 1999 *Revista da Ordem dos Advogados*, p. 721.

108 See J. Miranda & R. Medeiros, *Constituição Portuguesa Anotada*, Vol. I, 2005, p. 405.

Portuguese constitutional doctrine has understood that the Constitution should remain open to the recognition of new realities and to the increasing diversity of models of family. Therefore constitutional protection of the family can be extended to stable relationships between two people of the same sex.[109]

4.2. REGISTERED PARTNERSHIPS

The legislature seems to be left with registered partnership as a possible legal instrument for regulating the legal status of same-sex relationships. Is this model consistent with the Portuguese constitutional system? A solution to this problem must be sought.

The model of registered partnership was introduced for the first time in Denmark in 1989 as a means of providing legal protection to same-sex relationships and thus promoting social acceptance of these relationships.[110] Registered partnership was considered to be a new legal familial relationship. Although different from marriage, in name and the persons to whom it applied, it was very similar to it with regard to its effects, which are progressively being extended.[111] Other legal systems were quick to follow suit, firstly, those of other Nordic countries[112] and then in other countries such as The Netherlands,[113] Germany[114] and most recently the United Kingdom and Switzerland.

All the countries mentioned adopted this model of regulation of same-sex relationships basing it, to a greater or lesser extent, on the regime governing marriage. In fact, the laws on registered partnerships lay down detailed rules the establishment of the relationship, its effects on persons and property and its dissolution.

---

109 See J. Miranda & R. Medeiros, *Constituição Portuguesa Anotada*, Vol. I, 2005, p. 406; J. Canotilho & V. Moreira, *Constituição da República Portuguesa Anotada*, Vol. I, 2007, p. 568.

110 See I. Lund-Andersen, 'The Danish Registered Partnership Act', in K. Boele-Woelki *et al.* (eds.), *The Legal Recognition of Same-Sex Couples in Europe*, 2003, p. 13.

111 See I. Lund-Andersen, 'The Danish Registered Partnership Act', in K. Boele-Woelki *et al.* (eds.), *The Legal Recognition of Same-Sex Couples in Europe*, 2003, pp. 13, 17 *et seq.*

112 On registered partnerships in Sweden and Finland, see M. Savolainen, 'The Finish and the Swedish Partnership Acts – Similarities and Divergences', in K. Boele-Woelki *et al.* (eds.), *The Legal Recognition of Same-Sex Couples in Europe*, 2003, p. 24 *et seq.*

113 In The Netherlands, registered partnerships are not intended only for same-sex, but also for different-sex couples. On registered partnerships in the context of the Dutch legal system, see K. Boele-Woelki, 'Registered Partnership and Same-Sex Marriage in The Netherlands', in K. Boele-Woelki *et al.* (eds.), *The Legal Recognition of Same-Sex Couples in Europe*, 2003, pp. 45, especially, pp. 45–48.

114 On the 2001 reform that introduced the *Lebenspartnerschaft*, see K. Thorn, 'The German Law on Same-Sex Partnerships', in K. Boele-Woelki *et al.* (eds.), *The Legal Recognition of Same-Sex Couples in Europe*, 2003, pp. 84 *et seq.*

In most cases, registered partnerships appear to be little more than a substitute for marriage, although differences remain between the respective regimes.[115]

The creation of a new institution with a different name, but in all other respects similar to marriage should not be the path followed by the Portuguese legislature to achieve the objective of giving more effective legal protection to same-sex relationships. Firstly, because marriage in the Portuguese legal system enjoys a specific protection stemming from the *institutional guarantee* that it enjoys under the Constitution, contrary to any proposal to grant to same-sex partners an absolutely equal status to that of married couples.[116] Secondly, to accord an equal status in (almost all) material respects to that of married couples only with a different name could lead to some confusion[117] and to interpretative difficulties that should always to be avoided. Thirdly, the legislature must strive to regulate the specific characteristics of same-sex relationships in what that are unique and therefore deserve to be treated accordingly, eschewing the inappropriate solutions that could result from ignoring the differences from different-sex relationships, in particular those regarding the difference of gender within the family, the society[118] and the labour market.

The Portuguese legislature, in trying to ensure effective protection of those involved in same-sex relationships should seek to solve the legal problems raised by this model of cohabitation and therefore seek to create a specific legal regime for these situations which could take the form of registered partnerships, provided that they would not be considered a substitute for marriage or a 'second-class' marriage. By paying special attention to the specific features these relationships, the legislature would respect their difference reflecting the increasing social acceptance of these relationships.

On the path from *de facto* to *de jure* another step must be taken, the Portuguese legislature should chose the best direction to take in the light of the features and structuring principles of the Portuguese legal system.

---

115 Which, however, are still disputed. See H. Ytterberg, 'All Human Beings are Equal, but Some are More Equal than Others – Equality in Dignity without Equality in Rights?', in K. Boele-Woelki *et al.* (eds.), *The Legal Recognition of Same-Sex Couples in Europe*, 2003, pp. 1 *et seq.*

116 See J. Miranda & R. Medeiros, *Constituição Portuguesa Anotada*, Vol. I, 2005, p. 406.

117 See K. Thorn, 'The German Law on Same-Sex Partnerships', in K. Boele-Woelki *et al.* (eds.), *The Legal Recognition of Same-Sex Couples in Europe*, 2003, pp. 85, 87.

118 See K. Thorn, 'The German Law on Same-Sex Partnerships', in K. Boele-Woelki *et al.* (eds.), *The Legal Recognition of Same-Sex Couples in Europe*, 2003, p. 93.

SAME-SEX PARTNERS IN HUNGARY
Cohabitation and registered partnership

Orsolya Szeibert-Erdős*

1. INTRODUCTION

Same-sex partners can neither marry each other nor establish a registered partnership according to the Hungarian legal system currently in force. Nevertheless, they are permitted to live in an unmarried partnership within the framework of the current legislation in the field of informal cohabitation. This type of partnership is not regulated in the Family Act, Act No. IV. 1952, and so does not create any familial relationship between the partners. This cohabitation – élettárs in Hungarian – is defined in the Civil Code,[1] Act No. IV. 1959. The Code contains a number of limited and brief legal provisions with regards this cohabitation form.[2] Cohabitation was legally defined and regulated laconically in 1977 for the first time as a non-registered form of partnership restricted to different-sex partners. Later, in 1996 the gates of this informal partnership were opened for same-sex partners as a consequence of a decision of the Hungarian Constitutional Court.

Although this is the state of the law as of early 2008, some important steps have been taken since 2001. The most notable changes happened recently, especially in 2007. In December 2007 the Hungarian Parliament approved the Act on Registered Partnership, which will enter into force in January 2009. The Act makes it possible for same-sex and different-sex couples to enter into a registered partnership. Although there are some differences between the regulation of marriage and of registered partnership, the new Act orders the application of rules regarding marriage to apply correspondingly to registered partnership, at least as a main rule and for the relationship between the partners. The enactment of this Act is admittedly the most notable change in the regulation of same-sex partnerships, but many other changes have also taken place. The Constitutional Court has pronounced a number of judgments over the course of the last fifteen years affecting the legal position of homosexual persons and the adjudication of

* ELTE University of Budapest (Hungary), email: szeibert@ajk.elte.hu.

1 § 685/A Civil Code (*Polgári törvénykönyv*).

2 §§ 578/G (1)-(2) and 685. b) Civil Code.

homosexuality itself. Moreover, the recodification of the Civil Code has been going on since 2001. Inasmuch as the family law will comprise one part of the Civil Code, this process has involved the alteration and modernization of family law and especially the revision of the legal regime with respect to unmarried and/or registered partnership. Although some steps, decisions and accepted standpoints during this process had a positive effect on the legal acceptance of same-sex partnership as marriage, there were also negative steps and decisions, which go some way to explaining the delay of legal acceptance in Hungary.

2. THE CHANGE IN THE LEGAL STATUS OF HOMOSEXUAL COUPLES IN THE LIGHT OF THE CONSTITUTIONAL COURT'S DECISIONS

2.1. THE DECISION RESULTING IN THE ACCEPTANCE OF SAME-SEX INFORMAL COHABITATION AND THE REGULATION OF UNMARRIED PARTNERSHIP CURRENTLY IN FORCE

In 1995, the Constitutional Court had to deal with the institution of same-sex marriage and same-sex cohabitation.[3] A petition arrived to the Court alleging that the rule of the Family Act stating that only a man and a woman can enter into a marriage and the rule in the Civil Code stating that only a man and a woman can cohabit gives rise to sex discrimination. The Court analysed the institution of marriage and of cohabitation and stated very definitively that marriage must be restricted to different-sex couples. In the opinion of the Court the traditional purpose of marriage makes it impossible to permit same-sex couples to enter into marriage, also with a view to the fact that marriage is protected in the Hungarian Constitution.

In connection with cohabitation the Court took a more liberal stance, but it did not deal with the real function and purpose of cohabitation at all. The definition of unmarried partnership and the regulation for cohabitants was considered and the Court examined which legal rules contained rights and obligations for unmarried partners at that time. These were mostly rules in the field of social law, as well as civil and criminal procedural law. As a result of this investigation, the Constitutional Court stated that the differentiation between partners according to their gender violates the constitutional prohibition of discrimination, with certain exceptions. The exception applies if the law has been created with regard to

---

3 Decision of the Constitutional Court No. 14/1995 (III. 13.), *ABH* (*Alkotmánybírósági Határozatok*, Constitutional Court Decisions) 1995, p. 82.

either common children or to marriage with a third person. In these cases it is essential to distinguish between the forms of cohabitation according to the gender of the partners.

The Constitutional Court stayed the proceeding in this case so as to ensure that Parliament could resolve this unconstitutional situation. In 1996 the definition of cohabitation was extended to same-sex partners. Unmarried partners are two persons with an emotional and economic partnership who live together, without entering into a marriage, in a common household. Neither the establishment nor the termination of this partnership requires any registration procedure. The unmarried partnership comes into being in an informal way. Most of the time this does not cause any problem. However, there are other cases when the lack of the registration does create legal dispute. Sometimes the question arises whether the partners actually cohabited at all. In such cases evidence plays an enormous role and the court's task is to determine not only whether the partnership existed, but if it did exist the dates of its commencement and termination.

The court has to compare the cohabitation's definition and the facts of the concrete situation. Nowadays there is an established judicial practice in interpreting and applying the elements of the definition, but since this is always developing, this factual model cannot operate as safely as registration. Real importance is attributed to three elements of the definition: the emotional partnership, the economic partnership and whether the partners' relationship was recognised and obvious to third persons. Whether the couple lives together plays a decisive role in the decision, as does the economic partnership, which after analysis of the case law can be seen to be playing an increasing role. This last factor is balanced very critically and often the stated lack of economic co-operation ensures that the couple is regarded as not having reached the required level of commitment necessary for cohabitation. Sometimes the courts demand a higher level of co-operation than is often required of married partners!

Same-sex cohabitants have almost the same legal position as different-sex cohabitants, *e.g.* the Civil Code regulates the financial issues in the same way. Both groups of couples can enter into a cohabitation contract, but it occurs rarely. The statutory property regime is a partial community of property regime, namely the community of property of cohabitants. It resembles the matrimonial property of spouses, but there is a clear distinction between them. The cohabitants do not have any maintenance obligation according to the Civil Code, neither for the period of cohabitation, nor after the termination thereof. Nevertheless, judicial practice has developed differently; according to this development, the partners are obliged to maintain and take care of each other during the duration of the cohabitation since this is regarded as an integral element of cohabitation.

The parent-child relationship is not regulated by the Civil Code. Under the regime of the Family Act, parental responsibility does not depend on the marital status of the parents. The decisive factor is the establishment of the mother's or the father's legal parentage. Nevertheless, there are differences in the establishment of the paternal presumption. Actually, this is true only for different-sex couples.[4]

2.2. OTHER DECISIONS OF THE CONSTITUTIONAL COURT HAVING RELATION TO HOMOSEXUALITY

The fundamental premise that marriage can only entail a relationship between one man and one woman was repeated and affirmed by the Constitutional Court several times. Two decisions were handed down in October 2007,[5] which referred to the fact that marriage is the community of life between persons of different sex; a value protected by the Constitution. It was emphasized that the subject matter cannot be extended.

A decision of the Constitutional Court in May 1996 dealt with the question whether it should be forbidden (or at least restricted) for a minor to be a member of an association that is connected with homosexuality. The court procedure was initiated by the President of the Supreme Court. The aim of this procedure was to draw a line between two fundamental rights, on the one hand the right for a child to get the care and protection from the State that guarantees his or her proper physical, mental and moral development, and, on the other, a child's right to associate when he or she intends to be a member of an association that legally protects the interests of homosexuals. In its explanation the Constitutional Court stated that the freedom of association is a fundamental right, the restriction of which depends on two factors, namely the child's maturity to decide alone and the exact object of this decision.

The Constitutional Court emphasized that the State is obliged to protect the child from such dangers and risks that he or she is not able to appreciate due to his or her age or to measure the consequences of such a choice. The membership of an association requires taking a public stance and it thus can adversely affect the child's physical, mental and moral development, especially if the commitment is perceived in an inconsistent or negative way in the society.

Concerning the social perception of homosexual persons and of homosexuality itself, the Court declined to hold on the moral qualification of homosexuality.

---

4 About the legal status of cohabitants and the judicial practice in details in English: O. Szeibert-Erdős, 'Unmarried Partnerships in Hungary', in K. Boele-Woelki (ed.), *Common Core and Better Law in European Family Law*, 2005, pp. 313–330. In Hungarian: O. Szeibert-Erdős, 'Cohabitation', in A. Kőrös (ed.), *Családjogi Kézikönyv* (Family Law Handbook), 2007, pp. 850–898.

5 Decisions of the Constitutional Court No. 65/2007 (X. 18.) and No. 75/2007 (X. 19.), *ABH* 2007, pp. 940. and 943.

Nevertheless, it expressly stated that neither the peculiarities of homosexuality, nor the current social status of homosexual persons could be ignored when determining the child's right of association in that concrete situation. When weighing the child's decision to join an association, the problematic social integration of homosexuals must be taken into account. According to the decision, homosexuals are generally not accepted in Hungary at this time, which could even result in discrimination.

The 1996 decision stated that the State can limit the minor's right of association. This standpoint was severely criticised. Although the Constitutional Court emphasized its neutrality, many believed the decision to take a slanted stance. The starting point of these criticisms was that the moral development of the child could not be protected without deciding what is moral and is immoral.

This decision in its very detailed explanation also referred to its abovementioned decision handed down in 1995. The Constitutional Court admitted that same-sex partnership had been declared to be a value that required legal protection if the relationship was long-lasting and limited to special relationships. However, the Court confirmed a year later that the ground of this declaration was not the partnership's homosexual character, but the fact that cohabitation was a kind of partnership that was acknowledged in other fields of law. Besides, the differentiation between different-sex and same-sex partnerships seemed to be without any foundation.

In 1999 and 2002, the Constitutional Court decided two other relevant cases.[6] These changed certain rules of the Criminal Code in connection with homosexuality. The first of the decisions put an end to the regulation of incest, which was discriminatory towards same-sex fornication between brothers/sisters'. This was punished as a crime, in contrast to fornication between different-sex brothers/sisters. The 2002 decision equalised the age of consent for different-sex and same-sex relationships. Although these steps were taken in the field of criminal law, they are really important as they indicate the change in the social and legal perceptions towards homosexuality.

6 Decisions of the Constitutional Court No. 20/1999 (VI. 25.), *ABH* 1999, p. 159. and No. 37/2002 (IX. 4.), *ABH* 2002, p. 230.

3. CONCEPTIONS ABOUT THE SAME-SEX PARTNERSHIP IN THE COURSE OF THE CODIFICATION PROCESS

3.1. THE CONCEPT AND THE REGULATION PROGRAMME OF THE NEW CIVIL CODE

The Concept and the Regulation Programme of the recodified Civil Code was published in 2003.[7] The problem of unmarried partnership and the choice among the different alternative solutions was one of the most debated issues of family law. According to the Concept, there was a need to guarantee further rights for cohabitants, but only in a way that would not weaken the institution of marriage. This idea was based on the increasing number of cohabitants and the fact that cohabitating parents had the same parental rights as married parents. The aim was to grant maintenance rights and rights with regards the use of the common home to partners living in long-term partnerships. The Concept itself contains neither any willingness for the introduction of a registration method nor the institutionalisation of same-sex partnerships.

The Regulation Programme dealt in detail with the regulation itself. It affected the property issues of unmarried partners and definitively determined that there was no proposal to introduce the registered form of non-marital partnership. The issue of same-sex partnership remained outside the scope of the new Civil Code.

3.2. THE EXPERTS' PROPOSAL OF THE NEW CIVIL CODE

The slogan characterizing the Experts' Proposal of the new Family Law Book issued in 2005 was 'deliberate progress'.[8] This was especially true for non-marital partnership. The detailed rules of the Proposal were in accordance with the Concept, but they went one step further with regard to the registration of partnerships. Although the Proposal emphasized avoiding the introduction of a marriage-like 'registered partnership', the so-called 'optional registration' was drafted with the aim of granting a possibility for those partners (*e.g.* same-sex partners) who desired official registration. However, cohabitation would have preserved its

---

7 *Az új Polgári Törvénykönyv koncepciója és tematikája* (Concept and Regulation Programme of the New Civil Code), published in *Magyar Közlöny* (Hungarian Official Gazette), February 2003.

8 Among others the periodical *Családi Jog* (Family Law) published the Experts' Proposal in parts. The proposal about cohabitation was published in August 2005. A. Kőrös, '"*Fontolva haladás" – az új Ptk. Családjogi Könyve 1. Rész: Az élettársi jogviszony szabályozásának szakértői javaslata*' ('Deliberate progress' – Family Law Book of the new CC Part 1 Expert's Proposal for the regulation of cohabitation), 2005 *Family Law*, no. 2, pp. 1–10.

factual character even in these cases since this registration would only have had a declarative, and no constitutive, character. It would have served only as an evidence of the existence, duration and termination of unmarried partnership.

According to the Proposal's explanation the registration of unmarried partners would have been a special register, especially created with this single aim. The couple would have been able to jointly register their non-marital partnership in the registers maintained by the local government's notary. The registration would have been terminated on the couple's joint petition or upon the petition of either one of the cohabitants with notice being sent to the other partner. To avoid the polygamous registration, the Proposal contained the rule that only one partnership could have been recorded for one person at the same time. The Proposal did not connect any other legal effect to the fact of registration, apart from serving as evidence in the case of dispute.

3.3. THE ACTUAL PROPOSALS OF THE NEW CIVIL CODE

As of early 2008, there are now two proposals for the new Civil Code since the codification process has separated since late 2007. One official proposal is that of the Ministry of Justice[9] and one is of the Experts.[10] Their standpoints in the matter of registered partnership are slightly different. (Although the new Act has since been approved in the meantime, this fact that there are two proposals now can nonetheless still be important).

The Proposal of the Ministry of Justice would modify the institution of cohabitation and would introduce a new one, namely registered partnership. Nevertheless, it should be mentioned that this latter institution is a real registered partnership in terms of its content, but the Hungarian terminology is misleading. In Hungarian cohabitation is *élettárs*, so *élettárs* can roughly be translated as living in a factual non-registered unmarried partnership. Registered (non-marital) partnership was labelled in the Proposal as *bejegyzett élettársi kapcsolat*, that is to say registered cohabitation. It worth using the term registered partnership, rather than registered cohabitation.

The non-registered cohabitation has preserved its character since 2005 as it was formulated in the abovementioned Experts' Proposal. However, registered partnership has been drafted as a novel solution. According to the Experts' Proposal two persons – either same-sex or different-sex – can enter into registered partnership by declaring their intention before the registrar. The regulation in

9 It is available on the homepage of the Ministry, www.irm.gov.hu/download/ptk-normaszoveg-tervezet_20071029.pdf.

10 Published in: L. Vékás, *Szakértői javaslat az új Polgári Törvénykönyv tervezetéhez* (Experts' Proposal to the Draft of the new Civil Code), 2008, under edition.

case of marriage would be applied to the establishment and termination of the partnership. The rules with regard to maintenance, property issues, and for the use of the common household would be the same as for married partners and the surviving registered partner would inherit in exactly the same manner as surviving spouses according to the current system of intestate succession.

Although the Experts' Proposal of 2007 follows a different approach, the essence of the regulation resembles the Proposal of the Ministry. Non-marital partnership would be regulated as a family relationship in form of registered partnership and of cohabitation. Both forms of partnership would be open to both different-sex and same-sex partners without any discrimination. The aim is to realize the principle of equal treatment of persons living in the same kind of partnership. However, neither forms of unmarried partnership would result of certain legal effects of the marriage, namely the right to the partner's name, right of adoption and the paternal presumption based on the partnership itself.

According to the 2007 Experts' Proposal registered partnership would be registered in a special register by the registrar. Their property relationship, including maintenance and use of the common flat, would be identical to that applied to the married partners, but in other issues the rules for cohabitants would be applied for registered partners. Both the establishment and the termination of the partnership are regulated in more detail than in the Proposal of the Ministry. Registered partnership would be terminated not only if one partner dies or if one of the partners get married, but also by means of a dissolution procedure and by the registrar upon the common petition of the partners.

4. ACT ON REGISTERED PARTNERSHIP

In the summer and autumn of 2007 debate centred on same-sex marriage and same-sex registered partnership. While the Alliance of Free Democrats declared their intention to equalise the rights of same-sex partners with married partners, the Hungarian Socialist Party proclaimed that they were in favour of introducing same-sex registered partnership. The Bill itself was submitted in November and on 27th December the Hungarian Parliament approved the new Act on Registered Partnership, which will enter into force in January 2009. According to the literal translation, the institution will be called 'registered cohabitation', but this new form of partnership corresponds (in terms of its content) to the institution of registered partnership as this terminology is used in this context in Europe. (Registered partnership would be *bejegyzett partnerkapcsolat* in Hungarian but the Act uses the phrase *bejegyzett élettársi kapcsolat* that is to say registered cohabitation.)

Act No. CLXXXIV 2007 does not give any definition of the registered partnership. However, it states how to establish this form of partnership. The Family

Act follows the same method of regulation in case of marriage. Registered partnership can be created by two adults if they declare to enter into registered partnership with each other.[11] Minors are not allowed to enter into this partnership even with permission.[12]

One of the most important peculiarities of the partnership is that it is open both for same-sex and different-sex partners. It seems to be one institution, but in reality there are two institutions: registered partnership for different-sex couples and registered partnership for same-sex couples. Their function is far from identical since while same-sex couples only have the possibility to cohabit, a man and a woman are also able to get married. The explanation of the Act is very general and laconic, it refers to the fact that the family model based on marriage is increasingly chosen by fewer people, as it shown by statistical data. The question of why it seemed necessary to grant the right to registered partnership not only for same-sex partners can not be answered upon the mere explanation. It fixes that the increase of unmarried partnerships is a social tendency which is to be taken into attention just as the claim of same-sex partners for a legally regulated partnership. The consequence drawn by the legislature and put forward as a motive for the Act is that these two tendencies are connected.

Nevertheless, the question remains concerning the real purpose of the legislature: it seemed rational to meet the demands of the same-sex partners and of other couples who do not want to marry each other and at the same time do not want to cohabit either. Furthermore, it seemed to be political and social nonsense to introduce a marriage-like institution restricted to same-sex couples. The reactions and critics unambiguously indicate that society has understood the message of the Act: the emphasis has been laid on same-sex partnership.

4.1. THE COMPARISON BETWEEN MARRIAGE AND REGISTERED PARTNERSHIP

The Act contains four titles, as it regulates the establishment of registered partnership, its legal consequences, its termination and deals with the acts which are to be altered according to the new form of partnership. The process of establishment is the same as in case of marriage. The partners should declare their intention to enter into this partnership before the registrar who records the details and selects the day for the registration of the partnership, taking into account the parties' wishes.[13] The registered partnership is established by the declaration of the parties' identical intention before the registrar (identical to marriage). The

11 § 1(1).

12 § 1(2).

13 § 15 entering the § 26/G into the Act on Maintaining the Register.

registration is not a constitutive act, merely declarative. From this point of view the only difference between marriage and registered partnership is that a minor over 16 can marry with the permission of the guardianship authority. This is impossible when entering into a registered partnership.

The new Act alters the Act on Maintaining the Register stating that not only births, marriages and deaths have to be registered, but also registered partnerships.[14] This procedure follows the model of marriage. There are special regulations in connection with registration of the non-Hungarian citizen's registered partnership and with issue of certification of no impediment being necessary for the registered partnership's registration abroad.[15]

According to the Act on International Private Law, if a non-Hungarian citizen wishes to marry in Hungary, he or she has to certify that there is no impediment of marriage under his or her personal law. The Act on Registered Partnership refers to this rule, stating that the registrar can provide an exemption under the certification as in case of marriage. A Hungarian citizen, who wishes to enter into a registered partnership abroad, can claim for such a certificate by the registrar. He or she has to attach the declaration according to which there is no statutory impediment of entering into a registered partnership to his or her knowledge.

It is a really essential point that the same authority, *i.e.* the registrar, has competence to proceed in both ceremonies according to the same principles. The same is true of other formal criteria too, namely that the establishment of registered partnership should happen in public and solemnly; deviation from this rule is possible only at the parties' request.[16]

With regard to the legal effects, the Act orders that in questions not regulated by this Act, the rules of the Family Act concerning marriage are to be applied analogously.[17] This seems to be the key point: registered partnership results in the consequences of marriage as a main rule. Nevertheless, although many of the consequences of marriage are extended, this is not without exception. The property consequences are the same in their entirety, that is to say, the statutory property regime for registered partners is the community of property. Moreover, both for maintenance of the registered partner and for the use of the common flat, the rules to be applied for marriage and registered partnership are identical. The personal legal effects are also the same as a main rule, but the Act mentions two exceptions: registered partners – at least by their status – cannot use their partner's surname and they can not adopt a child together.[18]

14 § 15 entering § 35/A into Act on Maintaining the Register.

15 § 15 entering § 26/E and 26/F into Act on Maintaining the Register.

16 § 15 entering § 26/G into Act on Maintaining the Register.

17 § 2(1)-(2).

18 § 2(1) second sentence.

The regulation of the use of the surname for married couples in the Family Act is a modern one, being in force since January 2004. According to these rules, which are in line the international tendencies, not only the fiancée can take the man's surname, but the fiancé can choose to bear the woman's surname. Besides, they can have a common family name by connecting their family names. On the other hand, registered partners bear their own family name in spite of their status. The explanatory notes to the Act does not provide any motive for this, but the Experts' Proposal 2007 states that the rules for married partners' name are inherently connected to marriage pursuant to public opinion.

The prohibition of joint adoption means that registered partners are not permitted to adopt a child as adoptive parents together. Furthermore, step-parent adoption is also excluded, such that a registered partner cannot adopt the child of his or her registered partner and it is irrelevant whether the child is related by blood or was adopted.

Registered partnership can be terminated in a similar manner like a marriage, but there are some differences, too. The death of one partner terminates the partnership but it can be terminated by court. The court's action corresponds to divorce. If different-sex partners of registered partnership enter into a marriage, this results in the automatic termination of the registered partnership. An extra method of termination not available to spouses is the termination by public notary.[19] According to the explanation this option provides a quicker and a more flexible procedure. The termination process before the public notary is limited to those situations laid down in the Act. There are three cumulative requirements to be met: (a) the registered partners have to claim the termination of the partnership together without any undue influence, (b) they do not have common minor children or common children that require maintenance, *e.g.* child of legal age who is studying, and (c) they have arranged their property issues.[20] These issues are identical the issues required to be arranged by spouses wishing to divorce by virtue of mutual consent: maintenance, the right to use the common flat after termination and distribution of the common property. The Act stipulates in which cases it is impossible to initiate proceedings before the public notary and arranges in detail the regulations of the proceeding itself.[21] The aim is to guarantee a quick procedure by applying certain regulations of the civil procedure law.

The Act on Registered Partnership contains rules about the modification of the Family Act,[22] the Act on Maintaining the Register[23] and the Civil Code.[24] The tendency is unambiguous: registered partnership has been raised, or at least

19 § 3(1)-(2).
20 § 4(2).
21 § 4(3) and §§ 5–12 on procedural rules.
22 § 13.
23 §§ 14–15.
24 § 17.

almost been raised, to the level of marriage. This statement is supported by the regulation of void registered partnerships. According to the principle of monogamy, the Family Act declares marriage invalid if one of the parties has another existing marriage. This rule is amended by the Act such that an existing registered partnership will also result in a new marriage or registered partnership being regarded as void.[25] A similar rule is also apparent with regards the right to spousal maintenance after divorce ceasing not only by entering into a new marriage, but also by establishing a registered partnership.[26] Besides, the person of legal age being in need of maintenance can claim it from his or her relatives not only if he or she does not have a spouse after divorce, but also if he or she does not have a registered partner.[27] Of course, the minor with the right to maintenance precedes both the married partner and the registered partner.

The modification of the Civil Code affects two issues, namely if the guardian *ad litem* if the partner in suffering from a form of incapacity. The inheritance rules of the Code are also modified as if the registered partnership is terminated by a partner's death. Registered partnership also has the same property consequences as the marriage. The registered partner succeeds just like the widow/widower.[28]

4.2. THE COMPARISON BETWEEN REGISTERED PARTNERSHIP OF SAME-SEX PARTNERS AND OF DIFFERENT-SEX PARTNERS

Although registration has the almost same legal effects in both situations, there are some differences in relation to children. Although joint adoption is prohibited regardless of the gender of the registered partners, the rules of paternal legal status and of the common child's surname[29] are the same in a marriage and a in a different-sex registered partnership. The paternal presumption is statutorily established both in marriage and in registered partnership between man and woman.[30]

25 § 13 modifying § 7(1) Family Act and § 17(2) modifying 7(2) Family Act.
26 § 17(2) modifying § 22(2) Family Act.
27 § 17(2) modifying § 60(1) Family Act.
28 § 17(1).
29 § 13(4) modifying 42(1) Family Act.
30 §§ 13 and 17(2) modifying Family Act.

4.3. THREE STAGES: MARRIAGE, REGISTERED PARTNERSHIP ('REGISTERED COHABITATION') AND COHABITATION

There are seems to be a lot of possibilities for partners to choose their relationship form: for same-sex couples they can enter into a registered partnership or a factual cohabitation and different-sex couples are provided the same possibilities, alongside the possibility of marriage. With respect to different-sex couples, one can question whether there is a real need for three different choices. The difference emphasised between cohabitation and the other two registered forms of partnership. The regulation of cohabitation has always showed a very delicate balance between real social facts, *e.g.* an increase in the number of cohabitants and the legislature's desire to preserve the institution of marriage. This balancing act can be observed both in the Proposal of the Ministry and the Experts' Proposal.

Nevertheless, the same seems to be true for the Hungarian registered partnership. It illustrates a cautious balancing of the strong claim of same-sex partners to legalize their partnership and the fear of permitting same-sex partners into the institution of marriage. At least two signs of circumspection are apparent. One is the fact that registered partnership is not restricted to same-sex couples and the other is the Hungarian terminology used. As has been referred to above several times, the name of the new institution is actually registered cohabitation. This phrase allows someone to suppose at the first sight that there is only a slight difference between the registered and non-registered forms of cohabitation. As we can see, this interpretation does not square with the legal facts. The two 'forms of cohabitation' are far from each other not only in terms of family law, but also in inheritance law terms.

The Hungarian legislature has created an institution guaranteeing that same-sex couples are entitled to almost all of the rights and duties granted to spouses (as some exceptions exist). Nevertheless, the creation of this new institution could have been an onerous step which necessitated its mitigation. That is to say, it has 'only' been established as a registered form of cohabitation and 'not restricted' to homosexuals.[31]

[31] Despite the cautiousness, this institution is not supported by all. In late April 2008, the Christian Democratic People's Party announced to the press that they will initiate the annulment of the Act on Registered Partnership before the Constitutional Court, as it is contrary to the Hungarian Constitution which aims to protect the institution of marriage and the family, www.kdnp.hu/index.php?type=cikk&cikkid=3444.

5. CONCLUSION

As it has been shown, the codification process with respect to same-sex relationships has been accelerated. In 2001, experts seemed to be satisfied with the level of regulation for same-sex couples. Their ideas to widen the rights and duties of cohabitants stemmed from the conviction that the law has to mirror social change primarily in connection with different-sex partners. The optional registration meant a step further but only one cautious step as no special legal consequences were attached to the registration itself. (However, a conception emerged before 2007 according to which this not obligatory registration would have had some effects but only in inheritance law.)

Although the homosexual lobby and subsequently the liberal political conviction, considered this problem to be a topical one, it could have been felt that society itself was not ready to tolerate this kind of partnership. The explanations of the decisions of Constitutional Court showed this attitude very clearly. However, Act No. CXXV 2003 on Promoting Equal Treatment and Equal Chances, which was approved in December 2003, had important meaning for liberal movements. The Act prohibits both direct and indirect discrimination – among others – upon someone's sexual direction.[32] The explanation emphasises that the designation of sexual direction as a feature is in harmony with Direction (EC) No. 2000/78.

With having regard to the actual situation, some questions can be raised. One of them is whether the Act will enter into force in this form next year or whether the codification process of the Civil Code will amend the system by approving a less permissive regime. Another question is whether this Act will function in practice, that is to say, whether different-sex or same-sex partners will actually enter into registered partnership.

---

32 §§ 8 *m)* and 9.

SAME-SEX FAMILY UNIONS IN ISRAELI LAW

TALIA EINHORN*

1. INTRODUCTION

The legal problems encountered by same-sex couples in Israeli law are more complicated than those encountered in other democratic, developed countries. This is due to the fact that, in Israeli law, many areas of family law, first and foremost marriage and divorce, are governed by orthodox religious law, which does not recognize same-sex marriages at all and, furthermore, opposes such relationships, as well as any of their legal consequences. Nor is it possible for spouses to establish a registered partnership in Israel, since partnerships can only be established for commercial purposes.

Notwithstanding the fact that the legal system does not provide for civil marriage and divorce, a large spectrum of family unions has nonetheless developed, gaining state recognition in various respects, thanks to the liberal approach of the Israel Supreme Court.[1] However, a certain adaptation of the legal rules is also necessary for same-sex family unions to fit into this legal framework.

This article analyzes the subject from its different perspectives, along the timeline of any relationship, from the establishment of the family union to its end. It first explains the special Israeli legal framework, the understanding of which is indispensable to the appreciation of the problems encountered by same-sex spouses (Section 2). It then proceeds to analyze the establishment of same-sex family unions in Israel (Section 3); the status in Israel of same-sex family unions established by marriage abroad (Section 4); the status in Israel of same-sex

* Professor of Law, Sha'arei Mishpat College of Law / Tel-Aviv University Faculty of Management (Israel), email: taliaeinhorn@gmail.com.

1 The general developments in Israeli family law and international family law are discussed in T. Einhorn, 'Israeli International Family Law – the Liberalization of Israeli Substantive Family Law', in H.-E. Rasmussen-Bonne *et al.* (eds.), *Balancing of Interests – Liber Amicorum Peter Hay zum 70. Geburtstag*, 2005, pp. 141 *et seq.*; T. Einhorn, 'Family Unions in Israel – the Tensions between Religious Law and Secular Law and the Quest for Coherent Law', in T. Frantzen *et al.* (eds.), *Rett og tolerance – Festskrift til Helge Johan Thue*, 2007, pp. 697 *et seq. Cf.* also T. Einhorn, 'Israeli Private International Law, Part II, Chapter 6 – Family Law', in *International Encyclopedia of Laws – Private International Law* (looseleaf) *. Blanpain & B. Verschraegen (eds.)), 2008 (forthcoming), paras. 418 *et seq.*

registered partnerships established abroad (Section 5); the legal options regarding the choice of a family name for a same-sex family union (Section 6); same-sex spouses maintenance obligations (Section 7); same-sex spouses property relations (Section 8); child adoption by same-sex spouses (Section 9); fertility treatment/ surrogate motherhood agreements (Section 10); social rights owed by the State to same-sex spouses (Section 11); dissolution in Israel of a same-sex family union (Section 12); and succession (Section 13). It concludes with a critical evaluation of the legal situation (Section 14).

2. THE LEGAL FRAMEWORK

Israeli family law does not apply in all matters of family law a uniform system for all Israeli citizens with respect to both the applicable law as well as jurisdiction. Instead, it is divided between two different legal systems, the religious and the secular. This state of affairs goes back to the period when the Ottoman Empire controlled the Holy Land (1517–1917). Both the British Mandate (1917–1948), which replaced the Ottoman Empire, and the State of Israel, established after the British Mandate had ended, relied to a large extent on the system adopted by the Ottoman Empire.[2]

Key aspects of family law, i.e. those defined as 'matters of personal status', are subject to the personal law of the persons concerned. For Israeli citizens or residents this is their religious law, if they are Jewish, Muslim, Druze, or belong to one of the other eleven recognized religions.[3] For Israeli citizens, who are not members of one of the above religious communities, there is no generally applicable personal law. For non-resident foreigners, the law of their nationality applies (unless that law imports the law of their domicile, in which case the latter applies). In some matters (*e.g.*, maintenance), the law of domicile applies under Israeli legislation covering that matter specifically.

Some aspects of family law, such as adoption, succession, and matrimonial property, are regulated by secular, territorial legislation enacted by the *Knesset*.

Regarding jurisdiction, matters of marriage and divorce (with an exception regarding the dissolution of inter-faith marriages) are entrusted to the exclusive jurisdiction of the respective religious courts. Other 'matters of personal status'

---

2 For an extensive study *cf.* E. Vitta, *The Conflict of Laws in Matters of Personal Status in Palestine*, 1947.

3 They are: Eastern (Orthodox), Latin (Catholic), Gregorian Armenian, Armenian (Catholic), Syrian (Catholic), Chaldean (Uniate), Greek-Catholic – Melkite, Maronite, Syrian (Orthodox), Episcopal-Evangelical (since 1970) and Bahai (since 1971). The Second Schedule to the Palestine Order in Council, 1922, added by the Palestine (Amendment) Order in Council, 1939, Palestine Gazette 898, supplement 2, 459, included also the Jewish Community, which ceased to be organized as such upon the establishment of the State of Israel.

are subject to concurrent jurisdiction of the civil courts, which must, however, *ex officio* apply religious law, albeit under different rules of procedure and evidence.

The religious courts only adjudicate according to their religious law, except where a law passed by the *Knesset* is addressed to them as well.[4] In addition, they have to take account of some Israeli constitutional law principles and basic rights acquired thereunder.[5]

To the extent that a civil court has to decide a case according to religious law, it will follow a path which is quite different than that taken by a religious court called upon to decide the same case. In principle, according to the Interpretation Ordinance, 1945 (as well as its new version of 1954, and the Interpretation Law, 5741–1981), the religious laws (written or unwritten) of all recognized religious communities are an integral part of Israeli law and, consequently, within the judicial notice of the Court without need to be proved, as is the case with foreign law.[6] However, the difference in application is significant.[7] In particular, the civil courts apply different rules of procedure and evidence than those applied by the religious courts. The differences may lead to different results,[8] including cases of a

4 § 7, Women's Equal Rights Law, 5711–1951: 'All courts shall act in accordance with this Law; a tribunal competent to deal with matters of personal status shall likewise act in accordance therewith, unless all the parties are eighteen years of age or over and have consented before this tribunal, of their own free will, to have their case tried according to the laws of their community'; § 13(b), Spouses (Property Relations) Law, 5733–1973: 'In a matter dealt with by the Law, a religious court shall act in accordance with the provisions of this Law unless the parties have agreed before such court to litigate in accordance with religious law.'.

5 *Cf.*, *e.g.*, HCJ 1000/92 *Bavli* v. *The Great Rabbinical Court*, 48(2) *PD* (*Pisqei Din*, Collection of Judgments of the Israel Supreme Court) 221. In that case the Supreme Court held that: (1) the Rabbinical Court must take account of the equality between men and women and, consequently, it can no more apply the Jewish law rules which would have deprived the wife of most of the property acquired during the marriage; (2) Furthermore, the Rabbinical Court must recognize property rights acquired under Israeli civil law and protected under Israeli Constitutional Law, and cannot apply Jewish law to derogate from such rights. *Cf.* P. Shifman, 'The Rabbinical Courts – Where are They Heading?', 1994 *Mishpat Umimshal – Law and Government in Israel* 2, pp. 523 *et seq.* (in Hebrew).

6 In practice, however, courts occasionally require that the religious laws be proved by the parties on the basis of expert opinions. This may be done on the basis of Rule 258L(1), Civil Procedure Rules, which allows the Court to appoint an expert in family matters. Courts have accepted expert opinions as an *amicus curiae*, stating that they cannot be expected to have judicial notice of the religious laws of all religious communities – *cf.*, *e.g.*, CC (Civil Case) (Tel-Aviv) 778/50, 876/50 *A.B.* v. *M.B.*, 3 *PsM* (*Pesaqim Mehoziim*, Collection of District Court Judgments) 263 at p. 287, per Judge Zeltner, and Probate Case (Tel-Aviv) 115/54 *in re Testament of the deceased Michael Polak and re Grenzburg* v. *Eugenia Polak and Leib Bulein*, 12 *PsM* 129; Family Case (Tel-Aviv) 67250/00 *Minor* v. *Ploni*, tak-family electronic database 2001(1), 112 (25.2.01). *Cf.* I. Englard, *Religious Law in the Israel Legal System*, 1975, pp. 88 *et seq.*

7 *Cf.* M. Shava, 'The Nature and Scope of Jewish Law in Israel as Applied in the Civil Courts as Compared with its Application in the Rabbinical Courts', 1985 *The Jewish Law Annual* 5, pp. 173–194.

8 The question of how the decisions of the civil courts should relate to those made by the Rabbinical Courts has been discussed in CA 63/69 *Yossef* v. *Yossef*, 23(1) *PD* 804; Further Hearing 23/69 *Yossef* v. *Yossef*, 24(1) *PD* 792, given subsequently to the Rabbinical Court decision in the

'split status'.[9] In addition, whereas the civil courts may recognize the full effects of acts done outside the territory of Israel in compliance with foreign law (*e.g.*, civil marriages performed abroad), the religious courts consider themselves free from such restrictions, regarding religious law as having universal application to all persons subject to their jurisdiction.[10]

In 1995, Israel established a system of Family Courts, following the enactment of the Court for Family Affairs Law, 5795–1995 (hereinafter – 'Family Court Law'). Previously, the District Courts exercised jurisdiction in family law matters within the competence of the civil courts, and an appeal could be brought before the Israel Supreme Court as a matter of right. In contrast, the Family Courts are established in the same areas of jurisdiction as the Magistrates Courts, and their decisions are appealed to the District Courts. An appeal from the District Court to the Supreme Court is only possible after obtaining special permission from the Supreme Court. Consequently, there are fewer binding precedents of the Supreme Court, and much less harmony among court decisions handed down by different Family Court judges.

The Family Court Law applies to all familial and similar relations, regardless of whether the spouses were in fact married. There is still, however, some controversy whether the law applies to same-sex family unions, which will only be finally settled after the Supreme Court decides a case in this matter and makes a precedent binding on all other courts.[11]

The status, rights and obligations of same-sex spouses in Israel are examined against this background.

same matter: Case 4553/5713 [1953] *A.* v. *B.*, 1 *PDR* (Collection of Judgments of the Rabbinical Courts) 81. The Supreme Court held that decisions of the civil courts may be guided by decisions of the Rabbinical Courts in matters of personal status, but the latter are not binding upon them (*cf.* Further Hearing 23/69, at p. 810).

9 *Cf.* HCJ 51/69 *Rodnitzky* v. *The Rabbinical Court*, 24(1) *PD* 704. The Rabbinical Court considered the witnesses to a marriage incompetent (because, *inter alia*, they habitually desecrated the Sabbath) and, consequently, held the marriage invalid. In contrast, the Supreme Court determined the witnesses' competence under the Evidence Ordinance applicable in the civil courts and concluded that they were competent and the marriage – valid.

10 *Cf.* M. Silberg, *Personal Status in Israel*, 1957, pp. 255–259. *Cf.*, also, CA 238/53 *Cohen and Busslik* v. *The Attorney General*, 8 *PD* 4, 19, per Justice Silberg.

11 Recognition of same-sex spouses as coming within the scope of the Family Court Law was granted, *e.g.*, in Family Case (Tel-Aviv) 6960/03 *K.Tz.* v. *The Attorney General*, per J. Granit (21.11.04), tak-family 2004(4), 250, Family Case (Tel-Aviv) 3140/03 *R.A.* v. *L.M.* (16.2.2004), tak-Family 2004(1), 637, per J. Reish-Rothschild; Family Case 8510/01, per J. Alon-Laufer (12.8.01), reported in *LawData* database. Such recognition was denied, *e.g.*, in Family Case (Tel-Aviv) 16610/04 *Ploni* v. *the Attorney General* (8.5.05), per J. Geifman, faxdin 1228 (19.5.2005), 7/9.

3. SAME-SEX FAMILY UNIONS ESTABLISHED IN ISRAEL

Same-sex spouses cannot get married in Israel. Israeli law provides neither for a civil marriage nor for the establishment of a registered partnership. Non-Orthodox religious communities, such as the Reform Jewish Community, which would marry such spouses in a religious ceremony, are not authorized to perform religious marriages in Israel. Consequently, the only kind of family union that such spouses may establish in Israel is that of extra marital cohabitation. In Israeli law, such spouses are termed 'reputed spouses'.

Same-sex spouses are not the only type of 'reputed spouses'. In Israel there are three groups of unmarried couples who choose to live as reputed spouses: (1) those who cannot marry in Israel (inter-faith marriages, marriages prohibited by religious law); (2) those who are secular and do not wish to have a religious ceremony, or are wary of the difficulties, especially for women, of obtaining a Jewish divorce if the marriage fails; and (3) those who prefer, at least for the time being, a loose relationship, which does not impose upon them the whole set of effects which an established marriage entails.

Israeli law seems to have ignored the third, quite substantial group, and focused only on helping the first two. Accordingly, Israelis have seen an expansion of recognition of the effects of extra-marital cohabitation in Israeli secular law. To cover the cases in which spouses opted for becoming reputed spouses because they could not overcome the difficulty of obtaining the *get* (bill of divorce under Jewish law),[12] most rules have also been extended to reputed spouses who are concurrently officially married to others (with the exception of some rules, *e.g.* those governing succession, which are restricted to reputed spouses who are not married to another person at the time of death of their partner).[13]

In recent years, the rules have been gradually extended by the courts to same-sex reputed spouses. This extension is still subject to controversy, reflected in conflicting decisions of the Family Courts.

However, the Supreme Court has been very consistent in emphasizing that, unlike marriage, extra-marital cohabitation confers no status.[14] It is merely a

12 *Cf.* T. Einhorn, 'Jewish Divorce in the International Arena', in J. Basedow *et al.* (eds.), *Private Law in the International Arena – Liber Amicorum Kurt Siehr*, 2000, pp. 137 *et seq.*

13 Under the proposed draft civil codification, prepared by the Codification Committee, a 'spouse' for the purpose of succession will include reputed spouses, even if married, provided that the married spouse(s) had been separated at least three years from his or her lawfully wedded spouse, and the reputed spouses had cohabited for a period of at least three years before one of them passed away. The proposed draft can be viewed (in Hebrew) on the official webpage of the Ministry of Justice: http://www.justice.gov.il/NR/rdonlyres/7B5FF13D-B5EB-4E8E-83AE-7E47E5332948/0/yerosha.pdf.

14 *E.g.*, CA 384/61 *State of Israel* v. *Fessler*, 16 *PD* 102, 109; CA 356/78 *Steinitz* v. *Eged Members Pension Fund Ltd.*, 33(3) *PD* 556, 558; HCJ 693/91 *Efrat* v. *Commissioner of the Population Reg-*

contractual relationship. The contract need not be express, but may be implicitly deduced from the circumstances of living together as husband and wife in a common household. To the extent that the legislature did not define the rights of the reputed spouse specifically, those rights must be evaluated separately in every case, and for every act of legislation. Even here, however, interpretation has become rather flexible. In recent years, the court underlined that such relationships have become so common that it would be unjust to treat reputed spouses differently from married couples. Old cases in which reputed spouses had not been treated equally to lawfully married ones were therefore set aside. Although the Supreme Court is careful not to attach the word 'status' to extra-marital cohabitation, it nonetheless refers to such a relationship as an 'institution', using the same terminology that it uses for the 'institution' of marriage.

It is noteworthy that, according to Israeli law, it is possible to be entitled to the rights, and made subject to the obligations, of a reputed spouse within a very short period of time. In one case, three months of cohabitation sufficed for a woman to inherit the deceased spouse's share in the estate, despite evidence that the spouses kept their accounts and all other property separate, and the woman was still registered with the Ministry of the Interior as residing in her own apartment.[15]

4. SAME-SEX FAMILY UNIONS ESTABLISHED BY MARRIAGE IN A FOREIGN COUNTRY

Religious law limits the ability of spouses to marry in Israel, whether because of religious impediments to such a marriage, or because the spouses belong to different religious faiths. Consequently, already in the early days of the State, such spouses celebrated a civil marriage abroad and sought to have it recognized in Israel.

The *Funk-Schlesinger* case was the first, landmark decision to come before the Israel Supreme Court.[16] It concerned the civil marriage of an Israeli Jewish man with a Belgian Catholic woman, performed by the Belgian Consul in Cyprus. After having the marriage registered with the *registre matricule* at the Belgian embassy, the couple applied to be registered as married also in Israel. In his judgment for the majority of the Court, Justice Sussmann pointed out that:

> 'any state wishing to live within the family of nations must, to that end, give up some of its substantive law rules in cases having a foreign element (...). The fact that Jewish

istry, 47(1) *PD* 749, 787; CA 2000/97 *Lindorn* v. *Karnit Fund for Traffic Accident Victims* (19.2.99), 55(1) *PD* 12.

15 Succession Case (Tel-Aviv) 3696/90 *Amir* v. *Zager*, per Judge Kling, tak-district 91(3) 997 (16.9.91).

16 *Funk-Schlesinger* v. *Minister of the Interior*, HCJ 143/62, 17 *PD* 225 (22.2.1963).

> religious law considers mixed marriages void does not, in itself, compel the secular court to reach the same conclusion when it decides the question according to a foreign law. Only if the court reaches the conclusion that the marriage is offensive to Israeli external (international) public policy, that is if such a marriage is so offensive to public policy that it should be considered void irrespective of wherever it has been celebrated, then the court should give it no effect. However, religious impediments to marriage, important as they may be, should not be decisive in such cases. The Israeli public is divided into two camps – one which observes religious law or most of its commands, and another which emphasizes the difference between a state abiding by the rule of law and a state abiding by religious law [*halakha*]. The views of these two groups are entirely at odds with each other. Israeli public policy does not dictate that the judge will compel one camp to follow the views of the other. Life demands tolerance towards the other and showing consideration for differing views. Therefore, the yardstick of the judge must be the balance of *all* views prevailing in the public.'[17]

This general statement notwithstanding, the Supreme Court declined to rule on the validity in general of mixed (inter-faith) marriages and confined its ruling to the pertinent question, in that case the entering of the newly acquired marital status in the Israeli population registry.

The majority of the Supreme Court held that the registrar must enter any information provided by applicants into the population registry, unless it is manifestly incorrect (*e.g.* if the official is asked to register a 20 year old man as being 5 years of age). According to the Court, the registration is an administrative procedure, not a judicial one, designed to collect statistical data. Therefore, the registrar should have entered the marriage in the population registry, regardless of Israeli substantive family law rules that do not recognize such marriages. This ruling was also extended to marriages by proxy in Mexico or Paraguay, where the spouses remained in Israel and received their marriage certificate by post.[18] The effects of such marriages, however, were left to be decided on a case by case basis. Most recently, the Supreme Court suggested that it may be time to recognize such marriages as generally valid, as soon as they were validly celebrated abroad, calling upon the *Knesset* to resolve this matter definitively.[19]

In 2006,[20] several Israeli homosexual couples who had celebrated a civil marriage in Toronto, Canada, applied to be registered as married in Israel. The State authorities declined, arguing that, to be registered as such in Israel, a 'marriage' must be between a man and a woman. Other 'forms' recognized abroad do not fit within the existing concepts of Israeli law. A same-sex relationship can only be regarded in Israel as a 'social form' having some legal consequences, but not as a

17 *Ibid.*, pp. 256–257.

18 *Cf. Farkash* v. *Farkash*, Civil Appeal 778/77, 33(2) *PD* 469.

19 *Ploni* v. *Plonit*, HCJ 9607/03 (29.11.2006), tak-supreme 2006(4), 2765.

20 *Yossi Ben-Ari* v. *Commissioner of Population Registry, Ministry of the Interior*, HCJ 3045/05 (21.11.2006), tak-supreme 2006(4), 1725.

'legal form'. The Supreme Court rejected the State's linguistic and other claims, and ordered the Commissioner of the Population Registry to enter the same-sex marriages in the population registry. At the same time, the Court stated, as it had done before, that the registration is only a matter of state statistics (a pretext refuted by the single dissenting opinion). Therefore, the registration, in itself, is not indicative of whether or not Israeli law views this relationship as creating a family status. However, it does mean that Israeli law does not consider such a relationship as violating its *ordre public*. This point is of special importance in view of the series of court decisions, recognizing a variety of rights and obligations, which have been created by virtue of such a relationship.

5. REGISTERED PARTNERSHIPS ESTABLISHED IN A FOREIGN COUNTRY

Under Israeli law, there are no registered partnerships. Neither does the law provide for entering such partnerships in the Population Registry. Since Israeli law has recognized most effects of marriage even with respect to reputed spouses, registered partnerships, as such, do not offend *ordre public*. Israeli law should apply its conflicts rules by analogy to decide their various legal effects. Thus, the validity of a registered partnership should be governed by the law of the state under the laws of which it was registered.

6. FAMILY NAME

Each reputed spouse has a right to change his or her family name to that of the other spouse, even over the objection of the person who is lawfully married to the latter.[21] In 1996 the Names Law was amended so as to fall in line with the case law, which had already developed in this matter. The Names Law, as amended, enables a reputed spouse to apply to have his or her surname changed to that of the other spouse. In pratice, it is usually the woman who applies to change her surname.

These rules have also been applied to same-sex reputed spouses, who are entitled to have their surnames changed into that of the other spouse, or decide to use both surnames jointly (as may also be the case with lawfully wedded couples).

---

21 *Efrat* v. *Commissioner of Population Registry*, HCJ 693/91, 47(1) *PD* 749; *Nizri* v. *Commissioner of Population Registry*, HCJ 6086/94, 49(5) *PD* 693. In both cases the men were still lawfully married yet separated since years. In the first case, the marriage was closer to its end since the divorce proceedings had already been concluded and only the formal act of divorce was lacking. In the second case, the divorce proceedings were still ongoing and the wife objected to the reputed spouse changing her family name into that of her husband.

7. MAINTENANCE OBLIGATIONS

Maintenance of the spouse is a matter of personal status which is determined under religious law also by civil courts. The *Knesset* has enacted a secular law – the Family Law Amendment (Maintenance) Law, 5719–1959 – to complement, on a territorial basis, the religious rules applicable to maintenance. However, this law provides specifically that its provisions apply only to spouses to whom a personal law does not apply (*i.e.*, spouses who are not Jewish, Muslim, Druze, or members of one of the other recognized religious communities in Israel).[22]

7.1. SAME-SEX REPUTED SPOUSES

According to case law, during the period of cohabitation, a duty to maintain the reputed spouse may be based upon an implied contract deduced by the court from the circumstances of the cohabitation.[23] Following separation, however, the duty is, in principle, extinguished, and there are cases in which judges rejected such claims. There are, however, also court decisions which hold that reputed spouses may be obliged, according to the circumstances of the case, to pay maintenance to their cohabitant following separation (even if the spouses had signed an agreement to the effect that their relationship will not yield any of the rights acquired and obligations owed by reputed spouses)[24] and that, following separation, a reputed spouse may be entitled to 'rehabilitating', but not to permanent maintenance.[25]

7.2. SAME-SEX SPOUSES MARRIED ABROAD

Persons to whom a personal law applies (the majority of the population), are supposedly subject to their religious law, under which they have no duty to pay maintenance to same-sex spouses.

The Supreme Court has emphasized that a spouse has no universal right to maintenance.[26] Nonetheless, case law has mitigated this result in two types of cases: (a) if the spouse is unable to provide evidence regarding the personal law of the debtor, as a result of which a needy spouse may be deprived of economic

22 *Cf.* note 3 *supra.*
23 *Jaeger (Flink)* v. *Palevitz*, Civil Appeal 563/65, 20(3) *PD* 244.
24 *Plonit* v. *Ploni*, Family Case (Tel-Aviv) 51940/98, per J. Schochat, tak-family 2002(3) 13 (4.8.02).
25 *Ibid.*; *Magin* v. *Malka*, Family Case (Tel-Aviv) 63323/97, per J. Geifman, tak-family 2000(2) 21 (22.5.2000).
26 *Furer* v. *Furer*, Civil Appeal 592/83, 38(3) *PD* 561.

support. In such cases, the court will order spousal maintenance on the basis of the provisions of the Family Law Amendment (Maintenance) Law, since the granting of relief in the circumstances is compatible with the principles of the Basic Law: Human Dignity and Liberty;[27] (b) if, under his personal law, the husband owes no duty to pay maintenance to a wife whom he had married in a civil marriage, the court may nonetheless infer an agreement to pay maintenance on the basis of the support provided by that spouse prior to the breakdown of their marriage.[28]

Spouses who want to ensure their right to maintenance must therefore make a written agreement to that effect.[29]

8. PROPERTY RELATIONS

8.1. THE SPOUSES PROPERTY RELATIONS LAW

Unlike other aspects of Israeli family law, an effort was made by the Israeli legislature to regulate property relations by secular, territorial law. Accordingly, in 1973, the *Knesset* passed the Spouses (Property Relations) Law, 5733–1973 (hereafter – 'Spouses Property Relations Law'), which applies to all 'spouses' domiciled in Israel. The language of the Spouses Property Relations Law (including its choice of law rules) lends itself easily to being applied to same-sex couples as well. It uses 'spouse' in neutral terms, and does not require the spouses to be 'a man' and 'a woman', or 'husband' and 'wife' (as is the case, *e.g.*, in the Child Adoption Law, 5741–1981 (§3)[30]). Nonetheless, it is clear from the context, that the legislature had in mind only properly married spouses,[31] *i.e.*, spouses whose marriage is recognized by Israeli law.

---

27 *Nurit Solomon* v. *Dr. Eli Solomon*, Civil Appeal 7038/93, 51(2) *PD* 577.

28 *Bashbirakter* v. *Bashbirakter*, Family Court Case 12181/01 (Family Court, Tel-Aviv, per J. Shochat, 15.5.2002) (Nevo electronic database). In that case, the Court declined to apply the principles of the Basic Law: Human Dignity and Liberty as a basis for granting maintenance to the Jewish wife of a Moslem husband, since, according to the Court, these principles cannot substitute the personal law of the husband, under which the wife was not entitled to maintenance.

29 *Cf. Yaffa Gamliel* v. *The Supreme Rabbinical Court of Appeals*, HCJ 10605/02, 58(2) *PD* 529 (30.12.03).

30 *Cf.* Section 9 *infra*.

31 CA 640/82 *Cohen* v. *AG*, 39(1) *PD* 673. Justice Barak has more recently raised the question whether this rule is still valid, or whether the provisions of the Spouses Relations Law, or at least some of them, should be extended to reputed spouses (*cf.* Application Permission to Appeal 6854/00 *AG* v. *Michael Zemer*, tak-Supreme 2003(2), 3132 (20.7.2003)). However, the other two justices on the Panel were of the opinion that it did not. Since, so far, the Supreme Court has not decided this issue differently, the *Cohen* precedent applies.

The law applies to all couples married after 1st January 1974, a resources-balancing arrangement of all assets acquired during the marriage, when the marriage comes to an end. This means a separation of property with division of surplus upon dissolution of the marriage, due to death or divorce. The spouses may agree in writing upon a different arrangement, which must be approved by the competent authority (§§1, 2).[32] If the marriage breaks down, the arrangement will only be triggered by divorce (end of marriage), not beforehand.

8.2. SAME-SEX REPUTED SPOUSES

Since reputed spouses are not properly married, the Spouses Property Relations Law does not apply to them. According to the case law, which had developed before the Spouses Property Relations Law came into effect, and continued to develop thereafter, there is a presumption of community property covering all assets acquired for private use and all business assets acquired through mutual efforts.[33] Even if the assets have all been registered in the name of one reputed spouse, this would not in itself rebut the presumption.[34] Reputed spouses may deviate from this arrangement by making a contract which may (but need not) be approved by the Family Court under §3(c), Family Court Law, 5755–1995.[35]

Regarding same-sex reputed spouses, some Family Court judges consider themselves competent to approve reputed spouses' property contracts. Others, however, do not, holding that such spouses can be deemed neither 'spouses' nor 'reputed spouses', in the sense of the Family Court Law.[36] The Hebrew language lends some linguistic support to the latter decisions, since the term in Hebrew for a 'reputed spouse' is 'she who is known in the public as his wife'. Whereas some laws use the term 'spouse' in a neutral way, others mention specifically 'a man and a woman who live in a common household' (*e.g.*, §55, Succession Law). The Family Court Law defines 'spouse', as including 'she who is known in the public as his wife'. However, legal interpretation is not a matter of strict grammatical

32 In fact, the Supreme Court has also enforced a written agreement which had not been approved by the competent authority – *Yaffa Gamliel* v. *The Supreme Rabbinical Court of Appeals*, HCJ 10605/02 (30.12.03).

33 *Cf.* A. Ben-Dror, *Living Together: Without Marriage*, 2003, pp. 97 *et seq.* (in Hebrew), and all cases cited there.

34 *Cf. Blau* v. *Pozsh*, Civil Appeal 1717/98, 54(4) *PD* 376.

35 *Zemer* v. *The Attorney General*, Family Appeal (Tel-Aviv) 1002/00, tak-district 2000(2) 65535, per Deputy President, J. Porat (4.7.2000).

36 *Cf.* for approval – *K.Tz.* v. *The Attorney General*, Family Case (Tel-Aviv) 6960/03, per J. Granit (21.11.04), tak-family 2004(4), 250, and *R.A.* v. *L.M.*, Family Case (Tel-Aviv) 3140/03 (16.2.2004), tak-Family 2004(1), 637, per J. Reish-Rothschild. Approval denied, *e.g.*, in *Ploni* v. *the Attorney General*, Family Case (Tel-Aviv) 16610/04 (8.5.05), per J. Geifman, faxdin 1228 (19.5.2005), 7/9.

fastidiousness. The Family Court itself interprets this definition as relating also to 'he who is known in the public as her husband', notwithstanding the exact language used. Judged by other precedents in matters of same-sex spouses, including a precedent concerning succession,[37] the wording of the Succession Law notwithstanding, it is submitted that the Family Court, too, cannot pretend that Israeli law does not recognize same-sex reputed spouses as coming within the scope of Israeli family law. Same-sex spouses should be considered 'spouses' within the meaning of the Family Courts Law, and, consequently, their rights and obligations should be determined by the Family Court, as is the case with opposite-sex spouses.

However, it may be expected that judges will continue to give conflicting decisions regarding the jurisdiction of the family court, until the matter is finally settled in a binding precedent of the Supreme Court.

8.3. SAME-SEX SPOUSES MARRIED ABROAD

There are no reported cases concerning same-sex spouses who married abroad and were registered as married in Israel. In such cases, the Family Court will have to decide, as a preliminary matter, the question of the validity of the marriage, and whether or not such spouses are considered 'family members' within the meaning of this term in the Family Court Law and, consequently, subject to the jurisdiction of the Family Court, or whether such matters have to be heard by the general civil courts. However, in any case, it would be impossible to apply the resources-balancing arrangement provided by the Spouses Property Relations Law (except in the case of death), unless a divorce is obtained that would serve as a trigger to its enforcement.[38]

8.4. REGISTERED PARTNERSHIPS ESTABLISHED ABROAD

Failing a choice of law made by the partners, it is submitted that the property relations of a registered partnership (or analogous family unions established abroad),

[37] *E.g.*, HCJ 1779/99 *Kaddish-Brenner* v. *Minister of the Interior*, 54(2) *PD* 368 (29.5.2000), in which the Supreme Court ordered the Ministry of the Interior to register two lesbian spouses each as 'mother' of the child born to one of them and adopted by the other while domiciled in California, *cf.* Section 8 *infra*; CA 10280/01 *Yaros-Hakak* v. *The Attorney General*, 59(5) *PD* 64 (10.1.05), in which the Supreme Court held that a lesbian reputed spouse may adopt the child of the other spouse; CA (Nazareth) 3245/03 *A.M.* v. *The Attorney General*, tak-District 2004(4), 2532 (11.11.2004), awarding a same-sex reputed spouse rights in the estate of his spouse who had passed away intestate, identical to those that would have been given to opposite-sex spouses.

[38] Regarding the problem of obtaining a divorce, *cf.* Section 12 *infra*.

should be governed by the law of the state under the laws of which it was registered. The validity of a choice of law should also be governed by such law.

9. CHILD ADOPTION

9.1. ADOPTION UNDER ISRAELI LAW

Child adoption is covered by a secular, territorial law, the Adoption of Children Law, 5741–1981 (hereafter – 'the Adoption Law'). Although the Child Adoption Law, 5741–1981, does not mention 'reputed spouses', the Supreme Court held that a reputed spouse may adopt the daughter of her (opposite sex) spouse.[39] Such an adoption order has also been made with respect to a same-sex lesbian couple.[40] There is as yet no case law authorizing the adoption in Israel by reputed spouses of children who are not related to one of them. §3, Adoption Law, provides for adoption only by 'a husband and his wife together'. However, in February 2008 the Attorney General determined that the Adoption Law should nonetheless be interpreted as also relating to same-sex spouses or reputed spouses.[41] Accordingly, he directed the Ministry of Welfare to also accept and process adoption applications made by same-sex spouses with respect to children who are not related to them on an equal basis. The direction of the Attorney General has attracted sharp criticism from the religious political parties and Members of *Knesset*, and its implementation may still face opposition.

9.2. RECOGNITION OF A FOREIGN ADOPTION ORDER

In 1999, a case concerning a lesbian couple of Israeli citizens was brought before the Israel Supreme Court.[42] While residing for two years as students in Los Angeles, California, one of them gave birth following artificial insemination. The other spouse adopted the child. Both were entered in the Los Angeles civil register as the child's parents. Upon return to Israel, they applied to both be registered as the 'mother' of the child (the Israeli population registry admits the registration of 'father' and 'mother', but has no neutral category of 'parent', as in Los Angeles). The Commissioner of the Population Registry declined, arguing that he can enter the name of only one woman as being a child's 'mother' in the population registry.

39 *Plonit* v. *The Attorney General*, Civil Appeal 1165/01 (12.11.2002), 57(1) *PD* 69.

40 *Yaros-Hakak* v. *The Attorney General*, Civil Appeal 10280/01 (10.1.05), 59(5) *PD* 64.

41 A. Zino, 'The Attorney General: Allow Regular Adoptions by Same-Sex Spouses', *Ynet*, 10 February 2008), www.ynet.co.il/articles/0,7340,L-3505039,00.html (*ynet* is an Israeli Internet daily newspaper).

42 *Kadish-Brenner* v. *Minister of the Interior*, HCJ 1779/99 (29.5.2000), 54(2) *PD* 368.

In a majority opinion, the Supreme Court accepted the application of the lesbian spouses and ordered that each be registered as the 'mother' of the child. The Court, per Justice Dorner, reasoned that the status of a person should be recognized in an identical manner in all states. Recognition of the foreign status should be denied only if it is incompatible with the *ordre public*. This is especially true with respect to a foreign adoption order, which has to be considered valid in Israel, unless annulled by an Israeli court. Justice Beinish, on the other hand, restricted her reasoning to the duty of the Commissioner of the Population Registry to register whatever he is asked to register, since the only significance of the registration is the collection of statistical data.[43] According to Justice Beinish the legal effect of the adoption order remains open, to be decided in subsequent cases that will address this question directly rather than the registration of the adoption. Justice Zu'abi, in a minority opinion, considered that registering an adoption is different from the registration of a marriage. A marriage is just a ceremony, whereas the making of an adoption order requires a judicial decision. Consequently, it is also an Israeli judicial decision which should recognize it, rather than an act of an official of the Ministry of the Interior, who has no tools to verify the validity of the foreign certificate or court decision, and must accept almost any paper presented to him, even with the benefit of doubt.[44]

The criticism may be correct. However, as Israeli law is currently interpreted there is no way for a court to recognize a foreign adoption order. This situation is unacceptable, and consequently the Supreme Court did the best it could to remedy this situation in the best interests of the child.

Most recently, some doubt has been cast upon the future effects of the Supreme Court judgment in the *Kadish-Brenner* case. An application made by the Minister of the Interior in 2000 to have a Further Hearing in that case before the Israel Supreme Court has been withdrawn by the applicant in March, 2008.[45] Upon withdrawal of the application, the State made the following two declarations: (1) that the judgment of the High Court of Justice in this case will apply only to cases similar to the *Kadish-Brenner* case; (2) that the judgment applies only to the question of registration (which, as aforementioned, is a purely administrative matter in Israeli law), rather than to that of the status of the child (which is a matter of substance). This means that, unless a law is adopted by the *Knesset*, further judgments of the Supreme Court will be necessary to clarify this matter.

---

43 *Cf.* HCJ 143/62 *Funk Schlesinger* v. *Minister of the Interior*, 17 *PD* 229, regarding the registration in Israel of a civil marriage performed abroad; *cf.* Section 4 *supra*.

44 *Cf.* also the criticism of M. Shava, 'Registration and Recognition of a Foreign Adoption Order in a Lesbian Family: the Need to reexamine the Funk-Schlesinger Precedent and Determine its Limits', 2001 *Kiryat Ha-Mishpat* 1, pp. 103 *et seq.*

45 Further Hearing Court of Justice 4252/00 *Minister of the Interior* v. *Kadish-Brenner* (2.3.2008), tak-supreme 2008(1), 3883.

Another application to the High Court of Justice, brought in 2002 by homosexual reputed spouses, concerned the recognition of the adoption in the U.S.A. by the spouses, who have dual American and Israeli citizenship, of a Cambodian child in 2000, while being domiciled in the U.S.A. In April 2008, the State notified the Supreme Court that the child will be granted Israeli citizenship and registered in the population registry, on the basis of the American adoption order, as the son of the applicant spouses. In this case, the child was not related to either of the spouses. However, the State mentioned in its notification that its decision had been made 'considering the special circumstances of the case and the long time that the child had been staying in Israel without legal status'.[46] The statement made by the State means that also in the future, same-sex spouses will have to bring applications in the High Court of Justice for recognition of adoption orders given abroad, with respect to children who are not related to any of the adoptive parents.

10. FERTILITY TREATMENT / SURROGATE MOTHERHOOD AGREEMENTS

Upon the application of a lesbian reputed spouse, the Supreme Court avoided the regulations concerning in-vitro fertilization, to the extent that they authorized such treatment to married women but required a social worker's opinion before treating unmarried women.[47] The Court held the regulations to be unlawfully discriminatory in favor of married couples; the pertinent Israeli legislation regarding surrogate mothers – Agreements on the Transportation of Embryos (approval of agreements and status of the newly born infant) Law, 5756–1996 – makes the implantation of embryos in the surrogate mother conditional upon an agreement entered into between a married couple, on the one hand, and the surrogate mother, on the other. In 2006, however, the Committee appointed by law to approve the agreements, allowed a lesbian reputed spouse to have the fertilized egg of her spouse implanted into her uterus via in-vitro fertilization.[48]

Another problem arose in this matter with respect to the question of parenthood. Under Israeli law, no person, other than the biological parent, owes the duties and enjoys the rights of a parent towards a child. If a person, other than the

46 The case was reported by T. Zarhin, 'Precedent: The State recognized a child adopted by a couple of males abroad', *Ha'aretz* daily newspaper, 25 April 2008, p. 6 (News).

47 *Dr. Tal Yaros-Hakak* v. *Minister of Health*, HCJ 998/96, tak-supreme 1997(1), 939 (11.2.97).

48 The information was provided by a medical doctors' Internet forum on surrogacy (in Hebrew) – http://www.doctors.co.il/xID-5196,xCT-44,m-Doctors,a-Article.html (www.doctors.co.il is the leading Israeli internet database concerning health. It contains ca. 200 Discussion Forums, directed and managed by leading Israeli medical doctors and experts, among them also heads of hospital departments.).

biological father or mother, 'recognizes' a child as his or her own, such recognition is devoid of any legal effect. The only exception is adoption proper. However, another exception that seems to have emerged recently concerns the case of a lesbian couple, one of which is the biological mother, having donated the egg, and the other serving as a surrogate mother, having been impregnated through the implantation of embryo produced by the in vitro fertilization of the egg donated by her spouse. Following the birth of the child, both spouses applied to the Family Court to be declared the biological mothers of the child, however the Attorney General notified the Family Court that only the surrogate mother, who actually gave birth to the child, is recognized by the State as the biological mother of the child.[49]

11. SOCIAL RIGHTS

Reputed spouses are eligible, according to law, to collect the same pensions and social security benefits as married spouses (social security legislation defines a 'wife', as including the reputed wife, however, case law extended the rule to reputed husbands as well). Furthermore, whereas a widow who remarried is no longer eligible to collect social security benefits owed to her following the death of her first husband, the National Labor Court has held that this rule would not be applied to a widow who has, by the time of the decision, been a reputed spouse for over 20 years.[50] These rules apply also to same-sex spouses.[51]

12. DISSOLUTION OF A SAME-SEX FAMILY UNION

Under Israeli law, the religious courts have exclusive jurisdiction in matters of divorce between spouses who are both Jewish, Muslim, or Christian belonging to one of the recognized religious communities, or Druze.

49 The case has been reported by N. Sharvit, 'Mazuz [the Attorney General – TE] to the Court: A Couple of Lesbians Cannot Both be Registered as Biological Mothers', *Globes* daily newspaper, 6 April 2008, p. 25 (News).

50 *Social Security Institute v. Nehama Freiman*, Social Security Appeal 1407/04, per Deputy President. Barak, tak-national 2006(4), 395 (8.11.2006). In this case the woman was widowed in 1976, however in the past 20 years has been a reputed spouse (also giving birth to two children from that relationship), which prompted Social Security to attempt to stop making monthly payments due to widows, as would have been the case had she remarried. The National Labor Court decided in favor of Ms. Freiman, emphasizing that reputed spouses' relationships are generally lacking of stability.

51 A short list (in Hebrew) of social rights extended to same-sex reputed spouses has been reported by Y. Yoaz, 'Only do not apply for a family status', *Ha'aretz* daily newspaper, 17 May 2005. It can be viewed also on http://www.tehila.org.il/tehila/121-june05.htm. *Tehila* is a non-profit organization organized by parents of homo-lesbian persons.

In 1969, the *Knesset* enacted Matters of Dissolution of Marriage (Jurisdiction in Special Cases), 5729–1969, to provide for the dissolution of marriages between spouses belonging to different religious communities, to unrecognized communities, or to none. 'Dissolution of marriage' includes divorce, annulment of marriage and declaration of a marriage as void *ab initio* (§6).

In 2005, the Law has been amended to take account of certain aspects of international jurisdiction and it is now called Matters of Dissolution of Marriage (Jurisdiction in Special Cases and International Jurisdiction), 5729–1969 (hereafter – 'Dissolution of Marriage Law'). However, the Law does not apply to spouses who are both Jews, Muslims, Druzes, or members of the same recognized Christian Community, unless one or both of them are foreigners.[52] Consequently, by and large, matters of divorce of such couples have been left in the hands of the religious courts of their respective communities.

This means that, if the same-sex spouses both belong to one and the same religion of any of the above list, they cannot properly bring the relationship to an end, since their marriage is considered null and void, as well as devoid of any effect by religious law. Furthermore, it seems unlikely that divorce proceedings among same-sex spouses can be initiated with a religious court.

Only if the marriage is inter-faith can the Dissolution of Marriage Law apply to them. In most cases, the Family Court will be competent to decide these cases. Under this Law, the consent of both spouses is always considered good grounds for divorce (§5(c)). If they do not agree, the court is instructed to apply one of the following laws, listed according to priority (§5(a)):

(a) The substantive law of the common domicile of the spouses;
(b) The substantive law of the last common domicile of the spouses;
(c) The substantive law of the common state of citizenship of the spouses;
(d) The substantive law of the state where the marriage took place,

provided that the court will not apply a law which applies different laws to both spouses, or if, under such law, no divorce can be obtained. If none of the above laws applies, the Court may apply the substantive law of the state in which one of the spouses has his or her domicile, as may be deemed just by the court in the circumstances of the case (§5(b)).

If the spouses are Israeli citizens, domiciled in Israel, then the only viable option of all potentially applicable laws enumerated in §5(a) is the substantive law of the state in which the marriage took place.[53] This may yield harsh results, if the

52 The exceptions are listed in § 1(b) of the Dissolution of Marriages Law.

53 *Cf., e.g.*, Family Case (Haifa) 38030/99 *Gofman* v. *Gofman*, tak-Family 2001(3), 20, concerning the marriage of a Jewish husband and a wife who is not affiliated with any religion. The case was referred to the Family Court by the President of the Supreme Court (who, prior to the most

law of that state only provides for divorce under certain limited circumstances, which may make it difficult for such spouses to divorce.[54]

13. SUCCESSION

According to case law, a reputed spouse is entitled to the same rights as a spouse almost immediately following cohabitation, unless the deceased wrote a testament providing otherwise. A regular agreement determining the rights and obligations of the spouses will not suffice to deny a reputed spouse his or her inheritance rights. This is due to a narrow reading of §55, Succession Law.[55] Furthermore, the surviving reputed spouse is entitled, just like a married spouse, to maintenance out of the estate. According to case law, neither an agreement nor a testament to the contrary can abrogate this right.[56] Same-sex reputed spouses are likewise entitled to succeed their deceased cohabitant.[57]

14. EVALUATION

Israeli law has shown much flexibility in adapting a very traditional legal framework to the exigencies of modern life. Although matters of marriage and divorce are subject to the exclusive jurisdiction of religious courts, couples may nonetheless choose from among several arrangements – to have a religious marriage in Israel, live as reputed spouses, have a civil marriage abroad, have a Jewish religious marriage abroad (unlike Orthodox Judaism, Reform Judaism provides also for same-sex marriages), have a same-sex relationship, either as reputed spouses or, following a marriage abroad, be registered as married in Israel. All forms are

recent amendment of the Dissolution of Marriage Law, had exercised the jurisdiction to decide to whether the marriage will be dissolved by a civil court or by a religious court). Since at the time of the proceedings all spouses were domiciled in Israel, the Court decided to apply the Law of the state in which the spouses were married, *i.e.*, Russia.

54 *Cf.* the very pertinent criticism of Y. Ben-Menashe, 'Matters of Dissolution of Marriage (Special Cases) Law, 5729–1969 – Interim Conclusions – Achievements, Criticism and Reform Proposals', 1990/91 *Ha-Praklit* 39, pp. 201 *et seq.* (in Hebrew).

55 *Blau* v. *Pozsch*, Civil Appeal 1717/98, 54(4) *PD* 376 (7.9.2000). § 55, Succession Law, entitled 'quasi-will,' reads: 'Where a man and woman though not being married to one another, have lived together as husband and wife in a common household, then, upon the death of one of them, neither being married to another person, the deceased is deemed, subject to any contrary direction expressed or implied in the will of the deceased, to have bequeathed to the survivor what the survivor would have inherited on intestacy if they had been married to one another.'.

56 *Bar-Nahor* v. *Estate of Austerlitz*, Civil Appeal 7021/93, tak-supreme 94(3), 1512 (25.10.94).

57 *A.m.* v. *The Attorney General*, Civil Appeal (Nazareth) 3245/03 (11.11.2004), tak-district 2004(4), 2532.

acceptable, have their respectable place in society, and each person can reach self-fulfillment in his or her own way.

Not surprisingly perhaps, much is still to be done. In the absence of a civil marriage or divorce, or a system of familial registered partnership, the status, as well as the rights and obligations of same-sex spouses remain in a state of flux.

Same-sex family unions have so far not been recognized as conferring status. From a legal point of view, their relationship is considered purely contractual. Consequently, as shown in this article, the rights and obligations of same-sex spouses have remained unclear with respect to maintenance obligations, property relations and succession. If the same-sex spouses belong to the same religious community and were married abroad, they have no way of dissolving their marriage in Israel. Finally, the adoption in Israel of children by such spouses, whether related or unrelated to either of them, and the recognition of foreign child adoption orders, should be regulated by the legislature with clarity as to the consequences of such adoptions with respect to status, parenthood, and all other ensuing rights and obligations. The entry in the Population Registry of family unions established abroad and foreign adoption orders, without conferring status, is an unsatisfactory solution. It creates much vagueness with respect to the rights and obligations accruing to the spouses and their children, for the duration of the same-sex relationship, as well as upon its dissolution by separation or death.

It is to the credit of the Israel Supreme Court that it has done everything within it powers to make Israeli family law adapt to modern civil society, using principles borrowed from private international law, on the one hand, while not leaving any building block of the civil law unturned in search for remedies to help spouses of all sorts, on the other. More than anything, the Supreme Court has applied a political wisdom which enabled the settlement of many outstanding problems without drawing too much opposition from the religious camp. The Court has taken special care to ensure the protection of the best interests of children, not hesitating to overcome any legal obstacle along the way.

However, such development of family law by the Court, which recognizes concepts, but does not have a coherent system to define the ensuing rights and obligations, naturally also raises problems. For any non-traditional family union to be wholly and truly accepted by the Israeli legal system, the problems presented by it must be taken care of in a wholesome, conscientious manner, a challenge that cannot be met by case-law alone. This challenge has to be met by the *Knesset*, in the best interests of all Israeli citizens and residents.

IS THE UNION CIVIL?

Same-sex marriages, civil unions, domestic partnerships and reciprocal benefits in the USA

IAN CURRY-SUMNER* & SCOTT CURRY-SUMNER**

1. INTRODUCTION

The legal recognition of same-sex relationships has been a legislative Gordian knot for almost three decades in the United States of America. Few issues have been so polarising as the debate surrounding the opening of marriage to same-sex couples. The aim of this article is to provide a clear picture of the current state of affairs in the United States as regards the recognition of formalised same-sex relationships. In doing so, this article will provide an overview of relevant legislation prohibiting or permitting the legal recognition of same-sex relationships in all fifty states, as well as in the District of Columbia and at the federal level. Although a number of websites and other surveys have been produced over the years, these surveys are no longer up-to-date. Furthermore, this survey aims to provide a possible theoretical framework within which future research in this field can be placed. By identifying the trends, similarities and differences, this article will provide future academics in this field with possible hypotheses as to where the law may go in the future in those states that have not yet introduced such registration schemes.

This article is divided into six sections. After this introduction, the various states currently prohibiting the recognition of same-sex marriage and/or other forms of registration will be classified according to the source of the prohibition (§2). The subsequent section will be devoted to an analysis of the spectrum of registration schemes currently in force in jurisdictions across the country, namely reciprocal benefits (§3.1), domestic partnerships (§3.2), civil unions (§3.3) and

* Senior University Lecturer and Researcher, Private International Law, Comparative Law and Family Law, UCERF and Molengraaff Institute for Private Law, Utrecht University (The Netherlands), email: I.Curry-Sumner@law.uu.nl.

** University Lecturer, Common Law Systems, Private Law Department, Maastricht University (The Netherlands), email: s.currysumner@pr.unimaas.nl.

same-sex marriages (§3.4). The jurisdictions that are dealt with in these sections are obviously dealt with in much greater detail since they provide for some form of registration scheme. In total 11 jurisdictions will be dealt with in §3. Three states will form the basis of the analysis in §4, where the recognition of out-of-state same-sex marriages will be considered. After a few brief comparative remarks (§5), the article will conclude with a number of general remarks based on the overview provided (§6).

A number of choices have obviously had to be made in compiling a survey of this nature. This survey is limited to an overview of the law in the fifty states and the District of Columbia. The reason for this choice is twofold. Firstly, the sheer diversity of county, city and municipality ordinances is so great as to necessitate delineation of the ambit for this article. Secondly, the impact of county, city and municipality ordinances is much more limited than state-wide registration schemes. Although New York City may well be home to more than 8 million people and Vermont only 620,000, the legislation emanating out of Vermont is much more significant since this is state level legislation, instead of city level legislation. This distinction is crucial since all state level legislation is regarded as being of the highest order of legislation possible in a state, with the consequences attached thereto. This is not, however, the case as regards local government legislation, which can ultimately be superseded by state-wide level.[1] The inclusion of the District of Columbia is also justified since in this field it actually operates much more like a state than a city council, there being on authority higher in the legislative hierarchy than the federal government in the field of family law.

2. STATES PROHIBITING RECOGNITION OF SAME-SEX RELATIONSHIPS

2.1. FEDERAL LEVEL

Ever since the Supreme Court of Hawai'i ruled in 1993 that the State must show a 'compelling State interest' if it wished to continue to deny same-sex couples the right to marry, opponents of same-sex marriage have resorted to legislative action. Although the Hawaiian legislature eventually passed a constitutional amendment, after a popular vote, ensuring that the legislature had the power to reserve the definition of marriage to opposite-sex couples,[2] the aftermath of the case can still be seen today across the entire breadth of the United States.

---

1 W. Burnham, *Introduction to the law and legal system of the United States*, 2006.

2 Haw. Const. art. I, § 23: 'The legislature shall have the power to reserve marriage to opposite-sex couples'.

On the 21st September 1996, President Clinton signed the Defense of Marriage Act, or the Federal DOMA as it is commonly referred to, into law. The Bill received overwhelming support in both the House and the Senate. The passage of the DOMA legislation has now ensured that 'in determining the meaning of any Act of Congress or any ruling, regulation, or interpretation of the various administrative bureaus and agencies of the United States, the word "marriage" means only a legal union between one man and one woman as husband and wife, and the word 'spouse' refers only to a person of the opposite sex who is a husband or wife'.[3]

However, DOMA does two things. Not only does it define the term *marriage* and *spouse* for federal purposes, it also permits the states to deny recognition to other forms of unions.[4] It is evident from the legislative history accompanying the passage of this bill that the authority to enact such a law is to be found in the U.S. Constitution itself, which grants Congress the power to determine 'the effect' or 'the extent' of the full faith and credit clause.[5] Since its enactment, DOMA has engendered fierce debate with opponents arguing that Congress exceeded its power in enacting this legislation, and proponents arguing that it does not *enjoin* non-recognition, but simply grants States the *possibility* to refrain from recognition.[6]

What is perhaps most surprising about the entire DOMA debate is that it was actually founded on an incorrect reading of the constitutional full faith and credit clause.[7] Historically speaking, marriage has never been thought to be

3 1 U.S.C. § 7.

4 28 U.S.C. 1738C: 'No State, territory, or possession of the United States, or Indian tribe, shall be required to give effect to any public act, record, or judicial proceeding of any other State, territory, possession, or tribe respecting a relationship between persons of the same sex that is treated as a marriage under the laws of such other State, territory, possession, or tribe, or a right or claim arising from such relationship.'.

5 U.S. Const. art. IV, § 1: 'Full faith and credit shall be given to the public Acts, Records, and judicial Proceedings of every other State. And the Congress may be general Laws prescribe the Manner in which such Acts, records and proceedings shall be proved and the Effect thereof.'.

6 See, for example, M. Strasser, 'Defending marriage in light of the *Moreno-Cleburne-Romer-Lawrence* Jurisprudence: Why DOMA can't pass muster after *Lawrence*', 2005 *Creighton Law Review* 38, no. 2, p. 421. A bill currently in Congress would, if passed, remove jurisdiction from all federal courts to entertain challenges to DOMA: H.R. 724, 110th Congr., 1st Sess (2007). This Bill is the third in a series of similar bills, namely H.R. 3313, 108th Congr., 1st Sess. (2003) and H.R. 1100, 109th Congr., 1st Sess. (2005). In relation to the validity of a Canadian marriage for the purposes of US federal bankruptcy law, see *In re Kandu*, 315 B.R. 123 (Bankr. W.D. Wash. 2004) it was held that DOMA did not violate the 4th, 5th or 10th amendments to the US Constitution. See further E. Sack, 'The Retreat from DOMA: The Public Policy of Same-Sex Marriage and a Theory of Congressional Power Under the Full Faith and Credit Clause', 2005 *Creighton Law Review* 38, no. 2, p. 507.

7 Some have argued that this misunderstanding was the result of an overzealous press and student scholarly articles: see. P. Borchers, '*Baker* v. *General Motors*: Implications for interjurisdictional recognition of non-traditional marriages', 1998 *Creighton Law Review* 32, no. 1, pp. 152–153; J.L. Grossman, 'Resurrecting comity: revisiting the problem of non-uniform marriage laws', 2005 *Oregon Law Review* 84, p. 433; R.G. Spector, 'Same-sex marriages, domes-

encompassed by the full faith and credit clause. Questions of interstate marriage recognition have already been solved with resort to general principles of comity or marriage specific conflict of laws rules. According to general constitutional theory, states are not obliged to recognise each other's marriages on the basis of the stringent full faith and credit conditions. Nonetheless, debate concerning the validity of the federal DOMA has been completely overshadowed by the statutory and constitutional amendments of more than forty states that have now introduced their own mini-DOMA's.

Why then is this federal statute so important? Many federal laws use marital status as a connecting factor in attributing rights, duties and benefits. In 2004 the General Accounting Office, updating its 1997 Report, identified a total of 1,138 federal statutory provisions in which marital status is used as a factor in to determine the receipt of benefits, rights or privileges.[8] In enacting the Defense of Marriage Act, the federal Government effectively restricted these benefits to opposite-sex married couples; thereby denying these rights and benefits to same-sex couples, regardless of their status. Although many of these rights are extremely specific and rarely used, others deserve particular attention, including the right to receive a deceased spouse's social security benefits and survivors benefits,[9] the right to immigration benefits,[10] the right to income tax rate exemptions and deductions,[11] the right to file for joint bankruptcy, the right to petition for domestic violence protection orders,[12] the right to funeral and bereavement leave, the right to jointly file federal tax returns,[13] the right to make medical decisions on behalf of one's spouse, the right to spousal privilege in criminal proceedings,[14] inheritance rights[15] and the permission to make funeral decisions.

---

tic partnerships and private international law: At the dawn of a new jurisprudence in the United States', in A. Bonomi (ed.), *Yearbook of Private International Law. Volume 8*, 2006, pp. 169–187, p. 173; A. Koppelman, 'Interstate recognition of same-sex civil unions after *Lawrence* v. *Texas*', 2004 *Ohio State Law Journal* 65, p. 1265, and slightly more expanded version in A. Koppelman, 'Interstate recognition of same-sex marriages and civil unions: A Handbook for judges', 2005 *University of Pennsylvania Law Review* 153, p. 2143. For an opposite view see: L.A. Silverman, 'Vermont civil unions, full faith and credit, and marital status', 2001 *Kentucky Law Journal* 89, p. 1075.

8 GAO/OGC-97-16, 31 January 1997 and GAO-04-353R, 23 January 2004.

9 For example, 42 U.S.C. § 402.

10 For example, 8 U.S.C. § 1182.

11 See the whole of the Internal Revenue Code, *e.g.* 26 U.S.C. § 2.

12 For example, 18 U.S.C. § 2261, 42 U.S.C. § 10408 and 42 U.S.C. § 13981.

13 I.R.C. § 1.

14 Fed. R. Evid. 501. This rule actually contains two privileges, namely the privilege against adverse spousal testimony and the marital communications privilege, together commonly referred to as 'the spousal privileges'.

15 For example the exemption from estate tax, I.R.C. § 2001.

2.2. STATE LEVEL

It was, however, not only the federal legislature that feared the onslaught of same-sex marriages. No fewer than 45 States have since passed similar legislative amendments restricting their definition of marriage to that of one man and one woman. Nevertheless, it is important to identify a number of different categories.

2.2.1. State ban applies to same-sex marriages and other same-sex relationships

In Alabama,[16] Arkansas,[17] Georgia,[18] Idaho,[19] Kansas,[20] Kentucky,[21] Louisiana,[22] Michigan,[23] Nebraska,[24] North Dakota,[25] Ohio,[26]

16 Ala. Const. of 1901, Amendment 774. See also, Ala. Code § 30-1-19. This was also supported prior to these amendments by the Attorney General: Marriages-Marriage Licences, Ala. Op. Att'y Gen. No. 129 (20th April 2000).

17 Ark. Const. of 1874, Amendment 83. See also, Ark. Code Ann. § 9-11-208(b), § 9-11-208(c) and § 9-11-207. In *May* v. *Daniels*, 359 Ark. 1000, 194 S.W.3d 771 (Ark. 2004), the Supreme Court of Arkansas was faced with a pre-emptive challenge to the proposed constitutional amendment. The claimants alleged, *inter alia*, that the amendment was phrased using vague and misleading language. The court denied the petition.

18 Ga. Const. art. I, § 4. See also, Ga. Code Ann. § 19-3.3.1. In *Burns* v. *Burns*, 253 Ga. App. 600, 560 S.E. 2d 47 (Ga. Ct. App. 2002), the 2nd Division of the Georgia Court of Appeals held that a Vermont civil union did not constitute a marriage for the purposes of interpreting a visitation agreement. Although the constitutional amendment was in force at the time of the case, reference was made to the federal DOMA, as well as the state statutes in denying recognition of the civil union.

19 Idaho Const. art. III, § 28. See also, Idaho Code § 32-209.

20 Kan. Const. art. XV, § 16. See also, Kan. Stat. Ann. § 23-101(a) and § 23-115.

21 Ky. Const. § 233A. See also, Ky. Rev. Stat. Ann. § 402.005, § 402.20, § 402.040 and § 402.045: 'a legal status identical or substantially similar to that of marriage for unmarried individuals shall not be valid or recognized.'.

22 La. Const. art. XII, § 15. See also, La. Civ. Code Ann. art. 96 and art. 3520(B). In *Forum for Equality PAC* v. *McKeithen, 893 So.2d 715* (La. 2005), the Supreme Court of Louisiana reversed a district court decision (*Forum for Equal PAC* v. *McKeithen*, 886 So.2d 1172 (La. App. 1 Cir. 2004), in which Judge Morvant declared the amendment of the Louisiana Constitution to restrict marriage to same-sex couples unconstitutional.

23 Mich. Const. art I, § 25. See also, Mich. Comp. Laws § 551.1 and § 551.271. According to the Michigan Marriage Amendment: 'To secure and preserve the benefits of marriage for our society and for future generations of children, the union of one man and one woman in marriage shall be the only agreement recognized as a marriage or similar union for any purpose'. In *National Pride at Work Inc.* v. *Governor of Michigan*, 274 Mich. App. 147, 732 N.W. 2d 139 (Mich. Ct. App. 2007), the court had to interpret the phrase 'similar union'. The Michigan Court of Appeals held that the phrase precluded any body in Michigan from extending benefits to same-sex or opposite-sex unmarried relationships.

24 Neb. Const. art. I, § 29. See also, Neb. Rev. Stat. § 42-100.

25 N.D. Const. art. XV, § 28. See also, N.D. Cent. Code § 14-03-01 an § 14-03-08.

26 Ohio Const. art. XV, § 11. See also, Ohio Rev. Code Ann. § 3101.01. This statutory amendment also states that the 'recognition or extension by the state of the specific statutory benefits of a legal marriage to non-marital relationships between persons of the same sex or different sexes is against the strong public policy of this state': Ohio Rev. Code Ann. § 3101.01(c)(3).

Oklahoma,[27] South Carolina,[28] South Dakota,[29] Texas,[30] Utah,[31] Virginia[32] and Wisconsin[33] the State Constitution has been amended so as to prohibit the recognition of any union other than that of one man and one woman. These constitutional amendments not only prohibit the celebration of same-sex marriages, civil unions and other forms of registration within the state, but also proscribe the recognition of out-of-state marriages and non-marital registrations. Although these constitutional amendments have all been passed after state-wide referenda, the constitutionality of these amendments has begun to be brought into question. However, at present no state has overturned the constitutional amendment by virtue of its unconstitutionality.[34]

Although the amendment to the Alaskan Constitution is restricted to the non-recognition of same-sex marriages,[35] Section 25.05.013(b) of the Alaskan Statutes states, 'a same-sex relationship may not be recognized by the state as being entitled to the benefits of marriage'. It would therefore appear that same-sex couples claiming the benefits of marriage via a civil union or other form of civil recognition would be denied those benefits on the basis of this provision. A similar position is also taken in Florida where, despite the lack of a constitutional

27 Okla. Const. art. II, § 35. See also, Okla. Stat. Tit. 43, § 3.1. The constitutionality of both the state constitutional amendment, as well as the state statute restricting marriage to opposite-sex couples is currently being challenged: *Bishop* v. *Oklahoma*, 447 F.Supp.2d. 1239 (N.D. Okla. 2006). This cases involved two couples, one who wanted to celebrate a same-sex marriage in Oklahoma and another who filed for recognition of their Vermont civil union or their Canadian same-sex marriage in Oklahoma.

28 S.C. Const. art. XVII, § 15. See also, S.C. Code Ann. § 20-1-15. At the time of writing, Grossman argues that the statutes in South Carolina only prohibited same-sex marriages concluded in the state, and thus did not deal with the recognition of out-of-state marriages. Although this may indeed be the case, the constitutional amendment has changed this situation ensuring that same-sex marriages concluded out-of-state will not be recognised, see J.L. Grossman, 'Resurrecting comity: revisiting the problem of non-uniform marriage laws', 2005 *Oregon Law Review* 84, pp. 433, 478.

29 S.D. Const. art. XXI, § 9. See also, S.D. Codified Laws § 25—38 and § 25-1-1.

30 Tex. Const. art. I, § 32. See also, Tex. Fam. Code § 2.001 and § 6.204. § 6.204 also extends to a same-sex relationship other than marriage that is 'intended as an alternative to marriage or applies primarily to cohabitating persons and grants to the parties of the relationship legal protections, benefits, or responsibilities granted to the spouses of a marriage.'.

31 Utah Const. art. I, § 29. See also, Utah Code Ann. § 30-1-4.1. The statutory amendment also extends to same-sex relationships other than marriages.

32 Va. Const. art. I, § 15-A. See also, 15 Va. Code Ann. § 8, § 20-45.2 and § 20-45.3.

33 Wis. Const. art. XIII, § 13: 'a legal status identical to substantially similar to that of marriage for unmarried individuals shall not be valid or recognised in this state'.

34 Although at first instance (*Citizens for Equal Protection Inc.* v. *Bruning*, 368 F.Supp.2d. 980 (D. Neb. 2005)) the U.S. District Court held that the amendment to the Constitution of Nebraska was unconstitutional since it violated the equal protection clause, this decision was later reversed, *Citizens for Equal Protection Inc.* v. *Bruning*, 455 F.3d. 859 (8th Cir. 2006).

35 Alaska Const. art. I, § 25.

amendment, the state statutes prevent the recognition of any form of same-sex relationship, regardless of the terminology attached to it.[36]

Montana's Constitutional amendment is also restricted to the non-recognition of same-sex marriages.[37] The amendment to Montana's statutes is, however, slightly more debatable with regards to its ambit. Paragraph 4 of §451.022 reads,

> 'A contractual relationship entered into for the purpose of achieving a civil relationship (...) is void as against public policy.' [38]

One could argue, in attempting to have a civil union or domestic partnership recognised in Montana, that the benefit sought is not derived from a contractual relationship but from a legal status acquired in a foreign jurisdiction. Despite the appealing logic of this argument, it is unlikely that such an argument would succeed, and more-than-likely, that non-marital registered relationships will not be recognised in Montana on this basis.

A more convincing argument for the non-recognition of all registered same-sex relationships can be found in the statutory amendment to the Code of West Virginia, where it is stated,

> 'A public act, record or judicial proceeding of any other state, territory, possession or tribe respecting a relationship between persons of the same sex that is treated as a marriage under the laws of the other state, territory, possession, or tribe, or a right or claim arising from such relationship, shall not be given effect by this state.'[39]

From this text it would appear that the West Virginian legislature intended to deny recognition not only to same-sex married couples, but also those to those couples claiming a right granted to married couples on the basis of a 'public act, record or judicial proceeding' respecting the relationship between same-sex couples. A couple who has legally registered a domestic partnership in California would therefore not be entitled to marital benefits in West Virginia on the basis of their domestic partnership.

---

36 Fla. Stat. § 741.04 and § 741.212. The validity of these provisions, as well as the federal DOMA, is currently pending before judges in Florida in three separate cases: *Hunt* v. *Ake*, Case No. 8:04-CV-1852-T-30, *Sullivan* v. *Bush* Case No. 04–21118-CV and *Wilson* v. *Ake*, Case No. 8:04-CV-1680-T-30.

37 Mont. Const. art. XIII, § 7.

38 Mont. Code. Ann. § 40–1-103 and § 40–1-401.

39 W. Va. Code § 48–2-603.

2.2.2. State ban only applies to same-sex marriages

In Colorado,[40] Hawai'i,[41] Mississippi,[42] Missouri,[43] Nevada,[44] Oregon[45] and Tennessee[46] state-wide referenda have been held on whether the state definition of marriage should be restricted to opposite-sex couples. In all these states, the ensuing constitutional amendment was restricted to the non-recognition of same-sex marriages. Other forms of relationship are not mentioned. In two of these states, namely Hawai'i and Oregon, the legislature has gone on to introduce forms of non-marital registered relationship (see Sections 3 and 4).

In Arizona,[47] California,[48] Connecticut,[49] Delaware,[50] Illinois,[51]

---

40 Col. Const. art. II. See also, Col. Rev. Stat. § 14-2-104.

41 Haw. Const. art. I, § 23. This constitutional amendment simply grants the legislature the power to define the meaning of marriage. See also, Haw. Rev. Stat. § 572-1, § 572-1.6, § 572.C-1 and § 572.C-7.

42 Miss. Const. art. XIV, § 263A. See also, Miss. Code Ann. § 93-1-1.3.

43 Mo. Const. art. I, § 23. See also, Mo. Rev. Stat. § 451.022.

44 Nev. Const. art. I, § 21. See also, N.R.S. § 122.00.1.

45 Or. Const. art. XV, § 5a. See also, Or. Rev. Stat. § 106.010. The statutory restriction of marriage to same-sex couples was challenged in 2005 (prior to the enactment of the constitutional amendment). Gillette J., the judge at first instance, held that the denial of the *benefits* of marriage was contrary to Or. Const. art. I, § 20.However, this decision was reversed by the Supreme Court of Oregon. See *Li* v. *State of Oregon*, 338 Ore. 376, 110 P.3d 91 (Or. 2005).

46 Tenn. Const. art. XI, § 18. See also, Tenn. Code Ann. § 36-3-113.

47 Ariz. Rev. Stat. § 25-101 and § 25-112. In *Standhardt* v. *Arizona*, 206 Ariz. 276, 77 P.3d 451 (Ariz Ct. App. 2003), the Court of Appeals of Arizona held that the 'right to enter a same-sex marriage is not a fundamental liberty interest protected by due process.' (206 Ariz. 276, 285). In subsequently reviewing the denial of marriage licences to same-sex couples using a rational basis analysis the court held that there had been no infringement of the parties' equal protection rights.

48 Cal. Fam. Code § 308-5. This provisions has been challenged on the basis of its constitutionality: *Smelt* v. *Orange County*, 447 F.3d. 673 (9th Cir. 2006), partly validating and partly dismissing the first instance decision in the same case, *Smelt* v. *Orange County*, 347 F.Supp.2d. 861 (C.D. Cal. 2005). The decision in this case has been stayed pending the outcome of the so-called 'Marriage Cases': *Thomasson* v. *Newsom*, Case No. CGC 04-428794; *Proposition 22 Legal Defense & Education Fund* v. *City and County of San Francisco*, Case No. CPF 04-503943; *City & County of San Francisco* v. *State*, Case No. CGC 04-429539; *Woo* v. *Lockyer*, Case No. CPF 04-504030; *Tyler* v. *County of Los Angeles*, Case No. BS 088506; *Clinton* v. *State*, Case No. CGC 04-429548. Together these cases have been filed as *In re Coordinated Proceedings, Special Title [Rule 1550(c)], Marriage Cases*, No. 4365, 2005 WL 5833129 (Cal. Super. Ct., Mar. 14, 2005).

49 Conn. Gen. Stat. Ann. § 45a-727a. The non-recognition of same-sex marriages is Connecticut was also explicated in Attorney General Blumenthal's opinion on the 20th September 2005: for the text of the opinion see http://ct.gov/AG/cwp/view.asp?A=1770&Q=302438. Although in *Rosengarten* v. *Downes*, 71 Conn. App. 372, 802 A.2d 170 (Conn. App. Ct. 2002), the Appellate Court of Connecticut ruled that it was not empowered with 'plenary and general subject matter jurisdiction' to dissolve a Vermont civil union, this decision has since been called into question as a result of the enactment of civil unions legislation in the state (see § 5).

50 Del. Code Ann. § 101.

51 Ill. Comp. Stat. 5/201, 5/212 and 5/213.1. On the 15th February 2008, the Illinois Religious Freedom Protection and Civil Union Bill was submitted to the Illinois Senate, S.B. 2436, 95th

Indiana,[52] Iowa,[53] Maine,[54] Maryland,[55] Minnesota,[56] New Hampshire,[57] North Carolina,[58] Pennsylvania,[59] Vermont,[60] Washington[61] and Wyoming[62] the non-recognition of same-sex marriages has been codified by statutory amendment, without resorting to constitutional amendments and state-wide referenda. It is interesting to note that six of these states (California, Connecticut, Maine, New Hampshire, Vermont and Washington) have also introduced legislative schemes permitting same-sex couples to register their relationships (these schemes will be discussed in §4 and §5).

Even though the source of the proscription is irrelevant for an individual same-sex couple, it is important to note that the procedure for amending a state constitution is more arduous than a mere statutory amendment. As a result, same-sex couples in states that have passed constitutional amendments will

Congr. (2008). If passed this bill would introduce civil unions in Illinois for both same-sex and opposite-sex couples. This bill is similar to legislation filed in the House in 2007 (H.B. 1826, 95th Congr. (2007)), although this bill has not been scheduled for a vote by the full house. Two other bills have been introduced into the General Assembly, one aimed at amending the Illinois Constitution to restrict marriage to opposite-sex couples (S.B. 0008, 95th Congr. (2007)) and one to permit same-sex marriages (H.B. 1615, 95th Congr. (2007)). Neither bill has progressed to a full vote.

52 Ind. Code Ann. § 31–11-1-1. This statutory limitation was unsuccessfully challenged in *Morrison* v. *Sadler*, 821 N.E.2d 15 (Ind. Ct. App 2005).

53 Iowa Code § 595. This ban was struck down for a 24-hour period in Polk County by Judge Hanson in *Varnum* v. *Brien*, Case No. CV5965 (Iowa D.C. 2007). Although same-sex marriage licences were permitted between the 30th and 31st August 2007, the effects of the decision were constrained by a verbal statement from Judge Hanson who stayed his verdict pending an appeal to the Court of Appeals. In *Alons* v. *Iowa*, 698 N.W. 2d 858 (Iowa 2005), a same-sex couple had filed for the dissolution of their marriage at the district court in Woodbury County, Iowa. The court had granted the dissolution, despite the fact that the couple had actually entered into a civil union in Vermont. The plaintiffs (two state senators, four state representatives, a pastor and a church) filed for a writ of certiorari to have the decision annulled. The district court partly vacated the original decree and granted the following equitable relief: 'terminating the Vermont civil union, freeing the parties of any obligations incident tot hat union, declaring that the parties are single individuals with all rights or unmarried persons'. The Supreme Court of Iowa annulled the writ of certiorari since the plaintiffs had no standing to challenge the district court's decision.

54 Me. Rev. Stat. Ann. Tit. 19, § 701.

55 Md. Code Ann. [Family Law] § 2–201. In a 4–3 decision, the Court of Appeals of Maryland (the highest court in the state) decided that the statutory impediment on same-sex marriage is constitutional: *Conaway* v. *Deane*, 401 Md. 219, 932 A.2d 571 (Md. 2007).

56 Minn. Stat. § 517.03 and § 518.01.

57 N.H. Rev. Stat. Ann. § 457.1, § 457.2, § 457.3 and § 457.43.

58 N.C. Gen. Stat. § 51–1-2.

59 23 Pa. Cons. Stat. § 1704.

60 Vt. Stat. Ann. Tit. 15, § 1201(4) and § 23.

61 Rev. Code Wash. § 26.04.010(1), § 26.04.020(1)(c) and § 26.04.020(3). The constitutionality of this amendment has been challenged, albeit unsuccessfully, *Andersen* v. *King County*, 158 Wn.2d. 1, 138 P.3d 963 (Wash. 2006).

62 Wyo. Stat. Ann. § 20–1-101.

more-than-likely be confronted with the ramifications of that vote for many years to come.

2.2.3. No state ban currently in force

Only five states have passed neither a state constitutional amendment nor a legislative proposal restricting marriage to same-sex couples (Massachusetts, New Jersey, New Mexico, New York and Rhode Island). In all of these five states, same-sex relationships are granted some degree of recognition (discussed later in §4, §5, §6 and §7).

3. SPECTRUM OF STATE MECHANISMS FOR RECOGNISING SAME-SEX COUPLES

3.1. RECIPROCAL BENEFITS

At present only one state in the United States provides for a state-wide registry entitled 'reciprocal benefits', namely Hawai'i. Although the Oregon Family Council, Defence of Marriage Coalition and the Oregon House Conservatives introduced a reciprocal beneficiaries bill into the Oregon House of Representatives,[63] eventually House Bill 2007 was passed resulting in the introduction of domestic partnerships in the state (see Section 4). Furthermore, although bills to introduce a reciprocal beneficiary scheme have also been introduced in the Colorado Senate[64] and the Nevada Assembly,[65] neither has been successful. Nonetheless, in Nevada, at least, the issue has not been laid to rest entirely; a recent petition has been submitted to the Assembly by the Nevada System of Higher Education calling on the Assembly to introduce a system of reciprocal beneficiaries.[66]

Vermont also provides for a system of reciprocal benefits. However, according to §1301 of Title 15, Vermont Statutes Annotated, the purpose of the scheme is to 'provide two persons who are blood-relatives or related by adoption the opportunity to establish a consensual reciprocal beneficiaries relationship so they may receive the benefits and protections and be subject to the responsibilities that are granted to spouses' in specific areas. Consequently, the scheme is not open to unrelated same-sex couples and is therefore not functionally equivalent to the reciprocal beneficiary schemes discussed in this article.

63 Or. H.R. 3536, 74th Cong., 1st Sess. (2007).
64 Col. S. 166, 65th Cong., 2nd Sess. (2006).
65 Nev. Assembly 496, 71st Cong., 1st Sess. (2001).
66 See http://hr.unlv.edu/3dMemos/2007/PEBP%20Petition%2004-12-07.pdf.

3.1.1. *Hawai'i*

In 1993, the Hawaiian Supreme Court handed down perhaps one of the most momentous and groundbreaking judgments in its history.[67] On the 5th May 1993 in the case of *Baher* v. *Miike* (renamed from *Baehr* v. *Lewin* after Lawerence Miike became the new director of the Department of Health, the defendant in this case), the Hawaiian Supreme Court held that it was unconstitutional for the State to continue to deny same-sex couples the benefits of marriage, unless it could prove a compelling state interest.[68] Following this ruling, the case was remanded to the trial court. After an initial postponement, the case finally came before Judge Chang of the First Circuit Court of Hawai'i in September 1996.

In finding for the plaintiff, Judge Chang held that the State had not shown compelling evidence that such prejudice or harm to the majority would result from permitting same-sex marriages. Judge Chang went on to state that even if the State has satisfied this requirement, there was no proof that §572–1 had not been defined narrowly enough to avoid 'unnecessary abridgements of constitutional rights'.[69] Although the case was appealed to the Hawaiian Supreme Court, the case was declared moot in 1999 on the basis of the 1998 Constitutional amendment, and the decision was reversed.[70]

Nonetheless, this case served as fuel for the eventual introduction of the reciprocal beneficiary scheme introduced in July 1997. The legislature had hoped that by passing Act 383 (An Act relating to unmarried couples) the complaints of same-sex couples would be answered. The Act laid down a state-sanctioned registration scheme for those couples not entitled to marry.

This desire was not, however, shared by the homosexual community in Hawai'i. Since the introduction of reciprocal benefits on the islands, numerous calls have been made for the scheme to be replaced by civil unions. The latest attempt came in February 2007, when legislation to legalise civil unions was debated in both chambers of the Hawaiian State Legislature. After the hearing in the Hawaiian House Judiciary Committee, the Hawaiian House of Representatives declined to vote on the subject, in effect neutralising the bill.[71] Both the Senate and House Bills have been carried over to the 2008 legislative session.

---

67 See, for a more detailed analysis of the historical precursors to the legislation, W. Burnette, 'Hawaii's Reciprocal Beneficiaries Act: An effective step in resolving the controversy surrounding same-sex marriage', 1998 *Brandeis Law Journal* 37, pp. 83–85.

68 *Baher* v. *Lewin*, 74 Haw. 645, 852 P.2d 44 (Haw. 1993).

69 *Baehr* v. *Miike*, Civil No. 91–1394 (1st Circuit, Hawai'i 1996), especially at conclusions of law §§ 18 and 19.

70 *Baehr* v. *Miike*, 994 P.2d 566 (Haw. 1999).

71 Haw. H.R. 908, 24th Cong. (2007) and Haw. S. 1062, 24th Cong. (2007).

3.1.1.1. Establishment

A reciprocal beneficiary relationship is defined as 'a legal partnership between two people who are prohibited from marriage'.[72] Moreover, the scheme is open not only to same-sex couples, but also to those within the prohibited degrees of marriage.[73] It is, however, not possible to conclude a reciprocal beneficial relationship if either party is under the age of 18, nor if either party is already involved in a marriage or another reciprocal beneficiary relationship.[74] Furthermore, there are no state residency or U.S. citizenship requirements for registration to be permitted. To have the relationship registered both parties must provide their full consent and pay the required registration fee (currently set at $8).[75] As soon as all the procedural requirements have been met, the couple is provided with a notarised declaration of the relationship by the Department of Health.

3.1.1.2. Rights and duties

Hawai'i opted to explicitly enumerate those rights, duties and benefits that apply to reciprocal beneficiaries.[76] In doing so, it refrained from extending the 160 rights currently granted to opposite-sex married couples, and instead made a selection of rights which are subsequently extended to reciprocal benefits by means of amendment.[77] Of those rights that remain in force, the most important relate to the possibility to consent to a post-mortem examination,[78] the applicability of intestate law,[79] the right to hospital visitation rights,[80] the right to compensation in cases of wrongful[81] or accidental death,[82] certain property rights,

72 Haw. Rev. Stat. § 572C-2.

73 Haw. Rev. Stat. § 572C-4(3).

74 Haw. Rev. Stat. § 572C-4(1) and § 572C-4(2).

75 Haw. Rev. Stat. § 572C-5(a).

76 For a detailed explanation of the difference between enumeration and exclusion methods of ascribing rights and duties see, I. Curry-Sumner, *All's well that ends registered?*, 2005, pp. 290–292.

77 1997 Haw. Sess. Laws 383, sec. 4–73. A non-exhaustive list of rights granted by Hawaiian Statute to married couples can be found in *Baehr* v. *Miike*, op. cit. See also W. Burnette, 'Hawaii's reciprocal beneficiaries act: An effective step ion resolving the controversy surrounding same-sex marriage', 1998 *Brandeis Law Journal* 37, pp. 87–88.

78 Haw. Rev. Stat. § 453–15.

79 Haw. Rev. Stat. § 560:2–202 (elective share), § 560:2–301 (entitlement of spouse), § 560:2–802 and § 560:2–804.

80 Haw. Rev. Stat. § 323.

81 Haw. Rev. Stat. § 663–3.

82 Haw. Rev. Stat. § 88–85.

including joint tenancy,[83] holiday allowances equivalent to that of a spouse,[84] protection under Hawai'i domestic violence laws[85] and funeral leave.[86]

Originally the reciprocal benefits scheme also entitled parties to benefit from the medical insurance coverage of one's partner. The Act creating the reciprocal beneficiary scheme amended §431:10A of the Hawaiian Statutes, thus granting those involved in reciprocal beneficial relationships the opportunity to avail themselves of their partner's medical insurance.[87] In 1997, the Attorney General of Hawai'i delivered two opinions that stated that Section 4, Act 383 was limited to benefits derived from insurance companies and thus did not extend to protection offered via mutual benefit societies or health maintenance organisations.[88] In Hawai'i insurance companies, mutual benefit societies and health maintenance organisations can sell health care plans to Hawaiian employers directly. By restricting the application of the provisions to insurance companies, the Attorney General in effect wiped away the relevance of this provision, since the majority of employees in Hawai'i are not insured via insurance companies.

3.1.1.3. Termination

Either party may terminate a reciprocal beneficial relationship by filing a 'signed notarized declaration of the termination' with the director of health.[89] For the filing of the declaration, the parties must once again pay the required fee (currently set at $8). Once the declaration has been submitted, the director must issue a certificate of termination to each party and maintain a record of each declaration and certificate. Furthermore, a reciprocal beneficiary relationship may also be terminated by the subsequent issuance of a marriage license to either party.[90] After the termination of the relationship neither partner is entitled to claim alimony (or maintenance) from the other, nor any other of the rights and benefits enjoyed during the validity of the relationship.[91]

---

83 Haw. Rev. Stat. § 509–2.
84 Haw. Rev. Stat. § 79–7.
85 Haw. Rev. Stat. § 709–906.
86 Haw. Rev. Stat. § 79–13.
87 1997 Haw. Sess. Laws 383, sec. 4.
88 Section 4 of Act 383, Relating to Unmarried Couples, Op. Att'y Gen. 97–05 (1997) and Health Insurance Coverage for Reciprocal Beneficiaries, Op. Att'y Gen. 97–10 (1997).
89 Haw. Rev. Stat. § 572C-7(a).
90 Haw. Rev. Stat. § 572C-7(c) and (d).
91 Although not explicitly stated, this is implicit from the wording of the statute and can also be inferred from the relevant provisions on the applicability of intestate law, see Haw. Rev. Stat. § 560:2–802 and § 560:2–804.

3.2. DOMESTIC PARTNERSHIP

Although the term 'domestic partnership' has come to be associated with the East Coast of the U.S. and is often used to refer to registration schemes in states with substantially fewer rights than those states offering civil unions, this is not always the case. The term itself was first used in a legal action brought by Human Rights Campaign employee Larry Brinkin in 1982 against the Southern Pacific Railway Company. He was denied three days of paid leave by his employer upon the death of his partner of eleven years, since this right was only granted to a widow or widower. During this case, counsel for Mr. Brinkin argued that he had been involved in a 'domestic partnership' which was akin for all intents and purposes to a marriage. Although Mr. Brinkin lost his the case, the term 'domestic partnership' became popular in California to refer to unmarried couples living together as though they were married. Just three years later, the City of Berkeley became the first municipality in the country to enact a domestic partner registry and the first employer to offer domestic partner benefits. Although the term is also used in many municipality, city and county ordinances, this article will only focus on state-wide domestic partnership schemes.[92]

3.2.1. California

With this history in mind, it should come as no surprise that the first movement towards introducing a state-wide domestic partnership surfaced in California. In 1995, the first Bill aimed at introducing a state-wide registration scheme was submitted to the Californian Assembly. Although the Bill died in committee, it was an important step on the long and often arduous road to a full domestic partnership registry in the State.[93] Three similar bills were also introduced in 1997 and 1998, two of which despite being passed were subjected to the veto of the Governor Wilson.[94]

---

92 According to the 10th Amendment to the U.S. Constitution certain legislative powers are reserved to the individual states. In the latter half of the 20th century, many states have recognised the need for the local government to have more authority. The introduction of domestic partner registries is a classical example of how these local governments have seized this opportunity. See, V. Berger, 'Domestic partnership initiatives', 1991 *De Paul Law Review.* 40, p. 437; D. Weigel, 'Proposal for domestic partnership in the city of Detroit: Challenges under the law', 1997 *Detroit Mercy Law Review* 74, pp. 835–844. Although no recent statistics are available, due to the exponential increase in availability, in 1999 according to Lambda Legal Defense and Education Fund (New York) there were 123 colleges and universities, 37 labour unions, 476 private employees and 103 municipalities that offered domestic partnership benefits: S. Katz, 'Domestic partnership laws', in A. Bainham (ed). *International Survey of Family Law 1997*, 1999 pp. 485–505, p. 495.

93 Cal. A.B. 627, 1995–1996 Session (1995).

94 Cal. A.B. 54, 1997–1998 Session (1997), Cal. A.B. 1059, 1997–1998 Session (1997) and Cal. S.B. 75, 1999–2000 Session (1998). The last two bills were both vetoed by the resident Governor

Change came in 1999 with the passage of Assembly Bill 26 (A.B. 26). Although A.B. 26, like its counterpart Senate Bill 75, extended the partnership registry to all unmarried couples, it was later restricted to two categories, namely same-sex couples and those couples where both parties were older than 62 years of age.[95] The Governor found this proposition much more appealing, since it could not be regarded as providing a competitive alternative to marriage for opposite-sex couples. Governor Davis eventually signed the Bill into law on the 22nd September 1999. Although modest in scope, this legislation was immensely significant since it signalled the first time in U.S. legislative history that a state legislature had dealt with the issue of same sex registered relationships without pressure from the judiciary. From 1999 until 2005, the domestic partnership registry underwent constant amendment, revision and extension.[96]

The introduction of the California Domestic Partner Rights and Responsibilities Act of 2003 (or Assembly Bill 205) signalled a major shift in the legislature's approach to domestic partnerships. Although basic eligibility remained unaltered, the previous approach of enumerated rights was replaced by the wholesale presumption that domestic partners were to have all of the rights and responsibilities afforded to spouses under state law. Although certain exceptions were carved out, mainly regarding the creation and dissolution of domestic partnerships and certain tax issues, the presumption was a substantial step forward in the fight for the full legal equality of same-sex couples. Since the legislation dramatically changed the circumstances of existing domestic partnerships, the legislature directed the Secretary of State to inform all previously registered domestic partnerships of the changes and delayed the effect of the law for an additional year, until 1st January 2005.[97] Governor Davis signed the bill into law on 19th September 2003.[98]

(A.B. 1059 by Governor Wilson and S.B. 75 by Governor Davis).

95 This restriction was late relaxed so that either party had to have reached the age of 62, 2001 Cal. Stat. 893, sec. 3.

96 Cal. A.B. 25, 2001 Cal. Stat. 893 (extension of right and duties of domestic partners), Cal. A.B. 2216, 2001 Cal. Stat. 447 (intestate succession rights), Cal. S.B. 1049, 2001 Cal. Stat. 146 (survivor benefits for San Mateo), Cal. A.B. 2777, 2002 Cal. Stat. 373 (survivor benefits for the counties of Los Angeles, Santa Barbara and Marin), Cal. S.B. 1575, 2002 Cal. Stat. 412 (voiding wills in cases where domestic partners have assisted in drafting the will), Cal. S.B. 1661, 200, Cal. Stat. 901 (temporary disability).

97 For the text of the letter issued to all existing domestic partners, see Cal. Fam. Code § 299.3.

98 Again, this piece of legislation has also been substantially amended by virtue of Cal. A.B. 2208, 2004 Cal. Stat. 488 (clarifying health and disability insurance extension to domestic partners), Cal. S.B. 565, 2005 Cal. Stat. 416 (transfer of property without tax), Cal. S.B. 973, 2005 Cal. Stat. 418 (pension benefits), Cal. S.B. 1827, 2006 Cal. Stat. 802 (obligation to submit joint state tax returns), Cal. A.B. 2051, 2006 Cal. Stat. 856 ($23 domestic funding increase in registration fee), A.B. 102, 2007 Cal. Stat. 567 (possibility to change surname).

3.2.1.1. Establishment

Although the rights and duties attached to the status of domestic partner have since been extended, the conditions which need to be met before a domestic partnership can be registered have remained virtually unchanged since their enactment. Accordingly, two adults who have 'chosen to share one another's lives in an intimate and committed relationship of mutual caring' are permitted to register as domestic partners if they satisfy a number of procedural conditions.[99] Only two persons may be involved in one registered relationship (either a marriage or domestic partnership) at any one time, and may not be related to each other by blood in a way that would prevent them from being married to each other in the state of California.[100] Both persons, who must be over the age of eighteen, may either be (a) of the same-sex or (b) be of opposite-sex as long as one of the parties is over the age of 62 and either one of them meet the eligibility criteria under Title II, 42 U.S.C. §402(a) with regards old age benefits, or Title XVI, 42 U.S.C. §1381 with regards aged individuals.[101]

It is also a condition of the domestic partnership legislation that the parties have a common residence. Although §297(c) provides further clarification of the exact meaning of the term 'common residence', no geographical location is provided for this common residence, thus permitting out-of-state residents sharing the same residence to register a domestic partnership in California. The domestic partnership is established when both persons file a declaration of domestic partnership with the Secretary of State and the appropriate fee is paid.[102] After the form has been filed, the couple receives a copy of the form, a certificate of registration of domestic partnership, as well as a brochure entitled 'Your future together'.[103]

3.2.1.2. Rights and duties

According to §297.5, 'registered domestic partners shall have the same rights, protections, and benefits, and shall be subject to the same responsibilities, obligations, and duties under law, whether they derive from statutes, administrative regulations, court rules, government policies, common law, or any other provisions or sources of law, as are granted to and imposed upon spouses'. This there-

---

99 Cal. Fam. Code § 297(a).

100 Cal. Fam. Code § 297(b)(2) and § 297(b)(3).

101 Cal. Fam. Code § 297(b)(4) and § 297(b)(5).

102 Cal. Fam. Code § 298.5. At present the fee is set at $10, although same-sex partners must pay an extra $23. The additional $23 fee is used to develop and support a training curriculum specific to lesbian, gay, bisexual, and transgender domestic abuse support service providers, and to provide brochures specific to lesbian, gay, bisexual, and transgender domestic abuse.

103 For more information, see http://www.sos.ca.gov/dpregistry/index.htm.

fore ensures total parity between same-sex domestic partners and opposite-sex married couples. As a result domestic partners are also granted the same rights as spouses with regards, *inter alia*, rights and duties of spouses during the relationship, including the marital community of property and inheritance provisions,[104] adoption,[105] domestic violence,[106] and ex-spousal alimony.[107] Although until February 2008, with regards state tax returns, domestic partners had to use the same status as they use for their federal tax returns, *i.e.* unmarried,[108] this has since been amended.[109] As a result domestic partners are now permitted to file joint state tax returns. Accordingly, California now recognises domestic partners as functionally *identical* to spouses, in *everything* apart from name (as of course federal benefits).

3.2.1.3. Termination[110]

A domestic partnership may be terminated in one of two ways. Firstly, if specific requirements are met, a domestic partnership may be terminated by filing a Notice of Termination with the California Secretary of State. In order to qualify, all of the following requirements must be met:

- both parties have lived in California for six months prior to filing;
- the domestic partnership has lasted less than 5 years;
- no children were born prior or during the domestic partnership;
- no children were adopted during the domestic partnership;
- neither partner is pregnant;
- neither partner has any interest in real estate;
- neither partner is renting any land or building;
- except for automobile loans, the community obligations do not exceed $5,000;
- except for automobiles, the community property is worth less than $33,000;
- except for automobiles, neither partner has separate property totaling more than $33,000; and

---

104 Cal. Fam. Code, Division 4.

105 Cal. Fam. Code, Division 13. See also Cal. Fam. Code § 297.5(e).

106 Cal. Fam. Code, Division 10.

107 Cal. Fam. Code, Division 9.

108 Cal. Fam. Code § 297.5(g).

109 Cal. S.B. 1827, Cal. Stat. 802.

110 This article will not deal with conversion of 'old-style' Californian domestic partnerships into 'new-style' domestic partnerships, as provided for in Cal. Fam. Code § 299.3. According to the old-style domestic partnership legislation, a domestic partnership could be terminated by sending ones partner a notice (by registered mail) terminating the domestic partnership, or if either party subsequently married, or if the parties ceased to share a common residence. Since the 1st January 2005, these termination procedures have been repealed.

- both parties agree to waive may rights with regards support from the other partner, except insofar as it is included in the property settlement agreement dividing the community property and community obligations.[111]

If any of these conditions are not met, then either partner must initiate dissolution proceedings in the Superior Court.[112] These dissolution procedures are identical to the corresponding divorce proceedings. According to current Californian divorce law, a divorce may be granted if the parties have pleaded irreconcilable differences that have led to the irremediable breakdown of the marriage or that one of the parties is incurably insane.[113]

3.2.2. *Maine*

The 121st Maine Legislature passed Bill Number 1579, a domestic partner bill, in April 2004. This measure passed the House on 12th April 2004 with an 84 to 58 vote and the Senate on 27th April 2004 with an 18 to 14 vote. On 28th April 2004, Governor Baldacci signed law into effect; the law went into effect on 30th July 2004.

3.2.2.1. Establishment

Any mentally competent adult who satisfies the conditions laid down in §2710, Title 22, Maine Statutes may enter into a domestic partnership with one other person. Accordingly, neither partner may already be involved in a registered domestic partnership with anyone else or married to anyone else.[114] Furthermore, Maine imposes a 12-month residency requirement prior to the filing application. Through use of the word 'domiciled together' it is suggested that this 12-month period must be by virtue of a shared residence.[115] Although Title 22, Maine Statutes does not specify the age that someone must have attained in order to register a domestic partnership, use of the term 'adult' would tend to suggest that both parties must have attained the age of 18.[116] The domestic partnership register in Maine is unique in the U.S. in that it open to both same-sex and opposite-sex couples on an equal basis.

111 Cal. Fam. Code § 299(a).

112 Cal. Fam. Code § 299(d). The only distinction is that neither party need be a resident of or domiciled in California in order to file for dissolution of a domestic partnership, *i.e.* Cal. Fam. Code § 2320 does not apply to the dissolution of a domestic partnership.

113 Cal. Fam. Code § 2310.

114 Me. Rev. Stat. Ann. Tit. 22, § 2710.2.C and § 2710.2.D.

115 Me. Rev. Stat. Ann. Tit. 22, § 2710.2.B. This is further supported with reference to the 'common residence' in § 2710.3.

116 In accordance with Me. Rev. Stat. Ann. Tit. 19-A, § 101.1: '"Adult" means a person who is 18 years of age or older'. Although this provisions is restricted in its interpretation to Title 19-A, there is no reason to assume that the General Assembly had any other intention when using the word 'adult' with respect to the domestic partnership registry.

Registration of the partnership entails that the partners jointly file a declaration of domestic partnership with the Office of Vital Statistics, accompanied by the required filing fee (currently set at $35). The declaration must be under oath and their signatures must be notarised prior to filing the declaration. No ceremony is permitted. Once the registry has received the declarations they will be filed, with two copies returned to the parties at their common residence.[117]

3.2.2.2. Rights and duties

The aim of the 'Act to promote the financial security of Maine's families and children' was not the equalisation of the position of same-sex and opposite-sex couples. Instead the Act aimed to extend a limited number of rights, which were at that time restricted to opposite-sex married couples, to other couples that had evidenced 'a commitment to remain responsible indefinitely for each other's welfare'.[118] As a result, the Act only affected rights in the field of inheritance and medical decision-making. Accordingly, if a domestic partner dies without a will, trust, or other estate plan, the surviving domestic partner shall inherit the deceased partner's property in the same manner as a surviving spouse.[119] A domestic partner will, furthermore, also be considered the first next of kin, in the same manner as a spouse is the first next of kin, when determining who has the right to make funeral and burial arrangements.[120]

3.2.2.3. Termination

A domestic partnership is terminated if:

- either domestic partner gets married;[121]
- a notice of termination is filed indicating each partner's consent to the termination. This declaration must be signed by both domestic partners in the presence of a notary;[122] or

117 Me. Rev. Stat. Ann. Tit. 22, § 2710.3.

118 2003 Me. Laws 672, sec. 2 and 17.

119 Me. Rev. Stat. Ann. Tit 18-A, § 1-201.17, § 2-102. This means that a surviving domestic partner would inherit the entire estate, half the estate plus $50,000, or half the estate, depending on whether the deceased domestic partner has surviving children or parents.

120 Me. Rev. Stat. Ann. Tit. 22, § 2843-A.1.D. If parties neglected to register with the state but can show that they meet the definition of domestic partners in § 2710, this right will also be extended to them. This does not, however, extend to intestacy rights.

121 Me. Rev. Stat. Ann. Tit. 22, § 2710.4. It is not expressly stated that the partners must marry a third person. It is therefore to be expected that should an opposite-sex couple subsequently marry each other, this marriage will automatically terminate their domestic partnership.

122 Me. Rev. Stat. Ann. Tit. 22, § 2710.4.A.

- a notice under oath from either domestic partner that the other domestic partner was directly given a notice of intent to terminate the partnership. If giving notice by hand is not feasible, then a different way of giving notice may be accomplished as provided by the Maine Rules of Civil Procedure for commencement of a civil action. Termination under this method is not effective until 60 days after the notice has been given.[123]

3.2.3. *New Jersey*

Prior to the introduction of civil unions (see §5.3), domestic partnership was the only way option for same-sex couples wishing to have their relationship publicly recognised.[124] As of the 19th February 2007, this is no longer the case. Since this date, domestic partnerships are only allowed to be registered if both parties to the domestic partnership have attained the age of 62. Nonetheless, all those domestic partnerships entered into between 10th July 2004 and the 19th February 2007 remain unaltered with regards to the rights and responsibilities of domestic partnerships. All those domestic partners eligible to convert their domestic partnership into a civil union were given notice of this possibility prior to the entry into force of the civil union legislation. As a result of these legislative changes, domestic partnerships in New Jersey will remain outside the scope of this article.

3.2.4. *Oregon*

On the 8th July 2005, the Oregon Senate approved legislation to allow same-sex civil unions. As originally written, Senate Bill 1073 would have created civil unions and prohibited discrimination based on sexual orientation. However, on the 21st July, the House performed a series of moves aimed at torpedoing the bill, removing most of its language. Instead of containing anti-discrimination provisions and reference to civil unions, the bill referred to the state constitutional amendment and proposed to create a system of reciprocal benefits. The changes effectively killed momentum to pass the bill, which died in committee.

However, after the November 2006 mid-term elections Democrats won a majority of the formerly Republican-controlled house and in early 2007, Democrats re-introduced a bill in the House similar to original 2005 civil union legislation. The bill adopted the term 'domestic partnership' to describe these unions. This bill enjoyed a relatively easy passage through the legislature and passed the house on the 17th April 2007 (by a vote of 34–26) and the Senate on the 2nd May 2007 (by a vote of 21–9). Governor Kulongiski signed the Oregon Family Fairness

123 Me. Rev. Stat. Ann. Tit. 22, § 2710.4.B.

124 2003 N.J. Laws 246, 'An act establishing the rights and responsibilities of domestic partners, and revising parts of the statutory law'.

Acton the 9th May 2007. The law was scheduled to take effect on the 1st January 2008, but was delayed by a preliminary injunction. The injunction was finally lifted and the law came into force on the 1st February 2008. The first domestic partnerships took place on the 4th February 2008.

3.2.4.1. Establishment

Although a marriage in Oregon can be celebrated as soon as a person attains the age of 17,[125] a domestic partnership may only be concluded between parties both of whom who have reached the age of 18.[126] Furthermore, domestic partnership is only open to same-sex couples, one of whom must be resident in Oregon.[127] The prohibited degrees of relationship are, however, identical to those applicable to aspirant married couples.[128] Furthermore both facets of the principle of exclusivity are adhered to, namely that only two people may conclude a domestic partnership, and neither party may already be involved in a marriage, nor another domestic partnership.[129]

Two individuals wishing to become partners in a domestic partnership must complete and file a declaration of domestic partnership with the county clerk. In county clerk registers the declarations and returns a copy of the registered form, as well as a certificate of registered domestic partnership to the partners.[130] Signatures must be witnessed by a notary public.[131] The fee required varies per county, but is normally between $40-$50).

3.2.4.2. Rights and duties

According to sec. 9, 'Any privilege, immunity, right or benefit granted by statute, administrative or court rule, policy, common law or any other law to an individual because the individual is or was married, or because the individual is or was an in-law in a specified way to another individual, is granted on equivalent terms, substantive and procedural, to an individual because the individual is or was in a domestic partnership or because the individual is or was, based on a domestic partnership, related in a specified way to another individual.' As a result domestic

125 Or. Rev. Stat. § 106.010.
126 2007 Or. Laws § 99 sec. 3. The Act was also entitled the 'Oregon Family Fairness Act'.
127 2007 Or. Laws § 99 sec. 3(1).
128 Compare Or. Rev. Stat. § 106.020(b) and 2007 Or. Laws § 99 sec. 4(b).
129 Compare Or. Rev. Stat. § 106.020(a) and 2007 Or. Laws § 99 sec. 4(a).
130 Sec. 6(1) and 6(2), 2007 Act.
131 Sec. 6(5)(f), 2007 Act.

partners and spouses have been placed on an identical footing as regards the rights and duties incumbent on the parties to such relationships.[132]

3.2.4.3. Termination

If the domestic partnership was solemnized in Oregon and either party is a resident of or domiciled in Oregon at the time the suit is commenced, a suit for its annulment or dissolution may be maintained where the ground alleged is one set forth in §106.020 or §107.015.[133] When the civil union was not solemnized in Oregon or when any ground other than set forth in §106.020 or §107.015 is alleged, at least one party must be a resident of or be domiciled in Oregon at the time the suit is commenced and continuously for a period of six months prior thereto. In turn this means that civil unions will need to be dissolved when 'irreconcible differences have led to the irremediable breakdown of the marriage'.[134]

3.2.5. Washington

As already stated above, although Washington has not passed a constitutional amendment, the statutory definition of marriage has been amended so as to restrict it to marriages between opposite-sex couples. Furthermore, shortly after the Washington Supreme Court upheld the validity of this ban, two bills were submitted to the Washington Senate. The first would have opened up marriage to same-sex couples (and thus overturned the ban on same-sex marriage),[135] whilst the other bill aspired to introduce a domestic partnership registry.[136] The bill aimed at opening marriage to same-sex couples died in committee, whilst the domestic partnership bill received warm support in both the House (28 votes to 19) and the Senate (63 votes to 35). The Bill was eventually passed by the Senate on the 1st March 2007 and by the House on the 10th April 2007. Governor Gregoire signed the bill into law on the 21st April 2007, and the law entered into force on the 22nd July 2007, making Washington the fourth state to introduce a state-wide domestic partnership registry scheme.[137]

---

132 This extension of rights and benefits is, however limited to those rights and benefits extended at state level: sec. 9(5), 2007 Act.

133 Or. Rev. Stat. § 107.075(1) and (2).

134 Or. Rev. Stat. § 107.025(1). As a result of § 107.036, the doctrine of fault has been abolished in Oregon divorce law, expect for particular circumstances.

135 Wash. S. 5335, 60th Congr., 1st Sess. (2007), entitled Addressing Civil Marriage Equality.

136 Wash. S. 5336, 60th Congr., 1st Sess (2007), entitled Protecting individuals in domestic partnerships by granting certain rights and benefits.

137 2007 Wash. Laws 156.

In enacting this legislation, the legislature identified two separate groups that would be served by the legislation,

> 'The legislature finds that same sex couples, because they cannot marry in this state, do not automatically have the same access that married couples have to certain rights and benefits, such as those associated with hospital visitation, health care decision-making, organ donation decisions, and other issues related to illness, incapacity, and death. Although many of these rights and benefits may be secured by private agreement, doing so often is costly and complex.
> The legislature also finds that the public interest would be served by extending rights and benefits to different sex couples in which either or both of the partners is at least sixty-two years of age. While these couples are entitled to marry under the state's marriage statutes, some social security and pension laws nevertheless make it impractical for these couples to marry. For this reason, Chapter 156, Laws of 2007 specifically allows couples to enter into a state registered domestic partnership if one of the persons is at least sixty-two years of age, the age at which many people choose to retire and are eligible to begin collecting social security and pension benefits.'[138]

3.2.5.1. Establishment

The principle of exclusivity is also upheld in Washington's registration scheme, since the scheme is restricted to two persons of whom neither is married to someone other than the party to the domestic partnership and neither person is in a state registered domestic partnership with another person.[139] Although at first glance the phrase 'neither person is married to someone other than the party to the domestic partnership' would appear straight forward, a certain element of ambiguity does arise since the domestic partnership scheme in Washington is not only open to same-sex couples, but also to opposite-sex couples if either one of the parties is over the age of 62.[140] Read together, these provisions mean that married opposite-sex couples over the age of 62 are permitted to enter into a domestic partnership, despite the fact that they are already married to each other. Although there would be no advantage from doing so, it is strange that the legislature has not prevented this possibility.

Although the parties must also share a common residence, the geographical location of this residence does not have to be in Washington State. A couple living together in Oregon or Idaho are thus permitted to enter into a domestic partnership in Washington, subject to fulfilling all the other requirements. Furthermore, neither party may be a sibling, child, grandchild, aunt, uncle, niece, or nephew to the other person, nor may either person be nearer of kin to each other than sec-

138 Rev. Code Wash. § 26.60.010.
139 Rev. Code Wash. § 26.60.030(2) and § 26.60.030(3).
140 Rev. Code Wash. § 26.60.030(6).

ond cousins, whether of half or whole blood.[141]If all the abovementioned conditions are satisfied, the parties may file a signed, notarised declaration to the Secretary of State.[142] Once the declaration has been received, verified and a fee paid (currently set at $50),[143] the document is subsequently registered and a certificate of state registered domestic partnership is issued to each party.[144]

3.2.5.2. Rights and duties

Although the enumeration method has been used to ascribe rights to the Washingtonian domestic partners, the rights are all contained in Chapter 156, Laws of 2007. The rights and duties extended to domestic partners are:

- the extension of all employee benefits by virtue of the relationship,[145] including health care, life insurance, liability insurance, accidental death and dismemberment insurance, and disability income insurance;[146]
- the ability to grant informed consent for health care for a patient who is not competent;[147]
- the ability to be able to speak with health care providers who will now be able to disclose information about the other partner without that partner's authorisation;[148]
- a surviving domestic partner may bring a wrongful death action based on the death of the other partner;[149]
- title and rights to cemetery plots and rights of internment;[150]
- the ability to authorise autopsies and request copies of autopsy reports and records;[151]
- the right to control the disposition of the remains of a deceased partner;[152]
- the ability to consent to the removal of human remains from a cemetery plot;[153]

141 Rev. Code Wash. § 26.60.030(5).
142 Rev. Code Wash. § 26.60.040(1).
143 Rev. Code Wash. § 26.60.040(4).
144 Rev. Code Wash. § 26.60.040(2).
145 Rev. Code Wash. § 41.05.
146 Rev. Code Wash. § 41.05.065 and 2006 Wash. Laws 299, § 2.
147 Rev. Code Wash. § 7.70.065 and 2006 Wash. Laws 93, § 1.
148 Rev. Code Wash. § 70.02.050 and 2006 Wash. Laws 235, § 3.
149 Rev. Code Wash. § 4.20.020 and 1985 Wash. Laws 139, § 1, as well as Rev. Code Wash. § 4.20.060 and 1985 Wash. Laws 139, § 2.
150 For example, Rev. Code Wash. § 68.32.020, 68.32.040, § 68.32.060 and § 68.32.110 and 2005 Wash. Laws 365, § 92, § 94 and § 96.
151 Rev. Code Wash. § 68.50.100 and 2003 Wash. Laws 53, § 307, as well Rev. Code Wash. 68.50.101 and 1987 Wash. Laws 331, § 57.
152 Rev. Code Wash. § 68.50.160 and 2005 Wash. Laws 365, § 141.
153 Rev. Code Wash. § 68.50.200 and 2005 Wash. Laws 365, § 144.

- the ability to make anatomical gifts;[154]
- extension of intestate succession law when the domestic partner dies without a will;[155] and
- administration of an estate if the domestic partner died without a will or if the representative named in the will declines or is unable to serve.[156]

As a result, no rights are granted to domestic partners with respect to children rights,[157] domestic violence,[158] property relationships,[159] or maintenance (alimony).[160] However, these rights and duties have since been extended in 2008. Accordingly, approximately one third of all rights and duties attributed to married couples have been extended to domestic partners.[161]

3.2.5.3. Termination

A domestic partner may terminate the relationship by filing a notice of termination with the Secretary of State, coupled with the appropriate fee (currently set at $50). The notice must contain the notarised signature of one or both parties. If the form is, however, only signed by one party the party seeking termination must also file an affidavit with the Secretary stating that (a) the other party has been served in writing in the manner prescribed for the service of summons in a civil action, or (b) that the party seeking termination has not been able to find the other party after 'reasonable effort'.[162] If either of these methods for terminating a domestic partnership is used, the termination is deemed to be effective ninety days after the filing of the notice of termination and payment of the relevant fee.[163] A domestic partnership is also brought to an immediate end by the subsequent marriage of either party either with each other or with another person.[164]

---

154 Rev. Code Wash. § 68.50.550 and 1993 Wash. Laws 228, § 4.

155 Rev. Code Wash. § 11.04.015 and 1974 Wash. Laws (old) 117, § 6.

156 Rev. Code Wash. § 11.28.120 and 1995 Wash Laws (1st Supp.) 18, § 61.

157 For example, no extension of the uniform parentage act provisions to domestic partners: Rev. Code Wash. § 26.26.011 *et. seq.*

158 Although domestic partners benefit from the protection of the domestic violence protection by virtue of their shared residence, they are not explicitly mentioned as a group deserving of protection in the statutes: Rev. Code Wash. § 26.50.010.

159 Washington is one of the states to operate a matrimonial 'community of property' system: see Rev. Code Wash. § 26.16.030. This marital community is not applicable to domestic partners, unless they contract otherwise.

160 No extension of the rights listed in Rev. Code Wash. § 26.09.090.

161 2008 Wash. Laws 6.

162 Rev. Code. Wash. § 26.60.050(1)(a).

163 Rev. Code. Wash. § 26.60.050(2).

164 Rev. Code. Wash. § 26.60.050(4.

3.2.6. *District of Columbia*

Although the federal District of Columbia has recognised domestic partnerships since 11th June 1992, the scheme was not properly funded by Congress until the fiscal year 2002.[165] The original Act, entitled the *Health Care Benefits Expansion Act of 1992*,[166] authorised the Director of the Department of Health to amend Title 29 of the District of Columbia Municipal Regulations. As a result, the Director inserted a new Chapter 80 into the rules and thereby created the domestic partnership registry in the District of Columbia. Subsequent amendment to the provisions came in the form of the Domestic Partnership Equality Amendment Act of 2006, which came into effect on 4th April 2006.[167] In effect, this Act guarantees that in almost all cases a domestic partner will have the same rights as a spouse.[168]

3.2.6.1. Establishment

Unlike many of the other domestic partnership schemes, the institution created in District of Columbia is open to both same-sex and opposite-sex couples. Furthermore, domestic partnerships are also permitted between people who are related by blood (*e.g.*, siblings or a parent and adult child, provided both were single).[169] Nonetheless, the principle of exclusivity is still adhered to, both in terms of the prohibition on multiple simultaneous formal relationships, as well as with respect to the 'two persons' requirement.[170] The parties, both of whom must be over the age of 18, must also share a common residence.[171] The exact geographical location is not further specified, thus permitting out-of-state residents to register their partnership in the District of Columbia.[172]

---

165 Mayor's Order 2002-56, dated 4th March 2002.

166 D.C. Law 9-114.

167 D.C. Law 16-79.

168 See § 3.2.6.2.

169 The restrictions laid down in D.C. Mun. Regs. Tit. 29, § 8001.2 do not mention any restriction with regards the prohibited degrees of marriage.

170 D.C. Mun. Regs. Tit. 29, § 8001.2(b) and § 8001.2(d).

171 A number of evidential tools are nonetheless provided aimed at assisting the Registrars task of determining whether parties have a shared residence: D.C. Mun. Regs. Tit. 29, § 8004.1, namely (a) a current lease or rental agreement for residential property that names both applicants as occupants of the premises named in the lease or rental agreement; (b) a mortgage for residential property that names both applicants as mortgagors; (c) a deed for residential property that states that both applicants share title to the premises named in the deed; (d) utility bills for residential property that name both persons as being responsible for payment of the utility fees for the same address; or (e) an affidavit executed within the previous six months in which the parties each state under penalty of perjury that both domestic partners share the same residence.

172 D.C. Mun. Regs. Tit. 29, § 8001.2(a) and (c).

To become domestic partners, the parties must appear in person, provide documentation to establish that they satisfy the registration requirements, submit a single application for registration, and pay the appropriate fee (currently set at $45).

3.2.6.2. Rights and duties

The domestic partnership laws as they applied up until the recent amendment provided couples registered as domestic partners the same rights as family members to visit their domestic partners in the hospital and to make decisions concerning the treatment of a domestic partner's remains after the partner's death. Registration also granted District of Columbia Government employees a number of benefits. Furthermore, domestic partners were eligible for health care insurance coverage, could use annual leave or unpaid leave for the birth or adoption of a dependent child or to care for a domestic partner or a partner's dependents, and could make funeral arrangements for a deceased partner. Although a number of legislative amendments were made to the rights and duties after the implementation of the law in 2002, the substantial package of rights and duties remained more-or-less unaltered until 2006.[173]

As a result of the 2006 amendment, the methodology and ideology behind the institution has made a paradigm shift. Instead of using the *enumeration method*, the District of Columbia legislature has moved to an *exclusion method*, whereby all the rights and duties applied to married couples are now *mutatis mutandis* applicable to domestic partners, unless otherwise provided. The new law equates the position of domestic partners and spouses in many areas including, *inter alia*, mortgages, intestate succession, child support and premarital agreements.

3.2.6.3. Termination

A domestic partnership may only be terminated automatically when:

- either domestic partner dies;[174]
- one of the domestic partners marries another person or the domestic partners marry one another;[175] or

---

173 These minor amendments include: D.C. Law 15-17 (effective 21st June 2003, with regards health care benefits), D.C. Law 15-176 (effective 8th September 2004, with regards domestic partners treated the same as spouses in relation to deed recordation tax), D.C. Law 15-307 (effective from 8th April 2005, with regards exemption from excise tax on transfer of title) and D.C. Law 15-309 (effective from 8th April 2005, with regards the definition of 'spouse' in the Human Rights Act 1997).

174 .C. Mun. Regs. Tit. 29, § 8002.1(a).

175 D.C. Mun. Regs. Tit. 29, § 8002.1(b).

- one of the domestic partner abandons the domestic partnership or the partner's mutual residence.[176]

Alternatively if the parties wish to terminate their partnership they may also file for termination, either jointly or separately.[177] If only one partner files for termination that partner must serve notice of his or her intent to terminate the partnership on the other domestic partner.[178] A termination of domestic partnership statement filed pursuant to §8002.3 will become effective six months after the date the statement is filed with the Registrar.[179]

3.3. CIVIL UNION

3.3.1. *Connecticut*

On the 1st October 2005, Connecticut became the third US State to introduce a registry for same-sex couples entitled the 'civil union registry'. Unlike its predecessors, New Jersey and Vermont, Connecticut's decision to introduce a civil union registry was neither pre-empted nor mandated by a judicial decision. Nonetheless, cases did appear before the judiciary in Connecticut claiming that the inability for same-sex couples to marry was unconstitutional.

Even since the enactment of the Act concerning Civil Unions, same-sex couples continue to fight for the right to marry.[180] For example, eight same-sex couples brought a legal action before the state's courts, challenging the state's alleged discriminatory exclusion of same-sex couples from the right to marry. On 12th July 2006 a Superior Court judge court ruled against them arguing that: 'Civil union and marriage in Connecticut now share the same benefits, protections and responsibilities under law (...) The Connecticut Constitution requires that there be equal protection and due process of law, not that there be equivalent nomenclature for such protection and process.' In concluding, the judge held that denying same-sex couples the right to marry did not violate Connecticut's Constitution. This decision has been appealed to the Supreme Court of Connecticut and arguments were heard on the 14th May 2007; the decision is still pending.

---

176 D.C. Mun. Regs. Tit. 29, § 8002.1(c), in conjunction with § 8002.2.

177 D.C. Mun. Regs. Tit. 29, § 8002.3.

178 D.C. Mun. Regs. Tit. 29, § 8002.3(a) and § 8002.3(b).

179 D.C. Mun. Regs. Tit. 29, § 8002.4.

180 In *Kerrigan* v. *State of Connecticut*, 49 Conn. Super. 644, 909 A.2d 89 (Ct. Super Ct. 2006), eight same-sex couples petitioner to the court to declare that the distinction between civil union and marriage violated the Connecticut Constitution. The Court held 'that the Connecticut Constitution required that there be equal protection and due process of law, not that there be equivalent nomenclature for such protection'.

Activity has also been evident in the Connecticut Legislature with a bill having been introduced to the House on the 31st January 2007 aimed at providing same-sex couples with full marriage rights.[181] Although the bill passed the judiciary committee, the bill was never submitted to the full House or Senate, more than likely because Governor Rell said that she would veto any move to pass same-sex marriage legislation.

3.3.1.1. Establishment

Any two 'eligible persons' may enter into a civil union in Connecticut. This means persons over the age of eighteen,[182] who are of the same-sex,[183] and neither party is already married or involved in a civil union.[184] Although perhaps verging on the bounds of this article,[185] problems have arisen as regards the extent to which out-of-state registered relationships will be recognised with respect to this provision. In an opinion on the 20th September 2005, the Attorney General of Connecticut stated that,

> '1. Couples with a Vermont civil union or a California domestic partnership will be treated in Connecticut in the same way as a couple with a Connecticut civil union, but cannot also enter into a Connecticut civil union;
> 2. Same-sex couples with an out-of-state marriage, e.g. from Massachusetts or Canada, can enter into a Connecticut civil union, but the state of Connecticut will not recognize their marriage as valid; and
> 3. Couples with a form of domestic partnership other than from California might or might not be able to enter into a Connecticut civil union depending upon a comparison of the specific provisions of the out-of-state domestic partnership law to Connecticut law.'[186]

Furthermore, according to §§46b-38bb, in conjunction with §§46b-38cc, kindred are prohibited to the virtually the same extent from entering into civil unions as they are prevented from marrying.[187] Similarly to marriage, Connecticut also has no residency requirement for entering into a civil union. In order to register a civil

---

181 Conn. H.B. 7395, January Session 2007.
182 Conn. Gen. Stat § 46b-38bb(3).
183 Conn. Gen. Stat, § 46b-38bb(2).
184 Conn. Gen. Stat, § 46b-38bb(1).
185 This article is predominantly focused upon the substantive law issues arising in this field and does not address the conflict of laws aspects (except in so far as dealt with in § 4).
186 Op. Conn. Att'y Gen (20th September 2005). See http://ct.gov/AG/cwp/view.asp?A=1770&Q=302438.
187 According to Conn. Gen. Stat. § 46b-21 prohibits marriages between a man and his stepdaughter or stepmother (and likewise for a woman and her stepson or stepfather). However, these prohibitions are not extended to civil unions, those permitting civil unions between a man and his stepson or stepfather and likewise a woman and her stepdaughter or stepmother.

union, both parties must appear and make an application before the registrar of the town in which either: (1) the civil union is to be celebrated, or (2) either person to be joined in the civil union resides.[188] However, it would seem that parties may appear before the registrar separately since the law provides that 'if the license is signed and sworn to by the applicants on different dates, the earlier date shall be deemed the date of application.' The statute also requires that the 'license shall be completed in its entirety, dated, signed and sworn to by each applicant and shall state each applicant's name, age, race, birthplace, residence, whether single, widowed or divorced and whether under the supervision or control of a conservator or guardian.'[189]

Once the application has been filed, the couple has 65 days to enter into a civil union. The same individuals authorised to legally join two people in marriage are authorized to join two people in a civil union.[190] This means that religious officials may also preside over civil unions. They may do so 'in any town in the state',[191] although not for non-resident couples, since these civil unions must be celebrated at the place where the licence was issued.

3.3.1.2. Rights and duties

According to §46b-38nn, 'parties to a civil union shall have all the same benefits, protections and responsibilities under law, whether derived from the general statutes, administrative regulations or court rules, policy, common law or any other source of civil law, as are granted to spouses in a marriage.' Accordingly now significant changes were necessary to Connecticut's statutes. From 1st October 2005, all those laws granting rights to 'spouses', 'husbands' and 'wives' were equally extended to those involved in civil unions.

3.3.1.3. Termination

No specific dissolution laws were passed alongside the civil unions registry. Instead, all laws and regulations regulating Connecticut divorce law are equally applicable to those involved in a civil union. This means that either party must (a) have been resident in the state for at least 12 months immediately preceding the date of the filing of the complaint, (b) one of the parties was domiciled in Connecticut at the time of the civil union and returned to Connecticut with the intention of permanently remaining before the filing of the complaint; or (c) the cause for the dissolution of the marriage arose after either party moved into this state.

188 Conn. Gen. Stat. §46b-38gg.
189 Conn. Gen. Stat. §46b-38hh.
190 Conn. Gen. Stat. §46b-38dd(a).
191 Conn. Gen. Stat. §46b-38dd(a).

The grounds for the dissolution are also identical to those applicable for divorce in the state. This includes both fault and no-fault grounds. Unlike New Hampshire, it would appear that Connecticut does not restrict adultery to heterosexual sexual intercourse.[192]

3.3.2. *New Hampshire*

New Hampshire became the fourth state to recognize civil unions when Governor Lynch signed the bill into law on 31st May 2007. The law has been effective since 1st January 2008. The law itself is one of the shortest of all the ten states to have enacted registration schemes for same-sex couples. The move to introduce civil unions came without any court order or even the existence of a marriage lawsuit.

3.3.2.1. Establishment

Although the age to register a civil union is not markedly different from other states, namely 18, it is different from the applicable age limits set for marriage in New Hampshire.[193] At present, males may marry, subject to parental permission, from the age of 14 and females from the age of 13.[194] Although as regards the prohibited degrees of marriage, the prohibitions are fundamentally identical, one unexplainable difference is apparent, namely that civil unions are expressly prohibited with one's grandparent, although this restriction does not apply to marriages in the State.[195]

There is no residency requirement for marriage in New Hampshire and, by clear implication, no residency requirement for a New Hampshire civil union. Although complexities could occur with respect to the residency requirements in New Hampshire,[196] first indications would seem to point to this provision

192 For example, see *Swanson* v. *Swanson*, 128 Conn. 128, 20 A.2d 617 (Conn. Super. Ct. 1941. See also Conn. Gen. Stat § 46b-40(f): 'adultery means voluntary sexual intercourse between a married person and a person other than such person's spouse'.

193 N.H. Rev. Stat. § 457-A:2–4.

194 N.H. Rev. Stat. § 457:4–7.

195 N.H. Rev. Stat. § 457-A:3–4, compared with § 457:1–2.

196 The complexity is created by a 1979 New Hampshire Act that provides that non-residents may not marry in New Hampshire, 'if such [a] marriage would be void if contracted in [their home state]': N.H. Rev. Stat. § 457:44. Although this statute speaks only of marriages, the civil union legislation states that 'parties entering into a civil union shall be subject to the same requirements and conditions as contained in N.H. Rev. Stat. § 457' which includes the abovementioned restriction: N.H. Rev. Stat, § 457-A:2. If one interprets this restriction as a 'requirement or condition', then the possibility exists that same-sex couples will not be able to enter into a civil union in New Hampshire, if they reside in a state that expressly provides that a civil union would be void in that state. At the same time, this type of restriction – which exists in only a handful of states – has often not been enforced and may not be enforced in New Hampshire.

currently not being interpreted so as to prevent out-of-state couples from registering a civil union in New Hampshire.[197] As regards the formal ceremonial aspects, exactly the same procedure is applicable to the formation and registration of a civil union as that used to solemnise a marriage.[198] The only difference being that a minister, clergyman or clergywoman is not obliged to perform a civil union.[199]

3.3.2.2. Rights and duties

According to N.H. Rev. Stat. §457-A:6 and notwithstanding any law to the contrary, 'the parties to a civil union will be granted all the rights and subject to all the obligations and responsibilities provided for in the state law that apply to parties' who are married.

3.3.2.3. Termination

New Hampshire has also opted to apply its divorce legislation *mutatis mutandis* to the dissolution of a civil union.[200] This means that the divorce grounds will need to be applied to the dissolution of a civil union, namely the general 'irreconcilable differences'[201] ground and the fault-based grounds listed in N.H. Rev. Stat. §458. Although there are obviously certain advantages to the simple corresponding application of the divorce provisions to the dissolution of a civil union, many of these grounds will need to be 'reinterpreted' by the courts. Take, for example, adultery. In a 2003 case, the Supreme Court of New Hampshire held that a homosexual relationship between a married person and another did not constitute adultery within the meaning of N.H. Rev. Stat §458:7, II.[202] As the law currently stands a civil union partner could therefore only obtain dissolution of the civil union if his or her partner had sexual intercourse with a person of the opposite-sex!

A further issue also arises with respect to dissolving a New Hampshire civil union. According to New Hampshire law, the courts will only have jurisdiction to dissolve a civil union or a marriage if (a) both the parties were domiciled in New Hampshire when the action was commenced, (b) the plaintiff was so domiciled and the defendant was personally served with process within the state or (c) the

---

197 http://www.concordmonitor.com/apps/pbcs.dll/article?AID=/20080112/FRONTPAGE/801120399.

198 N.H. Rev. Stat. § 457-A:5, compared with § 457:31 and § 5-C:41–61.

199 N.H. Rev. Stat. § 457-A:5, last sentence.

200 N.H. Rev. Stat. § 457-A:7, in conjunction with § 458.

201 N.H. Rev. Stat. § 458:7-a.

202 *In the Matter of David G. Blanchflower and Sian E. Blanchflower*, 150 N.H. 226, 834 A.2d. 1010 (N.H. 2003). Thank you to Dan Krislov, Small and Lyons, Attorneys-at-law, Nashua, New Hampshire, for the confirmation of this interpretation.

plaintiff was domiciled in the state for one year prior to the action being filed.[203] If one reads these requirements in conjunction with the lack of residency requirements for registration of a civil union, one will immediately see the problem; although out-of-state couples may register their civil union in New Hampshire, they will have to reside at least one year in New Hampshire to be able to dissolve it!

3.3.3. *New Jersey*

On 14th June 2005, the New Jersey Court of Appeal (2–1 decision) held in the case of *Lewis* v. *Harris* that excluding same-sex couples from the right to marry did not violate the New Jersey Constitution.[204] On 25th October 2006, the New Jersey Supreme Court overturned the Court of Appeal, holding that it was unconstitutional to deny same-sex couples the rights and benefits provided of marriage.[205] The court reserved the question of whether those rights and benefits must be called marriage and directed the legislature to provide either marriage or another form of relationship recognition. In December 2006, the New Jersey legislature passed a civil unions law, which took effect in February 2007.

3.3.3.1. Establishment

For two persons to establish a civil union, they must satisfy all of the following criteria:

- neither may be a party to another civil union, domestic partnership or marriage recognised in the state of New Jersey;
- noth parties must be of the same sex and therefore be excluded from the marriage laws of New Jersey;
- both parties must have attained the age of eighteen, except as provided for in Section 10.[206]

These conditions therefore ensure that both aspects of the exclusivity principle are adhered to. Furthermore, although these are the only eligibility criteria

203 N.H. Rev. Stat. § 458:5.

204 *Lewis* v. *Harris*, 378 Super 168, 875 A.2d 259 (N.J. App. Div. 2005). In 2005, the Tax Court of New Jersey also determined that a same-sex marriage validly concluded in Canada was not entitled to recognition in New Jersey.

205 *Lewis* v. *Harris*, 188 N.J. 415, 908 A.2d 196 (N.J. 2006). The Supreme Court afforded the legislature and the executive 180 days to enact statutory amendments to achieve parity between same-sex and opposite-sex couples. For a case revolving around the moment at which this party should be regarded as taking effect, see *Quarto* v. *Adams*, 395 N.J. Super 802, 929 A.2d 1111 (N.J. Super. Ct. 2007).

206 N.J. Rev. Stat. § 37:1–30.

specifically applicable to civil unions, the marriage provisions have also been amended. It is there that one finds reference to those relatives not entitled to register a civil union; the list is identical for both opposite-sex marriages and same-sex civil unions.[207]

With regards to the procedure, the marriage or civil union license must be obtained from the registrar in the New Jersey municipality in which either applicant resides. Since there are no residency requirements imposed on aspirant civil union partners, should out-of-state residents wish to celebrate a civil union, they must file the declaration with the municipality where they intend to celebrate their civil union. Once the forms have been submitted, the relevant fee (currently set at $28) has been paid and the licence has been issued, the civil union is deemed to come into existence.[208]

3.3.3.2. Rights and duties

On the basis of the decision in *Lewis* v. *Harris,* §37:1–31.4.a states that 'civil union couples shall have all of the same benefits, protections and responsibilities under law, whether they derive from statute, administrative or court rule, public policy, common law or any other source of civil law, as are granted to spouses in a marriage.' Although thereafter a number of rights and benefits are explicitly mentioned, these are not to be regarded as exclusive. Instead the New Jersey legislature has opted for the exclusionary method, whereby all rights granted to married couples are extended to those involved in a civil union, unless stated otherwise.[209]

3.3.3.3. Termination

According to §37:1–31(b), the 'dissolution of civil unions shall follow the same procedures and be subject to the same substantive rights and obligations that are involved in the dissolution of a marriage'. This therefore means that §2:34–2 will apply to the grounds upon which a civil union may be terminated in New Jersey. Adultery is also a ground for divorce in New Jersey. However, in *S.B.* v. *S.J.B.*, the Superior Court of New Jersey held that a homosexual relationship did constitute adultery for the purposes of construing the New Jersey divorce statutes.[210] It is therefore to be presumed that this will also apply equally to the dissolution of civil unions.

---

207 N.J. Rev. Stat. § 37:1–1.

208 For a list of those judges competent to hear the case § 37:1–13.

209 N.J. Rev. Stat. § 37:1–32.5.

210 *S.B.* v. *S.J.B.*, 259 N.J. Super. 151, 609 A.2d 124 (N.J. Super Ct. 1992).

Jurisdiction will be founded if either party was a bona fide resident of New Jersey both at the time the cause of action arose, as well as at the time of the commencement of the action. However, no action may be filed for any cause other than adultery, unless one of the parties has been a bona fide resident for the year preceding the commencement of the action.[211]

3.3.4. *Vermont*

On 20th December 1999, the Vermont Supreme Court held in *Baker* v. *State*[212] that refusing to provide committed same-sex partners with the benefits and privileges granted to married couples violated the Vermont Constitution's Common Benefits Clause. In response to the court's decision, the Vermont legislature enacted a law permitting same-sex couples to enter into civil unions. As a result, Vermont became the first state in the United States to enact a registration scheme akin to marriage specifically for the registration of same-sex couples.

3.3.4.1. Establishment

Vermont also adheres to both facets of the principles of exclusivity, ensuring that civil unions in the state are only possible between two persons who are not already involved in another civil union or marriage.[213] Both parties must be of the same-sex and must have attained the age of 18.[214] There are no residency requirements imposed on aspirant civil union partners.[215] Those prohibited from registering a civil union on the basis of their affinity or consanguinity are identical to those prohibited from entering into a marriage.[216]

3.3.4.2. Rights and duties

Despite the fact that Vermont has chosen to enumerate all those rights and duties which are extended to partners in a civil union,[217] it has actually extended all state benefits to such couples. The first paragraph of §1204 states that 'Parties to a civil union shall have all the same benefits, protections and responsibilities under law, whether they derive from statute, administrative or court rule, policy, common

211 N.J. Rev. Stat. § 2A:34-10.
212 170 Vt. 194, 744 A.2d. 864 (Vt. 1999).
213 15 Vt. Stat. Ann. § 1202(1).
214 15 Vt. Stat. Ann. § 1202(3), in conjunction with 18 Vt. Stat. Ann. § 5163(a).
215 18 Vt. Stat. Ann. § 5160(a): 'The license shall be issued by the clerk of the town where either party resides or, if *neither is a resident* of the state, by any town clerk in the state'. (emphasis added).
216 15 Vt. Stat. Ann § 1203(a) and (b), compared with 15. Vt. Stat. Ann. § 1 and § 2.
217 15 Vt. Stat. Ann. § 1204.

law, or any other source of civil law, as are granted to spouses in a marriage'. This catch-all provision would appear to negate the need to then continue to specify all the individual rights and duties incumbent on civil union partners.

3.3.4.3. Termination

Also as regards the dissolution of the relationship, Vermont applies the law applicable to married couples *mutatis mutandis* to civil unions. As a result those wishing to dissolve their civil union in Vermont will have to show evidence satisfying one of the divorce grounds in 15 Vt. Stat. Ann. §551. This list includes 'adultery', which in Vermont has not yet been defined as either including or excluding 'homosexual activity'.[218] As a result, it is unclear whether a same-sex civil union partner can rely on the 'adultery' ground if his or her partner has engaged in 'extra-civil-union sex' with someone of the same sex.

4. MARRIAGE

4.1. MASSACHUSETTS

> 'The question before us is whether, consistent with the Massachusetts Constitution, the Commonwealth may deny the protections, benefits, and obligations conferred by civil marriage to two individuals of the same sex who wish to marry. We conclude that it may not. The Massachusetts Constitution affirms the dignity and equality of all individuals. It forbids the creation of second-class citizens.'[219]

Against this background, the Supreme Judicial Court of Massachusetts went on to hand down its momentous decision in the 2003 case of *Goodridge* v. *Department of Public Health.*[220] Interpreting the legislature's intent using the plain meaning of the marriage licensing statutes, the court recognised 'the long-standing statutory understanding, derived from the common law, that 'marriage' means the lawful union of a woman and a man. But that history cannot and does not foreclose the constitutional question.'[221]

---

218 This despite that in other jurisdictions this has been restricted, *e.g. Cohen* v. *Cohen*, 200 Misc. 19, 103 N.Y.S.2d 426 (N.Y. Super Ct. 1951). The statutory definition of adultery was later expanded so as to include homosexual activity.

219 *Goodridge* v. *Department of Public Health*, 440 Mass. 309, 312 (Mass. 2003).

220 *Goodridge* v. *Department of Public Health*, 440 Mass. 309, 798 N.E.2d 941 (Mass. 2003). In a later opinion, the Supreme Judicial Court also held that in implementing this decision, the Massachusetts legislature could not suffice with introducing civil unions: *Opinions of the Justices to the Senate*, 440 Mass. 1201, 802 N.E.2d 565 (Mass. 2004).

221 *Ibid.* at 320.

After pointing out that 'civil marriage is an esteemed institution, and the decision whether and whom to marry is among life's momentous acts of self-definition',[222] the court sketched the most important of the tangible and intangible benefits associated with marriage. According to the state constitution 'both the equality and liberty [provisions] guarantee, [that the] regulatory authority must, at very least, serve a legitimate purpose in a rational way; a statute must bear a reasonable relation to a permissible legislative objective.'[223] The court concluded that the marriage ban does not meet even this lowest standard of constitutional review, so there is no need to consider whether the case merits a stricter judicial scrutiny.[224]

The Department of Public Health provided three rationales for the ban: '(1) providing a 'favorable setting for procreation'; (2) ensuring the optimal setting for child rearing, which the department defines as 'a two-parent family with one parent of each sex'; and (3) preserving scarce State and private financial resources.'[225]

Taking these in turn, the court first analysed that with the civil marriage laws, 'it is the exclusive and permanent commitment of the marriage partners to one another, not the begetting of children, that is the *sine qua non* of civil marriage.'[226] Subsequently, the court explained that although protecting the welfare of children is a paramount State policy, '[r]estricting marriage to opposite-sex couples (...) cannot plausibly further this policy' of creating an optimal setting for child rearing because, among many other stated reasons, '[t]he "best interests of the child" standard does not turn on a parent's sexual orientation or marital status.'[227] Indeed, the court finds that 'excluding same-sex couples from civil marriage will not make children of opposite-sex marriages more secure, but it does prevent children of same-sex couples from enjoying the immeasurable advantages that flow from the assurance of "a stable family structure in which children will be reared, educated, and socialized".' Finally, the court dismissed the logic behind the Department's third rationale stating that a ban on same-sex marriage bears no rational relationship to the goal of economy, stating that it ignores the reality of many same-sex couples, including the named plaintiffs, who have children and other dependents in their care.[228]

After recognising that the decision marked 'a significant change in the definition of marriage',[229] the court gave reassurance that the definitional change would

222 *Ibid.*
223 *Ibid.* at 329.
224 *Ibid.* at 331.
225 *Ibid.*
226 *Ibid.*
227 *Ibid.* at 334.
228 *Ibid.* at 335.
229 *Ibid.* at 337.

'not disturb the fundamental value of marriage'[230] in U.S. society. The court also rejected the argument that expanding civil marriage in Massachusetts would lead to interstate conflict. Just as Massachusetts won't dictate to other states how they should respond to this decision, 'neither should considerations of comity prevent us from according Massachusetts residents the full measure of protection available under the Massachusetts Constitution'.[231] In the end, the court construed 'civil marriage to mean the voluntary union of two persons as spouses, to the exclusion of all others.'[232] As regards all conditions with respect to the establishment of a same-sex marriage, the rights and duties incumbent of the couple and the method applicable termination procedures, no difference is discernible between same-sex and opposite-sex marriages. Nonetheless, one important distinction is worth noting, namely that of residency.

According to the Supreme Judicial Court of Massachusetts, three categories of states must be distinguished from each other when determining the residency requirements for entry into a same-sex marriage in Massachusetts.[233] The first category of states are those states whose marriage licencing laws say that a marriage entered into by a same-sex couples at home would be void.[234] Any same-sex marriage celebrated by a resident from one of these states will be void in Massachusetts. The second category includes those states referred to as 'prohibited home states'. In these states, marriage licencing laws prohibit same-sex couples from marrying, but do not go so far as to declare such marriages to be 'void'.[235] Any same-sex marriage celebrated by a resident from one of these states will be voidable in Massachusetts. According to *Cote-Whitacre* v. *Department of Health*, same-sex couples who live in states from either of these two categories will not be permitted to marry in Massachusetts, unless they indicate an intent to reside in Massachusetts after marrying.[236] The third category includes those states whose marriage licencing laws are 'silent or ambiguous' on the question of marriage

---

230 *Ibid.*

231 *Ibid.* at 340.

232 *Ibid.* at 343. The dissent in the case rests on a standard, plain meaning analysis (*ibid.* at 351): 'The power to regulate marriage lies with the Legislature, not with the judiciary.'.

233 *Cote-Whitacre* v. *Department of Health*, 446 Mass. 350, 844 N.E.2d 623 (Mass. 2006).

234 Although the Supreme Judicial Court only dealt with one State, namely Maine, it is more than likely that 15 states satisfy this definition, namely Arizona, Arkansas, Delaware, Indiana, Kansas, Kentucky, Minnesota, Mississippi, Montana, Ohio, South Carolina, Tennessee, Texas and Utah.

235 Although the Supreme Judicial Court only deals with Connecticut, Vermont and New Hampshire, it is more than likely that 32 states satisfy this definition, namely Alabama, Alaska, California, Colorado, District of Columbia, Florida, Georgia, Hawai'i, Idaho, Illinois, Iowa, Louisiana, Maryland, Michigan, Missouri, Nebraska, Nevada, New Jersey, New York (from 6th July 2006 onwards), North Carolina, North Dakota, Oklahoma, Oregon, Pennsylvania, South Dakota, Virginia, Washington, West Virginia, Wisconsin and Wyoming.

236 *Cote-Whitacre* v. *Department of Health*, 446 Mass. 350, 359–361 (void home states) and 361–364 (prohibited home states).

because they do not expressly allow or expressly prohibit same-sex couples from marrying there. Thus far, it has been determined that Rhode Island does not prohibit same-sex marriages and that New York did not prohibit such marriages until the 6th July 2006.[237] In July 2007, the Massachusetts Department of Public Health also determined that New Mexico fits this definition.[238]

4.2. CALIFORNIA

On the 15th May 2008 the Californian Supreme Court finally gave its decision in the *In re Marriage Cases*. This case was a consolidated appeal of no fewer than six individual cases.[239] The main legal question put before the Supreme Court was whether it was unconstitutional to differentiate the formalised union of a different-sex couple, regarding this as a 'marriage' and the formalised union of a same-sex couple, regarding this as a 'domestic partnership'.[240] Although the Court acknowledged that there were indeed still minor differences between marriage, on the one hand, and domestic partnership, on the other,[241] it found that these two institutions existed as functional equivalents of each other.[242]

In answering this question the Court needed to determine the nature and scope of the right to marry. Referring to previous decisions of the Court,[243] the

237 *Cote-Whitacre* v. *Department of Health*, Case No. 04–2656, 2006 Mass. Super. Lexis 670 (Mass. Super Ct. 2007). This is a result of the decision of the New York Court of Appeals in *Hernandez* v. *Robles*, *supra*.

238 See http://www.mass.gov/Eeohhs2/docs/dph/vital_records/impediment.pdf.

239 *City and County of San Francisco* v. *State of California* (A110449 [Super. Ct. S.F. City & County, No. CGC-04–429539]); *Tyler* v. *State of California* (A110450 [Super. Ct. L.A. County, No. BS-088506]); *Woo* v. *Lockyer* (A110451 [Super. Ct. S.F. City & County, No. CPF-04–504038]); *Clinton* v. *State of California* (A110463 [Super. Ct. S.F. City & County, No. CGC-04–429548]); *Proposition 22 Legal Defense and Education Fund* v. *City and Council of San Francisco* (A110651 [Super. Ct. S.F. City & Council, No. CPF-04–503943]); *Campaign for California Families* v. *Newsom* (A110652 [Super. Ct. S.F. City & County, No. CGC-04–428794]).

240 *In re Marriage Cases*, No. S14799 (Cal. May 15, 2008).

241 Nine differences have been identified: (1) common residence requirement for domestic partners, not applicable to spouses, (2) application for lifting of the minimum age requirement not possible for domestic partners, (3) to register a domestic partnership the couple must file a declaration with the Secretary of State, whilst spouses must obtain a marriage licence from the county clerk, (4) possibility for confidential marriage in which marriage certificate and date of the marriage are not made public, not applicable to domestic partners, (5) summary dissolution for domestic partnership initiated by filing joint notice of termination with Secretary of State, for summary dissolution of a marriage is petitioned to the superior court, (6) residency requirements for dissolution are different providing for a *forum necessitates* for domestic partners, (7) differences with respect to the State Public Employee's Retirement System, (8) difference in interpretation with regards the property tax exemption for unmarried spouse of a veteran and (9) putative spouse doctrine does not apply to domestic partners.

242 *In re Marriage Cases*, No. S14799 (Cal. May 15, 2008), p. 45.

243 *In re Marriage Cases*, No. S14799 (Cal. May 15, 2008), pp. 49–51.

Supreme Court held that the right to marry is a fundamental constitutional right embodied in the Californian Constitution; a right that has over the decades changed with regards to its scope.[244] The Court, referring to *Perez*, noted that the examination of the right to marry must focus on 'the nature and substance of the interests' and explicitly referred to the repeated recognition that the right to marry represents 'the right of an individual to establish a legally recognised family with the person of one's choice, and, as such, is of fundamental significance both to society and to the individual'.[245] However, the Court also recognised that the role of civil marriage is not only to serve the interests of society. Instead, it recognised that the right to marry is a basic, constitutionally protected right, a fundamental right of all free men and women.

On this basis the Court found that the right to marry is an integral component of an individual's *personal autonomy* interest protected by the *privacy* provision of Article I, Section 1 and an individual's *liberty interest* protected by the *due process* clause of Article I, Section 7. Although the Court acknowledges that state marriage has always been limited to a union between one man and one woman, it also admits that tradition alone cannot be regarded as a sufficient justification for perpetuating (without examination) the restriction or denial of a *fundamental constitutional right.*

In moving to the particular case at hand, the Court argues that the State can transformed its own appreciation and understanding of homosexuality, admitting that the State now recognises that gay individuals are fully capable of entering into 'the kind of loving and enduring committed relationships that may serve as the foundation of a family'.[246] Furthermore, the court refused to accept the contentions of the Proposition 22 Legal Defense Fund and the Campaign for Californian Families that the right to marry was inextricably linked to the possibility to procreate. The Court stated,

> 'Men and women who desire to raise children with a loved one in a recognised family but who are physically unable to conceive a child with their loved one have never been excluded from the right to marry. Although the Proposition 22 Legal Defence Fund and the Campaign assert that the circumstances that marriage has not been limited to those who can bear children can be explained and justified by reference to the State's reluctance to intrude upon the privacy of individuals by inquiring into their fertility, if that were an accurate and adequate explanation for the absence of such a limitation it would follow that in instances in which the Stats is able to make a determination of an individual's fertility without such an inquiry, it would be constitutionally permis-

244 The Court refers particularly to the amendments to divorce, the minimum age requirements, the equalisation in the minimum age requirements and so forth in illustrating that the concept of marriage is not static, *id.*, pp. 25–26.

245 *In re Marriage Cases*, No. S14799 (Cal. May 15, 2008), p. 57.

246 *In re Marriage Cases*, No. S14799 (Cal. May 15, 2008), p. 68.

> sible for the State to preclude an individual who is incapable of bearing children from entering into marriage. There is, however, no authority whatsoever to support the proposition that an individual who is physically incapable of bearing children does not possess a fundamental constitutional right to marry.'[247]

Having established that same-sex couples were guaranteed the same substantive constitutional rights as different-sex couples to choose one's life partner and enter with that person into a committed, officially recognised and protected family relationship that enjoys all the constitutionally based incidents of marriage, the court moved on to the core question of whether it was legitimate for the State to assign different names to the individual institutions (*i.e.* marriage for different-sex couples and domestic partnership for same-sex couples). In drawing inspiration from the Perez case involving the prohibition on interracial marriages, the court held that in drawing a distinction is the name of the institutions, the State was withholding from same-sex couples the 'historic and rightly respected designation of marriage'.

Surprisingly the court in assessing the equal protection claim under the Californian Constitution argued that the claim must be analysed on the basis of the strict scrutiny test and not according to the rational basis standard of review.[248] What is perhaps even more surprising that this was accepted with regards to sexual orientation discrimination. This therefore places sexual orientation discrimination on the same level as sex and race discrimination in California; perhaps the most groundbreaking element of the decision, alongside the factual opening up of civil marriage to same-sex couples. In reaching the conclusion that the strict scrutiny standard must be applied the court first had to identify why sexual orientation was a 'suspect classification'. Reference was made to the Californian Court of Appeal's decision in *Sail'er Inn, Inc.* v. *Kirby*,[249] in which a three criteria test was outlined, in that the defining characteristic must

(a) be based upon an 'immutable trait';
(b) bear no relation to a person's ability to perform or contribute to society, and
(c) be associated with a stigma of inferiority and second class citizenship.

247 *Ibid*, pp. 72–73.

248 According to American constitutional analysis, traditionally two standards have been applied by the California courts in evaluating challenges made to legislation under the equal protection clause: (a) the rational basis standard and (b) the strict scrutiny standard. Over the course of time a third standard of review has developed in California entitled the 'intermediate scrutiny standard' (this is equivalent to standard applied by the U.S. Supreme Court is cases of sex or illegitimacy).

249 (1971) 5 Cal.3d. 1, at 18–19.

Although the Supreme Court agreed with the Court of Appeal's decision in that the last two criteria were indeed satisfied, it disagreed with the Court of Appeal's reasoning with regards to the first criterion.[250] The majority Supreme Court argued that regardless of whether sexual orientation is immutable, immutability is not a requirement for suspect classifications, since religion is also regarded as a suspect classification and religion is not immutable.

In applying the strict scrutiny test, the Court forced the State to provide a constitutionally compelling state interest in treating the two categories of individuals differently. Furthermore, the State must also show that the measures taken are not only related to that interest, but also that they are necessary to further that interest. In defending the disparate treatment, the State argued that the term 'marriage' has traditionally been defined as a union of one man and one woman. The court vehemently rejected this argument stating 'if we have learned anything from the significant evolution in the prevailing societal views and official policies toward members of minority race and toward women over the past half-century, it is that even the most familiar and generally accepted of social practices and traditions often mask an unfairness and inequality that frequently is not recognised or appreciated by those not directly harmed by those practices or traditions'.[251] The court eventually concluding that the State interest did not satisfy the constitutional compelling test since it was not clear that the measure taken was necessary to protect those rights currently enjoyed by those people who may marry; 'extending access to the designation of marriage to same-sex couples will not deprive any opposite-sex couple or their children of any of the rights and benefits conferred by the marriage statutes.'[252]

Although the Court holds that the necessary remedy to is strike Section 300 from the Californian Family Code and open civil marriage to same-sex couples, the Court does not provide any answer to question of what should happen with the current domestic partnerships and the institution of domestic partnership as such. Since the institution is also currently used by different-sex couples over the age of 62, it is unclear what the State will do with regards this point. Will California become similar to another New Jersey retaining domestic partnership for the elderly? Or will California progress towards the Massachusetts model and retain one institution open to all?

---

250 The Court of Appeal had argued that sexual orientation was not immutable and therefore sexual orientation was not a suspect classification, and thus not entitled to strict scrutiny analysis.

251 *In re Marriage Cases*, No. S14799 (Cal. May 15, 2008), p. 115.

252 *Ibid.*, p. 117.

5. RECOGNITION FOR OUT-OF STATE RELATIONSHIPS

5.1. NEW MEXICO

The validity in New Mexico of a same-sex marriage contracted in Massachusetts has not been challenged. New Mexico has not passed a constitutional amendment restricting marriage to opposite-sex couples, nor has it statutorily restricted marriage to such couples. The question therefore remains open

5.2. NEW YORK

New York is one of the five states not to have enacted any form of statutory restriction with regards same-sex marriage. As a result, the question currently remains open as to whether same-sex marriages legally performed in other jurisdictions will be recognised in New York. In 2004, both New York State Comptroller Hevesi,[253] and New York Attorney General Spitzer, issued opinions affirming the belief that out-of-state same-sex marriages should be recognised as valid in New York with respect to the state's retirement system and for all areas of the law, respectively.[254] Not long after these opinions, New York City Mayor Bloomberg also requested the state's five pension schemes to recognise those involved in same-sex marriages, civil unions and domestic partnerships for the purposes of city employee benefits. All three of these decisions are, however, being challenged in the courts.

In February 2008, the Fourth Department of the New York Appellate Division ruled that a same-sex marriage in Canada should be recognised in New York. In *Martinez* v. *County of Monroe*, the court reasoned as follows. Firstly, out-of-state opposite-sex marriages that would not have been legal in New York are only refused recognition if recognising them would violate the state's public policy. On this basis out-of-state same-sex marriages must be held to a similar standard.[255] It is therefore essential to determine whether the recognition of same-sex

253 See references in *Godfrey* v. *Hevesi*, 238 N.Y.L.J. 55.

254 The opinion was actually signed by the New York Solicitor General, Caitlin Halligan, although released via the Attorney General's Office, 2004 Op. Att'y Gen. No. I 2004–1 (3rd March 2004). For the full text, see http://www.oag.state.ny.us/press/2004/mar/mar03a_04.html.

255 Case No. 06–02591, Civ. 1562, 2008 NY Slip Op 909 (N.Y. App. Div. 4d Dep't. 2008). This follows decision of the Supreme Court of New York, Albany County in *Godfrey* v. *Hevesi*, op. cit. where a case was brought against the State Comptroller for his decision to recognise out-of-state marriages for the purposes of the State retirement system. The court held that it was not bound by *Hernandez* v. *Robles*, because that dealt with the in-state celebration of same-sex marriages, nor by *Langan* v. *St. Vincent's Hospital*, because that dealt with the recognition of out-of-state civil unions. See also *Godfrey* v. *Spano*, 15 Misc. 3d 809, 836 N.Y.S.2d 813 (2007).

marriages validly concluded in another jurisdiction is against the public policy of New York. In concluding that same-sex marriage recognition is not against the public policy of New York, the Appellate Division reversed the trial judge's ruling that Monroe Community College did not have to extend health benefits to an employee's same-sex spouse. Monroe County subsequently announced its intention to move for leave to appeal the decision to the Court of Appeals. Nonetheless, in the meantime, the decision has already begun its precedential working. Less than a month later, in *Beth R.* v. *Donna M.*, State Supreme Court Justice Drager issued a divorce licence to a same-sex couple married in Canada, citing *Martinez* v. *County of Monroe* as authority for the basis of her decision.[256]

Alongside the debate surrounding the recognition of same-sex marriages, case law has begun to develop on the basis of the recognition of out-of-state civil unions. In *Langan* v. *St. Vincent's Hospital of New York*, the claimant and the decedent had entered into a civil union in Vermont. The decedent was struck by a car while he was working for the claimant's insurance business, resulting in a serious leg injury. Whilst undergoing surgery on his leg, the decedent died. The claimant commenced a wrongful death action against the hospital where the surgery was performed. The Second Department of the Appellate Division held that a civil union partner could not sue the hospital to recover damages for wrongful death because he did not qualify as a surviving spouse,[257] thus reversing the original decision of the trial judge.[258]The claimant also filed for worker's compensation as the decedent's spouse pursuant to §16(1-a), Worker's Compensation Law. The Third Department of the Appellate Division rejected his claim stating that principles of comity did not require the New York courts to recognise a Vermont civil union.[259]

Furthermore, debate has also been intense regarding the right of New York residents to enter into same-sex marriages in New York.[260] In 2004, the mayor of the village of New Paltz was charged with solemnizing marriages for individuals who had not obtained marriage licences.[261] The mayor argued that the licensing requirement in the New York statute was unconstitutional and thus asked for

256 Case No. 350284/07.

257 25 A.D.3d 90, 802 N.Y.S.2d 476 (N.Y. App.Div. 2d Dep't. 2005).

258 196 Misc.2d. 440, reversed (2003).

259 849 N.Y.S.2d 105 (N.Y. App. Div. 3d Dep't. 2007).

260 In *Matter of Shields* v. *Madigan*, 5 Misc. 3d 901, 783 N.Y.S.2d 270 (N.Y. Sup. Ct. 2004), 20 petitioners were denied marriage licences and sought an order directing the town clerk to issue marriage licences. In noting the constitutional implications of this issue, the court held that 'marriage is a legal status subject to the control of the legislature … It is the legislature that is the appropriate body to engage in the studied debate that must necessarily precede the formulation of social policy with respect to same-sex marriage and the decision to extend any or all rights and benefits associated with marriage to same-sex couples' (783 N.Y.S.2d 270, 277). The decision was affirmed in 2006, *Matter of Shields* v. *Madigan*, 32 A.D.3d 1036, 820 N.Y.S.2d 890 (N.Y. App. Div. 2d Dep't. 2006).

261 *People* v. *West*, 4 Misc. 3d 605, 780 N.Y.S. 2d 723 (N.Y. Just, Ct. 2004).

dismissal of the charges in the interests of justice. In dismissing the charges Justice Katz noted the permanent injunction issued by Supreme Court Justice Kavanagh to prevent the issuance of more licences, as well as the constitutional implications of denying same-sex couples licences. In 2006, the Court of Appeals of New York (New York's highest court) held that the Constitution of New York does not compel the state to issue marriage licences to same-sex couples.[262] More recently, although a Senate Bill seeking to legalise same-sex marriage died in committee, an identical bill submitted to the House is now up for third reading, after being passed 85–65 votes.[263]

5.3. RHODE ISLAND

In the absence of a state DOMA, the question has been posed whether Rhode Island will recognise same-sex marriages from other states, despite the fact that its own residents cannot lawfully marry in their own state. On the 20th February 2007, Attorney General Lynch issued a public statement in which he declared that same-sex marriages lawfully concluded in Massachusetts would be entitled to recognition in Rhode Island.[264] In arriving at his conclusion, Attorney General Lynch identified the *public policy* of Rhode Island with respect to marriage, stating that

> 'Rhode Island has not enacted any legislation prohibiting same-sex marriages or stating a public policy against same-sex marriages even though they have been validly performed in neighbouring Massachusetts for approximately three years.'[265]

Furthermore, Rhode Island had passed legislation specifically enunciating its affirmative policy to prevent discrimination on the basis of sexual orientation. Taken together with other favourable conditions, such as the extension of health insurance benefits to domestic partners of state employees[266] and the courts recognition of *de facto* parental status for same-sex non-biological parents,[267] Lynch comes to the conclusion that same-sex marriages are not against the public policy of Rhode Island. Accordingly on the basis of the principles of full faith and credit and comity, a same-sex marriage validly concluded elsewhere will be recognised

262 *Hernandez* v. *Robles*, 7 N.Y.3d 338, 855 N.E.2d 1, 821 N.Y.S.2d 770 (N.Y. 2006). The decision to permit same-sex couples to marry, it was held, is a decision that must be taken by the legislature.
263 A.B. 8590 (2007), and the original Senate Bill: S.B. 5884 (2007).
264 R.I. Op. Att'y Gen. 2/20 (2007).
265 R.I. Op. Att'y Gen. 2/20 (2007), p. 4.
266 R.I. Gen. Laws § 36-12-1.
267 *Rubano* v. *DiCenzo*, 759 A.2d. 959 (R.I. 2000).

in Rhode Island. Whether this treatment extends to the recognition of civil unions, domestic partnerships and reciprocal benefits is unclear.

Although not technically binding, the opinion does provide a clear idea of the relevant legal principles involved specifically addressing the legal situation in Rhode Island. Furthermore, it makes a strong argument for supporting the view that there is nothing in the public policy of Rhode Island that would prevent the recognition of same-sex marriages. To add further fuel to the fire, the legislature has also been confronted with a number of specific attempts to either legalise same-sex marriages in the state or introduce a form of civil union.[268]

This open and liberal attitude has, however, recently been thrown into doubt as a result of the Supreme Court decision in *Chambers* v. *Ormiston*.[269] The case centred around a female same-sex couple legally married in Massachusetts. They filed for divorce in Rhode Island, and the Supreme Court had to determine whether or not they had subject-matter jurisdiction. In the 3–2 decision, the court held that in determining the meaning of the word 'marriage' in the divorce statutes, reference had to be made to the ordinary meaning of the word 'at the time of enactment'. In so doing, the court came to the conclusion that the ordinary meaning of the word marriage was to be understood as a legal union between 'one man and one woman'. As a result, the court held that it did not have subject-matter jurisdiction to grant a divorce. The effects of this case have yet to be determined, however, it is to be hoped that the heed will be taken of the court's reluctance to extent the ambit of the holding beyond the material facts of the case at hand.[270]

6. COMPARATIVE REMARKS

This article has attempted to provide a (brief) summary of the various statutory registration schemes currently available across the U.S. In doing so, the complexity of the substantive law situation is abundantly clear. This section compares the variety of registration schemes currently available throughout the United States. Despite the apparent lack of uniformity, a number of tentative conclusions and possible trends can, however, be identified.

268 S.B. 202 (2007) and H.B. 6081 (2007): Two bills in favour of same-sex marriage, and H.B. 5356 (2007), H.B. 5643 (2007) and S.B. 893 (2007): Three bills restricting the definition of marriage to opposite-sex couples and introducing civil unions. S.B. 687 (2007) and H.B. 6159 (2007): Two bills with the sole aim of restricting the definition of marriage to opposite-sex couples.

269 *Chambers* v. *Ormiston*, 935 A.2d 956 (R.I. 2007).

270 *Chambers* v. *Ormiston*, 935 A.2d 956, conclusion (R.I. 2007).

6.1. ESTABLISHMENT

In comparing the eligibility criteria for entry into the various relationship schemes provided for in the USA, a number of similarities and differences are evident. The overwhelming emphasis is, however, on the diversity of the solutions. No two schemes are entirely identical, although this is often the result of differences in the marriage laws between the states rather than the result of differences between the ethoses of the registration schemes themselves.[271] This section will focus on the five separate elements relating to the establishment or formation of the relationships, namely (i) the principle of exclusivity, (ii) the sex of the parties, (iii) the age of the parties, (iv) relevant residency requirements, and (v) the prohibited degrees of relationship.[272]

The only core principle common to all jurisdictions at this stage appears to be in relation to the principle of exclusivity. As mentioned above, the principle of exclusivity is comprised of two requirements. Firstly, only two persons may be involved in the relationship at any one time (the so-called principle of monogamy) and secondly that neither party to the relationship may already be involved in a marriage or other registered relationship (the so-called principle of exclusiveness).[273] Thus far, no jurisdiction has permitted those already involved in a marriage or registered relationship to enter into another registered relationship,[274] prior to terminating the previous relationship (the principle of exclusiveness). Moreover, no jurisdiction has yet to allow more than two persons to register a relationship (the principle of exclusiveness). All the surveyed jurisdictions adhere to this fundamental principle.

However, complete consistency ceases here. With respect to the sex of the parties, a variety of different approaches can be discerned. In Hawai'i, Maine and the District of Columbia the registration scheme is open to different-sex couples regardless of age, whereas in California, Washington, and the domestic partnership scheme in New Jersey, different-sex couples are only permitted to register if either one of the partners has attained the age of 62 (California and Washington) or both have attained this age (New Jersey). In the other States, namely Oregon, Connecticut, New Hampshire, Vermont, as well as the civil union scheme in New Jersey, registration is restricted to same-sex couples. Hence, in comparing

---

271 For the difference between external and international consistency see I. Curry-Sumner, *All's well that ends registered?*, 2005, pp. 257–259.

272 The formal procedure to register a partnership has been excluded from this comparison, since this section focuses on the *eligibility* criteria, rather than the procedural mechanism for registration.

273 For a fuller description of this principle, see I. Curry-Sumner, *All's well that ends registered?*, 2005, pp. 42 and 259–260.

274 At this point ignoring the loophole created in Washington regarding opposite-sex couples over the age of 62.

American jurisdictions, it is impossible to disentangle the age and sex requirements from each other; one is completely intertwined in the other.[275] Although no jurisdiction permits registration below the age of 18, in California, Washington and New Jersey (although only with the domestic partnership regime), a lower age limit of 62 has been introduced for different-sex partner registration.[276] The reason for this criterion is linked to the loss of social security benefits for widows and widowers upon remarriage. If a widow or widower remarries after having reached the age 62, he or she will lose his or her entitlement to social security benefits. In these states, registration therefore offers a possibility for elderly couples to enter into a secure relationship with their new partner, without risking the loss of important social security benefits. One other interesting point to note regarding the age limits imposed on aspirant registered partners is that they are not always identical to the equivalent ages imposed on aspirant spouses. For example in New Hampshire and Oregon the age to register a civil union and domestic partnership respectively is higher than the equivalent ages imposed in the marriage laws.[277] The reason for this could stem from the fact that the marital age limits are inherently linked to the ability to procreate (the age limit being linked to the age at which boys and girls are able to conceive children). Since these factors do not relevant in same-sex relationships, the reasons for the lower age limit do not apply, and hence the age is set at the age of majority.

Diversity is also present in the relevant residency requirements imposed on aspirant registered partners. Nonetheless, a certain trend is apparent. Every jurisdiction that has introduced a domestic partnership regime has also imposed a form of residency requirement, either by means of a common or shared residency requirement (California, Washington and District of Columbia), an individual residency requirement (Oregon) or a one year joint communal residency requirement (Maine). On the other hand, those states that have introduced reciprocal benefits or civil unions have not imposed any form of residency requirement, in line with the marriage laws in these states (Hawai'i, Connecticut, New Hampshire, New Jersey and Vermont). It could be that this distinction reflects a difference in the nature of the institutions. Whereas domestic partnership focuses on a common household and domesticity of the relationship, civil union addresses the actual relationship between the parties and is not focused on the living arrangements of the parties. It is in this aspect interesting to note that when Oregon changed the name of its relationship bill from 'civil union' to 'domestic partner-

275 This is a peculiarly American phenomenon, having not at all been witnessed with regards a similar comparison of European jurisdictions: I. Curry-Sumner, *All's well that ends registered?*, 2005, Chapter VIII.

276 In New Jersey this age limit also applies to same-sex registration of a domestic partnership.

277 New Hampshire: Civil unions are permitted once parties have attained 18 years of age; marriages are permitted from 14 years of age for males and 13 for females. Oregon: Marriages are permitted from 17 years of age, domestic partnerships from 18.

ship', a residency requirement was introduced.[278] Whether or not this can be regarded as a fundamental and inherent difference between these jurisdictions is, however, highly debatable. It is possible, the difference is simply the result of coincidence.

Regarding restrictions to the prohibited degrees of relationship, only Hawai'i and the District of Columbia permit those unable to get married because they are relatives to register their relationship. All other jurisdictions (California, Maine, Oregon, Washington, Connecticut, New Hampshire, New Jersey and Vermont) impose the same restrictions regarding degrees of relationship to registered relationships as are applied to marriages.[279]

Nonetheless, despite this overall non-uniform picture, if one looks at these those relationships bearing the same name, one is able to distil certain patterns or trends. There appears to be three distinct state groupings:

1. states that have introduced civil union statutes (CT, NH, NJ, VT, [OR]);
2. states that have introduced domestic partnerships statutes from same-sex couples and different-sex couples over the age of 62 (CA, NJ, WA);
3. states that have done neither of the above (HI, DC, ME).

In examining the first group of states, although the initiative underlying the establishment of civil unions is very different in these four states, since two registry systems were pre-empted by a judicial decision (New Jersey and Vermont) and two were the result of legislative initiatives (Connecticut and New Hampshire), the end results are very similar. Ultimately the aim of the legislation can be extrapolated from the original aims surrounding creation of the legislation. All those states to have introduced civil unions have done so on the same basis, namely by creating 'a state-regulated union created alongside marriage restricted to same-sex couples in which both parties have attained the age of 18 and are not related to each other within the prohibited degrees of relationships set forth in statute'.[280] In *Baker* v. *Vermont* and *Lewis* v. *Harris*, the Vermont and New Jersey Supreme Courts respectively held that it was unconstitutional to deny same-sex couples the rights and benefits of marriage. The question was left open whether marriage would be opened to same-sex couples, or a new institution would be

278 Senate Bill 1073, section 1: ' 'Civil union' means a civil contract that is solemnized in accordance with ORS 106.150 and that it entered into in person between two individuals of the same sex who are at least 17 years of age and who are otherwise capable', compared with House Bill 2007, section 3: ' "Domestic partnership" means a civil contract entered into in person between two individuals of the same sex who are at least 18 years of age, who are otherwise capable *and at least one of whom is resident in Oregon*.' (emphasis added).

279 At this point, the small difference noted in New Hampshire is regarded as so insignificant so as not to necessitate mention here.

280 This definition also applies in a European context, see See I. Curry-Sumner, *All's well that ends registered?*, 2005, p. 343.

created providing the same rights and benefits as marriage and in the same manner. In Connecticut and New Hampshire, the legislative intent was to create a registry scheme permitting 'same-sex couples to have the same rights, responsibilities and obligations as married couples'.[281]

In the jurisdictions that have introduced a domestic partnership scheme open to same-sex couples and different-sex couples over the age of 62 (*i.e.* California, New Jersey and Washington), a similar belief lay behind the original enactment of the statute. Although wanting to address the rights of same-sex couples, the legislature in all of these states found it politically difficult to introduce a registry scheme that would be restricted to same-sex couples. However, on the other hand, opening the scheme to different-sex couples resulted in other criticism since it would provide a competitive alternative to marriage for different-sex couples. In the end these states have all opted for a compromise solution. All same-sex couples may register their relationship, as may those different-sex couples over the age of 62 who wish to avoid the negative effects of remarriage on their social security benefits. In making this compromise, the fundamental argument for enacting a non-marital registration scheme is different than in those states that have introduced civil unions. The fact that New Jersey has since restricted its domestic partnership scheme can be explained with reference to the enactment of civil unions in the state. Same-sex partners now have the opportunity to enter into a 'marriage-like equivalent' and are thus no longer granted the opportunity to enter into a domestic partnership, along identical lines to different-sex couples.

One state, Oregon, causes slight problems in relation to this threefold distinction. Oregon has created an institution which is entitled 'domestic partnership', yet in all facets it resembles a 'civil union'. In this respect is it especially interesting to note that the original bill submitted to the Senate would have created a civil union registry.[282] However, the Republican-controlled House of Representatives effectively prevented the bill's passage. The subsequent compromise was the submission of an almost identical bill with the words 'domestic partnership' replacing the words 'civil union'. A rather cosmetic alteration since the content of the bill remained remarkably similar. One significant difference is the imposition of a residency requirement, expressly called for by the Republicans to ensure that Oregon would not become a home for same-sex registration tourism. In this respect, Oregon has really created a civil union in disguise.

The third and final category consists of Hawai'i, Maine and the District of Columbia. All three jurisdictions have created a relatively weak form of non-marital registered relationship, ensuring that only the minimum requirements are imposed on those wishing to register their relationship. In comparing these three

281 For Connecticut see, for example, the bill analysis accompanying Senate Bill 963. For New Hampshire see the title of the Act enacting civil unions.

282 See § 3.2.4.

jurisdictions, one is struck by the overwhelming non-uniformity of their schemes. Neither the reasons for the enactment of this legislation nor the choices made within this framework appear to resemble each other in any significant way.

Table 1. Eligibility criteria for registration schemes

Registration Scheme / Jurisdiction		Sex	Age	Residency	Prohibited Degrees	Exclusivity
RB	Hawai'i	Same and different sex	> 18	None	None	2 persons
DP	California	Same and > 62 different sex	> 18 (> 62 if different sex)	Common residence	Same as marriage	2 persons
	District of Columbia	Same and different sex	> 18	Common residence	None	2 persons
	Maine	Same and different sex	> 18	Common residence & > 12 months in ME	Same as marriage	2 persons
	New Jersey	Same and different sex	> 62	Common residence	Same as marriage	2 persons
	Oregon	Same-sex only	> 18	One party resident in OR	Same as marriage	2 persons
	Washington	Same and >62 different sex	> 18 (> 62 if different sex)	Common residence	Same as marriage	2 persons
CU	Connecticut	Same-sex only	> 18	None	Same as marriage	2 persons
	New Hampshire	Same-sex only	> 18	None	Same as marriage	2 persons
	New Jersey	Same-sex only	> 18	None	Same as marriage	2 persons
	Vermont	Same-sex only	> 18	None	Same as marriage	2 persons

Key: RB: Reciprocal Benefits; DP: Domestic Partnership; CU: Civil Union

6.2. RIGHTS AND DUTIES

With regard to the rights and duties attributed to non-marital registered partners, little uniformity can be deduced. At the one extreme, states such as Massachusetts, California and New Hampshire have extended all the rights and duties granted to married couples to those involved in same-sex equivalents. At the other end of the extreme, states such as Michigan and Alaska have passed constitutional and statutory amendments that deny same-sex couples *any* of the benefits granted to married couples.

Restricting comparison to those states that allow for some form of registration, one is able to deduce the utilisation of two different techniques. Some states have chosen to use an *enumeration* method to extend rights and benefits, explicitly stating each right, benefit, duty and responsibility that is granted to same-sex registered couples. Other states have instead opted for the *exclusion* method whereby *all* rights are extended, unless explicitly proscribed.[283] Table 2 provides an overview of the methods used.

Table 2. Rights and duties of registration schemes

Registration Scheme / Jurisdiction		Method	Extent
RB	Hawai'i	Enumeration	Weak
DP	California	<2005: Enumeration >2005: Exclusion	Strong
	District of Columbia	<2006: Enumeration >2006: Exclusion	Strong
	Maine	Enumeration	Weak
	New Jersey	Enumeration	Weak
	Oregon	Exclusion	Strong
	Washington	<2008: Enumeration >2008: Enumeration[284]	Weak
CU	Connecticut	Exclusion	Strong
	New Hampshire	Exclusion	Strong
	New Jersey	Exclusion	Strong
	Vermont	Exclusion[285]	Strong

Key: RB: Reciprocal Benefits; DP: Domestic Partnership; CU: Civil Union

Once again, three distinct groupings are discernible:

1. states that have introduced civil unions (CT, NH, NJ, VT, [OR]);
2. states that have introduced relationship schemes with weak benefits (HI, ME, NJ, WA);
3. states that have introduced domestic partnership with strong benefits (CA, DC).

The first category does not require much explanation. As already stated above, whether by virtue of a judicial decision or legislative proposal, the objective of all four pieces of legislation is to introduce a statutory institution identical (yet sepa-

283 See I. Curry-Sumner, *All's well that ends registered?*, 2005, pp. 298–299.

284 Legislative amendments in 2008 have resulted in more rights and duties being granted to domestic partners in Washington. However, these rights and duties are not extensive enough to constitute categorisation as 'strong registration'. For the precise categorisation criteria, see I. Curry-Sumner, *All's well that ends registered?*, 2005, pp. 291–298.

285 For a discussion of the exact method utilized by Vermont, see § 3.3.4.2.

rate) to marriage, restricted to same-sex couples. If one also takes on board the previous discussion with regards to Oregon actually being a civil union state, then one could argue that with respect to the rights and duties attributed to non-marital registered partners, Oregon also adopts a 'civil union' approach.

The second category consists of those states that have introduced partnership schemes with only limited rights and duties. These states have thus opted for a very different type of relationship scheme. Despite the apparent clarity of this grouping, the background surrounding the introduction of each State's legislation is very different. In Hawai'i the reciprocal benefits scheme was introduced as a palliative response to the calls for same-sex marriage. In the other three states this was not the case. What is perhaps most interesting in this category in the apparent divergence of the state with respect to each other. Since the introduction of these schemes, Hawai'i has restricted the rights and duties available, New Jersey has limited the eligibility criteria (but since introduced civil unions), Washington has extended the rights available, whereas Maine has not amended its legislation at all. This grouping is therefore perhaps the most fluid of all three groups and can therefore perhaps best be regarded as a 'temporary pit-stop' on the way to some other destination.

The third category is, however, slightly more difficult to explain. In these jurisdictions, the legislature has chosen to extend all the rights and benefits attributed to married couples to those involved in a non-marital registered relationship. In California and the District of Columbia this has been the result of legislative amendment in 2005 and 2006 respectively. In this respect, it is perhaps interesting to note that both jurisdictions *at the moment of creation* enumerated all the rights and duties attributed to domestic partners. However, both jurisdictions have gone on to extend those rights and duties to include all or virtually all the statewide rights and duties attributed to spouses. What is perhaps most remarkable is the fact that the legislatures in these states have not, however, tampered with the name of the institution.

6.3. TERMINATION

As regards the termination of these relationship forms, little uniformity can be deduced. States such as Hawai'i simply require notification to be sent by certified mail, whereas other states such as California require (in some cases) the parties to prove in court that the relationship has irremediably broken down. One clear uniform trend is, nonetheless apparent: those states that have introduced civil unions have regulated the termination of these relationships on exactly the same basis as the existing divorce rules, with the ensuing oddities with respect to adultery! It would also appear (rather logically) that the weaker the relationship form, the easier the dissolution procedure is.

6.4. THEORETICAL FRAMEWORK

On the basis of European research, it has been suggested that there are three models that can be distinguished with respect to non-marital registered relationships, the so-called pluralistic, dualistic and monistic models.[286] The question, which can therefore be posed, is whether this classification can also be applied to the registration schemes developed in the United States of America.

In the pluralistic model couples are offered two possibilities to formalise their relationship, irrespective of their gender, namely marriage or a form of non-marital registered relationship. It must, however, be noted that jurisdictions adhering to the pluralistic model tend to attain the end phase of this model by virtue of a two-stage process, thereby necessitating the division of the pluralistic model into two time-periods. The first time-period involves opening non-marital registration to both different and same-sex couples, whilst leaving marriage legislation entirely intact and unaltered. Once this has been achieved, the arguments for opening civil marriage to same-sex couples are strengthened, since the discrimination originally faced by same-sex couples, in not being able to marry, is simply replaced with a new form of discrimination; although different-sex couples are offered a choice of relationship forms, same-sex couples are not.[287] It is irrefutable that the option for different-sex couples to register their relationship along identical lines to same-sex couples in The Netherlands and Belgium, for example, played an important role in the pressure placed on these Governments to amend the laws prohibiting same-sex civil marriage.[288] This model can be represented diagrammatically.

Pluralistic model

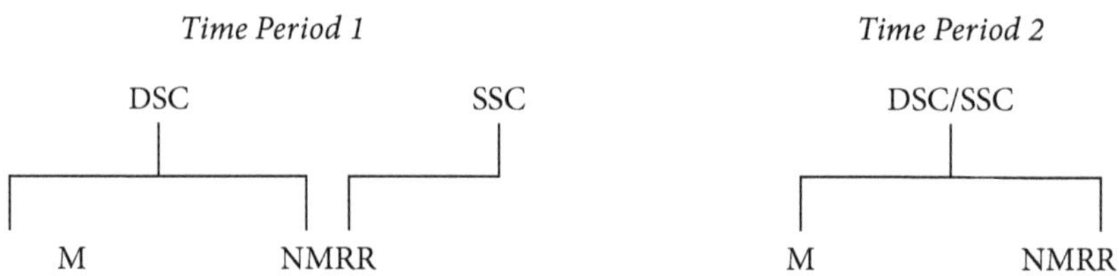

Key: DSC: *Different-Sex Couples*, SSC: *Same-Sex Couples*
M: *Marriage*, NMRR: *Non-Marital Registered Relationship*

---

[286] I. Curry-Sumner, *All's well that ends registered?*, 2005, pp. 266–278, 286–291, and 307–313.

[287] See, for example, Dutch Second Chamber, *Kamerstukken II* 1995–1996, 23 761, No. 7, p. 10.

[288] It is, therefore, argued that over the course of time, France will gradually come to debate the issue of opening civil marriage to same-sex couples. This issue has in fact already been raised in the courts as well as politically.

On the other hand, some jurisdictions have preferred the dualistic model, where couples are only provided with one institutionalised relationship form dependent on their sex: different-sex couples are able to marry, whilst same-sex couples are entitled to register their non-marital relationship. Diagrammatically illustrated:

Dualistic model

DSC — SSC
| — |
M — NMMR

A third possibility is the monistic model whereby couples, irrespective of their gender are presented with one institutionalised relationship form.

Monistic model

DSC/SSC
|
M

In relation to the American jurisdictions to have enacted registration schemes, it would appear that these models also hold true, although certain amendment is necessary. Massachusetts is perhaps the easiest State to begin with, having simply opened civil marriage to same-sex couples. It therefore has opted for the monistic model. Those states that have introduced civil unions (*i.e.* Connecticut, New Hampshire, New Jersey and Vermont) have all done so in a similar fashion to those European states that have adhered to the dualistic model.

State	**System**	**Model**
Massachusetts	Marriage	Monistic
Connecticut	Civil Union	Dualistic
New Hampshire	Civil Union	Dualistic
Vermont	Civil Union	Dualistic
Oregon	Domestic Partnership	Dualistic
California	Marriage / Domestic Partnership	Dualistic (and > 62) → monistic (?)
New Jersey	Civil Union / Domestic Partnership	Dualistic (and > 62)
Washington	Domestic Partnership	Dualistic (and > 62)
Maine	Domestic Partnership	Pluralistic (time phase 1)
District of Columbia	Domestic Partnership	Pluralistic (time phase 1)
Hawai'i	Reciprocal Benefits	Pluralistic (time phase 1)

One particular feature deserves particular attention, since it would appear that the terminology used to identify the relationship form is significant for the typology of the registration scheme in any particular State.

(a) Those states to have opened up *marriage* to same-sex couples (Massachusetts and California) would appear to be monistic states (assuming that California will indeed implement the holding of the Californian Supreme Court decision and subsequently remove domestic partnership).[289]
(b) 3 of the 4 States that have introduced *civil unions* have all done so on similar grounds, albeit for different reasons (Connecticut, New Hampshire and Vermont). In these States the legislature has created a parallel similar operating along identical lines to marriage. As already stated above, it is particularly interesting to note that Oregon, despite having introduced a form of domestic partnership, has done so along identical lines as those states to have introduced civil unions. This would appear to confirm the hypothesis that the terminology used to identify this new form of relationship is crucial. In Oregon the legislature refused to pass a Bill when it proposed to introduce *civil unions* (a term now associated with the dualistic system), whereas when the same Bill was reintroduced using the name *domestic partnership* (a term now associated with the pluralistic system), the objections were far less pronounced.
(c) Those States that have introduced *domestic partnerships* and *reciprocal benefits* have done so according to one of two different paths.
    (i) The first group consists of those States that have introduced domestic partnership for same-sex couples and different-sex couples over the age of 62 (California, New Jersey and Washington). It has been argued in this article that this group is, however, characterised by flux. All three States belonging to this group have, since enactment of domestic partnership, either introduced a new formalised registration system (New Jersey with civil union and California with marriage) or extensively expanded the rights and duties incumbent on the parties involved (Washington). If one considers the possibility for different-sex couples over the age of 62 as a specificity of these systems that should be removed from the analysis,[290] one is left with adherence to the dualistic model. In all these States, the State has begun with a registration with limited rights and duties, but has

[289] An alternative solution is obviously that the Californian legislature opens civil marriage to same-sex couples, and at the same time opens domestic partnership to different-sex couples. Although theoretically possible, there would appear to be no indication that this route will be followed.

[290] The argument for this is that the reason for these couples to utilise the domestic partnership regime is simply to avoid losing social security benefits. The legislature could alternatively choose to amend the social security legislation to ensure that these benefits would not be lost upon remarriage, and the need for different-sex domestic partnership would disappear.

since extended those rights and duties extensively ensuring that two of three States now attribute rights and duties via the exclusion method instead of the enumeration method.

(ii) The second group consists of those jurisdictions that have introduced domestic partnership or reciprocal benefits for same-sex couples *and* different-sex couples (District of Columbia, Hawai'i and Maine). These States have therefore all adhered to the pluralistic model of registration. In this group it is worth noting that all three states also originally used the enumeration method to attribute rights and duties to same sex partners, and that the package of rights and duties that was extended can be classified as being weak. It is, however, with respect to this group of jurisdictions that one can witness the most diversity of solution (*i.e.* with regards the prohibited degrees of relationship, the extent of the rights and duties attributed, the method used to attribute the rights and duties etc.).

7. CONCLUSION

With a country so divided on the issue of same-sex relationships, it would seem difficult, and possibly foolish, to propose possible solutions to the potential chaos that the United States may encounter in this field. Nevertheless, there are a couple of points that can be learnt from this brief summary of the state of affairs anno 2008.

Firstly, same-sex couples are increasingly gaining state recognition of their relationships. Although the road ahead would appear to be a long one, it does appear to be one which is slowly changing. Less than 10 years ago, same-sex couples were provided virtually no recognition anywhere in the country. Today, more than 10 jurisdictions provide for state-wide registration schemes and two states have even gone so far as to open marriage to same-sex couples. Although the fight has not been won, same-sex couples should take solace in the fact that a similar picture was also true of Europe ten years after Denmark became the first country in Europe to introduce 'registered partnerships'.[291]

Secondly, the states should pay more attention to ensuring that distinctions between marriage, on the one hand, and same-sex relationship recognition, on the other, serve a particular purpose. If the decision has been taken to extend all of the rights and benefits of marriage to same-sex couples, the conditions for establishment of the relationship should also mirror that institution; if a prohibition exists for one category, well-founded reasons should be provided as to why

[291] For an overview of the European situation, see I. Curry-Sumner, *All's well that ends registered?*, 2005.

this prohibition does not apply to the other category. Take, for example, the Oregon statute which ensures that opposite-sex couples may marry from 17 years of age, whereas same-sex couples can only register a domestic partnership from the age of 18. What is the reason for this difference? What purpose does this serve, other than to draw unnecessary distinctions?

Thirdly, it would appear crucial that more attention is paid to the terminological differences between the States. The name given to a State's registration scheme would appear to be representative not only of a State's political ideology with respect to same-sex relationships, but also representative of the type of registration scheme that is being created. This is of utmost importance as States pay increasing attention to the developments in sister states. The ever-increasing mobility of citizens across the United States will only lead to states being confronted with relationship forms from other states. Since 2002, the number of cases involving interstate recognition has begun to increase. As more states open their doors to same-sex recognition, more attention should be paid to the conflict of laws issues involved. Not only will the beast raise its ugly head with regards the recognition and termination of such relationships, but perhaps ever more frequently with regards the rights and duties associated with the relationship.[292]

The debate will, however, no doubt continue. Nonetheless, let us not forget the words of Chief Justice Deborah T. Poritz, in a powerful concurring and dissenting opinion in the case of *Lewis* v. *Harris*,

> 'What we name things matters, language matters (...) Labels set people apart surely as physical separation on a bus or in school facilities (...) By excluding same-sex couples from civil marriage, the State declares that it is legitimate to differentiate between their commitments and the commitments of heterosexual couples. Ultimately the message is that what same-sex couples have is not as important or as significant as 'real' marriage, that such lesser relationships cannot have the name of marriage.'

292 See I. Curry-Sumner & N. Maxwell, 'Same-sex, different statuts?', *Wayne State Law Review* (forthcoming).

COMPARATIVE SYNTHESIS

RESEARCH QUESTIONS IN FAMILY LAW DERIVED FROM A COMPARATIVE SYNTHESIS OF GENERAL TRENDS AND DEVELOPMENTS

KATHARINA BOELE-WOELKI, BENTE BRAAT, IAN CURRY-SUMNER, CHRISTINA JEPPESEN DE BOER, PIA LOKIN, MACHTELD VONK, NORA DE VRIES, WENDY SCHRAMA*

PRELIMINARY REMARK

This contribution summarizes the debates among the authors of this volume at the expert meeting which took place in Utrecht from 27th – 28th June 2008.[1] The meeting was aimed at enabling in-depth discussions of the issues that are addressed in the various contributions. The authors of this comparative synthesis all belong to the Utrecht Centre for European Research into Family Law (UCERF)[2] under whose auspices the expert meeting was organised.

1. ORGANIZATION AND STRUCTURE

The objective of the expert meeting was to identify similarities and differences based on the provided information, to explain, compare and evaluate the information provided. Each author prepared a 10-minute presentation of his/her article focussing on what he or she considered to be the most interesting or controversial issues of his or her paper. Furthermore, in order to stimulate debate, the authors were asked to prepare statements[3] and, if possible, to merge these statements into their presentation. The statements were submitted in advance. As a result, the expert meeting consisted of interactive sessions with ample time for

* Researchers at the Molengraaff Institute for Private Law, Utrecht University.

1 The G.J. Wiarda Institute for Legal Research of Utrecht University and the Royal Netherlands Academy of Art and Sciences (KNAW) granted financial support for the organization of the expert meeting.

2 See www.ucerf.nl.

3 Included at the end of this contribution.

discussion. The papers on similar topics were grouped together in three consecutive sessions:

(1) (Compulsory) arrangements regarding children
(2) Registration schemes for same-sex couples: new jurisdictions
(3) The effectiveness of the *pater est* rule consisting of
   (a) Children of cohabiting couples and the right to know
   (b) Assisted reproduction and the position of the known sperm donor.

The contents of all the contributions to this volume have been briefly summarized and compared in the introductory contribution "What comparative family law should entail" by Katharina Boele-Woelki.[4] The grouping of the articles and presentations in specific topics has not been used in writing this joint contribution. During the preparation of the expert meeting and more importantly during our discussions we noticed that some general notions, aspects and developments can be discerned which apply to all topics that have been addressed. These aspects that mark the current debates in family law around the globe at the dawn of the 21st century are grouped under the following headings: terminology and characterization (§2), constitutional framework (including religion) (§3), the role of the State (§4), party autonomy (including contracts) (§5), legal reform: by the legislature or by the courts? (§6) and the necessity of empirical research (§7). The many questions that under the different aspects have been raised illustrate the need for more research in (comparative) family law.

2. TERMINOLOGY AND CHARACTERIZATION

Apples and oranges are not comparable. In the field of comparative legal studies this old adage indicates that legal notions and concepts must be comparable. The search for the *tertium comparationis* refers to the problem of comparability which should have a certain quality. This quality depends on the presence of common elements in the rules, concepts or institutions to be compared whereby their structure, function and consequences are generally considered to be decisive. According to Zweigert/Kötz in particular, the function is the starting point and the basis of all comparative law. In their view different legal systems can only be compared if they solve the same factual problem, that is, answer the same legal need. In other words, the institutions of different legal systems can only be meaningfully compared if they perform the same task, if they serve the same function. This is the *tertium comparationis*.[5]

---

4 See pp. 1–24.
5 K. Zweigert & H. Kötz, *Introduction to Comparative Law*, 1998, p. 34.

In the field of comparative family law problems of comparability are also apparent. What is for example the meaning of the terms "parenthood" and "parentage" within the different jurisdictions? Which distinction can be drawn between rights and duties attached to the different concepts? More specifically – in the case of assisted reproduction – the question arises who is considered to be a surrogate mother, an egg donor or a sperm donor? Does a man who donates his sperm in a licensed clinic belong to the same legal category as a man who donates his sperm from the comfort of his own home? It is essential to know exactly who belongs to the different categories and which requirements must be fulfilled in order to categorize and distinguish the one from the other.

Another example which illustrates the necessity of carefully differentiating between different concepts and notions can be provided when looking at the relatively new phenomenon that the child resides on an alternating basis with both parents after their divorce. Can we talk about a shared or alternating residence when there is a division of care on a 40/60 or even 30/70 basis or must it always be on a 50/50 basis? When does alternating residence start and under which circumstances can we only speak of a contact arrangement? What is the conceptual difference between the one (alternating residence) and the other (a main residence in combination with a contact right)? Do financial factors also play a role? Arguably, the more time the child spends with a parent the lower the amount of child maintenance that this parent has to pay. In addition, geographical aspects might be of importance when considering the proximity of the parents' residences within the framework of joint parental responsibilities. The personal situations of the parents can differ significantly. Is it the distance or practical travelling time that is decisive when one of the parents wants to relocate with the child against the will of the other parent? Or is it only important that the moving parent has sufficient funds to allow the child to travel regularly? It should be kept in mind that in the United States, for instance, people easily move and travel over long distances, whereas in Denmark 80% of divorced parents remain in the same city after the dissolution of their marriage. This probably affects the way in which a legal system deals with the subject of alternating residence and requests for relocation.

Also in the field of formal relationships the name given to the couple's relationship can be misleading. Does marriage include same-sex couples? Does a registered partnership exclude different-sex couples? Is a same-sex marriage the same as a same-sex registered partnership? Is the essential element the protection or non-protection rather than the name? What is exactly in the name? Is the naming of a legal relationship important? From a strategic point of view it may sometimes be advisable to provide a "weaker" name to an institution in comparison to the institution of "marriage" in order to get the bill through Parliament, even if the institution at stake is similar to a marriage or entails many rights which are akin to marriage, such as, for instance, in the United Kingdom. The same development is noticeable in Hungary, where only the making available of the registration scheme for both same-sex and different-sex couples has gradually customized society with homosexuality. A different approach is applied in South Africa where there is no difference between a marriage under the Marriage Act and a marriage under the Civil Union Act. The dissolution of both relationships is called a divorce and the Divorce and Maintenance Acts apply in both cases. More generally and in view of the principles of equality, one might argue that the name of the formal institution which couples choose is essential. Moreover, the symbolic and emotional meaning of being married instead of being in a partnership or civil union should not be underestimated.

3. CONSTITUTIONAL FRAMEWORK (INCLUDING RELIGION)

The influence of constitutional rights as adopted in international, European or national legislation is of significant importance in the field of family law. In particular, the legal recognition of same-sex couples and the request of one parent against the will of the other parent to move with the children to another country demonstrate how difficult the balancing of interests and rights can be. In view of several constitutional rights the legal recognition of same-sex relationships is either prohibited or promoted. In particular, the constitutional protection of marriage naturally entails a more restricted approach. It limits the freedom to enact legislation recognizing lifestyles other than marriage. This can be clearly demonstrated in Hungary, Italy and Portugal where the marriage is protected by the constitution triumphs over the principle of equality. South Africa represents the other side of the spectrum. There a careful balancing has taken place between two constitutional rights: the freedom of religion, on the one hand, and the prohibition of discrimination on the basis of sexual orientation, on the other. As a result there is no difference between the Marriage Act and the Civil Union Act. The adopted two-track system for different and same-sex couples has only been enacted to accommodate religious concerns.

The right of the free movement of persons or, within the American setting, the right to travel, raises many questions if a request for relocation is to be decided. Recently, it has been confirmed by the European Court of Justice[6] that national legislation which places certain nationals of the EU Member State concerned at a

6 ECJ 14 October 2008, Case C-353/06 (Grunkin-Paul, Standesamt Niebüll).

disadvantage simply because they have exercised their freedom to move and to reside in another Member State is a restriction of the freedoms conferred by Article 18(1) of the EC Treaty on every citizen of the Union. Not only legislation can be considered to constitute an infringement of the free movement right, but also courts have to take this right into account. It is arguable that a prohibition on relocating forms an obstacle to the right to free movement.[7] How should the rights of mothers, fathers and children be balanced? Do the courts pay too much attention to the rights of the parents and too little to the rights of children? Are children heard? Does the child have a right to have contact with both parents? Also if one of the parents does not desire any contact? Do parents have a right to an equal amount of contact? Do they have the right to work wherever they want? Do they have the right to start a new family? In the last-mentioned case does the prohibition on any relocation infringe the right to marry as guaranteed in Article 12 of the Convention on Human Rights?

The debate on the constitutional dimensions of family law shows that an interdisciplinary cooperation between family law and (European) constitutional law experts is indispensable in order to provide clear answers. This should by and large be encouraged.

4. THE ROLE OF THE STATE

Another aspect which was reflected upon in the discussions on the contributions to this volume concerned the role of the State. How much State interference is desirable and in which cases? Who is to be protected? It has been submitted, for instance, that the State should be clear concerning its role with respect to the determination of paternity, more particularly that an unambiguous distinction is made between the social, genetic and legal elements of parentage. In many jurisdictions the question of what is the purpose of extending rights to fathers remains unanswered: Is it to ensure that all social fathers are protected, that the child is protected or that a firmer basis is provided for child support? More specifically, what is the State trying to achieve with child support: is it a commitment or attention to biology?

Also in the field of formal relationships the role of the State is not always clear. It is generally acknowledged that the *rationale* behind marriage cannot be limited to the idea of the protection of the weaker spouse. One must also consider the inseparable element of status in examining the institution of marriage. However,

7 However, the prohibition only lasts until the child reaches the age of majority.

should the status issue not be separated from the protection issue? Should the State not provide couples with many choices as to how to regulate their relationships? And even if they do not agree on anything that they should still be protected? In some countries this idea has been advanced but in a global world it might be difficult to have this kind of broad range of solutions because it is uncertain whether and how they will be recognized abroad. The question remains, however, why we always need to decide not to protect a certain group of persons (e.g. same-sex couples, social parents, known donors) in order to protect another group.

Finally, what is the role of the State if there are conflicts between parents concerning care and legal arrangements relating to children? It is generally presumed that parents solve their own problems. What happens, however, if they continue to disagree? Should the State assist parents in making decisions by providing alternative dispute resolution mechanisms? More specifically, is mandatory mediation the solution for relocation issues? Is increasing State interference in post-divorced families a general trend which is to be welcomed?

All in all it became clear that in respect of the debated topics the role of the State is sometimes questionable and not always clearly defined or not identifiable. Tension is also apparent in relation to the following aspect: the freedom of the parties to determine and agree on the rights and duties deriving from their relationship.

5. PARTY AUTONOMY (INCLUDING CONTRACTS)

Who determines the rules of family law – more distinctively the rights and duties within family relations? Generally, two aspects are decisive. First, which hierarchy of legal sources is to be taken into account and, second, in which area is party autonomy permitted? In respect of the legal sources the well-known common law/civil law divide is to be respected. How much weight is to be given to court decisions and how are statutory provisions to be interpreted? This topic is further elaborated under the next aspect which addresses the question of legal reform. Who is responsible for legal reforms: the legislature or the courts? In respect of the second aspect it is generally acknowledged that family law is – apart from property aspects and arrangements regarding children - to a very large extent mandatory law; hence party autonomy plays a relatively insignificant role. However, in some areas of the topics that were discussed agreements between the parties are gradually gaining legal importance. At least it is passionately debated what role party autonomy should play with respect to genetics. Should it really be the case that the paternity of a child rests only upon the will of the father? Should the State not be able to test everyone? On the other hand, at present perhaps not enough party autonomy is given to the biological father: why can he not deny his paternity in The Netherlands? In addition, should it not be possible to deny maternity? Moreover, in particular written contracts on parenthood in three-parent relationships not only raise legal questions (are they enforceable?) but also moral and ethical ones.

The discussions about the possibility of persons to determine, among themselves, their rights and duties within a family relationship also expose another outlook. What should happen if the parties do not agree in areas where they are encouraged to agree, such as the exercise of parental responsibilities after divorce? For example, the parents do not agree on the shared residence of the child, they cannot communicate with each other, but the court or the legislature imposes an alternating residence as the legal norm. Should the lack of an agreement on shared residence not be interpreted as an agreement that the child is to reside with one of the parents? Or – to provide another example – if the rationale behind marriage is the protection of the weaker party, it is arguable that in all cases the weaker party should be protected even when he or she has economically taken the wrong decisions. In this case should protection be imposed against the will of the other spouse? More generally, have a cohabiting couple always jointly made a choice not to marry? If one partner does not want to acquire that legal status and the protection it entails, the other has no choice.

As a result it is discernible that contracting in family relations has unquestionably increasingly gained more importance and acceptance. In which areas should party autonomy be permitted and why? What are its possibilities and limitations? These fundamental questions indisputably need further (comparative) research.

6. LEGAL REFORM: BY THE LEGISLATURE OR BY THE COURTS?

Who can determine which rules are to be applied in family relations? Primarily the answer depends on the legal system in question. Generally, it is known that in all civil law systems family law is codified, but also in common law systems family law issues are to a very large extent regulated by statute. Whereas the common law courts adhere to the notion of precedents, the civil law courts do not act so very differently. In both systems legal reforms are either initiated by the courts or by the government. However, the courts often decide that the legislature should take action because the current law for instance violates international obligations or because it does not provide answers to new developments in society. This can be demonstrated in the field of the recognition of same-sex relationships and also in respect of alternating residence and relocation. Regarding the latter only in a few jurisdictions have statutory rules been enacted.[8] So far the courts have dealt with any problems. The different legal standards provide judges with wide discretion. Due to the fact that the best interests of the child are too vague as a useful criterion in relation to both situations the outcomes are often inconsistent and unpredictable. Is it then not up to the legislature to formulate clear rules? Would, for instance, mandatory mediation be a step forward in relocation cases?

The (non-)recognition of same-sex relationships shows a different pattern. In many jurisdictions the courts decided that it was beyond their competence to legally recognize same-sex relationships. It should be the task of the legislature to introduce a new institution or to make marriage available to such relationships. It is striking to see that in this respect the courts in both the common law and the civil law systems have decided in a similar way. The courts paved the way for legal reform and, as a result, in the last twenty years or so more and more national legislatures have adopted legislation which is aimed at providing a legal status for same-sex couples.

Legal reform should preferably not be undertaken without empirical research. In the next section attention is finally paid to this fundamental requirement.

7. NECESSITY OF EMPIRICAL RESEARCH

In respect of many issues it has been submitted that we simply do not know how family relations work in practice. After a relationship has broken down, for instance, the parents increasingly agree on an alternative residence for the child; however, reliable data are not available. We do not know how often parents agree to care for the child on an alternating basis and how often such an arrangement is ordered by the courts, if this possibility exists. What are the legal arrangements? Which aspects are taken into account? How many children are affected? Why do the parents "share" the child? Is it considered to be convenient to be one week "on"

8 In France and Belgium the alternating residence of the child after a divorce between the parents should be the first option to be investigated by the courts. The CEFL Principles regarding Parental Responsibilities (Principle 3:20(2) and 3:21) and the ALI Principles on Family Dissolution (§ 2.08(1) and § 2.17(1)) also provide guidelines on alternating residence and relocation. Recently the Dutch Advocate General – who, according to the Dutch system, prepares the decision of the Dutch Supreme Court by analyzing the case in the form of a conclusion – referred to the CEFL Principles (Dutch Supreme Court 25 April 2008, LJN: BC5901). It concerned a request by a divorced mother to move with the children to Switzerland. The parents had joint parental responsibilities and the father objected.

and one week "off" duty? Does the arrangement cause difficulties in the long run? Is the child heard before the alternating residence is agreed upon and practised? How do parents communicate? Are all decisions always taken together? Which decisions are considered to belong to daily matters and which are important? Is there a relationship between an alternating residence and maintenance, and if so, which? Under which circumstances is the alternating residence changed into residence with one of the parents? How do children experience an alternating residence? What are the decisive factors which cause problems, if any? Is a shared residence in the best interest of the child? Actually, we have no idea how children experience an alternating residence or a relocation.

The necessity of sociological research has also been demonstrated in respect of the legal recognition of same-sex relationships at least in those jurisdictions where there is a possibility to choose between different types of relationships. Why do same-sex couples opt for a registered partnership or a marriage? Why do they not formalize their relationship? The latter question indisputably also applies to heterosexual couples. Another example concerns non-marital cohabitation. If, within such a relationship, a child is born, how often does the biological father recognize the child? In addition, how often do legal fathers, together with the birth mother, request parental responsibilities via the courts in those jurisdictions where this is necessary to acquire the status of the holder of parental responsibilities?

To date, these and many other questions remain unanswered. Qualitative and quantitative empirical/sociological research is therefore needed, preferably research that is undertaken in different jurisdictions where the results are comparable. This kind of research should be carried out with the assistance or even guidance of legal scholars and lawyers in order to determine whether the rules of family law still reflect the needs of society or whether and how they should be adjusted to societal changes.

FINAL REMARKS

The expert meeting in which, besides the authors, also a few other family law experts participated was positively evaluated. With no more than 30 participants it provided an excellent opportunity to really exchange and express ideas, opinions and concerns. The two-day meeting was mostly composed of extensive and passionate discussions. The authors were all well prepared and familiar with the views of their colleagues expressed in the respective contributions. In addition, the mix of experienced and young, but advanced family law experts also turned out to be stimulating. All in all, the Utrecht debates on family law around the globe were successful from both a professional and a personal perspective.

Annex: Statements of the authors participating in the expert meeting

Katharina Boele-Woelki: *What comparative family law should entail*

1. It is impossible to enter into a discussion about conclusions and recommendations, if a comparative study (in the field of family law) does not indicate the aim of the comparison, if it does not systematically present differences and similarities, if explanations for these are not provided and if the criteria which determine the evaluation are not specified.
2. It is a dangerous endeavor to pick and choose solutions, examples and arguments at random and present them merely with the intention to promote ideological or political ideas.
3. Comparative family law should include its international dimension.

Anna Singer: *Active parenting or Solomon's justice?*

1. Alternating residence provides the child a natural and unstrained contact with both parents when they are living apart from one another.
2. A possibility for the court to decide on alternating residence is a good way to emphasize that the parents have a joint responsibility for their child also after separation.
3. Court decisions on division of maintenance costs between the parents when the child has alternating residence would destroy the basis for cooperation between the parents.
4. Alternating residence is in effect dividing a child between two parents thereby reaching an equitable solution to an unsolvable problem.

Christina Jeppesen de Boer: *Parental relocation: Free movement rights and joint parenting*

1. The trend is that the possibilities for the resident parent to relocate are limited.
2. Strictly speaking, "the child's right to two parents" requires both parents to live in close proximity.

Theresa Glennon: *Divided parents, shared children: Conflicting approaches to relocation disputes in the USA*

1. Most US states use a version of a "best interests of the children" test to determine whether to permit a residential parent to relocate. Is a "best interests" test the right approach in the context of parental relocation? Does this focus give adequate protection to the interests of residential parents living their own lives? Should courts have the authority to block relocation, or should they simply determine which parent a child should live with after a relocation occurs?
2. Several US states and the ALI Principles for Family Dissolution use a different legal standard for relocation cases where the second parent has a substantial amount of contact with the child. Should the legal approach to relocation disputes change depending on the extent of the non-moving parent's involvement in the children's lives? What would be the possible beneficial and detrimental effects of this change?
3. The social science literature highlights some of the risks of divorce for children, but split in their emphasis on the importance of the relationship with the primary caregiver and the secondary caregiver. What can we learn from the social science literature on children and divorce, and is that literature useful in shaping legislative and judicial policy concerning relocation?
4. Scholars (including myself) have argued for three major shifts in the approach to relocation disputes: (1) the requirement of mandatory mediation; (2) judicial consideration of relocation by the other parent; and (3) the provision of compensatory funding by the parent who opposed relocation to the parent who is prevented from relocating. Do these proposals have merit, and should they be adopted?

Pierre de Vos: *A judicial revolution? The court-led achievement of same-sex marriage in South Africa*

1. The prohibition of discrimination on the basis of "sexual orientation" in a country's Constitution must – as a matter of logic, constitutional law and ethics – inevitably and inexorably lead to the extension of full marriage rights to same-sex couples.
2. When legal reform is considered in the field of family law regarding the protection of same-sex couples and their children, it is important to note that full equality require the extension of all the rights and duties as well as the status associated with traditional "marriage" to same-sex couples. This means that the provision of legislation that provides for "domestic partnerships" only – even when such partnerships attract all the legal consequences of marriage – will not be sufficient.
3. When courts are called upon to adjudicate on highly controversial matters such as the extension of full marriage rights to same-sex couples they run the

risk of creating damaging their own reputation. It is therefore better for such law reform to be led by democratically elected legislatures.

Orsolya Szeibert: *Same-sex partners in Hungary: Cohabitation and registered partnership*

1. From deliberate progress concerning the legal consequences of unmarried partnership during family law recodification to the approval of Act on Registered Partnership
2. Registered partnership for same-sex and different-sex partners: is it a marriage-like institution or rather registered cohabitation?

Ian Curry-Sumner/Scott Curry-Sumner: *Is the union civil? Same-sex marriages, civil unions, domestic partnerships and reciprocal benefits in the USA*

1. The name given to a registration scheme, although ultimately a political decision, is more determinative in the United States than in Europe when analysing the legal nature of the registration.
2. Despite the overall appearance of diversity, those jurisdictions to have enacted registration schemes for same-sex couples display remarkable uniformity.

Talia Einhorn: *Same-sex family unions in Israeli law*

1. In Israeli law, key areas of family law (e.g., marriage, divorce and maintenance), are governed by orthodox, religious law, which does not recognize same-sex marriages at all and, furthermore, opposes such relationships, as well as any of their legal consequences. Consequently, the legal problems encountered by same-sex couples in Israel are more complicated than those encountered in other democratic, developed countries.
2. The above statement notwithstanding, Israeli law has shown much flexibility in adapting a very traditional legal framework to the exigencies of modern life. The Israel Supreme Court has applied to such spouses the rules applying to "reputed spouses" (extra-marital cohabitation) which, although not conferring status, emulate in many respects the rules applying to lawfully married couples. In addition, it used principles borrowed from private international law, requiring the Ministry of the Interior to enter as married in the population registry same-sex spouses married abroad, and as adopted – children adopted by same-sex couples abroad. In order, however, to achieve a coherent and complete system defining the rights and obligations of same-sex spouses, the Court's decisions must be supplemented by legislation, a challenge which

has to be met by the Knesset, in the interests of all Israeli citizens and residents.

Matteo Bonini-Baraldi: *Family vs solidarity: recent epiphanies of teh Italian reductinist anomaly in the debate on de facto couples*

1. Is an informal procedure at the population registry a proper way for ensuring recognition of same-sex couples in the public sphere, with legal validity towards third parties?
2. It is necessary to emancipate from the binary logic which – in the Italian constitutional system – opposes the 'family' and 'social formations', a logic which descends from a limited reading of the constitutional text approved by the Constitutional Court.
3. "Solidarity" is not a fair substitute for "marital/conjugal life."
4. It does not make sense to pick and choose a few rights and to subordinate their exercise to a certain duration over time, sometimes three, sometimes nine years, solely on the grounds of the gender combination within the couple.
5. It is crucial to motivate whether a prevailing State interest exists, which could justify the *prima facie* violation of a fundamental freedom.
6. The question to be addressed should be: is it possible to demonstrate a rational or even necessary link between the objective served by the *status quo*, and current exclusion of same-sex couples from marriage? When this discussion will finally become of public domain in Italy, perhaps the answers will follow, more easily than expected]

Rosa Martíns: *Same-sex partnerships in Portugal: from de facto to de jure?*

1. Act 7/2001 establishes a minimum of protection of same-sex partners. However it makes no mention of the issues concerning the ownership of assets and to the regime covering the consequences of possible mingling of ownership of movable assets during the lifetime of the relationship, nor of the recognition of inheritance rights. These questions should be object of reflection when maintaining, modifying or creating a new legal regime for same-sex relationships.
2. Article 36(1) 2nd part, Constitution of the Portuguese Republic enshrines not only a right to marry, but also includes an *institutional guarantee* of marriage. From this *institutional guarantee* follows a protection that amounts to a ban on the legislature modifying the concept and the legal regime governing marriage in a manner leading to its abolition or even to detraction from its main features.

3. Even though men and women are considered to be citizens with equal rights and duties, the fact is that their real position before society and the labour market is quite unequal. This difference between sexes has a great influence in the legal regime of marriage.
4. The Portuguese legislature should seek to solve the legal problems raised by same-sex cohabitation and therefore seek to create a specific legal regime, paying special attention to the specific features these relationships, which could take the form of registered partnerships.

Wendy Schrama: *Family function over family form in the law on parentage? The legal position of children born in informal relationships*

1. Thirty years after the Marckx decision of the ECHR the relationship status of the parents of a child is still too important in the Dutch parentage law system. The difference between children born in and outside a formalised relationship in parentage law should be reduced.
2. The *pater est* rule, which is limited to the birth of a child during a marriage in the Dutch parentage law system, should be extended to children born to unmarried cohabiting couples.

Richard Blauwhoff: *Tracing down the historical development of the legal concept of the right to know one's origins: has 'to know or not to know' ever been the legal question?*

1. *Time/legal certainty*: An (adult) child's right to know is not contingent upon the passage of time, so a countervailing interest of the parent in privacy and in the prevention of 'stale claims' should not warrant legal protection either.
2. *Enforcement*: Only an exclusively informational judicial procedure can guarantee the right's procedural effectiveness. It acknowledges that a minor's interests in 'knowing' are distinguishable from status concerns while leaving disclosure to an 'independent authority' (rather than the parents alone).
3. *Enforcement/concept*: Giving principled precedence to the child's right to know necessarily involves compulsory DNA parentage testing since legal presumptions fall short of 'knowing'.
4. *Conceptual boundaries*: The right to know ends, where the right to establish contact with the biological parent begins.

Nancy Maxwell: *The Kansas case of K.M.H.: US law concerning the legal status of known sperm donors*

In the United States the general rule is that biological fathers are presumed to be the legal parents of any children they conceive through sexual intercourse with unmarried women. What should be the law concerning legal parenthood when unmarried women use known sperm donors to create children through assisted reproduction, particularly when U.S. case law indicates that these individuals are completely ignorant of the law and its consequences? (Or as stated at the end of my article: "Perhaps this is the ultimate question that legislators should consider when drafting statutes that add or subtract potential legal parents—what will be the law's impact on all interested parties when individuals continually create children through assisted reproduction, completely ignorant of the law and its consequences?")

Which factors should be relevant when a court considers the legal parentage of a known sperm donor?

1. A party alleges an oral agreement concerning the sperm donor's parentage
2. There is a written agreement concerning the sperm donor's parentage
3. The parties used a licensed physician to perform the insemination
4. The amount of contact between the child and the sperm donor
5. The sperm donor "openly and notoriously" recognizes the child as his
7. The mother "openly and notoriously" recognizes the child as the sperm donor's child
6. The perception that a child should have more than one parent
7. The perception that a child should have two different-sexed parents
8. The sperm donor's offer to financially support the child
9. The mother's acceptance of the sperm donor's financial support
10. The sperm donor being named as the "father" on the child's birth certificate
11. The sperm donor filing as a putative father in a Putative Father Registry
12. The mother signing legal documents acknowledging the sperm donor as the father

Machteld Vonk: *The role of formalised and non-formalised intentions in legal parent-child relationships in Dutch law*

1. The increased recognition of the rights of biological fathers on the one hand and of female same-sex families on the other hand creates tension between biological and social parenthood. Could this dilemma be solved by allowing a child to have three legal parents?
2. If surrogacy is not expressly forbidden in a jurisdiction, the transfer of parental rights from the surrogate mother to the commissioning parents should be properly regulated. The terms of a surrogacy contract may play a role in such a transfer of parental rights.

3. Common law is better equipped to adapt to new developments such as artificial insemination and surrogacy than civil law, because judges do not have to wait for the legislator to find solutions for legal questions that have not yet been addressed. What is the "value" of such casuistic judgements for a civil comparative lawyer who is looking for solutions in a common law system?

European Family Law Series

1. *Legal Recognition of Same-Sex Couples in Europe*, K. Boele-Woelki and A. Fuchs (eds.)
2. *European Family Law in Action Volume I: Grounds for divorce*, K. Boele-Woelki, B. Braat and I. Sumner (eds.)
3. *European Family Law in Action Volume II: Maintenance Between Former Spouses*, K. Boele-Woelki, B. Braat and I. Sumner (eds.)
4. *Perspectives for the Unification and Harmonisation of Family Law in Europe*, K. Boele-Woelki (ed.)
5. *Family Law Legislation of the Netherlands*, I. Sumner and H. Warendorf
6. *Indépendance et interdépendance patrimoniales des époux dans le régime matrimonial légal des droits néerlandais, français et suisse*, B. Braat
7. *Principles of European Family Law Regarding Divorce and Maintenance Between Former Spouses*, K. Boele-Woelki, F. Ferrand, C. González Beilfuss, M. Jänterä-Jareborg, N. Lowe, D. Martiny and W. Pintens
8. *Inheritance Law Legislation of the Netherlands*, I. Sumner and H. Warendorf
9. *European Family Law in Action Volume III: Parental Responsibilities*, K. Boele-Woelki, B. Braat and I. Curry Sumner (eds.)
10. *Common Core and Better Law in European Family Law*, K. Boele-Woelki (ed.)
11. *All's well that ends registered?*, I. Curry-Sumner
12. *Model Family Code – From a global perspective*, I. Schwenzer and M. Dimsey
13. *Harmonisation of Family Law in Europe. A Historical Perspective*, M. Antokolskaia
14. *Brussels II bis: Its Impact and Application in the Member States*, Katharina Boele-Woelki and Cristina González Beilfuss (eds.)
15. *Tensions between Legal, Biological and Social Conceptions of Parentage*, I. Schwenzer (ed.)
16. *Principles of European Family Law Regarding Parental Responsibilities*, K. Boele-Woelki, F. Ferrand, C. González Beilfuss, M. Jänterä-Jareborg, N. Lowe, D. Martiny and W. Pintens (eds.)
17. *Juxtaposing Legal Systems and the Principles of European Family Law on Divorce and Maintenance*, E. Örücü and J. Mair (eds.)
18. *Convergence and Divergence of Family Law in Europe*, M. Antokolskaia (ed.)
19. *European Challenges in Contemporary Family Law*, K. Boele-Woelki and T. Sverdrup (eds.)
20. *Children and their parents*, M. Vonk

21. *La capacité de l'enfant dans les droits français, anglais et écossais*, L. Francoz-Terminal
22. *Joint Parental Authority*, C.G. Jeppesen de Boer
23. *Debates in Family Law around the Globe at the Dawn of the 21st Century*, K. Boele-Woelki (ed.)

www.ingramcontent.com/pod-product-compliance
Ingram Content Group UK Ltd.
Pitfield, Milton Keynes, MK11 3LW, UK
UKHW051925100926
8556IPUK00022B/1375

9 789050 958752